Handy
DICTIONARY
of the
BIBLE

Statue of Rameses II at Temple of Luxor. He may have been either the Pharaoh of the Oppression or the Pharaoh of the Exodus. © MPS

Handy

DICTIONARY

of the

BIBLE

General Editor
MERRILL C. TENNEY

ZondervanPublishingHouse
Grand Rapids, Michigan

A Division of HarperCollins*Publishers*

Handy Dictionary of the Bible
Copyright 1965 by Zondervan Publishing House
Grand Rapids, Michigan

ISBN 0-310-33151-X

Requests for information should be addressed to:
Zondervan Publishing House
Grand Rapids, Michigan 49530

Printed in the United States of America

97   98 / LP / 21   20

PREFACE

Understanding the Bible is often difficult for the average reader because of the unfamiliar names of persons, places and objects to which it refers. The historical and cultural backgrounds are not readily known to modern-day readers and pre-suppose familiarity with information not easily found today. Consequently, the purpose of a Bible Dictionary is to make available resource information that will assist in understanding the specific portion of the Bible being studied.

The *Handy Dictionary of the Bible* is designed to perform this function. Its convenient size and easy-to-read type enhances its usability. While concise in content, it is amazingly complete in its handling of each of over five thousand entries. Additional features include informative photographs of key areas in Biblical lands, to assist in comprehending the setting in which many events took place. Of particular interest is the special section of archaeological photographs in the back of the book. We are indebted to the Matson Photo Service of Los Angeles, California for photographs used.

Little-known Bible facts come to light in this handy reference work.

THE PUBLISHERS

LIST OF ABBREVIATIONS

AD: after Christ
ASV: American Standard Version
BC: before Christ
c: approximately
cent: century
cf: see, compare
ch(s): chapter(s)
E: East(ern)
e g: for example
equiv: equivalent
ERV: English Revised Version
esp: especially
etc: and so forth
ff: following
ft: feet
Gr: Greek
Heb: Hebrew
i e: namely; that is
KJV: King James Version
LXX: Septuagint (Greek Translation
   of Old Testament)
I Macc: I Maccabees
II Macc: II Maccabees
marg: margin
MSS: manuscripts
mt(s): mount(s) (ain)
N: North(ern)
NE: Northeast(ern)
Nos: numbers
N-S: North-South
NT: New Testament
NW: Northwest(ern)
OT: Old Testament
q v: which see
RSV: Revised Standard Version
S: South(ern)
SE: Southeast(ern)
sq: square
SW: Southwest(ern)
vs: verse
viz: namely
W: West(ern)

Old Testament
Gen: Genesis
Exod: Exodus
Lev: Leviticus
Num: Numbers
Deut: Deuteronomy
Josh: Joshua
Judg: Judges
Ruth
I Sam: I Samuel
II Sam: II Samuel
I Kings
II Kings

I Chron: I Chronicles
II Chron: II Chronicles
Ezra
Neh: Nehemiah
Esth: Esther
Job
Ps: Psalms
Prov: Proverbs
Eccl: Ecclesiastes
S. of Sol: Song of Solomon
Isa: Isaiah
Jer: Jeremiah
Lam: Lamentations
Ezek: Ezekiel
Dan: Daniel
Hos: Hosea
Joel
Amos
Obad: Obadiah
Jonah
Mic: Micah
Nah: Nahum
Hab: Habakkuk
Zeph: Zephaniah
Hag: Haggai
Zech: Zechariah
Mal: Malachi

New Testament
Matt: Matthew
Mark
Luke
John
Acts
Rom: Romans
I Cor: I Corinthians
II Cor: II Corinthians
Gal: Galatians
Eph: Ephesians
Phil: Philippians
Col: Colossians
I Thess: I Thessalonians
II Thess: II Thessalonians
I Tim: I Timothy
II Tim: II Timothy
Titus
Philem: Philemon
Heb: Hebrews
Jas: James
I Pet: I Peter
II Pet: II Peter
I John
II John
III John
Jude
Rev: Revelation

Handy
DICTIONARY
of the
BIBLE

A

AARON (âr'ŭn, meaning uncertain), brother of Moses and Miriam (Num. 26:59; Exod. 6:20); three years older than Moses (Exod. 7:7). First referred to when Moses told God he could not be Israel's leader as he had no speaking ability, and God replied that Aaron would be his mouthpiece. Married Elisheba, sister of a prince of the tribe of Judah (Exod. 6:23; I Chron. 2:10), who bore Nadab, Abihu, Eleazar, and Ithamar.

He assisted Moses when he appeared before Pharaoh and during the 40 years wilderness journey. Helped Hur hold up Moses' hands in the battle with Amalek (Exod. 17:9-12). He had some weaknesses of character. At Sinai he made a golden calf while Moses tarried (Exod. 32); he and Miriam criticized Moses for marrying a Cushite woman (Num. 12:1,2). His authority was vindicated through miracle of rod (Num. 17). The authority of Aaron and Moses doubted at Meribah (Num. 20:12).

At Sinai he became high priest and head of the hereditary priesthood (Exod. 28:1), and his sons were consecrated to the priesthood (Lev. 8,9). When he died at the age of 123 on Mt. Hor, with Moses at his side, the high priesthood passed to his son, Eleazar (Num. 20:22-29; 33-38; Deut. 10:6; 32:50). Hebrews 5:4,5 refers to him as a type of Christ.

AARONITES (âr'ŭn-īts), descendants of Aaron who helped David (I Chron. 12:27).

AB (ăb), the fifth month of the Hebrew year (Num. 33:38).

ABADDON (à-băd'ŭn, ruin). In Job 31:12 it means "ruin;" in Job 26:6; Prov. 15:11; 27:20, "Sheol;" in Job 28:22, "death;" in Rev. 9:11, "Apollyon," who reigns over the infernal regions.

ABAGTHA (à-băg'thà), chamberlain of King Ahasuerus (Esth. 1:10).

ABANA(à-băn'à), a river of Damascus (II Kings 5:12).

ABARIM (ab'à-rīm, those beyond), either a region E of the Jordan or a mountain range NW of Moab (Num. 27:12).

ABBA (ab'à, Aramaic for father), Mark 14: 36; Romans 8:15; Galatians 4:6).

ABDA (ăb'dà, prob. servant of God).1. Father of Adoniram (I Kings 4:6). 2. A Levite (Neh. 11:17).

ABDEEL (ăb'dĕ-ĕl, servant of God), father of Shelemiah (Jer. 36:26).

ABDI (ăb'dī, prob. servant of God). 1. A Levite, the grandfather of Ethan (I Chron. 6:44). 2. A son of Elan (Ezra 10:26).

ABDIEL (ăb'dī-ĕl, servant of God), a Gadite chief (I Chron. 5:15).

ABDON (ab'dŏn). 1. A judge of Israel (Judg. 12:13-15). 2. Son of Shashak (I Chron. 8: 23,28). 3. Son of Jeiel (I Chron. 8:30). 4. Official of Josiah (II Chron. 34:20).

ABDON (City), Levite city in Asher (Josh. 21:30; I Chron. 6:74).

ABEDNEGO (à-bĕd'nē-gŏ, servant of Nego), a Hebrew living in Babylon (Dan. 1:7).

ABEL (à'bĕl, meaning uncertain), second son of Adam and Eve who was slain by his brother Cain (Gen. 4).

ABEL (à'bĕl, meadow). 1. A city in Ammon (II Sam. 20:14,18). 2. In I Samuel 6:18 KJV "the great stone of Abel" should probably be "stone."

ABEL-BETH-MAACHA (à'bĕl-bĕth-mă'à-kà), a town in Naphtali (II Sam. 20:15). Sheba fled there from King David (II Sam. 20: 14-22). Benhadad later seized it (I Kings 15:20) and Tiglath-pileser captured it (II Kings 15:29).

ABEL-CHERAMIM(à'bĕl-kĕr-à-mĭm, meadow of vineyards), a place in Ammon (Judg. 11:33).

ABEL-MAIM (à'bĕl-mà'ĭm, meadow of waters), variant of Abel-beth-maacah (II Chron. 16:4).

ABEL-MEHOLAH(à'bĕl-mē-hŏ'là, meadow of dancing), a town probably in the Jordan valley (Judg. 7:22).

ABEL-MIZRAIM (à'bĕl-mĭz'rā-ĭm), meadow or mourning of Egypt), a place E of the Jordan (Gen. 50:11).

ABEL-SHITTIM (à'bĕl-shĭt'ĭm, acacia-meadow), a place in Moab (Num. 33:49).

ABEL THE GREAT. In I Sam. 6:18 "the great stone of Abel" (KJV) should be "the great stone," as in ASV and the RSV.

ABEZ (à'bĕz), town in Issachar (Josh. 19:20).

ABI (à'bī), the mother of King Hezekiah (II Kings 18:2; II Chron. 29:1).

ABIA (à-bī'à), a variant for Abijah.

ABIASAPH (à-bī'à-săf, the father gathers), a Levite son of Korah (Exod. 6:24).

ABIATHAR (à-bī'à-thàr, father of abundance), son of |Ahimelech the high priest, whom he succeeded (I Sam. 22:20); loyal adviser of David (II Sam. 15:24; 17:15; 19:11); deprived of the high priesthood by Solomon because he favored Adonijah (I Kings 2:26,35).

ABIB (à'bĭb, an ear of corn), pre-exilic name for the first month of the year (Exod. 13:4; 23:15; 34:18).

ABIDA (à-bī'dà, the father knows), a son

of Midian (Gen. 25:4; I Chron. 1:33).

ABIDAN (à-bī′dăn, the father is judge), prince of the tribe of Benjamin (Num. 1:11).

ABIEL (ā′bĭ-ĕl, God is father). 1. Father of Kish (I Sam. 9:1). 2. One of David's mighty men (I Chron. 11:32).

ABIEZER (ā′bĭ-ē′zēr, father of help). 1. Head of a family in Manasseh (Judg. 6:11f). 2. One of David's mighty men (I Chron. 11:28).

ABIGAIL (ăb′ĭ-gāl, father is rejoicing). 1. Wife of Nabal, and, later, of David (I Sam. 25:3; 39-44). 2. Sister of David (I Chron. 2:16).

ABIHAIL (ăb′ĭ-hāl, the father is strength). 1. Father of Zuriel (Num. 3:35). 2. Wife of Abishur (I Chron. 2:29). 3. A Gadite (I Chron. 5:14). 4. Wife of Rehoboam (II Chron. 11:18). 5. Father of Queen Esther (Esther 2:15).

ABIHU (à-bī′hū, the father is he), second son of Aaron (Exod. 6:23). He and Nadab were slain for offering strange fire (Lev. 10).

ABIHUD (à-bī′hŭd, the father is majesty), grandson of Benjamin (I Chron. 8:3).

ABIJAH (à-bī′jà, Jehovah is Father). 1. Wife of Hezron (I Chron. 2:24). 2. Grandson of Benjamin (I Chron. 7:8). 3. Son of the prophet Samuel (I Sam. 8:2). 4. Descendant of Aaron (I Chron. 24:10). 5. Son of Jeroboam I (I Kings 14:1-18). 6. King of Judah, son and successor of Rehoboam (II Chron. 12:16). 7. Priest of Nehemiah's time (Neh. 10:7). 8. Mother of Hezekiah (II Chron. 29:1). 9. A priest (Neh. 12:4,7).

ABILENE (ăb′ĭ-lēn, meadow), a tetrarchy near Anti-Lebanon, ruled by Lysanias when John the Baptist began his ministry (Luke 3:1).

ABIMAEL (à-bĭm′ā-ĕl, God is father), a son or descendant of Joktan (Gen. 10:28).

ABIMELECH (à-bĭm′ē-lĕk, probably either the father is king or the father of a king). 1. A Philistine king of Gerar (Gen. 21:22-34). 2. Another king of Gerar (Gen. 26). 3. Son of Gideon by a concubine (Judg. 8:31). 4. Philistine king mentioned in the title of Psalm 34. 5. A priest in David's time (I Chron. 18:16).

ABINADAB (à-bĭn′à-dăb, father is generous). 1. A Levite in whose home the ark was kept for a time (I Sam. 7:1,2; 17:13). 2. Son of Jesse (I Sam. 16:8). 3. Son of Saul (I Sam. 17:13; 31:2). 4. A relative of Solomon (I Kings 4:11).

ABINOAM (à-bĭn′ō-ăm, the father is pleasantness), father of Barak (Judg. 4:6).

ABIRAM (à-bī′răm, the father is exalted). 1. A Reubenite who conspired against Moses (Num. 16). 2. Son of Hiel (I Kings 16:34).

ABISHAG (ăb′ĭ-shăg, the father wanders), a Shunamite woman who looked after David in his old age (I Kings 1:3,15; 2:17ff).

ABISHAI (à-bĭsh′ā-ī). Son of David's sister Zeruiah, and brother of Joab and Asahel. He was always intensely loyal to David (I Sam. 26:6-9; II Sam. 3:30; 16:9; I Chron. 18:12,13).

ABISHALOM (à-bĭsh′à-lŏm), variant of Absalom.

ABISHUA (à-bĭsh′ū-à). 1. Son of Phinehas (I Chron. 6:4,5,50). 2. A Benjamite (I Chron. 8:4).

ABISHUR (à-bĭsh′shēr, the father is a wall), son of Shammai (I Chron. 2:28,29).

ABITAL (à-bī′tăl, the father is dew), a wife of David (II Sam. 3:4; I Chron. 3:3).

ABITUB (à-bī′tŭb, the father is goodness), a Benjamite (I Chron. 8:8-11).

ABIUD (à-bī′ŭd), son of Zerubbabel (Matt. 1:13).

ABLUTION (See Washing).

ABNER (ăb′nēr, the father is a lamp), Saul's cousin and the commander-in-chief of his army (I Sam. 14:50). After Saul's death Abner made Ishbosheth king (II Sam. 2:8). Later he joined David, and was killed by Joab (II Sam. 3:26-30).

ABOMINATION OF DESOLATION, a term used to describe an utterly abhorrent and loathsome abomination (Dan. 9:27; 11:31; 12:11).

ABRAHAM (ā′brà-hăm, the father is high). A son of Terah and descendant of Shem whom God called out of Ur of the Chaldees to be the founder of the Hebrew nation (Gen. 12:1-6). He migrated first to Haran in Mesopotamia with his nephew Lot and his Father, Terah, and on the death of the latter entered Palestine. After short stays in Shechem, Bethel, and the Negeb he visited Egypt during a time of famine, and then returned to Hebron. In hope of God's promise of a son, he took as his wife Hagar, an Egyptian maid, who bore him Ishmael (Gen. 16). Later his wife Sarah bore Isaac, who became the heir of promise (Gen. 17:1). He died at the age of 175, and was buried in the cave of Machpelah in Hebron (Gen. 25:7-10).

ABRAHAM'S BOSOM was a Jewish symbol of blessedness after death (Luke 16:22,23).

ABRAM (See Abraham).

ABRECH (ăb′rĕk), probably an Egyptian word meaning to kneel (Gen. 41:43, ASV margin, RSV margin).

ABRONAH (à-brŏn′nà), in KJV Ebronah. Place where the Israelites camped (Num. 33:34,35).

ABSALOM (ăb′sà-lŏm, the father is peace). The third son of David, who rebelled against him, and lost his life as a result. Angry because his brother Amnon had ravished his sister Tamar, Absalom assassinated Amnon, and fled the kingdom (II Sam. 13:22-39). David finally recalled him, but refused to see him. Absalom proclaimed himself a candidate for the throne, and raised a revolt, but was defeated in battle, and killed by Joab, David's general (II Sam. 18:6-17). David mourned deeply over his death. Absalom was handsome and popular, and had succeeded in winning the favor of a large faction in Judea.

ABSTINENCE (ăb′stĭ-nĕns). The noun occurs once in KJV, and means abstinence from food (Acts 27:21); the verb occurs

six times, and means **to refrain from.**
The Jerusalem Council (Acts 15:20,29) commanded abstinence from "meats offered to idols, and from blood, and from things strangled, and from fornication." Abstinence was not commanded for its own sake, but was recommended to inculcate purity of diet and of life. Peter urged his friends to "abstain from fleshly lusts" (I Peter 2:11). God's people were told to abstain from idolatry (Exod. 34:15; Rom. 14:21; I Cor. 8:4-13).

ABYSS (à-bĭs'), means, in the NT, the **nether world, prison of disobedient spirits** (Luke 8:31, Rev. 9:1,2,11; 11:7; 17:8; 20:1-3), or the **world of the dead** (Rom. 10:7). The word does not occur in the KJV, but is translated **bottomless pit** in Revelation, and **deep** in Luke.

ACCAD (ăk'ăd), one of the ancient cities of Babylonia, perhaps identical with Agade, where Sargon I, the Semitic conqueror of the Semitic Accadians, made his capital in 2475 B. C. The identification uncertain.

ACCHO (ăk'ō), a seacoast town of Palestine, identified with the Ptolemais of the NT (Acts 21:7) and the modern Akka or Acre, eight miles N of Mt. Carmel and 30 miles S of Tyre.

ACELDAMA (à-sĕl'dà-mà), or Akeldama (a-kel'da-ma), the **field of blood,** the field purchased with the money which Judas received for betraying Christ (Acts 1:18,19). It was so named because it was purchased with blood-money, or perhaps because Judas' gruesome death occurred there.

ACHAIA (à-kā'yà), the Roman province which took in all of Greece south of Macedonia (Acts 19:21; Rom. 15:26; II Cor. 1:1; I Thess. 1:7,8), of which Corinth was the capital.

ACHAICUS (à-kā'ĭ-kŭs), a Corinthian Christian who visited Paul at Ephesus (I Cor. 16:17-19).

ACHAN (ā'kăn), an Israelite who took for himself part of the spoil of Jericho which had been devoted to God. Because of his theft the Israelites were defeated at Ai. When his sin was discovered, he and his family were stoned (Josh. 7:1-26).

ACHAR (ā'kàr). The same as Achan (I Chron. 2:7).

ACHAZ (ā'kăz). The same as Ahaz.

ACHBOR (ăk'bôr). 1. Father of a king of Edom (Gen. 36:38,39; I Chron. 1:49). 2. A messenger of King Josiah (II Kings 22:12,14).

ACHIM (ā'kĭm), an ancestor of Christ (Matt. 1:14).

ACHISH (ā'kĭsh), Philistine king of Gath, to whom David fled for protection (I Sam. 21:10-15).

ACHMETHA (ăk'mē-thà), ancient Ecbatana, modern Hamadan, capital of Media (Ezra 6:2).

ACHOR (ā'kôr), the valley where Achan was stoned (Josh. 7:24-26; Hos. 2:15).

ACHSA (ăk'sà). (See Achsah).

ACHSAH (ăk'sà), daughter of Caleb, who was married to Othniel, her cousin, in ful-

fillment of a promise that she would be given to the man that captured Kirjath-sepher (Josh. 15:16-19; Judg. 1:12-15).

ACHSHAPH (ăk'shăf), a city which Joshua captured (Josh. 12:7,20), located on the border of Asher (Josh. 19:24,25).

ACHZIB (ăk'zĭb). 1. A city of Judah (Josh. 15:44). 2. A town in Asher (Judg. 1:31; Josh. 19:29).

ACRE (ā'kêr), the amount of land a pair of oxen could plow in a day (I Sam. 14:14; Isa. 5:10).

ACROPOLIS (à-krŏp'ō-lĭs), the upper or higher city, citadel, or castle of a Greek municipality, especially the high rocky promontory in Athens where the treasury of the city and its finest temples were located.

ACROSTIC (à-krŏs'tĭc), a literary device by which the first letter of each line of poetry forms either a word or the successive letters of the alphabet. An outstanding example is the 119th psalm, in which each successive set of eight verses begins with a different letter of the Hebrew alphabet. The effect is not apparent in the English translation, but the Hebrew letters are given between the lines in order to preserve the construction.

ACTS OF THE APOSTLES. The NT book which gives the history of early Christianity from the ascension of Christ to the end of Paul's imprisonment in Rome. It is a selection of the deeds and words of the apostles illustrating the progress of the church in the first century. The traditional author is Luke, "the beloved physician" (Col. 4:14). The place of writing is not stated, but since the book ends abruptly with Paul awaiting trial in Rome, it was probably written there shortly after the latest event mentioned, about A. D. 62. Acts emphasizes the missionary growth of the church among the Gentiles, and the work of the Holy Spirit. Outline: 1. The origins of the church in Jerusalem (1:1-8:3). 2. The transition from the Jewish to the Gentile ministry, including the preaching to Samaria (ch. 8), the conversion of Paul (ch. 9), and the beginning of Gentile work in Caesarea (ch. 10) and Antioch (11,12). 3. The missionary journeys of Paul (13-28).

ADADAH (à-dā'dà), a city in Judah (Josh. 15:22).

ADAH (ā'dà, **ornament or morning**). 1. Wife of Lamech (Gen. 4:19,20,23). 2. Wife of Esau (Gen. 36:2,4,10,12,16).

ADAIAH (à-dā'yà, **Jehovah has adorned**). 1. A man of Boscath (II Kings 22:1). 2. A Levite (I Chron. 6:41-43). 3. Son of Shimshi (I Chron. 8:1,21). 4. A Levite (I Chron. 9:10-12). 5. Father of a man who helped make Joash king (II Chron. 23:1). 6. A man who married a foreign wife during the exile (Ezra 10:29). 7. Another man who did the same thing (Ezra 10:34). 8. A descendant of Judah (Neh. 11:5). 9. A Levite (Neh. 11:12).

ADALIA (ăd-à-lī'à), one of Haman's sons (Esth. 9:8).

ADAM (ăd'ăm, **of the ground**). The first human being. He was created in God's image (Gen. 1:27), placed in the Garden of Eden, and given dominion over the creatures of earth. Because he and his wife disobeyed God, they were thrust out of the Garden of Eden. Paul ascribes to him the origin of sin and death (Rom. 5:12-21).

ADAM (ăd'ăm, **red, or made**), a city in the Jordan valley where the Israelites entered the promised land (Josh. 3:16).

ADAMAH (ăd'à-mà, **red ground**), a city of Naphtali (Josh. 19:36). Location disputed.

ADAMANT (ăd'à-mănt), a stone harder than flint (Ezek. 3:9; Zech. 7:12).

ADAMI (ăd'à-mī, **earthy**), a place on the border of Naphtali (Josh. 19:33).

ADAR (ā'dàr), a place on the S border of Judah (Josh. 15:3). Rendered Addar in ASV and RSV.

ADBEEL (ăd'bè-èl, **languishing for God**), son of Ishmael (Gen. 25:13; I Chron. 1:29).

ADDAN (ăd'ăn), a place in Babylonia (Ezra 2:59).

ADDAR (ăd'àr, **threshing floor**). Grandson of Benjamin (I Chron. 8:3).

ADDER (See Animals – Reptiles).

ADDI (ăd'ī), an ancestor of Joseph (Luke 3:28).

ADDON (ăd'ŏn), the same place as Addan (Neh. 7:61).

ADER (ā'dèr), a Benjaminite (I Chron. 8:15).

ADIEL (ā'dī-èl). 1. Descendant of Simeon (I Chron. 4:36). 2. A priest (I Chron. 9:12). 3. Father of a man who supervised David's treasuries (I Chron. 27:25).

ADIN (ā'dĭn). 1. One whose family returned from exile with Zerubbabel (Ezra 2:15). 2. One whose posterity came back with Ezra (Ezra 8:6). 3. A family that sealed the covenant (Neh. 10:16).

ADINA (ăd'ĭ-nà), an officer of David (I Chron. 11:42).

ADINO (ăd'ĭ-nō), a Tachmonite (II Sam. 23:8).

ADITHAIM (ăd-ĭ-thā'ĭm), a city of Judah (Josh. 15:36).

ADJURATION (ăj-ŏŏ-rā'shŭn). The noun does not occur in the Bible, but the verb "adjure" is often found in both Testaments (I Sam. 14:24; I Kings 22:16; Mark 5:7). In every case, an appeal in the most impressive manner is meant.

ADLAI (ăd'là-ĭ), father of a man who oversaw David's cattle (I Chron. 27:29).

ADMAH (ăd'mà, **red earth**), a city destroyed with Sodom and Gomorrah (Deut. 29:23; Gen. 19:24-28).

ADMATHA (ăd'mà-thà), a prince of Persia and Media (Esth. 1:14).

ADNA (ăd'nà). 1. Son of Pahath-moab (Ezra 10:30). 2. A priest (Neh. 12:12-15).

ADNAH · (ăd'nà). 1. Follower of David (I Chron. 12:20). 2. An officer in the army of Jehoshaphat (II Chron. 17:14).

ADONI-BEZEK (à-dō'nī-bē'zĕk), a king of

Bezek who was captured and mutilated (Judg. 1:5-7).

ADONIJAH (ăd'ō-nī'jà, **my Lord is Jehovah**). 1. A son of David who tried in vain to seize the throne (I Kings 1:5-2:25). 2. A Levite (II Chron. 17:8). 3. A chieftain in Nehemiah's time (Neh. 10:14-16).

ADONIKAM (ăd-ō-nī'kăm), ancestor of a family that returned from exile with Zerubbabel (Ezra 2:13).

ADONIRAM (ăd-ō-nī'răm), an officer of David, Solomon, and Rehoboam, sometimes called Adoram or Hadoram (II Sam. 20:24; I Kings 4:6; 12:18).

ADONI-ZEDEK, ADONI-ZEDEC (KJV) (à-dō'nī-zē'dĕk, **lord of righteousness**), Amorite king of Jerusalem who with four other kings was defeated in battle and slain by Joshua at Gibeon (Josh. 10:1-27).

ADOPTION (à-dŏp'shŭn), to take a child of other parents and legally make it one's own child. Three instances are found in the OT: (Exod. 2:10; I Kings 11:20; Esth. 2:7,15). Paul uses the term a number of times to refer to God's taking repentant, believing sinners into His family, so that they become His children and heirs of the redemptive benefits of Christ (Rom. 8:16-18, 23; Gal. 4:1-3; Eph. 1:4,5).

ADORAIM (ăd'ō-răm), a fortress in Judah (II Chron. 11:9).

ADORAM (à-dō'răm), the same as Adoniram.

ADORATION (ăd-ō-rā'shŭn), homage paid to one held in high esteem, or worship (Dan. 3:5,6; Matt. 2:11).

ADRAMMELECH (ăd-răm'ĕ-lĕk, **Adar is king**). 1. Name given to Adar, the god brought to Samaria from Assyria by the Sepharvites (II Kings 17:31). 2. Son of Sennacherib, whom he slew (II Kings 19:37).

ADRAMYTTIUM (ăd'rà-mĭt'ĭ-ŭm), a port city of Mysia, in the Roman province of Asia (Acts 27:2).

ADRIA (ā'drĭ-à), same as Adriatic Sea, a body of water between Italy on the W and Dalmatia, Macedonia and Achaia on the E (Acts 27:27).

ADRIEL (ā'drĭ-ăl), son of Barzillai the Meholathite, to whom Merab, Saul's daughter, was given in marriage, although she had been promised to David (I Sam. 18:19).

ADULLAM (à-dŭl'ăm, **refuge**), a city between the hill country of Judah and the sea. David hid in one of the many caves near the city (I Sam. 22:1,2).

ADULLAMITE (à-dŭl'ăm-ĭt), used of Hirah, Judah's friend (Gen. 38:1,12,20).

ADULTERY (à-dŭl'tĕr-ê). In the OT, sexual intercourse, usually of a man, married or unmarried, always with the wife of another. The Ten Commandments forbid it (Exod. 20:14). The term is also used as a figure for idolatrous worship (Jer. 3:9; Ezek. 23:37). Jesus regards a lustful look as adultery (Matt. 5:27-30).

ADUMMIM (à-dŭm'ĭm), a pass on the road between Jerusalem and Jericho (Josh. 15:7; 18:17).

ADVENT (See Eschatology).

ADVERSARY (ăd'vẽr-sâr'ĕ), an enemy, personal, national, or supernatural (Exod. 23:22; Matt. 5:25).

ADVOCATE (ăd'vō-kāt, helper, Paraclete), the Holy Spirit, or Comforter in KJV (John 14:16,26; 15:26); Jesus Christ (I John 2:1).

AENEAS (ê-nê'ăs), a paralytic healed by Peter (Acts 9:32-35).

AENON (ê'nŏn, springs), a place near Salim where John the Baptist baptized (John 3:22,23).

AEON (ê'ŏn), a word meaning a period of time (Heb. 9:26), generally translated "world" (Rom. 12:2; II Tim. 4:10), or "aġe(s)" (Eph. 2:7; Col. 1:26).

AGABUS (ăg'á-bŭs), a prophet living in Jerusalem who prophesied a world-wide famine (Acts 11:27-30) and warned Paul he would be arrested in Jerusalem (Acts 21:10,11).

AGAG (ā'găg). 1. King of Amalek (Num. 24:7). 2. Another king of Amalek. Saul spared him when he should have killed him (I Sam. 15).

AGAGITE (ăg'á-gīt), Haman is thus called (Esth. 3:1,10; 8:5).

AGAPE (ăg'á-pā), a word meaning "love" and "love-feasts," which were followed by the Lord's Supper (I Cor. 11:20-34).

AGAR (ā'gär), name of Sarai's handmaid (Gal. 4:24,25).

AGATE (See Minerals).

AGE (See Aeon).

AGE, OLD, called the reward of filial obedience (Exod. 20:12). Respect for the aged is commanded (Lev. 19:32).

AGONY (ā'gō-nē, anguish), occurs only in Luke 22:44, of Jesus' agony in Gethsemane.

AGORA (ā'gō-rà, market place), in ancient cities the town meeting place, where the public met for the exchange of merchandise, information, and ideas ("Streets" Mark 6:56; Acts 17:17).

AGRAPHA (ăg'rà-fà, unwritten things), sayings ascribed to Jesus transmitted to us outside of the canonical Gospels. The number is not large, and most are obviously apocryphal or spurious. They are found in the NT outside the Gospels, ancient manuscripts of the NT, patristic literature, papyri, and apocryphal gospels.

AGRICULTURE, a word not used in the Bible, "husbandry" being used instead. It is as old as Adam, and was practiced by all ancient nations. In hilly countries like Palestine fields were irrigated and hills were terraced. The rainy season in Palestine extended from September to March, and seed was therefore sown in the fall. Seed was scattered broadcast. The vegetables commonly raised included peas, beans, lentils, lettuce, endive, leek, garlic, onion, cucumber, and cabbage. Wheat, barley, and rye were the staple cereals.

AGRIPPA I (à-grĭp'à), known in history as King Herod Agrippa I, and in the NT as Herod. He was the grandson of Herod the Great and ruled over the whole of Palestine from A. D. 40 to 44. He slew James to please the Jews and intended to do the same to Peter (Acts 12:2-4). He died in A. D. 44.

AGRIPPA II (à-grĭp'à), known in history as King Herod Agrippa II and in the NT as Agrippa. He was the son of Agrippa I, and ruled over only a small part of his father's territory. Paul appeared before him and Festus, as recorded in Acts 25:23-26:32. He died in A. D. 100.

AGUE (See Diseases, Malaria).

AGUR (ā'gûr, gatherer), the author or "collector" of the wise sayings in Proverbs 30.

AHAB (ā'hăb, father's brother). 1. Son of Omri and 7th king of the northern kingdom of Israel. He reigned 22 years, 873-851 B. C. Politically he was a very strong king, but religiously he was a failure. Jezebel, his wife, tried to crush Judaism and force idolatry on the nation. He fought against Ben-hadad, king of Syria, three times, and was mortally wounded in the third campaign. God raised up Elijah against him (I Kings 16:28-22:40).

AHARAH (à-hâr'àh), son of Benjamin (I Chron. 8:1).

AHARHEL (à-hâr'hĕl), a man of Judah (I Chron. 4:8).

AHASAI (à-hā'sī, my protector), a priest (Neh. 11:13).

AHASBAI (à-hăs'bī), father of one of David's heroes (II Sam. 23:34).

AHASUERUS (à-hăz'û-ê'rŭs). 1. Father of Darius the Mede (Dan. 9:1). 2. King of Persia mentioned in the book of Esther. There is much evidence that he was Xerxes, who reigned from 486 to 465 B. C. The Ahasuerus of Ezra 4:6 is probably also this same Xerxes, although sometimes identified with Cambyses, son of Cyrus.

AHAVA (à-hā'và), a river in Babylon (Ezra 8:15,21).

AHAZ (ā'hăz, he was grasped). 1. The 12th king of Judah in the divided monarchy; son of Jotham. He ruled from 735 to 715 B. C.; fostered idolatry in Judah and was one of the worst kings of Judah (II Kings 16; II Chron. 28). 2. Great-grandson of Jonathan (I Chron. 8:35,36).

AHAZIAH (ā'hà-zī'à, Jehovah hath grasped). 1. Son of Ahab and Jezebel; 8th king of Israel. He reigned 851-850 B. C. Like his parents, he was an idolater (I Kings 22: 51-53; II Kings 1:1-16). 2. Son of Jehoram and Athaliah. He was the 6th king of Judah in the divided monarchy and reigned only one year, 843 B. C. (II Chron. 22:2). He walked in all the idolatries of the house of Ahab (II Chron. 21:5-20).

AHBAN (à-băn), a Judahite (I Chron. 2:29).

AHER (ā-hẽr), a Benjamite (I Chron. 7:12).

AHI (ā'hī). 1. A Gadite (I Chron. 5:15). 2. An Asherite (I Chron. 7:34).

AHIAH (See Ahijah).

AHIAM (à-hī-ăm), one of David's heroes (II Sam. 23:33).

AHIAN (à-hī'ăn), a Manassite (I Chron. 7:19).

AHIEZER (à-hī-ê'zẽr). 1. A head of the

tribe of Dan (Num. 1:12; 2:25; 7:66). 2. A Gibeonite who followed David (I Chron. 12:3).

AHIHUD (à-hī′hŭd). 1. Prince of Asher (Num. 34:27). 2. Son of Ehud (I Chron. 8:7).

AHIJAH (à-hī′jà, **brother of Jehovah**). 1. A son of Jerahmeel, brother of Caleb (I Chron. 2:25). 2. Descendant of Benjamin (I Chron. 8:7). 3. A priest in Shiloh in the days of Saul (Ahiah, I Sam. 14:3). 4. A soldier in David's army (I Chron. 11:36). 5. A Levite in David's reign (I Chron. 26:20). 6. A scribe of Solomon (I Kings 4:3). 7. A prophet of Shiloh who foretold to Jeroboam that he would be king (I Kings 11:29-39) and to Jeroboam's wife that her son would die (I Kings 14:1-16). 8. Father of Baasha, King of Israel (I Kings 15:27). 9. A Jew in the days of Nehemiah (Neh. 10:26).

AHIKAM (à-hī′kàm, **my brother has risen up**), son of Shaphan the scribe in the days of Josiah (II Kings 22:12; 25:22; Jer. 40:5).

AHILUD (à-hī′lŭd), father of Jehoshaphat the recorder (II Sam. 8:16; 20:24).

AHIMAAZ (à-hĭm′à-àz, **brother of anger**). 1. Father-in-law of King Saul (I Sam. 14:50). 2. Son of Zadok the high priest; served as messenger for David in Absalom's rebellion (II Sam. 15:24-27; 17:15-22). 3. A commissary officer of Solomon (I Kings 4:15).

AHIMAN (à-hī′màn). 1. Giant son of Anak (Num. 13:22). 2. A Levite gatekeeper (I Chron. 9:17).

AHIMELECH (à-hĭm′ē-lĕk). Saul's high priest; slain by the king for helping David (I Sam. 21,22). 2. Son of Abiathar (II Sam. 8:17). 3. A Hittite (I Sam. 26:6).

AHIMOTH (à-hī′mŏth), son of Elkanah (I Chron. 6:25).

AHINADAB (à-hĭn′à-dàb), a commissary officer of Solomon (I Kings 4:14).

AHINOAM (à-hĭn′ō-àm). 1. Wife of King Saul (I Sam. 14:50). 2. One of David's wives (I Sam. 25:43; 27:3).

AHIO (à-hī′ō). 1. Son of Abinadab; helped bring the ark to Jerusalem (II Sam. 6:1-11). 2. A Benjamite (I Chron. 8:14). 3. A Gibeonite (I Chron. 8:31; 9:37).

AHIRA (à-hī′rà), prince of Naphtali (Num. 1:15; 2:29).

AHIRAM (à-hī′ràm), son of Benjamin (Num. 26:38).

AHIRAMITE (à-hī′rà-mīt), Num. 26:38.

AHISAMACH (à-hĭs′à-màk), A Danite (Exod. 31:6; 35:34).

AHISHAHAR (à-hĭsh′à-hàr), descendant of Benjamin (I Chron. 7:10).

AHISHAR (à-hī′shàr), an official over Solomon's household (I Kings 4:6).

AHITHOPHEL (à-hĭth′ō-fĕl, **brother of folly**), David's counselor who joined the conspiracy of Absalom. When his advice to Absalom that he pursue David immediately was disregarded, he went home and hanged himself (II Sam. 17:1-23).

AHITUB (à-hī′tŭb, **brother of goodness**). 1. Brother of Ichabod and son of Phinehas the son of Eli (I Sam. 14:3). 2. Father

of Zadok the high priest (II Sam. 8:17). 3. Father of another Zadok (I Chron. 6: 11,12), though he may be the same as 2.

AHLAB (à′làb), town of Asher (Jud. 1:31).

AHLAI (à′lī). 1. Father of one of David's soldiers (I Chron. 11:41). 2. Daughter of Sheshan who married her father's slave (I Chron. 2:31-35).

AHOAH (à-hō′à), son of Bela (I Chron. 8:4).

AHOHITE (à-hō′hīt), name given to descendants of Ahoah (II Sam. 23:9,28).

AHOLA (See Aholah).

AHOLAH (à-hō′là, **tent woman**), in God's parable to Ezekiel (Ezek. 23) a woman who represents Samaria, and with her sister Aholibah (Jerusalem) was accused of being unfaithful to Jehovah.

AHOLIAB (à-hō′li-àb), one who worked on the tabernacle (Exod. 31:6).

AHOLIBAH (See Aholah).

AHOLIBAMAH (à-hŏl′ĭ-bà′mà). 1. Wife of Esau (Gen. 36:2,18,25). 2. Edomite chieftain (Gen.'36:41).

AHUMAI (à-hū′mī), descendant of Judah (I Chron. 4:2).

AHURA MAZDA (à′hoo-rà màz′dà), the all wise spirit in the dualistic system of Zoroastrianism.

AHUZAM (à-hū′zàm), a Judahite (I Chron. 4:6).

AHUZZATH (à-hūz′àth), man who made a peace treaty with Isaac at Beersheba (Gen. 26:23-33).

AI (à′ī, ruin). 1. A city E of Bethel where Abraham pitched his tent when he arrived in Canaan (Hai, Gen. 12:8). It was the 2nd Canaanite city taken by the Israelites under Joshua (Josh. 7,8).

AIAH (à′yà). 1. A Horite (Ajah, Gen. 36: 24). 2. Father of Saul's concubine (II Sam. 3:7).

AIATH (à′yàth), feminine form of the city Ai (Isa. 10:28).

AIJA (à-ī′jà), another form of Ai (Neh. 11:31).

AIJALON (See Ajalon).

AIJELETH SHAHAR (à′jĕ-lĕth shà′hàr, **hind of the morning**), title of Psalm 22.

AIN (à′ĕn). 1. Landmark on the E border of the Promised Land (Num. 34:11). 2. City in S of Judah (Josh. 15:32).

AIN FESHKA, oasis on the W side of the Dead Sea, S of Khirbet Qumran.

AIN KAREM (à′ĕn kàr′ĕm), a Hebrew phrase meaning "the vineyards of Engedi" (S. of Sol. 1:14).

AIN KARIM (à′ĕn kàr′ĭm), a village in the hill country of Judea.

AJAH (à′jà), a Horite (Gen. 36:24).

AJALON, AIJALON (à′jà-lŏn). 1. City of Dan (Josh. 19:42). 2. Place in Zebulun (Judg. 12:12).

AKAN (à′kàn), descendant of the Horites of Mount Seir (Gen. 36:27).

AKELDAMA (See Aceldama).

AKHENATON (à′kĕn-à′t′n), name chosen by Amenhotep IV (1377-1360 B. C.) when he changed the religion of his country from polytheism to monotheism.

AKKAD (See Accad).

AKKUB (ăk'ŭb). 1. Son of Elioenai (I Chron. 3:24). 2. A Levite (I Chron. 9:17). 3. Another Levite (Neh. 8:7).

AKRABBIM (ăk-răb'ĭm), "ascent of" (Num. 34:4).

ALABASTER (ăl'a-băs'tẽr), stalagmitic carbonate of lime used by the ancients for vases and boxes for perfume and ointments (Matt. 26:7).

ALAMETH (ăl'a-mĕth). 1. Son of Becher (I Chron. 7:8). 2. Variant of Alemeth (I Chron. 8:36; 9:42).

ALAMMELECH (à-lăm'ĕ-lĕk), town of Asher (Josh. 19:26).

ALAMOTH (ăl'a-mŏth), musical term of uncertain meaning (Ps. 46:1; I Chron. 15:20).

ALCIMUS (ăl'sĭ-mŭs), high priest (I Macc. 7:9).

ALEMETH or ALMON (ăl'ĕ-mĕth, ăl'mŏn), a priests' city (I Chron. 6:60; Josh. 21:18).

ALEPH (a'lĕf), first letter of the Hebrew alphabet.

ALEXANDER THE GREAT. Son of Philip, King of Macedon. Lived from 356-323 B. C. He conquered the civilized world from Greece eastward to India. Described in Daniel 8.

ALEXANDRA (ăl-ĕg-zăn'drà), wife of Aristobulus, King of the Jews (105-104 B. C.).

ALEXANDRIA (ăl'ĕg-zăn'drĭ-à), a city founded by Alexander the Great in northern Egypt. It became the capital of the country and a great center of commerce and culture. Many thousands of Jews lived there.

ALGUM (See Plants of the Bible).

ALIAH (See Alvah).

ALIAN (See Alvan).

ALLEGORY. Description of a subject in the image of another rather than by direct statement (Gal. 4:24).

ALLELUIA (ăl-lē-lū'yà, praise ye Jehovah), same as Hallelujah, – an invitation to praise God (Ps. 104:35; 105:45).

ALLON (ăl'ŏn). 1. Prince of Simeon (I Chron. 4:37). 2. Town in Naphtali (Josh. 19:33). 3. Tree marking the burial place of Deborah (Gen. 35:8).

ALLON BACHUTH (See Allon 3).

ALMODAD (ăl-mŏ'dăd), son of Joktan (Gen. 10:26).

ALMON (ăl'mŏn), Levitical city in Benjamin (Josh. 21:18).

ALMON-DIBLATHAIM (ăl'mŏn-dĭb-là-thā'ĭm), one of the stops of the Israelites in their wilderness journeys (Num. 33:46,47,).

ALMOND TREE (See Plants).

ALMS (ăhms), charitable relief of the poor. Commended in both Testaments; it became legalistic among the Pharisees (Lev. 19:9, 10; Acts 9:36).

ALMUG (See Plants of the Bible).

ALOE (See Plants of the Bible).

ALOTH (a'lŏth), a district mentioned in I Kings 4:16.

ALPHA (ăl'fà), first letter of the Greek alphabet.

ALPHAEUS (ăl-fē'ŭs). 1. Father of Levi Mark 2:14). 2. Father of James the apostle (Matt. 10:3).

ALTAR (ăwl'tẽr, place of slaughter), a raised structure with a flat top, on which to place or sacrifice offerings to a deity. In OT times they were many and varied. The word is used 433 times in the KJV Bible. No sacrifices have been offered by the Jews since the destruction of the temple in A. D. 70.

ALTASCHITH (ăl-tăs'chĭth), a title notation in Psalms 57,58,59,75. Meaning uncertain.

ALUSH (a'lŭsh), a desert campsite of the Israelites (Num. 33:13,14).

ALVAH, ALIAH (ăl'và), prince of Edom (Gen. 36:40).

ALVAN, ALIAN (ăl'văn), a Horite (Gen. 36:23).

AMAD (a'măd), town of Asher (Josh. 19:26).

AMAL (a'măl), an Asherite (I Chron. 7:35).

AMALEK (ăm'a-lĕk), son of Eliphaz (Gen. 36:12).

AMALEKITES (à-măl'ĕk-ĭts), an ancient and nomadic marauding people dwelling mainly in the Negeb from the times of Abraham to Hezekiah, c. 2000-700 B. C. They are frequently mentioned in the history of Israel (Exod. 17:8ff.; Num. 14:45; I Sam. 15).

AMAM (a'măm), town in Judah (Josh. 15:26).

AMANA, AMANAH (See Abana).

AMANA (à-mä'nà), mountain near Lebanon (S. of Sol. 4:8).

AMARANTHINE (ăm-à-răn'thĭn, fadeth not away), an inheritance (I Pet. 1:4), glory (I Pet. 5:4).

AMARIAH (ăm'a-rī'àh). 1. Ancestor of Ezra (I Chron. 6:7,11,52; Ezra 7:3.). 2. A Levite (I Chron. 23:19). 3. Chief priest (II Chron. 19:11). 4. Levite (II Chron. 31:15). 5. A man guilty of intermarrying (Ezra 10:42). 6. Covenant signer (Neh. 10:3). 7. Levite (Neh. 12:2). 8. Son of Hezekiah (Zeph. 1:1).

AMARNA, TELL EL (à-mär'nà, tĕl ĕl, the hill amarna), the modern name for the ancient capital of Amenhotep IV (c. 1387-1366 B. C.), where in 1887 a large number of clay tablets containing the private correspondence between the ruling Egyptian Pharaohs and the political leaders in Palestine were discovered.

AMASA (à-mä'sà). 1. Captain of the rebel forces under Absalom. He was later killed by Joab (II Sam. 17:25; 20:4-12). 2. Prince of Ephraim (II Chron. 28:12f).

AMASAI (à-măs'ă-ĭ). 1. An officer who assured David of his loyalty to him (I Chron. 12:18). 2. A trumpeter (I Chron. 15:24). 3. Levite in the time of Hezekiah (II Chron. 29:12).

AMASHAI (à-măsh'à-ĭ), priest in Nehemiah's time (Neh. 11:13).

AMASIAH (ăm'à-sī'à), a captain under Jehoshaphat (II Chron. 17:16).

AMAZIAH (ăm-à-zī'à, whom Jehovah strengthens). 1. Ninth king of Judah; co-regent with his father Joash for at least a year; ruled for 29 years. The account of his life is found chiefly in II Kings 14 and II Chronicles 25. He was killed in a conspiracy. 2. Priest of Bethel in the reign of Jeroboam II (Amos 7:10-17). 3. A Simeonite (I Chron. 4:34,43). 4. Levite in the time of David (I Chron. 6:45,48).

AMBASSADOR, an envoy or messenger (II Chron. 35:21; Isa. 18:2; II Cor. 5:20).

AMBER (ăm′bĕr), used only to describe the color of divine glory (Ezek. 1:4,27; 8:2).

AMEN (ā-mĕn, **confirm, support**), it generally means "so let it be," "truly," "indeed."

AMETHYST (See Minerals).

AMI or **AMON** (ā′mī), servant of Solomon (Ezra 2:57).

AMINADAB (See Amminidab).

AMITTAI (à-mĭt′ī), father of Jonah (II Kings 14:25; Jonah 1:1).

AMMAH (ăm′ā), a hill around Gibeon (II Sam. 2:24).

AMMI (ăm′ī, **my people**), symbolic name given to Israel (Hos. 2:1).

AMMIEL (ăm′ĭ-ĕl). 1. A Danite (Num. 13:12). 2. Father of Machir (II Sam. 9:4,5; 17:27). 3. Father of Bathshua or Bathsheba (I Chron. 3:5). 4. Tabernacle porter (I Chron. 26:5).

AMMIHUD (à-mī′hŭd). 1. Father of a chief of Ephraim (Num. 1:10). 2. Father of Shemuel (Num. 34:20). 3. A Naphtalite (Num. 34:28). 4. King of Geshur to whom Absalom fled (II Sam. 13:37). 5. Son of Omri (I Chron. 9:4).

AMMINADAB (à-mĭn′à-dăb). 1. Aaron's father-in-law (Exod. 6:23). 2. Prince of Judah (Num. 1:7; 2:3). 3. Son of Kohath (I Chron. 6:22). 4. Kohathite who helped in the return of the ark (I Chron. 15:10,11).

AMMISHADDAI (ăm-ĭ-shăd′ī), father of a tribal leader in Moses' time (Num. 1:12; 2:25).

AMMIZABAD (à-mĭz′à-băd), son of one of David's captains (I Chron. 27:6).

AMMON (ăm′ŏn), son of Lot (Gen. 19:38). Father of the Ammonites.

AMMONITES (ăm′ŏn-ĭts), name given to the descendants of Ammon (Gen. 19:38). They occupied territory just east of Moab; a nomadic people. Capital was Rabbath-Ammon. People were fierce, warlike, idolatrous – their chief idol was Molech, hostile to Israel. (Judg. 11:13; I Sam. 11:2; Jer. 40:14; Ezek. 25:1-7).

AMNON (ăm′nŏn). 1. Son of David who violated his half-sister Tamar (II Sam. 13). 2. Man of Judah (I Chron. 4:20).

AMOK (ā′mŏk), priest who returned with Zerubbabel from exile (Neh. 12:7,20).

AMON (ā′mŏn). 1. Successor and son of king Manasseh and father of king Josiah (II Kings 21:19-26; II Chron. 33:21-25). 2. Governor of Samaria (I Kings 22:15-28). 3. Servant of Solomon (Neh. 7:57-59); sometimes called Ami (Ezra 2:57).

AMON (ā′mŏn), a city thought by most scholars to be the same as No (Jer. 46:25). It was the capital of Egypt. Thebes is the Greek name.

AMORITE (ăm′ō-rīt, **mountain dwellers**), a people descended from Canaan (Gen. 10:16), whose kingdom at one time occupied the larger part of Mesopotamia and Syria, with their capital at Haran. Amraphel was one of their kings (Gen. 14:1). They were a very wicked people. Moses defeated them in battle; Joshua ended forever their hostilities against Israel (I Sam. 7:14; Josh. 11:1-14).

AMOS (ā′mŏs, **burden-bearer**), a prophet whose ministry occurred in the reign of Jeroboam II (c. 786-746 B. C.). By trade he was a herdsman and dresser of sycamore-fig trees, and he lived in Tekoa, not far from Jerusalem. He sternly rebuked the luxurious and careless living of the people of Samaria, and warned the Israelites to abandon their idolatry and return to God. He foretold the captivity of Israel. In his book of 9 chapters he indicts foreign nations and Judah and Israel (1-2); condemns wicked Samaria (3-5); foretells judgment and promises restoration and prosperity (6-9).

AMOZ (ā′mŏz), father of Isaiah (II Kings 19:2,20).

AMPHIPOLIS (ăm-fĭp′ō-lĭs, a city pressed on all sides), city of Macedonia not far from Philippi. Paul passed through it (Acts 17:1).

AMPLIAS (ăm′plĭ-ăs), a Christian to whom Paul sent a greeting (Rom. 16:8).

AMRAM (ăm′răm). 1. Father of Moses (Exod. 6:18,20). 2. Son of Bani (Ezra 10:34). 3. Son of Dishon (I Chron. 1:41).

AMRAPHEL (ăm′rà-fĕl), king of Shinar, one of 4 kings who captured Lot and his goods (Gen. 14).

AMULET (ăm′ū-lĕt), anything worn as a charm against evil, disease, witchcraft, etc. (Isa. 3:20; Jer. 8:17).

AMUN (See Amon).

AMZI (ăm′zī). 1. Descendant of a man whom David set over the service of song (I Chron. 6:44-46). 2. Ancestor of a priest in the second Temple (Neh. 11:12).

ANAB (ā′năb), city of the Anakim (Josh. 11:21).

ANAH (ā′nà). 1. Mother of Esau's wife (Gen. 36:2,14,25). 2. Son of a prince of Edom (Gen. 36:20,29). 3. Son of Zibeon (Gen. 36:24).

ANAHARATH (à-nā′hà-răth), town in the territory of Issachar (Josh. 19:19).

ANAIAH (à-nī′ah). 1. A priest (Neh. 8:4). 2. A Jew in Nehemiah's time (Neh. 10:22).

ANAK (ā′năk), ancestor of the Anakim (Num. 13:22,28,33).

ANAKIM (ăn′à-kĭm), giants dwelling in Canaan (Gen. 6:4; Num. 13:22; Josh. 15:13,14).

ANAMIN (ăn′à-mĭm), a people descended from Mizraim (Gen. 10:13).

ANAMMELECH (à-năm′ĕ-lĕk), one of the gods worshiped by the heathen people settled in Samaria by the king of Assyria (II Kings 17:31).

ANAN (ā′năn), a returned exile who sealed the covenant with Nehemiah (Neh. 10:26).

ANANI (à-nā′ni), son of Elioenai, of the family of David (I Chron. 3:24).

ANANIAH (ăn′à-ni′áh). 1. Father of Maaseiah (Neh. 3:23). 2. Town of Benjamin (Neh. 11:32).

ANANIAS (ăn′à-ni′ás, **Jehovah has been gracious**). 1. Husband of Sapphira (Acts 5:1-11). Both were struck dead for lying to Peter about some money they were giving to the church. 2. A Christian of Damascus through whom Paul's sight was restored (Acts 9:10-19). 3. High priest before whom Paul was tried in Jerusalem (Acts 23:1-5).

ANAT (ā′nàt), Babylonian-Assyrian god.

ANATH (ā′nàth), father of Shamgar (Judg. 3:31).

ANATHEMA (à-nàth′ĕ-mà, **anything devoted**), anything cursed or consigned to damnation (Lev. 27:28,29; I Cor. 12:3; 16:22).

ANÂTHOTH (ăn′à-thŏth). 1. City of Benjamin (Josh. 21:18). 2. A Benjamite (I Chron. 7:8). 3. Man of Anathoth (Neh. 10:19).

ANCHOR. An appliance for holding a ship in a particular spot by mooring it to the bottom of the sea (Acts 27:29,30,40; Heb. 6:19).

ANCIENT OF DAYS. God, as He appeared in a vision to Daniel (Dan. 7:9,13,22).

ANCIENTS. Old men of experience.

ANDREW (ăn′drŏŏ, **manly**), brother of Simon Peter; lived at Capernaum; was a fisherman; led to Christ by John the Baptist (John 1:40-42); became an apostle (Matt. 10:2). Tradition says he was crucified on an X-shaped cross, now called a St. Andrew's cross.

ANDRONICUS (ăn′drō-ni′kŭs), a Christian to whom Paul sends a greeting (Rom. 16:7).

ANEM (ā′nĕm), city of Issachar (I Chron. 6:73).

ANER (ā′nèr). 1. Brother of Mamre (Gen. 14:13,24). 2. Levitical city in Manasseh (I Chron. 6:70).

ANGEL. A supernatural or heavenly being a little higher in dignity than man. Angels are created beings (Ps. 148:2-5); spirits (Heb. 1:14); do not marry (Luke 20:34-36). Created holy (Gen. 1:31; Jude 6), some fell from their state of innocence (II Peter 2:4), and of these some are held in chains (II Peter 2:4), while others are free to oppose the work of God. Both Testaments tell much about angels. Good angels worship God and assist, protect, and deliver God's people (Gen. 19:11; Ps. 91:11). Evil angels oppose God and try to defeat His will and frustrate His plans (Dan. 10:12,13; Matt. 4:3).

ANGEL OF THE LORD. An oft-recurring phrase in the OT, usually referring to deity and yet distinguished from Jehovah (Gen. 16:7-14; 22:11-18; 31:11,13).

ANIAM (à-ni′ăm), a Manassehite (I Chron. 7:19).

ANIM (ā′nĭm), city in S Judah (Josh. 15:50).

ANIMALS OF THE BIBLE. Birds and insects are treated in separate articles. This one treats, first, mammals and then non-mammalian animals, including sponges, corals, mollusks, and three other classes of vertebrates besides mammals, viz., fishes, amphibians, and reptiles. All the animals mentioned in the KJV are included.

I. Mammals. **Apes.** The apes that Solomon got from Tarshish were probably the rhesus monkey of India (I Kings 10:22). **Ass.** Asses, along with zebras and horses, belong to the horse family. The domesticated ass or donkey has served man for thousands of years. It is surer footed on mountain trails and better at carrying loads than the horse. In ancient times asses were used for farm work and as saddle animals, while horses were usually reserved for war. **Badger.** The badger as we know it is not found in Bible lands. Where it is referred to in the OT, the goat is probably meant, and this is the translation of the RSV. **Bats.** Although they are mammals, they are named along with birds in the Scriptures. They are classified as unclean. **Bears.** The "Syrian Brown Bear," Ursus syriacus, is the bear of the OT. They were once numerous in Palestine. **Behemoth.** It is thought that either the hippopotamus or the elephant is meant (Job 40:17,23). **Boar.** Psalm 80:13 speaks of the wild boar from the forest, but other references imply domesticated swine (Mark 5:11-13; Luke 15:15,16). Israelites were forbidden to eat swine flesh. **Camel.** Camels were used for riding, burden bearing, and carrying mail; their hair was used in cloth making; and in some areas their flesh and milk were esteemed. Abraham and Job were rich in camels. Oriental cities often had little gates for admitting late travelers, after the main gates had closed. They were called "needle's eyes." To pass, the camel had to kneel down, be unloaded, and crawl through on its knees. **Cattle.** Cattle figure prominently in the Bible. Bullocks were used for sacrifices. Calves were valued for food, sacrifice, and idolatrous worship. Milk, butter, cheese, and leather gave cattle much of their value. Oxen were used not only for food and sacrifice, but for draft animals. **Chamois.** The chamois referred to in Deut. 14:4-6 was probably the mountain sheep of Egypt and Arabia known as the Barbary Sheep. **Coney.** Conies resemble the rabbit, except that they have short legs and ears and no tail. They are rock dwellers; vegetarians, and their jaw action resembles cud-chewing, but they do not have the stomach of ruminants. **Dogs.** They were probably the first domesticated animals, but in ancient times were known less as a loved house dog than as a despised outcast with prowling and filthy habits (Prov. 26:11). **Dragons.** The word when used in the Bible sometimes means a serpent-like, symbolical animal (Ps. 74:13; Ezek. 32:2), and sometimes a literal animal, in some instances the crocodile, in others the jackal. John uses the word for

Satan. **Dromedary.** This is a one-humped camel. It has longer legs and travels faster than the two-humped camel. **Elephant.** Elephants were much used in the Maccabean wars. There are frequent references to ivory in the Bible. It was highly valued and was an item of luxury. **Fallow Deer.** This term is changed to roebuck, the male of the roe deer, in the RSV (Deut. 14:5; I Kings 4:22,23). **Fox.** In Scripture the word sometimes refers to the common fox of Palestine, which is a member of the dog family, and sometimes the jackal. **Gazelle.** This is a swift, small antelope found in hot, barren places in the Old World. It can run as much as 45 miles an hour. **Goats.** Goats and kids are mentioned almost 200 times in the Bible. Milk, butter, cheese, and meat are obtained from goats. They were offered in sacrifice, and their hair was made into cloth. **Greyhound.** Mentioned in Prov. 30:31. It is not certain what animal is referred to. **Hare.** Rabbits are not native to Palestine; there are at least two species of hares. Israelites were forbidden to eat them. **Hart.** The harts mentioned in the Bible may have been either the red deer of Europe and Asia or the Syrian deer. They must have been plentiful in Palestine, as they were a daily item of food at Solomon's table. **Hind.** These are female deer; male deer being called harts or stags. Their swiftness is referred to in Ps. 18:33 and Hab. 3:19. **Horse.** Horses were tamed in central Asia at least 4,000 years ago. God warned the Israelites not to rely upon horses for war. Solomon, especially, disobeyed God and multiplied them. They were used mostly for purposes of war, but were also sometimes used in agriculture (Isa. 28:24-29), in idolatrous processions (II Kings 23:11), and for riding (II Kings 9:14-37). **Hyena.** The word does not occur in the Bible, although hyenas were abundant in Palestine. **Ibex.** This is a type of bearded wild goat. **Jackal.** This was the wild dog of warmer parts of the Old World. Jackals hunted in small packs and lived as scavengers. **Leopard.** Also called a panther, its color is tawny with black spots. It is a fierce, fearless, and very intelligent animal. **Leviathan.** It is not certain what animal is referred to. The crocodile has been suggested. Psalm 104:26 may refer to the sperm whale. **Lion.** In ancient times lions were numerous in Palestine, Syria, and Asia Minor, and they are often mentioned in Scripture. Their size and majestic bearing have won them the title, "King of Beasts." In the Bible the lion is often used as a symbol of might. **Mouse.** The mice mentioned in Scripture probably included a number of small rodents. The Philistines were ravaged by a scourge of mice when they took the ark from the Israelites. **Mole.** In Lam. 4:3 the RSV has "jackals"; in Isa. 2:20 the blind rat or mole rat of Southeastern Europe instead of the true mole of America is probably meant. **Monster.** In the ASV and

RSV "jackals" is used in place of "sea monsters." In Gen. 1:21 the RSV uses "sea monsters" instead of "great whale." **Mule.** A mule is a cross between a male donkey and a female horse. It is almost always sterile. Mules have been used since earliest times. Israelites were forbidden to breed them (Lev. 19:19), but they made use of them (II Sam. 13:29). **Pygarg.** The word means "white-rumped," and probably applies to some antelope such as the addax. The RSV translates it "ibex." **Roe.** This word appears in the KJV, but not in the RSV, where the word "gazelle" is used instead in most instances. **Satyr.** In Isa. 13:21 and 34:14 the KJV and RSV use "satyr" where the ASV uses "wild goat." Satyrs were half man and half goat in the myths of ancient Greece. In Lev. 17:7 and II Chron. 11:15 the same word is translated "devils." **Sheep.** Sheep are oftener mentioned in the Bible than any other animal. They were perhaps the earliest animal domesticated. Sheep were kept for their milk even more than for their flesh. They also provided wool, skins, and meat, and their horns were used for carrying oil and wine and as trumpets. They were also much used for sacrifice. The lamb is used as a symbol of Christ. **Swine.** The words "hog" and "pig" are not used in the Bible, but swine are often mentioned. They were regarded as unclean, and Israelites were forbidden to eat them. **Unicorn.** A fabulous animal with one horn. Instead of "unicorn" the ASV and RSV use "wild ox," which was possibly the auroch, an animal once plentiful in Palestine. When seen in profile, it appeared to have but a single horn, hence its name. **Weasel.** This is a small, slender-bodied, carnivorous animal that feeds on birds, mice, rats, and other vermin. For Israelites it was an unclean animal (Lev. 11:29). **Whale.** The word is used in the Jonah story for a great fish, although the ASV and RSV use "whale" at Matt. 12:40. The "great whales" of the KJV in Gen. 1:21 is "great sea-monsters" in the ASV. **Wolf.** This no longer seen in Palestine, although abundant in ancient times.

II. Non-Mammalian Animals. **Sponges.** Sponges were used for a variety of purposes in ancient times: padding for shields and armor, bathing, scrubbing floors, and drinking. **Corals.** They were highly valued by Hebrews and were sometimes ranked with precious stones (Job 28:18; Lam. 4:7; Ezek. 27:16). **Mollusks.** They included most of the shellfish except the crustaceans. Tyrian purple was made from the genera Murex and Purpura. Pearls are mentioned several times in the NT (Matt. 7:6; 13:45, 46). **Fishes.** While there are many references to fish in the Bible, no particular species is ever named. Fishing is often referred to, and fish were an important food staple in all Mediterranean lands. **Amphibians.** Two species of frogs and three of toads are reported from Egypt. One frog, rana esculenta, is found all over Europe, Syria, Palestine, and Egypt. **Reptiles.** The Northern Viper or Adder is common in Europe and Africa. The word adder is used for several different Hebrew words, and therefore it is difficult to identify the species meant. **Asp.** This refers to a poisonous reptile, very probably the Egyptian Cobra. **Chameleon.** Various species are found in Africa and Asia. The Nile Monitor attains a length of about 6 feet. **Cockatrice.** Some dreaded reptile is evidently meant in Isa. 11:8 and 59:5. **Gecko.** Probably a nocturnal lizard (Lev. 11:30). **Lizard.** Mentioned only in Lev. 11:30, and may refer to a gecko, crocodile, chameleon, or a lizard. **Serpent.** No single species mentioned in the Bible can be identified with certainty. **Tortoise.** An unclean animal (Lev. 11:29), rendered "great lizard" in the RSV. **Viper.** Probably a poisonous serpent.

ANISE (See Plants of the Bible).

ANKLET, an ornament for the ankles worn by women.

ANNA (ăn′à, grace), a widow and prophetess who at the age of 84 recognized Jesus as the Messiah when He was brought into the Temple (Luke 2:36-38).

ANNAS (ăn′ăs, gracious), high priest from A. D. 6 to about 15. Five of his sons and his son-in-law Caiaphas were also high priests. He is referred to as high priest in Luke 3:2 and Acts 4:6, but that is probably because as head of the family he was the most influential priest and still bore the title.

ANOINT. A practice common in the East, anointing was of three kinds: ordinary – after bathing, as a mark of respect (Luke 7: 46), for burial (Mark 14:8, 16:1), for shields; sacred – both things and people, such as prophets (I Kings 19:16), priests (Exod. 28:41), and kings (I Sam. 9:16); and medical – for the sick and wounded (Isa. 1:6; Luke 10:34). The words "Messiah" and "Christ" mean "the anointed one."

ANTELOPE (See Animals, Gazelles).

ANTICHRIST (against Christ). The word is found only in the writings of John (I John 2:18,22; 4:3; II John 7), and may mean either an enemy of Christ or one who usurps Christ's name and rights, but the idea conveyed by the word appears throughout Scripture. The OT reveals the general Jewish belief that in the end time some hostile person or power would bring an attack against God's people, but it would be crushed by Jehovah or His Messiah (Ps. 2; Ezek. 38,39; Zech. 12-14). Jesus warns against false Christs (Matt. 24:24; Mark 13:22). II Thess. 2:1-12 gives a full description of the working of Antichrist, under the name of the "Man of sin."

ANTI-LEBANON (See Lebanon).

ANTIOCH (ăn′tĭ-ŏk). 1. Antioch in Syria, the capital of Syria, built in 301 B. C., on the left bank of the Orontes. In 65 B. C. the Romans took the city and made it the capital of the Roman province of Syria. It became the third largest city in the Roman empire, with a population of 500,000. Paul and Barnabas labored there, and it was from there that Paul and his companions set out on his three missionary journeys. It was the first Gentile church. 2. Antioch near Pisidia, a town in S Asia Minor, situated in Phrygia, not far from Pisidia. Paul and Barnabas preached there on their first missionary journey (Acts 13:14-14:19). Paul must have visited the church there on his second and third missionary journeys (Acts 16:6; 18:23).

ANTIOCHUS (ăn-tĭ′ŏ-kŭs, withstander). 1. Antiochus III, the Great (223-187 B. C.), king of Syria; gained control of Palestine in 198 B. C. 2. Antiochus IV (Ephiphanes), son of Antiochus III (175-163 B. C.); his attempt to Hellenize the Jews led to the Maccabean revolt. 3. Antiochus V (Eupator), son of the above; after a brief reign he was slain.

ANTIPAS (ăn′tĭ-pàs), a contraction of Antipater. 1. An early Christian martyr of Pergamum (Rev. 2:13). 2. Herod Antipas, son of Herod the Great, he ruled Galilee and Perea from 4 B. C. to A. D. 39. See Herod.

ANTIPATER (See Herod).

ANTIPATRIS (ăn-tĭp′à-trĭs, belonging to Antipater), a city built by Herod the Great on the road between Jerusalem and Caesarea and named after his father. Paul was briefly imprisoned there (Acts 23:31).

ANTITYPE, that which is represented by a type.

ANTONIA, TOWER OF, a fortress castle connected with the Temple at Jerusalem, built by Herod the Great. It was garrisoned by Roman soldiers who watched the temple area (Acts 21:30ff).

ANTOTHIJAH (ăn′tŏ-thi′jà), son of Shashak, a Benjamite (I Chron. 8:24,25).

ANTOTHITE (ăn′tŏth-it), inhabitant of Anathoth (I Chron. 11:28; 12:3).

ANTS (See Insects).

ANUB (à′nŭb), son of Coz of the tribe of Judah (I Chron. 4:8).

ANVIL (ăn′vil), the word occurs in several senses in the OT; only once with the meaning of "anvil" (Isa. 41:7).

APELLES (à-pĕl′ĕz), a Roman Christian (Rom. 16:10).

APES (See Animals).

APHARSATHCHITES (àf′àr-săth′kĭts), colonists in Samaria who protested to Darius against the rebuilding of the Temple in Jerusalem (Ezra 4:9; 5:6; 6:6).

APHARSITES (à-fär′sĭts), Samaritans who protested the rebuilding of the Temple in Jerusalem (Ezra 4:9).

APHEK (à′fĕk, strength, fortress). 1. City NE of Beirut (Josh. 13:4). 2. City in Asher (Josh. 19:30; Judg. 1:31). 3. Town in the Plain of Sharon (Josh. 12:18). 4. Town in the Plain of Jezreel (I Sam. 4:1; 29:1).

APHEKAH (à-fē′kà), city in Judah (Josh. 15:53).

APHIAH (à-fī′à), ancestor of Saul (I Sam.

9:1).

APHIK (See Aphek).

APHRAH (ăf′rà), a town mentioned in parallelism with Gath in Micah 1:10.

APHSES (ăf′sēz), a Levite (I Chron. 24:15).

APOCALYPSE (See Apocalyptic Literature).

APOCALYPTIC LITERATURE. There are two types, canonical and uncanonical. The first includes Daniel and Revelation which give revelations of the secret purposes of God, the end of the world, and the establishment of God's Kingdom on earth. The second appeared between c. 200 B. C. and A. D. 200 and also purports to give revelations of the last times, the salvation of Israel, the last judgment, and the hereafter. Outstanding apocalypses are I Enoch, Jubilees, Assumption of Moses, Second Esdras, Apocalypse of Baruch, Second Enoch. The Testaments of the Twelve Prophets, the Psalms of Solomon (17th and 18th), and the Sibylline Oracles are also usually included in a discussion of apocalyptic literature. Certain characteristics mark them. They deal with the future; imitate the visions of the prophets; are written under the names of OT worthies; use symbolism; are Messianic.

APOCRYPHA (à-pŏk′rĭ-fà, **hidden, spurious**). Books and chapters interspersed among the canonical books of the OT in the Vulgate, but not found in the Hebrew OT. The Roman Catholic Church received as canonical at the Council of Trent (1546) all of these books except I and II Esdras and the Prayer of Manasseh. From the time of Luther Protestants have rejected their canonicity. They include: I and II Esdras, Tobit, Judith, Additions to the Book of Esther, The Wisdom of Solomon, Ecclesiasticus, Baruch, Epistle of Jeremiah, The Prayer of Azariah and the Song of the Three Young Men, Susanna, Bel and the Dragon, The Prayer of Manasseh, I and II Maccabees.

APOLLONIA (ăp′ō-lō′nĭ-à, **pertaining to Apollo**), a town of Macedonia 38 miles E of Thessalonica (Acts 17:1).

APOLLOS (à-pŏl′ŏs, **belonging to Apollo**), a learned Alexandrian Jew, instructed in the Christian faith by Aquilla and Priscilla at Ephesus, subsequently went to Corinth where he became a mighty preacher of the gospel. Before long an Apollos party arose which was a rival to the Pauline party, but there does not appear to have been any feeling of rivalry between Paul and Apollos. (Acts 18:26-28; I Cor. 3:4; I Cor. 16:12; Titus 3:13.)

APOLLYON (See Abaddon).

APOSTASY (à-pŏs′tà-sē, **a falling away**). There are many warnings against apostasy in the Bible (II Thess. 2:3; Jude). Among apostates in the Bible are Saul (I Sam. 15:11; Hymenaeus and Alexander (I Tim. 1:19,20); Demas (II Tim. 4:10).

APOSTLE (à-pŏs′l, **one sent forth, messenger**), one chosen and sent with a special commission as the fully authorized representative of the sender. The name appears in a twofold sense, as the official name of those 12 disciples chosen by Jesus to be with Him during His ministry, see Him after His resurrection, and to lay the foundations of His Church; and, in a broader sense, to designate Christian messengers commissioned by a community (Acts 13:3). Jesus is once called an apostle (Heb. 3:1). The names of the 12 are Simon Peter (Cephas, Bar-jona), Andrew, John, Philip, James, Bartholomew (maybe the same as Nathanael), Thomas (Didymus), Matthew (Levi), Simon Zelotes, Jude (Lebbaeus, Thaddeus), James the Less, Judas Iscariot (Matt. 10). Matthias took the place of Judas Iscariot (Acts 1:15-26). Paul was called to be an apostle (Acts 9; I Cor. 1:1; II Cor. 10-12). Scripture tells us little of the missionary work of most of the apostles, and tradition reveals little that is trustworthy. It appears that the majority died martyrs' deaths. In the early church they exercised and claimed a unique authority to teach and lay the foundations of the Church. Their office was not, and could not be, passed on to others. It was unique.

APOSTOLIC AGE, the period in the history of the Christian Church when the Apostles were alive.

APOTHECARY (à-pŏth′ĕ-kà-rē), a word that refers not to the selling of drugs, but to the making of perfumes (Exod. 30:25,35; 37:29; II Chron. 16:14; Neh. 3:8).

APPAIM (ăp′â-ĭm), son of Nadab (I Chron. 2:30).

APPAREL (See Dress).

APPEAL (à-pēl′). Moses provided for lower and higher courts (Exod. 18:26; Deut. 17: 8-13). In NT times the Sanhedrin was the highest court of the Jews; but every Roman citizen could appeal to the emperor, as Paul did (Acts 25:11).

APPEARING (See Eschatology).

APPELLATIO (ăp′ĕ-lā′tĭ-ō), the judicial process of appealing to a higher magistrate, as Paul did in Festus' court (Acts 25:1-12).

APPHIA (ăf′ĭ-à, ăp′fĭ-à), a Christian of Colossae (Philem. 2).

APPIAN WAY (ăp′ĭ-ăn), an ancient Roman road on which Paul traveled (Acts 28: 13-16).

APPII FORUM (ăp′ĭ-ī fō′rŭm), a town on the Appian Way c. 40 miles from Rome where Paul was met by Christians from Rome (Acts 28:15).

APPIUS, MARKET OF (See Appii Forum).

APPLE (See Plants).

APPLE OF THE EYE, the eyeball; symbolizing that which is precious and protected.

APRON (See Dress).

AQABAH, GULF OF (à′kà-bà), the eastern arm of the Red Sea, where Solomon's seaport was located (I Kings 9:26).

AQUEDUCT (ăk′wĕ-dŭkt), a channel made of stone to convey water to places where the water is to be used. Many fine Roman aqueducts survive.

AQUILA (ăk'wĭ-là, **eagle**), a Jewish Christian, a tentmaker by trade, who with his wife Priscilla labored with Paul at Corinth and was of help to Apollos and many others (Acts 18:2,18,26; Rom. 16:3,4; I Cor. 16:19; II Tim. 4:19).

AR (àr), a city or district of Moab (Num. 21:15; Deut. 2:9,18,19; Isa. 15:1).

ARA (ā'rà), an Asherite (I Chron. 7:38).

ARAB (ăr'ăb), city of Judah (Josh. 15:52).

ARABAH (ăr'à-bà, **desert plain**), name applying to the rift running from Mt. Hermon to the Gulf of Aqabah. It is a narrow valley of varying breadth and productivity. The Israelites made stops there in their wilderness wanderings, and Solomon got iron and copper from its mines. (Deut. 1:1,7; 11:30; Josh. 3:16; I Sam. 23:24; Jer. 39:4.)

ARABIA (à-rā'bĭ-à, **steppe**). Originally the N part of the peninsula between the Red Sea and the Persian Gulf (Isa. 21:13; Ezek. 27:21), but later the entire peninsula (Neh. 2:19; Acts 2:11; Gal. 1:17; 4:25). Its ill-defined border, proximity, and plundering population made it a major factor conditioning the history of Israel.

ARAD (ā'răd). 1. Descendant of Benjamin (I Chron. 8:15). 2. City c. 17 miles S of Hebron (Josh. 12:14; Judg. 1:16).

ARAH (ā'rà). 1. An Asherite (I Chron. 7:39). 2. Father of a family that returned from exile (Ezra 2:5; Neh. 7:10). 3. Jew whose granddaughter became the wife of Tobiah the Ammonite (Neh. 6:18).

ARAM (ā'răm). 1. Son of Shem (Gen. 10: 22,23). 2. Son of Kemuel, Abraham's nephew (Gen. 22:21). 3. An Asherite (I Chron. 7:34). 4. In KJV, for the Greek form of Ram (Matt. 1:3,4, ASV, RSV), called Arni in ASV, RSV of Luke 3:33. 5. Place in Gilead (I Chron. 2:23). 6. The name of Syria (Num. 23:7), and usually so designated (II Sam. 8:5; I Kings 20:20; Amos 1:5). The Aramaean people spread from Phoenicia to the Fertile Crescent, and were closely related to Israel, with whom their history was intertwined.

ARAMAIC (ăr'à-mā'ĭk), a Semitic language, closely related to Hebrew, which developed various dialects and spread to all of SW Asia. Aramaic portions in the OT are: Dan. 2:4-7:28; Ezra 4:8-6:18; 7:12-26; Jer. 10:11. Aramaic words occur in the NT (Mark 5:41; 15:34; Matt. 27:46; Rom. 8:15; Gal. 4:6; I Cor. 16:22). Aramaic was the colloquial language of Palestine from the time of the return from the exile.

ARAN (ā'răn), son of Dishan (Gen. 36:26,28).

ARARAT (ăr'à-răt), name applied to Armenia (II Kings 19:37; Isa. 37:38) and to its mountain range (Gen. 8:4). Noah's ark is supposed to have rested on Mt. Ararat (Gen. 8:4). The region is now part of Turkey.

ARATUS (ăr'à-tŭs), Greek poet from whom Paul quotes in Acts 17:28. He lived c. 270 B.C.

ARAUNAH (à-rô'nà), a Jebusite who sold a threshing floor to David to erect an altar (II Sam. 24:16-24). Called Ornan in I Chron. 21:15-25.

ARBA (àr'bà), giant ancestor of Anak (Josh. 14:15; 15:13; 21:11).

ARBATHITE (àr'bà-thīt), a native of Beth-arabah (II Sam. 23:31; I Chron. 11:32).

ARBITE (àr'bĭt), one of David's mighty men (II Sam. 23:35).

ARCH (See Architecture).

ARCHAEOLOGY (àr-kē-ŏl'ō-jĭ). Study of the material remains of the past by excavating ancient buried cities and examining their remains, deciphering inscriptions, and evaluating the language, literature, art, architecture, monuments, and other aspects of human life and achievement. Biblical archaeology is concerned with Palestine and the countries with which the Hebrews and early Christians came into contact. Modern archaeology began with Napoleon's expedition to Egypt, on which many scholars accompanied him to study Egyptian monuments (1798), and with the work of Edward Robinson in Palestine (1838, 1852). Discoveries of great importance which throw much light upon the Patriarchal Period are the Mari Tablets, the Nuzi Tablets, the Tell-el Amarna Tablets, and the Ras Shamra Tablets. The discovery of the Dead Sea Scrolls and the excavation of Qumran are the most recent archaeological finds of importance. Archaeology is of great help in better understanding the Bible, in dealing with critical questions regarding the Bible, and in gaining an appreciation of the ancient world.

ARCHANGEL (See Angels).

ARCHELAUS (àr'kē-lā'ŭs), son of Herod the Great; he ruled over Judea, Samaria, and Idumea from 4 B. C. to A. D. 6 (Matt. 2:22).

ARCHERS (àr'cherz), hunters or warriors with bow and arrow, weapons universally used in ancient times (Gen. 21:20; Judg. 5:11; I Sam. 20:17-42; Isa. 21:17). "Arrow" is often used figuratively (Job 6:4; Jer. 9:8), as is also "bow" (Ps. 7:12; 64:3).

ARCHEVITES (àr'kē-vīts), colonists in Samaria who complained to the king of Persia about the Jews' rebuilding of Jerusalem (Ezra 4:9).

ARCHI (àr'kĭ), perhaps the name of a clan in Ephraim (Josh. 16:2).

ARCHIPPUS (àr-kĭp'ŭs, **master of the horse**), an office bearer in the church at Colossae (Col. 4:17; Philem. 2).

ARCHITE (àr'kĭt), member of a clan in Ephraim (Josh. 16:2; I Chron. 27:33).

ARCHITECTURE. The materials of architecture in antiquity were wood, clay, brick (formed of clay, whether sun-baked or kiln-fired), and stone. The determining factor in the choice of material used was local availability. The homes of the poor had no artistic distinction. The wealthy and the nobility, however, adorned their palatial homes ornately with gold and ivory. Architectural remains – temples, city gates, arches, ziggurats, pyramids – survive intact in great abundance, and archaeology has uncovered the foundations of countless buildings. Each country had its own distinctive style of architecture. No architecture has surpassed that of Greece, although the temple of Solomon and the one rebuilt by Herod were universally admired.

ARD (ärd), son or grandson of Benjamin (Gen. 46:21; Num. 26:40).

ARDITE (är'dīt), descendant of Ard (Num. 26:40).

ARDON (är'dŏn), son of Caleb (I Chron. 2:18).

ARELI (à-rē'lī), founder of the Arelite tribal family (Gen. 46:16; Num. 26:17).

AREOPAGITE (är'ē-ŏp'à-jĭt), -gĭt), a member of the Areopagus (Acts 17:34).

AREOPAGUS (är-ē-ŏp'à-gŭs, hill of Ares). 1. The rocky hill of the Greek god of war Ares on the Acropolis at Athens. 2. The name of a council which met on Mars' Hill. In NT times it was primarily concerned with morals and education. Paul was brought before it (Acts 17:19).

ARETAS (är'ē-tās, virtuous), a Nabatean king, father-in-law of Herod Antipas (II Cor. 11:32).

ARGOB (är'gŏb). 1. A region in Bashan taken by the Israelites under Moses (Deut. 3:4) and given to the half-tribe of Manasseh (Deut. 3:13). 2. II Kings 15:25 refers either to a place or a person. The Heb. text is uncertain.

ARIDAI (à-rĭd'ā-ī), son of Haman killed by the Jews (Esth. 9:9).

ARIDATHA (à-rĭd'à-thà), another son of Haman killed by the Jews (Esth. 9:8).

ARIEH (à-rī'ē), either a person or a place. The text is uncertain (II Kings 15:25).

ARIEL (är'ĭ-ĕl, lion of God). 1. Leader under Ezra (Ezra 8:16,17). 2. In II Sam. 23:20 and I Chron. 11:22 the KJV, ASV, and RSV have varying readings because of the uncertainty of the text. 3. Figurative name for Jerusalem (Isa. 29:1,2,7).

ARIMATHEA (är'ĭ-mà-thē'à), home of Joseph who buried Jesus in his own tomb (Matt. 27:57; Mark 15:43). Its location is in doubt, but it is conjectured to be Ramathaim-zophim, c. 20 miles NW of Jerusalem.

ARIOCH (är'ĭ-ŏk). 1. King of Ellasar in Syria and confederate with Chedorlaomer (Gen. 14:1,4,9). 2. Captain under Nebuchadnezzar (Dan. 2:14-25).

ARISAI (à-rĭs'à-ī), son of Haman (Esth. 9:9).

ARISTARCHUS (är'ĭs-tär'kŭs, best ruler), a Thessalonian traveling companion of Paul (Acts 19:29; 20:4; 27:2; Col. 4:10; Philem. 24).

ARISTOBULUS (à-rĭs'tō-bū'lŭs, best counselor), a Roman Christian greeted by Paul (Rom. 16:10).

ARK (ärk). 1. Noah's ark was built of gopherwood and was 450 by 75 by 30 feet. Nothing is known about what happened to it after Noah abandoned it (Gen. 6-8). 2. The basket of bulrushes in which Moses was abandoned is also called an ark (Exod.

2:2-5). 3. The ark of the covenant was a chest containing the tables of the law, resting in the tabernacle or in the temple. It was made of wood and gold, and a mercy seat of gold was placed on top of it. Poles were used for carrying it. It was made after the golden calf was destroyed (Deut. 10:1). Besides the tables of the law, it later also contained the book of Law (Deut. 31:26), manna (Exod. 16:33), and Aaron's rod (Num. 17:10). The Israelites took it with them on their wilderness journeys. It rested in various places until David brought it to Jerusalem. For the Israelites it symbolized the presence of God. It is unknown what happened to it when the Temple was destroyed. Also called the ark of testimony (Exod. 25:16,22) and ark of God (I Sam. 3:3).

ARKITES (är'kīts), descendants of Canaan from Arka, a Phoenician town (Gen. 10:17; I Chron. 1:15).

ARM, used as a figure for might (Isa. 53:1; Ezek. 30:25).

ARMAGEDDON (är-mà-gĕd'ŏn, **Mount Megiddo**), a word found only in Rev. 16:16, for the final battleground between the forces of good and evil. Located on the S rim of Esdraelon, the scene of many decisive battles in the history of Israel (Judg. 5:19,20; 6:33; I Sam. 31; II Kings 23:29,30).

ARMENIA (är-mē'nĭ-à), a mountainous country N of Assyria, to which Sennacherib's sons fled after they murdered him (II Kings 19:37; Isa. 37:38).

ARMLET, BRACELET, an ornament usually for the upper arm, worn by both men and women (Exod. 35:22; Num. 31:50; II Sam. 1:10; Isa. 3:20).

ARMONI (är-mō'nī), son of Saul slain by the Gibeonites (II Sam. 21:8-11).

ARMOR-BEARER, adjutant who bore the armor of an officer and guarded him (Judg. 9:54; I Sam. 31:4; II Sam. 23:37).

ARMORY, a depository for weapons and valuables (Neh. 3:19; S. of Sol. 4:4).

ARMS, ARMOR. Hebrew offensive weapons: sword (Gen. 3:24; Exod. 17:13); rod – a stick loaded at one end (Ps. 23:4); sling (I Sam. 17:40,49; II Kings 3:25); bow and arrows (II Sam. 22:35); spear, lance, javelin or dart (Josh. 8:18; Judg. 5:8). Defensive armor: shield (Eph. 6:16); helmet (I Sam. 17:5); coat of mail (I Sam. 17:5,38); greaves (I Sam. 17:6); girdle (II Sam. 20:8).

ARMY. In Israel males (except Levites) were subject to military duty at the age of 20 (Num. 1:3,17). Army divisions were subdivided into thousands and hundreds, with respective officers (Num. 31:14). Until Israel got its first king it had no standing army, but whenever there was need God raised up men of special ability to save the country from its enemies. Down to the time of Solomon Israel's armies were composed mostly of footmen (I Sam. 4:10); later horsemen and chariots were added (II Sam. 8:4; I Kings 10:26,28,29). The

Roman army was composed of legions divided into cohorts, maniples, and centuries (Acts 10:1; 21:31).

ARNAN (àr'nàn), descendant of Solomon (I Chron. 3:21).

ARNON (àr'nòn), river flowing into the E side of the Dead Sea a little N of its center. It was the boundary between the Moabites and the Amorites in the time of Moses (Num. 21:13); later, between Israel and the Moabites (Deut. 2:24; Josh. 12:1).

AROD (à'ròd), ancestor of Arodites (Num. 26:17).

AROER (à-rō'ẽr, naked). 1. Town of Gad (Num. 32:34; Josh. 13:25). 2. Reubenite town on the Arnon (Deut. 2:36; Josh. 13:9). 3. Town in the S part of Judah (I Sam. 30:28).

ARPAD (àr'pàd), city near Hamath (II Kings 18:34; 19:13; Isa. 10:9; Jer. 49:23).

ARPHAXAD (àr-făk'sàd), son of Shem and ancestor of Abraham (Gen. 10:22; 11:10-13).

ARROW (See Arms).

ART. The six major arts are music, the dance, architecture, sculpture, painting, and literature. They can be classified as spatial (architecture, sculpture, painting) and temporal (music, literature), with the dance extending over both categories. Because of the commandment against representational art (Exod. 20:4), Israel did little with painting and sculptoring. Phoenician craftsmen helped Israel in its major architectural works. Dancing was practiced. Music reached a high development; but Israel's literature was not surpassed in all antiquity.

ARTAXERXES (àr-tà-zürk'sẽz), a proper name or possibly title, for several kings of Persia. Two, or possibly three, Persian kings are so named in the OT: the pseudo-Smerdis of Ezra 4:7-23; "Longimanus," who granted the requests of Ezra (7:6) and Nehemiah (2:1-8) to go to Jerusalem; and possibly another king who reigned before 516 B. C. (Ezra 6:14).

ARTEMAS (àr'tē-màs), a companion of Paul at Nicopolis (Titus 3:12).

ARTEMIS (àr'tē-mis), the Greek goddess of hunting, corresponding to the Roman Diana. Her largest and most famous temple was at Ephesus; it was regarded as one of the wonders of the ancient world (Acts 19:23-41).

ARTIFICER (See Occupations).

ARTILLERY (àr-til'ẽr-ē), a word referring to Jonathan's bow and arrows (I Sam. 20:40).

ARTISANS (See Occupations).

ARUBOTH (à-rŭb'ŏth), region in Judah assigned to provide food for Solomon (I Kings 4:10).

ARUMAH (à-rōō'mà), place near Shechem where Abimelech lived (Judg. 9:41).

ARVAD (àr'vàd), island off the coast of Phoenicia (Ezek. 27:8,11). Its people were descended from Ham (Gen. 10:18).

ASA (à'sà, healer). 1. Third king of Judah, reigning from 964-923 B. C. (I Kings 15:9-24; II Chron. 14:16). He began his reign

with a religious reformation (II Chron. 14:3-5; 15:1-17), and was a very godly king, in spite of his idolatrous ancestors. The first 10 years of his reign were peaceful; after that he was engaged in war with Zerah the Ethiopian (II Chron. 14:9-15) and the northern kingdom (I Kings 15). He died of a severe disease of the feet because he did not trust in the Lord (II Chron. 16:12-14). 2. Levite (I Chron. 9:16).

ASADIAH (à-sà-dī'à), ancestor of Baruch (Baruch 1:1).

ASAHEL (às'à-hèl). 1. Nephew of David; a valiant soldier (I Chron. 27:7); he was killed by Abner (II Sam. 2:18-23). 2. A teaching Levite (II Chron. 17:8). 3. Temple overseer (II Chron. 31:13). 4. Priest (Ezra 10:15).

ASAHIAH (às'à-hī'à), officer sent by Josiah to Huldah the prophetess about the Law (II Kings 22:12-14).

ASAIAH (à-sā'yà, whom Jehovah made). 1. A Simeonite (I Chron. 4:36). 2. Levite in the time of David (I Chron. 6:30). 3. A Shilonite (I Chron. 9:5). 4. Chief Levite in David's day who helped bring the ark to Jerusalem (I Chron. 15:6,11).

ASAPH (à'sàf). 1. A Levite in charge of music in the time of David and Solomon. Twelve psalms are credited to him (50,73-83). 2. Father of Hezekiah's recorder (II Kings 18:18). 3. Official under Persian king (Neh. 2:8). 4. In I Chron. 26:1 read Ebiasaph (cf. ch. 9:19).

ASAREEL (à-sà'rē-èl, ASV Asarel), descendant of Judah (I Chron. 4:16).

ASARELAH (às'à-rē'là, ASV Asharelah), Levite in David's time (I Chron. 25:2). Called Jesharelah in v. 14.

ASCENSION OF CHRIST (See Acts 1:6-11; Mark 16:19, Luke 24:50-52). The name given to that event in which Christ left the earth and returned to the Father. It was an actual physical return, and brings important benefits to believers.

ASENATH (às'ẽn-àth), wife of Joseph (Gen. 41:45-52) and mother of Manasseh and Ephraim.

ASER (à'sẽr), Greek form of Asher (q.v.).

ASHAN (à'shàn), city first assigned to Judah (Josh. 15:42), then to Simeon (Josh. 19:7; I Chron. 4:32), then became a Levitical city (I Chron. 6:59).

ASHBEA (àsh'bē-à), Judahite (I Chron. 4:21).

ASHBEL (àsh'bèl), son of Benjamin (Num. 26:38).

ASHCHENAZ (See Ashkenaz).

ASHDOD (àsh'dŏd, stronghold), one of the five chief cities of the Philistines (Josh. 13:3). Center of Dagon (fish-god) worship; ark taken there but returned (I Sam. 5:1-7); conquered by Uzziah (II Chron. 26:6); destruction predicted by Amos (1:8); captured by Sargon II of Assyria (Isa. 20:1); tried to hinder Jews in Nehemiah's time (Neh. 4:7-9; 13:23,24). Called Azotus in LXX and NT (Acts 8:40).

ASHDODITES (people of Ashdod).

ASHDOTH PISGAH (àsh'dŏth-piz'gà), slopes

or springs of Pisgah, a mt. range NE of the Dead Sea (Deut. 3:17; 4:49; Josh. 12:3).

ASHER, or **ASER** (ăsh′ẽr, ā′sẽr, happy, Aser in KJV of NT). 1. 8th son of Jacob (Gen. 30:12,13; 35:26). 2. Tribe descended from Asher (Josh. 19:24-31); territory in NW corner of Palestine.

ASHERAH (à-shē′rà). 1. Canaanite goddess. 2. Images of the goddess Asherah, whose worship was lewd (Exod. 34:13; I Kings 16:29-33).

ASHES. Figurative expression denoting grief, penitence, humiliation (Gen. 18:27; Esth. 4:3), destruction (Ezek. 28:18).

ASHIMA (à-shī′mà), god of Hamath, whose worship was brought to Samaria by king of Assyria c. 715 B. C. (II Kings 17:30).

ASHKELON, ASKELON, ASCALON (ăsh′kẽ-lŏn, ăs′kẽ-lŏn), one of the 5 chief cities of the Philistines, 12 miles N of Gaza; taken by tribe of Judah (Judg. 1:18), but retaken by Philistines, who held it through most of OT period; denounced by Amos (1:6-8), Zephaniah (2:4,7) and Zechariah (9:5). Destroyed A.D. 1270.

ASHKENAS (See Ashkenaz).

ASHKENAZ (ăsh′kē-năz). 1. Descendant of Noah (Gen. 10:3; I Chron. 1:6). 2. People associated with Ararat mentioned in Jer. 51:27).

ASHNAH (ăsh′nà), two towns of Judah (Josh. 15:33; 15:43).

ASHPENAZ (ăsh′pē-năz), head of eunuchs in court of Nebuchadnezzar (Dan. 1:3,7).

ASHRIEL (See Asriel).

ASHTAROTH or **ASTAROTH** (ăsh′tà-rŏth), city in Bashan, probably so named from having a temple to the goddess Ashtoreth (Deut. 1:4; Josh. 9:10; 12:4).

ASHTEROTH-KARNAIM (ăsh′tē-rŏth-kàr-nā′im), region of the Rephaim in Abraham's time (Gen. 14:5). Exact site unknown.

ASHTORETH (ăsh′tŏ-rěth), goddess of the Canaanites; male consort was apparently Baal, and the two were worshipped with lewd rites. Sometimes worshipped by Israelites (Judg. 2:11-23; I Sam. 7:3,4; I Kings 11:4-8). Josiah destroyed her places of worship (II Kings 23:13,14).

ASHUR (ăsh-ẽr′), descendant of Judah (I Chron. 2:24; 4:5).

ASHURBANIPAL (à-shōō-bā′nē-pàl, Ashur creates a son), king of Assyria, reigned from 668-626 B. C.; great lover of learning – his library (over 22,000 tablets) survives.

ASHURITES (ăsh′ur-īts), people belonging to Ishbosheth, son of Saul (II Sam. 2:9).

ASHURNASIRPAL II (à-shōōr-năs′ĭr-pàl), ruthless king of Assyria, reigned early in 9th cent. B. C.

ASHVATH (ăsh′văth), descendant of Asher (I Chron. 7:33).

ASIA (ā′zhà). 1. Continent E of Europe. 2. In NT for Asia Minor (Acts 19:26) – present-day Turkey, or Roman proconsular Asia in SW part of Asia Minor (Acts 20:4; I Cor. 16:19).

ASIARCHS (ā′shĭ-àrks, **chiefs of Asia**), civil and priestly officials of the Roman province

of Asia chosen yearly to preside over the national games and theatrical displays (Acts 19:31).

ASIEL (ā′sĭ-ĕl), Simeonite prince (I Chron. 4:35).

ASNAH (ăs′nà), head of a family that returned from the captivity (Ezra 2:50).

ASNAPPER (ăs-năp′ẽr), king of Assyria, usually identified with Ashurbanipal (Ezra 4:10).

ASP (See Animals).

ASPATHA (ăs-pā′thà), son of Haman (Esth. 9:7).

ASRIEL (ăs′rĭ-ĕl). 1. Descendant of Manasseh (Num. 26:31; Josh. 17:2). 2. Son of Manasseh, Ashriel (I Chron. 7:14).

ASS (See Animals).

ASSIR (ăs′ẽr). 1. Cousin of Moses (Exod. 6:24). 2. Ancestor of Samuel (I Chron. 6:23). 3. Son of Jeconiah (I Chron. 3:17).

ASSOS (ăs′ŏs), seaport of Mysia in Asia Minor (Acts 20:13,14).

ASSUR, ASSHUR (ăs′ûr, ăsh′ûr), the god of the Assyrians; the reputed founder of the Assyrians; the capital of Assyria; often the nation Assyria. (Gen. 10:11; I Chron. 1:17; Hosea 14:3).

ASSURANCE, a word meaning firmness of mind; confidence; trust (Isa. 32:17; Col. 2:2).

ASSYRIA (à-sĭr′ĭ-à), in KJV sometimes Asshur, Assur; its first capital was Assur, later, Nineveh. Originally located between the upper Tigris and Zab rivers, at its height it included all the land between the Black and Caspian Seas, Persian Gulf, and the Mediterranean Sea (including Egypt). Its people were Semites. Its kings often made war on Israel (II Kings 15:19, 29; 16:7,9; II Chron. 28:20); finally took the northern kingdom into captivity in 721 B. C. (II Kings 17:6; 18:11). Nineveh was taken in 612 B. C.

ASTARTE (See Ashtaroth, Ashtoreth).

ASTROLOGERS (ăs-trŏl′ō-jẽrz), those who try to find out the influence of the stars upon human affairs and of foretelling events by their positions and aspects. (Dan. 2:27; 4:7; 5:7,11; Isa. 47:12,13).

ASTRONOMY. There are many passages in the Bible which refer to some aspect of the subject (Gen. 1:16; Ps. 147:4; Ps. 19:1-6; Job 22:12; Isa. 13:10; Amos 5:8; I Cor. 15:41). Among astronomical problems that are unsolved are the long day of Joshua (Josh. 10:12-14), the return of the shadow on the sundial of Ahaz (Isa. 38:8), and the star that led the wise men to Bethlehem (Matt. 2:2).

ASUPPIM (à-sŭp′ĭm), storehouses at the S gate of the Temple (I Chron. 26:15,17; Neh. 12:25).

ASYNCRITUS (à-sĭng′krĭ-tŭs), Christian friend of Paul in Rome (Rom. 16:14).

ATAD (ā′tăd), name of a place E of the Jordan (Gen. 50:10,11).

ATARAH (ăt′à-rà), wife of Jerahmeel (I Chron. 2:26).

ATAROTH (ăt′à-rŏth). 1. City near Gilean

(Num. 32:3,34). 2. City on the border between Ephraim and Benjamin (Josh. 16:2). 3. Place on E border of Ephraim (Josh. 16:7). 4. Place near Bethlehem (I Chron. 2:54).

ATER (ā'tēr). 1. Ancestor of an exiled family (Ezra 2:16; Neh. 7:21). 2. Another such ancestor (Ezra 2:42; Neh. 7:45). 3. Jewish leader who sealed the covenant with Nehemiah (Neh. 10:17).

ATHACH (ā'thăk), city of Judah (I Sam. 30:30).

ATHAIAH (à-thī'à), son of Uzziah (Neh. 11:4).

ATHALIAH (ăth'à-lī'à). 1. The only woman who ever reigned over Judah. She was the wife of Jehoram king of Judah. She reigned for 6 years and was slain as she left the Temple. Her story is told in II Kings 8:18, 25-28; 11:1-20; II Chron. 22:1-23:21; 24:7. 2. A Benjamite (I Chron. 8:26). 3. Father of a returned exile (Ezra 8:7).

ATHENS (ăth'ĕnz), capital of Attica. Named after its patron goddess Athene. It centered around a rocky hill called Acropolis. The Athenians defeated the Persians in 490 and 480 B. C., and then built a small empire. Period of greatest glory was during the rule of Pericles (459-431). In 146 B. C. the Romans made it part of the province of Achaea. It continued to remain a great educational and cultural center. Paul visited there on his second missionary journey (Acts 17).

ATHLAI (ăth'là-i), a man who divorced his foreign wife (Ezra 10:28).

ATONEMENT (à-tōn'mĕnt, **to cover, cancel**), satisfactory reparation for an offense or injury; that which produces reconciliation (Exod. 30:16). In the Bible it means the covering of man's sins through the shedding of blood; in the OT, the blood of sacrificed animals; in the NT, the blood of man's Redeemer, Jesus Christ.

ATONEMENT, DAY OF, a Hebrew festival, instituted by Moses, and held on the 10th day of the 7th month, involving abstinence from labor, fasting, penitence and sacrifice for sin. The day marked the only entry of the high priest into the Holy of Holies (Lev. 16).

ATROTH (ăt'rŏth), town built by Gadites E of Jordan (Num. 32:35).

ATTAI (ăt'à-i). 1. Judahite (I Chron. 2:35, 36). 2. Gadite (I Chron. 12:11). 3. Brother of Judah king, Abijah (II Chron. 11:20).

ATTALIA (ăt'à-lī'à), seaport town of Pamphylia in S Asia Minor (Acts 14:25).

ATTIRE (See Dress).

AUGUSTUS CAESAR (ô-gŭs'tŭs sē'zẽr), 1st Roman emperor (27 B.C.-A.D. 14). Jesus was born during his reign (Luke 2:1).

AUL (ôl), obsolete variant of awl; a sharp piercing tool (Exod. 21:6; Deut. 15:17).

AUTHORIZED VERSION (See Bible, Translations of).

AVA (ă'và), region in Assyria from which people were brought to colonize Samaria (II Kings 17:24,31).

AVEN (ā'vĕn, **vanity**). 1. City of Heliopolis in Egypt (Ezek. 30:17). 2. Places of idolatry in Bethel (Hosea 10:5,8). 3. Place in Syria dedicated to heathen worship; perhaps Baalbek (Amos 1:5).

AVENGER (à-vĕn'jẽr), kinsman who felt obligated to avenge the death of man (Num. 35:11-34).

AVIM, AVIMS, AVITES (ā'vĭm, ā'vĭmz, ā' vĭts). 1. Ancient inhabitants of Gaza (Deut. 2:23; Josh. 13:3). 2. City of Benjamin (Josh. 18:23).

AVITH (ā'vĭth), capital city of Hadad in Edom (Gen. 36:35).

AWL (See Aul).

AX, chopping instrument (I Kings 6:7; Jer. 10:3).

AYIN (ā'yĕn). 1. 16th letter of Hebrew alphabet. 2. Place on N boundary of Palestine (Num. 34:11). 3. Town in Judah (Josh. 15:32).

AZAL (See Azel).

AZALIAH (ăz'à-lī'à), father of Shaphan the scribe (II Kings 22:3).

AZANIAH (ăz'à-nī'à), Levite (Neh. 10:9).

AZAREEL, AZARAEL (à-zā'rē-ĕl). 1. Levite (I Chron. 12:6). 2. Musician (I Chron. 25:18). 3. Captain in David's army (I Chron. 27:22). 4. Man who divorced his foreign wife (Ezra 10:41). 5. Priest (Nah. 11:13). 6. Musician (Neh. 12:36).

AZAREL (Same as Azareel).

AZARIAH (ăz'à-rī'à, **Jehovah hath helped**). 1. Man of Judah (I Chron. 2:8). 2. King of Judah. See Uzziah. 3. Son of Jehu (I Chron. 2:38). 4. Son of Ahimaaz (I Chron. 6:9). 5. Levite (I Chron. 6:36). 6. Son of Zadok (I Kings 4:2). 7. High priest (I Chron. 6:10). 8. Son of Nathan (I Kings 4:5). 9. Prophet (II Chron. 15:1-8). 10. Sons of King Jehoshaphat (II Chron. 21:2). 11. Son of Jehoram (II Chron. 22:6). 12. Son of Jeroham (II Chron. 23:1). 13. Son of Johanan (II Chron. 28:12). 14. Levite (II Chron. 29:12). 15. High priest (II Chron. 26:16-20). 16. Son of Hilkiah (I Chron. 6:13,14). 17. Opponent of Jeremiah (Jer. 43:2). 18. Jewish captive of Babylon (Dan. 1:7). 19. Son of Maaseiah (Neh. 3:23). 20. Levite (Neh. 8:7). 21. Priest (Neh. 10:2). 22. Prince of Judah (Neh. 12:32,33).

AZAZ (ā'zăz), Reubenite (I Chron. 5:8).

AZAZEL (à-zā'zĕl, KJV, **scapegoat**). Word of uncertain meaning found only in Lev. 16: 8,10,26 in connection with one of the goats chosen for the service of the Day of Atonement. It has been interpreted both personally and impersonally as meaning 1) an evil spirit, 2) removal, 3) devil.

AZAZIAH (ăz'à-zī'à). 1. Harper (I Chron. 15:21). 2. Chief of Ephraim (I Chron. 27:20). 3. Levite (II Chron. 31:13).

AZBUK (ăz'bŭk), father of a Nehemiah (Neh. 3:16).

AZEKAH (à-zē'kà), town in NW Judah (Josh. 10:10,11; 15:35; I Sam. 17:1).

AZEL (ā'zĕl). 1. Descendant of Jonathan (I Chron. 8:37; 9:43). 2. Place near Jerusalem (Zech. 14:5).

AZGAD (ăz'găd), ancestral head of a family of postexilic Jews (Ezra 2:12; 8:12).

AZIEL (ĕ'zĭ-ĕl), Levite (I Chron. 15:20).

AZIZA (à-zĭ'zà), man who divorced his foreign wife (Ezra 10:27).

AZMAVETH (ăz-mā'vĕth). 1. One of David's heroes (II Sam. 23:31). 2. Benjamite (I Chron. 12:3). 3. David's treasurer (I Chron. 27:25). 4. Descendant of Jonathan (I Chron. 8:36). 5. Place N of Anathoth (Ezra 2:24; Neh. 12:29).

AZMON (ăz'mŏn), town on S border of Judah (Num. 34:4,5; Josh. 15:4).

AZNOTH-TABOR (ăz'nŏth-tā'bôr), place near Mt. Tabor (Josh. 19:34).

AZOR (ā'zôr), post-exilic ancestor of Christ (Matt. 1:13,14).

AZOTUS (à-zō'tŭs), also called Ashdod, one of the 5 chief Philistine cities, half way between Joppa and Gaza. Home of Anakim; assigned to Judah; Uzziah broke down its walls (II Chron. 26:6); Sargon besieged

it (Isa. 20:1); opposed rebuilding of the walls of Jerusalem (Neh. 4:7); Philip preached there (Acts 8:40).

AZRIEL (ăz'rĭ-ĕl). 1. Chieftain of Manasseh (I Chron. 5:24). 2. Naphtalite (I Chron. 27:19). 3. Man in Jeremiah's time (Jer. 36:26).

AZRIKAM (ăz'rĭ-kăm). 1. Son of Neariah (I Chron. 3:23). 2. Descendant of Saul (I Chron. 8:38; 9:44). 3. Levite (I Chron. 9:14). 4. Officer of Ahaz (II Chron. 28:7).

AZUBAH (à-zū'bà). 1. Wife of Caleb (I Chron. 2:18,19). 2. Mother of Jehoshaphat (I Kings 22:42).

AZUR (See Azzur).

AZZAH (See Gaza).

AZZAN (ăz'ăn), father of a prince of Issachar (Num. 34:26).

AZZUR (ăz'ĕr). 1. Father of Hananiah (Jer. 28:1). 2. Father of Jaazaniah (Ezek. 11:1). 3. Signer of the covenant (Neh. 10:17).

B

BAAL (bā'ăl, **lord, possessor, husband**). 1. Appears in the OT with a variety of meanings: "master" or "owner" (Exod. 21:28,34; Judg. 19:22), "husband" (Exod. 21:3; II Sam. 11:26). 2. Usually, however, it refers to farm god of the Phoenicians and Canaanites, responsible for crops, flocks, fecund farm families. Each locality had its own Baal. The Baalim were worshipped on high places with lascivious rites, self-torture, and human sacrifice. Altars to Baal were built in Palestine; Jezebel in Israel and Athaliah in Judah championed Baal worship (I Kings 16:31,32; II Chron. 17:3). 3. Descendant of Reuben (I Chron. 5:5). 4. Benjamite (I Chron. 8:30). 5. In composition it is often the name of a man and not of Baal, e.g. Baal-hanan (I Chron. 1:49).

BAALBEK (băl'bĕk, **city of Baal**), city of Coele-Syria, c. 40 miles NW of Damascus, famous for its ruins.

BAALE OF JUDAH (bā'ăl-jŏŏ'dà), town on N border of Judah, same as Baalah and Kiriath-baal and Kirjath-jearim (II Sam. 6:2; I Chron. 13:6).

BAAL-GAD (bā'ăl-găd, **Gad is Baal**), place near Mt. Hermon (Josh. 11:17; 12:7; 13:5).

BAAL-HAMON (bā'ăl-hā'mŏn), place where Solomon had a vineyard (S. of Sol. 8:11).

BAAL-HANAN (bā'ăl-hā'năn). 1. King of Edom (Gen. 36:38). 2. Overseer of David (I Chron. 27:28).

BAAL-HAZOR (bā'ăl-hā'zôr), place near Ephraim (II Sam. 13:23).

BAAL-HERMON (bā'ăl-hûr'mŏn), place marking NW limit of Manasseh (Judg. 3:3).

BAALI (bā'à-lĭ, **my lord**), name often given to Jehovah by Israel (Hos. 2:16).

BAALIS (bā'à-lĭs), king of Ammonites (Jer. 40:14).

BAAL-MEON (bā'ăl-mē'ŏn), city on frontiers of Moab (Num. 32:38), called Beth-meon in Jer. 48:23 and Beon in Num. 32:3.

BAAL-PEOR (bā'ăl-pē'ôr, **Baal of Peor**), Mo-

abite deity worshiped on Mt. Peor (Num. 25:1-9; Ps. 106:28).

BAAL-PERAZIM (bā'ăl-pe-rā'zĭm), place near valley of Rephaim (II Sam. 5:18-20).

BAAL-SHALISHA (bā'ăl-shăl'ĭ-shà), place in Ephraim (II Kings 4:42-44).

BAAL-TAMAR (bā'ăl-tā'màr), place in Benjamin near Gibeah and Bethel (Judg. 20:33).

BAAL-ZEBUB (bā'ăl-zē'bŭb, **Baal, or lord of flies**), name under which Baal was worshiped by the Philistines of Ekron (II Kings 1:2,3,6).

BAAL-ZEPHON (bā'ăl-zē'fŏn), place near Red Sea (Exod. 14:2,9; Num. 33:7).

BAANA (bā'à-nà). 1. Officers of Solomon (I Kings 4:12). 2. Father of Zadok (Neh. 3:4).

BAANAH (bā'à-nà, **son of oppression**). 1. Israelite who with his brother murdered Ish-bosheth (II Sam. 4). 2. Father of Heleb (II Sam. 23:29; I Chron. 11:30). 3. Jew who returned from the captivity (Ezra 2:2). 4. An officer of Solomon (I Kings 4:16).

BAARA (bā'à-rà), wife of Shaharaim (I Chron. 8:8).

BAASEIAH (bā'à-sē'yà), ancestor of Asaph the musician (I Chron. 6:40).

BAASHA (bā'à-shà, **boldness**), 3rd king of Israel; exterminated house of Jeroboam; made war on Asa, king of Judah (I Kings 15:16-21); idol-worshiping; reigned 24 years; after his death his whole house was killed by Zimri (I Kings 16:1-12).

BABEL, TOWER OF (bā'bĕl, **gate of God**), tall brick structure built on plain of Shinar not long after the Deluge (Gen. 11:1-9). Babylonian ziggurats were probably imitations of this tower.

BABYLON (băb'ĭ-lŏn), Greek form of "Babel;" name of city and country of which it was the capital. First mentioned in Gen. 10:10; Hammurabi became ruler in 18th cent.; reached height of power under Nebuchadnezzar II (605-562 B. C.); conquered by Cyrus of Persia, 539 B. C.; often mentioned in prophecy (Isa. 13:1, 19; 14:22; 21; 46; 47; Jer. 50; 51); famous for hanging gardens, temples, palace; ruins remain. In NT the symbol of opposition to God (I Pet. 5:13; Rev. 14:8).

BACA (bā′kà, balsam tree), unknown valley of Palestine (Ps. 84:6); refers figuratively to an experience of sorrow turned into joy.

BACHRITES (băk′rīts), family of Ephraim (Num. 26:35).

BADGER (See Animals).

BAG, sack or pouch made for holding anything. Many kinds are mentioned in Scripture (Deut. 25:13; II Kings 5:23; Matt. 10:10 "scrip").

BAHURIM (bà-hū′rĭm), place on the road from Jerusalem to Jericho (II Sam. 16:5; 19:16).

BAJITH (bā′jĭth, house), may be textual error for bath, "daughter" (Isa. 15:2).

BAKBAKKAR (băk-băk′ĕr), Levite (I Chron. 9:15).

BAKBUK (băk′bŭk), head of a family that returned from the captivity (Ezra 2:51).

BAKBUKIAH (băk′bū-kī′à), Levite (Neh. 11:17).

BAKER (See Occupations and Professions).

BALAAM (bā′lăm, perhaps devourer), son of Beor from Pethor on the Euphrates (Deut. 23:4), a diviner employed by king Balak to curse Israel, but God caused him to bless instead (Num. 22-24); tried to turn Israelites from Jehovah (Num. 31), and was killed by them. In NT he is held up as an example of the pernicious influence of hypocritical teachers who attempt to lead God's people astray (Jude 11; II Peter 2:15).

BALAH (bā′là), town in SW Palestine (Josh. 19:3).

BALAK (bā′lăk, devastator), king of Joab who hired Balaam to curse the Israelites (Num. 22-24; Judg. 11:25).

BALANCE (băl′ăns), instrument for weighing (Lev. 19:36; Ezek. 45:10; Micah 6:11).

BALD LOCUST (See Insects).

BALDNESS. Israelites were forbidden to shave the head (Lev. 21:5; Deut. 14:1) as a sacrifice to the deity; but shaving of the head was done as a mark of mourning for the dead (Lev. 21:5; Isa. 15:2). Nazirites who completed a vow offered their shaven hair to Jehovah (Num. 6:18; cf. Acts. 18:18; 21:24).

BALM (bàm), odoriferous resin used as an ointment for wounds (Jer. 51:8).

BAMAH (bā′mà), high place of idolatrous worship (Ezek. 20:29).

BAMOTH-BAAL (bā′mŏth-bā′ăl), place near Arnon river (Num. 21:19; 22:41 RSV).

BAND, a company of men (Acts 10:1; 27:1).

BANI (bā′nī, posterity). 1. Gadite (II Sam. 23:36). 2. Levite (I Chron. 6:46). 3. Descendant of Judah (I Chron. 9:4). 4. Levite (Neh. 3:17). 5. Levite (Neh. 9:4). 6. Levite (Neh. 11:22). 7. Levite (Neh. 10:13). 8. Man who signed covenant (Neh. 10:14). 9. Ancestor of Jews who returned from captivity (Ezra 10:29). 10. Descendant of

a Bani (Ezra 10:38).

BANK. A primitive kind of banking was known in ancient times. Israelites could not charge each other interest (Exod. 22:25), but could charge Gentiles (Deut. 23:20).

BANNER. Banners, ensigns, or standards were used in ancient times for military, national, and ecclesiastical purposes very much as they are today (Num. 2:2; Isa. 5:26; 11:10; Jer. 4:21).

BANQUET (băng′kwĕt). Social feasting was common among the Hebrews. There were feasts on birthdays (Gen. 40:20), marriages (Gen. 29:22), funerals (II Sam. 3:35), grape-gatherings (Judg. 9:27), sheep-shearing (I Sam. 25:2,36), sacrifices (Exod. 34:15), and on other occasions. Often a second invitation was sent on the day of the feast (Luke 14:17). Guests were welcomed with a kiss (Luke 7:45) and their feet were washed (Luke 7:44). Banquets were often enlivened with music, singing, and dancing (Luke 15:23-25).

BAPTISM (băp′tĭzm). The word baptizo in Jewish usage first appears in the Mosaic laws of purification (Exod. 30:17-21; Lev. 11:25), where it means washing or cleansing. Jews baptized proselytes. John's baptism was connected with repentance so that Jews might be spiritually prepared to recognize and receive the Messiah, and it differed from the baptism of Jesus (Luke 3:16; John 1:26). Christian baptism symbolizes union with Christ (Gal. 3:26,27), remission of sins (Acts 2:38), identification with Christ in His death to sin and resurrection to new life (Rom. 6:3-5), and becoming a member of the body of Christ (I Cor. 12:13). The blessings of baptism are received by faith (Rom. 6:8-11).

BAR- (bàr), an Aramaic word meaning "son;" in the NT used as a prefix (Matt. 16:17).

BARABBAS (bàr-ăb′ás, son of the father), a prisoner released by Pilate at the trial of Jesus (Matt. 27:16; Mark 15:15).

BARACHEL (bàr′à-kĕl), father of Elihu, friend of Job (Job 32:2,6).

BARACHIAS (bàr′à-kī′ăs), father of Zachariah, priest slain between Temple and altar (Matt. 23:35).

BARAK (bàr′ăk, lightning), Israelite who defeated Sisera at the command of Deborah the judge (Judg. 4,5; Heb. 11:32).

BARBARIAN (bàr-bàr′ĭ-ăn). Originally, any-one who did not speak Greek (Rom. 1:14); later, one who was not a part of the Graeco-Roman culture (Col. 3:11).

BARBER (See Occupations and Professions).

BAR-JESUS (bàr′jē′sŭs, son of Jesus), Jewish magician in court of Sergius Paul (Acts 13:6-12).

BAR-JONA (bàr′jō′nà, son of Jonah), surname of the Apostle Peter (Matt. 16:17).

BARKOS (bàr′kŏs), founder of a family that returned from the captivity (Ezra 2:53).

BARLEY (See Plants).

BARNABAS (bàr′nà-băs, son of exhortation or consolation), Levite from Cyprus (Acts 4:36); early friend and co-worker of Paul

(Acts 9:27); worked with Paul at Antioch (Acts 11:22-26) and on Paul's 1st missionary journey (Acts 13-14); went to Jerusalem council with Paul (Acts 15); left Paul because he would not take Mark on 2nd missionary journey (Acts 15:36-41). Paul speaks highly of him in epistles (I Cor. 9:6; Gal. 2:1,9,13; Col. 4:10).

BARREL (băr′ĕl), a large earthenware water jar (I Kings 17:12-16; 18:33).

BARSABAS (băr-săb′ăs, son of Sabas). 1. Surname of Joseph (Acts 1:23) and of Judas (Acts 15:22).

BARTHOLOMEW (băr-thŏl′ŏ-mū, son of Tolmae), one of the 12 apostles (Matt. 10:3); perhaps Nathanael (John 1:45).

BARTIMAEUS (băr′tĭ-mē′ŭs, son of Timaeus), blind man healed by Jesus (Mark 10:46-52).

BARUCH (băr′ŭk, blessed). 1. Trusted friend and amanuensis of Jeremiah (Jer. 32:12; 36;4ff). 2. Man who helped Nehemiah rebuild walls of Jerusalem (Neh. 3:20). 3. Priest (Neh. 10:6). 4. Judahite (Neh. 11:5).

BARUCH, BOOK OF, Jewish apocryphal book found in the LXX, purporting to be a treatise by Jeremiah's scribe Baruch to Jewish exiles in Babylon.

BARZILLAI (băr-zĭl′ă-ĭ, made of iron). 1. Wealthy Gileadite who was friendly to David (II Sam. 17:27-29; 19:31-40). 2. Returning exile in Ezra's time (Ezra 2:61, 62). 3. A Meholathite whose son married Saul's daughter (II Sam. 21:8).

BASEMATH (băs′ē-măth), see Bashemath.

BASHAN (bă′shăn, smooth, fertile land), region E of the Sea of Galilee from Gilead to Mt. Hermon; fertile and noted for fine cattle (Deut. 32:14; Ezek. 39:18); assigned to tribe of Manasseh (Josh. 13:29,30). Included in kingdom of Herod the Great and his son Philip.

BASHAN-HAVOTH-JAIR (bă′shăn-hă′vŏth-jă′ĭr), group of unwalled towns in the NW part of Bashan (Num. 32:41; Deut. 3:14; Josh. 13:30).

BASHEMATH (băsh′ē-măth). 1. Wife of Esau (Gen. 26:34). 2. Ishmael's daughter (Gen. 36:3,4,13,17). Called Mahalath in Gen. 28:9. 3. Solomon's daughter, called Basmath (I Kings 4:15).

BASIN (bă′sin), a wide hollow vessel for holding water for washing and other purposes (Exod. 24:6; "bowls," Zech. 9:15; John 13:5).

BASKET (băs′kĕt), baskets were made of various materials – leaves, reeds, rushes, twigs, ropes; and were of various sizes and shapes (Deut. 26:2; "pots," Ps. 81:6; Matt. 14:20; John 6:13).

BASMATH (băs′măth), (I Kings 4:15; elsewhere spelled Bashemath).

BASTARD (băs′tĕrd, child of incest), bastards and their descendants to the 10th generation were excluded from the assembly of the Lord (Deut. 23:2); had no claim to paternal care or the usual privileges and discipline of legitimate children.

BAT (See Animals).

BATH (See Weights and Measures).

BATH, BATHING, BATHE. Bathing for physical cleanliness or refreshment is not often mentioned in the Bible, where most references to bathing are to partial washing. Bathing in the Bible stands chiefly for ritual acts – purification of ceremonial defilement (Exod. 30:19-21; Lev. 16:4,24; Mark 7:3,4).

BATHRABBIM (băth′răb′ĭm), name of a gate of Heshbon (S. of Sol. 7:4).

BATH-SHEBA (băth-shē′bă, daughter of Sheba), wife of Uriah the Hittite, a soldier in David's army, with whom David committed adultery (II Sam. 11). After Uriah's murder David married her and had 4 sons by her (II Sam. 5:14; I Chron. 3:5) after the first one died; Nathan and Solomon were two of them (Matt. 1:6; Luke 3:31).

BATH-SHUA (băth′shōō-ă). 1. In KJV Gen. 38:2 and I Chron. 2:3 have "daughter of Shua." 2. In I Chron. 3:5, the mother of Solomon. Probably a scribal error for Bath-sheba.

BATTERING RAM (See War, Warfare).

BATTLE. In ancient Israel military science was relatively simple. A force was usually divided into two attacking divisions, the one in the rear serving as a reserve. Spearmen probably formed the first line, bowmen or archers the second, and slingers the third. Sometimes a battle was preceded by duels between individuals (I Sam. 17:3ff; II Sam. 2:14ff). The faint-hearted were exempt (Deut. 20:8). The ark was often taken along to insure victory.

BATTLE-AX (See Arms and Armor).

BATTLE-BOW (See Arms and Armor).

BATTLEMENT, parapet surmounting ancient fortified buildings and city walls; required on roofs of houses (Deut. 22:8).

BAVAI (băv′ă-ĭ), man who helped rebuild walls of Jerusalem (Neh. 3:18).

BAYTREE (See Plants).

BAZLITH (băz′lĭth), ancestor of a family which returned from captivity (Ezra 2:52).

BAZLUTH (băz′lŭth), same as Bazlith (Ezra 2:52).

BDELLIUM (dĕl′ĭ-ŭm), fragrant gum or resin listed with precious stones (Gen. 2:12; Num. 11:7).

BEALIAH (bē′ă-lī′ă), Benjamite (I Chron. 12:5).

BEALOTH (bē′ă-lŏth). 1. Town in S Judah (Josh. 15:24). 2. Place in N Israel (I Kings 4:16, "Aloth" in KJV).

BEAM (bĕm), large long piece of timber prepared for use for house (I Kings 7:3) or weaver's loom (Judg. 16:14). Used in figurative sense by Jesus (Matt. 7:3; Luke 6:41).

BEAN (See Plants).

BEAR (See Animals).

BEARD (bērd), among Semites a badge of manly dignity; plucked out or cut off as a sign of mourning; Israelites forbidden to shave corners of their beards, probably because it was a heathen religious act;

shaved in leprosy (Lev. 14:9); shaved in Egypt (Gen. 41:14).

BEAST (bēst). 1. A mammal, not man, distinguished from birds and fishes (Gen. 1:29,30). 2. A wild, as distinguished from a domesticated animal (Lev. 26:22; Isa. 13:21,22). 3. Any of the inferior animals, as distinguished from man (Ps. 147:9; Eccl. 3:19). 4. Apocalyptic symbol of brute force – sensual, lawless, and God-opposing (Dan. 7; Rev. 13:11-18).

BEATITUDES (bē-ăt'ĭ-tūds, blessedness), a word not found in the English Bible, but meaning either (1) the joys of heaven, or (2) a declaration of blessedness. Beatitudes occur frequently in the OT (Ps. 32:1,2; 41:1). The Gospels contain isolated beatitudes by Christ (Matt. 11:6; 13:16; John 20:29), but the word is most commonly used of those in Matt. 5:3-11 and Luke 6:20-22, which set forth the qualities that should characterize His disciples.

BEBAI (bē'bā-ī). 1. Ancestor of a family that returned from the captivity (Ezra 2:11). 2. One of this family.

BECHER (bē'kẽr). 1. Second son of Benjamin (Gen. 46:21; I Chron. 7:6). 2. Son of Ephraim (Num. 26:35).

BECHORATH (bē'kō-răth), ancestor of Saul (I Sam. 9:1).

BED. In ancient times the poor generally slept on the ground, their outer garment serving as both mattress and blanket. Sometimes a rug or a mat was used as a bed. Bedsteads were early known (Deut. 3:11); and the wealthy had elaborate beds (Amos 6:4; Esther 1:6).

BEDAD (bē'dăd), father of Hadad (Gen. 36:35).

BEDAN (bē'dăn). 1. Hebrew judge (I Sam. 12:11). 2. Manassehite (I Chron. 7:17).

BEDEIAH (bē-dē'yà), man who divorced foreign wife (Ezra 10:35).

BEE (See Insects).

BEELIADA (bē'ē-lī'à-dà), son of David (I Chron. 14:7).

BEELZEBUB (See Baalzebub).

BEELZEBUL (See Baalzebub).

BEER (bēẽr). 1. Encampment of Israel (Num. 21:16-18). 2. Place to which Jotham fled (Judg. 9:21).

BEERA (bē-ē'rà), descendant of Asher (I Chron. 7:37).

BEERAH (bē-ē'rà), Reubenite prince (I Chron. 5:6).

BEER-ELIM (bē'ẽr-ē'lĭm), village of Moab (Isa. 15:8).

BEERI (bē-ē'rī). 1. Hittite (Gen. 26:34). 2. Father of Josea (Jos. 1:1).

BEER-LA-HAI-ROI (bē'ẽr-là-hī'rŏī), a well where the Lord appeared to Hagar (Gen. 16:7,14).

BEEROTH (bē-ē'rŏth, wells), Canaanite town that deceived Israel (Josh. 9:3ff); assigned to Benjamin (Josh. 18:25).

BEERSHEBA (bē'ẽr-shē'bà, well of seven), place in S Judah where Abraham made a covenant with Abimelech and dug well (Gen. 21:31); God appeared to Jacob there

(Gen. 46:1); and Elijah fled there (I Kings 19:3); Amos (8:14) rebuked its people.

BEETLE (See Insects).

BEGGAR (bĕg'ãr). Professional beggars were unknown in Mosaic times, since the law made ample provision for the poor. Later it became more prevalent; and in the NT beggars appear more frequently (Mark 10: 46-52; Luke 16:19-31; John 9:8,9; Acts 3: 1-11).

BEHEMOTH (See Animals).

BEKAH (See Weights and Measures).

BEL (băl, lord), the Baal of the Babylonians (Isa. 46:1); called Merodach by Hebrews (Jer. 50:2). See Baal.

BELA, BELAH (bē'là, destruction). 1. Place near the S of the vale of Siddim, called also Zoar (Gen. 14:2). 2. King of Edom (Gen. 36:32). 3. Reubenite chief (I Chron. 5:8). 4. Son of Benjamin (Gen. 46:21).

BELIAL (bē'lĭ-ăl), not a proper noun in the OT, but a word meaning "worthlessness," "wickedness," "lawlessness." (Deut. 13:13; Judg. 19:22; I Sam. 25:25). Personified in II Cor. 6:15.

BELL. Bells of gold were attached to the official robe of the high priest (Exod. 28:33-35; 39:25). Bells were attached to the necks of domesticated animals (Zech. 14:20).

BELLOWS (bĕl'ōs), device made of skins for blowing fire (Jer. 6:29).

BELSHAZZAR (bĕl-shăz'ãr, may Bel protect the king), son of Nabonidus, grandson of Nebuchadnezzar, last king of the Neo-Babylonian Empire. During a drunken feast Daniel told him that God had found him wanting; and shortly thereafter Babylon fell to the Medo-Persians and Belshazzar was slain (Dan. 5:1-30).

BELTESHAZZAR (bĕl'tē-shăz-ãr, may Bel protect his life), name given to Daniel by Nebuchadnezzar's steward (Dan. 1:7; 2:26; 4:8).

BEN (bĕn, son), Levite (I Chron. 15:18).

BENAIAH (bē-nā'yà, Jehovah has built). 1. Levite, son of Jehoiada, a priest (II Sam. 8:18); captain of David's bodyguard (II Sam. 23:23); very brave (II Sam. 23: 20,21; I Chron. 11:22,23); supervised coronation of Solomon (I Kings 1:38f). 2. One of David's mighty men (II Sam. 23:30). 3. Simeonite prince (I Chron. 4:36f). 4. Levite harpist (I Chron. 15:18). 5. Priest, trumpeter (I Chron. 15:24). 6. Ancestor of Jahaziel the prophet (II Chron. 20:14). 7. Temple overseer (II Chron. 31:13). 8. Four Israelites who put away their foreign wives (Ezra 10:25,30,35,43). 9. Pelatiah's father (Ezek. 11:13).

BEN-AMMI (bĕn'ăm'ī, son of my people), son of one of Lot's daughters; progenitor of Ammonites (Gen. 19:38).

BENE-BERAK (bĕn'ē-bē'răk), town of Dan a few miles SE of Jaffa (Josh. 19:45).

BENE-JAAKAN (bĕn'ē-jā'à-kăn), desert encampment of Israelites (Num. 33:31; Deut. 10:6).

BENEVOLENCE, DUE (bĕn-ĕv'ō-lĕns), euphemism for conjugal rights (I Cor. 7:3).

BENHADAD (bĕn-hā'dăd, **son of Hadad**), titular name for the rulers of Syria, who were thought to be descended from the Syrian god Hadad. 1. King of Damascus, contemporary with Asa, king of Judah (I Kings 15:18), whom he helped against Baasha (I Kings 15:18-21). 2. Probably the son of 1. Contemporary with Ahab of Israel, by whom his army was routed (I Kings 20:26ff). 3. Son of Hazael; contemporary of Amaziah, king of Judah, and Jehoahaz of Israel; oppressed 10 tribes, but defeated by Joash, son of Jehoahaz (II Kings 13:3-13).

BENHAIL (bĕn-hā'ĭl), prince of Judah (II Chron. 17:7).

BEN-HANAN (bĕn'hā'năn), Judahite (I Chron. 4:20).

BENINU (bĕ-nī'nū), Levite who signed covenant with Nehemiah (Neh. 10:13).

BENJAMIN (bĕn'jà-mĭn, **son of my right hand**). 1. Youngest son of Jacob; called Benoni by dying mother Rachel, but renamed Benjamin by Jacob (Gen. 35:16-20); went to Egypt with family (Gen. 43). 2. Great-grandson of 1 (I Chron. 7:10). 3. Israelite who married a foreign wife (Ezra 10:32).

BENJAMIN, TRIBE OF, tribe named for Jacob's youngest son; fame foretold by Jacob (Gen. 49:27; Judg. 20:16); territory between Judah and Ephraim (Josh. 18:11-28); punished for frightful sin (Judg. 19-21). King Saul and the apostle Paul were Benjamites (I Sam. 9:1,2; Phil. 3:5).

BENO (bĕ'nō), son of Jaaziah (I Chron. 24:26,27).

BEN-ONI (bĕn'ō'nī), name given Benjamin by his dying mother (Gen. 35:18). See Benjamin.

BEN-ZOHETH (bĕn'zō'hĕth), Judahite (I Chron. 4:20).

BEON (bĕ'ŏn), Reubenite town (Num. 32:3); called Beth-Baal-Meon in Joshua 13:17.

BEOR (See Balaam).

BERA (bĕ'rà), king of Sodom (Gen. 14:2,8).

BERACHAH (bĕr'à-kà), Benjamite who joined David at Ziklag (I Chron. 12:3).

BERACHAH, VALLEY OF (bĕr'à-kà, **valley of blessing**), place in Judah where Jehoshaphat praised God for victory (II Chron. 20:26).

BERACHIAH (bĕr-à-kī'à, **Jehovah blesses**). Sometimes Berechiah. 1. Descendant of David (I Chron. 3:20). 2. Father of Asap (I Chron. 9:16). 3. Levite (I Chron. 9:16). 4. Custodian of the ark (I Chron. 15:23). 5. Ephraimite (II Chron. 28:12). 6. Father of a builder in days of Nehemiah (Neh. 3:4,30; 6:18). 7. Father of the prophet Zechariah (Zech. 1:1,7).

BERAIAH (bĕr'à-i'à), son of Shimhi of Benjamin (I Chron. 8:21).

BEREA or **BEROEA** (bĕr-ē'à), city in SW Macedonia (Acts 17:10-14; 20:4); church founded there by Paul on 2nd missionary journey.

BERED (bĕ'rĕd, **to be cold**), place in the

vicinity of Kadesh-barnea (Gen. 16:14).

BERI (bē'rī), Asherite (I Chron. 7:36).

BERIAH (bē-rī'à). 1. Son of Asher (Gen. 46:17); Beriites descended from him (Num. 26:44).

BERIITES (bē-rī'ĭts), descendants of Beriah, an Asherite (Gen. 46:17).

BERITES (bē'rĭts), people who followed Sheba in revolt against David (II Sam. 20:14).

BERNICE (bĕr-nī'sē, **victorious**), eldest daughter of Herod Agrippa I (Acts 12:1); married to Herod of Chalcis and to King Ptolemy of Sicily; caused scandal by living with her brother Agrippa (Acts 25:23; 26:30); became mistress of Vespasian and Titus.

BERODACH-BALADAN(bē-rō'dăk-băl'à-dăn, **Marduk has given a son**), king of Babylon, also called Merodach-baladan; sent letter and present to Hezekiah (Isa. 39:1).

BEROTHAH, BEROTHAI (bē-rō'thà, bē-rō'thī, **wells**), town located between Hamath and Damascus (Ezek. 47:16). May be same as Hadadezer (II Sam. 8:8).

BERYL (bĕr'ĭl, **yellow jasper**), precious stone in the high priest's breastplace (Exod. 28:20; 39:13). Also referred to in Dan. 10:6; Rev. 21:20).

BESAI (bē'sī), founder of a family which returned to Jerusalem (Ezra 2:49; Neh. 7:52).

BESODEIAH (bĕs'ō-dē'yà), father of Meshullam, a builder under Nehemiah (Neh. 3:6).

BESOM (bē'zŭm, **broom**), word used metaphorically for utter destruction (Isa. 14:23).

BESOR (bē'sòr), brook near Gaza (I Sam. 30:9,10).

BETAH (bē'tà), city of Syria captured by David (II Sam. 8:8). Called "Tibhath" in I Chron. 18:8.

BETEN (bē'tĕn), city on border of Asher (Josh. 19:25).

BETH (bēth, **house**), second letter of the Hebrew alphabet and the Hebrew number 2.

BETHABARA (bĕth'ăb'à-rà, **house of the ford**), place on the E bank of the Jordan where John baptized (John 1:28).

BETHANATH (bĕth'à'năth), city near Naphtali (Josh. 19:38; Judg. 1:33).

BETH-ANOTH (bĕth'à'nŏth), town in Judah (Josh. 15:59).

BETHANY (bĕth'à-nē, **house of affliction; house of unripe figs**). 1. Bethabara of John 1:28 (KJV) is in the best MSS rendered "Bethany." 2. Town 2 miles SE of Jerusalem; home of Mary, Martha, and Lazarus (John 11:18); place of ascension of Jesus (Luke 24:50,51).

BETH-ARABAH (bĕth'ăr'à-bà, **house of the desert**), town assigned to Judah on N end of Dead Sea (Josh. 15:6,61; 18:22). Called Arabah in Josh. 18:18.

BETHARAM (bĕth'à'răm), town E of Jordan belonging to Gad (Josh. 13:27). Called "Bethharan" in Num. 32:36.

BETHARABEL (bĕth'ăr'bĕl, **house of Arbel**), town destroyed by Shalmaneser, perhaps in Naphtali (Hos. 10:14).

BETHAVEN (bĕth'à'vĕn, **house of vanity**),

town in N Benjamin (Josh. 18:12). The word is used figuratively by Hosea (4:15; 10:5).

BETHAZMAVETH (bĕth'ăz-mā'vĕth), village of Benjamin (Neh. 7:28).

BETH BAAL MEON (bĕth bā'ăl mē'ŏn), place E of the Jordan assigned to Reuben (Josh. 13:17). Same as Baal-meon (Num. 32:38) and Beon (Num. 32:3).

BETHBARAH (bĕth'bär'ă, house of the ford), ford of Jordan (Judg. 7:24).

BETH-BIREI (bĕth'bir'ī), town of Simeon (I Chron. 4:31). "Bethlebaoth" in Josh. 19:6 and "Lebaoth" in Josh. 15:32.

BETHCAR (bĕth'kär), place W of Mizpah (I Sam. 7:11).

BETH DAGON (bĕth'dā'gŏn, house of Dagon). 1. Town of Judah (Josh. 15:41). 2. Town of Asher (Josh. 19:27).

BETH-DIBLATHAIM (bĕth-dĭb'lă-thā'ĭm, town in Moab (Jer. 48:22). Also called "Almondiblathaim" (Num. 33:46) and "Diblath" (Ezek. 6:14).

BETHEL (bĕth'ĕl, house of God). 1. Town 12 miles N of Jerusalem, originally known as "Luz" (Gen. 28:19). Abraham encamped near it (Gen. 12:8; 13:3); God met Jacob there (Gen. 28:10-22) and Jacob built an altar there, calling the place "El-bethel" (Gen. 35:7). Assigned to Benjamin (Josh. 18:21,22); captured by Joseph's descendants (Judg. 1:22-26); ark abode there (Judg. 20: 26-28). Jeroboam set up golden calf there (I Kings 12:26-30). Amos and Hosea denounced it (Amos 3:14; called Beth-aven, "house of idols," Hos. 4:15). Josiah restored worship of Jehovah (II Kings 23: 15-23). 2. City in S Judah (I Sam. 30:27). "Bethul" in Josh. 19:4.

BETHEMEK (bĕth'ē'mĕk), town of Asher (Josh. 19:27).

BETHER (bĕ'thĕr), range of mountains mentioned in S. of Sol. 2:17.

BETHESDA (bĕ-thĕs'dă, house of grace), a spring-fed pool in Jerusalem (John 5:1-16) into which the sick went for healing.

BETHEZEL (bĕth'ē'zĕl), town in S Judah (Mic. 1:11).

BETHGADER (bĕth'gă'dĕr), place in Judah (I Chron. 2:51).

BETHGAMUL (bĕth'gă'mŭl), city in Moab (Jer. 48:23).

BETH-GILGAL (bĕth'gĭl'găl), probably same as Gilgal (Neh. 12:27-29).

BETH-HACCEREM (bĕth'hă-kē'rĕm), town of Judah (Neh. 3:14).

BETH-HARAN (bĕth'hă'răn), fortified city E of the Jordan (Num. 32:36).

BETH-HOGLAH (bĕth'hŏg'lă), village of Benjamin (Josh. 15:6; 18:19,21).

BETH-HORON (bĕth'hŏ'rŏn, place of a hollow), twin towns a few miles apart about 11 miles NW of Jerusalem (Josh. 16:3,5; 18:13); assigned to Ephraim and given to the Kohathites (Josh. 21:22).

BETH-JESHIMOTH (bĕth-jĕsh'ĭ-mŏth, house of desert), town 9 miles SE of Jericho (Josh. 12:3; 13:20; Num. 33:49).

BETH-LE-APHRAH (bĕth'lĕ-ăf'ră), name of

place perhaps in Philistine plain (Mic. 1:10).

BETHLEBAOTH (bĕth'lĕ-bā'ŏth), town of Simeon (Josh. 19:6); "Beth-birei" in I Chron. 4:31.

BETHLEHEM (bĕth'lĕ-hĕm, house of bread). 1. Town 5 miles SW of Jerusalem. Called Ephrath in Jacob's time; after conquest of Canaan called Bethlehem-judah (Ruth 1:1) to distinguish it from Bethlehem of Zebulun. Burial place of Rachel (Gen. 35:16,19); home of Ibzan (Judg. 12:8-10), Elimelech (Ruth 1:1,2) and Boaz (Ruth 2:1,4). David anointed there (I Sam. 16:13); known as "city of David" (Luke 2:4,11). Jesus born there (Matt. 2:1; Luke 2:15-18). 2. Town of Zebulun (Josh. 19:15).

BETH-LEHEM-JUDAH (See Bethlehem).

BETH-LE-JESHIMOTH or **BETHJESIMOTH** (bĕth'jĕsh'ĭ-mŏth), town assigned to Reuben (Josh. 13:20).

BETH-MAACHAH (bĕth'mā'ă-kă), town to which Joab pursued Sheba (II Sam. 20: 14,15).

BETH-MARCABOTH (bĕth'mär'kă-bŏth), town of Simeon (I Chron. 4:31).

BETH-MEON (bĕth'mē'ŏn), city of Moab (Jer. 48:23), same as Beth-baal-meon (Josh. 13:17).

BETHNIMRAH (bĕth'nĭm'ră), fortified city of Gad E of the Jordan (Num. 32:3,36).

BETHPALET or **BETH-PHELET** (bĕth'pă' lĕt or bĕth'fĕ'lĕt), town in S Judah (Josh. 15:27).

BETHPAZZEZ (bĕth'păz'ĕz), town of Issachar (Josh. 19:21).

BETHPEOR (bĕth'pē'ŏr), place in Moab where Israel encamped (Deut. 3:29) and Moses was buried (Deut. 34:6).

BETHPHAGE (bĕth'fă-jē), village NW of Bethany (Mark 11:1; Luke 19:29).

BETHRAPHA (bĕth'ră'fă), son of Eshton a Judahite (I Chron. 4:12).

BETHREHOB (bĕth're'hŏb), town in N of Palestine inhabited by Aramaeans who fought against David (II Sam. 10:6).

BETHSAIDA (bĕth'sā'ĭ-dă, house of fishing). 1. City on Sea of Galilee, probably close to Capernaum (John 1:44; 12:21); home of Peter, Andrew, Philip; upbraided by Jesus (Matt. 11:20-23; Luke 10:13-15). 2. Town on E side of Sea of Galilee, in Gaulonitis; rebuilt by Philip the tetrarch and made his capital. Jesus fed 5000 people there (Luke 9:10-17).

BETHSAH or **BETHSHEAN** (bĕth'shăn or bĕth'shē'ăn, house of quiet), city of Manasseh 14 miles S of the Sea of Galilee in the valley of Jezreel. Dates back to 3500 B. C. After Saul died, the Philistines fastened his body to the wall of Bethshan (I Sam. 31:8-12). Solomon included it in one of his commissary districts (I Kings 4:12).

BETHSHEMESH (bĕth'shĕ'mĕsh, house of the sun). 1. Town of NW Judah near Philistine border (Josh. 15:10; I Sam. 6:12); Levite city (Josh. 21:16; I Chron. 6:59); cows brought ark to it (I Sam. 6); there Joash king of Israel made Amaziah of Judah prisoner (II Kings 14:11-13; II Chron. 25: 21-23). 2. City of Issachar (Josh. 19:22). 3. City of Naphtali (Josh. 19:38; Judg. 1:33). 4. Idol city in Egypt (Jer. 43:13), the Egyptian city On, the Greek Heliopolis.

BETHSHITTA (bĕth'shĭt'à), town between the valley of Jezreel and Zererah in the Jordan valley (Judg. 7:22).

BETHTAPPUA (bĕth'tăp'ū-à), town c. 5 miles W of Hebron (Josh. 15:53).

BETHUEL or **BETHUL** (bĕ-thū'ĕl or bĕth'ūl, abode of God). 1. Son of Nahor and Milcah, nephew of Abraham, and father of Rebekah and Laban (Gen. 22:22,23; 24:15, 24,27; 28:2). 2. Town in the S of Simeon (Josh. 19:4; I Chron. 4:30); same as Chesil (Josh. 15:30).

BETHUL (See Bethuel).

BETHZUR (bĕth'zûr, house of rock), fortress town in Judah, 4 miles N of Hebron (Josh. 15:58; II Chron. 11:7; Neh. 3:16); called Bethsura in Maccabean times.

BETONIM (bĕt'ō-nĭm), town of Gad, E of the Jordan (Josh. 13:26).

BEULAH (bū'là, married), poetic name for restored Israel (Isa. 62:4).

BEZAI (bē'zā-ī). 1. Head of a family that returned with Zerubbabel (Ezra 2:17; Neh. 7:23). 2. Probably a later member of the same family (Neh. 10:18).

BEZALEEL (bē-zăl'ē-ĕl, in the shadow of God). 1. Judahite empowered by the Spirit to work in metals, wood, and stone for the tabernacle (Exod. 31:2; 35:30). 2. Jew who divorced his foreign wife (Ezra 10:30).

BEZEK (bē'zĕk). 1. Town in Judah where Adoni-bezek was defeated (Judg. 1:1-5). 2. Town c. 14 miles NE of Samaria (I Sam. 11:8).

BEZER (bē'zĕr, strong). 1. Levitical city of refuge in territory of Reuben (Josh. 21:36). 2. Asherite hero (I Chron. 7:37).

BIBLE. The name given to the collection of the Old and New Testament books. The word "Bible" comes from Gr. **biblia** (books) which, although a plural noun, came to be used in the Latin as a singular. Thus "The Books" because by common consent "The Book." The plural term **biblia** stresses the fact that the Bible is a collection of books; that the word came to be used in the singular emphasizes the fact that there is in these books a wonderful unity. The names "Old" and "New Testament" have been used since the close of the 2nd century to distinguish the Jewish and Christian Scriptures. Most of the OT is written in Hebrew; a few parts are in Aramaic (Ezra 4:8-7:18; 7:12-26; Jer. 10:11; Dan. 2:4-7:28). Except for a few words and sentences which are in Aramaic, the NT was composed in Greek, the language of ordinary intercourse in the Hellenistic world. The Protestant Bible contains 66 books, 39 in the OT and 27 in the NT. The Roman Catholic OT contains 46 books, plus additions to Esther and Daniel. Jews accept as canonical only the 39 books accepted by Protestants. The additional books are

known by Protestants as the Apocrypha. They were a part of the Greek OT known as the Septuagint. All branches of the Christian church are agreed on the NT canon. Although written over a period of more than 1000 years, the Bible has come to us in a remarkable state of preservation. The recently discovered Dead Sea Scrolls, some dating as far back as the 2nd and 3rd centuries B. C., bear witness to a text remarkably like the Hebrew text we have today. For the NT the evidence for the text includes 4500 Greek manuscripts, dating from about A. D. 125 to the invention of printing; versions, some of which go back to c. A. D. 150; and quotations of Scripture in the writings of the Church Fathers, beginning with the end of the first century. The chapter divisions we have today were made in 1228 and the verse divisions in 1551. Translations of the Bible began to appear very early. The Septuagint was made c. 250-150 B. C.; the NT appeared in Latin and Syriac c. A. D. 150. The Bible, in whole or in part, is now available in more than 1100 languages and dialects. The theme of the Bible in both Testaments is the redemption of man. The OT tells about the origin of man's sin and the preparation God made for the solution through His own Son the Messiah. The NT describes the fulfilment of God's redemptive plan.

BIBLE, ENGLISH VERSIONS. John Wycliffe (1320-1384) first made the whole Bible available in English. Until then the people had only parts of the Old and New Testaments. His translation, made with the assistance of others, was made from the Latin Vulgate, not the original Hebrew and Greek. The NT appeared in 1380; the OT in 1382. Since printing was not known until the next century, copies of the Wycliffe Bible had to be made by hand. The common people eagerly received it, but the church opposed it, and after Wycliffe's death disinterred and burned his bones. Laws were passed prohibiting the reading of the Bible in the vernacular, with the penalty of death. William Tyndale (1494-1536), driven out of England by the church because he planned a new translation of the Bible in English, had the NT published in Germany in 1525 and then smuggled into England, where the church publicly burned it when it could secure copies. His NT was made directly from the Greek and was the first printing of either Testament in English. He began a translation of the OT from the Hebrew text, but did not live to complete it. He was betrayed by an English Roman Catholic and burned at the stake, his last words being, "Lord, open the king of England's eyes."

While Tyndale was still in prison, an English Bible, printed on the Continent, appeared in England. It was the rendering of Miles Coverdale, although in the NT and in those parts of the OT done by

Tyndale, it was no more than a slight revision of the latter's work. This was the first complete printed Bible in the English language. Two years later it was licensed by the king and was distributed with royal approval. The first Bible actually printed in England was the Thomas Matthew Bible, in 1537. The next to appear was a revision of the Matthew Bible, by Coverdale. It came out in 1539 and was called the Great Bible because of its large size and sumptuousness. Protestants who fled England when Mary Tudor became queen in 1553 brought out the Genevan Bible in 1560, which enjoyed a long popularity. During the reign of Queen Elizabeth, in 1568, the Bishops' Bible appeared, so called because a number of bishops were involved in its production. Catholic scholars brought out the Rheims NT in 1582 and the Douai OT in 1609, 1610, both based on the Latin Vulgate.

The most famous of all English versions, the King James Version, was the work of about 50 scholars and was published in 1611 during the reign of King James I. This work was actually a revision of the Bishops' Bible on the basis of the Hebrew and Greek. In spite of its quality, it was many years before it won universal acceptance. The English Revised Version was made necessary for a number of reasons: in the course of time the language of the KJV had become obsolete; a number of Greek manuscripts were discovered that were far superior to those available to the KJV translators; and improvement in the knowledge of Hebrew made possible a more accurate rendering of the OT. The English translators were assisted by American scholars. The NT appeared in 1881 and the OT in 1885. The American Standard Version, published in 1901, is a revision of the English Revised Version.

The discovery of thousands of Greek papyri in the sands of Egypt revealed that the NT was written in the everyday language of the people, and this has resulted in bringing out many translations in the spoken English of today, among which those of Weymouth (1903), Moffatt (1913, 1914), Goodspeed (1923), and Phillips (1958) have been the most popular. The Revised Standard Version, which is a revision of the ASV, appeared in 1946 (NT) and 1952 (OT); and the NT part of the New English Bible in 1961.

BICHRI (bik'rī), father of Sheba (II Sam. 20:1).

BIDKAR (bid'kär), officer in army of Joram, king of Israel (II Kings 9:25).

BIGTHA (big'thá), chamberlain of Ahasuerus (Esth. 1:10).

BIGTHAN or **BIGTHANA** (big'thăn or big-thä'na), chamberlain of Ahasuerus (Esth. 2:21-23).

BIGVAI (big'vā-ī, fortunate). 1. Man who returned from the captivity (Ezra 2:2; Neh. 7:19). 2. Ancestor of family that returned

from the captivity (Ezra 2:14; Neh. 7:19). 3. Probably the same as 2(Ezra 8:14).

BILDAD (bil'dăd), "comforter" of Job; made three speeches (Job 8; 18; 25).

BILEAM (bil'ē-ăm), town in W of Manasseh (I Chron. 6:70). May be same as Ibleam of Josh. 17:11; Judg. 1:27; II Kings 9:27.

BILGAH (bil'gá). 1. Head of 15th course of priests (I Chron. 24:14). 2. Priest who returned with Zerubbabel (Neh. 12:5).

BILGAI (bil'gá-i), priest in Nehemiah's time (Neh. 10:8).

BILHAH (bil'há, foolish). 1. Rachel's maidservant; Jacob's concubine; mother of Dan and Naphtali (Gen. 29:29; 30:1-8). 2. Town of Simeon (I Chron. 4:29). Balah in Josh. 19:3.

BILHAN (bil'hăn, foolish). 1. Horite; son of Ezer (Gen. 36:27; I Chron. 1:42). 2. Early Benjamite (I Chron. 7:10).

BILSHAN (bil'shăn), Jewish leader who returned from the captivity (Ezra 2:2; Neh. 7:7).

BIMHAL (bim'hăl), Asherite (I Chron. 7:33).

BINDING AND LOOSING. The carrying of a key or keys was a symbol of the delegated power of opening and closing. The apostles were given power to bind and to loose. Peter loosed the feet of the lame man at the Gate Beautiful (Acts 3:1-10) and Paul bound the sight of Bar-Jesus (Acts 13:8-11).

BINNUI (bin'û-i). 1. Levite (Ezra 8:33). 2. Man who divorced his foreign wife (Ezra 10:30). 3. Another who divorced his foreign wife (Ezra 10:38). 4. Alternate spelling of Bani (cf. Ezra 2:10; Neh. 7:15). 5. Rebuilder of Jerusalem (Neh. 3:24; 10:9). 6. Levite (Neh. 12:8).

BIRDS. 360-400 different kinds are found in Palestine, and of these, 26 are found only there. The Bible lists about 50 classifying them as clean and unclean (Lev. 11: 13-19; Deut. 14:11-19). Birds are mentioned in all but 21 books of the Bible. The following birds are specifically noted: bittern, chicken, cock, cormorant, crane, crow, cuckoo, cuckow (KJV name for cuckoo), dove, eagle, falcon, fowl (used of all flying birds), gier eagle, glede, great owl, hawk, hen, heron, hoopoe (same as lapwing), kite (same as falcon), lapwing, little owl, nighthawk, ospray, ossifrage, ostrich, owl, partridge, peacock, pelican, pigeon, quail, raven, screech owl, sea mew (same as cuckoo), sparrow, stork, swallow, swan, turtledove, vulture.

BIRSHA (bir'shà), king of Gomorrah (Gen. 14:2,10).

BIRTH. The Heb. ceremonies connected with childbirth are given in Lev. 12.

BIRTHRIGHT. In Israel the birthright included a double portion of the inheritance (Deut. 21:15-17), and the privilege of priesthood; but God at Sinai set apart the tribe of Levi instead of the firstborn for that service.

BIRZAVITH (bir-zā'vith), an Asherite or a village of Asher (I Chron. 7:31).

BISHLAM (bĭsh'lăm), officer of Cambyses (Ezra 4:7).

BISHOP (bĭsh'ŭp, **overseer**), same as elder or presbyter (Titus 1:5,7; I Tim. 3:1; 4:14); an overseer (Acts 20:17,28; I Peter 5:2); ruler (Rom. 12:8).

BITHIAH (bĭ-thī'á, **daughter of Jehovah**), daughter of Pharaoh and wife of Mered of Judah (I Chron. 4:18).

BITHRON (bĭth'rŏn), region in Gad (II Sam. 2:29).

BITHYNIA (bĭ-thĭn'ĭ-á), region in N Asia Minor; where the Holy Spirit forbade Paul to preach (Acts 16:6-10); destination of I Peter (I Pet. 1:1).

BITTER HERBS. Used at Passover Feast to remind Israelites of servitude in Egypt (Exod. 12:8; Num. 9:11).

BITTERN (See Birds).

BITUMEN (bĭ-tū'mĕn), mineral pitch used for waterproofing (Exod. 2:3; Gen. 6:14) and for mortar in the tower of Babel (Gen. 11:3). Found along Dead Sea, Euphrates, and other places.

BIZJOTHJAH (bĭz-jŏth'jà), town in S Judah (Josh. 15:28).

BIZTHAH (bĭz'thà), chamberlain in court of Ahasuerus (Esth. 1:10).

BLAINS (See Diseases).

BLASPHEMY (blăs'fĕ-mè), in Jewish law, cursing or reviling God or the king (Ps. 74:10; Isa. 52:5; Rev. 16:9,11,21). Blasphemy of God was punished by stoning (Lev. 24:16). Naboth (I Kings 21:10-13), Stephen (Acts 6:11), and Jesus (Matt. 9:3) were falsely accused of blasphemy.

BLASTUS (blăs'tŭs), chamberlain of Herod Agrippa I (Acts 12:20).

BLESS, BLESSING. To bless is to make happy, or to pray for the happiness of someone, or to guard and protect, or to glorify. God blesses (Gen. 1:22,28; 2:3; Ps. 33:12). Well-known blessings: Num. 6:22-27; II Cor. 13:14.

BLESSING, THE CUP OF, the communion cup set apart for the Lord's Supper (I Cor. 10:16).

BLINDNESS (See Diseases).

BLOOD. Israelites forbidden to eat blood (Gen. 9:4). Often synonymous with life (Gen. 9:4; Lev. 17:11,14; Deut. 12:23). No forgiveness of sins without shedding of blood (Heb. 9:22). Christ's blood saves (I Cor. 11:25; Eph. 2:13; I Peter 1:2,19).

BLOOD, AVENGER or REVENGER OF. One who took it upon himself to avenge the blood of a slain kinsman. This was often done in ancient Israel and is done among primitive peoples today. (Gen. 9:6; Num. 35:6).

BLOOD, ISSUE OF (See Diseases).

BLOODY SWEAT (See Diseases).

BOANERGES (bō'á-nûr'jĕz, **sons of thunder**), title given James and John (Mark 3:17).

BOAR (See Animals).

BOAZ (bō'ăz), Bethlehemite in the days of the judges; kinsman and husband of Ruth (Ruth 2-4). Listed in the genealogy of Jesus (Matt. 1:5).

BOAZ AND JACHIN (See Temple).

BOCHERU (bŏ'kè-rōō), descendant of Saul (I Chron. 8:38).

BOCHIM (bō'kim, **weepers**), place near Gilgal where Israelites were rebuked (Judg. 2:1-5).

BOHAN (bō'hăn), descendant of Reuben after whom a stone was named (Josh. 15:6; 18:17).

BOIL (See Diseases).

BOLSTER, a pillow (Gen. 28:11,18; I Sam. 19:13).

BONDMAID, BONDMAN (See Occupations).

BONE, used in both a literal and figurative sense in Scripture, – figurative for strength, kinship (Gen. 29:14). Dry bones are a picture of hopeless death (Ezek. 37:1-12).

BOOK. In ancient Assyria and Babylonia most books were written on soft clay which was then baked. In Egypt papyrus was used several thousand years before the time of Christ. C. 200 B. C. skins of animals began to be used. Books made of papyrus and parchment were in roll form. The codex (book with pages) was invented in the 2nd cent. A. D. Israel used papyrus and parchment.

BOOTH, a temporary shelter made of branches of a tree (Gen. 33:17; Lev. 23:42; Job 27:18).

BOOTY. Spoils of war. Property and persons were sometimes preserved, and sometimes completely destroyed (Josh. 6:18-21; Deut. 20:14,16-18). Abraham gave a tenth (Gen. 14:20); David ordered that booty be shared with baggage guards (I Sam. 30:21-25).

BOOZ (See Boaz).

BORROW, BORROWING. The law of Moses gives careful directions concerning the responsibility of those who borrow (Exod. 22:1-15).

BOSCATH (See Bazkath).

BOSOM (bŏŏz'ŭm). In Scripture the word is generally used in an affectionate sense (Isa. 40:11; John 1:18). Sometimes it is almost synonymous with "heart" (Eccl. 7:9; Ps. 35:13).

BOSOR (Same as Beor, See Balaam).

BOSSES, convex projection in center of shield (Job 15:26).

BOTCH (See Diseases).

BOTTLE. A container made of goat-skin (Job 32:19; Matt. 9:17), earthenware (Jer. 19:1,10,11), or glass (Ps. 56:8).

BOTTOMLESS PIT (See Abyss).

BOUNDARY STONES. Stones used to mark the boundary of property (Josh. 13:21); to remove them was forbidden (Deut. 27:17).

BOW (See Arms and Armor).

BOW (See Rainbow).

BOWELS, the word is used to translate a number of Heb. words. 1. Literally (II Chron. 21:15-19). 2. Generative parts of the body (Gen. 15:4; Ps. 71:6). 3. Seat of the emotions, "heart" (See Lam. 1:20; Phil. 1:8).

BOWL (bōl), a vessel, usually hemispherically shaped, to hold liquids (Amos 6:6; Zech. 4:3).

BOX, BOX TREE (See Plants).

BOZEZ (bō'zĕz), one of two rocky crags near Gibeah (I Sam. 14:4).

BOZKATH or **BOSCATH** (bŏz'kăth), town in S Judah (Josh. 15:39).

BOZRAH (bŏz'rà, sheepfold). 1. City of Edom (Gen. 36:33; Jer. 49:13,22). 2. City of Moab c. 75 miles S of Damascus (Jer. 48:24).

BRACELET, properly a circlet for the wrist or arm worn by both sexes, sometimes as a mark of royalty (Gen. 24:22,30; II Sam. 1:10). In Exod. 35:22 it may be "brooches."

BRAMBLE (See Plants).

BRANCH, title for the Messiah as the offspring of David (Jer. 23:5; 33:15; Zech. 3:8). Symbol of prosperity (Gen. 49:22).

BRASS, next to silver and gold, the most frequently mentioned metal in Scripture. KJV usually uses "brass" (an alloy of copper and zinc) when it should be "copper" or "bronze" (an alloy of copper and tin). Gen. 4:22; II Sam. 22:35; Job 28:2; Dan. 2:31-39.

BRAY. 1. To utter harshly (Job 30:7). 2. To beat small, usually in a mortar (Prov. 27:22).

BRAZEN SEA, an immense laver in front of the temple for washing sacrifices and hands of priests (II Kings 25:13; I Chron. 18:8).

BRAZEN SERPENT, serpent of "brass" made by Moses in the wilderness. When people were bitten by poisonous serpents, they looked at it and were saved from death (Num. 21:4-9). A type of Christ saving us from the effects of sin (John 3:14-16).

BREAD, the universal staff of life. Wheat was generally used, but barley was a substitute among the poor. Flour was ground by hand between two stones. Flour, yeast, salt, olive oil and water or milk were the ingredients. Some bread was made without yeast, such as the "unleavened bread" of The Passover (Exod. 12:15-20). Dough placed in the oven was only about 1/4 inch thick, and was therefore quickly baked. "Bread" is often used figuratively for food in general (Gen. 3:19; Matt. 6:11). In the Tabernacle the loaves of shew-bread indicated the presence of the Lord among His people.

BREAD, SHEW (See Bread).

BREECHES (See Dress).

BRICK, building material made of clay dried in the sun. Earliest mention of brick in the Bible is found in the story of the Tower of Babel (Gen. 11:3). Ancient bricks were generally square and were much larger than ours. Bricks were either baked in the sun or in kilns.

BRIDE, BRIDEGROOM (See Wedding).

BRIDECHAMBER (See Wedding).

BRIDGE. The word is not found in the English Bible. Bridges were hardly known among the Israelites, who generally crossed streams by a ford (Gen. 32:22) or a ferry (II Sam. 19:18).

BRIDLE, the word appears in a literal and figurative sense (Prov. 26:3; Ps. 32:9; James 1:26; 3:2; Rev. 14:20).

BRIER (See Plants).

BRIMSTONE, properly "sulphur" (Gen. 19: 24). Also used figuratively for punishment and destruction (Job 18:15; Ps. 11:6; Rev. 21:8).

BRONZE, an alloy of copper and tin. The word is not found in Scripture, but probably the "steel" used for making metallic bows was really bronze (II Sam. 22:35; Job 20:24). (See Brass).

BROOK, a small stream, usually one which flows only during the rainy season (Deut. 2:13; I Kings 18:40; II Sam. 15:23).

BROTHER. 1. Kinsman of same parents (Gen. 27:6), or the same father (Gen. 28:2), or the same mother (Judg. 8:19). 2. A man of the same country (Exod. 2:11; Acts 3:22). 3. Member of the same tribe (II Sam. 19:12). 4. An ally (Amos 1:9). 5. One of a kindred people (Num. 20:14). 6. Co-religionist (Acts 9:17; Rom. 1:13). 7. Fellow office-bearer (Ezra 3:2). 8. Someone of equal rank or office (I Kings 9:13). 9. Any member of the human race (Matt. 7:3-5; Heb. 2:17). 10. Someone greatly beloved (II Sam. 1:26). 11. Relative (Gen. 14:16; Matt. 12:46).

BROTHERS OF OUR LORD. James, Joses, Simon, and Judas are called the Lord's brothers (Matt. 13:55); He also had sisters (Matt. 13:56); John 7:1-10 states that His brothers did not believe in Him. There are differences of opinion as to whether the "brothers" were full brothers, cousins, or children of Joseph by a former marriage.

BUCKET or **PAIL**, the word is used figuratively in Isa. 40:15 and Num. 24:7.

BUKKI (bŭk'ī). 1. Prince of the tribe of Dan (Num. 34:22). 2. High priest of Israel (I Chron. 6:5,51; Ezra 7:4).

BUKKIAH (bŭ-kī'à), Levite (I Chron. 25: 4,13).

BUL (bōōl), 8th month of Jewish ecclesiastical year (I Kings 6:38).

BULL (See Animals: Cattle).

BULLOCK (See Animals: Cattle).

BULRUSH (See Plants).

BUNAH (bū'nà), descendant of Judah (I Chron. 2:25).

BUNNI (bŭn'ī), 3 Levites mentioned in Nehemiah had this name (9:4; 10:15; 11:15).

BURDEN, a heavy load (literal or figurative) – Num. 11:11; Matt. 11:30.

BURIAL. Among the Israelites corpses were wrapped in cloth or bound in bands (Matt. 27:59; John 11:44); in the case of the wealthy the body was anointed with spices and perfumes (John 12:7; 19:39);. Burial was either in the ground or a cave (Matt. 27:60). Often mourners were hired to join with the friends in lamentation (Jer. 9:17).

BURNING. God's judgments have often been accompanied with fire (Gen. 19:24-28; Lev. 10:1-6; Num. 16:2,35).

BURNT OFFERING (See Offerings).

BUSH (See Plants).

BUSHEL (See Weights and Measures).

BUSINESS (See Trade and Travel).

BUTLER (See Occupations and Professions).

BUTTER. Used in both literal (Ps. 55:21) and figurative sense (Job 29:6; Gen. 18:8).

BUZ (bŭz). 1. Son of Nahor (Gen. 22:21). 2. Gadite (I Chron. 5:14).

BYBLOS (See Gebal).

BYWAYS, literally "crooked paths," travelled to avoid danger (Judg. 5:6).

C

CAB (căb), a measure of capacity, a little less than 2 quarts (II Kings 6:25).

CABBON (kăb'ŏn), town in Judah (Josh. 15:40), perhaps same as Machbena (I Chron. 2:49).

CABUL (kā'bŭl). 1. City of Asher c. 9 miles SE of Acre; still inhabited (Josh. 19:27). 2. District in N Galilee ceded by Solomon to Hiram of Tyre (I Kings 9:13; II Chron. 8:2).

CAESAR (sē'zēr). 1. Name of a Roman family of which Caius Julius Caesar was the most prominent. 2. Title of Roman emperors after Julius Caesar (Matt. 22:17; Luke 23:2; John 19:15; Acts 17:7). Several Caesars are referred to in the NT (Luke 2:1; 3:1; 20:22; Acts 11:28; 25:8).

CAESAREA (sĕs'à-rē'à), seaport city built by Herod the Great c. 25 miles NW of Samaria in honor of Augustus Caesar; became the Roman capital of Palestine; home of Cornelius the Roman centurion (Acts 10) and Philip, the evangelist (Acts 8:40; 21:8); Paul imprisoned there for two years (Acts 23:31-26:32). Now called Kaysariyeh.

CAESAREA PHILIPPI (sĕs'à-rē'à fī-lĭp'ī, Caesarea of Philip), city enlarged by Philip the tetrarch and named by him in honor of the Roman emperor. Peter confessed Jesus to be the Messiah there (Matt. 16: 13-17).

CAGE. 1. Basket to keep live birds (Jer. 5:27). 2. Prisoner cage, "ward" (Ezek. 19:9 ASV, RSV). 3. Haunt (Rev. 18:2).

CAIAPHAS, JOSEPH (kā'yà-făs), high priest from A. D. 18-36; plotted against and took part in condemnation of Jesus (Matt. 26: 3-5; 26:57; John 18:28); took part in trial of Peter and John (Acts 4:6-22).

CAIN (kān). 1. First son of Adam and Eve; murdered his brother Abel (Gen. 4). 2. Progenitor of the Kenites (Josh. 15:57). 3. Village in Judah (Josh. 15:57).

CAINAN (kā-ī'năn). 1. Son of Enos (Gen. 5:9-14; I Chron. 1:2; Luke 3:37). 2. Son of Arphaxad (Luke 3:36).

CALAH (kā'là), ancient city of Assyria on the Tigris built by Nimrod, grandson of Ham, son of Noah (Gen. 10:6-12).

CALAMUS (See Plants).

CALCOL (See Chalcol).

CALDRON, pot for boiling meat (Jer. 52: 18,19).

CALEB (kā'lĕb, dog). 1. Son of Jephunneh; prince of Judah; one of 12 men sent into Canaan to spy out the land (Num. 13:6), and with Joshua brought back a good report; entered the Promised Land (Josh. 14:15; Num. 13;14). 2. Son of Hezron, son of Judah (I Chron. 2:18,19,42), probably the same as "Chelubai" of I Chron. 2:9.

CALEB-EPHRATAH (kā'lĕb-ĕf'rà-tà), place

where Hezron died (I Chron. 2:19,24). Reading is doubtful.

CALENDAR. During the Bible period time was reckoned solely on astronomical observations. Days, months, and years were determined by the sun and moon. 1. Days of the week were not named by the Jews, but were designated by ordinal numbers. The Jewish day began in the evening with the appearance of the first stars. Days were subdivided into hours and watches. The Hebrews divided nights into three watches (Exod. 14:24; Judg. 7:19; Lam. 2:19). 2. The seven-day week is of Semitic origin. Egyptians had a week of 10 days. The Jewish week had its origin in the Creation account, and ran consecutively irrespective of lunar or solar cycles. This was done for man's physical and spiritual welfare. The Biblical records are silent regarding the observance of the Sabbath day from creation to the time of Moses. Sabbath observance was either revived or given special emphasis by Moses (Exod. 16:23; 20:8). 3. The Hebrew month began with the new moon. Before the exile months were designated by numbers. After the exile names adopted from the Babylonians were used. Synchronized Jewish sacred calendar: 1. Nisan (March-April) (7). 2. Iyyar (April-May) (8). 3. Sivan (May-June) (9). 4. Tammuz (June-July) (10). 5. Ab (July-August) (11). 6. Elul (August-September) (12). 7. Tishri (September-October) (1). 8. Heshvan (October-November) (2). 9. Kislev (November-December) (3). 10. Tabeth (December-January) (4). 11. Shebat (January-February) (5). 12. Adar (February-March) (6). 4. The Jewish calendar had two concurrent years, the sacred year, beginning in the spring with the month Nisan, and the civic year, beginning with Tishri, numbered as in parentheses above. The sacred year was instituted by Moses, and consisted of lunar months of 29-1/2 days each, with an intercalary month, called Adar Sheni, every 3 years. Every 7th year was a sabbatical year for the Jews–a year of solemn rest for landlords, slaves, beasts of burden, and land, and freedom for Hebrew slaves. Every 50th year was a Jubilee year, observed by family reunions, canceled mortgages, and return of lands to original owners (Lev. 25:8-17).

CALF, young bull or cow; used for food and for sacrifice; calves used for sacrifice were usually males a year old.

CALF, GOLDEN (See Calf Worship).

CALF WORSHIP, was a part of the religious worship of almost all ancient Semitic peoples. Bulls symbolized strength, vigor, and endurance. Aaron made a golden calf

(Exod. 32:4), and Jeroboam set up 2 golden calves in his kingdom (I Kings 12:29).

CALKER, one who makes a boat waterproof (Ezek. 27:9,27).

CALL, one of the most common verbs in the Bible, used principally with one or another of 4 different meanings: to speak out in the way of prayer (Jer. 33:3); to summon or appoint (Jer. 1:15); to name a person or thing (Gen. 1:5); to invite men to accept salvation (Heb. 3:1).

CALNEH (kăl'nĕ), one of the cities founded by Nimrod after the Flood (Gen. 10:10); in the S part of Mesopotamia.

CALNO (kăl'nō), city which tried to resist the Assyrians (Isa. 10:9).

CALVARY (kăl'và-rē, skull). The Latin is calvaria; the Hebrew, "Golgotha" (Matt. 27:33; Mark 15:22; John 19:17). A place not far from the walls of Jerusalem where Christ was crucified and near which He was buried (Luke 23:33). The exact site is a matter of dispute.

CAMEL, draught animal of Semitic peoples (II Kings 8:9); source of wealth; regarded as unclean by Israelites (Lev. 11:4); hair used for cloth (II Kings 1:8 RSV; Matt. 3:4).

CAMEL'S HAIR, mentioned only in Matt. 3:4 and Mark 1:6, where it is said that John the Baptist wore a garment of camel's hair. Such garments are still used in the Near East.

CAMON or **KAMON** (cā'mŏn), town in Gilead near Mazareth (Judg. 10:5).

CAMP, ENCAMPMENT, a group of tents intended for traveling or for temporary residence as in case of war. Israel in the wilderness was given precise instructions as to the order and arrangements of its camp, both at rest and in traveling (Num. 2, 3).

CAMPHIRE (kăm'fīr), Asiatic thorny shrub with fragrant white flowers (S. of Sol. 1:14; 4:13).

CANA of Galilee (kā'nà of găl'ĭ-lē), town in Galilee near Nazareth (John 2:1-11; 4: 46-54; 21:2).

CANAAN, CANAANITES (kā'nà, kā'nàn-ĭts). 1. Son of Ham; descendants occupied Canaan (Gen. 9:18,22; 10:6). 2. Canaan was one of the old names for Palestine, the land of the Canaanites dispossessed by the Israelites. In the Amarna letters (c. 1400 B. C.) the name is applied to the Phoenician coast. In the Hexateuch the Canaanites include the whole pre-Israelite population, even E of the Jordan. The Canaanites were of Semitic stock, and were part of a large migration of Semites from NE Arabia in the 3rd millennium B. C. The Israelites were never able completely to exterminate them.

CANAANITE, SIMON THE, one of the 12 apostles (Matt. 10:4).

CANANAEAN (kā'nà-nē'ăn), the description of Simon "the Zealot" in Matt. 10:4. Cananaean is Aramaic for Zealot. KJV has "Canaanite," but this is wrong.

CANDACE (kăn'dà-sĕ), the Queen of Ethiopia mentioned only in Acts 8:27. The name seems to have been a general designation of Ethiopian queens, like "Pharaoh" for Egyptian kings.

CANDLESTICK, a word found in the KJV which could usually more accurately be rendered "lampstand," because the "lights" were not candles at all, but olive-oil lamps.

CANE, probably the sweet calamus (Isa. 43:24; Jer. 6:20).

CANKER (kăn'kĕr, gangrene), a word that may mean "cancer" (II Tim. 2:17).

CANKERWORM, name given to larval stage of the locust; very voracious (Joel 1:4; 2:25).

CANNEH (kăn'ĕ), city, perhaps Calneh, with which Tyre traded (Ezek. 27:23).

CANONICITY. By the canon is meant the list of the books of the Bible accepted by the Christian church as genuine and inspired. The Protestant canon includes 39 books in the OT and 27 in the New. The Roman Catholic canon has 7 more books and some additional pieces in the OT. The Jews have the same OT canon as the Protestants. The OT canon was formed before the time of Christ, as is evident from Josephus (Against Apion 1:8), who wrote c. A. D. 90. We know very little of the history of the acceptance of the OT books as canonical. There is much more documentary evidence regarding the formation of the NT canon. The Muratorian Canon (c. A. D. 170), which survives only as a fragment, lists most of the NT books. Some of the books were questioned for a time for various reasons, usually uncertainty of authorship, but by the end of the 4th century our present canon was almost universally accepted, and this was done not by arbitrary decree of bishops, but by the general concensus of the church.

CANTICLES (See Song of Solomon).

CAPERNAUM (kà-pûr'nà-ŭm, village of Nahum), town on NW shore of Sea of Galilee where Jesus made His headquarters during His ministry in Galilee (Matt. 4:13; Mark 2:1), and where He performed many striking miracles (Matt. 8:5-13; Mark 2:1-12; John 4:46-54). The town has completely disappeared and its very site is a matter of debate.

CAPH (kăf), the 11th letter of the Hebrew alphabet corresponding to our "k." As a numeral it is "eleven."

CAPHTOR (kăf'tôr), place from which the Philistines originally came (Amos 9:7), probably from the island of Crete.

CAPPADOCIA (kăp'à-dō'shĭ-à), province in E part of Asia Minor; its people were Aryans (Acts 2:9; I Peter 1:1).

CAPTAIN, a title usually expressing leadership, not necessarily military as the "captain of the temple" (Acts 4:1). The term does not refer to specific grades or ranks in a military organization.

CAPTIVITY. The term Captivity has reference to the captivity of the Ten Tribes in

722 B. C. and to the captivity of Judah in 586 B. C. Both came in stages. After a series of invasions by the Assyrian kings Tiglath-pileser (II Kings 15:29; I Chron. 5:26) and Shalmaneser (II Kings 17:3,5), Sargon II (II Kings 17:6,7) took the Ten Tribes captive, and Esarhaddon and Ashurbanipal imported to the region of Samaria some conquered peoples from the East (Ezra 4:2,10). The Southern Kingdom was taken into captivity by the Babylonian king, Nebuchadnezzar, over a period of years. In 605 B. C. he took to Babylon some members of the nobility, including Daniel the prophet (II Chron. 36:2-7; Jer. 45:1; Dan. 1:1-3); in 597 B. C. he carried off King Jehoiachin and thousands of the nobility and leading people (II Kings 24:14-16), among them the prophet Ezekiel; in 586 B. C. he destroyed Jerusalem and deported into Babylonia all but the poorest of the land (II Kings 25:2-21); 5 years later still another group was taken into Babylonia. Ezra and Nehemiah describe the return of the captives, which took place in 538 B. C., when Cyrus king of Persia, to whom Babylonia fell the year before, issued a decree permitting the return of the Jews (Ezra 1:1-4), of whom 43,000 returned with Zerubbabel (Ezra 2:64). In 458 B. C. 1800 returned with Ezra.

CARAVAN, company of travelers united together for a common purpose or for mutual protection and generally equipped for a long journey, especially in desert country or through foreign and presumably hostile territory. Gen. 32, 33; I Sam. 30:1-20.

CARBUNCLE, a precious gem, perhaps a ruby or emerald; used in high priest's breastplate (Exod. 28:17; 39:10).

CARCAS (kàr'kàs), chamberlain in service of Ahasuerus (Esth. 1:10).

CARCASE (ASV and modern English, carcass), the dead body of a man or beast. Jews were ceremonially unclean if they touched a carcass (Lev. 11:8-40; Deut. 14:8; Num. 6:6,7; 9:10).

CARCHEMISH (kàr'kè-mìsh), city of the Hittites located on the W bank of the Euphrates 63 miles NE of Aleppo (Isa. 10:9). There Nebuchadnezzar won a great victory over Pharaoh Necho in 605 B. C. (Jer. 46:2; II Chron. 35:20).

CAREAH (kà-rè'á), more often "Kareah;" father of Johanan and Jonathan in Jeremiah's time (Jer. 40:8,13,15,16; 42:1,8; 43: 2,4,5).

CARMEL (kàr'mèl, garden). 1. Mountainous promontory jutting into the Mediterranean W of the Sea of Galilee. 2. Town of Judah c. 7 miles S of Hebron (Josh. 15:55; I Sam. 25:2,5).

CARMELITE (kàr'mèl-ìt), native of Judaean Carmel (I Sam. 27:3; I Chron. 11:37).

CARMI (kàr'mè). 1. Son of Reuben (Gen. 46:9; Num. 26:6). 2. Descendant of Judah and father of Achan (Josh. 7:1; I Chron. 4:1).

CARNAL (kàr'nàl), human nature corrupted by sin (Rom. 7:14; II Cor. 10:4; Heb. 7:16). The OT expression "lying carnally" describes adultery (Lev. 18:20) and fornication (Lev. 19:20).

CARPENTER (See Occupations, Professions).

CARPUS (kàr'pùs), friend of Paul (II Tim. 4:13).

CARRIAGE, baggage (I Sam. 17:22; Isa. 10:28).

CARSHENA (kàr'shè-nà), Medo-Persian prince (Esth. 1:14).

CARTS, light, small, usually two-wheeled vehicles for carrying people or freight (I Sam. 6:7-16; Amos 2:13).

CASIPHIA (cà-sìf'ì-à), place where exiled Levites lived (Ezra 8:17).

CASLUHIM (kàs'lù-hìm), people descended from Mizraim (Gen. 10:13,14; I Chron. 1:11,12).

CASSIA (See Plants).

CASTLE, fortified building or stronghold (Neh. 7:2 - KJV has "palace"). Where KJV has "castles," ASV sometimes, more correctly, uses encampments (I Chron. 6:54).

CASTOR AND POLLUX (kàs'tèr, pòl'ùks, sons of Zeus), sons of Zeus by Leda; considered tutelary deities favorable to sailors (Acts 28:11).

CATACOMBS, subterranean burial places used by the early church. Most are in Rome, where they extend for 600 miles.

CATERPILLAR (See Insects).

CATHOLIC EPISTLES, term applied to the Epistles of James, Peter, John, and Jude, probably because most of them are not addressed to individual churches or persons, but to the universal church.

CATTLE (See Animals).

CAUDA (kow'dà), small island c. 25 miles S of Crete (Acts 27:16 in KJV "Clauda").

CAUL. 1. Membrane covering stomach and part of liver (Lev. 3:4; 4:9). 2. Covering of heart or breast (Hos. 13:8). 3. Either bag or purse, or net for woman's hair (Isa. 3:18). RSV has "headband."

CAVE, hollowed-out place in the earth, usually in limestone, used as dwellings, places of refuge, burial, storehouses, cisterns, stables for cattle (Gen. 19:30; I Kings 19:9; Judg. 6:2; Matt. 27:60; John 11:38).

CEDAR (See Plants).

CEDRON (sè'dròn, in ASV more properly "Kidron"), ravine and winter brook flowing southward between Jerusalem and Mt. of Olives to Dead Sea; became burial ground (II Kings 23:6) and dumping place for destroyed idols (I Kings 15:13; II Chron. 29:16; 30:14; John 18:1).

CEILING (KJV and ERV "cieling"), in I Kings 6:15 the reference is to the walls of the Temple.

CELLAR, place for storage of wine (I Chron. 27:27).

CENCHREA (sèn'krè-à), eastern port of Corinth; had Christian church (Rom. 16:1).

CENSER, vessel for burning incense (Num. 16:6,7,39). Censers in Temple were made of gold (I Kings 7:50; II Chron. 4:22).

CENSUS, a numbering and registration of a people. The Bible tells of a number of censuses (Exod. 38:26; Num. 1:2,3; 26:51; I Chron. 21:1-6; 27:24; I Kings 5:15; II Chron.

2:17,18; Ezra 2; Luke 2:1).

CENTURION (cĕn-tū'rĭ-ŏn, **hundred**), commander of 100 soldiers in Roman army (Matt. 8:5-13; Acts 10; 22:25; 23:17).

CEPHAS (sē'fås, **rock**), name given by Jesus to Apostle Peter (John 1:42).

CHAFF, refuse of grain which has been winnowed (Job 21:18; Ps. 1:4; Isa. 17:13; Hos. 13:3; Zeph. 2:2); also dry grass (Isa. 5:24) and straw (Jer. 23:28). Often used figuratively for something worthless (Ps. 1:4; Matt. 3:12).

CHAIN, used as mark of distinction (Gen. 41:42; Dan. 5:7,16,29), for ornaments in the tabernacle (Exod. 28:14,22; 39:15,17,18), for fetters (Ps. 68:6; 149:8; Isa. 45:14); also used figuratively for oppression (Lam. 3:7; Ps. 73:6; 149:8).

CHALCEDONY (kăl-sĕd'ō-nē, kăl-sē-dō'nē), precious stone, perhaps agate (Rev. 21:19).

CHALCOL (kăl'kŏl), a wise man (I Kings 4:31; I Chron. 2:6).

CHALDAEA or **CHALDEA** (kăl-dē'à), country of which Babylon was the capital (Gen. 11:31; Job 1:17; Isa. 48:20; Jer. 50:10).

CHALDEAN (kăl-dē'ån), coming from Chaldaea.

CHALDEAN ASTROLOGERS (See Wise Men).

CHALDEES (kăl-dēz, kăl'dēz), people of Chaldea.

CHAMBERING, acts of illicit intercourse (Rom. 13:13).

CHAMBERLAIN (chăm'bĕr-lĭn). In the OT the eunuch in charge of a king's harem (Esth. 1:10,12,15; 2:3,14,15,21). In Acts 12:20 the chamberlain is an attendant on a lord in his bedchamber. In Rom. 16:23 he is a steward.

CHAMBERS OF IMAGERY, rooms in the Temple where 70 elders of Israel worshiped idols with incense (Ezek. 8:12).

CHAMELEON (See Animals).

CHAMOIS (See Animals).

CHANAAN (See Canaan).

CHANCELLOR (chăn-sĕl-lĕr), a Persian official in Palestine (Ezra 4:8,9,17).

CHANGERS OF MONEY, men who exchanged one currency for another at a premium (Matt. 21:12; Mark 11:15; John 2:14,15).

CHAPMAN (chăp'măn), a peddler (II Chron. 9:14).

CHARASHIM (kăr'å-shĭm, **craftsmen**), valvey E of Joppa between Ono to the N and Lod (Lydda) to the S (I Chron. 4:14).

CHARCHEMISH, CARCHEMISH (kăr'kē-mĭsh, kăr-kē'mĭsh), Hittite capital on the Euphrates.

CHARGER, dish or platter (Num. 7:13-85; Exod. 25:29; 37:16; Matt. 14:8,11).

CHARIOT (chăr'ĭ-ŭt), a two-wheeled vehicle for war, racing, processions, etc. (Gen. 41:43; 46:29; I Kings 18:44; II Kings 5:9; Acts 8:28). Used by enemies of Israel (Exod. 14:7-15:19; I Sam. 13:5), but not by Israel until time of David (II Sam. 8:4; I Kings 9:19; 10:26).

CHARITY (chăr'ĭ-tē), in the Bible never means giving to the poor, but a God-inspired love for the welfare of others (I Cor. 13). It is a translation of the Gr. agape, which means divine, unmotivated, spontaneous, self-giving love (John 3:16; I John 4:8).

CHARRAN (See Haran).

CHASTE, CHASTITY (chăst, chăs'tĭ-tē, **pure, consecrated**), the word originally meant pure in a ritual sense, but later developed a moral sense; virtuous; pure in thought and act (II Cor. 11:2; I Peter 3:2; Titus 2:5; I John 3:3).

CHASTISEMENT (chăs'tĭz-mĕnt, **discipline**), the word has many connotations: punishment (Jer. 30:14), discipline (Heb. 12:8), instruction (Acts 7:22; 22:3; II Tim. 3:16).

CHEBAR (kē'băr), river or canal in Chaldea on whose banks Ezekiel had visions (Ezek. 1:1; 3:23; 10:15,20,22; 43:3).

CHECKER WORK, ornamentation for the capitals of 2 pillars in Solomon's temple (I Kings 7:17).

CHEDORLAOMER (kĕd'ŏr-lā-ō'mûr), king of Elam against whom Abraham fought (Gen. 14:1,4,5,9,17).

CHEESE. Milk of cows, goats, or sheep was stored in skins, and because of the warm climate it would soon curdle and become cheese.

CHELAL (kē'lăl), man who put away his foreign wife (Ezra 10:30).

CHELLUH (kĕl'û), man who put away his foreign wife (Ezra 10:35).

CHELUB (kē'lŭb, **Caleb**). 1. Brother of Shuah (I Chron. 4:11). 2. Father of head of gardeners in David's time (I Chron. 27:26).

CHELUBAI (kē-lōō'bī), son of Hezron, elsewhere called Caleb (I Chron. 2:9).

CHEMARIM (kĕm'å-rĭm), Zeph. 1:4; idolatrous priests (II Kings 23:5; Hosea 10:5).

CHEMOSH (kē'mŏsh), god of Moab (Num. 21:29; Jer. 48:7,13,46); also worshiped by Ammonites (Judg. 11:24); Solomon introduced his worship into Jerusalem to please a foreign wife (I Kings 11:7,33).

CHENAANAH (kē-nā'å-nà). 1. Father of false prophet Zedekiah (I Kings 22:11,24; II Chron. 18:10,23). 2. Benjamite (I Chron. 7:10).

CHENANI (kē-nā'nī, kĕn'å-nī), Levite who helped returned exiles (Neh. 9:4).

CHENANIAH (kĕn'å-nī'à). 1. Chief Levite in David's time (I Chron. 15:22,27). 2. An Izharite, perhaps same as 1 (I Chron. 26:29).

CHEPHAR-HAAMMONI (kē'făr-hā-ăm'ō-nī), town of Benjamin, site unknown (Josh. 18:24).

CHEPHIRAH (kē-fī'rà), Hivite town (Josh. 9:17) in territory of Benjamin (Josh. 18:26).

CHERAN (kē'răn), Horite (Gen. 36:26; I Chron. 1:41).

CHERETHIM, CHERETHITES (kĕr'ē-thĭm, kĕr'ē-thĭts), Philistine tribe in S Palestine (I Sam. 30:14; Ezek. 25:16; Zeph. 2:5) from which David drew his bodyguard (II Sam. 8:18; 15:18).

CHERITH (kē'rĭth), brook where, at God's command, Elijah hid himself (I Kings 17:1-5).

CHERUB (chĕr'ŭb), pl., **CHERUBIM** (chĕr'ŭ-bĭm), KJV has cherubims. Outside the Bible, the English plural is cherubs. Cherubim are living heavenly creatures in winged human-animal form with the faces of lion, ox, man, and eagle. Guardians of Eden (Gen. 3:24); two golden cherubim were placed on the mercy seat above the ark (Exod. 25:18-22); curtains of the tabernacle were embroidered with cherubim (Exod. 26:1); God dwelt between cherubim (Num. 7:89; I Sam. 4:4) and rides on them (II Sam. 22:11); Solomon placed 2 cherubim in Holy of Holies (I Kings 6:23-28; 8:7). See Rev. 4:6,9.

CHERUB (kē'rŭb), unknown place in Babylonia from which exiles returned (Ezra 2:59).

CHESALON (kĕs'à-lŏn), landmark on N border of Judah, W of Jerusalem (Josh. 15:10).

CHESED (kē'sĕd, kĕs'ĕd), son of Nahor and nephew of Abraham (Gen. 22:22).

CHESIL (kē'sĭl, kĕs'ĭl), town in S of Judah, near Hormah and Ziklag (Josh. 15:30).

CHEST. 1. Receptacle for money to repair the Temple (II Kings 9,10; II Chron. 24:8,10,11). 2. Trunk (Ezek. 27:24).

CHESTNUT TREE (See Plants).

CHESULLOTH (kē-sŭl'ŏth), town in Issachar (Josh. 19:18).

CHEZIB (kē'zĭb), town in lowland of Judah (Gen. 38:5). Perhaps same as Achzib 1.

CHICKEN (See Birds).

CHIDON (kī'don), name for threshing floor where Uzza died for touching ark (I Chron. 13:9). Called Nachon in II Sam. 6:6. Near Jerusalem.

CHILD, CHILDREN. Among Israelites children were greatly desired (Gen. 15:2; 30:1; I Sam. 1:11,20); the firstborn belonged to God and must be redeemed (Num. 3:40-51); from the time of Abraham males were circumcised (Gen. 17:12; 21:4); discipline was firm (Prov. 22:15) and respect for parents commanded (Exod. 21:17). Jesus' love for children is often seen in the Gospels (Matt. 9:23-26; Mark 5:35-43). The Bible offers many attractive pictures of childhood: Moses (Exod. 2:1-10); Samuel (I Sam. 1:20-3:19); Jesus (Luke 2:7-40).

CHILDBEARING, an expression found only in I Tim. 2:15, a verse of uncertain meaning.

CHILDREN OF GOD. 1. Angelic beings (Job 1:6; 2:1; 38:7). 2. Men, by creation (Luke 3:38; Isa. 64:8). 3. Israel in covenant relation to God (Exod. 4:22). 4. Individual Israelites (Hos. 1:10). 5. Gentiles (Isa. 19:25). 6. Jesus (Matt. 3:17; 17:5; Luke 1:35). 7. God's redeemed ones (John 1:12; 14:6).

CHILDREN OF ISRAEL (See Israel).

CHILEAB (kĭl'ē-ăb), son of David (II Sam. 3:3).

CHILION (kĭl'ĭ-ŏn), son of Elimelech and Naomi; married Orpah (Ruth 1:2-5; 4:9,10).

CHILMAD (kĭl'măd), place (site unknown) which traded with Tyre (Ezek. 27:23).

CHIMHAM (kĭm'hăm), Gileadite friend of David (II Sam. 19:37-40).

CHINNERETH, CHINNEROTH (kĭn'ē-rĕth, -rŏth). 1. Fortified city on NW shore of the Sea of Galilee (Josh. 19:35). 2. District in Galilee (I Kings 15:20). 3. Ancient name for Sea of Galilee (Num. 34:11; Deut. 3:17; Josh. 11:2).

CHIOS (kī'ŏs), island in Aegean Sea 12 miles W of Smyrna (Acts 20:15).

CHISLEV (kĭz'lĕv, KJV Chisleu), 9th month of the Hebrew ritual year (Neh. 1:1; Zech. 7:1).

CHISLON (kĭz'lŏn), Benjamite (Num. 34:21).

CHISLOTH-TABOR (kĭs'lŏth-tā'bēr), same place as Chesulloth (Josh. 19:12).

CHITTIM, KITTIM (kĭt'ĭm), descendants of Javan (Gen. 10:4; I Chron. 1:7, Kittim); Cyprus and its inhabitants, and eventually also the islands and coasts of the Mediterranean (Isa. 23:12; Jer. 2:10; Ezek. 27:6).

CHIUN (kī'ŭn), the god Saturn (Amos 5:26). Prabably same as Rephan.

CHLOE (klō'ē), Christian woman, apparently of Corinth (I Cor. 1:11).

CHORASHAN (kŏr'ăsh'ăn), place S of Judah (I Sam. 30:30).

CHORAZIN (kō-rā'zĭn), city c. 2 miles N of Capernaum (Matt. 11:21; Luke 10:13).

CHOZEBA (kō-zē'bà), town of Judah (I Chron. 4:22).

CHRIST, JESUS (krist, jē'zŭs, Gr. Iesous, for Heb. Jeshua, Jehoshua, Joshua, Jehovah is salvation; Heb. mashiah, Gr. Christos, anointed). Christ signifies Anointed One (Acts 10:38); Jesus signifies Saviour (Matt. 1:21,25; Luke 1:31).

I. Comprehensive Life and Work. The Scriptures teach the pre-existence of Jesus (John 1:1). All things have been created and are maintained in existence by Him (Col. 1). Moses and the prophets spoke of Him in OT times (John 5:46; Luke 24:27,44). In OT times He appeared as the Angel of Jehovah (Gen. 18:1-19; Judg. 13). By His incarnation He took on human nature to reveal God more fully (John 1:14,18) and to redeem men (Mark 10:45). He is still the God-man, and in heaven He represents the saints before God (I John 2:1; Heb. 7:25). Some day He will return for His people, judge all men, and usher in His eternal kingdom, where there will be no sin and death.

II. The Earthly Ministry. The Messiah foretold in the OT came in the fulness of time (Gal. 4:4). God providentially supplied the proper background for His appearing and mission. The hand of God may be seen in using Augustus to make possible the birth of Jesus in the place appointed by prophetic announcement (Luke 2:1-7; Mic. 5:2). The shepherds and the Magi from the East illustrate the joy of humble folk in seeing the Saviour and the desire of Gentiles to share in the benefits of the incarnation. Christ was not simply a messenger from God like an OT prophet, but the eternal Son of God taking on human nature, yet free from any taint of sin. He had a divine and a human nature united in one person. The boy Jesus grew up in a normal way, developing in body and advancing in knowledge and wisdom. He performed no miracles until after He began His public ministry. At His baptism the Holy Spirit anointed Him to enable Him to fulfil His ministry. Immediately following his baptism Satan tempted Him to break His dependence on the Father and rely upon special consideration as the Son of God. His ministry was a brief one, about 2-1/2 or 3-1/2 years. The Gospel of John supplements the Synoptic Gospels in telling about the place of Jesus' ministry. A large part of his Gospel reports His ministry in Judea, whereas the Synoptic Gospels stress His ministry in Galilee, although there are also notices of visits to Tyre and Sidon (Matt. 15:21-28), Caesarea-Philippi (Matt. 16:13ff), the Decapolis (Mark 7:31), Samaria (Luke 9:51-56), and Perea (Mark 10:1). During His Galilean ministry Jesus made Capernaum His headquarters. From there He went forth to the surrounding country healing the sick, casting out demons, and preaching the coming of the kingdom of God. By the kingdom of God is meant the rule of God over His willing creatures. The kingdom is both a present and a future reality. Entrance into the present aspect of the kingdom comes through faith in the Son of God. The final phase will be inaugurated when Jesus comes again in power and glory. A characteristic teaching method of Jesus was the parable. This He used to veil the truth from His enemies, who were hoping to hear Him say something incriminating so they could arrest Him, and to reveal the truth to His friends more clearly. During the earlier phase of His ministry Jesus ministered mainly to the multitude. He was popular with it until He refused to be made king after the feeding of the 5,000 and made clear that He was not the political redeemer they were looking for, but was Bread from heaven. The multitude then abandoned Him, and He spent a large part of His remaining ministry teaching the Twelve, chiefly about His coming death and resurrection. Somehow even those closest to Him could not see the necessity of His death, even when they recognized Him as Messiah and the Son of the living God, as Peter did at Caesarea Philippi. His chief opponents were the scribes and Pharisees, who resented His rejection of the traditions they kept so carefully and who were shocked when He claimed to be deity and declared men's sins forgiven. They made common cause with their opponents, the Sadducees, and with the Herodians to destroy Jesus. From the days of the transfiguration on, He moved steadily toward Jerusalem to fulfil His mission at the cross. At least a quarter of the Gospel material is devoted to Passion Week and the resurrection story, showing that for the early church the events of this period were of supreme importance. Christ came to die; but His resurrection was the Father's attestation to the truth of the claims Christ made about Himself.

III. Names, Titles, and Offices. The name **Jesus** means Saviour (Matt. 1:21) and is the same as the Hebrew name Joshua. It is usually joined with other terms; when it stands alone it is doubtless for the purpose of emphasizing His humanity. **Christ**, meaning "anointed one," is the Greek equivalent of the Hebrew word **Messiah**. Often it is used with the definite article, which gives it the force of "the promised Christ." Sometimes Jesus forbade people to make Him known as the Messiah (Matt. 16:20). Jesus knew that if this title should be used freely of Him among the Jews, it would excite the populace to expect in Him a political Messiah. Since this was not the purpose of Jesus He suppressed the use of the term except among the apostles (Matt. 16:16). The name **Emmanuel** occurs only once (Matt. 1:23), and means "God with us." Because of the years He spent in Nazareth Jesus was often called the Nazarene (Luke 24:19). When Jesus referred to Himself His most usual method of identification was to use the title **Son of Man**. This may occasionally lay stress on Jesus' humanity, but in the main it serves to point to His transcendence as a heavenly figure (Dan. 7:13). The designation **Son of God** sets off the uniqueness of this particular Son. It is to be noticed that whenever Jesus spoke of the Father He recognized a unique relationship to Him, one that human beings cannot share. The title **Son of David** (Matt. 21:9; Luke 18:38) is a distinctly Messianic title pointing to Him as the one who fulfilled the Davidic covenant. A few passages proclaim outright that Jesus is **God** (John 1:1,18; 20:28; Rom. 9:5; Titus 2:13; Heb. 1:8). The term **Lord** (Acts 2:36; 10:36; Rom. 10:9; I Cor. 8:6; Phil. 2:11) denotes the sovereignty of Christ, His headship over the individual believer, the church as a body, and all things. The title **Word** (John 1:1,14; I John 1:1) points to Jesus as the revealer of God. The designation **Servant** (Phil. 2:7) illustrates that the early church regarded Jesus as fulfilling the Servant of Jehovah role in Himself (see Matt. 12: 17-21). The name **Saviour** suggests the reason for Jesus coming into the world (Luke 2:11; John 4:42). Jesus' saving mission is also declared in the expression, **Lamb of God** (John 1:29,36). Jesus is referred to as **High Priest** in Hebrews and **Mediator** between God and man in I Tim. 2:5. Paul uses the title **Last Adam** (I Cor. 15:45) in contrast to the first Adam, suggesting the undoing of the consequences of sin brought on by Adam's transgression.

IV. Character. To describe Jesus in all the perfections of His character would be impossible. Certain perfections deserve special mention, but it cannot be said that

He was noted for these above others. He had **integrity**. He was truth incarnate. He had **courage** – both physical courage and the courage of conviction. He had **compassion** as He dealt with people. He clothed Himself with **humility**. His character was crowned with **sinlessness** – not simply the absence of sin, but a positive holiness in all that He said and did.

V. **Influence**. The influence of Jesus, in spite of the brevity of His life, is seen in the NT, where every book centers in Him. When He comes into a human life, He brings to it a new point of reference and a new set of values. Sinners are transformed by Him. He is the conscience of the world. He has mightily affected society in its organized state. He has taught the world the dignity of human life, improved the status of women, brought about the abolition of slavery, stimulated interest in social work. The arts owe their sublimest achievements to the desire to honor Him. Even moralists and philosophers who do not acknowledge His deity nevertheless acknowledge the excellence of His moral teaching.

CHRISTIAN (krĭs'chăn, krĭst'yăn). The meaning is "adherent of Christ." The disciples were first called Christians in Antioch (Acts 11:26).

CHRISTIANITY. The word does not occur in the Bible, but was first used by Ignatius, in the first half of the 2nd century. It designates all that which Jesus Christ brings to men of faith, life, and salvation.

CHRISTMAS, the anniversary of the birth of Christ, and its observance; celebrated by most Protestants and by Roman Catholics on Dec. 25; by Eastern Orthodox churches on Jan. 6; and by the Armenian church on Jan. 19. The first mention of its observance on Dec. 25 is in the time of Constantine, c. A. D. 325. The date of the birth of Christ is not known. The word Christmas is formed of Christ plus Mass, meaning a religious service in commemoration of the birth of Christ. It is not clear whether the early Christians thought of or observed Christmas, but once introduced the observance spread throughout Christendom. Some Christian bodies disapprove of the festival.

CHRONICLES, I and II. Heb. name is "The words (affairs) of the days," meaning "The annals." Jerome first entitled them "Chronicles." Originally they formed a single composition, but were divided into I and II Chronicles in the LXX, c. 150 B. C. They stand last in the Heb. canon. Ancient tradition and modern scholarship suggest that they were written by Ezra some time c. 450 B. C. The work consists of 4 parts: genealogies, to enable the Jews to establish their lines of family descent (I Chron. 1-9); the kingdom of David, as a pattern for the ideal theocratic state (I Chron. 10:29); the glory of Solomon (II Chron. 1-9); the history of the southern kingdom

(II Chron. 10-36).

CHRONOLOGY, NEW TESTAMENT. In ancient times historians were not accustomed to record history under exact dates, but were satisfied when some specific event was related to the reign of a noted ruler or a famous contemporary. Our method of dating events in reference to the birth of Christ was started by Dionysius Exiguus, a monk who lived in the 6th century. The birth of Christ may be dated in the latter part of the year 5 B. C., as it is known that Herod the Great died in 4 B. C., and according to the Gospels Jesus was born some time before the death of the king. Luke gives the age of Jesus at His baptism as "about thirty years" (3:23). This would bring the baptism at c. A. D. 26 or 27. Since Herod began the reconstruction of the temple in 20 B. C., the "forty and six years" mentioned by the Jews during the first Passover of Jesus' public ministry (John 2:13-22) brings us to A. D. 27 for this first Passover. The ministry of John the Baptist began about the middle of A. D. 26. The time of the crucifixion is determined by the length of the ministry of Jesus. Mark's Gospel seems to require at least 2 years. John's Gospel explicitly mentions 3 Passovers (2:23; 6:4; 11:55). If the feast of 5:1 is also a Passover, as seems probable, then the length of the ministry of Jesus was full three years and a little over. This places the crucifixion at the Passover of A. D. 30. As for the Apostolic Age the chronological data are very limited and uncertain. The death of Herod Agrippa I, one of the fixed dates of the NT, is known to have taken place in A. D. 44. This was the year of Peter's arrest and miraculous escape from prison. The proconsulship of Gallio was between 51 and 53, and this would bring the beginning of Paul's ministry at Corinth to c. A. D. 50. The accession of Festus as governor, under whom Paul was sent to Rome, probably took place c. 59,60.

The following chronological table is regarded as approximately correct:

Birth of Jesus	5 B. C.
Baptism of Jesus – late A. D. 26 or early 27	
First Passover of Ministry	27
Crucifixion of Jesus	30
Conversion of Saul	34 or 35
Death of Herod Agrippa I	44
Epistle of James	before 50
First Missionary journey	48-49
Jerusalem Conference	49 or 50
Second Missionary journey	
	begun spring 50
Paul at Corinth	50-52
I and II Thessalonians from Corinth	51
Galatians from Corinth (?)	early 52
Arrival of Gallio as Proconsul	May 52
Third Missionary journey	begun 54
Paul at Ephesus	54-57
I Corinthians from Ephesus – spring 57	
II Corinthians from	
Macedonia	fall 57

Romans from Corinth — winter 57-58
Paul's arrest at Jerusalem — Pentecost 58
Imprisonment at Caesarea — 58-60
On Island of Malta — winter 60-61
Arrival at Rome — spring 61
Roman Imprisonment — 61-63
Colossians, Philemon,
Ephesians — summer 62
Philippians — spring 63
Paul's release and further work — 63-65
I Timothy and Titus — 63
Epistle to the Hebrews — 64
Synoptic Gospels and Acts — before 67
I and II Peter from Rome — 64-65
Peter's death at Rome — 65
Paul's second Roman imprisonment — 66
II Timothy — 66
Death at Rome — late 66 or early 67
Epistle of Jude — 67-68
Writings of John — before 100
Death of John — 98-100

CHRONOLOGY, OLD TESTAMENT. The chronology of the OT presents many complex and difficult problems. Often the data are completely lacking, and where they exist, they are not adequate or plain. Even where the data are abundant, the exact meaning is not immediately clear, and there are therefore many interpretations possible. For the period from the creation to the Deluge the only Biblical data are the ages of the patriarchs in the genealogical tables of Genesis 5 and 7:11. Extra-Biblical sources for this period are almost completely lacking. For the period from the Deluge to Abraham we are again dependent upon the genealogical data in the Bible. The numbers vary in the Masoretic text, the LXX, and the Samaritan Pentateuch. The construction of an absolute chronology from Adam to Abraham is not now possible on the basis of the available data. The patriarchs may be dated c. 2100-1875; the Exodus c. 1445 B. C.; the beginning of the conquest of Canaan c. 1405. An accurate chronology of the period of the judges is impossible, as the length of the period is unknown, and a number of the judges undoubtedly exercised control at the same time. The United Monarchy began c. 1050 B. C.; the Divided Monarchy in 931 B. C. The kingdom of Israel went into the Assyrian captivity c. 722 B. C.; and the kingdom of Judah into the Babylonian captivity in 586 B. C. Judah returned from the Babylonian captivity in 538 B. C. Nehemiah returned to Babylon in 433 B. C.

CHUB (kŭb), ally of Egypt (Ezek. 30:5).
CHUN (kŭn), Aramean city (I Chron. 18:8), called "Berothai" in II Sam. 8:8.
CHURCH. The English "church" derives from the Greek kuriakos (belonging to the Lord), but it stands for another Greek word, ekklesia (whence "ecclesiastical"), denoting an assembly. In ancient Greece the ekklesia meant the assembled citizens of a community. In the LXX it is the translation of qahal, meaning "convocation," "assembly" (Deut. 23:2; I Sam. 19:20;

II Chron. 20:5; Ps. 149:1; Ezra 10:8). In the NT the word is used to describe local groups of believers (Acts 5:11; 7:38; 8:1; Rom. 16:1; I Cor. 1:2; I Thess. 1:1), and all believers in universal fellowship (I Cor. 10:32). The church is not primarily a human structure, but the church of Jesus Christ (Matt. 16:18), or of the living God (I Tim. 3:15). It is the fellowship of the people of God; the bride of Christ (Eph. 5:25; the body of Jesus Christ (Rom. 12:5; I Cor. 12:12; Eph. 4:4,12,16).

CHUSHAN RISHATHAIM (kū'shăn rish'á-thā'im), Mesopotamian king (Judg. 3:5-11).
CHUZA (kū'zá), steward of Herod Antipas whose wife Joanna was among women who ministered to Jesus and His disciples (Luke 8:3).
CILICIA (sĭ-lĭsh'ĭ-á), country in SE Asia Minor. Its chief city was Tarsus, birthplace of Paul (Acts 21:39; 22:3; 23:34). It became a Roman province in 100 B. C. The gospel reached it early (Acts 15:23), probably through Paul (Acts 9:30; Gal. 1:21), who confirmed the churches established there (Acts 15:41).
CINNAMON (See Plants).
CIRCUMCISION (sir-kŭm-sĭ'shŭn, a cutting around), the cutting off of the foreskin, a rite instituted by God as the sign of the covenant between Him and Abraham and his descendants (Gen. 17:10) that He would be their God, and they were to belong to Him, worshiping and obeying only Him. It was made a legal institution in the wilderness by Moses (Lev. 12:3; John 7:22, 23). Every male child was circumcised on the 8th day after its birth. Other nations also practiced the rite (Egyptians, Arabians, etc.). The Christian church refused to force Gentiles to be circumcised (Acts 15:5; Gal. 5:2).
CISTERN (sĭs'tẽrn), an artificial reservoir dug in the earth or rock for the collection and storage of water from rain or spring (Prov. 5:15; Eccl. 12:6; Isa. 36:16; Jer. 2:13). Cisterns were a necessity in Palestine with its long, dry, rainless summers. Empty cisterns were sometimes used as prisons (Gen. 37:22; Jer. 38:6; Zech. 9:11).
CITIES OF REFUGE, six cities set apart by Moses and Joshua as places of asylum for those who had accidentally committed manslaughter. There they remained until a fair trial could be held. If proved innocent of willful murder, they had to remain in the city of refuge until the death of the high priest (Num. 35; Deut. 19:1-13; Josh. 20).
CITIES OF THE PLAIN (circle of the Jordan), cities near the Dead Sea, including Sodom, Gomorrah, Admah, Zeboiim, and Zoar. Lot lived in Sodom (Gen. 13:10-12). They were destroyed because of their wickedness (Gen. 19). They were probably at the S end of the Dead Sea, and it is believed that the sea covers the site.
CITIZENSHIP (Gr. politeuma, commonwealth), in the NT "citizen" means usually

no more than the inhabitant of a city (Judg. 9:2-20; Acts 21:39) or a country (Luke 15:15; 19:14). Roman citizenship brought with it certain privileges, such as the right of appeal to the emperor and exemption from shameful punishments; and it could be acquired by birth, purchase, or through special service and favor (Acts 16:37-39; 22:25-29; 23:27). Paul brings out that Christians are citizens of a heavenly commonwealth, and ought to live accordingly (KJV "conversation" Phil. 1:27; 3:20).

CITY. In ancient times cities owed their origin not to organized manufacture, but to agriculture. Usually they were built on the side of a mountain or the top of a hill, and where a sufficient supply of water was assured. Cities always had walls, many of them 20-30 ft. thick, which were protected sometimes with moats and towers. Gates of the city were closed at night (Josh. 2:5,7). Within the walls, the important features of a city were the Tower or Stronghold; a High Place, where sacrifices were offered and feasts held; the Broad Place by the Gate, an open area just inside the city gate serving the purpose of social intercourse in general; and the streets, which were narrow, winding, unpaved alleys, rarely cleaned, and never lighted. Little is known about the way city government was administered.

CITY OF DAVID. 1. Jebusite stronghold of Zion captured by David and made by him his royal residence (II Sam. 5:6-9). 2. Bethlehem, the home of David (Luke 2:4).

CLAUDA (klô'dà), small island off SW coast of Crete (Acts 27:16).

CLAUDIA (klô'dĭ-à), Christian at Rome (II Tim. 4:21).

CLAUDIUS (klô-dĭ-ūs), 4th Roman emperor (41-54). He banished all Jews from Rome (Acts 18:2). The famine foretold by Agabus took place in his reign (Acts 11:28).

CLAUDIUS LYSIAS (klô-dĭ-ūs lis'ĭ-às), chief captain of Roman forces in Jerusalem who rescued Paul from fanatical Jewish rioters (Acts 21:31; 24:22). To protect Paul he sent him to Caesarea.

CLAY, substance widely used in ancient times for making brick, mortar, pottery, and, in some countries, tablets for inscriptions.

CLAY TABLETS, were made of clay which, while still wet, had wedge-shaped letters imprinted on them with a stylus, and then were kiln-fired or sun-dried. They were made of various shapes, and were often placed in a clay envelope. Vast quantities have been excavated in the Near East. The oldest go back to 3000 B. C.

CLEANTHES (klè-ăn'thēz), Greek Stoic philosopher of 3rd cent. B. C. whose poem, **Hymn to Zeus**, is quoted by Paul (Acts 17:28).

CLEMENT (klĕm'ĕnt), Christian fellow-laborer of Paul's (Phil. 4:3).

CLEOPAS (klè'ô-pàs), one of two disciples with whom Jesus walked on the resurrection day (Luke 24:18).

CLEOPHAS (klè'ô-fàs), husband of one of the Marys (John 19:25).

CLERK (See Occupations, Professions).

CLOAK (See Dress).

CLOSET, private room or storage closet (Luke 12:3).

CLOTH, CLOTHES, CLOTHING (See Dress).

CLOUD. Most references to clouds in the Bible are metaphoric or figurative, symbolizing calamity (Ezek. 30:3), danger (Isa. 44:22), mystery (Job 3:5), presence of God (Isa. 19:1), etc.

CLOUD, PILLAR OF, symbol of the presence and guidance of God in the wilderness journeys of the Israelites (Exod. 13:21,22).

CLOUT (See Dress).

CNIDUS (nĭ'dŭs), city of Caria, at the SW corner of Asia Minor, past which Paul sailed on his journey to Rome (Acts 27:7).

COAL. The Bible never refers to true mineral coal, which has not been found in Palestine proper. The references are always either to charcoal or to live embers of any kind. Hebrews usually used charcoal for warmth or cooking. Isa. 47:14; John 18:18; 21:9.

COAT (See Dress).

COCK (See Birds).

COCKATRICE (See Animals).

COCK CROWING, when referring to time is the period between 12 and 3 a.m. (Matt. 26:34; Mark 13:35).

COCKLE (See Plants).

COELE SYRIA (sĕl'ē-sĕr'ĭ-à, hollow Syria), name for that part of Syria that lay between the Lebanon and Anti-Lebanon Mts.

COFFER (kŏf'ẽr), box used by Philistines to return Ark of Israelites (I Sam. 6:8, 11,15).

COFFIN, probably box in which mummy was placed (Gen. 50:26).

COIN (See Money).

COL-HOZEH (kŏl-hō'zè), father of Shallum (Neh. 3:15) and Baruch (Neh. 11:5).

COLLAR (See Dress).

COLLEGE, quarter of Jerusalem near the Fish Gate (II Kings 22:14; II Chron. 34:22).

COLLOP (kŏl'ŭp), slice of meat or fat (Job 15:27).

COLONY, settlement of Roman citizens, authorized by the government, in conquered territory; served as a garrison (Acts 16:12).

COLOSSAE (kŏ-lŏs'ē), city of Phrygia, c. 12 miles from Laodicea and Hierapolis (Col. 1:2). Philemon and Onesimus were members of the church there (Col. 4:9).

COLOSSIANS, BOOK OF (kŏ-lŏsh'ănz), epistle written by Paul in prison; although he does not say where (Col. 4:3,10,18), most likely in Rome, c. A. D. 62. It was written to combat a serious Judaic-Gnostic error. Outline: 1. Salutation and thanksgiving (1:1-8). 2. Doctrinal section (1:9-2:5). 3. Practical exhortations (2:6-4:6). 4. Concluding salutations (4:7-18).

COLT (See Animals).

COMFORTER, THE (See Holy Spirit).

COMMANDMENT, used in the English Bible to translate a number of Heb. and Gr. words meaning law, ordinance, statute, word, judgment, precept, saying, charge, etc.

COMMANDMENTS, TEN. In Heb. the Ten Commandments are called the ten words (Exod. 34:28; Deut. 4:13) or the words (Exod. 20:1; Deut. 5:22). They are God's precepts given to Moses on Mt. Sinai. The Bible contains 2 accounts of how they were given (Exod. 20:1-17; Deut. 5:6-21). They were written on 2 tables of stone (Exod. 31:18; 32:15-19; 34:1-4,27-29; Deut. 10:1-5). There is uncertainty as to how they are to be numbered and how they were divided between the two tables. They were not intended to be a "yoke of bondage" to the Israelites, but a wise provision for God's people to enable them to enter a life of joyful fellowship with their God. The first four deal with man's relationship to God; the others, with his relationship to other people. All except the 4th are repeated in the NT and are expected to be obeyed by Christians. Indeed, Jesus shows that God's interpretation is stricter than that of the Jews. Except as the NT deepens and extends its principles, the Decalogue represents the high-water level of morality. Jesus says that love is the fulfilment of the law (Matt. 22:35-40).

COMPEL, as used by Jesus in Luke 14:23 does not mean physical force, but zeal and moral urgency.

CONANIAH (còn'á-ni'á, **Jehovah has founded**). 1. Levite (II Chron. 31:12,13). 2. Another Levite (II Chron. 35:9).

CONCISION (còn-sizh'ûn, mutilation, cutting), circumcision that is wholly ceremonial and without regard for its spiritual significance (Phil. 3:2).

CONCUBINE, a woman lawfully united in marriage to a man in a relation inferior to that of the regular wife (Gen. 16:1; 22:24; Judg. 8:31; II Sam. 3:7; 5:13). Law of Moses allowed it (Exod. 21:7-11; Deut. 21:10-14). A number of prominent OT figures had concubines – Abraham (Gen. 25:6), Jacob (Gen. 35:22), Gideon (Judg. 8:31), David (II Sam. 5:13), Solomon (I Kings 11:3), Rehoboam (II Chron. 11:21).

CONCUPISCENCE (còn-kū'pĭ-sèns), intense longing for what God would not have us to have (Rom. 7:8; Col. 3:5; I Thess. 4:5).

CONDUIT (kòn'dū-ĭt), a channel for conveying water from its source to the place where it was delivered (II Kings 20:20; Isa. 7:3).

CONEY (See Animals).

CONFECTION, a compound of perfume or medicine (not sweetmeats) (Exod. 30:35).

CONFECTIONARY, a perfumer; found only in I Sam. 8:13.

CONFECTIONER (See Occupations, Professions).

CONFESSION, to acknowledge one's faith in anything, as in the existence and authority of God, or the sins of which one has been guilty (Matt. 10:32; Lev. 5:5; Ps. 32:5); to concede or allow (John 1:20; Acts 24:14; Heb. 11:13); to praise God by thankfully acknowledging Him (Rom. 14:11; Heb. 13:15).

CONGREGATION, the Hebrew people viewed in their collective capacity as God's people or as an assembly of the people summoned for a definite purpose (I Kings 8:65). Sometimes it refers to an assembly of the whole people; sometimes to a part (Num. 16:3; Exod. 12:6; 35:1; Lev. 4:13).

CONIAH (kō-nī'á, **Jehovah is creating**), a form of the name Jehoiachin (Jer. 22: 24,28; 37:1).

CONSCIENCE, awareness that an action conforms to or is contrary to one's standard of right and wrong (Acts 23:1; I Tim. 1:5; Heb. 13:18). Important NT passages that deal with it are Rom. 2:14,15 and I Cor. 8:10. The NT stresses the need of having a good conscience toward God.

CONSECRATION, an act by a person or thing dedicated to the service and worship of God, like Levites (Exod. 13:2; Num. 3:12), objects (Josh. 6:19), nations (Exod. 19:6).

CONVERSATION, a word often used in the KJV to signify conduct or manner of life, especially with respect to morals (Phil. 1:27; 3:20).

CONVERSION (kòn-vèr'zhûn, a turning), a turning, which may be literal or figurative, ethical or religious, either from God, or, more frequently, to God. It implies a turning from and a turning to something, and is therefore associated with repentance (Acts 3:19; 26:20) and faith (Acts 11:21). On its negative side it is turning from sin, and on its positive side it is faith in Christ (Acts 20:21). Although it is an act of man, it is done by the power of God (Acts 3:26). In the process of salvation, it is the first step in the transition from sin to God.

CONVICTION, means to convince or prove guilty. It is the first stage of repentance, experienced when the evil nature of sin has been brought home to the penitent, and it has been proved to him that he is guilty of it. The word does not appear in the KJV, but both Testaments give many examples of it, most notably Psalm 51.

CONVOCATION (kòn-vō-kà'shûn), a religious festival during which no work could be done (Num. 10:2; Isa. 1:13; 4:5).

COOS (kō'òs, summit), island off the coast of Caria in S Asia Minor (Acts 21:1).

COPING (kōp'ĭng), parapet on house roof (I Kings 7:9).

COPPERSMITH. The word should be rendered "worker in brass" (II Tim. 4:14).

COR (See Weights and Measures).

CORAL (kòr'ál), ranked by Hebrews with precious stones (Job 28:18; Ezek. 27:16).

CORBAN (kòr'bàn, an offering), an offering, bloody or unbloody, made to God (Lev. 1:2,3; 2:1; 3:1; Num. 7:12-17; Mark 7:11).

CORD. In the ancient East cords were made of skins of animals, vines, bark of trees, flax; the word is also used figuratively in the Bible (Job. 36:8; Prov. 5:22; Eccles. 4:12).

CORIANDER (See Plants).

CORINTH (còr'inth, ornament), Greek city on isthmus between the Peloponnesus and the mainland; destroyed by Romans in 146 B. C. and rebuilt in 46 B. C.; capital of the Roman province of Achaia. Paul founded a church there (Acts 18:1; 20:2,3) wrote two epistles to it.

CORINTHIANS (kŏ-rin'thĭ-ănz), First and Second Epistles. I Corinthians was written by the Apostle Paul in Ephesus on his 3rd missionary journey (Acts 19; I Cor. 16:8,19), probably in 56 or 57. He had previously written a letter to the Corinthians which has not come down to us (I Cor. 5:9), and in reply had received a letter in which he was asked a number of questions. Paul had also heard of factions in the church from the servants of Chloe (1:11). These circumstances led to the writing of I Corinthians. Outline: 1. Factions in the church (1-4). 2. Incestuous marriage (5). 3. Disputes of Christians brought before heathen courts (6). 4. Phases of the subject of marriage (7). 5. Meat offered to idols (8-10). 6. Head coverings for women; proper observance of the Lord's Supper (11). 7. Spiritual gifts (12-14). 8. Resurrection of the body (15). 9. Collection for the poor of Jerusalem; closing remarks (16).

II Corinthians was written by Paul somewhere in Macedonia on his 3rd missionary journey as a result of a report concerning the church brought to him by Titus. Outline: 1. Some thoughts on the crisis through which the church has just passed (1-7). 2. Collection for the poor (8,9). 3. Defense of Paul's ministry against the attacks of his enemies and a vindication of his apostleship (10-13).

CORMORANT (See Birds).

CORN (See Plants, Wheat).

CORNELIUS (kŏr-nĕl'yŭs, of a horn), Roman centurion stationed at Caesarea, and the first Gentile convert (Acts 10,11).

CORNERSTONE, foundation stone upon which a building is started. The word is used in both a literal and a figurative sense in Scripture (Ps. 118:22; Job 38:6; Isa. 28:16; Zech. 10:4, etc.). Christ is the Cornerstone of the Church (Matt. 21:42; Eph. 2:20; I Peter 2:5-7).

CORNET, a wind instrument with a curved horn, the sound being a dull monotone (I Chron. 15:28; Ps. 98:6; Dan. 3:5,10,15; Hos. 5:8).

COS, COOS (kŏs), island in Aegean Sea; mentioned in connection with Paul's 3rd missionary journey (Acts 21:1).

COSAM (kŏ'săm), ancestor of Christ (Luke 3:28).

COSMETICS, any of the various preparations used for beautifying the hair and skin (II Kings 9:30; Jer. 4:30; Ezek. 23:40).

COTTON, originally designated muslin or calico; later included linen (Esth. 1:6;

Isa. 19:9).

COUCH, a piece of furniture for reclining, but sometimes only a rolled-up mat (Amos 6:4; Matt. 9:6).

COULTER (kŏl'tẽr), a plowshare (I Sam. 13:19-21).

COUNCIL (koun'sĕl). 1. Group of people gathered for deliberation (Gen. 49:6; II Kings 9:5). 2. The Jewish Sanhedrin (Matt. 26:59; Acts 5:34) and lesser courts (Matt. 10:17; Mark 13:9).

COUNSELLOR (koun'sĕ-lẽr), one who gives counsel; a member of the Sanhedrin (Mark 15:43; Luke 23:50).

COURSE OF PRIESTS AND LEVITES. David divided the priests and Levites into 24 groups, called courses in Luke 1:8, each with its own head (I Chron. 24:1ff). Each course officiated a week at a time.

COURT. 1. Enclosed yard of a building (II Sam. 17:18; II Kings 20:4; Jer. 32:2). 2. System of courts was set up by Moses and his successors (Exod. 18:25,26).

COVENANT, a mutual agreement between 2 or more persons to do or refrain from doing certain acts; sometimes the undertaking of one of the parties. In the Bible God is regarded as the witness of this pact (Gen. 31:50; I Sam. 20:8). In the OT there are 3 different types of covenant. 1. A two-sided covenant between human parties, both of which voluntarily accept the terms of the agreement (I Sam. 18:3,4; Mal. 2:14; Obad. 7). 2. A one-sided disposition imposed by a superior party (Ezek. 17:13,14). In this God "commands" a covenant which man, the servant, is to obey (Josh. 23:16). 3. God's self-imposed obligation, for the reconciliation of sinners to Himself (Deut. 7:6-8; Ps. 89:3,4). Covenants of God: 1. Edenic, God's promise of redemption (Gen. 3:15). 2. Noachian, for the preservation of the race (Gen. 9:9). 3. Abrahamic, granting blessings through Abram's family (Gen. 15:18). 4. Sinaitic, designating Israel as God's chosen people (Exod. 19:5,6). 5. Levitical, making reconciliation through priestly atonement (Num. 25:12,13). 6. Davidic, Messianic salvation promised through David's dynasty (II Sam. 23:5). The prophets foretold a New Covenant (Jer. 31:31-34) which would center in a person (Isa. 42:6; 49:8). In the New Covenant man is placed in right relationship to God through Christ (Heb. 7:22; 8:6-13; II Cor. 3:6-18).

COVERING THE HEAD, in ancient Greece only immoral women appeared in the streets with their heads uncovered. Paul, in I Cor. 11:15, means that Christian women cannot afford to disregard social convention; it would hurt their testimony.

COVETOUSNESS (kŭv'ĕt-ŭs-nĕs). 1. Desire to have something (I Cor. 12:31). 2. Inordinate desire for what belongs to another (Exod. 20:17; Rom. 7:7).

COW (See Animals: Cattle).

COZ (kŏz), Judahite (I Chron. 4:8).

COZBI (kŏz'bĭ), Midianite woman slain by

Phineas (Num. 25:16-18).

CRACKNEL, a light, crisp biscuit, of a curved or hollowed shape (I Kings 14:3).

CRAFT, CRAFTSMAN (See Occupations, Professions).

CRAFTINESS, CRAFTY, guile, cunning (Dan. 8:25; Luke 20:23).

CRANE (See Birds).

CREATION. The Bible clearly teaches that the universe, and all matter, had a beginning, and came into existence through the will of the eternal God (Gen. 1,2). The Bible gives no information as to how long the original creation of matter occurred, or the first day of creation began, or the sixth day ended. It appears that God ceased His creative activity after the 6th day and now rests from His labors. The Bible does not support the view that everything now existing has come into its present condition as a result of natural development. God determined that plants and animals were to reproduce "after their kind." The Scriptures do not say how large a "kind" is, and nothing in the Bible denies the possibility of change and development within the limits of a particular "kind." The two creation accounts in Gen. 1,2 supplement each other. Gen. 1 describes the creation of the universe as a whole; while Gen. 2 gives a more detailed account of the creation of man and says nothing about the creation of matter, light, heavenly bodies, plants and animals, except to refer to the creation of animals as having taken place at an earlier time.

CREATURE, that which has been created (Rom. 1:25; 8:39; Heb. 4:13).

CREATURE, LIVING, symbolical figure presented first in Ezek. 1:5ff, and again in Rev. 4:6-9; 5:6,8,11; 6:1,3,5-7 ASV. The living creatures in Revelation are somewhat modified from those in Ezekiel's vision.

CREED, a succinct statement of faith epitomizing the basic tenets of religious faith. Such passages as Matt. 16:16 and I Tim. 3:16 give the Biblical foundation for the Christian creed. There are 3 ancient creeds: the Apostles' Creed, the Nicene Creed, and the Athanasian Creed. The Reformers also prepared creeds.

CREEK, modern translations use "bay" for the KJV "creek" in Acts 27:39, identified as St. Paul's Bay, c. 8 miles NW of the town of Zaletta on the island of Malta.

CREEPING THING (See Animals, Insects).

CRESCENS (krĕs'ĕnz, increasing), companion of Paul (II Tim. 4:10).

CRETE, CRETAN (krēt, krē'tăn), an island in the Mediterranean, 165 miles long, 6-35 miles wide, forming a natural bridge between Europe and Asia Minor. It was the legendary birthplace of Zeus. Paul and Titus founded a church there (Titus 1:5-14). The Cretans in the OT are called Cherethites (I Sam. 30:14; Ezek. 25:16). Cretans were in Jerusalem on the Day of Pentecost (Acts 2:11). According to Paul they were not of a high moral character (Titus 1:12).

CRIB, rack for the feeding of domestic livestock (Job 39:9; Prov. 14:4; Isa. 1:3; Luke 2:7).

CRIMSON, brilliant red dye obtained from a bug (II Chron. 2:7,14; Jer. 4:30; Isa. 1:18).

CRISPING PIN, pin for curling the hair (Isa. 3:22).

CRISPUS (krĭs'pŭs), former ruler of Jewish synagogue at Corinth, converted by Paul (Acts 18:8; I Cor. 1:14).

CROP, pouch-like enlargement in gullet of many birds in which food is partially prepared for digestion (Lev. 1:16).

CROSS. The cross existed in 4 different forms: 1. The Latin, with the cross beam near the upper part of the upright beam. 2. St. Andrew's, in the shape of an "X." 3. St. Anthony's, in the form of the letter "T." 4. The Greek, with the cross beams of equal length. Sometimes the cross was a simple upright. Crucifixion was practiced, especially in times of war, by the Phoenicians, Carthaginians, Egyptians, and the Romans. Before he was crucified a prisoner was scourged with a lash. Crucifixion was by tying or nailing. Death by crucifixion resulted not from loss of blood but from heart failure. Victims did not usually succumb for 2 or 3 days. Death was hastened by the breaking of the legs. Sometimes a fire was built beneath the cross that its fumes might suffocate the sufferer. The word cross is often used figuratively to represent the gospel (Gal. 6:14) or suffering (Eph. 2:16).

CROW (See Birds).

CROWN, a band encircling the head to designate honor, worn by priests, kings, queens (Exod. 28:36-38; II Chron. 23:11; Esther 2:17). In the NT two Gr. words for crown are used: **stephanos** and **diadema**, the first referring to a garland or chaplet such as was worn by a victorious athlete (II Tim. 4:8; Rev. 2:10), the other the crown worn by kings (Rev. 19:12). Jesus had a crown of thorns placed on His head to ridicule Him (Matt. 27:29). The variety of thorns used is not known.

CROWN OF THORNS (See Crown).

CRUCIFIXION (See Cross).

CRUSE (krōōs), a small, porous, earthen vessel to hold liquids (I Sam. 26:11,12,16; I Kings 19:6).

CRYSTAL, probably rock crystal or crystallized quartz (Job. 28:17; Rev. 4:6; 21:11; 22:1).

CUBIT (See Weights and Measures).

CUCKOO (See Birds).

CUCKOW (See Birds).

CUCUMBER (See Plants).

CUMMIN (See Plants).

CUNEIFORM (cŭn-nē'ĭ-fôrm), a system of writing by symbolic wedge-shaped characters upon clay tablets used chiefly in the Mesopotamian area in ancient times. More than half a million such clay tablets have been found.

CUP, a word used in a literal and figurative

sense. Cups were of various forms and designs, and made of a variety of materials: gold, silver, earthenware, copper, bronze, etc. Figuratively, the cup symbolizes prosperity or malediction (Ps. 11:6; 16:5; 17:4); drunkenness (Prov. 23:31); blessing (I Cor. 10:16); one's lot in life (Ps. 11:6; 16:5).

CUPBEARER, palace official who served wine at a king's table (Gen. 40:1ff; I Kings 10:5).

CURSE, to wish harm or evil upon someone; on the divine level, to impose judgment (Gen. 3:14,17). The cursing of one's parents brought the death penalty (Lev. 20:9). Christians are exhorted to bless and not to curse (Matt. 5:11; Luke 6:28; Rom. 12:14).

CURTAINS. 1. Curtains which covered the tabernacle (Exod. 26:1ff; 38:9ff). 2. Figuratively, the heavens (Isa. 40:22).

CUSH (kūsh). 1. Son of Ham, one of the three sons of Noah (Gen. 10:6-8; I Chron. 1:8-10). 2. Benjamite (Ps. 7 title). 3. Territory in region of Tigris and Euphrates (Gen. 2:13 ASV).

CUSHI (kū'shī), member of the Cushite people. 1. A Cushite (II Sam. 18:21-32). 2. Contemporary of Jeremiah (Jer. 36:14). 3. Father of the prophet Zephaniah (Zeph. 1:1).

CUSTOM, when not referring to a tax, usually means "manner," "way," or "statute" Gen. 31:35; Judg. 11:39; Jer. 32:11). In NT it means "manner," "usage" (Luke 1:9; Acts 6:14), and "religious practices."

CUSTOM, RECEIPT OF. The Romans imposed tribute or taxes upon the Jews as upon all their subjects for the maintenance of their provincial government. Matthew was a tax collector, or publican, and left his work to follow Jesus (Matt. 9:9).

CUTHA or **CUTH** (kū'thȧ, kūth), city, probably NE of Babylon, from which Sargon, king of Assyria, brought immigrants to repopulate the area of Samaria when he had sacked in 722 B. C. (II Kings 17:24-30).

CUTTINGS (cuttings in the flesh), a heathen practice, including tattooings, gashes, castrations, etc., usually done in mourning for the dead and to propitiate deities, but forbidden to the Israelites (Deut. 14:1).

CYLINDER SEALS, a cylinder, measuring from 1-1/2 to 3 inches long and usually made of clay, on which inscriptions were made.

CYPRESS (See Plants).

CYPRUS (sī'prŭs, copper), island in the E Mediterranean just off the coast of Syria and Cilicia, 148 miles long and c. 40 miles wide. Rich in copper deposits. Many Jews lived there. Home of Barnabas (Acts 4:36). Evangelized by Paul, Barnabas, and Mark (Acts 13:4; 15:39).

CYRENE, CYRENIAN (sī'rē'nī, wall), city in N Africa, W of Egypt, c. 10 miles from the coast. Originally a Greek city, it passed into the hands of the Romans. Simon, who helped Jesus carry His cross, came from there (Luke 23:26). People from Cyrene were in Jerusalem on the day of Pentecost (Acts 2:10). Jews from the synagogue of the Cyrenians disputed with Stephen (Acts 6:9).

CYRENIUS (sī-rē'nĭ-ŭs), full name is Publius Sulpicius Quirinius; Syrian governor for Rome at the time of Christ's birth. At that time Rome regarded Syria-Palestine as one province. Most famous because of the controversy concerning the census which Luke says occurred "when Cyrenius was first governor of Syria." He was apparently governor of Syria twice, the first 6 or 5 B. C., the second A. D. 6-10. Such a taxation census was made every 14 years.

CYRUS (cī'rŭs), founder of Persian Empire; captured Babylon in 539 B. C., thus ending the neo-Babylonian empire; instituted kindly policy of repatriation for captive peoples, and allowed the Jews to return to Palestine (II Chron. 36:22,23; Ezra 1: 1-14; Isa. 44:28; 45:1-7). Died in 530 B. C.

D

DABAREH (dăb'ȧ-rē), erroneous spelling of Daberath (Josh. 21:28).

DABBASHETH (dăb'ȧ-shĕth), town on W border of Zebulun (Josh. 19:10).

DABERATH (dăb'ē-răth), Levitical city in Issachar (Josh. 19:12; I Chron. 6:72).

DAGON (dā'gŏn, fish?), pagan deity with body of fish, head and hands of man. Probably god of agriculture. Worshiped in Mesopotamia and Canaan; temples in Ashdod (I Sam. 5:1-7), Gaza (Judg. 16:21-30), and in Israel (I Chron. 10:10). Samson destroyed the temple in Gaza (Judg. 16:30).

DALAIAH (dȧl'ā-ī'ȧ). 1. Descendant of David (I Chron. 3:24). 2. Priest (I Chron. 24:18). 3. Prince who interceded for preservation of Jeremiah's scroll (Jer. 36:12,25). 4. Founder of returned family (Ezra 2:60; Neh. 7:62). 5. Father of Shemaiah (Neh. 6:10).

DALE, THE KINGS. 1. Place near Jerusa-

lem where Abram met Melchizedek (Gen. 14:17). 2. Absalom's memorial (II Sam. 18:18).

DALMANUTHA (dăl-mȧ-nū'thȧ), village on W coast of the Sea of Galilee, adjoining Magdala (Matt. 15:39; Mark 8:10).

DALMATIA (dăl-mā'shȧ, deceitful), province on NE shore of Adriatic Sea called also Illyricum (Rom. 15:19; II Tim. 4:10).

DALPHON (dăl'fŏn), Haman's son (Esth. 9:7).

DAMARIS (dăm'ȧ-rĭs), convert of Paul (Acts 17:34).

DAMASCUS (dȧ-măs'kŭs), ancient city of Syria, more than 4000 years old; 2000 feet above sea level; watered by Abana and Pharpar rivers (II Kings 5:12); at E foot of Anti-Lebanon mts. Played an important part in Biblical history. David conquered it (II Sam. 8:5,6; I Chron. 18:3-6). Rulers who played prominent part in history of Israel and Judah: Rezon (I Kings 11:23-25), Ben-hadad (I Kings 15:16-21), Hazael (II Kings 8:15; 13:22-25), Ben-hadad II (II Kings 13:24,25). During NT times Damascus was ruled by Arabia under Aretas (II Cor. 11:32). Paul converted near Damascus (Acts 9:1-18) and preached there (Acts 9:22). Captured by Moslems in A. D. 635 and made the seat of the Mohammedan world.

DAMNATION, when referring to the future it means primarily eternal separation from God with accompanying awful punishments (Matt. 5:29; 10:28; 23:33; 24:51). The severity of the punishment is determined by the degree of sin (Luke 12:36-48), and is eternal (Mark 3:29; II Thess. 1:9; 66:24; Jude 6,7).

DAN (CITY), northernmost city of Palestine; originally Leshem (Josh. 19:47; Judg. 18:29); captured by Danites and renamed Dan (Judg. 18). "From Dan to Beersheba" (Judg. 20:1; I Sam. 3:20) means the whole length of Palestine.

DAN (TRIBE OF), tribe to which Dan the 5th son of Jacob gave origin and the territory allotted to it in Canaan. Danites were given an area lying between Judah and the Mediterranean Sea, occupied by the Philistines, but failure to conquer the Philistines made them move northward where they conquered Leshem and renamed it Dan (Josh. 19:47; Judg. 18:1-29). Samson was a Danite (Judg. 13:2,24). Jeroboam set up a golden calf in Dan (I Kings 12:25-33). Pul took many Danites into captivity (I Chron. 5:26).

DANCING, used to express joy, as at a birth or wedding (Job 21:11; Jer. 31:4; Matt. 11:17; Luke 15:25); to celebrate victory (Exod. 15:20,21; Judg. 11:34; I Sam. 18:6); to worship (II Sam. 6:14; Ps. 149:3). Often the source of dissipation and harm (Exod. 32:19; Mark 6:22). In Hebrew dancing the sexes did not intermingle, and usually the dancing was done by women. Men danced solo (II Sam. 6:14-16) and in groups (I Sam. 30:16).

DANIEL (dăn'yĕl, **God is my judge**). 1. David's 2nd son (I Chron. 3:1; – Chileab, II Sam. 3:3). 2. A post-exilic priest (Ezra 8:2; Neh. 10:6). 3. Prophet of Judah and author of the Book of Daniel; among hostages deported to Babylon by Nebuchadnezzar in 605 B. C., where he was called Belteshazzar and held influential positions under Nebuchadnezzar, Belshazzar, Darius, and Cyrus. The last known event in his life took place in the 3rd year of Cyrus (536 B. C.), when he was given a vision of the course of world history and the final judgment (Dan. 10-12:4).

DANIEL, BOOK OF, a prophetic book which stands among the "writings" in the Hebrew OT (which consists of "the law, prophets, and writings") because while he had the gift of a prophet (Matt. 24:15), his position was that of a governmental official. The book is apocalyptic in character and abounds in symbolic and figurative language, and

as a result it has been subject to many different interpretations. The first half of the book (chs. 1-6) consists of six narratives on the life of Daniel and his friends: their education, his revelation of Nebuchadnezzar's dream-image, the trial by a fiery furnace, his prediction of Nebuchadnezzar's madness, his interpretation of the handwriting on the wall, and his ordeal in the lion's den. The second half (7-12) consists of four apocalyptic visions, predicting the course of world history. There are references to the book in the NT (Matt. 24:15; Luke 1:19,26; Heb. 11:33,34). Chs. 2:4b-7:28 are composed in Aramaic; the rest is in Hebrew. His book was designed to inspire Jewish exiles with confidence in Jehovah (4:34-37).

DAN-JAAN (dăn'jä'ăn), place, probably in Dan, covered by David's census (II Sam. 24:6).

DANNAH (dăn'ă), town in Judah probably near Hebron (Josh. 15:49).

DARA, DARDA (dăr'ă, dăr'dă), member of a family of noted wise men (I Kings 4:31; I Chron. 2:6).

DARIC (dăr'ĭk), Persian gold coin used in Palestine after the return from the captivity (Ezra 2:69; Neh. 7:70-72 ASV, RSV). Worth c. $5.00.

DARIUS (dă-rī'ŭs), a common name for Medo-Persian rulers. 1. Darius the Mede (Gubaru), son of Ahasuerus (Dan. 5:31; 9:1); made governor of Babylon by Cyrus, but he seems to have ruled for only a brief time (Dan. 10:1; 11:1); prominent in the Book of Daniel (6:1,6,9,25,28; 11:1). 2. Darius Hystaspes, 4th and greatest of the Persian rulers (521-486 B. C.); reorganized government into satrapies and extended boundaries of empire; great builder; defeated by Greeks at Marathon 490 B. C.; renewed edict of Cyrus and helped rebuild the temple (Ezra 4:5; 24; 5:5-7; 6:1-12; Hag. 1:1; 2:1,10,18; Zech. 1:1,7; 7:1). Died in 486 B. C. and was succeeded by Xerxes, grandson of Cyrus the Great. 3. Darius, the Persian, last king of Persia (336-330 B. C.); defeated by Alexander the Great in 330 B. C. (Neh. 12:22). Some scholars identify him with Darius II (Nothus), who ruled Persia and Babylon (423-408 B. C.).

DARKNESS, used in the Old and the New Testaments in both a literal and a figurative sense; associated with evil, danger, crime, the mysterious (Exod. 20:21), ignorance (Job 37:19), agency of eternal punishment (Matt. 22:13), spiritual blindness (Isa. 9:2).

DARKON (dăr'kŏn), descendant of Solomon's servant, Jaala, who returned with Zerubbabel from exile (Ezra 2:56).

DATHAN (dă'thăn), Reubenite who with his brothers rebelled against Moses (Num. 16:1-15).

DAUGHTER, a word of various uses in the Bible, it refers to both persons and things, often without regard to kinship or sex. l. Daughter (Gen. 11:29) or female descendant (Gen. 24:48). 2. Women in general (Gen. 28:6; Num. 25:1). 3. Worshipers of the true God (Ps. 45:10; Isa. 62:11; Matt. 21:5; John 12:15). 4. City (Isa. 37:22). 5. Citizens (Zech. 2:10).

DAVID (da'vid, beloved or, as in ancient Mari, chieftain), Israel's greatest and most loved king, described in I Sam. 16 through I Kings 2:11 (I Chron. 11-29), plus many of the Psalms. Born in 1040 B. C. (II Sam. 5:4), the youngest son of Jesse of Bethlehem (I Sam. 16:10,11); took care of his father's sheep (I Sam. 16:11; 17:34-36); anointed king by Samuel (I Sam. 16:13); played harp for Saul (I Sam. 16:18,23); killed Goliath (I Sam. 17:45-51); became loved friend of Jonathan (I Sam. 18:1-3); Saul, jealous, tried to take his life (I Sam. 18:13-16,28-19:1); driven into outlawry by Saul (I Sam. 19:11; 21:10); fled to Philistine Gath (I Sam. 21) and lived in wilderness cave of Adullam (I Sam. 22); joined by Abiathar and a variety of malcontents (I Sam. 22:2); pursued by Saul (I Sam. 23; Ps. 7:4; I Sam. 26); after the death of Saul at Mt. Gilboa in 1010 B. C. he was declared king over Judah (II Sam. 2-4). In 1003 B. C. all Israel acclaimed him king (II Sam. 5:1-5; I Chron. 11:10; 12:38). After the defeat of the Philistines (II Sam. 5: 18-25) he captured the Jebusite stronghold of Jerusalem and made it his religious capital by bringing the ark to Jerusalem (II Sam. 6; I Chron. 13; 15:1-3); organized worship (I Chron.15,16); expanded kingdom on all sides (II Sam. 8; 10; 12:26-31); planned temple (II Sam. 7; I Chron. 17; 22:7-10); had family problems (II Sam. 12-19; I Kings 1); sinned with Bathsheba (II Sam. 11: 1-12:23; Ps. 51; fought Philistines (II Sam. 21:15-22); made Solomon his successor (I Kings 1,2); died after reigning 40 years (II Sam. 2:11; 5:4; I Chron. 29:27). Wrote 73 psalms; ancestor of Jesus (Matt. 1:1; 22:41-45).

DAVID, CITY OF. 1. Portion of Jerusalem occupied by David in 1003 B. C.; 2500 feet above sea-level. Originally a Canaanite city (Ezek. 16:3), it dates back to the 3rd millennium. Solomon enlarged the City of David for the temple and other buildings, and later kings enlarged the city still more (II Chron. 32:4,5,30; II Kings 20:20; Isa. 22:9-11). 2. Bethlehem (Luke 2:11).

DAY, a word having various meanings in the Bible, denoting time from sunrise to sunset (Ps. 74:16), time in general (Judg. 18:30; Obad. 12; Job 18:20), length of life (Gen. 5:4), the time of opportunity (John 9:4), etc.

DAY OF ATONEMENT, an annual Hebrew feast when the high priest offered sacrifices for the sins of the nation (Lev. 23:27; 25:9). It was the only fast period required by Mosaic law (Lev. 16:29; 23:31). It was observed on the 10th day of the 7th month; a day of great solemnity and strictest conformity to the law.

DAY OF CHRIST, a term used in the NT

to indicate the redemptive ministry of Jesus, both while in the flesh and upon His return. Sometimes called "that day" (Matt. 7:22) and "the day" (I Cor. 3:13).

DAY OF THE LORD, in the OT the day of divine defeat of evil and the triumph of the kingdom of God (Isa. 2:12; 13:6; Ezek. 13:5; Zeph. 1:14); in the NT a day when Christ comes and brings judgment upon unbelievers (Matt. 10:15; Rom. 2:5,6; II Peter 3:7,12) and deliverance and joy to God's people (Matt. 16:27; 24:30; John 6:39; II Cor. 1:14; Phil 1:6,10). It will culminate in the new heaven and the new earth (Isa. 65:17; 66:22; Rev. 21:1).

DAYSMAN (dāz'mǎn, to act as umpire), a mediator or arbitrator (Job 9:33). In Job it means that no human being is worthy of acting as a judge of God.

DAYSPRING (da'spring, to break forth), poetic name for dawn (Job 38:12).

DAYSTAR (light-giving), the planet Venus; seen as a morning star, heralding the dawn (Isa. 14:12; II Peter 1:19; Rev. 22:16).

DEACON, DEACONESS (dē'kŭn, dē'kŭn-ĕs, servant), in the KJV the word "deacon" appears only in Phil. 1:1 and four times in I Tim. 3; but the Greek word so rendered occurs c. 30 times in the NT. In most cases there is no technical meaning relating to a specialized function in the church. The word means basically a servant. Paul uses the word of himself and of Epaphras (Col. 1:7,23,25). The word in the NT is usually connected with the supply of material needs and service (Rom. 15:25; II Cor. 8:4). The diaconate, as a church office, is based by inference upon Acts 6:1-8; but at least two of the seven men were evangelists. Qualifications given in I Timothy 3 show that they were not considered ordinary lay members of the church. This is evident in Phil. 1:1. It does not appear from the NT that deaconesses were ever church officers. See Rom. 16:1.

DEAD SEA, called in Scripture the Salt Sea (Gen. 14:3), Sea of the Arabah or East Sea (Joel 2:20; Zech. 14:8). It measures 47 by 10 miles and occupies a geologic fault that extends from Syria through the Red Sea into Africa. It is 1300 feet below sea level, and in its deepest place is 1300 feet deep. Has no outlet; therefore its salt concentration is four times that of ocean water; is slowly expanding; is often mentioned in the Bible (Num. 34:12; I Chron. 18:12; II Chron. 20:1,2; Ezek. 47:18).

DEAD SEA SCROLLS, discovered, in 1947, by Arabic Bedouin, in caves a mile or so W of the NW corner of the Dead Sea, at Qumran. So far MSS have been found in 11 caves, and they are mostly dated as coming from the last century B. C. and the first century A. D. At least 382 MSS are represented by the fragments of Cave Four alone, c. 100 of which are Biblical MSS. These include fragments of every book of the Hebrew Bible except Esther. Some of the books are represented in many copies. Not all the MSS are in fragments; some are complete or nearly complete. In addition to Biblical books, fragments of apocryphal and apocalyptic books, commentaries, Thanksgiving Psalms, and sectarian literature have been found. Near the caves are the remains of a monastery of huge size, the headquarters of a monastic sect of Jews called the Essenes. The discoveries at Qumran are important for Biblical studies in general. They are of great importance for a study of the OT text, both Hebrew and the LXX. They are also of importance in relation to the NT, as they furnish the background to the preaching of John the Baptist and Jesus. There is no evidence that either John the Baptist or Jesus was a member of the group.

DEATH, refers to cessation of natural life (Gen. 25:11; Lev. 16:1; Deut. 34:5; Matt. 8:22; 15:37), the departure of the spirit from the body (II Tim. 4:6), laying aside the body (II Cor. 5:1); inevitable (Josh. 23:14). In the spiritual sense death is a separation from God (Luke 1:79; I John 3:14). The righteous and wicked go on forever, the righteous to everlasting good (Isa. 35:10; 45:17; Dan. 7:14, 12:2; Rev. 7:17), the evil to eternal torment (Jer. 20:11; Dan. 12:2; Matt. 25:46; Mark 3:29; II Thess. 1:9; Jude 7). The Bible does not teach the annihilation of the wicked. Jesus has conquered death and removed its sting (John 5:24; I Cor. 15:53-57; I John 5:12; Rev. 1:18). The second death is final separation from God (Rev. 20:6,14).

DEBIR (de'bēr). 1. City of Judah, c. 10 miles SW of Hebron; captured by Joshua from the Anakim (Josh. 10:38,39); later became a Levitical city (Josh. 21:15; I Chron. 6:58). 2. King of Eglon; defeated by Joshua at Gibeon (Josh. 10:1-11). 3. Town E of Jordan on border of Gad (Josh. 13:24-26). 4. Town on road between Jerusalem and Jericho (Josh. 15:7).

DEBORAH (dĕb'ō-rà, bee). 1. Rebekah's nurse (Gen. 24:59; 35:8). 2. Fourth of Israel's judges; prophetess; urged Barak to fight Sisera (Judg. 4:4-14); composed and sang a song of triumph (Judg. 5).

DEBT (a sum owed, an obligation), under Mosaic law Jews were not allowed to exact interest from other Jews (Exod. 22:25). The poor were protected against usurers by special laws (Exod. 22:25-27). Debtors unable to pay could have their property, family, and even person seized (Lev. 25: 25-41), and could be thrown into prison (Matt. 18:21-26). The word also has reference to moral obligation (Matt. 6:12; Rom. 8:12).

DECALOGUE (dĕk'à-lŏg, ten words), the Ten Commandments given by God to Moses at Sinai (Exod. 20); inscribed on tablets of stone (Deut. 4:13) and placed in the ark of the covenant (Deut. 10:2). Jesus approved the law (Matt. 5:18; 22:40) and fulfilled it (Matt. 5:27-48; 23:23).

DECAPOLIS (dē-kăp'ō-lĭs, ten cities), league of 10 Greek cities E of the Jordan established after the Romans occupied the area (65 B. C.). They had their own coinage, courts, and army.' Later a few other cities were added.

DECISION, VALLEY OF, place where God will some day gather all nations for judgment (Joel 3:2,12,14).

DECREE, an official ruling or law (Dan. 2:9; Esth. 1:20; Jonah 3:7; Acts 16:4; Rev. 13:8).

DEDAN (dē'dän). 1. An Arabian people descended from Noah (Gen. 10:6,7); lived in NW part of the Persian Gulf. 2. A descendant of Abraham by Keturah (Gen. 25:3).

DEDICATION (to sanctify, consecrate), the setting apart of things or people for God's use: tabernacle (Num. 7), temple (I Kings 8), city wall (Neh. 12:27), private dwellings (Deut. 20:5), people (Exod. 19:14).

DEDICATION, FEAST OF, annual Jewish feast celebrating the restoration of the temple following its desecration by Antiochus Epiphanes. Jesus delivered a discourse at this feast (John 10:22ff).

DEEP, the ocean (Neh. 9:11); chaos (Gen. 1:2), deepest part of sea (Gen. 49:25), abyss (Luke 8:31; Rev. 9:1; 11:7).

DEFILE (dē-fīl), to profane, pollute, render unclean. Could be ceremonial (Gen. 34; Lev. 13:46; 18; Num. 5; Ezek. 18:11) or moral (Matt. 15:20; Mark 7:15; I Cor. 8:7; II Cor. 7:1). The idea of ceremonial defilement does not exist in the NT.

DEGREE (dĕ-grē). The word degrees occurs in the titles of Psalms 120 to 134, but the reason is uncertain. Also used to mean rank or order (I Chron. 15:18; 17:17; Ps. 62:9; Luke 1:52; James 1:9).

DEGREES, SONGS OF, title given Psalms 120-134. Uncertainty exists as to the origin of the title. Various theories are held.

DEKAR (dē'kàr), father of one of Solomon's purveyors (I Kings 4:7-9).

DELAIAH (dē-lā'yà, freed by Jehovah). 1. Descendant of David (I Chron. 3:1-24). 2. Head of 23rd course of priests (I Chron. 24:18). 3. Prince who tried to save Jeremiah's roll from destruction (Jer. 36:12,25). 4. Ancestor of tribe that returned under Zerubbabel (Ezra 2:60; Neh. 7:62). 5. Father of Shemaiah (Neh. 6:10).

DELILAH (dē-lī'là, dainty one), Philistine woman who lured Samson to his ruin (Judg. 16:4-20).

DELUGE (See Flood).

DEMAS (dē'màs, popular), fellow laborer with Paul (Col. 4:14; Philem. 24) who later deserted him (II Tim. 4:10).

DEMETRIUS (dē-mē'trĭ-ŭs, belonging to Demeter). 1. Disciple praised by John (III John 12). 2. Silversmith at Ephesus who made trouble for Paul (Acts 19:23-27).

DEMONS, evil spirits (Matt. 8:16; Luke 10: 17,20); invisible, incorporeal; form hierarchy (Eph. 6:10-12); have superhuman intelligence; are opposed to God; take possession of people, bringing upon them such evils as blindness (Matt. 12:22), insanity (Luke 8:26-36), dumbness (Matt. 9:32,33), and suicidal mania (Mark 9:22). Two classes: those who are free (Eph. 2:2; 6:11,12) and those who are imprisoned in the abyss (Luke 8:31; Rev. 9:1-11; 20:1-3).

DENARIUS (See Money).

DEPRAVITY (dĕ-prăv'ĭ-tė), the loss of man's original righteousness and love for God and the moral corruption of man so that he has an irresistible bias toward evil. In this state he can do nothing perfectly pleasing to God, and without the saving grace of God no salvation is possible.

DEPUTY (dĕp'ū-tė), one appointed to rule under a higher authority, as a regent in place of a king (I Kings 22:47) or a Roman consul or proconsul (Acts 13:7; 18:12; 19:38).

DERBE (dûr'bė), city in SE corner of Lycaonia, in Asia Minor (Acts 14:20).

DESERT, a waste, desolate, uncultivated, and often arid, place (Deut. 32:10; Job 24:5).

DESIRE OF ALL NATIONS, some expositors refer the prophecy to Christ's first advent; others, to the second advent; still others deny a Messianic application altogether and hold it means the precious gifts of all nations (Hag. 2:7).

DESOLATION, ABOMINATION OF, a phrase found in Dan. 11:31 and 12:11 which most expositors take to refer to the idolatrous desecration of the temple by Antiochus Epiphanes in 168 B. C., when heathen sacrifices were offered on the altar. Christ takes the phrase from Daniel and applies it to what was to take place when the Roman armies advanced against Jerusalem (Luke 21:20).

DEUEL (dū'ĕl), Gadite (Num. 1:14; 7:47; 10:20). In Num. 2:14 the name is Reuel.

DEUTERONOMY (dū'tẽr-ŏn'ō-mē, second law), the Jewish name for it is "words," from the opening expression, "These are the words which Moses spake." Mosaic authorship is claimed in 31:9,24,26. The book contains three farewell addresses of Moses, given by him in sight of Canaan, which he was forbidden to enter, and a renewal of Israel's covenant with God. Outline: 1. First discourse (1-4). 2. Second discourse (5-26). 3. Third discourse (27-30). 4. Last counsels; parting blessings (31-34).

DEVIL (slanderer), one of the principal titles of Satan, the arch-enemy of God and of man. It is not known how he originated, unless Isa. 14:12-20 and Ezek. 28:12-19 give us a clue, but it is certain that he was not created evil. He rebelled against God when in a state of holiness and apparently led other angels into rebellion with him (Jude 6; II Peter 2:4). He is a being of superhuman power and wisdom, but not omnipotent or omniscient. He tries to frustrate God's plans and purposes for human beings. His principal method of attack is by temptation. His power is limited and he can go only as far as God permits. On the Judgment Day he will be cast into hell to remain there forever.

DEVOTED THING, that which is set apart

unto the Lord, and therefore no longer belongs to the former owner (Josh. 6:17-19).

DEW, in the dry summers and autumns of Palestine dew was a great blessing to the land (Gen. 27:28; Judg. 6:37-40), while the absence of it was regarded as a misfortune (II Sam. 1:21; I Kings 17:1). Often used as a symbol of blessing (Gen. 27:28) and of refreshment (Deut. 32:2; Job. 29:19; Ps. 133:3; Isa. 18:4).

DIADEM, the Hebrew word is usually rendered "mitre" or "turban," and was a headdress worn by men (Job 29:14), women ("hoods," Isa. 3:23), priests (Ezek. 21:26), and kings (Isa. 28:5; 62:3). Very different from the crown (Gr. **stephanos**), which was given to victorious athletes. Diadems were made of silk cloth and were covered with gems.

DIAL, a sundial, used to tell time during the day (II Kings 20:11; Isa. 38:8).

DIANA (dï-ăn'à), the Roman goddess of the moon; identified with Artemis, her Greek counterpart; usually represented as a virgin huntress. The Diana of the Ephesians (Acts 19:24-35) was a combination of the Greek Artemis and the Semitic goddess Ashtoreth, the patroness of the sexual instinct. Her images were lascivious. Her special worship was centered in the great temple at Ephesus.

DIASPORA (dï-ăs'pô-rà, that which is sown), the name applied to the Jews living outside of Palestine and maintaining their religious faith among the Gentiles. By the time of Christ the diaspora must have been several times the population of Palestine.

DIBLAIM (dĭb-lá'ĭm), father-in-law of Hosea, the prophet (Hos. 1:3).

DIBLATH (dĭb'lăth), probably an early copyist's error for Riblah, a town c. 50 miles S of Hamath (Ezek. 6:14).

DIBON, DIBON-GAD (dï'bŏn). 1. Place in Moab c. 10 miles E of the Dead Sea; given by Moses to Reuben (Josh. 13:9,17). Dibon-gad (Num. 33:45) was the place where the Moabite Stone was found. 2. Town in S. Judah (Neh. 11:25).

DIBRI (dĭb'rē), Danite (Lev. 24:11-16).

DIDRACHMA (See Money).

DIDYMUS (dĭd'ĭ-mŭs, twin), surname of Thomas (John 11:16; 20:24; 21:2).

DIKLAH (dĭk'là), son of Joktan (Gen. 10:27; I Chron. 1:21).

DILEAN (dĭl'ē-ăn), town in lowlands of Judah (Josh. 15:38).

DIMNAH (dĭm'nà), Levite town in Zebulun (Josh. 21:35). May be same as Rimmon (I Chron. 6:77).

DIMON (dï'mŏn), town in Moab, generally called "Dibon" (q.v.), but in Isa. 15:9 twice written Dimon, c. 4 miles N of Aroer.

DIMONAH (dï-mō'nà), town in S of Judah (Josh. 15:22), probably the same as the "Dibon" of Neh. 11:25).

DINAH (dï'nà), daughter of Jacob and Leah (Gen. 30:21); violated by Shechem.

DINAITE (dï'nà-ĭt), a people brought from

Assyria to colonize Samaria (II Kings 17:24; Ezra 4:7-10).

DINHABAH (dĭn'hȧ-bà), city of Bela, king of Edom (Gen. 36:32).

DIONYSIUS, THE AREOPAGITE (dī-ô-nĭsh'ĭ-ŭs, the ăr'ē-ŏp'ȧ-gīt), member of the Areopagus, Athenian supreme court; converted by Paul (Acts 17:34).

DIOSCURI (dī-ŏs'kū-rē, sons of Zeus), twin sons of Zeus named Castor and Pollux; regarded by sailors as guardian deities (Acts 28:11).

DIOTREPHES (dī-ŏt'rĕ-fēz, nurtured by Zeus), domineering Christian leader condemned by John (III John 9,10).

DISCERNING OF SPIRITS, the ability to discern between those who spoke by the Spirit of God and those who were moved by false spirits (I Cor. 12:10).

DISCIPLE (learner), a pupil of some teacher. The word implies the acceptance in mind and life of the views and practices of the teacher (Matt. 9:14; 22:16; John 9:28). Sometimes it refers to the Twelve Apostles (Matt. 10:1; 11:1), but more often simply to Christians (Acts 6:1,2,7; 9:36).

DISEASES to which the Bible refers appear to have been mostly diseases that now exist. I. Diseases with primary manifestations in skin were of two kinds, those which were believed to require isolation and those not requiring isolation. A. Those requiring isolation: leprosy (Exod. 4:6), syphilis (Prov. 7:22,23), smallpox (perhaps Job's boils), boil or carbuncle (Hezekiah's - II Kings 20:7), anthrax (Exod. 9:3), scabies (Deut. 28:27). B. Skin diseases not requiring isolation: inflammation (Lev. 22:22). II. Diseases with primary internal manifestations. A. Plague - bubonic (I Sam. 5:9; 6:5) and pneumonic (II Kings 19:35). B. Consumption: tuberculosis (Lev. 21:20), typhoid fever, malaria (Lev. 26:16; Deut. 28:22), diarrhea, dysentery, and cholera (Acts 28:8). III. Diseases caused by worms and snakes: intestinal roundworm infection (Acts 12:21-23), guinea worm, snakebite (Acts 28:3,6). IV. Diseases of the eyes: epidemic blindness (II Kings 6:18), infirmity (Gal. 4:13). V. Nervous and mental diseases. Miscellaneous medical disorders and therapy: excessive menstrual flow (Luke 8:43,44), gangrene (II Tim. 2:17), dropsy (Luke 14:2), dumbness (Luke 1:20-22,64), coronary occlusion (II Sam. 24:10), cretinism (Lev. 21:20), lameness (Luke 14:21), palsy or paralysis (Matt. 9:2). Physicians mentioned in the NT; Matt. 9:12; Luke 4:23; Col. 4:14.

DISH, usually made either of baked clay or of metal. Orientals ate from a central platter or dish (Matt. 26:23).

DISHAN (dī'shăn), son of Seir (Gen. 36:21).

DISHON (dī'shŏn). 1. Horite chief (Gen. 36:21). 2. Descendant of Seir the Horite (Gen. 36:25). The two may, however, be the same.

DISPENSATION (dĭs-pĕn-sā'shŭn, law or arrangement of a house), in I Cor. 9:17;

Eph. 3:2 and Col. 1:25 it means "stewardship," "office," "commission" – words involving the idea of administration. In Eph. 1:10 the word dispensation refers to God's plan of salvation. The NT uses the word in a twofold sense: with respect to one in authority, it means an arrangement or plan; with respect to one under authority, it means a stewardship or administration.

DISPERSION (See Diaspora).

DIVES (dī'vēz, rich), name applied to the rich man in the parable of the rich man and Lazarus (Luke 16:19-31) in the Vulgate.

DIVINATION (dĭv-ĭ-nā'shŭn), the practice of foreseeing or foretelling future events or discovering hidden knowledge; forbidden to Jews (Lev. 19:26; Deut. 18:10; Isa. 19:3; Acts 16:16). Various means were used: reading omens, dreams, the use of the lot, astrology, necromancy, and others.

DIZAHAB (dĭ'zà-hăb), place in region of Sinai where Moses gave farewell address (Deut. 1:1).

DOCTOR (teacher), usually master or teacher (Luke 2:46; 5:17).

DODAI (dō'dī), officer in David's army (I Chron. 27:4).

DODANIM (dō'dȧ-nĭm), son of Javan (Gen. 10:4).

DODAVAH (dō'dȧ-và), Eliezer's father (II Chron. 20:37).

DODO (dō'dō). 1. Grandfather of Tola (Judg. 10:1). 2. Son of Ahohi (II Sam. 23:9). 3. Father of one of David's mighty men (II Sam. 23:24).

DOEG (dō'ĕg), Edomite herdsman of Saul who reported to the king that Ahimelech the priest had helped David. In revenge Saul had Doeg slay Ahimelech and the inhabitants of Nob (I Sam. 22:11-23).

DOG (See Animals).

DOOR, often used in the NT in a figurative sense, many times referring to Christ (John 10:1,2,7; Rev. 3:20), but also to opportunity (Matt. 25:10; Acts 14:27; I Cor. 16:9), and freedom and power (Col. 4:3).

DOORKEEPER, keeper of doors and gates in public buildings, temples, walled cities, etc., often called "porter." (II Kings 7:10; I Chron. 23:5; Ps. 84:10; Ezra 7:24; Mark 13:34).

DOPHKAH (dŏf'kà), station of Israelties between Red Sea and Sinai (Num. 33:12).

DOR (dŏr), Canaanite city on coast of Palestine, c. 8 miles N of Caesarea (Josh. 12:23).

DORCAS (dŏr'kàs, gazelle), Christian woman living at Joppa whom Peter raised from the dead (Acts 9:36-43).

DOTHAN (dō'thăn, two wells), place c. 13 miles N of Shechem where Joseph was sold (Gen. 37:17) and Elisha saw vision of angels (II Kings 6:13-23).

DOUGH, used in making bread or cake (Exod. 12:34,39; Jer. 7:18; Hos. 7:4).

DOVE (See Birds).

DOVE COTE, opening of pigeon-house (Isa. 60:8).

DOVE'S DUNG, used as food in famine (II Kings 6:25). See Plants.

DOWRY (dou're), price paid by suitor to parents of prospective bride (Gen. 29:15-20; 34:12; I Sam. 18:25); and money which bride brought to her husband (I Kings 9:16).

DRACHMA (See Money).

DRAGON, imaginary creature of great size and frightening aspect (Job 30:29; Ps. 44:19; Isa. 13:22); Satan (Rev. 12:9; 20:2).

DRAM (See Weights and Measures).

DRAUGHT HOUSE, privy or water-closet (II Kings 10:27).

DRAWER OF WATER, one who brought water from a well or a spring to a house (Deut. 29:11; Josh. 9:23-27).

DREAM. There are numerous instances in the OT of God revealing something to people by means of dreams (Gen. 20:3; 28:12; 37:5-11; 40:5; Dan. 2; 4; Matt. 1:20). Some of these dreams were given to persons outside the chosen family, e.g. Abimelech of Gerar (Gen. 20:3), Laban (Gen. 31:24), Pharaoh (Gen. 41:1-36). God gave to some men the gift of interpreting dreams (Gen. 40:5-23; Dan. 4:19-27). Dreams may lead people astray (Deut. 13:1-3).

DRESS. Scriptural statements and archaeological finds reveal much about the kind of clothing worn by the people of Biblical times. In unspoiled Arab areas the basic forms of clothing worn today are very much the same as those worn in Biblical times. Among the Hebrews clothes expressed the innermost feelings and desires of the people. Clothes were made of various materials: skin (Matt. 7:15), hair (Matt. 3:4), wool (Gen. 38:12), linen (Prov. 31:13), cotton (Isa. 19:9). The dress of men consisted of: **inner-tunic** or **undershirt** (KJV "breeches," Exod. 28:42); **tunic-coat**, a shirt-like outer garment worn in the home and on the street (Luke 3:11); **girdle**, or **belt** (John 21:7; Acts 12:8), made of cloth or leather; **cloak, mantle,** or **robe** –a large, loose-fitting garment worn over all other articles of clothing (I Sam. 24:11; I Chron. 15:27); **headdress** (Exod. 28:40; Job 29:14); **shoes** and **sandals** (Gen. 14:23; Acts 12:8). The dress of women was similar to that worn by men except that it was longer and of finer material, and included also a veil (Gen. 38:14), and ornaments (Isa. 3:18-23). Phylacteries, consisting of small leather cases containing passages of Scripture from the OT were worn by male Jews at morning prayers beginning c. the 2nd century B. C.

DRINK. Beverages of the Jews were water (Gen. 24:11-18), wine (Gen. 14:18; John 2:3), and milk (Judg. 4:19).

DRINK OFFERING, offering of oil and wine to God accompanying many sacrifices (Exod. 29:40,41).

DROMEDARY (See Animals).

DROPSY (See Diseases).

DROSS, refuse separated from molten ore or metal. Often used figuratively of what is worthless (Isa. 1:22,25; Ezek. 22:18,19).

DRUNKENNESS, a major vice in antiquity, even among the Hebrews, but more so among the wealthy. Drunkenness is forbidden by the Scriptures (Lev. 10:9; Deut. 21:20; Prov. 23:21; I Cor. 5:11; 6:10; Gal. 5:21). Among drunken people in the OT are Noah (Gen. 9:21), Lot (Gen. 19:33,35), Nabel (I Sam. 25:36), Uriah (II Sam. 11:13). Sometimes used figuratively (Isa. 29:9).

DRUSILLA (droo-sil'a), daughter of Herod Agrippa I; married first to Azizus, king of Emesa; later to Felix, procurator of Judea (Acts 24:24,25).

DUKE, in general the leader of a clan or a tribal chief (Gen. 36:15; Exod. 15:15); also a prince (Josh. 13:21).

DUMAH (du'ma, silence). 1. Son of Ishmael (Gen. 25:14-16). 2. Town in S of Judah (Josh. 15:52-54). 3. Place (unknown) connected with Seir or Edom (Isa. 21:11,12).

DUMBNESS (See Diseases).

DUNG, laws were made regarding excrement of human beings and animals used in sacrifice (Deut. 23:12-14; Exod. 29:14; Lev. 8:17). Dry dung was often used as fuel (Ezek. 4:12-15); also fertilizer (Isa. 25:10; Luke 13:8).

DUNG GATE, gate in Jerusalem wall that led out to the valley of Hinnom where rubbish was dumped (Neh. 3:14).

DURA (du'ra), plain of Babylon where Nebuchadnezzar set up his image (Dan. 3:1).

DWARF (thin, small, withered), could not officiate at the altar (Lev. 21:20).

DYERS, DYEING (See Occupations).

E

EAR (physical organ of hearing), priests had blood applied to ear at consecration (Exod. 29:20; Lev. 8:24) and lepers at cleansing (Lev. 14:14). Piercing of the ear of a slave denoted permanent servitude (Exod. 21:6; Deut. 15:17).

EARNEST, something of value given by a buyer to a seller, to bind the bargain; a token of what is to come (II Cor. 1:22; Eph. 1:14).

EARRING, worn by both men and women either on the nose or on the ears (Gen. 24:47; Isa. 3:21; Ezek. 16:12).

EARTH, a word with a variety of meanings: as a material substance (Gen. 2:7), territory (Gen. 28:15), whole earth (Gen. 12:3), country (Gen. 13:10; 45:18), inhabitants of world (Gen. 6:11), world (Gen. 1:1).

EARTHQUAKE. Actual earthquakes recorded in Scripture: I Kings 19:11; Amos 1:1; Zech. 14:5; Matt. 28:2. Also used figuratively of God's judgment (Judg. 5:4; Ps. 77:18; Isa. 29:6).

EAST (place of the sunrise, east), a significant direction for the Hebrews (Exod. 38:13; Num. 3:38; 10:14; Ezek. 10:19; 11:23; 43:2,4). "Children of the east" means people of lands E of Palestine (Job 1:3).

EASTER (passover), rendered **Easter** in Acts 12:4 KJV, but should be **Passover**, as in

ASV. The day on which the church celebrates the resurrection of Jesus Christ.

EAST SEA, or the Dead Sea, the E boundary of Judah (Josh. 15:5).

EAST WIND, hot, dry wind coming from the E (Jer. 4:11); destructive (Gen. 41:6; Ezek. 17:10); used as a means of judgment by God (Isa. 27:8; Jer. 18:17).

EBAL (ē'bȧl). 1. Son of Shobal (Gen. 36:23; I Chron. 1:40). 2. Mt. 3077 feet high in Samaria, opposite Mt. Gerizim; curses recited from it (Deut. 27:4-26). 3. Son of Joktan (I Chron. 1:22).

EBED (ē'bĕd, servant). 1. Father of Gaal (Judg. 9:26-45). 2. Son of Jonathan (Ezra 8:6).

EBED-MELECH (ē'bĕd-mē-lĕk, servant of the king), Ethiopian eunuch who pulled Jeremiah out of a miry dungeon (Jer. 39:15-18).

EBEN-EZER (ĕb'ĕn-ē'zĕr, stone of help), town of Ephraim where Israelites were defeated by Philistines (I Sam. 5:1). Later, after defeating Philistines, the Israelites erected a memorial stone, calling it Ebenezer (I Sam. 7:12).

EBER (ē'bĕr, beyond). 1. Son of Shelah (Gen. 10:24; 11:14; I Chron. 1:18). 2. Gadite (I Chron. 5:13). 3. Benjamite (I Chron. 8:12). 4. Another Benjamite (I Chron. 8:22). 5. Head of priestly family (Neh. 12:20).

EBIASAPH (ē-bī'ȧ-sȧph), son of Elkanah (Exod. 6:24; I Chron. 6:23; 9:19).

EBRONAH (ē-brō'nȧh), Hebrew encampment in wilderness (Num. 33:34). Site uncertain.

ECBATANA (ĕk-bȧt'ȧ-nȧ), capital of Media, where Cyrus issued decree authorizing rebuilding of temple called Achmetha (Ezra 6:2).

ECCLESIASTES (ē-klē-zĭ-ăs'tēz, preacher). Heb. title qoheleth, an official speaker in an assembly – the Preacher; Gr. Ekklesiastes. Traditionally ascribed to Solomon. Author seems to speak from standpoint of general rather than special revelation; examines life from every angle to see where satisfaction can be found, and finds it only in God. In the meantime we are to enjoy the good things of life as gifts of God, but in everything we must remember the Creator. Two divisions of thought in the book: the futility of life; the answer of practical faith.

ECUMENICISM (ĕk'ū-mĕn'ĭ-cĭsm, derived from Gr. olkoumene, the whole inhabited world), a movement among Christian religious groups – Protestant, Eastern Orthodox, Roman Catholic – to bring about a closer unity in work and organization. The word is not found in the Bible, but Biblical backing for the movement is found in John 17 where Jesus prays for the unity of His Church.

EDAR (ē'dȧr), tower near which Jacob encamped on way back to Canaan (Gen. 35:21).

EDEN (ē'd'n, delight). 1. Place in which God planted a garden in which He put Adam and Eve. Exact site is unknown, but traditionally in the Tigris-Euphrates area. 2. Region in Mesopotamia conquered

by Assyrians (II Kings 19:12; Isa. 37:12). 3. Gershonite (II Chron. 29:12; 31:15).

EDER (ē'dĕr). 1. City in S Judah near Edom (Josh. 15:21), possibly same as Adar. 2. Son of Mushi (I Chron. 23:23; 24:30).

EDOM (ē'dŏm, red). 1. Name given to Esau because he sold his birthright for red pottage (Gen. 25:30). 2. Descendants of Esau (Ps. 83:6) and their country (Judg. 11:17; Num. 34:3). Located at SE border of Palestine. Capital: Sela (Petra). Original inhabitants were Horites (Gen. 14:6).

EDOMITES (ē'dŏm-īts, red), descendants of Esau (Deut. 23:7); refused to allow Israelites to pass through territory (Num. 20:14-21); Saul fought them (I Sam. 14:47); David conquered them (II Sam. 8:14); continual enemies of Israel (I Kings 11:14-22; II Chron. 21; 25; Isa. 34:5-8; 63:1-4; Jer. 49:17). Made part of Israel by Maccabeans.

EDREI (ĕd'rē-ī, strong). 1. A chief city of Og, king of Bashan (Deut. 1:4; Josh. 12:4). Assigned to Manasseh (Josh. 13:12,31). Located c. 10 miles NE of Ramoth-Gilead. 2. City of Naphtali, location unknown (Josh. 19:37).

EDUCATION (See Schools).

EGG (whiteness), appears only in the plural form (Deut. 22:6; Job 39:14; Isa. 10:14).

EGLAH (ĕg'lȧh, heifer), wife of David (II Sam. 3:5; I Chron. 3:3).

EGLAIM (ĕg'lȧ-im), place in Moab (Isa. 15:8).

EGLON (ĕg'lŏn). 1. City of Canaan located between Gaza and Lachish (Josh. 10:3,5, 23); captured by Joshua (Josh. 10:36,37; 12:12); assigned to Judah (Josh. 15:39). 2. King of Moab who captured Jericho from Israelites (Judg. 3:12,13,14,21).

EGYPT (ē'jipt), country NE of Africa; also called country of Ham (Ps. 105:23,27); watered by Nile, the longest river in the world (4000 miles), the annual overflow of which is of the greatest importance to the country because of the almost complete absence of rain. Country divided into Upper and Lower Egypt, Lower Egypt including the delta area. Nile valley and delta bounded by desert. Called Mizraim by Israelites. Ruler called Pharaoh. Religion polytheistic; gods: Ptah, Ra, Thum, Amon. History begins c. 3000 B. C. Powerful empire in OT times; granary of Roman empire and cultural center in NT times. Held Israel in bondage for centuries until appearance of Moses (Exod. 1-14). Often in contact with Israel (I Kings 3:1; 14:25,26).

EGYPT, RIVER OF, the dividing line between Canaan and Egypt (Gen. 15:18; Num. 34:5), the southern boundary of Judah (Josh. 15:4,47). Not really a river, but a wady of the desert near the border of Egypt.

EHI (ē'hī), son of Benjamin (Gen. 46:21).

EHUD (ē'hŭd, union). 1. Descendant of Benjamin (I Chron. 7:10; 8:6). 2. Judge of Israel who murdered Eglon King of Moab (Judg. 3:15-30).

EKER (ē'kĕr), son of Ram (I Chron. 2:27).

EKRON (ĕk'rŏn, eradication), most northern of the five chief cities of the Philistines;

located on boundary between Judah and Dan (Josh. 15:11; 19:43); assigned to Judah (Josh. 15:45); ark carried to Ekron (I Sam. 5:10).

EL (èl, **God**), generic word for God in the Semitic languages; Canaanite chief god was El; name borrowed by Hebrews from Canaanites, although they usually used plural form Elohim. Often used in compounds.

ELA (ē′là), father of commissary officer of Solomon (I Kings 4:18 RSV).

ELADAH (èl′à-dàh), descendant of Ephraim (I Chron. 7:20).

ELAH (ē′làh, **terebinth**). 1. Chief of Edom (Gen. 36:41). 2. Valley in which David killed Goliath (I Sam. 17:2,19; 21:9). 3. King of Israel, son of Baasha; killed by Zimri (I Kings 16:8-10). 4. Father of Hoshea, the last king of Israel (II Kings 15:30; 17:1; 18:1,9). 5. Son of Caleb (I Chron. 4:15). 6. Benjamite (I Chron. 9:8).

ELAM (ē′làm). 1. Son of Shem (Gen. 10:22; I Chron. 1:17). 2. Son of Shashach (I Chron. 8:24). 3. Son of Meshelemiah (I Chron. 26:3). 4. Ancestor of family which returned from exile (Ezra 2:31; Neh. 7:34). 5. Another ancestor of a returned family (Ezra 2:31; Neh. 7:34). 6. Father of two sons returned from exile (Ezra 8:7). 7. Ancestor of man who married a foreign woman (Ezra 10:2,26). 8. Chief who sealed covenant with Nehemiah (Neh. 10:14). 9. Priest who took part in dedication of the wall (Neh. 12:42).

ELAM (ē′làm), country situated on the E side of the Tigris opposite Babylonia; was one of the earliest civilizations; figures prominently in Babylonian and Assyrian history. Some of its people were brought to Samaria by the Assyrians (Ezra 4:9,10). Elamites at Jerusalem on day of Pentecost (Acts 2:9).

ELASAH (èl′à-sàh). 1. Man who married foreign woman (Ezra 10:22). 2. Son of Shaphan; took letter to exiles in Babylon for Jeremiah (Jer. 29:3).

ELATH, ELOTH (ē′làth, ē′lôth, **lofty trees**), town on Gulf of Aqaba (Deut. 2:8) in Edom, near Ezion-geber, Solomon's seaport (I Kings 9:26).

EL-BETHEL (èl-bèth′èl, **the God of the House of God**), name given by Jacob to Luz because God there revealed Himself to him (Gen. 35:7).

ELDAAH (èl-dā′àh), son of Midian (Gen. 25:4).

ELDAD (èl′dàd, **God has loved**), one of Moses' 70 elders (Num. 11:24-29).

ELDER (èld′èr), the older men of a community; highly respected because of their wisdom and experience by Hebrews (Lev. 19:32; Deut. 32:7; Job 32:6); became heads of families and clans (Deut. 22:15; Exod. 3:16; 19:7). Became rulers of synagogue. Joined the priests and scribes against Jesus (Matt. 27:12). Appointed for each congregation (Acts 14:23). Terms "elders" and "bishops" used interchangeably in NT

(Acts 20:17,28). Qualifications of elders given in I Tim. 3:1-7 and Titus 1:6-9.

ELEAD (ē′lè-àd), Ephraimite (I Chron. 7:21).

ELEADAH (See Eladah).

ELEALEH (ē′lè-à′lè), town of Reuben c. 1 mile N of Heshon (Num. 32:3,37; Isa. 15:4; 16:9; Jer. 48:34).

ELEASAH (ē′lè-à-sàh). 1. Hezronite (I Chron. 2:39,40). 2. Benjamite (I Chron. 8:37; 9:43).

ELEAZAR (ē-lè-à′zàr, **God has helped**). 1. 3rd son of Aaron (Exod. 6:23); became high priest (Num. 3:32; 20:28); assisted Moses (Num. 26:1,2; 31:13-54; 32:28); helped Joshua divide promised land (Josh. 14:1; 19:51). 2. Son of Abinadab who was sanctified to keep the ark (I Sam. 7:1). 3. Son of Dodai (II Sam. 23:9,10; I Chron. 11:12-14). 4. Son of Mahli (I Chron. 23:21,22; 24:28). 5. Levite (Ezra 8:32-34). 6. Priest (Neh. 12:42). 7. Ancestor of Joseph, the husband of Mary (Matt. 1:15).

ELECT (è-lèct, **chosen**), those chosen by God for some special purpose (Ps. 106:23; Isa. 43:20; 45:4). Among the elect mentioned in Scripture are Moses, Israelites, Christ, angels, Christ's disciples.

ELECTION (**choice, selection**), God's eternal decree to choose from sinners deserving condemnation those whom He will save, providing salvation through Christ and the Holy Spirit. The source of election is in God alone (John 6:37,44; Eph. 1:4), and the cause is His compassionate mercy and His own glory. The objects of election are individual men (Matt. 22:14; John 15:19; Rom. 8:29; 9:13,15,18,22).

EL-ELOH-ISRAEL (èl′ē-lò′hè-iz′rà-èl), name of an altar erected by Jacob near Shechem (Gen. 33:20).

ELEMENTS (**rows, series, alphabet, first principles of a science, physical elements, primary constituents of the universe, heavenly bodies, planets, personal cosmic powers**). In Heb. 5:12, first principles; Gal. 4:3,9, **heathen deities and practices**; Col. 2:8,20, rudiments.

ELEPH (ē′lèf), town of Benjamin, near Jerusalem (Josh. 18:28).

ELEPHANT (See Animals).

ELEUSIS (èl′ū-sis), place in Attica where worshipers of Demeter were initiated into religious mysteries involving rebirth.

ELEVEN, THE, the 11 apostles who remained after the defection of Judas (Mark 16:14; Luke 24:9,33; Acts 2:14).

ELHANAN (èl-hà′nàn). 1. Son of Jaareoregim (also called Jair), who slew Lahmi, brother of Goliath (II Sam. 21:19; I Chron. 20:5). 2. One of David's heroes (II Sam. 23:24; I Chron. 11:26).

ELI (ē′li), descendant of Aaron; acted as both judge and high priest in Israel (I Sam. 1-4; 14:3; I Kings 2:27); failed to discipline his sons, and trouble befell him; priesthood given to the line of Zadok (I Kings 2:27).

ELI, ELI, LAMA SABACHTANI (ā'lēē, ä'lēē, lämä sà-bàk'tà-nēē, my God, my God, why hast Thou forsaken me), one of the seven cries of Jesus from the cross (Matt. 27:46; Mark 15:34).

ELIAB (ē-lī'ăb). 1. Leader of the tribe of Zebulun (Num. 1:9; 2:7; 7:24,29; 10:16). 2. Reubenite, father of Nathan and Abiram (Num. 16:1,12; 26:8,9; Deut. 11:6). 3. David's oldest brother (I Sam. 16:6; 17:13,28). 4. Levite (I Chron. 15:18,20; 16:5). 5. Gadite warrior who joined David at Ziklag (I Chron. 12:9). 6. Levite ancestor of Samuel (I Chron. 6:27). Called Elihu (I Sam. 1:1) and Eliel (I Chron. 6:34).

ELIADA (ē-lī'à-dà). 1. Son of David (II Sam. 5:16; I Chron. 3:8). 2. Benjamite general (II Chron. 17:17). 3. Father of Rezon (I Kings 11:23). KJV had Eliadah.

ELIAH (ē-lī'à). 1. Son of Jeroham (I Chron. 8:27). 2. Israelite who divorced foreign wife (Ezra 10:26).

ELIAHBA (ē-lī'à-bà), member of David's guard (II Sam. 23:32; I Chron. 11:33).

ELIAKIM (ē-lī'à-kim, God sets up). 1. Master of Hezekiah's household; sent by the king to negotiate with invading Assyrians (II Kings 18:17-37; Isa. 36:1-22) and then to seek help of Isaiah the prophet (II Kings 19:2; Isa. 37:2). 2. Original name of king Jehoiakim (II Kings 23:34; II Chron. 36:4). 3. Priest (Neh. 12:41). 4. Ancestor of Jesus (Matt. 1:13). 5. Another and earlier ancestor of Jesus (Luke 3:30).

ELIAM (ē-lī'ăm). 1. Father of Bathsheba (II Sam. 11:3). Called Ammiel in I Chron. 3:5. 2. Son of Ahithophel (II Sam. 23:34).

ELIAS (ē-lī'ăs), Greek form of the name Elijah, used in KJV in all occurrences in the NT.

ELIASAPH (ē-lī'à-săf). 1. Head of Gadites in wilderness sojournings (Num. 1:14; 2:14; 7:42,47; 10:20). 2. Levite; prince of Gershonites (Num. 3:24).

ELIASHIB (ē-lī'à-shib, God restores). 1. Head of 11th priestly course (I Chron. 24:12). 2. Judahite (I Chron. 3:24). 3. High priest (Neh. 3:1,20,21; 13:4,7,28). 4. Levite who put away his foreign wife (Ezra 10:24). 5. Man who married a foreign wife (Ezra 10:27). 6. Another man who married a foreign wife (Ezra 10:36). 7. Ancestor of man who helped Ezra (Ezra 10:6; Neh. 12:10,22,23).

ELIATHAH (ē-lī'à-thà), leader of temple musicians (I Chron. 25:4,27).

ELIDAD (ē'lī'dăd), Benjamite prince (Num. 34:21).

ELIEL (ē'lī-ĕl, ē-lī'ĕl, God is God). 1. Ancestor of Samuel (I Chron. 6:34). Called Eliab in I Chron. 6:27. 2. Chief of Manasseh (I Chron. 5:24). 3. Son of Shimhi (I Chron. 8:20). 4. Son of Shashak (I Chron. 8:22). 5. Captain in David's army (I Chron. 11:46). 6. One of David's heroes (I Chron. 11:47). 7. Gadite; perhaps same as 5 or 6 (I Chron. 12:11). 8. Chief of Judah; perhaps same as 5 (I Chron.

15:9). 9. Chief Levite (I Chron. 15:11). 10. Levite overseer (II Chron. 31:13).

ELIENAI (ĕl-ĭ-ē'nī), Benjamite (I Chron. 8:20).

ELIEZER (ĕl-ĭ-ē'zēr, God is help). 1. Steward of Abraham (Gen. 15:2). Perhaps same as servant mentioned in Gen. 24. 2. Son of Moses and Zipporah (Exod. 18:4; I Chron. 23:15,17; 26:25). 3. Grandson of Benjamin (I Chron. 7:8). 4. Priest (I Chron. 15:24). 5. Reubenite chief (I Chron. 27:16). 6. Prophet who rebuked Jehoshaphat (II Chron. 20:37). 7. Chieftain sent to induce Israelites to return to Jerusalem (Ezra 8:16). 8. Priest who put away foreign wife (Ezra 10:18). 9. Levite who did the same (Ezra 10:23). 10. Son of Harim who did the same (Ezra 10:31). 11. Ancestor of Jesus (Luke 3:29).

ELIHOENAI (ĕl-ĭ-hō-ē'nī, to Jehovah are my eyes). See also Elioenai. 1. Man who returned with Ezra (Ezra 8:4). 2. Korahite doorkeeper of tabernacle (I Chron. 26:3). In KJV, Elioenai; ASV, RSV, Eliehoenai.

ELIHOREPH (ĕl-ĭ-hō'rĕf), scribe of Solomon (I Kings 4:3).

ELIHU (ē-lī'hū, He is my God). 1. Great-grandfather of Samuel (I Sam. 1:1). Called Eliel in I Chron. 6:34. 2. Manassehite (I Chron. 12:20). 3. Tabernacle porter (I Chron. 26:7). 4. Brother of David (I Chron. 27:18). Also called Eliab. 5. One of Job's friends (Job 32:2-6; 34:1; 35:1; 36:1).

ELIJAH (ē-lī'jà, Jehovah is God). See also Elias. 1. Benjamite (I Chron. 8:27 ASV, RSV; called Eliah in KJV). 2. Son of Harim (Ezra 10:21). 3. Man who put away his foreign wife (Ezra 10:26 ASV, RSV; called Eliah in KJV). 4. Tishbite. Predicts to Ahab that there will be a drought; he is fed by ravens, and then taken care of by a widow at Zarephath (I Kings 17:17-24). After three years he proposes to Ahab a test as to whether the Canaanite Baal or the Israelite Jehovah is the true God (18:17-40). On Mt. Carmel the god Baal is thoroughly discredited and 450 prophets of Baal are slain. Jezebel vows vengeance on the prophet (19:1-8) and he flees into the wilderness, where he hears the still, small voice of the Lord. He anoints Elisha to succeed him as prophet. He rebukes Ahab for the murder of Naboth (21:17-29). He tells Ahab's son, Ahaziah, that he will die (II Kings 1). He is taken up to heaven in a whirlwind (II Kings 2:1-15). John the Baptist is called Elijah (Matt. 11:14; 17:10-13; Luke 1:17). Elijah appears to Jesus on the Mt. of Transfiguration (Matt. 17:3,4; Mark 9:4,5; Luke 9:30-33).

ELIKA (ē-lī'kà), one of David's mighty men (II Sam. 23:25).

ELIM (ē'lim, terebinths), 2nd stopping-place of Israelites in the wilderness (Exod. 15:27; 16:1; Num. 33:9,10).

ELIMELECH (ē-lim'ē-lĕk, my God is king), husband of Naomi (Ruth 1:2,3; 2:1,3; 4:3,9).

ELIOENAI (ĕl-ĭ-ō-ē'nī). Son of Neariah (I Chron. 3:23,24). 2. Simeonite prince (I Chron. 4:36). 3. Benjamite (I Chron. 7:8).

4. Man who put away his foreign wife (Ezra 10:22). 5. Man who divorced foreign wife (Ezra 10:27). 6. Priest, perhaps same as 4 (Neh. 12:41).

ELIPHAL (ē-lī'fál), one of David's mighty men (I Chron. 11:35). Perhaps same as Eliphelet in II Sam. 23:34.

ELIPHALET (ē-lif'à-lèt), son of David (II Sam. 5:16; I Chron. 14:7).

ELIPHAZ (ēl'ī-fàz, God is gold). 1. Son of Esau by Adah (Gen. 36:4-16; I Chron. 1: 35,36). 2. Chief of Job's three friends (Job 2:11); in his speeches he traces all affliction to sin.

ELIPHELEH (ē-lif'ē-lèh), Levite musician (I Chron. 15:18,21).

ELIPHELET (ē-lif'ē-lèt). See also Eliphalet. 1. Son of David (I Chron. 3:8). 2. Another son of David (I Chron. 3:6). 3. Son of Ahasbai (II Sam. 23:34). 4. Benjamite (I Chron. 8:39). 5. Jewish leader who returned with Ezra (Ezra 8:13). 6. Man who put away his foreign wife (Ezra 10:33).

ELISABETH (See Elizabeth).

ELISHA (ē-lī'shà, God is salvation), son of Shaphat; anointed Elijah's successor (I Kings 19:16-21); had a long ministry during the reigns of Jehoram, Jehu, Jehoahaz, and Joash, kings of Israel; performed miracles (II Kings 4-6).

ELISHAH (ē-lī'shà, God saves), son of Javan, whose name was given to an ancient land and its people, not identified (Gen. 10:4; I Chron. 1:7; Ezek. 27:7).

ELISHAMA (ē-lish'à-mà, God has heard). 1. Grandfather of Joshua (Num. 1:10; 2:18; 7:48,53; 10:22; I Chron. 7:26). 2. Son of David (II Sam. 5:16; I Chron. 3:8). 3. Another son of David, who is also called Elishua (I Chron. 3:6; cf. II Sam. 5:15). 4. Judahite (I Chron. 2:41). 5. Father of Nethaniah (II Kings 25:25; Jer. 41:1). Nos. 4 and 5 may be same person. 6. Secretary to Jehoiakim (Jer. 36:12,20,21). 7. Priest (II Chron. 17:8).

ELISHAPHAT (ē-lish'à-fàt), officer who supported Jehoiada (II Chron. 23:1).

ELISHEBA (ē-lish'ē-bà), wife of Aaron (Exod. 6:23).

ELISHUA (ēl-ī-shū'à), son of David (II Sam. 5:15; I Chron. 14:5). Called Elishama in I Chron. 3:6.

ELIUD (ē-lī'ûd), ancestor of Christ (Matt. 1:14,15).

ELIZABETH (ē-liz'à-bèth, God is my oath), wife of Zacharias (Luke 1:5-57); mother of John the Baptist; kinswoman to Mary.

ELIZAPHAN (ēl-ī-zā'fàn, e-liz'à-fan). 1. Son of Uzziel (Num. 3:30; I Chron. 15:8). 2. Prince of Zebulun (Num. 34:25).

ELIZUR (ē-lī'zēr), Reubenite prince (Num. 1:5; 2:10; 7:30-35; 10:18).

ELKANAH (ēl-kā'nà, God has possessed). 1. Father of Samuel (I Sam. 1:1-2:21). 2. Son of Korah (Exod. 6:23,24; I Chron. 6:23). 3. Official at court of Ahaz (II Chron. 28:7). 4. Warrior of David (I Chron. 12:6). 5. In addition, several Levites bear the name Elkanah (I Chron. 6:22-28; 33-38; 9:16).

ELKOSH (ēl'kŏsh), birthplace of Nahum the prophet (Nahum 1:1).

ELLASAR (ēl-lā'sàr), city-state in Babylonia in time of Abraham (Gen. 14:1,9).

ELMODAM (ēl-mō'dăm), ancestor of Christ (Luke 3:28).

ELNAAM (ēl-nā'àm), father of two of David's soldiers (I Chron. 11:46).

ELNATHAN (ēl-nā'thàn, God has given). 1. Grandfather of Jehoiachin (II Kings 24:8). 2. Son of Achbor (Jer. 26:22). May be same as 1. 3. Levites who helped Ezra (Ezra 8:16).

ELOHIM (ē-lō'hĭm), the most frequent Hebrew word for God; plural "elohim" (Gen. 1:1). Used of heathen gods (Exod. 18:11), angels (Ps. 8:5), judges (Exod. 21:6), and Jehovah.

ELON (ē'lŏn). 1. Hittite whose daughter Esau married (Gen. 36:2). 2. Son of Zebulon (Gen. 46:14; Num. 26:26). 3. Judge (Judg. 12:11,12).

ELON (place). 1. Town of Dan (Josh. 19:43). Elon-beth-hanan in I Kings 4:9.

ELPAAL (ēl-pā'àl), Benjamite (I Chron. 8: 11,12,18).

ELPALET (ēl-pā'lèt, ēl'pà-lèt). See Eliphalet (I Chron. 3:6).

EL SHADDAI (ēl shăd'ī), probably "Almighty God," the name by which God appeared to Abraham, Isaac, and Jacob (Exod. 6:3).

ELTEKEH (ēl'tē-kè), city of Dan (Josh. 19:44).

ELTEKON (ēl'tē-kŏn), city of Judah (Josh. 15:59).

ELTOLAD (ēl-tō'làd), city in S Judah assigned to Simeon (Josh. 15:30; 19:4). Tolad in I Chron. 4:29

ELUL (ē-lŏŏl'), 6th month of Hebrew year, c. Aug., Sept. (Neh. 6:15).

ELUZAI (ē-lū'zà-ī), Benjamite (I Chron. 12:5).

ELYMAS (ēl'ī-màs), Greek name of the Jew Bar-Jesus (Acts 13).

ELZABAD (ēl-zà'bàd, ēl'zà-bàd). 1. Gadite (I Chron. 12:12). 2. Levite (I Chron. 26:7).

EMBALM (ēm-bàm), embalming was of Egyptian origin; Jacob and Joseph were embalmed (Gen. 50:2,26).

EMBROIDERY; artistic needlework and fine weaving were highly prized by the Hebrews and their neighbors (Judg. 5:30; Josh. 7:20). The hangings of the temple and the robes of the priests were decorated with embroidery (Exod. 26:37; 27:16; 28:33,39; 39:29).

EMIM (ē'mĭm), the original inhabitants of Moab (Deut. 2:10,11).

EMMANUEL (ē-măn'ū-ĕl, God with us), name of child which virgin would bear (Isa. 7:14) and at whose birth salvation would be near. Micah 5:2 takes Him to be the Messiah.

EMMAUS (ē-mā'ùs), village seven miles from Jerusalem (Luke 24:7-35).

EMMOR (ēm'ŏr), father of Sychem (Acts 7:16). Same as Hamor.

ENAM (ē'năm), city in lowland of Judah, possibly translated "open place" (Gen. 38: 14,21). Not identified.

ENAN (ē'năn), father of Ahira (Num. 1:15; 2:29).

ENCAMPMENT, places where Israelites encamped on way from Egypt to Canaan (Num. 33). Also headquarters of armies (I Sam. 13:16; II Chron. 32:1).

ENCHANTMENT, the use of any form of magic, including divination; forbidden to God's people (Deut. 18:10; Acts 8:9,11; 13:8,10; 19:19).

ENDOR (ĕn'dŏr, **spring of habitation**), village c. seven miles SE of Nazareth (I Sam. 28:7).

EN-EGLAIM (ĕn-ĕg'lā-ĭm), place by the Dead Sea (Ezek. 47:10). Site unknown.

EN-GANNIM (ĕn-găn'ĭm). 1. Town in lowland of Judah (Josh. 15:34). 2. Levite town in Issachar (Josh. 19:21; 21:29).

EN-GEDI (ĕn-gĕ'dī, **fountain of wild goat**), oasis on W coast of Dead Sea in territory of Judah (Josh. 15:62); Hazazon-tamar in Gen. 14:7.

ENGRAVER. Engraving was highly developed by Israelites and surrounding peoples (Gen. 38:18; Esth. 3:12; Jer. 22:24).

EN-HADDAH (ĕn-hăd'à), town on border of Issachar (Josh. 19:21).

EN-HAKKORE (ĕn-hăk'ō-rē), spring of Samson (Judg. 15:19).

EN-HAZOR (ĕn-hä'zŏr), fortified city in Naphtali (Josh. 19:37).

EN-MISHPAT (ĕn-mĭsh'păt), the older name for Kadesh (Gen. 14:7).

ENOCH (ē'nŭk, **consecrated**). 1. Cain's eldest son (Gen. 4:17). 2. City built by Cain (Gen. 4:17). 3. Father of Methuselah (Gen. 5: 21,22); walked with God (Gen. 5:24); translated to heaven (Gen. 5:18-24; Heb. 11:5).

ENOCH, BOOKS OF, apocalyptic literature written by various authors and circulated under the name of Enoch; written c. 150 B. C. to A. D. 50.

ENOS (ē'nŏs), son of Seth (Gen. 4:26; 5:6-11).

ENOSH (ē'nŏsh), son of Seth (I Chron. 1:1; Gen. 4:26; 5:6-11).

EN-RIMMON (ĕn-rĭm'ŏn), place S of Jerusalem (Zech. 14:10; Neh. 11:29).

EN-ROGEL (ĕn-rō'gĕl, **fountain of feet**), place on border between Benjamin and Judah (Josh. 15:7; 18:16).

ENTAPPUAH (ĕn-tăp'ū-à), town of Manasseh in land of Tappuah (Josh. 17:7,8).

EPAENETUS (ĕp-ē'nē-tŭs, **praised**), convert of Paul (Rom. 16:5).

EPAPHRAS (ĕp'á-frás), Colossian Christian; visited Paul in prison (Col. 1:4,7,8; 4:12).

EPAPHRODITUS (ê-păf-rō-dī'tŭs, **lovely**), messenger sent by church at Philippi to Paul in Rome (Phil. 2:25-30; 4:18).

EPHAI (ē'fī, **gloomy**), Netophathite; sons warned Gedaliah (Jer. 40:8-16; 41:3).

EPHER (ē'fĕr). 1. Grandson of Abraham (Gen. 25:4; I Chron. 1:33). 2. Judahite (I Chron. 4:17). 3. Manassehite (I Chron. 5:23,24).

EPHESDAMMIM (ê-fĕs-dăm'ĭm, **boundary of blood**), place between Shocoh and Azekah in Judah, where David killed Goliath (I Sam. 17:1). Called Pas-dammim in I Chron. 11:13.

EPHESIANS, EPISTLE TO THE, written by

Paul (1:1; 3:1) while a prisoner (3:1; 4:1; 6:20), probably at Rome (Acts 28:30,31). Written to a number of churches, including Ephesus (1:1). Sets forth the blessings the believer has in Christ. Outline: Doctrine (redemptive blessings, Jew and Gentile one body in Christ, Paul the messenger of this mystery). 1-3. Practical exhortations (Christians to walk as God's saints; their duties as God's family; the Christian warfare). 4-6.

EPHESUS (ĕf'ē-sŭs, **desirable**), capital of the Roman province of Asia; near seacoast on Cayster River; great commercial city; famous for temple of Diana. Paul founded church there and wrote epistle to it (Acts 19, 20; I Cor. 16:8). One of seven letters in Revelation written to it (Rev. 2:1-7).

EPHLAL (ĕf'lăl), Judahite (I Chron. 2:37).

EPHOD (ĕf'ŏd). 1. Sacred vestment originally worn by the high priest (Exod. 28:4ff; 39:2ff). Later, other persons wore them too (I Sam. 2:18; 2:28; 14:3; 22:18). 2. Manasseh prince (Num. 34:23).

EPHPHATHA (ĕf'á-thà), Aramaic word meaning "be opened" (Mark 7:34).

EPHRAIM (ē'frâ-ĭm, **double fruit**). 1. Son of Joseph and Asenath (Gen. 41:50-52); progenitor of tribe called by his name which settled in the central country of Palestine and later became part of N Kingdom (I Kings 12; Isa. 7:2; 11:13; Ezek. 37:15-22). 2. City N of Jerusalem (II Sam. 13:23; John 11:54). 3. Gate of Jerusalem (II Kings 14:13; II Chron. 25:23).

EPHRAIM, MOUNT OF (ē'frâ-ĭm), mountainous part of Ephraim (Josh. 17:15).

EPHRAIM, WOODS OF, place in Gilead where David defeated forces of Absalom (II Sam. 18:6).

EPHRAIMITE (ē'frâ-ĭm-ĭt), member of tribe of Ephraim (Josh. 16:10; Judg. 12).

EPHRAIN (ē'frâ-ĭn), town taken from Jeroboam by Abijah (II Chron. 13:19).

EPHRATH (ĕf'răth). 1. Place where Rachel was buried (Gen. 35:16). 2. Wife of Caleb (I Chron. 2:19,20). 3. Ancient name of Bethlehem (Mic. 5:2).

EPHRON (ē'frŏn). 1. Hittite who sold field of Machpelah to Abraham (Gen. 23:8,9). 2. Mt. c. 6 miles NW of Jerusalem (Josh. 15:9). 3. City taken from Jeroboam by Abijah (II Chron. 13:19).

EPICUREANS (ĕp-ĭ-kū-rē'ănz), followers of Epicurus, the Greek philosopher (341-270 B. C.), who taught that the chief purpose of man is to achieve happiness; materialistic; denied life after death (Acts 17:16-33).

EPISTLE (ē-pĭs'l, **letter**), formal letters containing Christian doctrine and exhortation, referring particularly to the 21 epistles of the NT, divided into Pauline and General epistles. Not all the epistles of the apostles have survived (I Cor. 5:9).

ER (ûr). 1. Son of Judah (Gen. 38:3,6,7). 2. Son of Shelah (I Chron. 4:21). 3. Ancestor of Jesus (Luke 3:28).

ERAN (ē'răn), grandson of Ephraim (Num. 26:36).

ERASTUS (ė-ràs'tŭs, **beloved**). 1. Convert of Paul (Acts 19:22). 2. Corinthian Christian (Rom. 16:23).

ERECH (ē'rēk), Babylonian city founded by Nimrod (Gen. 10:10); located 40 miles NW of Ur.

ERI (ē'rī), son of Gad (Gen. 46:16).

ESAIAS (See Isaiah).

ESAR-HADDON (ē'sår-hăd'ŏn, **Ashur has given a brother**), son and successor of Sennacherib; ruled 681-669 B. C. (II Kings 19:37; Isa. 37:38); restored city of Babylon; conquered Egypt; brought deportees into Samaria (Ezra 4:2); took Manasseh captive (II Chron. 33:11).

ESAU (ē'saw, **hairy**), firstborn of twin brothers, Esau and Jacob, sons of Isaac and Rebecca (Gen. 25:24,25); sold his birthright for a mess of pottage to his brother (Gen. 25:30-34); married two Hittite women (Gen. 26:34); sought to kill Jacob for tricking him out of Isaac's blessing (Gen. 27); later reconciled to Jacob (Gen. 32:7-33:15). Scripture sometimes uses Esau as the name of the land of Edom in which his descendants lived (Gen. 36:8).

ESCHATOLOGY (ĕs-kà-tŏl'ō-gē, **doctrine of last things**), division of systematic theology dealing with the doctrine of last things such as death, resurrection, second coming of Christ, end of the age, divine judgment, and the future state. The OT teaches a future resurrection and judgment day (Job 19:25,26; Isa. 25:6-9; 26:19; Dan. 12:2,3). The NT interprets, enlarges, and completes the OT eschatology. It stresses the 2nd coming of Christ (I Cor. 15:51,52), the resurrection (Rom. 8:11; I Cor. 15), and the final judgment when the unsaved are cast into hell (Rev. 20) and the righteous enter into heaven (Matt. 25:31-46). Christians differ on how the millennium in Rev. 20:1-6 is to be interpreted, dividing themselves into amillennialists, postmillennialists, and premillennialists.

ESDRAELON (ĕs-drà-ē'lŏn), valley of Jezreel which lies between Galilee on the N and Samaria on the S; assigned to Issachar and Zebulun; scene of important battles in Bible history (Judg. 4; I Sam. 31; II Kings 23:29).

ESDRAS, BOOKS OF (See Apocrypha).

ESEK (ē'sĕk, **contention**), well dug by Isaac's servants in valley of Gerar (Gen. 26:20).

ESH-BAAL (ĕsh'bā-ăl, **man of Baal**), or Ishbosheth, son of Saul; ruled two years, and then murdered by David's men (II Sam. 2:8-10; 4:5-12). Originally called Eshbaal (I Chron. 8:33; 9:39).

ESHBAN (ĕsh'bān), Horite (Gen. 36:26; I Chron. 1:41).

ESHCOL (ĕsh'kŏl, **cluster**). 1. Amorite who helped Abram (Gen. 14:13,24). 2. Valley near Hebron famous for large grapes (Num. 13:23,24).

ESHEAN (ĕsh'ē-ăn), city near Hebron (Josh. 15:52).

ESHEK (ē'shĕk), descendant of Jonathan (I Chron. 8:38-40).

ESHTAOL (ĕsh'tā-ŏl), town 13 miles NW of Jerusalem (Josh. 15:33), assigned to Dan (Josh. 19:41); scene of Samson exploits (Judg. 13:24,25; 16:31).

ESHTEMOA (ĕsh'tē-mō-à). 1. City S of Hebron assigned to Levites (Josh. 21:14; I Sam. 30:28). 2. Son of Ishbah (I Chron. 4:17). 3. Maacathite (I Chron. 4:19).

ESHTEMOH (ĕsh'tē-mō), city of Judah (Josh. 15:50).

ESHTON (ĕsh'tŏn), descendant of Judah (I Chron. 4:11,12).

ESLI (ĕs'lī), ancestor of Christ (Luke 3:25).

ESROM (ĕs'rŏm), son of Perez (Matt. 1:3; Luke 3:33).

ESSENES (ė-sĕnz'), Jewish religious sect not mentioned in the Bible, but described in Josephus, Philo, and Dead Sea Scrolls; most lived communal, celibate lives; observed Law strictly; practiced ceremonial baptisms; apocalyptic; opposed Temple priesthood.

ESTHER (ĕs'tèr, Ishtar, Babylonian goddess, star), Jewess; cousin of Mordecai; became queen of Ahasuerus (Xerxes I, 486-465 B. C.); saved her countrymen from destruction.

ESTHER, BOOK OF, last of historical books of the OT; author unknown; probably written c. 400 B. C. Peculiar features of book: no mention of the name of God; no mention of prayer. Tells of Jewish girl Esther who became queen of Persia and saved her people from destruction. Outline. 1. Esther becomes queen (1-2:17). 2. Jewish danger (2:18-3:15). 3. Jews saved (4-10). In the LXX there are several interpolations scattered through the story.

ETAM (ē'tăm). 1. Town in Judah between Bethlehem and Tekoa (I Chron. 4:3). 2. Village of Simeon (I Chron. 4:32). 3. Place where Samson lived (Judg. 15:8,11).

ETERNAL LIFE, participation in the life of Jesus Christ, the eternal Son of God (John 1:4; 10:10; 17:3; Rom. 6:23), which reaches its fruition in the life to come (Matt. 25:46; John 6:54; Rom. 2:7; Titus 3:7). It is endless in its duration and divine in quality.

ETERNITY, refers to the endless past, the unending future, or to God's present experience of all time; one of the attributes of God (Jer. 1:5; Ps. 90).

ETHAM (ē'thăm), encampment of Israel in wilderness journeys (Exod. 13:20; Num. 33:6-8).

ETHAN (ē'thăn). 1. Wise man in Solomon's time (I Kings 4:31; Ps. 89 title). 2. Son of Zerah (I Chron. 2:6,8). 3. Descendant of Gershon (I Chron. 6:42-43). 4. Levite singer (I Chron. 6:44; 15:17,19).

ETHBAAL (ĕth'bā'ăl), king of Sidon; father of Jezebel (I Kings 16:31).

ETHER (ē'thèr), town in Judah between Libnah and Ashan (Josh. 15:42).

ETHIOPIA (ė-thī-ō'pĭ-à), country extending S of Egypt northward, including Nubia, Sudan, and N if not S modern Ethiopia. Moses married Ethiopian woman (Num.

12:1). In NT times it was ruled by a queen whose name or title was Candace (Acts 8:27).

ETHIOPIAN EUNUCH (ē-thī-ō'pī-ǎn ū'nŭk), treasurer of Candace, queen of the Ethiopians (Acts 8:26-39); became Christian through Philip.

ETHNAN (ĕth'nǎn), Judahite (I Chron. 4:7).

ETHNI (ĕth'nī), Gershonite Levite leader of song (I Chron. 6:41).

EUBULUS (ū-bū'lŭs), Roman Christian who sent greeting with Paul (II Tim. 4:21).

EUERGETES (ū-ûr'jē-tēz), "benefactors," a title of honor (Luke 22:25).

EUNICE (ū'nĭs, ū-nī'sē), mother of Timothy (II Tim. 1:5).

EUNUCH (ū'nŭk), castrated male, used as custodians of royal harems and court officials (Dan. 1:3; Acts 8:27; II Kings 20:18; Jer. 41:16; Esth. 1:10-15; 2:21). Not practiced by Jews; eunuchs not allowed to enter congregation (Deut. 23:1).

EUODIAS (ū-ō'dĭ-ás, fragrant), Christian woman at Philippi (Phil. 4:2).

EUPHRATES (ū-frā'tēz), river in Mesopotamia 1780 miles long from Armenia to Persian Gulf. Called "the river," "the great river" (Isa. 8:7; Deut. 1:7). Limit of possessions of David and Solomon (I Chron. 18:3; II Sam. 8:3-8; I Kings 4:21; II Chron. 9:26).

EUROCLYDON (ū-rŏk'lĭ-dŏn), E wind raising mighty waves on Mediterranean; shipwrecked Paul (Acts 27:14).

EUTYCHUS (ū'tĭ-kŭs, fortunate), youth who fell asleep while Paul preached and fell out of window to his death; was restored to life by Paul (Acts 20:9,10).

EVANGELIST (ē-vǎn'jē-list, one who announces good news). 1. One who preached the good news of Jesus Christ from place to place (Acts 8:25; 14:7; I Cor. 1:17). 2. Writer of one of the four Gospels.

EVE (ēv), the first woman; Adam's wife; mother of all living (Gen. 3:20). Deceived by Satan, she brought sin into the world.

EVENING SACRIFICE, one of two daily offerings prescribed in Mosaic ritual (Exod. 29:38-42; Num. 28:3-8).

EVI (ē'vī), king of Midian (Num. 31:8).

EVIL (ē'vīl), that which is not in harmony with the divine order, both moral and physical (Gen. 3; Job 2:10; Ps. 23:4; Luke 16:25).

EVIL-MERODACH (ē'vīl-mē-rō'dǎk), king of Babylon (562-560 B. C.); murdered by brother-in-law; released Jehoiachin (II Kings 25:27-30; Jer. 52:31-34).

EVIL SPIRITS (See Demons).

EWE (ū), female sheep.

EXCOMMUNICATION (ĕks-kŏ-mū-ni-kā'shŭn), disciplinary exclusion from church fellowship. Jews had temporary and permanent excommunication. Early church practiced it (I Cor. 5:5; I Tim. 1:20).

EXECUTIONER, commander of the king's bodyguard who executed his sentence (Gen. 37:36; Jer. 39:9; Dan. 2:14).

EXILE, usually refers to the period of time during which the Southern Kingdom (Judah) was forcibly detained in Babylon. Began in reign of Jehoiakim (609-598 B. C.) and ended with decree of Cyrus permitting Jews to return to Palestine (536 B. C.).

EXODUS (ĕk'sō-dŭs, a going out), departure of Israel from Egypt under Moses (Exodus).

EXODUS, BOOK OF, 2nd book of the Bible. "Exodus" means "a going out," referring to departure of Israel from Egypt. Date is not altogether certain—from 1280 to 1447 B. C. Outline. 1. Israel in Egypt (1:1-12:36). 2. The Journey to Sinai (12:37-19:2). 3. Israel at Sinai (19:3-40:38).

EXORCISM (ĕk'sôr-sĭzm, to adjure), the expelling of demons by means of magical formulas and ceremonies (Matt. 12:27; Mark 9:38; Acts 19:13).

EXPIATION (ĕx-pī-ā'shŭn), the act or means of making amends or reparation for sin.

EYE, used both literally and figuratively (Exod. 21:26; Ps. 19:8; Eph. 1:18).

EYES, PAINTING OF, ancients painted eyelids to enhance the beauty of the feminine face (Jer. 4:30; Ezek. 23:40).

EYESALVE, a preparation for the eyes; also used figuratively for restoration of spiritual vision.

EZEKIEL (ē-zēk'yĕl, God strengthens), Hebrew prophet of the Exile; of priestly family (Ezek. 1:3); deported to Babylon with Jehoiachin in 597 B. C.; contemporary of Jeremiah and Daniel; lived with Jewish exiles by the canal Chebar (Ezek. 1:1,2; 3:15); ministry falls into two periods: the first ends with the siege of Jerusalem in 587 B. C. (24:1,27), the 2nd begins with the news of Jerusalem's fall (Ezek. 33: 21,22).

EZEKIEL, BOOK OF, written by the prophet in captivity to warn and comfort Israel and to show it was not forsaken. The last part looks forward to the coming of the Kingdom of God. Outline. 1. Denunciation of Judah and Israel (1-24). The prophecies of this section were uttered before the fall of Jerusalem. Dated 593-588 B. C. 2. Oracles against foreign nations (25-32). Dated 587-571 B. C. 3. The future restoration of Israel (33-48). Dated 585-573 B. C.

EZEL (ē'zĕl), stone marking final meeting place of David and Jonathan (I Sam. 20:19).

EZEM (ē'zĕm), or Azem, town near Edom assigned to Simeon (Josh. 15:29; 19:3; I Chron. 4:29).

EZER (ē'zĕr, help). 1. Horite chief (Gen. 36:21; I Chron. 1:38). 2. Descendant of Hur (I Chron. 4:4). 3. Ephraimite (I Chron. 7:21). 4. Gadite warrior (I Chron. 12:9). 5. Man who helped repair wall of Jerusalem (Neh. 3:19). 6. Levite singer (Neh. 12:42).

EZION-GEBER (ē'zī-ŏn-gē'bêr), city near Elath on Gulf of Aqabah; encampment of Israelites (Num. 33:35,36). Solomon and Jehoshaphat built fleets of ships there (I Kings 9:26ff; II Chron. 8:17,18; 20:35,36; I Kings 22:48,49).

EZNITE (ĕz'nīt), designation of Adino, one of David's chief captains (II Sam. 23:8).

EZRA (ĕz′rȧ, help). 1. Judahite (I Chron. 4:17). 2. Priest who returned from Babylon to Jerusalem with Zerubbabel (Neh. 21:1). In Neh. 10:2 spelled Azariah. 3. Jewish priest, descendant of Eleazar, and scribe who is the main character of the Book of Ezra and the co-worker of Nehemiah. With the permission of Artaxerxes, king of Persia (458 B. C.) he returned to Jerusalem with 1800 Jews to carry out a religious reform. He compelled Jews who had married foreign wives to divorce them. Thirteen years later (446 B. C.) he appeared in Jerusalem with Nehemiah; he read and interpreted the law of Moses before the people, assisted in the dedication of the wall, and helped Nehemiah bring about a religious reformation.

EZRA, BOOK OF, so named because Ezra is the principal person mentioned in it; he may also be its author, as Jewish tradition says. The Book of Ezra continues the narrative after Chronicles, and tells the story of the return from Babylon and the rebuilding of the temple. The purpose of the author is to show how God fulfilled His promise given through prophets to restore His exiled people to their own land and raised up great men to rebuild the temple, re-establish the old forms of worship, and end compromise with heathenism. The period covered is 536-458 B. C. Outline. 1. Narrative of the return of the Jews from Babylonia under Zerubbabel and the restoration of worship in the rebuilt temple (1-6). 2. Second group of exiles return with Ezra, and Ezra's religious reforms (7-10).

EZRAHITE (ĕz′rȧ-hit), designation of Ethan and Heman (I Kings 4:31; titles of Pss. 88,89).

EZRI (ĕz′rī), overseer of David (I Chron. 27:26).

F

FABLE, a narrative in which animals and inanimate objects speak as if they were human beings. There are two fables in the OT (Judg. 9:7-15 and II Kings 14:9), though the word "fable" does not appear. In the NT it has the meaning of fiction, a story that is improbable or untrue (I Tim. 1:4; 4:7; II Tim. 4:4; Titus 1:14; II Pet. 1:16).

FACE, the translation of three Heb. words: 'ayin, eye, 'āph, nose, pānim, face, and of the Greek pro′sopon, face. Sometimes it might mean person, presence, or favor. To hide one's face meant to reject (Ps. 27:9); to cover the face was a sign of condemnation (Esth. 7:8); to fall on one's face indicated submission or humiliation (Gen. 17:3).

FAIR has the meaning of beautiful (Acts 7:20), clean (Zech. 3:5), persuasive (Prov. 7:21). It is not used to describe complexion.

FAIR HAVENS, a small bay on the S coast of Crete, about 5 miles E of Cape Matala, where Paul stayed for a short time on his way to Rome (Acts 27:8-12).

FAIRS occurs only in the KJV; the ARV translates it "wares" (Ezek. 27:12,14, 16,19,27).

FAITH has both an active and a passive sense in the Bible. The former meaning relates to one's loyalty to a person or fidelity to a promise; the latter, confidence in the word or assurance of another. In the OT (KJV) the word faith occurs only twice (Deut. 32:20; Hab. 2:4), and the word believe appears less than thirty times. Faith is taught by the examples of the servants of God who committed their lives to Him in unwavering trust and obedience. OT faith is never mere assent to a set of doctrines or outward acceptance of the Law, but utter confidence in the faithfulness of God and a loving obedience to His will.

In the NT faith and believe occur almost 500 times. The NT makes the claim that the promised Messiah had come, and that Jesus of Nazareth was the promised Messiah. To believe on Him meant to become a Christian, and was pivotal in the experience of the individual. Jesus offered Himself as the object of faith, and made plain that faith in Him was necessary for eternal life.

The first Christians called themselves believers (Acts 2:44), and endeavored to persuade others to believe in Jesus (Acts 6:7; 28:24). In the epistles of Paul faith is contrasted with works as a means of salvation (Rom. 3:20-22). Faith is trust in the person of Jesus, the truth of His teaching, and the redemptive work which He accomplished at Calvary.

Faith may also refer to the body of truth which constitutes the whole of the Christian message (Jude 3).

FAITHFULNESS, an attribute both of God and man, implying loyalty, constancy, and freedom from arbitrariness or fickleness (II Cor. 1:18; Gal. 5:22; II Tim. 2:2).

FALCON (See Birds).

FALL, THE. The fall of man as related in Genesis 3 is the historical choice by which man sinned voluntarily, and consequently involved all the human race in evil (Rom. 5:12f.; I Cor. 15:22). By the fall man was alienated from God. Man was created in God's own image, with a rational and moral nature like God's, with no inner impulse to sin and with a will free to choose the will of God. Yielding to the outward temptation turned him from God, and created an environment in which sin became a potent factor. Redemption from the fall is accomplished through the second Adam, Jesus Christ (Rom. 5:12-21; I Cor. 15:21,22,45-49).

FALLOW DEER (See Animals).

FALLOW GROUND is untilled ground (Jer.

4:3; Hos. 10:12).

FALSE CHRISTS. Jesus warned His disciples that imitators and pretenders would follow Him who would try to deceive His followers (Matt. 24:5-11,23-25; Mark 13:6, 21,23; Luke 21:8).

FALSE PROPHET. Any person pretending to possess a message from God, but not possessing a divine commission (Jer. 29:9). The false prophet is mentioned in the Book of Revelation (Rev. 19:20) and is usually identified with the two-horned beast of Revelation 13:11-18.

FAMILIAR SPIRIT is the spirit of a dead person or a demon whom mediums claimed that they could summon for consultation (Deut. 18:11). The word familiar has the sense of the Latin familiaris, "belonging to one's family," and hence ready to serve as a slave. Such spirits were supposed to be able to reveal the future (Isa. 8:19; I Sam. 28:7). Israelites were forbidden to consult such spirits (Lev. 19:31) under penalty of death (Lev. 20:6).

FAMILY. The concept of the family in the Bible differs from the modern institution. The Hebrew family was larger than families today, including the father of the household, his parents, if living, his wife or wives and children, his daughters and sons-in-law, slaves, guests and foreigners under his protection. Marriage was arranged by the father of the groom and the family of the bride, for whom a dowry, or purchase money was paid to her father (Gen. 24). Polygamy and concubinage were practiced, though not favored by God. The husband could divorce the wife, but she could not divorce him.

The father of a family had the power of life and death over his children. To dishonor a parent was punishable by death (Exod. 21:15,17). The NT concept followed that of the OT. Parents and children, husbands and wives, masters and slaves were enjoined to live together in harmony and love (Eph. 5:22-6:9).

FAMINE was frequent in ancient Palestine because of failure of rain, or destructive storms, or plagues of insects, especially locusts, or war. (See Gen. 12:10; 41:56; I Kings 17:1; 18:2; II Kings 6:25). Famine could be a judgment of God on wickedness (Jer. 14:12,15). The term is used figuratively of a scarcity of the word of God (Amos 8:11).

FAN, a fork with two or more prongs used to throw grain into the air after threshing, that the chaff might be blown away (Isa. 30:24; Matt. 3:12).

FARMING was the chief occupation of the people of Israel after the conquest of Canaan. Each family received a piece of ground marked by boundaries that could not be removed (Deut. 19:14). Plowing took place in the autumn, when the ground was softened by the rains. Grain was sown during the month of February; harvest began in the spring, and usually lasted

from Passover to Pentecost. The grain was cut with a sickle, and gleanings were left for the poor (Ruth 2:2). The grain was threshed out on the threshing-floor, a saucer-shaped area of beaten clay 25 or more feet in diameter, on which animals dragged a sledge over the sheaves to beat out the grain. The grain was winnowed by tossing it into the air to let the chaff blow away, and was then sifted to remove impurities (Ps. 1:4). Wheat and barley were the most important crops, but other grains and vegetables were cultivated as well.

FARTHING (See Money).

FASTING, or abstinence from food and water for a longer or shorter period was a regular accompaniment of certain aspects of worship, and is frequently mentioned in the Bible. The only fast required by the Law was that of the Day of Atonement (Lev. 16:29,31; Jer. 36:6). Fasts were held on special occasions for national penitence or to avert impending calamities (I Sam. 7:6).

Fasting was practiced by strict Jews of Jesus' day (Luke 2:37; 18:12), and Jesus Himself fasted in the wilderness during the period of temptation (Matt. 4:2). The church observed it on occasions when special prayer was necessary (Acts 13:2,3; 14:23). Jesus sanctioned fasting, but did not command it (Mark 2:18-22).

FAT. The layer of fat around the kidneys and other viscera of sacrificial animals which was forbidden for food, but which was burned as an offering to Jehovah (Lev. 4:31). Sometimes the word is used in the KJV as equivalent to "vat," a receptacle into which the grape juice flowed when pressed from the fruit (Joel 2:24; Isa. 63:2).

FATHER has various meanings in the Bible. It may denote (1) an immediate male progenitor (Gen. 42:13), or (2) a male ancestor, immediate or remote (Gen. 17:4; Rom. 9:5), or (3) a spiritual ancestor (Rom. 4:11; John 8:44), or (4) the originator of a mode of life (Gen. 4:20), or (5) an advisor (Judg. 17:10), or a source (Job 38:28). God is called the Father of the universe (Jas. 1:17) and the Creator of the human race (Mal. 2:10).

FATHOM (See Weights and Measures).

FATLING. A clean animal fattened for offering to God (Ps. 66:15; II Sam. 6:13).

FEAR may be either apprehension of evil or awe of just authority. The disciples were afraid when they saw Jesus walking on the water, and thought He was a ghost (Matt. 14:26); "the fear of the Lord" (Prov. 9:10) is the proper reverence accorded to God.

FEASTS were the sacred festivals of Judaism which were occasions of public worship. There were seven in all. The Passover, or Feast of Unleavened Bread was established before the giving of the Law to celebrate the Exodus from Egypt. It began on the 14th day of Nisan, and continued for a week (Lev. 23:5-8). Attendance was required of all male Jews (Deut. 16:16).

The Feast of Pentecost or Feast of Weeks was celebrated fifty days after the Passover. The feast lasted one day, and marked the completion of the wheat harvest, at which two loaves of bread made from the new grain were offered to God (Deut. 16:9-12).

The Feast of Trumpets or New Moon was held on the first day of the seventh month (October), and began the civil year of the Jews (Lev. 23:23).

The Day of Atonement was observed ten days later as a day of national penitence and mourning. The high priest confessed the sins of the community, and entered into the Most Holy Place with the blood of the offering to make atonement for the people (Lev. 23:26-32).

The Feast of Tabernacles was the last of the feasts prescribed by the Law. It began five days after the Day of Atonement (Lev. 23:34; Deut. 16:13), and lasted eight days. It commemorated the entrance into the Promised Land after the wandering in the wilderness.

The Feast of Lights originated with the cleansing of the Temple under the Maccabees, and was observed for eight days beginning with the 25th day of Kislev (December).

The Feast of Purim was a memorial to the deliverance of the Jews by Esther from the plot of Haman (Esther 9:1-10).

FELIX was the Roman procurator of Judea from A. D. 52 to 60, under whose administration Paul was imprisoned (Acts 23:24-24:27).

FELLOES, the exterior parts of the rim of a wheel (I Kings 7:33).

FELLOW, a contemptuous name for an unnamed person (Judg. 18:25), or a friend or equal (Heb. 1:9).

FELLOWSHIP, a social or business partnership (II Cor. 6:14-18); membership in a local church (Acts 2:42); partnership in the work of the gospel (II Cor. 8:4).

FENCED CITY. An allusion to the custom of enclosing settlements with walls for protection against invasion (Deut. 3:5).

FERTILE CRESCENT. A modern description of the territory from the Persian Gulf to Egypt, which is watered by the Euphrates, Tigris, Orontes, Jordan, and Nile rivers.

FESTIVALS (See Feasts).

FESTUS, PORCIUS was the Roman governor who succeeded Felix in the province of Judea (Acts 24:27). He presided at the hearing of the apostle Paul when he made his defense before Herod Agrippa II (Acts 24:27-26:32). When Paul appealed to Caesar, Festus sent him to Rome. The date of Festus' accession is uncertain, probably A. D. 59/60. He died in office in A. D. 62.

FETTERS, chains or shackles for the feet of prisoners, generally made of bronze or of iron (Judg. 16:21; Ps. 105:18; 149:8).

FEVER (See Diseases).

FIELD. The Biblical field was generally not enclosed, but was marked off from its neighbors by boundary markers. "Field of Moab" (Gen. 36:35) means any plot in the territory of Moab.

FIG (See Plants).

FILLET. "Fillets" (Exod. 27:10,11; 38:10-19) were the rods between the columns that supported the hangings of the Tabernacle.

FINING-POT is the crucible in which ore is melted to be purified from dross (Prov. 17:3; 27:21).

FIR (See Plants).

FIRE. An emblem of the presence of God (Ezek. 1:27) and a means of judgment (Gen. 19:24). The offerings of the Tabernacle were consumed by fire (Lev. 9:24); "strange fire" was forbidden (10:1,2). Fire was used for cooking (John 21:9), for warmth (18:18), and for the disposal of rubbish (15:6). Fire was an emblem of testing (I Cor. 3:12-15) and of judgment (Rev. 1:14).

FIREBRAND, a remnant of a burnt stick (Amos 4:11), torches used as weapons (Prov. 26:18), and burning wood used for light (Judg. 7:16).

FIREPAN, a vessel for carrying live coals (Exod. 27:3).

FIRKIN (See Weights and Measures).

FIRMAMENT, the expanse of sky surrounding the earth, made to divide the waters from the waters (Gen. 1:6). The Hebrew word (raqia) does not denote a solid substance, but thinness or expanse.

FIRST BEGOTTEN, a term applied to the Lord Jesus Christ in Hebrews 1:6 and Revelation 1:5.

FIRSTBORN, the first offspring of a family, generally used of men (Exod. 13:11-15), but sometimes of animals. The firstborn succeeded his father as head of the house, and received a double portion of the inheritance (Deut. 21:17).

FIRST DAY OF THE WEEK (See Sunday).

FIRST FRUITS. The first fruits were the first part of the crops that were offered to God as thanksgiving for His goodness (Exod. 23:19; Lev. 23:17; Deut. 26:1-11).

FISH (See Animals).

FISH GATE, an ancient gate on the E side of Jerusalem near Gihon where Tyrians held a fish market (II Chron. 33:14; Neh. 13:16).

FISHING (See Occupations and Professions).

FISHHOOK, a metal hook used both to catch fish (Matt. 17:27) and to keep them captive (Amos 4:2).

FISH POOL. See Song of Solomon 7:4.

FITCH (See Plants).

FLAG (See Plants).

FLAGON, a large container for wine (Isa. 22:24). In II Samuel 6:19 the Hebrew means "raisins."

FLAX (See Plants).

FLEAS (See Insects).

FLEECE is the shorn wool of a sheep (Deut. 18:4).

FLESH. 1. The soft part of the body of men or animals. 2. All living creatures (Gen. 6:18). 3. Humanity in general (Num. 16:22). 4. Intellect and volition contrasted with emotional desire (Matt. 26:41). 5. Human nature deprived of the Holy Spirit and dominated by sin (Rom. 7:14; Col. 2:18; I John 2:16).

FLESH-HOOK, a metal implement used for handling large pieces of flesh at the altar of sacrifice (Exod. 27:3; 38:3; I Chron. 28:17).

FLIES (See Insects).

FLINT (See Minerals).

FLOCK, a collection of sheep under the care of a shepherd, sometimes including goats as well (Gen. 27:9; 30:32). Used figuratively of Christ's disciples (Luke 12:32; I Pet. 5:2,3).

FLOOD, DELUGE. "The Flood" refers to the deluge of Noah (Gen. 6:13-8:19) which God sent to destroy a hopelessly depraved race of men (Isa. 54:9; Matt. 24:37-39; Luke 17:26,27; Heb. 11:7; I Pet. 3:20), and through which Noah and his family were preserved in the ark. According to Genesis, the waters covered all visible territory (Gen. 7:19) and lasted for more than a year. All living persons except Noah and his family were destroyed. The date of the Flood is uncertain, but it must have preceeded the time of Abraham by a number of centuries.

"Flood" is used once of the Euphrates River (Josh. 24:3, KJV), or of any mass of water (Exod. 15:8; Ps. 24:2).

FLOUR, fine-crushed and sifted grain, generally wheat, rye, or barley (Judg. 6:19).

FLOWER (See Plants).

FLUTE (See Music).

FLY (See Insects).

FOAL (See Animals).

FODDER, the mixed food of cattle (Job 6:5).

FOOD. Various kinds of food were used in Bible times. The staple of diet was bread made from wheat, barley, or rye. Vegetables such as beans, lentils, melons, onions, cucumbers, and gourds were eaten freely. Fruits abounded; grapes, figs, pomegranates are mentioned frequently (Deut. 23:24; Num. 13:23). Fish and meat were included in the Jewish diet with certain restrictions: beef and lamb or goat were "clean," camel, rabbit, and pork were forbidden, together with shellfish and eels, carnivorous birds, and reptiles of all kinds. Insects were forbidden for certain types of grasshoppers or locusts (Lev. 11:1-45). Honey, spices and salt were included in daily diet. Milk and cheese were the chief dairy products (Deut. 32:14; I Sam. 17:18).

FOOL in Scripture connotes conceit and pride, or deficiency in judgment rather than mental inferiority (Eccl. 10:14; Ps. 14:1; Matt. 23:17).

FOOT, that part of the body on which men and animals walk, or that part of furniture on which it stands. The base of the laver was called its foot (Exod. 30:18).

FOOTMAN, a member of the infantry, or a runner used for dispatching messages (I Sam. 22:17).

FOOTSTOOL, a literal support for the feet

(II Chron. 9:18), a figure of subjection (Ps. 110:1; Isa. 66:1; Matt. 5:35).

FORD, a shallow place in a stream where men and animals could cross on foot (Gen. 32:22; Isa. 16:2).

FOREHEAD, the part of the face above the eyes, often revealing the character of the person: shamelessness (Jer. 3:3), courage (Ezek. 3:9), or godliness (Rev. 7:3).

FOREIGNER. Among the Jewish people, anyone outside the nation was regarded as inferior (Gen. 31:15), and possessed restricted rights. He could not eat the Passover (Exod. 12:43), enter the sanctuary (Ezek. 44:9), become king (Deut. 17:15), or intermarry on equal terms (Exod. 34:12-16). They could be included in the nation by accepting the Law and its requirements. In the NT the word is applied to those who are not members of God's kingdom (Eph. 2:19).

FOREKNOWLEDGE (See Election).

FOREORDINATION (See Election).

FORESKIN, the fold of skin cut off in the process of circumcision (Gen. 17:11,14).

FOREST. In ancient times, most of the hills of Palestine were covered with trees. The forest of Lebanon yielded the cedar and fir lumber which Hiram of Tyre sold to Solomon (I Kings 5:8-10).

FORGIVENESS is a relationship established between man and God or between man and man by the giving up of resentment or claim to requital on account of an offense. The offense may be a deprivation of a person's property, rights, or honor; or it may be a violation of moral law. Forgiveness is conditioned on repentance and the willingness to make reparation. The ground of forgiveness of sin is the atoning death of Christ (Col. 1:14; 3:13). Christ claimed the authority to forgive sins (Mark 2:5,7; Luke 7:48,49).

FORK, probably an ancient type of pitchfork (I Sam. 13:21).

FORNICATION, unlawful sexual intercourse of an unwed person (I Cor. 6:9,18). It was commonly associated with heathen worship (Jer. 2:20; 3:6), and was used as a figure of disloyalty to God (Ezek. 16:3-22).

FORT, FORTRESS, the citadel around which ancient settlements were built (Num. 13:28; Deut. 1:28), and within which the inhabitants took refuge in time of war (II Sam. 5:9).

FORTUNATUS, a Corinthian Christian, a friend of Paul (I Cor. 16:17).

FORUM APPII, "the market of Appius," a place 43 miles SE of Rome, where Paul was met by friends (Acts 28:15).

FOUNDATION, the footing or wall on which a building is erected. Used figuratively of the foundation of faith (I Cor. 3:10,11) or of the church (Eph. 2:20).

FOUNTAIN, a spring of water, greatly prized in an arid land like Palestine (Deut. 8:7). Used figuratively of eternal life (John 4:14; Rev. 21:6).

FOUNTAIN GATE, a gate in the walls of

Jerusalem (Neh. 2:14; 3:15; 12:37).

FOWL (See Birds).

FOWLER, a bird-catcher (Ps. 91:3; 124:7; Hos. 9:8).

FOX (See Animals).

FRANKINCENSE, a resin obtained from a tree growing in Arabia (Isa. 60:6; Jer. 6:20) which was burned for incense (Exod. 30:34-38). It was one of the gifts presented to the infant Jesus by the Magi (Matt. 2:11, 15). (See Plants).

FREEMAN, a slave who has been granted his freedom (I Cor. 7:22), or a free man as contrasted with a slave (Gal. 4:22,23).

FREEWILL OFFERINGS (See Offerings).

FRET. The verb means to be irritated, angry, or nervous (Ps. 37:1,7,8); the noun refers to a painful type of leprosy (Lev. 13:51,52).

FRINGE, the tassel of twisted cords fastened to the outer garments of Israelites (Num. 15:38; Deut. 22:12).

FROG (See Plagues, Animals).

FRONTLET, a small leather case bound to the forehead, containing a series of passages from the Law. Frontlets were worn by male Jews during the time of morning prayer except on Sabbaths and festivals.

FROST appeared in winter on the high elevations in Bible lands (Job 37:10; 38:29).

FRUIT. Fruits mentioned in the Bible are grapes, pomegranates, figs, olives, and apples. The word is often used metaphorically of product or result (Deut. 7:13; Prov. 1:31; Gal. 5:22).

FRYING PAN, properly a saucepan for boiling or baking (Lev. 2:7; 7:9).

FUEL. Wood, charcoal, dried grass, and even the dung of animals was used for fuel (Ezek. 4:12,15; Matt. 6:30; John 18:18).

FULLER (See Occupations and Professions).

FULLER'S FIELD, a field outside Jerusalem where fullers washed the cloth that they were processing (Isa. 7:3; 36:2).

FULLER'S SOAP, an alkali used for cleaning new cloth (Mal. 3:2).

FUNERAL, the ceremonies used in disposing of a dead human body. In Palestine the body was buried within a few hours after death in a tomb or cave. The body was washed, anointed with spices, and wrapped in cloths (John 12:7; 19:39,40). Refusal of proper burial was utter disgrace (Jer. 22:19).

FURLONG (See Weights and Measures).

FURNACE. The word does not refer to a device for central heating, but either to a smelter for metals (Prov. 17:3; Ezek. 22:22), or for a baking oven (Lev. 2:4).

FURNITURE. The principle reference to furniture in the Bible concerns the articles in the Tabernacle and Temple. Common people had little furniture; kings had bedsteads (Deut. 3:11) and tables (Judg. 1:7).

FUTURE LIFE (See Immortality, Eschatology).

G

GAAL (gāal, loathing), son of Ebed, who led the men of Shechem in a revolt against Abimelech, the son of Gideon (Judg. 9: 26-41).

GAASH (gāāsh, quaking), a hill near Mt. Ephraim where Joshua was buried (Judg. 2:9).

GABA (gā'-bà), a Benjamite city (Josh. 18:24).

GABBAI (gāb'ā-ī, collector), a chief of Benjamin (Neh. 11:8).

GABBATHA (gāb'à-thà, height, ridge), the place called "the Pavement" (John 19:13) where Jesus was tried before Pilate.

GABRIEL (gā'bri-ĕl, man of God), an angel who served as a messenger of God (Dan. 8:16; 9:21; Luke 1:11, 19, 26-38).

GAD (gād, fortune). 1. The seventh son of Jacob (Gen. 30:9-11). The tribe of Gad settled on the E side of the Jordan after the conquest of Canaan. 2. The prophet and biographer of David (I Sam. 22:5; II Sam. 24:11-18; I Chron. 29:29). 3. A Canaanite god of fortune (Josh. 11:17; 12:7; 13:5; 15:37).

GADARA, GADARENES (gād'à-rà, gād-à-rēnz), one of the cities of the Decapolis near the SE end of the Sea of Galilee, near which the demoniacs lived whom Jesus healed (Mark 5:1; Luke 8:26,37; Matt. 8:28, Gr. text).

GADDI (gād'ī), Manasseh's representative among the twelve spies (Num. 13:11).

GADDIEL (gād'dī-ĕl), Zebulun's representative among the twelve spies (Num. 13:10).

GADI (gā'dī), father of Menahem, a king of Israel (II Kings 15:14-20).

GAHAM (gā'-hàm), a son of Nahor by his concubine Reumah (Gen. 22:24).

GAHAR (gā'hàr), a family of the Nethinim who returned with Zerubbabel to Jerusalem (Ezra 2:47).

GAIUS (gā'yûs). 1. A Macedonian disciple who traveled with Paul (Acts 19:29). 2. A man of Derbe who accompanied Paul from Macedonia to Asia (Acts 20:4). 3. A Corinthian whom Paul baptized (I Cor. 1:14). 4. The addressee of III John (III John 1, 5-8).

GALAL (gā'lāl), the name of two Levites, mentioned in I Chronicles 9:15, and in 9:16, Nehemiah 11:17.

GALATIA (gà-lā'shǐ-à), originally a territory in north-central Asia Minor where the Gauls settled; later the name of a Roman province in central Asia Minor, organized in 25 B. C. The cities of Antioch of Pisidia, Iconium, Lystra, and Derbe belonged within this province. Paul's use of the term (I Cor. 16:1; Gal. 1:2; II Tim. 4:10) and Peter's allusion (I Pet. 1:1) probably refer to the province as a whole.

GALATIANS, EPISTLE TO THE, is a short but important letter of Paul, containing a protest against legalism and a clear statement of the gospel of God's grace. It was written shortly after the close of the first missionary journey to the churches of Galatia (Gal. 1:1) to counteract the propaganda of certain Jewish teachers who insisted that to faith in Christ must be added circumcision and obedience to the Mosaic Law (2:16; 3:2-3; 4:10,21; 5:2-4;6:12). After the introduction to the Epistle (1:1-10) Paul attempted to vindicate his apostolic authority (1:11-2:21), and then proceeded to explain the meaning of justification by faith (3:1-4:31), concluding with a discussion on the nature of the Christian life of liberty (5:1-6:10). The conclusion (6:11-17) and benediction (6:18) constituted a personal appeal to the Galatians to return to their initial faith.

GALBANUM (găl'bà-nŭm), a gum resin used in the sacred incense (Exod. 30:34).

GALEED (găl'ē-ĕd, **a heap of witnesses**), the name given by Jacob to the heap of stones which he and Laban raised as a memorial of their compact (Gen. 31:47,48).

GALILEAN (găl'ĭ-lē'ăn), a native of Galilee (Matt. 26:69; John 4:45; Acts 1:11, 5:37).

GALILEE (găl'ĭ-lē, **the ring ór circuit**), the most northerly of the three provinces of Palestine (Galilee, Samaria, Judea), Measuring approximately 50 miles N to S and 30 miles E to W, it was bounded in the W by the coastal plain along which ran the road from Egypt to Phoenicia, and the caravan routes from the coast to Damascus and the East crossed its southern part through the valley of Esdraelon. The northern part had been settled by Gentiles after the captivity of Israel, and in Jesus' day their descendants still lived there (Matt. 4:13-15). Galileans spoke with a peculiar accent (Matt. 26:73), and were despised by the Jews of the south (John 7:52). From 4 B. C. to A. D. 39 Galilee was governed by Herod Antipas (Luke 3:1; 13:32), who built the city of Tiberias. Jesus exercised the larger part of his ministry in Galilee, especially in the cities surrounding the lake.

GALILEE, SEA OF, called also "the Sea of Gennesaret" (Luke 5:1), or "the Sea of Chinnereth" (Num. 34:11; Deut. 3:17) from the Hebrew meaning "harp-shaped," the shape of the sea, or "the Sea of Tiberias" because Herod's capital was on its shores (John 6:1; 21:1). The lake is 13 miles long and 8 miles wide, filled with sweet and clear water, and full of fish. Because it was located in a pocket in the hills, it was subject to sudden violent storms.

GALL. 1. The secretion of the human gallbladder (Job 16:13). 2. The poison of serpents (20:14). 3. A bitter and poisonous herb (Jer. 9:15), perhaps used as an anodyne to deaden pain (Matt. 27:34).

GALLERY, a balcony of the temple in Ezekiel's vision (Ezek. 41:16; 42:3,5,6).

GALLEY (See Ship).

GALLIM (găl'ĭm, **heaps**), a town of Benjamin (Isa. 10:30; I Sam. 25:44).

GALLIO (găl'ĭ-ō), Junius Annaeus Gallio, the Roman proconsul of Achaia when Paul was

in Corinth (A. D. 51). He refused to hear any accusations against Paul, and discharged him as innocent (Acts 18:12-17).

GALLOWS, in Biblical usage a pole on which criminals were impaled (Esth. 5:14; 6:4).

GAMALIEL (gȧ-mā'lĭ-ĕl, **reward of God**). 1. Chief of tribe of Manasseh (Num. 1:10; 2:20; 10:23). 2. An eminent Pharisee and teacher of the Law, the teacher of Paul (Acts 22:3). He was broadminded and tolerant toward early Christians (5:34-39).

GAMES. Little is known of the amusements of the Hebrews. There are references to dancing (Jer. 31:13; Luke 15:25), and the play of children is mentioned in Scripture (Zech. 8:5; Matt. 11:16,17; Luke 7:32). Paul alludes to athletic contests (I Cor. 9:24,25; Eph. 6:12) and the author of Hebrews speaks of the race (Heb. 12:1,2).

GAMMADIM (gă'mȧ-dĭm, probably **valiant men**), the garrison in the watchtowers of Tyre (Ezek. 27:11).

GAMUL (gă'mŭl), the head of the twenty-second course of priests (I Chron. 24:17).

GARDEN, a cultivated piece of ground planted with flowers, vegetables, shrubs, or trees, fenced with a mud or stone wall (Prov. 24:31) or with thorny hedges (Isa. 5:5). Gardens were sometimes used for burial places (Gen. 23:17; II Kings 21:18,26; John 19:41). The future state of the saved is figuratively represented by a garden (Rev. 22:1-5).

GARDENER (See Occupations and Professions).

GAREB (gă'rĕb, scabby). 1. One of David's warriors (II Sam. 23:38; I Chron. 11:40). 2. A hill near Jerusalem (Jer. 31:39).

GARLICK, GARLIC (See Plants).

GARMENTS (See Dress).

GARMITE (gàr'mĭt), a name applied to Keilah (I Chron. 4:19).

GARNER (gàr'nẽr), a barn or storehouse (Ps. 144:13; Joel 1:17; Matt. 3:12).

GARRISON, a fortress manned by soldiers, used chiefly for the occupation of a conquered country (I Sam. 10:5; 13:3; 14:1,6; II Sam. 8:6,14).

GASHMU (găsh'mū), sometimes called Geshem, an Arabian who opposed Nehemiah's restoration of Jerusalem (Neh. 6:6; 2:19; 6:1,2).

GATAM (gă'tăm), grandson of Esau, an Edomite chief (Gen. 36:11,16; I Chron. 1:36).

GATE, the opening to enclosed buildings, grounds, or cities. Gates were generally made of wood, plated with metal to resist fire (Ps. 107:16; Isa. 45:2). They swung on pivots set in the walls, and were closed with bars of wood or metal (Nah. 3:13; I Kings 4:13). They were shut at night, and opened in the morning (Deut. 3:5; Josh. 2:5,7).

Business was conducted at the city gate (Neh. 3:3,28); announcements were made at the gates (Jer. 7:2); law was dispensed at the gate by the elders of the city (Ruth 4:1,2,11; Prov. 22:22; II Sam. 19:8); to sit in the gate meant the attainment of an eminent position (Prov. 32:23).

GATH (găth, winepress), a city of the Philistines (I Sam. 6:17), home of Goliath (I Sam. 17:4), and scene of some of David's exploits (21:10-15). Its location is uncertain.

GATH-HEPHER (găth-hē'fẽr, winepress of the well), a town on the border of Zebulun (Josh. 19:12,13, ASV) and birthplace of Jonah the prophet (II Kings 14:25).

GATH-RIMMON (găth-rĭ'mŭn, winepress of Rimmon). 1. A city of Dan on the Philistine plain (Josh. 19:45). 2. A town of Manasseh, W of Jordan, assigned to Levites (Josh. 14:25).

GAULANITIS (gŏl-ăn-i'tis), a province NE of the Sea of Galilee, ruled by Herod Antipas.

GAZA (gä'zà, strong), one of the five chief Philistine cities, and the most southwesterly toward Egypt. It was an important stop on the caravan route. Originally a Canaanite city (Gen. 10:19) Gaza was assigned by Joshua to Judah (Josh. 15:47), and was occupied later (Judg. 1:18). It was captured by the Philistines (Judg. 13:1) and controlled by them until the time of Hezekiah (II Kings 18:8). Samson was imprisoned and died in Gaza (Judg. 16:1,21). It is mentioned once in the NT in connection with Philip's ministry to the Ethiopian eunuch (Acts 8:26).

GAZELLE (See Animals).

GAZER (See Gezer).

GAZEZ (gā'zĕz), the name of the son and of the grandson of Ephah (I Chron. 2:46).

GAZZAM (găz'ăm), one of the Nethinim, whose descendants returned from exile (Ezra 2:48; Neh. 7:51).

GEBA (gē'bà, hill), a town in the territory of Benjamin (Josh. 18:24 ASV, RSV), assigned to the Levites (Josh. 21:17). Jonathan defeated the Philistines at Geba (I Sam. 13:3). Asa fortified the city (I Kings 15:22), and in Hezekiah's time it was the northernmost city of Judah (II Kings 23:8). Men from Geba returned after the exile (Ezra 2:26).

GEBAL (gē'băl, border). 1. A seaport of Phoenicia north of Sidon, the modern Jebeil, 25 miles north of Beirut. The land of the Gebalites is mentioned in Joshua 13:5,6. The town was renowned for its expert stonemasons (I Kings 5:17,18 ASV) and for shipbuilding (Ezek. 27:9). 2. A land between the Dead Sea and Petra (Ps. 83:6-8).

GEBER (gē'bẽr). 1. One of Solomon's purveyors in Ramoth-Gilead (I Kings 4:13). 2. The son of Uri (I Kings 4:19).

GEBIM (gē'bĭm), a place near Anathoth (Isa. 10:31).

GECKO (See Animals).

GEDALIAH (gĕd'à-lī'à). 1. Son of Shaphan, governor of Mizpah, and friend of Jeremiah (II Kings 25:22-25; Jer. 40:5-16), assassinated by Ishmael, son of Nethaniah (Jer. 41:1-3). 2. A priest of the sons of Jeshua (Ezra 10:16). 3. Grandfather of Zephaniah (Zeph. 1:1). 4. One of the six sons of Jeduthun (I Chron. 25:8,9). 5.

A son of Pashur (Jer. 38:1-6).

GEDER (gē'dẽr), a Canaanite city captured by Joshua (Josh. 12:13).

GEDERAH (gē-dē'rà, wall), the modern Jedireh, located between the valleys of Sorek and Aijalon in the hills of Judah.

GEDOR (gē'dôr, wall). A city in the hill-country of Judah (Josh. 15:58). 2. An unknown town where Jeroham lived (I Chron. 12:7). 3. A descendant of Benjamin (I Chron. 8:31; 9:37). 4. Descendants of Judah (I Chron. 4:4,18).

GEHAZI (gē-hā'zĭ, valley of vision), the servant of Elisha (II Kings 4:8-37; 5:1-27; 8:4-6). He was punished for avarice by becoming a leper.

GEHENNA (gē-hĕn'à, valley of Hinnom), a valley on the W and SW of Jerusalem which formed part of the border between Judah and Benjamin (Josh. 15:8; 18:16; Neh. 11:30,31). It later became the place of pagan sacrifice (II Chron. 28:3; 33:6; Jer. 32:35). Josiah defiled it by making it the city dump, where fires were kept constantly burning to consume the refuse (II Kings 23:10). Jewish apocalyptic writers called it the entrance to hell, and it became a figure of hell itself. Jesus used the term in this sense (Matt. 5:22 ASV; 18:9; 23:15). See Hades, Hell.

GELILOTH (gē-lī'lŏth), a place on the border of Benjamin (Josh. 18:17).

GEMALLI (gē-măl'ĭ, camel rider), father of Ammiel, and one of the twelve spies (Num. 13:12).

GEMARIAH (gĕm'à-rī'à, accomplishment of the Lord). 1. Son of Shaphan the scribe and friend of Jeremiah (Jer. 36:10-25). 2. A son of Hilkiah, sent as ambassador to Nebuchadnezzar (Jer. 29:3).

GENEALOGY (jĕn'ē-ăl'ō-jē), a list of ancestors or descendants, or the study of lines of descent. The genealogies of the Bible show biological descent, the right of inheritance, succession to an office, or ethnic and geographical relationships. There are numerous genealogical lists in Genesis (5:1-32; 10:1-32; 11:10-32; 35:22-39; 36:1-43; 46:8-27) and in I Chronicles 1-9. Some family genealogies of the Restoration are given in Ezra (2:1-63; 8:1-20) and in Nehemiah (7:7-63). In the NT "genealogies" seems to refer to an excessive concern for pagan or Gnostic series of angelic beings (I Tim. 1:4; Titus 3:9).

GENEALOGY OF JESUS CHRIST. Two genealogies are given in the NT: in Matthew 1:1-17 and in Luke 3:23-28. Matthew traces the descent of Jesus from Abraham and David, and divides it into three sets of fourteen generations. He omits three generations after Joram, namely Ahaziah, Joash, and Amaziah (I Chron. 3:11,12). Contrary to Hebrew practice, he names five women: Tamar, Rahab, Ruth, Bathsheba, and Mary. The sense of "begat" in Hebrew genealogies is not exact: it indicated immediate or remote descent, an adoptive relation, or legal heirship. Luke's genealogy moves from Jesus to Adam, agreeing with I Chronicles 1:1-7,24-28 between Abraham and Adam. From David to Abraham he agrees with Matthew; from Jesus to David he differs from Matthew. Perhaps Matthew gives the line of legal heirship, while Luke gives the line of physical descent.

GENERATION (jen′ẽr-a′shŭn), in the OT the translation of two Hebrew words, (1) **toledhoth,** referring to lines of descent from an ancestor (Gen. 2:4; 5:1; 6:9; Ruth 4:18), and (2) **dor,** meaning a period of time (Deut. 32:7; Exod. 3:15; Ps. 102:24), or all the men living in a given period (Judg. 3:2), or a class of men having a certain quality (Ps. 14:5), or a company gathered together (Ps. 49:19).

In the NT **generation** translates four Greek words, all having reference to descent: (1) **genea,** for lines of descent from an ancestor (Matt. 1:17); or all the men living in a given period (Matt. 11:16); or a class of men having a certain quality (Matt. 12:39); or a period of time (Acts 13:36); (2) **genesis,** meaning genealogy (Matt. 2:17); (3) **gennema,** meaning brood or offspring (Matt. 3:7; 12:34; 23:33); or **genes,** clan, race, kind, nation (I Pet. 2:9).

GENESIS (jĕn′ĕ-sis), the first book of the Bible. The name is derived from a Greek word meaning "origin" or "beginning," which is the title of the book in the Greek Septuagint. It contains the beginnings of physical life (1-2), the growth of civilization to the Flood (3-8), and the descendants of Noah to Abraham (9-11:26). Genesis 11:27 through 50:26 traces the history of Abraham and Lot; Ishmael and Isaac; Jacob and Esau; and Joseph and his brethren in Egypt.

GENNESARET (gĕ-nĕs′á-rĕt). 1. "The land of Gennesaret" is a plain on the northwest shore of the Sea of Galilee (Matt. 14:34; Mark 6:53). 2. "The Lake of Gennesaret" is the same as the Sea of Galilee (Luke 5:1). See **Galilee, Lake of.**

GENTILES (jĕn′tĭlz, Heb. **goy,** or **goyim, nation, people**). Usually it means a non-Israelite people (Judg. 4:2; Isa. 11:10; 42:1; Mal. 1:11).

GENTILES, COURT OF THE, the outer part of the Temple, which the Gentiles might enter.

GENUBATH (gĕ-nū′băth, Heb. **genuvath, theft**), a son of Hadad the Edomite (I Kings 11:20).

GERA (gē′rá, **grain**), a name common to tribe of Benjamin. (1) A son of Benjamin (Gen. 46:21). (2) A grandson of Benjamin (I Chron. 8:3,5). (3) The father of Ehud (Judg. 3:15). (4) A son of Ehud (I Chron. 8:7). (5) Father of Shimei (II Sam. 16:5).

GERAH (See Weights and Measures).

GERAR (gē′rár, **circle, region**), a town in the Negev, located on an inland caravan route. Abraham and Isaac both lived there (Gen. 20:1,2; 26:1-33).

GERASA (gē-rá′sà), a city east of the Jordan midway between the Sea of Galilee and the Dead Sea, the modern Jerash. The city is not mentioned in the NT, but the adjective **Gerasene** is mentioned in Mark 5:1.

GERGESA (gûr-gē′sà), a place probably midway of the Sea of Galilee, where the bank is steep (Matt. 8:28 KJV, and RSV margin; Mark 5:1 RSV margin; Luke 8:26,37 ASV, RSV margins).

GERIZIM (gē-ri′zim), a mountain of Samaria, 2849 feet high, SW of Mt. Ebal. It was the site of the recital of the blessing of the Law (Deut. 27:11-26). There the Samaritans built a temple and established worship (John 4:20-21).

GERSHOM (gûr′shŏm, **to cast out,** or **stranger**). (1) The first son of Moses (Exod. 2:22). (2) The oldest son of Levi (I Chron. 6:16). (3) One of the "heads of houses" who returned with Ezra from Babylon (Ezra 8:2). (4) The father of the Levite who became priest to the Danites in Laish (Judg. 18:30).

GERSHON (gûr′shŏn), oldest of the three sons of Levi (Gen. 46:11). His descendants during the wilderness wanderings were responsible for the care and transportation of the Tabernacle (Num. 3:23-26).

GERZITES (gûr′zits), **GIZRITES** (gĭz′rĭts), or **GERIZZITES** (gē′rĭz′ĭts), a tribe named with the Geshurites and the Amalekites (I Sam. 27:8).

GESHAM (gē′shăm), a descendant of Caleb (I Chron. 2:47).

GESHEM (gē′shĕm), an Arabian who opposed the work of Nehemiah (Neh. 2:19; 6:1,2), identical with Gashmu (6:6).

GESHUR (gē′shûr, **bridge**). 1. A country in Syria on the western border of Bashan E of the Jordan (Deut. 3:14; II Sam. 3:3). 2. A district in southern Palestine near Philistine territory (Josh. 13:2; I Sam. 27:8).

GETHER (gē′thẽr), the third son of Aram (Gen. 10:23; I Chron. 1:17).

GETHSEMANE (gĕth-sĕm′á-nè, probably Aramaic for **oil-press**), a place on the Mt. of Olives in which was a garden where Jesus prayed (Matt. 26:36; Mark 14:32; John 18:1).

GEUEL (gē-ū′ĕl), a representative from the tribe of Gad sent to spy out Canaan (Num. 13:15).

GEZER (gē′zẽr, **portion**), a fortified town 18 miles NW of Jerusalem. Its king was defeated by Joshua (Josh. 12:12), and its inhabitants were reduced to slave labor (16:10). The city was later assigned to the Levites (21:21).

GHOR, THE, the upper level of the Jordan valley, about 150 feet above the river channel.

GHOST (gŏst), the human spirit as distinguished from the body. To "give up the ghost" means to breathe one's last, to die (Job 11:20; Gen. 25:8; 35:29; 49:33; Matt. 27:50; John 19:30). "Holy Ghost" in KJV is translated "Holy Spirit" in ASV, RSV. Unlike modern usage, it does not refer to an apparition.

GIAH (gī'à), an unknown place near Hebron (II Sam. 2:24).

GIANTS, men of exceptional height and strength, called nephilim (Gen. 6:4 ASV, RSV, Num. 13:33), and rephaim (Deut. 2:11,20, ASV, RSV). Representatives of the giants were Og, king of Bashan (Josh. 12:4; 13:12), and Goliath, whom David slew (I Sam. 17).

GIBBAR (gib'ár), a man whose children returned from captivity with Zerubbabel (Ezra 2:20).

GIBBETHON (gib'ē-thŏn), a city W of Gezer in the territory of Dan (Josh. 19:44), given to the Levites (21:23).

GIBEA, (gĭb'ē-à), a grandson of Caleb (I Chron. 2:49).

GIBEAH (gĭb'ē-à). 1. An unknown city in the hill-country of Judah (Josh. 15:57). 2. A city in Benjamin on the E side of the N-S road a few miles north of Jerusalem, where Saul's palace was located (Judg. 19:12; 20:10; I Sam. 13:2; 15:34; Isa. 10:29). First mentioned in the civil war with the Benjaminites (Judg. 19-20); capital of early United Kingdom (I Sam. 22:6). 3. A town in the hill country of Ephraim (Josh. 24:33 RSV). 5. A hill where the ark was kept until David took it to Jerusalem (II Sam. 6:3,4 KJV; cf. I Sam. 7:1).

GIBEONITES (gĭb'ē-ŏn-īts), the inhabitants of Gibeon; Hivites (Josh. 9:3,7), or Horites (Gen. 36:20; Deut. 2:12). Reduced to slavery by Joshua because they negotiated a treaty by deceit (Josh. 9).

GIBLITES (gĭb'līts), the inhabitants of Gebal or Byblos (Josh. 13:5). See Gebal.

GIDDALTI (gĭ-dăl'tī), a leader of music (I Chron. 25:4,29).

GIDDEL (gĭd'ĕl). 1. One of the Nethinim who returned from exile (Ezra 2:47; Neh. 7:49). 2. Sons of Giddel (Ezra 2:56; Neh. 7:58).

GIDEON (gĭd'ē-ŏn, feller or hewer), son of Joash, who lived in Ophrah near Mt. Gerizim (Judg. 6:1-9:6). Called by God to liberate Israel from the Midianites (6:17-23), he overturned the altar of Baal and cut down the sacred grove. He summoned the tribes to his aid. By a series of tests he reduced the force to 300 picked men (Judg. 7:1-8) with which he routed the Midianites and freed the entire land from their domination. He refused to be made king, but judged Israel for 40 years (8:22-28).

GIDEONI (gĭd'ē-ō'nī, cutter down), a prince of Benjamin (Num. 7:60), whose son ruled them (10:24).

GIDOM (gī'dŏm, desolation), an isolated place E of Bethel (Judg. 20:45).

GIER EAGLE (See Birds).

GIFT, GIVING. At least eleven words are used in the Bible to mean giving: eshkar, a reward (Ps. 72:10); minhah, an offering to a superior (Judg. 3:15); mattan, that given to gain a favor (Gen. 34:12), or as an act of submission (Ps. 68:29); mattena' and mattanah, an offering (Gen. 25:6; Dan. 2:6); shohadh, a bribe (Deut. 16:19); in the NT,

dosis and doron, anything given (Luke 21:1, James 1:17); doma, a present (Matt. 7:11); charis and charisma, special endowment (Rom. 1:11; I Tim. 4:14).

GIFTS, SPIRITUAL, or charismata, a theological term meaning any endowment that comes through the grace of God (Rom. 1:11). They are discussed by Paul in I Corinthians 12-14, and include the power to speak in an unlearned tongue (I Cor. 14:1-33), power to exorcise demons (Acts 13:7-12), ability to heal the sick (I Cor. 12:9), prophecy (Rom. 12:6), keenness of wisdom and knowledge (I Cor. 12:4-8). Each individual is responsible for the exercise of his own gift (I Pet. 4:10). Gifts are distributed by the Holy Spirit (Heb. 2:4).

GIHON (gī'hŏn, burst forth). 1. One of the four rivers in Eden (Gen. 2:8-14), supposed by some to be the Nile. The real identity is uncertain. 2. A spring located near Jerusalem (I Kings 1:32-40).

GILALAI (gĭl'à-lī), a musician who assisted in the dedication of the wall of Jerusalem (Neh. 12:36).

GILBOA (gil-bō'à, bubbling). A range of hills on the E side of Esdraelon, named for a never failing spring. In a battle on Mt. Gilboa Saul was defeated, and committed suicide (I Chron. 10:1-8).

GILEAD (gil'ē-ăd, rugged), the land owned by Israel E of the Jordan river, extending from the S end of the Sea of Galilee to the N end of the Dead Sea and E to the desert. In Moses' time it was thickly forested, and contained good grazing lands. Jacob camped at Gilead (Gen. 31:21,23). In the conquest of Canaan Gilead was allotted to Reuben, Gad, and the half-tribe of Manasseh (Deut. 3:13). Gilead was famous for its balm (Jer. 8:22; 46:11; 51:8), which was exported to Egypt (Gen. 37:25) and to Tyre (Ezek. 27:17). The Gileadites in later years fell into gross idolatry (Hos. 6:8; 12:11); were conquered by Syria (II Kings 10:32-34); and were led into captivity by Tiglath-pileser (II Kings 15:27-29).

GILGAL (gil'găl, circle of stones), the first camp of Israel after crossing the Jordan (Josh. 4:19,20). It became one of the border cities of Judah (15:7), and was visited by Samuel when he judged Israel (I Sam. 7:16). Here Saul was confirmed king (I Sam. 11:15) and later lost his kingdom (13:8-15).

The Gilgal of Elijah and Elisha (II Kings 2:1; 4:38) may be another town nearer Bethel.

GILOH (gī'lō), home of Ahithophel, one of David's counsellors (II Sam. 15:12; Josh. 15:51).

GIMZO (gĭm'zō, place of lush sycamores), a town off the Jerusalem Highway, 3 miles SW of Lydda (II Chron. 28:18).

GIN, a trap to catch game (Amos 3:5), or a plot to deceive and destroy (Ps. 140:5; 141:9; Job 18:9; Isa. 8:14).

GINATH (gī'năth, protector), the father of Tibni (I Kings 16:21).

GINNETHO (See Ginnethon).

GINNETHON (gĭn'ē-thŏn), a priest who returned to Jerusalem with Zerubbabel (Neh. 10:6; 12:4).

GIRDLE (See Dress).

GIRGASHITES (gûr'gà-shītes), a Hamitic tribe of Canaan conquered by Joshua (Gen. 10:15,16; Deut. 7:1).

GISPA (gĭs'pà, listener), an overseer of the Nethinim (Neh. 11:21).

GITTAH-HEPHER (See Gath-hepher).

GITTAIM (gĭt'ā-ĭm, two wine presses), a town of Benjamin to which the Beerothites fled (Neh. 11:31,33; II Sam. 4:3). The site is unknown.

GITTITES (gĭt'īts, of Gath), natives of Gath (Josh. 13:1-3; II Sam. 6:8-11; 15:18; 21:19).

GITTITH (gĭt'ĭth), a word found in the titles of Psalms 8, 81, 84. It may denote a musical instrument imported from Gath, or may be the title of a tune.

GIZONITE (gī'zō-nĭt), the title of one of David's bodyguard (I Chron. 11:34).

GLASS was manufactured as early as 2500 B. C. by the Egyptians, and later by the Phoenicians, who promoted its commercial use, especially in jewelry. The Hebrews seem to have been unacquainted with it, for it is mentioned only once in the OT (Job 28:17). The glass mentioned by Paul (II Cor. 3:18) and by James (Jas. 1:23, 24) was properly not glass at all, but the mirror of polished bronze. The allusions in Revelation 21:18,21 refer to crystal glass.

GLEAN, the Hebrew custom of allowing the poor to follow the reapers, and to gather the grain or grapes that remained after the harvest (Judg. 8:2; Ruth 2:2,16; Isa. 17:6).

GLEDE (See Birds).

GLORY, concerning God, the exhibition of His divine attributes and perfections (Ps. 19:1) or the radiance of His presence (Luke 2:9); concerning man, the manifestation of his commendable qualities, such as wisdom, righteousness, self-control, ability, etc. Glory is the destiny of believers (Phil. 3:21; Rom. 8:21; I Cor. 15:43).

GNASH, to grind the teeth together as an expression of rage (Job 16:9), hatred (Ps. 37:12); frustration (Ps. 112:10). In the NT it expresses anguish and failure rather than anger (Matt. 8:12; 13:42,50; 25:30).

GNAT (See Insects).

GOAD, a long wooden pole fitted with a sharp point for prodding oxen (Judg. 3:31; Acts 26:14 ASV, RSV).

GOAT (See Animals).

GOATH (gō'ăth), an unknown place west of Jerusalem (Jer. 31:39).

GOB (gŏb, pit, cistern), the site of two of David's battles with the Philistines (II Sam. 21:18).

GOD. The Bible contains no definition of God, but contains many allusions to His being and attributes. God is Spirit, or discarnate person (John 4:24), infinite in power (Dan. 4:35), complete in wisdom, absolutely truthful (Heb. 6:18), perfectly holy (Lev.

11:44). He has revealed Himself through nature (Rom. 1:20) and through His Son (Heb. 1:1,2). There is only one true God (Deut. 6:4). Other gods are mentioned in the Bible as false (Judg. 6:31; I Kings 18:27; I Cor. 8:4-6), or as demonic (I Cor. 10:19-22).

GODLINESS, the piety toward God and the rectitude of conduct which spring from a proper relationship with Him (II Tim. 3:5).

GOLAN (gō'lăn), a city in the half tribe of Manasseh in Bashan, appointed to be a city of refuge and assigned to the Levites (Deut. 4:43).

GOLD (See Minerals).

GOLDSMITH (See Occupations and Professions).

GOLGOTHA (gŏl'gō-thà, skull), the place of the crucifixion of Christ, located outside of Jerusalem (Matt. 27:33; Mark 15:22) on the public road (John 19:20).

GOLIATH (gō-lī'ăth, exile), one of the last of the giants, more than nine feet tall (I Sam. 17). Another by the same name was killed by Elhanan (II Sam. 21:19).

GOMORRAH (gō-mô'rà, submersion), one of the five "cities of the plain" located at the S end of the Dead Sea, and now submerged under its waters. They were destroyed by an explosion of gases that overwhelmed them under a rain of hot salt and sulphur, after which they sank into the sea because of the subsidence of the land (Gen. 19:24-28).

GOPHER WOOD (gō'fer wŏŏd), the wood from which Noah's ark was made (Gen. 6:14), most probably cypress.

GOSHEN (gō'shĕn, mound of earth). 1. The NE section of the Nile delta, where the Israelites under Jacob settled while Joseph was prime minister (Gen. 46). 2. A district of S Palestine between Gaza and Gibeon (Josh. 10:41). 3. A town in the SW part of the mountains of Judah (Josh. 15:51).

GOSPEL. The English word gospel is derived from the Anglo-Saxon word godspell, which meant "good news." As now used, it means the message of Christianity and the books in which the story of Christ's life and teaching is found (Rom. 1:15,16). In the NT the word is never applied to a book but to the message (Rom. 1:1; I Thess. 2:2,9; Acts 20:24; Eph. 6:15).

GOSPELS, THE FOUR. Because they contain the basic facts of Jesus' life, the writings of Matthew, Mark, Luke, and John are called the Gospels. The first three are called "Synoptic" because they "see the whole together," and present similar views of the life and teaching of Christ. Matthew presents Christ as the Messiah; Mark emphasizes His activity and the popular reaction to Him; Luke stresses His humanitarian interests; and John's Gospel is a collection of selected memoirs, carefully organized to induce belief (John 20:30,31).

GOURD (See Plants).

GOVERNOR (gŭv'ẽr-nôr), a word applied to

Governor, an official who rules a land on behalf of a king or emperor to whom he is subordinate. The term is applied to Joseph (Gen. 42:6), Gedaliah (Jer. 40:5), and in the NT to the Roman procurators of Judea, Pilate, Felix, Festus (Matt. 27:2; Acts 23:24; 26:30).

GOZAN (gō'zăn), a city located in NE Mesopotamia on the Habor River, to which the Israelites were deported by the Assyrians (II Kings 17:6; 18:11; 19:12; I Chron. 5:26).

GRACE, a term employed by the Biblical writers with a wide variety of meaning: charm, sweetness, loveliness (Ps. 45:2); the attitude of God toward men (Titus 2:11); the method of salvation (Eph. 2:5) the opposite of legalism (Gal. 5:4); the impartation of spiritual power or gifts (I Cor. 12:6; II Tim. 2:1); the liberty which God gives to men (Jude 4).

GRAFF, GRAFT, a horticultural process by which the branches of a cultivated tree may be inserted into the trunk of a wild tree (Rom. 11:17ff.).

GRAIN (See Plants).

GRANARY (grăn'ĕrĕ), a storehouse for grain and other dry crops (Matt. 3:12; Luke 3:17). See Garner.

GRAPE (See Plants).

GRASS. A general term for many kinds of green plants (Gen. 1:11,12; Matt. 6:30), including weeds.

GRASSHOPPER (See Insects).

GRATE, a copper network, placed under the top of the great altar, to hold the sacrifice while burning (Exod. 27:4; 35:16; 38:4,5).

GRAVE, a place of interment for the dead. Sometimes graves were mere holes in the earth (Gen. 35:8; I Sam. 31:13); sometimes, natural caves (Gen. 23:1-9); sometimes artificial chambers hollowed out of rock (Matt. 27:60). Graves were often marked by flat whitewashed stones (Matt. 23:27).

GRAVE CLOTHES. Preparatory to burial, the body was washed and anointed with spices, then wrapped in a winding sheet, bound with grave-bands, and the head wrapped in a square cloth (John 11:44; 19:40).

GRAVEN IMAGE, a carved image of wood, stone, or metal, generally used as an idol (Isa. 44:9-17; 45:20; Deut. 7:5).

GREAT OWL (See Birds).

GREAVES (See Arms, Armor).

GREECE (GRECIA), the peninsula and archipelago of islands between the Adriatic and Aegean Seas, called in Genesis 10:2 Javan in the early catalog of nations, and Achaia in the NT (Acts 18:12; 19:21; Rom. 15:26; II Cor. 1:1).

GREEK LANGUAGE was a branch of the Indo-European family from which most of the languages of Europe are descended. The Attic dialect spoken in Athens and its colonies on the Ionian coast was combined with other dialects in the army of Alexander the Great, and was spread by his conquests through the East. Greek was widely spoken in Palestine, and became the chief language of the early church (Acts 21:37).

GREEK VERSIONS. There are four translations of the Hebrew OT into Greek: (1) the Septuagint, originating in Alexandria about 275 B. C.; (2) the version of Aquila (c. A. D. 125), produced by the Jews when Christians took over the Septuagint; (3) the version of Theodotion, a second century revision of the Septuagint; and (4) the version of Symmachus, an idiomatic translation, probably of the second century.

GREYHOUND (See Animals).

GRIND, to pulverize grain between two millstones (Matt. 24:41; Luke 17:35).

GROVE, a mistranslation of the Hebrew asherah, emblem of the goddess of fertility, symbolized by the trunk of a tree. The reforming kings of Judah destroyed these idolatrous emblems (I Kings 15:13; II Kings 17:10; 21:3; 23:4).

GUARD, the translation of a number of Hebrew and Greek words: (1) tabbah, slaughterer (Gen. 37:36; II Kings 25:8; Dan. 2:14); (2) ruts, runner, trusted messengers of a king (I Kings 14:27,28); (3) mishmar, watch (Neh. 4:22); (4) mishma'ath, guard (II Sam. 23:23); (5) spekoulator, "executioner," a guard, a spy (Mark 6:27); (6) koustodia, watch (Matt. 27:65).

GUDGODAH (gŭd-gō'dà, cleft), a place in the wilderness journeys of Israel (Deut. 10:7), location unknown.

GUEST CHAMBER, a room in which to eat (I Sam. 9:22; Mark 14:14; Luke 22:11).

GUILT, the deserving of punishment because of infraction of a law. Guilt could be the result of unconscious sin (Lev. 5:17), or could be incurred by the group for the sin of an individual (Josh. 7:10-15). There are degrees of guilt (Luke 12:47,48; Acts 17:30), but in the sight of God all men are guilty of sin (Rom. 3:19).

GUNI (gū'nī), the name of a family of Naphtali (Gen. 46:24; Num. 26:48; I Chron. 7:13). 2. The head of a Gadite family (I Chron. 5:15).

GUNITE (gū'nīt), the family of Guni (Num. 26:48).

GUR (gŭr), the place of Amaziah's death, NE of Samaria (II Kings 9:27).

GUR-BAAL (gŭr bā'ăl, sojourn of Baal), a town probably located S of Beersheba (II Chron. 26:7).

GUTTER, the channel or tunnel through which David's soldiers obtained access to the Jebusite fortress of Jerusalem (II Sam. 5:8).

H

HAAHASHTARI, HAASHTARI (hă'à-hăsh'tà-rī, hă-ăsh'tà-rī, the Ahashtarite), son of Naarah (I Chron. 4:6).

HABAIAH (hà-bā'yà, Jehovah has hidden),

priest whose descendants were excluded from priesthood (Ezra 2:61).

HABAKKUK (hà-băk'ŭk, embrace), prophet of the book which bears his name; wrote when the temple was still standing (2:20; 3:19), between c. 605-587 B. C., probably during the reign of the Judean king Jehoiakim. Outline. 1. Perplexity of the prophet as to why the sinful Jews are not punished, and why God should use a heathen nation to punish the Jews (1). 2. God's answer that the proud Chaldeans will themselves be punished (3). 3. Prayer of Habakkuk (3).

HABAZINIAH (hăb-à-zī-nī'à), ancestor of the Rechabites in Jeremiah's time (Jer. 35:3).

HABERGEON (hăb'ẽr-jŭn, coat of mail (II Chron. 26:14; Neh. 4:16).

HABIRU (hà-bī'rū), a people mentioned in Mari, Nuzi, and Amarna tablets; fundamental meaning seems to be "wanderers," of mixed racial origin, including both Semites and non-Semites. Connection with Hebrews is obscure.

HABOR (hā'bòr), tributary of Euphrates to which Shalmanezer banished the northern tribes of Israel (II Kings 17:6; 18:11).

HACHALIAH (hăk'à-lī'à), father of Nehemiah (Neh. 1:1; 10:1).

HACHILAH (hà-kī'là), hill near Ziph and Maon where David hid from Saul (I Sam. 23:19; 26:1,3).

HACHMONI (hăk'mō-ni), father of Jehiel and Jashobeam (I Chron. 27:32; 11:11).

HADAD (hā'dăd, fierceness). 1. Grandson of Abraham (Gen. 25:15; KJV has Hadar). 2. Early king of Edom (I Chron. 1:50). 3. Earlier king of Edom (Gen. 36:35; I Chron. 1:46). 4. Edomite prince (I Kings 11:14-25). 5. Supreme god of Syria, – deity of storm and thunder.

HADADEZER, HADAREZER (hăd-ăd-ē'zẽr, hăd-ăr-ē'zẽr, Hadad is a help), king of Zobah defeated in battle by David (II Sam. 8:3ff; 10:15-19).

HADAD-RIMMON (hā-dăd-rĭm'ŏn, Hadad and Rimmon, two Syrian divinities), a place of mourning in valley of Megiddo (Zech. 12:10).

HADAR (hā'dàr). 1. Son of Ishmael (Gen. 25:15). 2. King of Edom (Gen. 36:39). See Hadad.

HADASHAH (hà-dăsh'à), town of Judah (Josh. 15:37).

HADASSAH (hà-dăs'à), Esther (Esth. 2:7,15).

HADATTAH (hà-dăt'à), town in S of Judah; or a description of Hazor (Josh. 15:25).

HADES (hā'dēz, not to be seen), the place or state of the dead, the equivalent of the Hebrew Sheol, which is variously rendered "grave," "hell," "pit." (See Sheol). The NT word, generally translated "hell," does not necessarily imply a place of torment, but connotes the grim and cheerless aspect of death (Acts 2:27; Rev. 1:18; 6:8; 20:13,14). It may include the idea of retribution (Luke 16:23).

HADID (hā'dĭd), village in Benjamin c. 3 miles E of Lydda (Ezra 2:33; Neh. 7:37;

11:34).

HADLAI (hăd'lī), father of Amasa (II Chron. 28:12).

HADORAM (hà-dō'răm). 1. Son of Joktan (Gen. 10:27; I Chron. 1:21). 2. Son of king of Hamath (I Chron. 18:9-11). 3. Rehoboam's superintendent of men under taskwork (II Chron. 10:18).

HADRACH (hā'drăk), Syrian country (Zech. 9:1).

HAGAB (hā'găb), ancestor of Nethinim who returned with Zerubbabel (Ezra 2:46).

HAGAR (hā'gàr, flight), Egyptian handmaid of Sarah who bore Abraham a son as proxy for Sarah (Gen. 16:1-16); driven out by Sarah and Abraham (Gen. 21:1-21); her story an allegory of the difference between law and grace (Gal. 4:21-5:1).

HAGARENES, HAGARITES (hā'gàr-ēnz, hā'gàr-īts), descendants of Ishmael with whom Saul made war (I Chron. 5:10,18-22; 27:31).

HAGGAI (hăg'à-ī, festal), prophet to the Jews in 520 B. C.; little known of his personal history; contemporary with Zechariah and Darius Hystaspes. Outline. 1. Call and encouragement to build (1). 2. The Messianic hope (2).

HAGGERI (hăg'ē-ri), father of Mibhar (I Chron. 11:38).

HAGGI (hăg'ī), son of Gad (Gen. 46:16; Num. 26:15).

HAGGIAH (hà-gī'à), Levite (I Chron. 6:30).

HAGGITH (hăg'ĭth), wife of David (II Sam. 3:4) and mother of Adonijah (I Kings 1:5-31).

HAGIOGRAPHA (hăg-ĭ-ŏg'rà-fà, holy writings), 3rd division of Heb. OT: Psalms, Proverbs, Job, Song of Solomon, Ruth, Lamentations, Ecclesiastes, Esther, Daniel, Ezra-Nehemiah, I and II Chronicles.

HAI (hā'ī). 1. Town E of Bethel and near Beth-aven (Gen. 12:8; 13:3; Josh. 7,8). Spelled Ai in KJV. 2. City of the Ammonites (Jer. 49:3).

HAIL. 1. Hail storms in the Near East often do considerable damage to crops (Exod. 9:23,24; Josh. 10:11). Used figuratively for divine retribution. 2. A greeting (Matt. 26:49).

HAIR, regarded by Jews as a mark of beauty and sometimes of pride; baldness was despised (II Kings 2:23; Isa. 3:24; Jer. 47:5). Nazarites and women wore hair long (Num. 6:5; Luke 7:38). Israelites could not cut the corners of their beards (Lev. 19:27).

HAKKATAN (hăk'à-tăn), father of Johanan who returned with Ezra (Ezra 8:12).

HAKKOZ (hăk'ŏz). KJV sometimes has Koz, once Coz. 1. Descendant of Aaron (I Chron. 24:10; Ezra 2:61; Neh. 3:4,21). 2. Judahite (I Chron. 4:8).

HAKUPHA (hà-kū'fà), ancestor of Nethinim (Ezra 2:51; Neh. 7:53).

HALAH (hā'là), district in Media to which Israelites were taken captive (II Kings 17:6; 18:11; I Chron. 5:26).

HALAK (hā'lăk), mountain marking S limit of Joshua's conquests (Josh. 11:17; 12:7).

HALHUL (hăl'hŭl), town near Hebron in

Judah (Josh. 15:58).

HALI (hā'lī), town of Asher (Josh. 19:25).

HALL. 1. Court of the high priest's palace (Luke 22:55). 2. Official residence of a Roman governor (Matt. 27:27; Mark 15:16).

HALLEL (hă-lăl', praise). Psalms 113-118 called the "Egyptian Hallel;" Ps. 136, "the Hallel." Psalms 120-136 often called the "Great Hallel."

HALLELUJAH (hăl'ĕ-lōō'yȧ, praise ye Jehovah), liturgical ejaculation urging all to praise Jehovah. Occurs at the beginning of Psalms 106, 111-113, 117, 135, 146-150 and at the close of 104-106, 113, 115-117, 135, 146-150.

HALLOHESH (hă-lō'hĕsh), father of Shallum (Neh. 3:12); covenanter (Neh. 10:24), perhaps the same man.

HALLOW (hăl'ō, to render or treat as holy), to set apart for sacred use; to hold sacred; to reverence as holy (Exod. 20:11; Matt. 6:9).

HAM (hăm). 1. Son of Egypt; provoked father by immodest act (Gen. 9:21-27). 2. City E of Jordan (Gen. 14:5). 3. Descendants of Ham (Ps. 78:51; 105:23; 106:22). In these passages "Ham" is used as another name for Egypt.

HAMAN (hā'măn), prime minister of Ahasuerus, king of Persia (Esther 3:1,10;7:7-10).

HAMATH (hā'măth, fortification), a very old city on the Orontes in Syria (Gen. 10:18; Num. 13:21; I Kings 8:65); now called Hama.

HAMATH-ZOBAH (hā'măth-zō'bȧ), a place mentioned in II Chron. 8:3.

HAMMATH (hăm'ăth, hot spring). 1. Fortified city of Naphtali, c. 1 mile S of Tiberias (Josh. 19:35). 2. Founder of Rechabites (RSV I Chron. 2:55).

HAMMEDATHA (hăm-ē-dā'thȧ), father of Haman the Agagite (Esth. 3:1).

HAMMELECH (hăm'ē-lĕk), a proper name in the KJV, but should be "the king" as in RSV.

HAMMER, a tool used for a variety of purposes: smoothing metals (Isa. 41:7), driving tent pins (Judg. 4:21), forging (Isa. 44:12), etc. Sometimes used figuratively for any crushing power (Jer. 23:29; 50:23).

HAMMOLEKETH (hă-mŏl'ē-kĕth), sister of Gilead (I Chron. 7:18).

HAMMON (hăm'ŏn). 1. Place c. 10 miles S of Tyre (Josh. 19:28). 2. City of Naphtali (I Chron. 6:76).

HAMMOTH-DOR (hăm'ŏth-dôr), city of Naphtali (Josh. 21:32).

HAMMURABI (hăm-ŏŏ-rä'bē), king of Babylon (1728-1686 B. C.); not the same as Amraphel of Gen. 14:1-12; great builder and lawgiver (Code of Hammurabi).

HAMONAH (hă-mō'nä), prophetic name of city near which Gog is defeated (Ezek. 39:16).

HAMON-GOG, VALLEY OF (hā'mŏn-gŏg, multitude of God), prophetic name for place E of Dead Sea where "multitude of Gog" will be buried (Ezek. 39:11-15).

HAMOR (hā'môr, ass), father of Shechem (Gen. 34:2ff).

HAMUEL (hăm'ū-ĕl), Simeonite (I Chron. 4:26).

HAMUL (hā'mŭl), son of Perez; ancestor of Hamulites (Gen. 46:12).

HAMUTAL (hă-mū'tăl), wife of Josiah; mother of Jehoahaz and Zedekiah (II Kings 23:31; 24:18).

HANAMEEL (hăn'ȧ-mĕl), cousin of Jeremiah the prophet (Jer. 32:7-12).

HANAN (hā'năn, gracious). 1. Benjamite (I Chron. 8:23). 2. Son of Azel (I Chron. 9:44). 3. Son of Maachah (I Chron. 11:43). 4. Temple servant who returned with Zerubbabel (Ezra 2:46; Neh. 7:49). 5. Interpreter of the Law (Neh. 8:7). 6. Covenanters with Nehemiah (Neh. 10:10,22,26). 7. Influential Jerusalem Jew (Jer. 35:4).

HANANEEL (hă-năn'ē-ĕl, God is gracious), tower in Jerusalem wall (Jer. 31:38; Zech. 14:10).

HANANI (hȧ-nā'nī, gracious). 1. Son of Heman (I Chron. 25:4,25). 2. Seer who rebuked Asa (II Chron. 16:7-10). 3. Priest who married a foreigner (Ezra 10:20). 4. Brother of Nehemiah (Neh. 1:2; 7:2). 5. Musical priest (Neh. 12:36).

HANANIAH (hăn-ȧ-nī'ȧ, Jehovah is gracious). 1. Son of Heman (I Chron. 25: 4,23). 2. Captain of Uzziah's army (II Chron. 26:11). 3. Father of Zedekiah (Jer. 36:12). 4. Benjamite (I Chron. 8:24). 5. Grandfather of Irijah (Jer. 37:13). 6. Hebrew name of Shadrach (Dan. 1:6,7). 7. Son of Zerubbabel (I Chron. 3:19,21). 8. Man who married a foreign woman (Ezra 10:28). 9. Perfumer (Neh. 3:8). 10. Wall repairer (Neh. 3:30). 11. Governor of castle (Neh. 7:2). 12. Perhaps same as 11 (Neh. 10:23). 13. Head of priestly house (Neh. 12:12,41). 14. False prophet in days of Zedekiah (Jer. 28:10ff).

HAND, often used figuratively for power (Gen. 9:2,5), liberality (Deut. 15:8), ordination (I Tim. 4:14), and many other things.

HANDBREADTH (See Weights and Measures).

HANDICRAFT, trade requiring manual skill.

HANDKERCHIEF, sometimes translated "napkin," used for a variety of purposes (Luke 19:20-23; John 11:44; 20:7; Acts 19:12).

HANDLE, door knob (S. of Sol. 5:5).

HANDMAID or HANDMAIDEN, female slave or servant.

HANDS, IMPOSITION OF, a ceremony having the idea of transference, identification, and devotion to God (Exod. 29:10,15,19; Lev. 16:21; Acts 8:14-17; II Tim. 1:6).

HANDSTAFF, rod carried in hand (Ezek. 39:9).

HANES (hā'nĕz), place in Egypt (Isa. 30:4).

HANGING, not a form of capital punishment in Bible times. Where used, except in II Sam. 17:23; Matt. 27:5, it refers to the suspension of a body from a tree or post after the criminal had been put to death (Gen. 40:19,22; Deut. 21:22).

HANGINGS, material hung in the tabernacle so as to preserve the privacy and sacredness of that which was within (Exod.

27:9-19; Matt. 27:51).

HANIEL (hăn'ĭ-ĕl). An Asherite (I Chron. 7:39).

HANNAH (hăn'ȧ, grace), mother of Samuel (I Sam. 1;2).

HANNATHON (hăn'nȧ-thŏn), city in N Zebulon (Josh. 19:14).

HANNIEL (hăn'ĭ-ĕl). 1. Prince of Manasseh (Num. 34:23).

HANOCH (hăn'nŏk). 1. Grandson of Abraham by Keturah (Gen. 25:4; I Chron. 1:33). 2. Son of Reuben (Gen. 46:9; Exod. 6:14; I Chron. 5:3).

HANUN (hā'nŭn, favored). 1. King of Ammon who provoked David to war (II Sam. 10:1-5; I Chron. 19:1-5). 2. Two men who helped repair wall of Jerusalem (Neh. 3:13,30).

HAPHRAIM (hăph-rā'ĭm), city of Issachar, near Shunem (Josh. 19:19).

HARA (hā'rȧ), place in Assyria to which Israelites were exiled by Assyrians (I Chron. 5:26).

HARADAH (hăr-ā'dȧ), encampment of Israelites in wilderness (Num. 33:24).

HARAN (hā'răn). 1. Brother of Abraham (Gen. 11:27,28). 2. Son of Caleb (I Chron. 2:46). 3. Gershonite Levite (I Chron. 23:9).

HARAN or CHARRAN (hā'răn, chär'răn), city in N Mesopotamia, on Balikh river, a branch of the Euphrates. Abraham lived there before going to Canaan (Gen. 11:31), and he sent his servant there to find a wife for Isaac (Gen. 24:4). Also mentioned in II Kings 19:12; Isa. 37:12; Ezek. 27:23.

HARARITE (hā'rȧ-rīt, mountain dweller), area in hill country of either Judah or Ephraim (II Sam. 23:11,33; I Chron. 11:34).

HARBONA, HARBONAH (hăr-bō'nȧ, hărbō'nȧ), chamberlain of Ahasuerus (Esth. 1:10; 7:9).

HARE (See Animals).

HAREPH (hā'rĕf), son of Caleb (I Chron. 2:51).

HARETH, HERETH (hā'rĕth), forest in Judah where David stayed (I Sam. 22:5).

HARHAIAH (hăr-hā'yȧ), father of Uzziel, a goldsmith (Neh. 3:8).

HARHAS (hăr'hăs), grandfather of Shallum (II Kings 22:14). In II Chron. 34:22 "Hasrah."

HARHUR (hăr'hŭr), head of family that returned with Zerubbabel (Ezra 2:51; Neh. 7:53).

HARIM (hā'rĭm). 1. Priest (I Chron. 24:8). 2. Family that returned with Zerubbabel (Ezra 2:39; Neh. 7:35). 3. Family of priests (Ezra 2:39; 10:21; Neh. 7:42; 12:15). 4. Family that married foreign wives (Ezra 10:31). 5. Father of worker on the wall (Neh. 3:11). 6. Man who sealed covenant (Neh. 10:27).

HARIPH (hā'rĭf), family which returned with Zerubbabel (Neh. 7:24). This man with this name sealed covenant with God (Neh. 10:19).

HARLOT, both common and religious harlotry very prevalent in ancient times; both kinds were forbidden to the Israelites (Lev. 19:29; 21:7,9,14; Deut. 23:18). Paul warned against fornication with harlots (I Cor. 6:15,16).

HARNEPHER (hăr'nē-fēr), Asherite (I Chron. 7:36).

HAROD (hā'rŏd, trembling), spring beside which Gideon encamped (Judg. 7:1).

HARODITE (hā'rŏd-ĭt), patronymic of Shammah and Elika (II Sam. 23:25).

HAROEH (hā-rō'ĕ), grandson of Caleb (I Chron. 2:52).

HAROSHETH OF THE GENTILES (hā-rō'shĕth), town in N Palestine c. 16 miles NW of Megiddo; home of Sisera (Judg. 4:2,13,16).

HARP (See Music).

HARROW (hā'rō), instrument for dragging or leveling off a field (Job 39:10; "breaking clods," Isa. 28:24; Hosea 10:11).

HARROWS, instrument of iron to cut conquered peoples (II Sam. 12:31; I Chron. 20:3).

HARSHA (hăr'shȧ), head of a family of Nethinim which returned with Zerubbabel (Ezra 2:52; Neh. 7:54).

HART (See Animals).

HARUM (hā'rŭm), father of Aharhel (I Chron. 4:8).

HARUMAPH (hȧ-rōō'măf), father of Jedaiah (Neh. 3:10).

HARUPHITE (hȧ-rōō'fīt), designation of Shephatiah (I Chron. 12:5).

HARUZ (hā'rŭz), father-in-law of Manasseh, king of Judah (II Kings 21:19).

HARVEST. Economy of Israelites was strictly agricultural; therefore harvest time was a very significant event for them. Laws governed harvest operations (Lev. 23:10,14,22; 25:5). In NT the term is used for the gathering in of the redeemed (Matt. 13:39).

HASADIAH (hăs'ȧ-dī'ȧ), son of Zerubbabel (I Chron. 3:20).

HASENUAH (hăs-ē-nū'ȧ). 1. Benjamite (I Chron. 9:7). 2. Father of assistant overseer of Jerusalem (Neh. 11:9).

HASHABIAH (hăsh-ȧ-bī'ȧ, whom Jehovah esteems). 1. Ancestor of Ethan (I Chron. 6:45). 2. Ancestor of Shemaiah (I Chron. 9:14; Neh. 11:15). 3. Son of Jeduthun (I Chron. 25:3). 4. Civil official in David's time (I Chron. 26:30). 5. Overseer of tribe of Levi (I Chron. 27:17). 6. Chief of Levites (II Chron. 35:9). 7. Levite teacher (Ezra 8:19). 8. Chief priest (Ezra 8:24). 9. Worker on the wall (Neh. 3:17). 10. Priest (Neh. 12:21). 11. Ancestor of Uzzi (Neh. 11:22). 12. Chief of Levites (Neh. 3:17; 12:24).

HASHABNAH (hȧ-shăb'nȧh), man who sealed covenant with Nehemiah (Neh. 10:25).

HASHABNIAH (hăsh-ăb-nī'ȧ). 1. Father of Hattush (Neh. 3:10). 2. Levite (Neh. 9:5).

HASHBADANA (hăsh-băd'ȧ-nȧ), man who stood by Ezra as he read the law (Neh. 8:4).

HASHEM (hā'shĕm), father of some of David's mighty men (I Chron. 11:34).

HASHMANNIM (hăsh'măn-nĭm, translated "heaven of heavens," meaning unknown (Ps. 68:33).

HASHMONAH (hăsh-mō'nȧ), encampment of Israelites in wilderness (Num. 33:29,30).

HASHUB (See Hasshub).

HASHUBAH (hà-shōō'bà), son of Zerubbabel (I Chron. 3:20).

HASHUM (hā'shŭm). 1. Family which returned from exile (Ezra 2:19; 10:33; Neh. 7:22). 2. Priest who stood at side of Ezra when he read law (Neh. 8:4). 3. Chief of people who sealed the covenant (Neh. 10:18). May be same as 2.

HASHUPHA (hà-shōō'fà), family which returned from exile with Zerubbabel (Ezra 2:43; Neh. 7:46).

HASMONAEANS (See Maccabees).

HASRAH (hăs'rà), grandfather of Shallum (II Chron. 34:22); "Harhas" in II Kings 22:14.

HASSENAAH (hăs-ē-nā'à), father of sons who built fish gate in Jerusalem (Neh. 3:3).

HASSHUB (hāsh'ŭb, **considerate**). 1. Father of Levite who returned from exile (I Chron. 9:14). 2. Worker on wall of Jerusalem (Neh. 3:11). 3. Another worker on the wall (Neh. 3:23). KJV "Hashub." 4. One who sealed covenant (Neh. 10:23). KJV has Hashub. May be same as 2 or 3.

HASUPHA (See Hashupha).

HAT (See Dress).

HATACH (hā'tăk), chamberlain (Esth. 4:5-10).

HATHATH (hā'thăth), son of Othniel (I Chron. 4:13).

HATIPHA (hà-tī'fà), head of family of Nethinim (Ezra 2:54; Neh. 7:56).

HATITA (hà-tī'tà), ancestor of family of porters which returned from exile (Ezra 2:42; Neh. 7:45).

HATSI HAM MENUCHOTH (hà-tsī-hăm-mĕn-ū'kŏth), marginal reading on I Chron. 2:54 in KJV which is eliminated in ASV.

HATTIL (hăt'il), family which returned from exile (Ezra 2:57; Neh. 7:59).

HATTIN, HORNS OF (hăt'tĕn, **hollows**), hill near village of Hattin on which, tradition says, Christ delivered the Sermon on the Mount.

HATTUSH (hăt'ŭsh). 1. Descendant of Zerubbabel (I Chron. 3:22). 2. Man who returned from Babylon (Ezra 8:2). 3. Worker on the wall (Neh. 3:10). May be same as 2. 4. Man who sealed covenant (Neh. 10:4). May be same as 2 or 3. 5. Priest who returned with Zerubbabel (Neh. 12:2).

HAURAN (hà'ō-ràn), plateau E of Jordan and N of Gilead (Ezek. 47:16,18). Called Bashan in ancient times; in time of Romans, Auranitis.

HAVILAH (hăv'ĭ-là, **sand land**). 1. Son of Cush (I Chron. 1:9). 2. Son of Joktan (Gen. 10:29; I Chron. 1:23). 3. Land encompassed by Pishon river (Gen. 2:11,12). 4. One of the boundaries of the Ishmaelites (I Sam. 15:7).

HAVOTH-JAIR (hă-vŏth-jā'ĭr), group of villages which Jair, son of Manasseh, took (Num. 32:41).

HAWK (See Birds).

HAZAEL (hăz'à-ĕl, **God sees**), king of Syria (841-798 B. C.); killed and succeeded Benhadad (II Kings 8:7-15); oppressed Israel (II Kings 13:22); besieged Jerusalem (II Kings 12:17,18).

HAZAIAH (hà-zā'yà), Judahite (Neh. 11:5).

HAZAR (hā'zàr), often prefixed to descriptive place names; also used for encampments of nomads.

HAZAR-ADDAR (hā'zàr-ăd'ár), place on S boundary of Judah (Num. 34:4. In Josh. 15:3 "Addar").

HAZAR-ENAN (hā'zàr-ē'nàn), place on NE corner of Canaan (Num. 34:9,10).

HAZAR-GADDAH (hā'zàr-găd'à), town in S of Judah, near Simeon (Josh. 15:27).

HAZAR-HATTICON (hā'zàr-hăt'ĭ-kŏn), place near Damascus (Ezek. 47:16).

HAZARMAVETH (hā'zàr-mā'vĕth, **village of death**), son and descendants of Joktan (Gen. 10:26; I Chron. 1:20).

HAZAR-SHUAL (hā'zàr-shōō'ăl), town in S Judah (Josh. 15:28; 19:3; I Chron. 4:28; Neh. 11:27).

HAZAR-SUSAH (hā'zàr-sū'sà), city of Simeon (Josh. 19:5); site uncertain.

HAZAZON-TAMAR (hā'à-zŏn-tā'mĕr), town on W coast of Dead Sea (Gen. 14:7). KJV has "Hazezon-tamar."

HAZEL (hā'z'l), KJV has "almond tree," which is better (Gen. 30:37).

HAZELELPONI, ZELELPONI (hăz'ĕ-lĕl-pō'nĭ, zĕl-ĕl-pō'nĭ), Jewish woman (I Chron. 4:3).

HAZERIM (hà-zē'rĭm), should be "villages" (Deut. 2:23).

HAZEROTH (hà-zē'rŏth), encampment of Israelites in wilderness (Num. 11:35;12:16).

HAZEZON-TAMAR (hăz'ĕ-zŏn-tā'mĕr), another spelling for Hazazon-tamar, q.v.

HAZIEL (hā'zĭ-ĕl), Levite (I Chron. 23:9).

HAZO (hā'zō), son of Nahor (Gen. 22:22).

HAZOR (hā'zŏr, **enclosed place**). 1. City c. 5 miles W of waters of Merom, ruled by Jabin (Josh. 11:1,10); conquered by Joshua and, later, by Deborah and Barak (Judg. 4; I Sam. 12:9); fortified by Solomon (I Kings 9:15); its inhabitants taken into exile by Assyria (II Kings 15:29). 2. Town in S of Judah (Josh. 15:23). 3. Another town in S Judah (Josh. 15:25). 4. Town N of Jerusalem (Neh. 11:33). 5. Region in S Arabia (Jer. 49:28-33).

HAZOR-HADATTAH (hā'zŏr-hà-dăt'à, **new Hazor**), town in S Judah (Josh. 15:25).

HE (hā), 5th letter of Heb. alphabet, pronounced like English h; also used for number 5.

HEAD, used literally and in a variety of figurative ways (Isa. 7:8; 9:14,15; Ezek. 9:10; Eph. 5:23).

HEADBAND, HEADDRESS (See Dress).

HEAD OF THE CHURCH. Christ, who gives the church life, direction, strength (Eph. 1:22; 5:23; Col. 1:18).

HEADSTONE (See Cornerstone).

HEART. In the Bible regarded as the seat of the intellect, feelings, and will (Gen. 6:5; 18:5; Ps. 119:2), innermost being (Gen. 6:6), whole moral nature of fallen man (Jer. 17:9).

HEARTH. Brand (Ps. 102:3), fire pan (Zech. 12:6), hearth on altar (Lev. 6:9), brazier

(Jer. 36:22,23), burning mass (Isa. 30:14).

HEATH, shrub growing on W slopes of Lebanon (Jer. 17:6; 48:6).

HEATHEN (hēē'th'n, **people, nation**), usually refers to Gentiles. God's interest in the heathen seen esp. in Jonah and in NT.

HEAVEN. 1. One of the two great divisions of the universe, the earth and the heavens (Gen. 1:1; 14:19); stars and planets (Gen. 1:14-17; Ezek. 32:7,8). 2. Abode of God (Gen. 28:17; Ps. 80:14; Isa. 66:1; Matt. 5:12) and of the good angels (Matt. 24:36). 3. Inhabitants of heaven (Luke 15:18; Rev. 18:20).

HEAVE OFFERING (See Offerings).

HEAVE SHOULDER (See Offerings).

HEAVING AND WAVING (See Offerings).

HEBER (hē'bĕr, associate). 1. Great-grandson of Jacob (Gen. 46:17). 2. Kenite whose wife Jael killed Sisera (Judg. 4:11-21). 3. Son of Ezrah (KJV "Ezra") (I Chron. 4:18). 4. Benjamite (I Chron. 8:17). 5. Gadite (I Chron. 5:13). 6. Benjamite (I Chron. 8:22). 7. Father of Peleg and Joktan (Luke 3:35).

HEBREW OF THE HEBREWS, pureblooded, very strict Jew (Phil. 3:4-6).

HEBREWS, EPISTLE TO THE. Authorship uncertain; authors suggested: Paul, Timothy, Barnabas, Apollos; place of writing also uncertain; probably written before 70 A. D.; written to Christians in danger of lapsing from faith. Outline. 1. Pre-eminence of Christ (1:1-4:13). Christ superior to angels and to Moses. 2. Priesthood of Christ (4:14-10:18). Christ a priest like Melchizedek. 3. Perseverance of Christians (10:19-12:29). 4. Postscript: Exhortations, personal concerns, benediction (13:1-25).

HEBREW, HEBREWS, designation for Abraham and descendants, the equivalent of Israelites. Abraham is first in OT to be called Hebrew (Gen. 14:13). Origin of word uncertain; may be same as Habiru of Amarna tablets; may come from "Eber," the father of Peleg and Joktan (Gen. 10:24,25), or from a Heb. root meaning "to pass over" (from the crossing of the Euphrates by Abraham).

HEBREW LANGUAGE. The NW branch of the Semitic language family; has close affinity to Ugaritic, Phoenician, Moabitic, and the Canaanite dialects; sister languages include Arabic, Akkadian, and Aramaic. Except for a few passages in Ezra, Daniel, and Jeremiah, it is the language of the OT.

HEBRON (hē'brŏn, league). 1. Ancient city c. 19 miles SW of Jerusalem; encampment of Abraham (Gen. 13:18); spies found Anakim there (Num. 13:22); given to Caleb (Josh. 14:6-15); capital of David for 7-1/2 years (II Sam. 2:11). 2. Son of Kohath (Exod. 6:18). 3. Town in Asher (Josh. 19:28). 4. Descendant of Caleb (I Chron. 2:42,43).

HEDGE, enclosure of stones or thorns (Isa. 5:5; Hos. 2:6; Matt. 21:33).

HEGAI or **HEGE** (hĕg'á-ī, hē'gē), eunuch in charge of Ahasuerus' harem (Esth. 2:3, 8,15).

HEIFER, young cow (Gen. 15:9; Deut. 21:3).

HEIFER, RED (See Animals).

HEIR (See Inheritance).

HELAH (hē'là), wife of Ashur (I Chron. 4:5,7).

HELAM (hē'lăm), place in Syrian desert E of Jordan where David defeated forces of Hadarezer (II Sam. 10:16,17).

HELBAH (hĕl'bà), town in Asher (Judg. 1:31).

HELBON (hĕl'bŏn), city of N Syria (Ezek. 27:18).

HELDAI (hĕl'dà-ī). 1. Commander of David (I Chron. 27:15). 2. Returned Jewish exile (Zech. 6:9-15). Spelled "Helem" in 6:14.

HELEB (hē'lĕb), one of David's valiant men of war (II Sam. 23:29).

HELED (hē'lĕd), brave soldier (I Chron. 11:30).

HELEK (hē'lĕk), son of Gilead (Num. 26:30; Josh. 17:2).

HELEM (hē'lĕm). 1. Asherite (I Chron. 7:35), called Hotham in verse 32. 2. Ambassador (Zech. 6:14); same as Heldai (Zech. 6:10).

HELEPH (hē'lĕf), village of Naphtali (Josh. 19:33).

HELEZ (hē'lĕz). 1. Judahite (I Chron. 2:39). 2. Able soldier of David (II Sam. 23:26; I Chron. 11:27; 27:10).

HELI (hē'lī), father of Joseph, the husband of Mary (Luke 3:23); or perhaps the father of Mary, the mother of Jesus.

HELIOPOLIS (hē-li-ŏp'ō-lis, **city of the sun**), city near S end of Nile Delta called "On" in the Bible (Gen. 41:45; 46:20).

HELKAI (hĕl'ka-ī), priest (Neh. 12:15).

HELKATH (hĕl'kăth), town in S Asher (Josh. 19:25). Later called Hukok (I Chron. 6:75).

HELKATH HAZZURIM (hĕl'kăth hăz'ū-rim), plain near pool of Gibeon where soldiers of Joab and Abner fought (II Sam. 2:12-16).

HELL, place and condition of retribution for unredeemed man; eternal (Matt. 18:8,9); unquenchable (Matt. 3:12; Mark 9:44) fire; lake of fire (Rev. 20:14); fire and worm (Mark 9:48); place of torment (Rev. 14:10); place of outer darkness (Matt. 8:12; 22:13; 25:30).

HELLENISTS (hĕl'ĕn-ĭsts), Jews who made Greek their tongue (Acts 6:1; 9:29). See RSV.

HELMET (See Arms, Armor).

HELON (hē'lŏn), father of Eliab (Num. 1:9).

HELPMEET, helper (Gen. 2:18).

HELPS, one of the gifts of the Spirit, probably the ability to perform helpful works in a gracious manner (I Cor. 12:7-11,28-31).

HEMAM (hē'măm), grandson of Seir the Horite (Gen. 36:22). "Homam" in I Chron. 1:39.

HEMAN (hē'măn, faithful). 1. Wise man (I Chron. 2:6). 2. Levite musician of David (I Chron. 6:33; 25:5). 3. Ps. 88 attributed to Heman the Ezrahite, who may be same as 1.

HEMATH (hē'măth), father of Rechabites (Jer. 35:2-18). In Amos 6:14 "Hemath" should be "Hamath;" in I Chron. 2:55 "Hemath" should be "Hammath" (ASV).

HEMDAN (hĕm'dăn), Horite (Gen. 36:26).

HEMLOCK (See Plants).

HEM OF A GARMENT, fringes or tassels on the borders of the Jewish outer garment (Num. 15:38,39).

HEN (hĕn), son of Zephaniah (Zech. 6:14).

HENA (hĕn'ȧ), city on S bank of Euphrates, c. 180 miles NW of Babylon (II Kings 18:34; 19:13; Isa. 37:13).

HENADAD (hĕn'ȧ-dăd), Levite whose descendants helped Zerubbabel (Ezra 3:9) and Nehemiah (Neh. 3:18,24).

HENOCH (See Enoch).

HEPHER (hē'fẽr, pit, well). 1. Founder of Hepherites (Num. 26:32). 2. Son of Ashhur (KJV Ashur) (I Chron. 4:5,6). 3. One of David's brave soldiers (I Chron. 11:36). 4. Royal city in Canaan conquered by Joshua (Josh. 12:17).

HEPHZIBAH (hĕf'zĭ-bȧ, my delight is in her). 1. Wife of Hezekiah (II Kings 21:1). 2. Symbolical name given to Zion (Isa. 62:4).

HERB (See Plants).

HERD. Herds of cattle were used in plowing, threshing, sacrifice (Gen. 18:17; Job 1:3; 42:12).

HERDMAN, person in charge of cattle (Gen. 13:7) or pigs (Matt. 8:33); despised in Egypt (Gen. 46:34), but honored in Israel (Gen. 47:6; I Chron. 27:29).

HERES (hē'rĕz, sun). 1. District around Aijalon (Judg. 1:35). 2. Place E of the Jordan (Judg. 8:13 ASV, RSV). 3. Egyptian city, translated "city of destruction" (Isa. 19:18), undoubtedly Heliopolis.

HERESH (hē'rĕsh), Levite (I Chron. 9:15).

HERESY (hĕr'ĕ-sĕ, choose). 1. Sect, not necessarily representing a departure from orthodox doctrine (Acts 5:17; 24:5,14; 28:22). 2. Doctrine or sect representing a departure from sound doctrine (II Peter 2:1).

HERMAS (hûr'măs), Roman Christian (Rom. 16:14).

HERMES (hûr'mēz). 1. Greek god (messenger), same as Mercury in Latin (Acts 14:12). 2. Friend of Paul at Rome, called Hermas (Rom. 16:14).

HERMOGENES (hûr-mŏj'ē-nēz, born of Hermes), professed Christian who deserted Paul (II Tim. 1:15).

HERMON (hûr'mŏn, sacred mountain), mt. marking S terminus of Anti-Lebanon range; 30 miles SW of Damascus; 9,000 ft. above sea level; marks N boundary of Palestine; has three peaks. Has borne several names: "Shenir" or "Senir" (Deut. 3:9), "Sirion" (Deut. 3:9), "Sion" (Deut. 4:48). Probably mt. of Transfiguration (Matt. 17:1). Seat of Baal worship (Judg. 3:3). Modern Jebel esh Sheikh.

HEROD (hĕr'ŭd). Idumean rulers of Palestine (47 B. C.-A. D. 79). Line started with Antipater, whom Julius Caesar made procurator of Judaea in 47 B. C. 1. Herod the Great, first procurator of Galilee, then king of the Jews (37-4 B. C.); built Caesarea, temple at Jerusalem; slaughtered children at Bethlehem (Matt. 2:1-18). At his death his kingdom was divided among his three sons: Archelaus, Herod Antipas, and Philip.

2. Archelaus ruled over Judaea, Samaria, and Idumea (4 B. C.-A. D. 6), and was removed from office by the Romans (Matt. 2:22). 3. Herod Antipas ruled over Galilee and Perea (4 B. C.-A. D. 39); killed John the Baptist (Matt. 14:1-12); called "fox" by Jesus (Luke 13:32). 4. Philip, tetrarch of Batanaea, Trachonitis, Gaulanitis, and parts of Jamnia (4 B. C.-A. D. 34). Best of the Herods. 5. Herod Agrippa I; grandson of Herod the Great; tetrarch of Galilee; king of Palestine (A. D. 41-44); killed James the apostle (Acts 12:1-23). 6. Herod Agrippa II. King of territory E of Galilee (c. A. D. 53-70); Paul appeared before him (Acts 25:13-26:32).

HERODIANS (hē-rō'dĭ-ănz), supporters of the rule of the Herods and of Rome (Matt. 22:16; Mark 12:13; 3:6).

HERODIAS (hē-rō'dĭ-ăs), granddaughter of Herod the Great who had John the Baptist put to death (Matt. 14:3-6; Mark 6:17; Luke 3:19).

HERODION (hē-rō'dĭ-ŏn), Christian kinsman of Paul (Rom. 16:11).

HERON (hĕr'ŏn), large aquatic bird Jews could not eat (Lev. 11:19; Deut. 14:18).

HESED (hē'sĕd, mercy), father of one of Solomon's officers (I Kings 4:10).

HESHBON (hĕsh'bŏn, reckoning), Moabite city c. 20 miles E of Jordan; ruled by Sihon, but Israel took it from him (Num. 21:21-31); assigned to Reuben (Num. 32:37; Josh. 13:17), later given to Levites (Josh. 21:39; I Chron. 6:81).

HESHMON (hĕsh'mŏn), town in S Judah (Josh. 15:27).

HETH (hĕth), progenitor of the Hittites (Gen. 10:15; 23:3; 27:46).

HETHLON (hĕth'lŏn), place just N of Mt. Lebanon (Ezek. 47:15).

HEXATEUCH (hĕk'sȧ-tūk), a term referring to the Pentateuch and Joshua as though it were a literary unit.

HEZEKI (hĕz'ē-kī), Benjamite (I Chron. 8:17).

HEZEKIAH (hĕz'ē-kī'ȧ, Jehovah has strengthened), 13th king of Judah (c. 724-695 B. C.); son of Ahaz; great religious reformer and prosperous ruler; Isaiah prophesied and Sennacherib's army was destroyed in his reign; his son Manasseh succeeded him. His story is told in II Kings 18-20, II Chron. 29-32, and Isa. 36-39.

HEZION (hē'zĭ-ŏn), grandfather of Benhadad, king of Syria (I Kings 15:18).

HEZIR (hē'zẽr). 1. Head of 17th course of priests (I Chron. 24:15). 2. Covenanter with Nehemiah (Neh. 10:20).

HEZRAI (hĕz'rā-ī), Carmelite hero of David (II Sam. 23:35). I Chron. 11:37 has Hezro.

HEZRO (See Hezrai).

HEZRON (hĕz'rŏn). 1. Son of Perez (Gen. 46:12. 2. Son of Reuben (Gen. 46:9). 3. Place on S border of Judah (Josh. 15:3).

HIDDAI (hĭd'ā-ī), one of David's heroes (II Sam. 23:30). Same as Hurai of I Chron. 11:32.

HIDDEKEL (hĭd'ē-kĕl), Hebrew name of Tigris river (Gen. 2:14).

HIEL (hī'ĕl), man who rebuilt Jericho and brought God's curse on himself (I Kings 16:34).

HIERAPOLIS (hī-ĕr-ăp'ō-lĭs, sacred city), ancient Phrygian city near Colossae (Col. 4:13).

HIEROGLYPHICS (See Writing).

HIGGAION (hĭ-gā'yŏn), musical term probably meaning "solemn sound" (Ps. 9:16; 92:3).

HIGH PLACES, places of worship on high ground (Num. 22:41; I Kings 11:7), often associated with licentiousness (Hos. 4:11-14; Jer. 3:2) and human sacrifice; Israelites commanded to destroy high places of Canaanites (Num. 33:52; Deut. 33:29), but they did not entirely do so and often they themselves used them for the worship of Baalim; at times Jews worshiped Jehovah on high places (I Kings 3:2,4).

HIGH PRIEST (See Priest).

HILEN (hī'lĕn), Levitical city in Judah (I Chron. 6:58); spelled "Holon" in Josh. 15:51; 21:15.

HILKIAH (hĭl-kī'à, portion of Jehovah). 1. Father of Eliakim (II Kings 18:18). 2. Merarite Levite (I Chron. 6:45). 3. Merarite Levite (I Chron. 26:11). 4. High priest who found book of the Law and sent it to Josiah (II Kings 22,23; II Chron. 34:14). 5. Priest who returned with Zerubbabel (Neh. 12:7). 6. Father of Jeremiah (Jer. 1:1). 7. Father of Gemariah who stood by Ezra at Bible reading (Neh. 8:4).

HILL COUNTRY, any region of hills and valleys, but in Scripture generally the higher part of Judaea (Luke 1:39,65).

HILLEL (hĭl'ĕl), father of Abdon (Judg. 12:13,15).

HIN (See Weights and Measures).

HIND (See Animals).

HINGE, contrivance enabling a door or window to swing in its place (I Kings 7:50); often used figuratively for something of great importance.

HINNOM, VALLEY OF (hĭn'ŏm), dumping ground SW and S of Jerusalem. The Greek equivalent, gehenna, became the word for "hell" (James 3:6). See Gehenna.

HIP AND THIGH, expression denoting thoroughness with which Samson slew Philistines (Judg. 15:8).

HIRAH (hī'rà), Adullamite (Gen. 38:1,12,20).

HIRAM (hī'răm). 1. King of Tyre in reigns of David and Solomon, to whom he sent food, gold, and building material for the temple (II Sam. 5:11; I Kings 9:11-14). 2. Worker in brass for Solomon's temple (I Kings 7:13,14; 40-45; II Chron. 2:13,14; 4:11-16). "Huram" in II Chron. 4:11; Huramabi, "Huram, my father," in II Chron. 2:13; 4:16.

HIRELING, laborer who works for his wages (Deut. 24:15; Matt. 20:1-6).

HITTITES (hĭt'īts), descendants of Ham, through Canaan's 2nd son Heth (Gen. 10:15; I Chron. 1:13); often referred to in the OT (Gen. 10:15; 26:34; Josh. 9:1; Judg. 3:5,6; I Kings 11:1; Ezra 9:1); prominent all

through 2nd millennium B. C.; their stronghold, Carchemish, fell to the Assyrians in 717 B. C.; archaeology has uncovered ten thousand tablets at their ancient capital, Boghaz-koy, and their civilization is now well known.

HIVITES (hī'vīts), one of the seven nations of Canaan conquered by Joshua (Josh. 24:11); often mentioned in the OT (Josh. 11:3; Judg. 3:3; II Sam. 24:7); last referred to when Solomon raised a levy from their remnants to do task work for him (II Chron. 8:7). Some scholars think they may be the same as the Horites.

HIZKIAH, HIZKIJAH (hĭz-kī'à, hĭz-kī'jà), found twice in KJV, but in each case should be "Hezekiah," as in ASV. 1. Ancestor of Zephaniah (Zeph. 1:1). 2. Covenanter with Nehemiah (Neh. 10:17).

HOBAB (hō'băb, beloved), brother-in-law of Moses (Num. 10:29; Judg. 4:11 (KJV has "father-in-law").

HOBAH (hō'bà), place N of Damascus (Gen. 14:15).

HOD (hŏd), Asherite (I Chron. 7:37).

HODAIAH (hō-dā'yà), descendant of David (I Chron. 3:24).

HODAVIAH (hō-dà-vī'à). 1. Chief in Manasseh (I Chron. 5:24). 2. Benjamite (I Chron. 9:7). 3. Levite whose descendants returned with Zerubbabel (Ezra 2:40). Also called Hodevah (Neh. 7:43) and Judah (Ezra 3:9).

HODESH (hō'dĕsh), wife of Shaharaim, a Benjamite (I Chron. 8:9).

HODEVAH (See Hodaviah).

HODIAH (hō-dī'à), man who married sister of Naham (I Chron. 4:19).

HODIJAH (hō-dī'jà). 1. Levite (Neh. 8:7; 9:5 10:10,13). 2. Leader in Nehemiah's time (Neh. 10:18).

HOGLAH (hŏg'là), daughter of Zelophehad (Num. 26:33; 27:1-11; 36:1-12; Josh. 17:3,4).

HOHAM (hō'hăm), Amorite king who entered into a league against Joshua (Josh. 10:3).

HOLINESS, HOLY, basic meaning is "separateness;" anything separated from common and dedicated to sacred use; holiness originates in God and is communicated to things, places, times, and persons engaged in His service; God demands that His people be holy, i.e., separated unto Him (Num. 15:40,41; Deut. 7:6). Jesus is the Holy One of God (Mark 1:24; Luke 4:34; John 6:69).

HOLON (hō'lŏn). 1. Levitical city in hill country of Judah (Josh. 15:51); called Hilen in I Chron. 6:58). 2. Moabite town (Jer. 48:21).

HOLY OF HOLIES (See Tabernacle).

HOLY GHOST (See Holy Spirit).

HOLY PLACE (See Tabernacle).

HOLY SPIRIT, 3rd person of the Godhead (Matt. 28:19; II Cor. 13:14). He dwells in Christians (John 14:17), convicts of sin (John 16:8), inspires the Scriptures and speaks through them (Acts 1:16; II Peter 1:21), intercedes for believers (Rom. 8:26). Has attributes of personality: will (I Cor. 12:11), mind (Rom. 8:27), thought, knowledge, words (I Cor. 2:10-13), love (Rom.

15:30). Can be treated as a person: lied to and tempted (Acts 5:3,4,9), resisted (Acts 7:51), grieved (Eph. 4:30), blasphemed against (Matt. 12:31). Equated with the Father and the Son (Matt. 28:19; II Cor. 13:14).

HOMAM (hō'măm), grandson of Seir (I Chron. 1:39). KJV has Hemam in Gen. 36:22.

HOMER (See Weights and Measures).

HONEY, a common food in Palestine (II Sam. 17:29); found in clefts of rocks (Deut. 32:13; Ps. 81:16) and on the ground (I Sam. 14:25-27). A standard of comparison for pleasant things (S. of Sol. 4:11; 5:1; Prov. 16:24; 5:3; Ezek. 3:3).

HOOD (See Dress).

HOOK, used for fishing (Job 41:1; Matt. 17:27), hanging curtains (Exod. 26:32,37; 27:10,17), pruning (Joel 3:10; Mic. 4:3), hanging meat (Ezek. 40:43).

HOOPOE (See Birds).

HOPE, a gift of the Holy Spirit (I Cor. 13:8,13); not mere expectation and desire, but trust and confidence (Rom. 15:13). Christ our hope (I Tim. 1:1); depends on resurrection of Christ (I Cor. 15:19).

HOPHNI (hŏf'nī), unworthy son of Eli (I Sam. 1:3; 2:34; 4:4,17).

HOR (hŏr, **mountain**). 1. Mt. on edge of Edom where Aaron died and was buried (Num. 20:22-29; 33:37-41). 2. Mt. on N boundary of Palestine (Num. 34:7,8). Site unknown.

HORAM (hō'răm), king of Gezer (Josh. 10:33).

HOREB (hō'rĕb, **drought, desert**), used interchangeably with "Sinai," the scene of many events in life of Moses (Exod. 3:1; 17:6; 33:6; Deut. 1:2). Elijah fled to it (I Kings 19:8).

HOREM (hō'rĕm), city in Naphtali (Josh. 19:38).

HOR-HAGIDGAD (hŏr-hă-gĭd'găd), Israelite encampment (Num. 33:32,33), called Gudgodah in Deut. 10:7).

HORI (hō'rī). 1. Son of Seir (Gen. 36:22, 29,30; I Chron. 1:39). 2. Simeonite spy (Num. 13:5).

HORIM (See Horites).

HORITE, HORIM (hō'rīt, hō'rĭm), people conquered by Chedorlaomer (Gen. 14:6); may be same as Hivites (Gen. 34:2; Josh. 9:7); thought to be Hurrians, from highlands of Media.

HORMAH (hŏr'mà, **devoted place**), town between Gaza and Beer-sheba (Num. 14:45; Deut. 1:44); originally called "Zephath" (Judg. 1:17).

HORN, first made of animal horns, later of metal (Num. 10:2); for giving signals (Josh. 6:5) and containers (I Sam. 16:1). Projections of corners of altar were called "horns of the altar" (Exod. 27:2; I Kings 1:50). A symbol of strength and honor (Ps. 18:2; Dan. 7:7; Luke 1:69).

HORNET (See Insects).

HORONAIM (hŏr-à-nā'ĭm), place in Moab (Isa. 15:5; Jer. 48:3,5,34).

HORONITE (hŏr'ō-nīt), appellation of San-

ballat (Neh. 2:10,19; 13:28).

HORSE (See Animals).

HORSE GATE, one of the gates of Jerusalem (Neh. 3:28-32; Jer. 31:38-40).

HORSE LEECH, bloodsucking worm which clings to the flesh (Prov. 30:15).

HOSAH (hō'sà). 1. Town in Asher (Josh. 19:29). 2. Levite porter (I Chron. 16:38; 26:10,11,16).

HOSANNA (hō-zăn'à, **save now**), originally a prayer, "Save, now, pray" (Ps. 118:25); chanted when Jesus entered Jerusalem (Matt. 21:9-15; Mark 11:9,10).

HOSEA (hō-zē'à, **salvation**), 8th cent. B. C. prophet during reigns of Uzziah, Jothan, Ahaz of Judah, and Hezekiah and Jeroboam II of Israel (Hos. 1:1), contemporary with the prophets Isaiah, Amos, and Micah. Outline. 1. Hosea's unhappy marriage and its results (1-3). 2. Priests condone immorality (4). 3. Israel's sin will be punished unless she repents (5). 4. Israel's sin is thoroughgoing; her repentance halfhearted (6). 7. Inner depravity and outward decay (7). 8. Nearness of judgment (8). 9. Impending calamity (9). 10. Israel's guilt and punishment (10). 11. God pursues Israel with love (11). 12. Exhortation to repentance, with promised restoration (12-14).

HOSHAIAH (hō-shā'yà, **Jehovah has saved**). 1. Man who assisted at dedication of wall (Neh. 12:32). 2. Father of Jezaniah (Jer. 42:1) or Azariah (Jer. 43:2).

HOSHAMA (hòsh'à-mà), son of Jeconiah or Jehoiachin (I Chron. 3:18).

HOSHEA (hō-shē'à, **salvation**). 1. Joshua's earlier name (Num. 13:8,16). 2. Son of Azaziah (I Chron. 27:20). 3. Son of Elah (II Kings 15:30; 17:1-6; 18:1). 4. Covenanter with Nehemiah (Neh. 10:23).

HOSPITALITY, commanded in Mosaic law (Lev. 19:34); illustrations: Gen. 14:17-19; 18; 19; 24:15-28; 29:1-14; 43:15-34; Exod. 2:15-22; Judg. 13:2-23; Matt. 14:15-21; Luke 10: 38-42).

HOST, Army (Gen. 21:22); angels (Ps. 103:21; Josh. 5:14); heavenly bodies (Deut. 4:19); creation (Gen. 2:1); God of hosts (I Sam. 17:45); one who shows hospitality (Rom. 16:23; Luke 10:35).

HOSTAGE, hostages taken by Jehoash (II Kings 14:14).

HOTHAM (hō'thăm), Asherite (I Chron. 7:32).

HOTHAN (hō'thăn), Aroerite (I Chron. 11:44).

HOTHIR (hō'thěr), Kohathite (I Chron. 25:4,28).

HOUGH (hŏk, **to hamstring an animal**), Josh. 11:6,9; II Sam. 8:4.

HOUR, may be a point of time (Matt. 8:13), or a period (Rev. 17:12). Israelites reckoned days from sunset to sunset; Romans reckoned hours from midnight to noon, as we do.

HOUSE. 1. Family line (Exod. 2:1; Num. 12:7). House of God: Bethel (Gen. 28:17), tabernacle (Exod. 34:26; Deut. 23:18), temple (I Kings 6:1). 2. Houses in Palestine were usually made of native material. The very poor often lived in caves cut out of limestone ridges (I Sam. 24:3; I Kings 18:4; 19:9). Nomadic people lived in tents, often made of goat or camel hair (Gen. 4:20). Large ones had two or more center poles (Exod. 26:32). Where rocks abounded houses were made of limestone. Along the Mediterranean houses were made of clay. Window openings were narrow and high up in the walls. Roofs were made of alternating layers of clay and straw. Walls continued several feet above the roof line (Deut. 22:8; Josh. 2:6). A stairway led from the street to the roof. In larger houses there would be a court yard. Sheep and goats were often kept on the ground floor, while the family lived upstairs. Wealthier homes had rooms built around an open court. The rich built mansions and palaces (Amos 5:11; John 18:15).

HUKKOK (hŭk'ŏk), border town of Naphtali (Josh. 19:34).

HUKOK (See Helkath).

HUL (hŭl), son of Aram (Gen. 10:23).

HULDA (hŭl'dȧ, weasel), prophetess in reign of Josiah (II Kings 22:14-20; II Chron. 34:22-28).

HUMANITY OF CHRIST (See Christ).

HUMILITY, freedom from pride, lowliness, meekness, modesty; Christians commanded to be humble (Phil. 2:3,4; Rom. 12:10; I Cor. 13:4-6; I Peter 5:5,6).

HUMTAH (hŭm'tȧ), town of Judah near Hebron (Josh. 15:54).

HUPHAM (hū'fȧm), son of Benjamin; founder of Huphamites (Num. 26:39).

HUPHAMITES (See Hupham).

HUPPAH (hŭp'ȧ), priest in David's time (I Chron. 24:13).

HUPPIM (hŭp'ĭm), probably same as Hupham.

HUR (hûr, whiteness). 1. One who, with Aaron, held up Moses' hands (Exod. 17:10, 12). 2. Grandfather of Bezaleel, chief workman in the tabernacle (Exod. 31:2, 35:30; 38:22). 3. Midianite king (Num. 31:1-8). 4. In KJV, the father of an officer (I Kings 4:8). 5. Father of Rephaiah (Neh. 3:9).

HURAI (hū'rā-ĭ), one of David's heroes (I Chron. 11:32). Called Hiddai in II Sam. 23:30.

HURAM (hū'răm, **noble-born**). 1. Benjamite (I Chron. 8:5). 2. King of Tyre (II Chron. 2:3,11,12). Usually called Hiram. 3. Tyrian artificer (II Chron. 2:13; 4:11,16).

HURI (hū'rī), Gadite (I Chron. 5:13).

HURRIANS (See Horites).

HUSBANDMAN (hŭz'bånd-mȧn), farmer, whether owner or tenant.

HUSBANDRY (See Occupations and Professions).

HUSHAH (hū'shȧ), son of Ezer (I Chron. 4:4).

HUSHAI (hū'shī), Archite; counselor of David who overthrew counsels of Ahithophel (II Sam. 15:32,37; 16:16-18; 17:5-15; I Chron. 27:33).

HUSHAM (hū'shăm), king of Edom (Gen. 36:34,35; I Chron. 1:45,46).

HUSHATHITE, THE (hū'shăth-ĭt), patronymic of Sibbecai, one of David's heroes (II Sam. 21:18; I Chron. 11:29; 20:4; 27:11).

HUSHIM (hū'shĭm). 1. Son of Dan (Gen. 46:23), called Shuham in Num. 26:42.

HUSKS, pods of carob tree (Luke 15:16).

HUZ (hŭz), son of Nahor (Gen. 22:21).

HUZZAB (hŭz'ăb), word of uncertain meaning; may be noun or verb (Nahum 2:7).

HYACINTH (hī'ȧ-sĭnth). 1. Deep purple (Rev. 9:17). KJV has "jacinth." 2. A precious stone (Rev. 21:20). RV has "sapphire."

HYENA (See Animals).

HYKSOS (hĭk'sŏs), a W Semitic people who ruled an empire embracing Syria and Palestine; conquered Egypt c. 1700 B. C.

HYMENAEUS (hī'mė-nē'ŭs), apostate Christian excommunicated by Paul (I Tim. 1:19, 20; II Tim. 2:16-18).

HYMN (See Music).

HYPOCRISY (hĭ-pŏk'rĭ-sė), play-acting, with special reference to religion (Matt. 7:5; 23:28; Mark 12:15; Luke 12:1; I Tim. 4:2; I Peter 2:1).

HYSSOP (See Plants).

I

IBHAR (ĭb'hȧr), son of David (II Sam. 5:15; I Chron. 14:5).

IBLEAM (ĭb'lė-ȧm), town given to the tribe of Manasseh (Josh. 17:11). Ahaziah slain there (II Kings 9:27). Generally identified with Bileam (I Chron. 6:70).

IBNEIAH (ĭb-nē'yȧ), Benjamite (I Chron. 9:8).

IBNIJAH (ĭb-nī'jȧ), Benjamite (I Chron. 9:8).

IBRI (ĭb'rī), Merarite Levite (I Chron. 24:27).

IBZAN (ĭb'zȧn), 10th judge of Israel (Judg. 12:8-10); had 30 sons and 30 daughters.

ICHABOD (ĭk'ȧ-bŏd, **inglorious**), son of Phinehas, Eli's son (I Sam. 4:19ff).

ICONIUM (ī-cō'nĭ-ŭm), city in S central part of Asia Minor; visited by Paul (Acts 13:51; 14:1-22; 16:2; II Tim. 3:11).

IDBASH (ĭd'băsh), man of Judah (I Chron. 4:3).

IDDO (ĭd'ō). 1. Son of Zechariah (I Chron. 27:21). 2. Head of Nethinim (Ezra 8:17). 3. Levite (I Chron. 6:21). 4. Seer and prophet (II Chron. 9:29; 12:15; 13:22). 5. Father of Abinadab (I Kings 4:14). 6. Grandfather of the prophet Zechariah (Zech. 1:1,7; Ezra 5:1; 6:14).

IDOL (See Idolatry).

IDOLATRY (ī-dŏl'ȧ-trē). All the nations surrounding ancient Israel were idolatrous, and Israel also often fell into this sin, as a consequence of which God punished the nation severely. Idols were made of various materials: silver, gold, wood, stone, etc. (Isa. 40:19,20; 44:9-20; Jer. 10:9). Even Christians are warned to be on their guard against idolatry (I Cor. 5:10; Gal. 5:20).

IDUMAEA (ĭd'ū-mē-ȧ), **pertaining to Edom**), Greek and Roman name for Edom

(Mark 3:8).

IGAL (i'găl). 1. Spy of Issachar (Num. 13:7). 2. One of David's heroes (II Sam. 23:36). 3. Descendant of Jeconiah (I Chron. 3:22).

IGDALIAH (ig'dà-lĭ'à), father of the prophet Hanan (Jer. 35:4).

IGEAL (ĭ'gĕ-ăl), son of Shemaiah (I Chron. 3:22).

IIM (i'im). 1. Town in S Judah (Josh. 15:29). 2. Town E of the Jordan (Num. 33:45).

IJE-ABARIM (i'jè-ăb'à-rĭm), encampment of Israel (Num. 33:44).

IJON (i'jŏn), town of Naphtali (I Kings 15:20; II Chron. 16:4); c. 8 miles NW of Banias.

IKKESH (ik'ĕsh), father of one of David's heroes (II Sam. 23:26; I Chron. 11:28).

ILAI (ĭ'lā-ĭ), one of David's heroes (I Chron. 11:29); called Zalmon in II Sam. 23:28.

ILLYRICUM (il-lĭr'ĭ-kŭm), Roman province on E coast of Adriatic. Paul preached there (Rom. 15:19). Now part of Yugoslavia.

IMAGE (See Idolatry).

IMAGE, NEBUCHADNEZZAR'S. Symbolic figure seen by Nebuchadnezzar in a dream the meaning of which was interpreted by Daniel (Dan. 2).

IMAGE OF GOD. Man is created by God in His own image (Gen. 1:26,27; 5:1,3; 9:6; I Cor. 11:7; Eph. 4:24; Col. 3:10; James 3:9). The image is not corporeal but rational, spiritual, and social. The fall of man destroyed, but did not obliterate the image. Restoration of the image begins with regeneration.

IMAGE WORSHIP (See Idol).

IMLAH (im'là), father of the prophet Micaiah (I Kings 22:8,9; II Chron. 18:7,8).

IMMANUEL (ĭ-măn'ū-ĕl, God is with us), a child borne by a maiden whose birth was foretold by Isaiah, and who was to be a sign to Ahaz (Isa. 7:14); at his birth salvation would be near. Many prophecies cluster around this child (Isa. 8:9,10; 9:6,7; 11:1; Micah 5:2,3; Matt. 1:22,23).

IMMER (im'ẽr). 1. Head of 16th course of priests (I Chron. 24:14; Ezra 2:37; 10:20). 2. Priest (Jer. 20:1). 3. Place in Babylonia (Ezra 2:59).

IMMORTALITY. The Biblical concept of immortality is not simply the survival of the soul after bodily death, but the self-conscious continuance of the whole person, body and soul together, in a state of blessedness, due to the redemption of Christ and the possession of "eternal life." The Bible nowhere attempts to prove this doctrine, but everywhere assumes it as an undisputed postulate. The condition of believers in their state of immortality is not a bare endless existence, but a communion with God in eternal satisfaction and blessedness. Job 19:23-27; Ps. 16:9-11; 17:15; 49:15; 73:24; Isa. 26:19; Dan. 12:2; Hos. 13:14; Matt. 10:28; Luke 23:43; John 11:25f; 14:3; II Cor. 5:1,10.

IMMUTABILITY (ĭ-mū-tà-bil'ĭ-tè, unchangeableness), the perfection of God by which He is devoid of all change in essence, attributes, consciousness, will, and promises. Mal. 3:6; Ps. 33:11; 102:26.

IMNA (im'nà), Asherite (I Chron. 7:35).

IMNAH (im'nà). 1. Son of Asher (Num. 26:44; I Chron. 7:30). 2. Levite (II Chron. 31:14).

IMPRECATORY PSALMS. Psalms – especially Nos. 2,37,69,109,139,143 – which contain expressions of an apparent vengeful attitude towards enemies. For some people these Psalms constitute one of the "moral difficulties" of the OT.

IMPUTATION (See Impute).

IMPUTE (im-pūt), to attribute something to a person, or reckon something to the account of another. Aspects of the doctrine found in the NT: the imputation of Adam's sin to his posterity; the imputation of the sin of man to Christ; the imputation of Christ's righteousness to the believer. Gen. 2:3; I Pet. 2:24; Rom. 3:24; 5:15; Gal. 5:4; Titus 3:7.

IMRAH (im'rà), Asherite (I Chron. 7:36).

IMRI (im'rī). 1. Judahite (I Chron. 9:4). 2. Father of Zaccur (Neh. 3:2).

INCARNATION (in-kär-nà'shŭn, becoming flesh), the doctrine that the eternal Son of God became human, and that He did so without in any manner or degree diminishing His divine nature (John 1:14; Rom. 8:3; I Tim. 3:16).

INCENSE (in'sĕns), an aromatic substance made of gums and spices to be burned, especially in religious worship. The ingredients for Temple incense were specified (Exod. 30:23f). Burned morning and evening in the Temple (Exod. 30:1-10), and taken into the Holy of Holies on the Day of Atonement (Lev. 16:12,13). It symbolized prayer (Ps. 141:2; Rev. 5:8; 8:3,4).

INDIA (in'dĭ-à), country on the E limit of kingdom of Ahasuerus (Esth. 1:1; 8:9).

INFLAMMATION (See Diseases).

INHERITANCE (in-hĕr'ĭ-tàns). In the OT the word is used literally to refer to inherited property (Deut. 21:15-17; Num. 27:8; Ruth 3:12,13); the land of Canaan promised to Abraham and his descendants (I Kings 8:36; Num. 34:2; Deut. 4:21,38); Jehovah Himself (Jer. 10:16); Israel (Deut. 4:20); in the NT it usually refers to the kingdom of God with all its blessings (Matt. 25:34; I Cor. 6:9; Gal. 5:21), both present and eschatological (Rom. 8:17-23; I Cor. 15:50; Heb. 11:13; I Peter 1:3,4).

INK. Any liquid used with pen or brush to form written characters (Jer. 36:18; II Cor. 3:3; II John 12; III John 13).

INN, a lodging place for travellers. Inns in the modern sense were not very necessary in ancient times, since travelers found hospitality the rule (Exod. 2:20; Judg. 19:15-21; II Kings 4:8; Acts 28:7; Heb. 13:2). Ancient inns were usually mere shelters for man and beast, although often strongly fortified.

INNOCENTS, SLAUGHTER OF, the slaughter, by Herod the Great, of children in Bethlehem (Matt. 2:16-18).

I.N.R.I., the initials of the Latin superscription on the cross of Jesus, standing for **IESUS NAZARENUS, REX IUDAEORUM,** Jesus of Nazareth, King of the Jews (Matt. 27:37; Mark 15:26; Luke 23:38; John 19:19).

INSECTS OF THE BIBLE. Among the many kinds of insects mentioned in the Bible are the following: grasshoppers, locusts, crickets, scale insects, moths, butterflies, flies, fleas, ants, bees, hornets, scorpions, spiders, wasps.

INSPIRATION, the special influence of the Holy Spirit guiding certain persons to speak and write what God wanted communicated to others, without suspending their individual activity or personality (I Cor. 2:13; II Tim. 3:16; I Peter 1:10,11; II Peter 1:19-21).

INTEREST (in'tẽr-ẽst). The law of Moses forbade loaning at interest to a fellow Israelite (Exod. 22:25), but permitted charging interest to a foreigner (Deut. 23:20). Taking of interest was condemned by the prophets (Ezek. 18:8,13,17; Jer. 15:10). Reference to interest in the NT: Matt. 25:27; Luke 19:23.

INTERMEDIATE STATE. Period of time which elapses between death and the resurrection. For the righteous it is one of blessedness (II Cor. 5:8); for the wicked it is one of conscious suffering (Luke 16:19-31).

IPHEDEIAH (if-ê-dē'yà), descendant of Benjamin (I Chron. 8:25).

IR (ir), Benjamite (I Chron. 7:7,12).

IRA (ī'rà). 1. Chief minister of David (II Sam. 20:26). 2. One of David's mighty men (II Sam. 23:26; I Chron. 11:28). 3. One of David's heroes (II Sam. 23:38; I Chron. 11:40).

IRAD (ī'răd), son of Enoch (Gen. 4:18).

IRAM (ī'răm), chief of Edom (Gen. 36:43; I Chron. 1:54).

IR-HA-HERES (ir-hà-hē'rĕz), city of Egypt, translated "city of destruction" (Isa. 19:18). Site unknown.

IRI (ī'rī), Benjamite (I Chron. 7:7,12).

IRIJAH (i-rī'jà), captain who arrested Jeremiah (Jer. 37:13).

IR-NAHASH (ir-nà'hàsh), town of Judah, founded by Tehinnah (I Chron. 4:12). Site uncertain.

IRON; used at least as far back as 2700 B. C.; came into general use in Palestine in 13th cent.; during period of judges the Israelites had to go to the Philistines to get iron tools made or repaired (I Sam. 13:20), and even in the time of Saul they had no chariots or weapons of iron (I Sam. 13:22). David's conquest of the Philistines brought extensive iron industries to Israelites. Iron ore was brought from Spain, the Lebanon range (Jer. 11:14; Deut. 4:20; 8:9; I Kings 8:51), and probably Egypt (Deut. 4:20). Among things made of iron were vessels (Josh. 6:19,24), threshing instruments (Amos 1:3); axes (II Sam. 12:31), other tools (I Kings 6:7), weapons (Num. 35:16), armor (II Sam. 23:7), chariots (Josh.

17:16), gates (Acts 12:10), prison bars (Ps. 107:10,16); Isa. 10:34). The word is often used figuratively in Scripture (Deut. 28:23, 48; Ps. 107:10; Dan. 2:33; Jer. 1:18).

IRON (ī'rŏn), fortified city of Naphtali (Josh. 19:38).

IRPEEL (ir'pī-ĕl), city of Benjamin (Josh. 18:27).

IRRIGATION (ir-i-gà'shŭn), practiced in Palestine (Eccl. 2:5,6; Isa. 58:11) and Egypt (Deut. 11:10).

IR-SHEMESH (ir-shē'mĕsh), city of Dan (Josh. 19:41).

IRU (ī'rōō), son of Caleb (I Chron. 4:15).

ISAAC (ī'zàk, **one laughs**), only son of Abraham by Sarah (Gen. 17:19); circumcised (Gen. 21:4); almost offered as sacrifice by father (Gen. 22); married Rebekah (Gen. 24) and had two sons, Jacob and Esau (Gen. 25:20,26); lied about wife (Gen. 26:10); blessed sons (Gen. 27); died at Mamre (Gen. 35:27-29).

ISAIAH (ī-zā'yà, **salvation of Jehovah**), prophet of Judah during reigns of Uzziah, Jotham, Ahaz, and Hezekiah (Isa. 1:1); son of Amoz; had two sons (Isa. 7:3; 8:3); ministry began in the year Uzziah died (Isa. 6:1); highly regarded especially by Hezekiah (II Kings 19:1-11); preeminently the prophet of redemption; foretold coming of the Messiah (9:6; 25:1; 28:29; 53; etc.); first of major prophets; author of Book of Isaiah. Outline: 1. Introduction (1). 2. Denunciation of Jerusalem (2-5). 3. Temple vision (6). 4. Book of Immanuel (7-12). 5. Prophecies against the nations (13-23). 6. Prophecies of judgment and future blessing (24-35). 7. Historical events (36-39). 8. Book of Consolation (40-66).

ISCAH (is'kà), daughter of Haran (Gen. 11:29).

ISHBAH (ĭsh'bà), Judahite (I Chron. 4:17).

ISHBAK (ĭsh'bàk), son of Abraham and Keturah (Gen. 25:2).

ISHBI-BENOB (ĭsh'bī-bē'nŏb), giant slain by Abishai (II Sam. 21:16,17).

ISH-BOSHETH (ĭsh-bō'shĕth, **man of shame**), originally called Eshbaal; succeeded Saul his father as king and reigned for two years, but was slain by David's men (II Sam. 2:8-32; 4:5-12).

ISHI (ĭsh'ī, **my husband**), symbolic name expressive of the ideal relation between God and Israel (Hos. 2:16).

ISHI (ĭsh'ī, **salutary**). 1. Judahite (I Chron. 2:31). 2. Another Judahite (I Chron. 4:20). 3. Descendant of Simeon (I Chron. 4:42). 4. Manassehite (I Chron. 5:24).

ISHIAH (ĭ-shī'à). 1. Man of Issachar (I Chron. 7:3). 2. Levite (I Chron. 24:21). 3. Another Levite (I Chron. 23:20, Jesiah in KJV). 4. One of David's heroes (Jesaiah, I Chron. 12:6).

ISHIJAH (ĭ-shī'jà), man who put away his foreign wife (Ezra 10:31).

ISHMA (ĭsh'mà), Judahite (I Chron. 4:3,4).

ISHMAEL (ĭsh'mà-ĕl, **God hears**). 1. Son of Abraham by Sarah's handmaid Hagar (Gen. 16); circumcised (Gen. 17:26); cast out on

Sarah's insistence (Gen. 21); progenitor of Ishmaelites (Gen. 17:20; 25:12-16). 2. Descendant of Jonathan (I Chron. 8:38; 9:44). 3. Father of Zebadiah (II Chron. 19:11). 4. Son of Jehohanan (II Chron. 23:1). 5. Judahite who slew Gedaliah (II Kings 25:25; Jer. 40:7-16; 41:1-18).

ISHMAELITE (ĭsh'mȧ-ĕl-ĭt), a descendant of Ishmael; Ishmaelites were nomads (Gen. 37:25-28; 39:1).

ISHMAIAH (ĭsh-mā'yȧ). 1. Gibeonite (I Chron. 12:4). 2. Chief of Zebulunites (I Chron. 27:19).

ISHMEELITE (See Ishmaelite).

ISHMERAI (ĭsh'mė-rī), Benjamite (I Chron. 8:18).

ISHOD (ī'shŏd), Manassite (I Chron. 7:18).

ISHPAN (ĭsh'păn), son of Shashak (I Chron. 8:22).

ISHTAR (ĭsh'tär), Semitic goddess worshipped in Phoenicia, Canaan, Assyria, and Babylonia, and sometimes even by the Israelites, called Ashtoreth or Ashtaroth (Judg. 2:13; 10:6; I Kings 11:5; II Kings 23:13); worship usually accompanied by lascivious rites.

ISHTOB (ĭsh'tŏb), place in Palestine which supplied Ammonites with soldiers against David (II Sam. 10:6,8).

ISHUAH (ĭsh'ū-ȧ), son of Asher (Gen. 46:17).

ISHUAI (ĭsh'ū-ī). 1. Son of Asher (Num. 26:44, Jesuai in KJV). 2. Son of Saul (I Sam. 14:49; Ishui in KJV).

ISHUI (ĭsh'ū-ī). See ISHUAI, of which Ishui is another spelling in KJV.

ISLAND, ISLE. 1. Dry land, as opposed to water (Isa. 42:15). 2. Body of land surrounded by water (Jer. 2:10). 3. Coastland (Gen. 10:5; Isa. 20:6). 4. The farthest regions of the earth (Isa. 41:5; Zeph. 2:11).

ISMACHIAH (ĭs'mȧ-kī'ȧ), overseer of the temple (II Chron. 31:13).

ISMAIAH (ĭs-mā'yȧ). 1. Gibeonite (I Chron. 12:4). 2. Zebulunite chief (I Chron. 27:19).

ISPAH (ĭs'pȧ), Benjamite (I Chron. 8:16).

ISRAEL (ĭz'rā-ĕl, one who strives with God). 1. Name given to Jacob (Gen. 32:28; 35:10). 2. Name given collectively to 12 tribes of Israel (Exod. 3:16). 3. Name given to N kingdom after revolt of 10 tribes (I Sam. 11:8; I Kings 14:19,29). 4. Name given to all who have faith of Abraham (Ps. 73:1; Isa. 45:17; John 1:47; Rom. 11:13-36; Gal. 6:15,16).

ISRAELITE (See Israel).

ISSACHAR (ĭs'ȧ-kär). 1. Son of Jacob and Leah; descendants formed tribe of Issachar. 2. Korahite (I Chron. 26:5).

ISSUE (See Diseases).

ISUAH (See Ishuah).

ISUI (See Ishui).

ITALIAN BAND, cohort of Italian soldiers stationed in Caesarea when Peter preached to Cornelius (Acts 10:1).

ITALY (ĭt'ȧ-lĭ), country between Alps and Messina with Rome as its capital (Acts 10:1; 18:2; 27:1; Heb. 13:24).

ITCH (See Diseases).

ITHAI (ĭth'ȧ-ī), Benjamite (I Chron. 11:31, called Ittai in II Sam. 23:29).

ITHAMAR (ĭth'ȧ-mȧr), youngest son of Aaron; founded priestly family (Exod. 6:23; I Chron. 6:3; 24:1).

ITHIEL (ĭth'ĭ-ĕl). 1. Friend of Agur (Prov. 30:1). 2. Benjamite (Neh. 11:7).

ITHMAH (ĭth'mȧ), Moabite hero (I Chron. 11:46).

ITHNAN (ĭth'năn), town in S of Judah (Josh. 15:23). Not identified.

ITHRA (ĭth'rȧ), father of Amasa (I Chron. 2:17, Jether in KJV).

ITHRAN (ĭth'răn). 1. Horite (Gen. 36:26; I Chron. 1:41). 2. Asherite (I Chron. 7:37).

ITHREAM (ĭth'rē-ăm), son of David by Eglah (II Sam. 3:5; I Chron. 3:3).

ITHRITE (ĭth'rīt), family from which two of David's heroes came (II Sam. 23:38; I Chron. 11:40).

ITTAH-KAZIN (ĭt'ȧ-kā'zĭn), place on border of Zebulun (Josh. 19:13). Site unknown.

ITTAI (ĭt'ȧ-ī). 1. One of David's heroes (II Sam. 23:29; I Chron. 11:31). 2. Gathite who became a loyal follower of David (II Sam. 15:18-22; 18:2,5).

ITURAEA (ĭt'ū-rē'ȧ, pertaining to Jetur), region NE of Palestine; its people descended from Jetur, son of Ishmael, and from whom the name Iturea is derived (Gen. 25:15); ruled by Philip (Luke 3:1).

IVAH (ī'vȧ), city, probably in Syria, captured by the Assyrians (II Kings 18:34; 19:13; Isa. 37:13).

IVORY (ī'vō-rĭ), imported into Palestine from India; widely used by the rich (Amos 3:15; 6:4; I Kings 22:39; Ps. 45:8). Solomon's throne made of ivory (I Kings 10:18).

IZCHAR (See Izhar).

IZHAR (ĭz'här). 1. Levite (Exod. 6:18; Num. 3:19; I Chron. 6:18,38). 2. Descendant of Judah (I Chron. 4:7).

IZRAHIAH (ĭz-rȧ-hī'ȧ), chief of tribe of Issachar (I Chron. 7:3).

IZRAHITE (ĭz'rȧ-hīt), patronymic of Shamhuth (I Chron. 27:8).

IZRI (ĭz'rĭ), chief of one of the Levitical choirs (I Chron. 25:11). Called Zeri in v. 3.

J

JAAKAN (jā'ȧ-kăn), descendant of Esau (I Chron. 1:35-42).

JAAKOBAH (jā-ȧ-kō'bȧ), Simeonite prince (I Chron. 4:36).

JAALA, JAALAH (jā'ȧ-là, jā'ȧ-là), man whose descendants returned from Babylon (Ezra 2:56).

JAALAM (jā'ȧ-lăm), son of Esau (Gen. 36: 2,5,18).

JAANAI (jā'ȧ-nī), son of Gad (I Chron. 5:11,12).

JAARE-OREGIM (jā'ȧ-rē-ŏr'ē-jĭm), father of Elhanan, who slew the giant brother of Goliath (II Sam. 21:19). Spelled Jair in

I Chron. 20:5.

JAASAU (jā'à-sāū), man who divorced foreign wife (Ezra 10:37).

JAASIEL, JASIEL (jà-ā'sĭ-ĕl, jā'sĭ-ĕl), son of Abner (I Chron. 11:47; 27:21).

JAAZANIAH (jà-ăz'à-nī'à, Jehovah hears), also called Azariah (Jer. 43:2). 1. Manassehite who slew Gedaliah and led Israelites into Egypt (Jer. 43:1-7). Jeremiah calls him Jezaniah (40:8; 42:1) and Azariah (43:2). 2. Son of Jeremiah (not prophet) (Jer. 35:1-11). 3. Leader in idolatrous worship (Ezek. 8:10-12). 4. Prince denounced by Ezekiel (Ezek. 11:1-3).

JAAZER, JAZER (jā'à-zèr, jā'zèr, helpful), Ammonite stronghold E of the Jordan, probably c. 14 miles N of Heshbon; assigned to Gad (Josh. 13:24,25); later given to Levites (Josh. 21:39).

JAAZIAH (jà'àz-ī'à), Levite (I Chron. 24:20,26).

JAAZIEL (jà-ā'zĭ-ĕl), temple musician (I Chron. 15:18), called Aziel in v. 20.

JABAL (jā'bàl), son of Lamech (Gen. 4: 20-22).

JABBOK (jăb'ŏk, flowing), river E of the Jordan c. halfway between the Dead Sea and the Sea of Galilee; marked boundary of kingdoms of Sihon and Og (Gen. 32:22; Num. 21:24; Josh. 12:2).

JABESH (jā'bĕsh). 1. Father of King Shallum (II Kings 15:8-13). 2. Short term for Jabesh-Gilead (I Chron. 10:12).

JABESH-GILEAD (jā'bĕsh-gĭl'ē-àd, dry),city E of the Jordan, 10 miles SE of Bethshan in area of Manasseh (Num. 32:33). Its men were killed when they refused to attend the sacred assembly at Mizpeh (Judg. 21:8-15); its people buried the remains of Saul and Jonathan (I Sam. 31:1-13).

JABEZ (jā'bĕz). 1. Judahite of noble character (I Chron. 4:9). 2. Town in Judah (I Chron. 2:55).

JABIN (jā'bĭn, able to discern). 1. King of Hazor; defeated and slain by Joshua (Josh. 11). 2. Another king of Hazor; defeated by Barak (Judg. 4; I Sam. 12:9; Ps. 83:9).

JABNEEL (jăb'nē-ĕl). 1. Town in N border of Judah, just S of Joppa (Josh. 15:11), modern Jabna. Called Jabneh in II Chron. 26:6. Later called Jamnia. 2. Frontier town of Naphtali (Josh. 19:33).

JABNEH (jăb'nè), same as Jabneel 1.

JACHAN (jā'kăn), descendant of Gad (I Chron. 5:13).

JACHIN, JACHIN AND BOAZ (jā'kĭn). 1. Son of Simeon (Gen. 46:10). Jarib in I Chron. 4:24. 2. Leader of 21st course of priests (I Chron. 24:17). 3. Jachin and Boaz were the names of two symbolic pillars in porch of Solomon's temple (I Kings 7:15-22; II Chron. 3:15-17).

JACINTH (jā'sĭnth, hyacinth), precious stone, probably blue sapphire, in foundation of New Jerusalem (Rev. 21:20).

JACKAL (See Animals).

JACOB (jā'kŭb, supplanter). 1. Son of Isaac and Rebekah; younger twin brother of Esau (Gen. 25:21-26) from whom he se-

cured the birthright by giving him a bowl of soup (Gen. 25:29-34); got Isaac's blessing through fraud (Gen. 27:1-41); fled to Haran and on way had vision of ladder (Gen. 27:42-28:22); served Laban for many years and married his daughters, Leah and Rachel (Gen. 29:1-30); had 12 sons and a daughter by his wives and their maids, Zilpah and Bilhah (Gen. 29-31); fled from Laban (Gen. 31); wrestled with angel of the Lord at Peniel (Gen. 32:24-32); friendship with Esau restored (Gen. 33); went to Egypt during time of famine (Gen. 42-46) and died there (Gen. 49). 2. Patronymic of Israelites (Num. 23:10; Ps. 59: 13). 3. Father of Joseph, husband of Mary (Matt. 1:15,16).

JACOB'S WELL, well near base of Mt. Gerizim where Jesus talked with a Samaritan woman (John 4).

JADA (jā'dà), Judahite; son of Onam (I Chron. 2:26,28).

JADAU (jā'dō), Israelite who married foreign woman during captivity (Ezra 10:43).

JADDUA (jà-dū'à). 1. Prince who sealed covenant (Neh. 10:21). 2. Son of Jonathan; priest who returned from Bàbylon (Neh. 12:11).

JADON (jā'dŏn), one who helped in rebuilding of Jerusalem wall (Neh. 3:7).

JAEL (jā'ĕl, wild goat), wife of Heber; killed Sisera with tent pin (Judg. 4:18-23).

JAGUR (jā'gèr), town in S Judah (Josh. 15:21).

JAH (jà), contraction of **Jahweh**, occuring in poetry (Ps. 68:4) and in compounds of proper names.

JAHATH (jā'hăth). 1. Grandson of Judah (I Chron. 4:1,2). 2. Great-grandson of Levi (I Chron. 6:16-20). 3. Levite (I Chron. 23: 10,11). 4. Levite (I Chron. 24:22). 5. Merarite Levite (II Chron. 34:8-12).

JAHAZ (jā'hăz), **JAHAZA** (jà-hā'zà), **JAHAZAH** (jà-hā'zà), place N of Arnon river in Moab taken from Sihon (Num. 21:21-25) and assigned to Reuben (Josh. 13:18; 21:36).

JAHAZIAH (jà-hā'zĭ-à), Israelite who opposed Ezra in matter of divorcing foreign wives (Ezra 10:15).

JAHAZIEL (jà-hā'zĭ-ĕl). 1. Soldier who joined David at Ziklag (I Chron. 12:1-4). 2. Priest (I Chron. 16:6). 3. Levite (I Chron. 23:2,19). 4. Levite prophet (II Chron. 20:14ff). 5. Ancestor of family which returned from captivity (Ezra 8:5).

JAHDAI (jà'dā-ī), descendant of Caleb (I Chron. 2:47).

JAHDIEL (jà'dĭ-ĕl), Manassite (I Chron. 5:24).

JAHDO (jā'dō), Gadite (I Chron. 5:14).

JAHLEEL (jà'lē-ĕl), son of Zebulun; founder of Jahleel clan (Num. 26:26).

JAHMAI (jà'mà-ī), grandson of Issachar; chieftain (I Chron. 7:1,2).

JAHWEH (See God).

JAHZAH (jà'zà), town in Reuben (I Chron. 6:78).

JAHZEEL (jà'zē-ĕl), **JAHZIEL** (jà'zĭ-ĕl), son of Naphtali (Gen. 46:24); Jaziel in I Chron. 7:13).

JAHZERAH (jà'zè-rà), priest (I Chron. 9:12).

JAIR (jà'ẽr). 1. Son of Manasseh (Num. 32:40,41). 2. Judge; Gileadite (Judg. 10:3,4). 3. Father of Elhanan who slew Goliath the Gittite (II Sam. 21:19 marg.). 4. Father of Mordecai (Esth. 2:5).

JAIRUS (jà'ĭ-rŭs), synagogue ruler whose child Jesus raised from death (Mark 5:22).

JAKAN (jà'kăn), Horite (I Chron. 1:42). Same as Akan in Gen. 36:27 and Jaakan in Gen. 36:20,21,27.

JAKEH (jà'kè), father of Agur, a writer of proverbs (Prov. 30:1).

JAKIM (jà'kim). 1. Benjamite (I Chron. 8:12,19). 2. Head of 12th course of priests (I Chron. 24:12).

JALON (jà'lŏn), Judahite (I Chron. 4:17).

JAMBRES (jăm'brēz), magician who opposed Moses before Pharaoh (II Tim. 3:8).

JAMES (jāmz). 1. Son of Zebedee and Salome (Matt. 27:56; Mark 1:19; 15:40); elder brother of Apostle John (Matt. 17:1; Mark 3:17; 5:37); one of the apostles (Matt. 17:1); may have been cousin of Jesus; fisherman (Luke 5:10,11); with Jesus at transfiguration (Matt. 17:1-8) and in Gethsemane (Matt. 26:36-46); with John given surname Boanerges (Mark 3:17); angered other apostles (Mark 10:41); killed by Herod Agrippa I (Acts 12:2). 2. James the Less; apostle (Matt. 10:3; Acts 1:13); son of Alphaeus. 3. James, the Lord's brother (Matt. 13:55; Mark 6:3; Gal. 1:19); did not accept Jesus' claims during His ministry (John 7:5), but did after the resurrection (I Cor. 15:7); head of church in Jerusalem (Acts 12:17; 21:18; Gal. 1:19; 2:9,12); presided at Jerusalem council (Acts 15:13; 21:18); gave advice to Paul (Acts 21); Josephus says he was martyred by Jewish High Priest (c. A. D. 62). 4. Father of Apostle Judas (not Iscariot) (Luke 6:16; Acts 1:13).

JAMES THE LESS (See James 2).

JAMES, EPISTLE OF. Written by James (1:1), most likely the brother of the Lord, to Jewish Christians, to comfort them in trials and warn and rebuke them regarding errors and sins into which they had fallen. Outline: 1. Comfort (1). 2. Warnings against specific sins of which they are guilty, such as pride, favoring the rich, misuse of the tongue, believing in faith without works (2-4). 3. Exhortation to patience in suffering and prayer (5).

JAMIN (jà'min). 1. Son of Simeon (Gen. 46:10). 2. Judahite (I Chron. 2:27). 3. Teacher of the Law under Ezra (Neh. 8:7).

JAMLECH (jăm'lĕch), Simeonite prince (I Chron. 4:34).

JANNA (jăn'à), ancestor of Christ (Luke 3:23,24).

JANNES (jăn'ĕz), Egyptian magician who opposed Moses (II Tim. 3:8).

JANOAH (jà-nō'à), JANOHAH (jà-nō'hà) in KJV of Joshua. 1. Town of Naphtali (II Kings 15:29). 2. Town on boundary of Ephraim (Josh. 16:6,7).

JANUM (jà'nŭm), town in Judah (Josh. 15:53).

JAPHETH (jà'fĕth, **God will enlarge**), son of Noah (Gen. 5:32; 6:10; 7:13; 10:21); had seven sons (Gen. 10:2); descendants occupied "isles of Gentiles" (Gen. 10:5); blessed by Noah (Gen. 9:20-27).

JAPHIA (jà-fī'à). 1. King of Lachish killed by Joshua (Josh. 10:3). 2. Son of David (II Sam. 5:15; I Chron. 3:7). 3. City in E border of Zebulun (Josh. 19:12).

JAPHLET (jăf'lĕt), Asherite (I Chron. 7:32).

JAPHLETI (jăf'lè-tī), clan on W border of Ephraim (Josh. 16:1-3).

JAPHO (jà'fō), Hebrew form of Joppa, border town in Dan (Josh. 19:46).

JARAH (jà'rà), descendant of Gibeon (I Chron. 9:42), Jehoaddah in I Chron. 8:36.

JAREB (jà'rĕb), Assyrian king to whom Ephraim went for help (Hos. 5:13).

JARED (jà'rĕd), father of Enoch (Gen. 5:18-20).

JARESIAH (jăr'ē-sī'à), Benjamite (I Chron. 8:27).

JARHA (jàr'hà), Egyptian slave of Sheshan (I Chron. 2:34,35).

JARIB (jà'rib). 1. Son of Simeon, also called Jachin (I Chron. 4:24; Gen. 46:10 marg.). 2. Israelite chief who helped Ezra (Ezra 8:15-20). 3. Man who divorced foreign wife (Ezra 10:18).

JARMUTH (jàr'mŭth). 1. City of Judah 16 miles W by S of Jerusalem (Josh. 15:35); identified with Yarmuk. 2. Levite city of Issachar (Josh. 21:28,29). Ramoth in I Chron. 6:73; Remeth in Josh. 19:21.

JAROAH (jà-rō'à), Gadite (I Chron. 5:14).

JASHEN (jà'shĕn), father of some of David's heroes (II Sam. 23:32); Hashem in I Chron. 11:34).

JASHER, BOOK OF (jà'shẽr), author of book quoted in Josh. 10:13; II Sam. 1:18; LXX of I Kings 8:53.

JASHOBEAM (jà-shŏ'bè-ăm). 1. Hero who joined David at Ziklag (I Chron. 12:6). 2. One of David's chieftains (I Chron. 11:11); Adino in II Sam. 23:8, Jashebasebet in margin of ASV. 3. Hachmonite; may be same as 2 (I Chron. 27:2,3).

JASHUB (jà'shŭb). 1. Son of Issachar (Num. 26:24). Gen. 46:13 has **Job** in KJV. 2. Shear-Jashub, a son of Isaiah (Isa. 7:3). 3. Man who married foreign wife (Ezra 10:29).

JASHUBI-LEHEM (jà-shōō'bĭ-lè'hĕm), word of doubtful meaning; probably a member of tribe of Judah (I Chron. 4:22,23).

JASON (jà'sŭn), Christian friend of Paul (Acts 17:5-9; Rom. 16:21).

JATHNIEL (jăth'nĭ-ĕl), Levite porter of temple (I Chron. 26:2).

JATTIR (jàt'ẽr), Levite town in Judah (Josh. 15:20,48; I Chron. 6:57; I Sam. 30:27).

JAVAN (jà'văn), son of Japheth; father of Elishah, Tarshish, Kittim, and Dodanim (Gen. 10:2; I Chron. 1:5,7). Javan is same as Greek Ionia, with whom the Hebrews traded (Joel 3:4-6).

JAVELIN (See Arms, Armor).

JAZER, JAAZER (jà'zẽr). (See Jaazer).

JAZIZ (jà'ziz), overseer of David's flocks (I Chron. 27:31).

JEALOUSY, WATER OF, holy water mixed with dust given by priest to woman accused of infidelity; it brought curse if she was found guilty (Num. 5:11-31).

JEARIM (je-à-rim), hill on N border of Judah (Josh. 15:10).

JEATERAI (jè-ăt'ê-rī), Gershonite Levite, grandson of Iddo (I Chron. 6:21).

JEBERECHIAH (jè-bĕr'ê-kī'à), father of Zechariah, a scribe (Isa. 8:2).

JEBUS (jē'bŭs), name of Jerusalem when in possession of Jebusites (Josh. 15:63; Judg. 19:10); taken by Israelites (Judg. 1:8), but stronghold not captured until David's time (II Sam. 5:7,8).

JEBUSITES (jĕb'ū-zīts), Canaanite tribe living at Jebus (Gen. 10:16; 15:21; Num. 13:29; Josh. 11:3). Joshua killed their king (Josh. 10:23-27).

JECAMIAH, JEKAMIAH (jĕk'à-mī'à). 1. Judahite (I Chron. 2:41). 2. Son of King Jeconiah (I Chron. 3:17,18).

JECOLIAH, JECHOLIAH (jĕk-ô-lī'à), mother of King Uzziah (II Chron. 26:3; II Kings 15:2).

JECONIAH (jĕk'ô-nī'à), variant of Jehoiachin; king of Judah, captured by Nebuchadnezzar (II Kings 24:1-12). Contracted to Coniah in Jer. 22:24,28; 37:1).

JEDAIAH (jè-dā'yà, Jehovah knows). 1. Simeonite (I Chron. 4:37,38). 2. Priest who returned with Zerubbabel (Neh. 3:10; 12: 6,19). 3. Priest (I Chron. 9:10; 24:7; Ezra 2:36; Neh. 7:39). 4. Priest in Nehemiah's time (Zech. 6:14).

JEDIAEL (jè-dī'à-ĕl). 1. Benjamite (I Chron. 7:6,11). 2. One of David's heroes (I Chron. 11:45). 3. Temple doorkeeper (I Chron. 26:1,2).

JEDIDAH (jè-dī'dà), mother of King Josiah (II Kings 22:1).

JEDIDIAH (jĕd-ï-dī'à, beloved of Jehovah), name that Nathan gave to Solomon (II Sam. 12:24,25).

JEDUTHUN (jè-dū'thŭn, praise), Levite appointed by David as head of musicians in the tabernacle (I Chron. 25:1-3).

JEEZER (jè-ē'zĕr), chief in tribe of Manasseh (Num. 26:30; Abiezer in Josh. 17:2).

JEGAR-SAHADUTHA (jē'gàr-sà-hà-dū'thà), name given by Laban to heap of stones set up as memorial of covenant between him and Jacob; called Galeed by Jacob (Gen. 31:47,48).

JEHALELEEL, JEHALELEL (jè-hăl'ê-lĕl). 1. Descendant of Judah (I Chron. 4:16). 2. Merarite Levite (II Chron. 29:12).

JEHDEIAH (jè-dē'yà). 1. Descendant of Moses (I Chron. 24:20). 2. Man in charge of David's asses (I Chron. 27:30).

JEHEZEKEL (jè-hĕz'ê-kĕl), priest in David's time (I Chron. 24:16).

JEHIAH (jè-hī'à), doorkeeper of ark in David's time (I Chron. 15:24).

JEHIEL (jè-hī'ĕl). 1. Levite musician (1 Chron. 15:18,20; 16:5). 2. Gershonite Levite (I Chron. 23:8; 29:8). 3. Son of Hachmoni (I Chron. 27:32). 4. Son of Jehoshaphat (II Chron. 21:2). 5. Levite who helped

Hezekiah in reformation (II Chron. 29:14). 6. Overseer of offerings in Hezekiah's time (II Chron. 31:13). 7. Temple ruler in days of Josiah (II Chron. 35:8). 8. Father of Obadiah (Ezra 8:9). 9. Father of Shechaniah (Ezra 10:2). 10. Priest who put away foreign wife (Ezra 10:21).

JEHIELI (jè-hī'ê-lī), Gershonite Levite in David's day (I Chron. 26:21,22).

JEHIZKIAH (jè-hīz-kī'à), Israelite chief in days of Ahaz, king of Judah (II Chron. 28:12).

JEHOADAH (jè-hō'à-dà), descendant of King Saul (I Chron. 8:36); Jarah in I Chron. 9:42.

JEHOADDAN (jè-hō-ăd'ăn), wife of King Joash of Judah (II Chron. 25:1); Jehoaddin in II Kings 14:2 ASV.

JEHOAHAZ (jè-hō'à-hăz, Jehovah has grasped). 1. Son and successor of Jehu; 11th king of Israel; reigned 17 years, c. 815-800 B. C. (II Kings 10:35; 13:1); maintained calf-worship of Jeroboam; defeated in battle by kings of Syria; succeeded by his son Jehoash (II Kings 13:2-9, 22-25). 2. King of Judah, 608 B. C.; son of Josiah, whom he succeeded; reigned only three months; died in Egypt (II Kings 23:30-34); also called Shallum (I Chron. 3:15; Jer. 22:10-12). 3. Variant form of name of Ahaziah, king of Judah (II Chron. 21:17). 4. Full name of Ahaz, king of Judah.

JEHOASH, JOASH (jè-hō'ăsh, jō'ăsh). 1. Grandson of Benjamin (I Chron. 7:8). 2. Descendant of Judah (I Chron. 4:22). 3. Father of Gideon (Judg. 6; 12). 4. Keeper of David's cellars of oil (I Chron. 27:28). 5. Israelite who joined David at Ziklag (I Chron. 12:3). 6. Son of King Ahab (I Kings 22:26). 7. King of Judah from 884-848 B. C. (II Kings 11-13; II Chron. 24,25). 8. King of Israel from 848-832 B. C. (II Kings 13:10-13; 14:8-16; II Chron. 25: 17-24).

JEHOHANAN (jè-hō-hà'năn), 1. Doorkeeper of tabernacle (I Chron. 26:3). 2. Officer of Jehoshaphat (II Chron. 17:15). 3. Father of Ishmael who assisted Jehoiada (II Chron. 23:1). 4. Man who married foreign wife (Ezra 10:28). 5. Priest (Neh. 12:13). 6. Levite singer at dedication of new wall (Neh. 12:42).

JEHOIACHIN (jè-hoi'à-kĭn, Jehovah establishes), son and successor of King Jehoiakim; next to last king of Judah; reigned three months in 597 B. C. (II Chron. 36:9); also called Coniah (Jer. 22:24,28; 37:1), Jeconiah, and Jechonias (Matt. 1:11,12); burned prophecies of Jeremiah (Jer. 36: 23,32); deported to Babylon (II Chron. 36:10), where after 37 years of captivity he was released by Evil-merodach (II Kings 25:27).

JEHOIADA (jè-hoi'à-dà, Jehovah knows). 1. Father of Benaiah, one of David's most faithful officers (II Sam. 23:22; I Kings 4:4). 2. Grandson of the preceding (I Chron. 27:34). 3. Descendant of Aaron who aided David at Ziklag (I Chron. 12:27).

4. High priest; wife hid Joash; plotted overthrow of Queen Athaliah (II Chron. 23; II Kings 11).

JEHOIAKIM (jė-hoi'ȧ-kĭm, **Jehovah sets up**), son of Josiah, godly king of Judah; originally named "Eliakim," but name changed to Jehoiakim by Pharaoh Necho by whom he was made king and to whom he paid tribute; rebelled three years later; died ignoble death (II Kings 23:34-37; 24:1-6; II Chron. 36:4-8).

JEHOIARIB, JOIARIB (jė-hoi'ȧ-rĭb, joi'ȧ-rĭb). Priest in days of David (I Chron. 24:7). 2. Priest who returned from exile (I Chron. 9:10). 3. Man who helped Ezra (Ezra 8:16,17). 4. Judahite (Neh. 11:5). 5. Priest (Neh. 11:10; 12:6).

JEHONADAB (jė-hŏn'ȧ-dȧb). 1. Son of David's brother Shimeah (II Sam. 13:3). 2. Kenite who helped Jehu abolish Baal-worship in Samaria (II Kings 10:15f). See also Jonadab.

JEHONATHAN (jė-hŏn'ȧ-thăn). 1. Overseer of David's property (I Chron. 27:25). 2. Levite (II Chron. 17:8). 3. Priest (Neh. 12:18).

JEHORAM (jė-hō'răm, **Jehovah is exalted**). 1. Son of Jehoshaphat of Judah, whom he succeeded as king in 849 B. C.; slew own brothers; married Athaliah, daughter of Ahab and Jezebel (I Kings 22; II Chron. 18); an idolater; denounced by Elijah; died horrible death (II Kings 9:14-26).

JEHOSHABEATH (jė-hō-shăb'ė-ăth), name of Jehosheba (q.v.) as found in II Chron. 22:11).

JEHOSHAPHAT (jė-hŏsh'ȧ-făt, **Jehovah is judge**), in KJV of NT Josaphat. 1. Priest in David's time (I Chron. 15:24). 2. Recorder of David and Solomon (II Sam. 8:16, etc.). 3. Solomon's purveyor (I Kings 4:17). 4. 4th king of Judah; son and successor of King Asa; reigned 25 years, beginning c. 871 B. C. (II Chron. 17-20); took away high places and taught people law of the Lord; rebuked for joint enterprises with Ahab and Ahaziah; died c. 850 B. C., and his son Jehoram succeeded to throne. 5. Father of Jehu who destroyed house of Ahab (II Kings 9:2,14).

JEHOSHAPHAT, VALLEY OF (jė-hŏsh'ȧ-făt, **Jehovah judges**), valley where all nations shall be gathered by Jehovah for judgment (Joel 3:2,12); may be symbolical.

JEHOSHEBA (jė-hŏsh'ė-bȧ, **Jehovah is an oath**), daughter of King Jehoram; wife of high priest Jehoiada; hid Joash from Athaliah (II Kings 11:2).

JEHOSHUA, JEHOSHUAH (jė-hŏsh'ū-ȧ, **Jehovah saves**), variant spelling for Joshua (Num. 13:16; I Chron. 7:27).

JEHOVAH (jė-hō'vȧ), English rendering of Hebrew tetragram YHWH, name of God of Israel; original pronunciation unknown, because out of reverence for God's name it was never pronounced. When the vowel points were added to the Hebrew consonantal text, the Jewish scribes inserted into YHWH the vowels for Adonai, and read Adonai (Lord) instead. The name is derived from the verb "to be," and so implies eternity of God. There are 10 combinations of the word "Jehovah" in the OT.

JEHOVAH-JIREH (jė-hō'vȧ-jī're, **Jehovah will provide**), name given by Abraham to place where he was ready to sacrifice Isaac (Gen. 22:14).

JEHOVAH-NISSI (jė-hō'vȧ-nĭs'ĭ, **Jehovah is my banner**), name given by Moses to altar he built as memorial of victory over Amalekites (Exod. 17:15).

JEHOVAH-SHALOM (jė-hō'vȧ-shā'lŏm, **Jehovah is peace**), name Gideon gave to altar at Ophra (Judg. 6:24).

JEHOVAH-SHAMMAH (jė-hō'vȧ-shă'mȧ, **Jehovah is there**), name given to heavenly Jerusalem in Ezekiel's vision (Ezek. 48:35m).

JEHOVAH-TSIDKENU (jė-hō'vȧ-tsĭd-kē'nū), **Jehovah is our righteousness**), name given king who is to rule over Israel (Jer. 23:6) and His city (Jer. 33:16).

JEHOZABAD (jė-hŏz'ȧ-băd). 1. Conspirator against King Joash (II Chron. 24:26). 2. Porter of tabernacle (I Chron. 26:4). 3. Benjamite army commander (II Chron. 17:18).

JEHOZADAK (jė-hŏz'ȧ-dăk, **Jehovah is righteous**), high priest at time of Babylonian captivity (I Chron. 6:14,15; Neh. 12:26); Josedech in Haggai and Zechariah; Jozadak in Ezra and Nehemiah.

JEHU (jė'hū). 1. Judahite (I Chron. 2:38). 2. Simeonite (I Chron. 4:35). 3. Benjamite (I Chron. 12:3). 4. Prophet; rebuked Baasha (I Kings 16:1,7,12) and Jehoshaphat (II Chron. 19:1-3). 5. 10th king of Israel; son of Jehoshaphat; slew Joram (II Kings 9:24-26), Ahaziah, king of Judah, and Jezebel, also worshipers of Baal; began dynasty which lasted more than 100 years.

JEHUBBAH (jė-hŭb'ȧ), Asherite (I Chron. 7:34).

JEHUCAL (jė-hū'kăl), man sent by King Zedekiah to Jeremiah for prayers (Jer. 37:3); in Jer. 38:1, Jucal.

JEHUD (jė'hŭd), town in Dan, c. 7 miles E of Joppa (Josh. 19:45).

JEHUDI (jė-hū'dĭ, **a Jew**), prince in Jehoiakim's court (Jer. 36:14,21).

JEHUDIJAH (jė'hū-dī'jȧ, **Jewess**), not a proper noun as in KJV, but adjective: Jewess (I Chron. 4:18).

JEHUSH (jė'hŭsh), Benjamite (I Chron. 8:39).

JEIEL (jė-i'ĕl). 1. Reubenite (I Chron. 5:7). 2. Benjamite (I Chron. 9:35). 3. One of David's mighty men (I Chron. 11:44). 4. Levite musician (I Chron. 15:18,21). 5. Levite (II Chron. 20:14). 6. Scribe of Uzziah (II Chron. 26:11). 7. Chief of Levites (II Chron. 35:9). 8. Man who married foreign wife (Ezra 10:43).

JEKABZEEL (jė-kăb'zė-ĕl), place re-inhabited by Judahites (Neh. 11:25).

JEKAMEAM (jėk'ȧ-mē-ăm), head of a Levitical house (I Chron. 23:19; 24:23).

JEKAMIAH (jĕk'ȧ-mī'ȧ). 1. Judahite (I Chron. 2:41). 2. Son of King Jeconiah

(Jehoiachin); in AV Jecamiah (I Chron. 3:18).

JEKUTHIEL (jĕ-kū'thĭ-ĕl), Judahite (I Chron. 4:18).

JEMIMA (jĕ-mī'mà), daughter of Job born after restoration from affliction (Job 42:14).

JEMUEL (jĕ-mū'ĕl), son of Simeon (Gen. 46:10; Exod. 6:15). Called Nemuel in Num. 26:12 and I Chron. 4:24).

JEPHTHAH (jĕf'thà, he opens), 9th judge of Israelites; history given in Judg. 11: 1-12:7; driven from home by brothers because of his illegitimacy, but called back by Israel to fight Amorites, whom he defeated; sacrificed daughter because of rash promise. KJV has Jephthae in Heb. 11:32, where he is listed among the heroes of faith.

JEPHUNNEH (jĕ-fŭn'ĕ). 1. Father of Caleb (Num. 13:6). 2. Son of Jether (I Chron. 7:38).

JERAH (jē'rà), Arabian tribe descended from Joktan (Gen. 10:26; I Chron. 1:20).

JERAHMEEL (jĕ-rà'mĕ-ĕl, God pities). 1. Descendant of Judah (I Chron. 2:9,25-27, 33,42). 2. Merarite Levite (I Chron. 24:29). 3. Officer sent to arrest Jeremiah (Jer. 36:26).

JERASH (See Gerasa).

JERED (jē'rĕd). 1. Son of Mahalaleel (I Chron. 1:2). 2. Judahite (I Chron. 4:18).

JEREMIAH (jĕr'ĕ-mī'à, Jehovah founds, or exalts). In KJV of NT "Jeremy" and "Jeremias" (Matt. 2:17; 16:14). One of greatest Hebrew prophets (c. 640-587 B. C.); born into priestly family of Anathoth, 2-1/2 miles NE of Jerusalem; called to prophetic office by a vision (Jer. 1:4-10), and prophesied during last five kings of Judah (Josiah, Jehoahaz II, Jehoiakim, Jehoiachin, Zedekiah); probably helped Josiah in his reforms (II Kings 23); warned Jehoiakim against Egyptian alliance; prophetic roll destroyed by king (Jer. 36); persecuted by nobility in days of last king (Jer. 36,37); Nebuchadnezzar kind to him after the destruction of Jerusalem (Jer. 39:11,12); compelled to go to Egypt with Jews who slew Gedaliah, and there he died (Jer. 43:6,7).

Six other Jeremiahs are briefly mentioned in the OT: 1. Benjamite who came to David at Ziklag (I Chron. 12:4). 2,3. Gadites (I Chron. 12:10,12). 4. Manassite (I Chron. 5:24). 5. Father of wife of King Josiah (II Kings 23:30,31). 6. Rechabite (Jer. 35:3).

JEREMIAH, BOOK OF. Written by the prophet Jeremiah; dictated to his secretary Baruch (ch. 36); LXX about 1/8 shorter than the Hebrew book; material not arranged in chronological order. Outline: I. Jeremiah's oracles against the theocracy (1:1-25:38). A. Prophet's call (1:1-19). B. Reproofs and admonitions (2:1-20:18). C. Later prophecies (21:1-25:38). II. Events in the life of Jeremiah (26:1-45:5). A. Temple sermon and Jeremiah's arrest (26:1-24). B. Yoke of Babylon (27:1-29:32). C. Book of Consolation (30:1-33:26). D. Experiences of Jeremiah before Jerusalem fell (34:1-36:32).

E. Jeremiah during siege and destruction of Jerusalem (37:1-39:18). F. Last years of Jeremiah (40:1-45:5). III. Jeremiah's oracles against foreign nations (46:1-51:64): Egypt, Philistines, Moab, Ammonites, Edom, Damascus, Kedar and Hazor, Elam, Babylon. IV. Appendix: The fall of Jerusalem and related events (52:1-34).

JEREMOTH (jĕr'ĕ-mŏth). 1. Benjamite (I Chron. 7:8). 2. Another Benjamite (I Chron. 8:14). 3. Merarite Levite (I Chron. 23:23; 24:30). 4. Chief of musicians (I Chron. 25:4,22). 5. Prince of Naphtali (I Chron. 27:19). 6. Three men who put away foreign wives (Ezra 10:26,27,29).

JERIAH (jē-rī'à), head of Levitical house (I Chron. 23:19; 24:23; 26:31).

JERIBAI (jĕr'ĭ-bī), one of David's heroes (I Chron. 11:46).

JERICHO (jĕr'ĭ-kō, moon city), city 5 miles W of the Jordan and 7 miles N of Dead Sea, c. 800 feet below sea level; an oasis with tropical climate. There are three Jerichos: the OT city, the NT city, and a modern town, all near each other. Probably the oldest city in the world; strategically located to control ancient trade route from the E to Palestine; destroyed by Joshua (Josh. 6); given to Benjamin (Josh. 18:21); rebuilt by Hiel (I Kings 16:34). OT Jericho excavated by John Garstang and Kathleen Kenyon.

JERIMOTH (jĕr'ĭ-mŏth). 1. Benjamite (I Chron. 7:7). 2. Another Benjamite (I Chron. 12:5). 3. Son of David (II Chron. 11:18). 4. Temple overseer (II Chron. 31:13). 5. Levite musician (I Chron. 25:4). 6. Merarite (I Chron. 24:30).

JERIOTH (jĕr'ĭ-ŏth), wife of Caleb (I Chron. 2:18).

JEROBOAM I (jĕr'ō-bō'ăm, the people become numerous), 1st king of Israel after division of kingdom, overseer of public works under Solomon (I Kings 11:28); told by the prophet Ahijah that he would become king of 10 tribes (I Kings 11:29-40); fled to Egypt because Solomon sought to kill him (I Kings 11:40); became king with Shechem as capital (I Kings 12:1-25); built centers of worship with golden calves at Dan and Bethel (I Kings 12:25-33); downfall foretold by the prophet Ahijah (I Kings 13,14).

JEROBOAM II (jĕr-ò-bō'ăm), 13th king of Israel (c. 785-754 B. C.); son and successor of Jehoash, king of Israel; successful in war with adjacent nations, and extended territory of Israel; moral corruption and idolatry prevalent during his reign; contemporary prophets: Hosea, Joel, Jonah, Amos; succeeded by son Zechariah (II Kings 14:23-29).

JEROHAM (jē-rō'hăm, may he be pitied). 1. Grandfather of Samuel (I Sam. 1:1). 2. Benjamite (I Chron. 8:27). 3. Another Benjamite (may be same as preceding) (I Chron. 9:8). 4. Priest (I Chron. 9:12; Neh. 11:12). 5. Father of two of David's recruits at Ziklag (I Chron. 12:7). 6. Father of Azarel (I Chron. 27:22). 7. Father of Azariah (II Chron. 23:1).

JERUBBAAL (See Gideon).

JERUBBESHETH (See Gideon).

JERUEL (jĕ-rŏŏ'ĕl), wilderness in vicinity of En-gedi (II Chron. 20:16).

JERUSALEM (jĕ-rŏŏ'sȧ-lĕm, name probably means peace), city 33 miles E of Mediterranean and 14 miles W of Dead Sea, on a rocky plateau 2550 feet high; average temperature, 63 degrees; Kidron Valley on E side, Valley of Hinnom (Gehenna) on W and S sides, and Tyropoeon Valley passes through the city running N and S; E of the Kidron Valley are Gethsemane and the Mount of Olives; the city is supplied with water from springs and wells, with water stored in reservoirs built in the city; hills in the city: Western, Temple, Ophel, and Mt. Acra; ancient Jebusite city located on hill S of Ophel (SE corner of Jerusalem) and was 1250 by 400 feet (I Chron. 11:4-8); walls of the city extended northward and southward several times; present walls date from Suleiman the Magnificent (A. D. 1542); temple stood on Mt. Zion (Rock Moriah); same as the Salem of Melchizedek (Gen. 14:18); also called Salen (Ps. 76:2), Jebus (Judg. 19:10,11), "City of David," Zion (I Kings 8:1; II Kings 14:20); City of Judah (II Chron. 25:28), City of God (Ps. 46:4); city of Great King (Ps. 48:2); Holy City (Neh. 11:1).

JERUSALEM, NEW, city of God referred to in Rev. 3:12 and Rev. 21:2 as coming down out of heaven from God. Gal. 4:26 describes the New Jerusalem as the mother of believers.

JERUSHA, JERUSHAH (jĕ-rŏŏ'shȧ), wife of King Uzziah and mother of King Jotham (II Kings 15:33; II Chron. 27:1).

JESAIAH, JESHAIAH (jĕ-sā'yȧ, jĕ-shā'yȧ). 1. Musician in David's reign (I Chron. 25:3,15). 2. Levite (I Chron. 26:25). 3. Grandson of Zerubbabel (I Chron. 3:21). 4. Son of Athaliah (Ezra 8:7). 5. Descendant of Merari (Ezra 8:19). 6. Benjamite (Neh. 11:7).

JESHANAH (jĕsh'ȧ-nȧ or Je-shȧ'na), town near Bethel, in Ephraim (II Chron. 13:19).

JESHARELAH (jĕsh'ȧ-rē'lȧ), ancestral head of course of musicians (I Chron. 25:14), called Asarelah in verse 2.

JESHEBEAB (jĕ-shĕb'ē-ăb), ancestral head of 14th course of priests (I Chron. 24:13).

JESHER (jĕ'shēr), son of Caleb (I Chron. 2:18).

JESHIMON (jĕ-shī'mŏn), desert area N of Dead Sea (Num. 21:20; 23:28; I Sam. 23: 19,24).

JESHISHAI (jĕ-shĭsh'ȧ-ī), Gadite (I Chron. 5:14).

JESHOHAIAH (jĕsh-ō-hā'yȧ), prince in Simeon (I Chron. 4:36).

JESHUA, JESHUAH (jĕsh'ū-ȧ, Jehovah is salvation). 1. Joshua, son of Nun (Neh. 8:17). 2. Head of 9th course of priests (I Chron. 24:11). 3. Family which returned with Zerubbabel (Ezra 2:6; Neh. 7:11). 4. Levite (II Chron. 31:15). 5. High priest who

returned with Zerubbabel (Ezra 2:2; Neh. 7:7), called "Joshua" in Hag. 1:1 and Zech. 3:1ff. 6. Leading Levitical family (Ezra 2:40; 3:9; Neh. 7:43). 7. Town in S of Judah (Neh. 11:26).

JESHURUN, JESURUN (jĕsh'ū-rŭn, jĕs'ū-rŭn, upright one), poetical or ideal title of Israel; usually used as title of honor (Deut. 33:5,26; Isa. 44:2).

JESIAH (jĕ-sī'ȧ). See Isshiah.

JESIMIEL (jĕ-sĭm'ĭ-ĕl), prince of Simeon (I Chron. 4:36).

JESSE (jĕs'ē), grandson of Boaz (Ruth 4:18-22); son of Obed; father of David (I Sam. 17:12-14); lived at Bethlehem.

JESUI (jĕs'ū-ī), or sometimes Isui, or Ishuai. 1. Asherite (Gen. 46:17; Num. 26:44; I Chron. 7:30). 2. Son of Saul (I Sam. 14:49).

JESUS, JESUS CHRIST (See Christ).

JETHER (jē'thēr, abundance). 1. In Exod. 4:18 KJVm, for Jethro, father-in-law of Moses. 2. Gideon's eldest son (Judg. 8: 20,21). 3. Father of Amasa (I Chron. 2:17). 4. Judahite (I Chron. 2:32). 5. Judahite (I Chron. 4:17). 6. Asherite, same as Ithran(?) (cf. I Chron. 7:37 with vs. 38).

JETHETH (jē'thĕth), Edomite chieftain Gen. 36:40; I Chron. 1:51).

JETHLAH (jĕth'lȧ), town of Dan (Josh. 19:42).

JETHRO (jĕth'rō, excellence), priest of Midian and father-in-law of Moses (Exod. 3:1); personal name probably Reuel (Exod. 2:18; 3:1); father of Zipporah, whom Moses married (Exod. 3:1,2); advised Moses (Exod. 18:14-24).

JETUR (jē'tēr), son of Ishmael and descendants (Gen. 25:15; I Chron. 1:31); Itureans of NT times.

JEUEL (jē-ū'ĕl). 1. Judahite (I Chron. 9:6). 2. Levite (II Chron. 29:13, Jeiel). 3. Leader in Ezra's company (Ezra 8:13), Jeiel in KJV.

JEUSH (jē'ŭsh). 1. Son of Esau (Gen. 36:5). 2. Benjamite (I Chron. 7:10). 3. Gershonite Levite (I Chron. 23:10,11). 4. Descendant of Jonathan (I Chron. 8:39), Jehush in KJV. 5. Son of Rehoboam (II Chron. 11:19).

JEUZ (jē'ŭz), Benjamite (I Chron. 8:10).

JEW (jōō), after division of kingdom the word denoted a member of the S kingdom in contrast to a member of N kingdom; after Babylonian Captivity, all Hebrews were called Jews (Matt. 27:11; Acts 2:5).

JEWEL, JEWELRY. Articles of jewelry in OT times: diadems, bracelets, necklaces, anklets, rings for fingers, gold nets for hair, pendants, head-tire gems, amulets and pendants with magical meanings, jeweled perfume and ointment boxes, crescents for camels; used for personal adornment and utility and for religious festivals. Not much said about jewelry in NT; most condemnatory (I Tim. 2:9; James 2:2). The New Jerusalem is adorned with jewels (Rev. 21:19).

JEZANIAH (jĕz-ȧ-nī'ȧ), Maacathite captain when Jerusalem fell (II Kings 25:23; Jer.

40:7,8).

JEZEBEL (jĕz'ĕ-bĕl), daughter of Ethbaal, priest of Astarte, king of Tyre and Sidon; wife of Ahab, king of Israel (c. 874-853 B. C.); killed prophets of Jehovah (I Kings 18:13); opposed Elijah (I Kings 19:1,2); caused murder of Naboth (I Kings 21); slain by Jehu (II Kings 9:30-37). In Rev. 2:20 a symbol of spiritual fornication.

JEZER (jĕ'zĕr), Naphtalite founder of a tribal family (Gen. 46:24; Num. 26:49; I Chron. 7:13).

JEZIAH (jĕ-zī'à), man who put away foreign wife (Ezra 10:25).

JEZIEL (jĕ'zi-ĕl), Benjamite (I Chron. 12:3).

JEZLIAH (jĕz-lī'à), Benjamite (I Chron. 8:18).

JEZOAR (jĕ-zō'ĕr), Judahite (I Chron. 4: 5-7).

JEZRAHIAH (jĕz-rà-hī'à). 1. Descendant of Issachar called Izrahiah (I Chron. 7:3). 2. Musician (Neh. 12:42).

JEZREEL (jĕz're-ĕl, **God sows**). 1. City on border of Issachar, 5 miles N of Jerusalem (Josh. 19:18; I Sam. 29:1). 2. Town in hill country of Judah (I Sam. 25:43; 27:3). 3. Judahite (I Chron. 4:3). 4. Son of prophet Hosea (Hos. 1:4,5).

JIBSAM (jib'săm), descendant of Issachar (I Chron. 7:2).

JIDLAPH (jid'lăf), son of Nahor and Milcah (Gen. 22:22).

JIMNA (jĭm'nà), son of Asher (Num. 26:44).

JIPHTAH (jif'tà), unidentified town in Shephelah of Judah (Josh. 15:43).

JIPHTHAH-EL (jif'thà-ĕl), valley on N border of Zebulun (Josh. 19:14,27).

JOAB (jō'ăb, **Jehovah is father**). 1. Son of Zeruiah, the half-sister of David (II Sam. 2:18); brother of Asahel and Abishai (I Chron. 2:16); slew Abner (II Sam. 3:22-39); became David's commander-in-chief (I Chron. 11:4-9); defeated Syria, Edom, Ammon (II Sam. 10-12); brought about murder of Uriah (II Sam. 11); killed Absalom (II Sam. 18:9-15) and Amasa (II Sam. 20:4-13); supported Adonijah (I Kings 1); killed at order of Solomon (I Kings 2:28-34). 2. Judahite (I Chron. 4:14). 3. Founder of family of returned exiles (Ezra 2:6; 8:9; Neh. 7:11). 4. Village, apparently in Judah (I Chron. 2:54). In KJV name is "Ataroth, the house of Joab."

JOAH (jō'à). 1. Son of Obed-edom (I Chron. 26:4). 2. Levite (I Chron. 6:21). 3. Recorder under King Hezekiah (II Kings 18:18, 26; Isa. 36:3,11,22). 4. Recorder under King Josiah (II Chron. 34:8).

JOAHAZ (jō'à-hăz), father of Joah, recorder of King Josiah (II Chron. 34:8).

JOANNA (jō-ăn'à). 1. Wife of Chuza, Herod's steward (Luke 8:2,3). 2. Ancestor of Christ (Luke 3:27). Lived c. 500 B. C.

JOASH, I (jō'ăsh, **Jehovah has given**), shorter form of "Jehoash." 1. Father of Gideon (Judg. 6:11). 2. Son of Ahab (I Kings 22:26; II Chron. 18:25). 3. Benjamite (I Chron. 12:3). 4. Judahite (I Chron. 4:22). 5. Son of Ahaziah, king of Judah; became

8th king and ruled 40 years; first restored religion of Jehovah, then apostatized; had Zechariah murdered; murdered by servants (II Kings 12:20; II Chron. 24:25). 6. Son of Jehoahaz, called also Jehoash, king of Israel; reigned c. 800-784 B. C.; friendly to Elisha the prophet; succeeded by son, Jeroboam II (II Kings 13:10-13; II Chron. 26:17).

JOASH, II (jō'ăsh). 1. Benjamite (I Chron. 7:8). 2. Officer of David (I Chron. 27:28).

JOATHAM (jō'à-thăm), son of Uzziah; king of Judah (Matt. 1:9).

JOB (jōb, meaning uncertain), chief character of Book of Job, one of the wisdom books of the OT and great literary masterpiece, written in form of poetry; author unknown and date unknown, but many scholars favor Solomonic age; deals with justice of God in His dealings with human beings. Outline: 1. Prologue (1,2). 2. Job's complaint (3). 3. Debates between Job and three friends (4-31). 4. Speech of Elihu (32-37). 5. Voice of God (38-41). Job's submission and restoration (42).

JOBAB (jō'băb, howl). 1. Son of Joktan (Gen. 10:29; I Chron. 1:23). 2. 2nd king of Edom (Gen. 36:33; I Chron. 1:44,45). 3. King of Madon (Josh. 11:1; 12:19). 4. Benjamite (I Chron. 8:9). 5. Benjamite (I Chron. 8:18).

JOCHEBED (jŏk'ĕ-bĕd), daughter of Levi, wife of Amram and mother of Moses (Exod. 6:20; Num. 26:59).

JOED (jō'ĕd), Benjamite (Neh. 11:7).

JOEL (jō'ĕl, **Jehovah is God**). 1. Author of 2nd of Minor Prophets books. Nothing is known of his life. See Joel, Book of. 2. Son of Samuel (I Sam. 8:2; I Chron. 6:33). 3. Simeonite prince (I Chron. 4:35). 4. Reubenite chief (I Chron. 5:4-8). 5. Gadite chief (I Chron. 5:12). 6. Ancestor of Samuel (I Chron. 6:36). 7. Chief of Issachar (I Chron. 7:3). 8. One of David's mighty men (I Chron. 11:38). 9. Levite (I Chron. 15: 7,11,17). 10. Officer of David (I Chron. 27:20). 11. Levite (II Chron. 29:12). 12. Man who married foreign wife (Ezra 10:43). 13. Benjamite overseer (Neh. 11:9).

JOEL, BOOK OF (jō'ĕl). Dates suggested range from c. 830 to 350 B. C.; no clear indication in book of time of writing; background of book a locust plague, regarded by prophet as punishment for sin, causes him to urge nation to repent of its sins and predict a worse visitation, the future Day of the Lord. Outline: 1. Locust plague and its removal (1:1-2:27). 2. Future day of the Lord (2:28-3:21). a. Spirit of God to be poured out (2:28-32); b. judgment of the nations (3:1-17); c. blessing upon Israel following judgment (3:18-21).

JOELAH (jō-e'là), one of David's recruits at Ziklag (I Chron. 12:7).

JOEZER (jōè'zĕr), one of David's soldiers (I Chron. 12:6).

JOGBEHAH (jŏg'beà), city in Gilead assigned to Gad (Num. 32:35; Judg. 8:11).

JOGLI (jŏg'lī), Danite (Num. 34:22).

JOHA (jō'hà). 1. Benjamite (I Chron. 8:16).

2. One of David's mighty men (I Chron. 11:45).

JOHANAN (jō-hā′năn, Jehovah has been gracious). 1. Jewish leader who tried to save Gedaliah from plot to murder him (Jer. 40:13,14); took Jews, including Jeremiah, to Egypt (Jer. 40-43). 2. Son of King Josiah (I Chron. 3:15). 3. Son of Elioenai (I Chron. 3:24). 4. Father of Azariah, high priest in Solomon's time (I Chron. 6:9,10). 5. Benjamite; joined David at Ziklag (I Chron. 12:4). 6. Gadite; captain in David's army (I Chron. 12:12,14). 7. Ephraimite chief (II Chron. 28:12). 8. One of those who left Babylon with Ezra (Ezra 8:12). 9. Son of Tobiah, who married a Jewess in days of Nehemiah (Neh. 6:18). 10. Son of Eliashib (Ezra 10:6). 11. High priest, grandson of Eliashib (Neh. 12:22).

JOHN (jŏn, Jehovah has been gracious). 1. John the Baptist (q.v.). 2. The apostle, the son of Zebedee, and brother of James. (See JOHN, THE APOSTLE). 3. John Mark (q.v.). 4. Father of Simon Peter (John 1:42; 21:15,17, called Jonas in KJV). 5. Jewish religious dignitary who called Peter and John to account for their preaching about Jesus (Acts 4:6). 6. Father of Mattathias (I Macc. 2:1). 7. Eldest son of Mattathias (I Macc. 9:36). 8. Father of Eupolemus (I Macc. 8:17; II Macc. 4:11). 9. John Hyrcanus, son of Simon (I Macc. 13:53; 16:1). 10. Jewish envoy (II Macc. 11:17).

JOHN, THE APOSTLE. Son of Zebedee and Salome, and brother of James (Matt. 4:21; 27:56; Mark 15:40; Acts 12:1,2); lived in Galilee, probably in Bethsaida (Luke 5:10; John 1:44); fisherman (Mark 1:19,20); became disciple of Jesus through John the Baptist (John 1:35); called as apostle (Mark 1:19,20; Luke 5:10); one of three apostles closest to Jesus (others, Peter and James); at raising of Jairus' daughter (Mark 5:37; Luke 8:51); transfiguration (Matt. 17:1; Mark 9:2; Luke 9:28); Gethsemane (Matt. 26:37; Mark 14:33); asked Jesus to call fire down on Samaritans, and given name Boanerges (sons of thunder) (Mark 3:17; Luke 9:54); mother requested that John and James be given places of special honor in coming kingdom (Mark 10:35); helped Peter prepare Passover (Luke 22:8); lay close to Jesus' breast at Last Supper (John 13:25); present at trial of Jesus (John 18:15,16); witnessed crucifixion of Jesus (John 19: 26,27); recognized Jesus at Sea of Galilee (John 21:1-7); active with Peter in Apostolic church (Acts 3:1-4:22; 8:14-17). Lived to old age; 4th Gospel, three epistles, and Revelation attributed to him.

JOHN THE BAPTIST (jŏn băp′tĭst), forerunner of Jesus; son of Zacharias and Elizabeth, both of priestly descent (Luke 1:5-25, 56-58); lived as Nazirite in desert (Luke 1:15; Matt. 11:12-14,18); began ministry beyond Jordan in 15th year of Tiberias Caesar (Luke 3:1-3); preached baptism of repentance in preparation of coming of Mes-

siah (Luke 3:4-14); baptized Jesus (Matt. 3:13-17; Mark 1:9,10; Luke 3:21; John 1:32); bore witness to Jesus as Messiah (John 1:24-42); imprisoned and put to death by Herod Antipas (Matt. 14:6-12; Mark 6:17-28); praised by Jesus (Matt. 11:7-14); Luke 7: 24-28); disciples loyal to him long after his death (Acts 18:25).

JOHN, EPISTLES OF. The First Epistle of John. Evidently written by author of 4th Gospel; date uncertain, but apparently late in 1st century; purpose: to warn readers against false teachers (Gnostic) and exhort them to hold fast to Christian faith and fulfill Christian duties, especially love; false teachers called anti-Christs (2:18,22; 4:3); plan of Epistle is difficult to follow, but thoughts repeated often are the necessity of doing righteousness as an evidence of divine sonship, the necessity of love for the brethren, and believing that Jesus is the Christ come in the flesh.

The Second Epistle of John. Written to exhort readers to hold fast to the commandments which they had received, to warn against false teachers who deny that Christ is come in the flesh, and to tell them that he will soon visit them. "Elect lady" may be woman or church.

The Third Epistle of John. Addressed to Gaius to commend him for his Christian life and hospitality to evangelists sent by John and to censure Diotrephes for his bad conduct.

JOHN, THE GOSPEL OF. Early tradition and internal evidence of the Gospel show that this book was written by the apostle John. Early tradition also places the writing of the book sometime toward the close of the 1st century A. D., in Asia Minor. The author states his purpose in 20:30,31: to show that Jesus is the Christ, the Son of God, and that those believing this might have life in His name. Some of the characteristics which distinguish the Gospel from the others are: an emphasis on the deity of Christ; stress upon the King rather than upon the kingdom; non-parabolic teaching; emphasis upon the coming and work of the Holy Spirit. Outline: 1. Incarnate Word (1:1-18). 2. Testimony to Jesus' Messiahship (1:19-2:11). 3. Christ's self-revelation through words and deeds (2:12-12:50). 4. Christ's self-revelation in His crucifixion and resurrection (13-21).

JOHN MARK (See Mark).

JOIADA (joi′á-dá, Jehovah knows). 1. Repaired walls of Jerusalem (Neh. 3:6; in KJV Jehoiada). 2. Son of Eliashib (Neh. 12:10; 13:28).

JOIAKIM (joi′á-kĭm), father of Eliashib (Neh. 12:10,12,26).

JOIARIB (joi′á-rĭb). 1. Teacher in Ezra's time (Ezra 8:16). 2. Judahite (Neh. 11:5). 3. Priest who returned with Zerubbabel (Neh. 12:6,7).

JOKDEAM (jŏk′dā-ăm), town in Judah (Josh. 15:56).

JOKIM (jō′kĭm), Judahite (I Chron. 4:22).

JOKMEAM (jŏk'mē-ăm), town in Ephraim (I Chron. 6:68). KJV wrongly has Jokneam in I Kings 4:12, ASV.

JOKNEAM (jŏk'nē-ăm), town in or near Mt. Carmel (Josh. 12:22).

JOKSHAN (jŏk'shăn), son of Abraham and Keturah (Gen. 25:2,3).

JOKTAN (jŏk'tăn), tribe descended from Shem (Gen. 10:25,26,29; I Chron.1:19,20,23).

JOKTHEEL (jŏk'thē-ĕl), 1. Town in Judah (Josh. 15:38). 2. Place in Edom, probably Petra (II Kings 14:7).

JONA (See Jonah, Jonas).

JONADAB (jŏn'à-dăb). 1. Son of Shimeah (II Sam. 13:3). 2. Son of Rechab (II Kings 10:15ff).

JONAH (jō'nà, dove). 1. Prophet of Israel; son of Amittai; predicted victory over Syria through Jeroboam II, who reigned 790-750 B. C.; author of Book of Jonah (II Kings 14:25; Jonah 1:1).

JONAH, BOOK OF, written to show that God's gracious purposes are not limited to Israel, but extend to the Gentile world; a great work on foreign missions (4:11); while found among the Minor Prophets, there is little prophecy in it. Outline: 1. Jonah's commission, disobedience, and punishment (1:1-16). 2. Jonah's deliverance (1:17-2:10). 3. Jonah preaches; Nineveh repents and is spared (3). 4. God's mercy defended (4).

JONAN (jō'năn), ancestor of Jesus (Luke 3:30).

JONAS (jō'nàs). 1. Prophet Jonah (Matt. 12:39-41; 16:4; Luke 11:29-32). 2. Name given in KJV to the father of Apostle Peter in John 21:15,16. In John 1:42 KJV has Jona.

JONATH-ELEM-RECHOKIM, UPON (jō'năth ē'lĕm rē-hō'kĭm), probably the melody to which Ps. 56 was written.

JONATHAN (jŏn'à-thăn, Jehovah has given). 1. Levite; became priest of Micah in Ephraim, and later of Danites (Judg. 17,18). 2. Son of King Saul. See separate article, following. 3. Son of high priest Abiathar (II Sam. 15:27,36; 17:17,20; I Kings 1:42,43). 4. Son of Shimea (II Sam. 21:21). 5. One of David's mighty men (II Sam. 23:32). 6. Son of Uzziah (I Chron. 27:25). 7. Jerahmeelite (I Chron. 2:32,33). 8. David's "uncle" (I Chron. 27:32). 9. Father of Ebed (Ezra 8:6). 10. Son of Asahel (Ezra 10:15). 11. Priest (Neh. 12:11). 12. Priest (Neh. 12:14). 13. Levite (Neh. 12:35). 14. Scribe (Jer. 37:15,20). 15. Son of Kareah (Jer. 40:8). 16. Son of Mattathias (I Macc. 2:5; 9-13). 17. Son of Absalom (I Macc. 13:11). 18. Priest (II Macc. 1:23).

JONATHAN, son of Saul, king of Israel (I Sam. 13:16; 14:49; I Chron. 8:33); defeated Philistines in battle (I Sam. 13,14); loyal friend of David, friendship with whom has become symbol of noblest love for another, and for whom he risked his own life (I Sam. 19:1-7;20); killed by Philistines with Saul at Mt. Gilboa (I Sam. 31:2-10).

JOPPA (jŏp'pà), once in KJV Japho (Josh. 19:46); ancient walled town on coast of Palestine, c. 35 miles NW of Jerusalem; assigned to Dan; mentioned in Amarna letters; seaport for Jerusalem. In NT times Peter there raised Dorcas to life (Acts 9:36f) and received vision of sheet filled with animals (Acts 10:1ff; 11:5ff). Now called Jaffa.

JORAH (jō'rà), family which returned with Zerubbabel (Ezra 2:18). Called Hariph in Neh. 7:24.

JORAI (jō'rā-ī), Gadite (I Chron. 5:13).

JORAM (jō'răm), same as longer form Jehoram. 1. Son of king of Hamath (II Sam. 8:10). 2. Levite (I Chron. 26:25). 3. Son of Ahab, king of Israel (II Kings 8:29). 4. King of Judah (II Kings 8:21-24; 11:2; I Chron. 3:11; Matt. 1:8). 5. Priest (II Chron. 17:8).

JORDAN RIVER (jôr'd'n, descender), most important river of Palestine; flows through a rift extending from Lebanon to the Dead Sea (and beyond); very circuitous, so that although the distance from the Sea of Galilee to the Dead Sea is 70 miles, the river is 200 miles in length; valley through which it runs is 160 miles long, 2 to 15 miles wide, and at the Dead Sea is 1300 feet below sea level; 3 to 10 feet deep and c. 100 feet wide (Gen. 13:10; Josh. 2:7; Judg. 3:28; Matt. 3:13). Important events associated with Jordan: Israel crossing under Joshua (Josh. 3), work of John the Baptist (Matt. 3:6; Mark 1:5), baptism of Jesus (Matt. 3:13; Mark 1:9).

JORIM (jō'rĭm), ancestor of Jesus (Luke 3:29).

JORKOAM (jôr'kō-ăm), place in Judah; ASV, Jorkeam (I Chron. 2:44).

JOSABAD, JOZABAD (jŏs'à-băd, jŏz'à-băd). 1. Recruit of David at Ziklag (I Chron. 12:4). 2. Two Manassites (I Chron. 12:20). 3. Levite (II Chron. 31:13). 4. Levite (Ezra 8:33). 5. Priest who put away foreign wife (Ezra 10:22).

JOSEPH (jō'zĕf, may God add). 1. Son of Jacob and Rachel (Gen. 30:22-24); Jacob's favorite child (Gen. 37:3,4); sold into Egypt by his brothers (Gen. 37); imprisoned for resisting temptation of Potiphar's wife (Gen. 39); promoted by Pharaoh to position next to the king because of interpreting dreams (Gen. 40,41); saved Egypt and his own family from famine (Gen. 42-45); settled family in Egypt (Gen. 47); bones brought to Shechem; ancestor of two tribes Manasseh and Ephraim. Man of great nobility of character; magnanimous; forgiving; faithful to duty. 2. Issacharite; father of one of 12 spies (Num. 13:7). 3. Head of course of musicians (I Chron. 25:2,9). 4. Man who divorced foreign wife (Ezra 10:42). 5. Priest (Neh. 12:14). 6. Three ancestors of Jesus (Luke 3:24,26,30). 7. Son of Zacharias (I Macc. 5:18,55-62). 8. Husband of Mary, mother of Jesus (Matt. 1:16; Luke 3:23); carpenter (Matt. 13:55); lived in Nazareth (Luke 2:4); Davidic descent (Matt. 1:20); went to Bethlehem with Mary for census, and Jesus born there (Luke 2:4-6);

took Jesus and Mary to Egypt (Matt. 2: 13-18); took 12-year old Jesus to Jerusalem (Luke 41-45). 9. One of the brethren of Jesus (Matt. 13:55). KJV has "Joses." 10. Jew of Arimathaea; member of Sanhedrin (Matt. 27:57; Mark 15:43); secret disciple of Jesus (John 19:38); had Jesus buried in his own tomb (Matt. 25:57-60; Luke 23:50-53; John 19:38). 11. Christian considered by apostles to replace Judas Iscariot (Acts 1:21,23,26). 12. Personal name of Barnabas (Acts 4:36; in KJV Joses).

JOSEPH BARSABAS (jŏ'sĕf bàr-sàb'ăs), early disciple of Christ considered by apostle to take place of Judas Iscariot. Matthias was chosen (Acts 1:21,26).

JOSES (jŏ'sĕz). 1. One of brethren of Jesus (Mark 6:3). 2. Name of Barnabas (Acts 4:36).

JOSHAH (jŏ'shà), descendant of Simeon (I Chron. 4:34).

JOSHAPHAT (jŏsh'à-făt). 1. One of David's mighty men (I Chron. 11:43). 2. Priest (I Chron. 15:24), Jehoshaphat in KJV.

JOSHAVIAH (jŏsh'à-vī'à), son of Alnaam (I Chron. 11:46).

JOSHBEKASHAH (jŏsh'bē-kā'shà), leader of the 17th course of musicians (I Chron. 25:4,24).

JOSHEB-BASSEBET (jŏ'shĕ-bà'sĕ-bĕt), one of David's mighty men (II Sam. 23:8 ASV), probably corruption of Jashobeam, as in I Chron. 11:11.

JOSHUA (jŏsh'ū-à, **Lord is salvation**. Later **Jeshua, Jesus**). 1. Ephraimite, son of Nun (I Chron. 7:27); assistant of Moses; repulsed Amalekite attack (Exod. 17:9); one of 12 spies (Num. 13:8); succeeded Moses (Deut. 31; Josh. 1); entered, conquered, and apportioned Canaan (Joshua); buried at Timnath-serah (Josh. 24:29). KJV has Jesus in Acts 7:45; Heb. 4:8. 2. Native of Bethshemesh (I Sam. 6:14). 3. Governor of Jerusalem (II Kings 23:8). 4. High priest who returned with Zerubbabel, called Jeshua (Ezra 2:2; 3:2-9; Neh. 7:7).

JOSHUA, BOOK OF, 6th book of Bible; first of "historical books" in English, but first of prophets in Heb. OT. Tells how Joshua, Moses' successor, conquered Canaan, as promised by God (Josh. 1:1; 24:31). Author not named; date uncertain, but probably prior to 1200 B. C. Outline: 1. Conquest of Canaan (1-12). 2. Apportionment of territory to tribes (13-22). 3. Joshua's farewell address (22-24).

JOSIAH (jŏ-sī'à, **Jehovah supports him**). 1. 16th king of Judah; son and successor of Amon; ascended throne when eight years old, and ruled 31 years (c. 640-609 B. C.); outstanding righteous ruler; suppressed idolatry; repaired temple; found book of Law and had it publicly read; defeated in battle and killed by Pharaoh Necho at Megiddo (II Kings 22,23; II Chron. 34,35). KJV had Josias in Matt. 1:10,11. 2. Son of Zephaniah (Zech. 6:10), may be same as Hen of v. 14.

JOSIBIAH (jŏs'ĭ-bī'à), Simeonite (I Chron.

4:35).

JOSIPHIAH (jŏs'ĭ-fī'à), ancestor of family which returned with Ezra (Ezra 8:10).

JOT (jŏt), smallest letter of Heb. alphabet, similar to our apostrophe sign, '. Used figuratively for something of apparently small moment (Matt. 5:17,18).

JOTBAH (jŏt'bà), Levitical city in Judah, just S of Hebron (II Kings 21:19).

JOTBATH (jŏt'băth), encampment of Israel (Deut. 10:7).

JOTBATHAH (jŏt'bà-thà), encampment of Israel (Num. 33:33,34; Deut. 10:7). KJV has Jotbath in Deut. 10:7.

JOTHAM (jŏ'thăm, **Jehovah is perfect**). 1. Son of Gideon; speaker of the 1st Bible parable (Judg. 9:5-57). 2. Judahite (I Chron. 2:47). 3. Eleventh king of Judah; son of Uzziah, whose regent he was for a time; successful, righteous king (II Kings 15: 5-38; II Chron. 27); contemporary of Isaiah (Isa. 1:1), Hosea (Hos. 1:1), Micah (Mic. 1:1); ancestor of Jesus (Matt. 1:9, KJV has Joatham).

JOURNEY, SABBATH DAY'S, 3000 feet (Acts 1:12).

JOY, emotion excited by expectation or acquisition of good; attribute of God (Ps. 104:31); one of the fruits of the Spirit (Gal. 5:22,23,24); not the same as happiness, which depends largely on happenings, as it may be experienced even in affliction (II Cor. 13:9; Col. 1:11; James 1:2; I Peter 1:8).

JOZABAD (jŏz'à-băd, **Jehovah endows**). 1. Gederathite; joined David at Ziklag (I Chron. 12:4, Josabad in KJV). 2. Two Manassites who also joined David (I Chron. 12:20). 3. Levites (II Chron. 31:13). 4. Chief Levite (II Chron. 35:9). 5. Levite who assisted Ezra (Ezra 8:33). 6. Man who put foreign wife away (Ezra 10:22). 7. Another such man (Ezra 10:23). 8. Levite who helped Nehemiah (Neh. 8:7). 9. Chief Levite in Nehemiah's time (Neh. 11:16).

JOZACHAR (jŏz'à-kàr), assassin of Joash, king of Judah (II Kings 12:20,21; II Chron. 24:26).

JOZADAK (jŏz'à-dăk), father of priest who returned with Zerubbabel (Ezra 3:2, etc.). Called Josedech in Haggai and Zechariah.

JUBAL (jōō'băl), son of Lamech; inventor of harp and pipe (Gen. 4:21).

JUBILEE (jōō'bĭ-lē, **trumpet**), celebrated by Israelites every 50 years; announced by blowing of trumpet. Features: Israelite slaves freed from bondage; ancestral lands returned to original owner; land lay fallow that year (Lev. 25).

JUBILEES, BOOK OF, Jewish apocalyptic book written in inter-testamental period.

JUCAL (jōō'kăl), prince who put Jeremiah in prison (Jer. 38:1).

JUDA (See Judah).

JUDAEA (See Judea).

JUDAH (jōō'dà, **praised**). 1. Son of Jacob and Leah (Gen. 29:35); saved Joseph's life (Gen. 37:26-28); had twin sons by Tamar

(Gen. 38:12-30); leader among brothers (Gen. 43:3; 46:28; 49:8-12); received blessing of Jacob (Gen. 49:9,10); ancestor of David (Ruth 4:18-22) and of Christ (Matt. 1:3-16). 2. Hebrew tribe descended from Judah, Jacob's son; acquired most of S Palestine (Josh. 15:20-63); prominent throughout history of Israel. Well-known Judahites: Caleb (Num. 13:6; 34:19), Othniel (Judg. 3:8-11); David and Solomon (I Sam. 17:12). KJV has Juda in NT. 3. Name of five individuals mentioned in Ezra-Nehemiah, not all from same tribe: Ezra 3:9; 10:23; Neh. 11:9; 12:8; 12:34.

JUDAH, KINGDOM OF, began when 10 N tribes withdrew from Rehoboam (c. 912) and lasted until Jerusalem fell in 587 B. C.; 50 years later Cyrus, king of Persia, permitted the Jews to return (I Kings 12-22; II Kings; II Chron. 11-36; Ezra; Nehemiah). Consisted of tribes of Judah and Benjamin. One dynasty ruled throughout.

JUDAISM (jōō'dà-iz'm), the religious system held by the Jews. Its teachings come from the OT.

JUDAS, JUDA (jōō'dàs, jōō'dà, **praised**). 1. Ancestor of Christ (Luke 3:30 ASV). 2. Galilean insurrectionist (Acts 5:37). 3. Brother of our Lord (Matt. 13:55). 4. Apostle (Luke 6:16). 5. Man with whom Paul lodged (Acts 9:11). 6. Barsabbas; leading Jerusalem Christian (Acts 15:22,27,32).

JUDAS ISCARIOT ("man of Kerioth"); probably from S of Judah; chosen apostle (Matt. 10:4; Mark 3:19; Luke 6:16); treasurer of apostolic company (John 12:6; 13:29); covetous for money (Matt. 26:6-13); betrayed Jesus (Matt. 26:47-49); hanged himself (Matt. 27:3-5; Acts 1:17,18).

JUDAS BARSABAS (See Judas).

JUDAS OF GALILEE (See Judas).

JUDE (jōōd), writer of last of NT epistles; brother of James (1:1); probably brother of Jesus (Mark 6:3).

JUDE, EPISTLE OF; author calls himself brother of James; both probably brothers of Jesus, and did not accept His claims until after the resurrection. Date: prior to A. D. 81. Occasion for writing: appearance of an alarming heresy with immoral tendencies, perhaps Gnosticism. Outline: 1. Introduction (1-4). 2. Condemnation of false teachers (5-16). 3. Admonitions (17-23). 4. Doxology (24,25).

JUDEA, JUDAEA (jōō-dē'à), term used for Palestine province to which tribes of Judah and Benjamin returned from Babylonian captivity (Ezra 5:8; 9:9). Since most of the exiles belonged to the tribe of Judah, they came to be called Jews and their land Judea. Under Romans it was ruled by a procurator, whose immediate superior was the proconsul of Syria, and whose official residence was Caesarea. Geographically c. 55 miles N to S, and about the same distance E and W; from Mediterranean to the Dead Sea, and Joppa to S portion of Dead Sea (Luke 3:1).

JUDGE, a civil magistrate; Moses organized judiciary of Israel (Exod. 18:13-26; Deut. 1:9-17); prophets complained about courts corrupted by bribery (Isa. 1:23; Amos 5:12; Micah 3:11).

JUDGES, THE, leaders and deliverers of Israelites from death of Joshua to king Saul (Othniel, Ehud, Shamgar, Deborah, Barak, Gideon, Abimelech, Tola, Jair, Jephthah, Ibzan, Elon, Abdon, Samson). Eli the high priest and Samuel the prophet also functioned as judges. See Book of Judges.

JUDGES, BOOK OF. Seventh book of the OT; takes its title from the men who ruled Israel from death of Joshua to Samuel, their principal function being that of military deliverers to the oppressed Hebrews; no claim to authorship in book, and no clear indication of date of writing of book; covers period of c. 300 years. Outline: 1. Introduction (1:1-2:10). 2. Main body of book, describing cycles of failure, oppression, and relief by judges. Activities of 13 judges described (2:11-16:31). 3. Appendix (17-21).

JUDGMENT (jŭj'mĕnt), referring in Bible sometimes to the pronouncing of a formal opinion or decision by men, but more often to a calamity regarded as sent by God, by way of punishment, or a sentence of God as the judge of all. The history of Israel is the story of a succession of judgments upon enemies of God's people and upon His covenant nation when they flouted His will. "Day of Jehovah" a day of punishment for all the unjust, even those who boast of belonging to the people of the covenant (Isa. 2:12; Amos 5:18; Hos. 5:8,9); purpose of judgment of God's people is their purification, not destruction. Jesus warns against uncharitable judgments (Matt. 7:1); so also Paul (Rom. 14; I Cor. 8-10). Final Judgment referred to in Matt. 11:20-24; 25:31-46; John 16:11; present world will be shaken and destroyed (Matt. 24:29-35); entrusted to Christ (Matt. 3:11,12; John 5:22; Rom. 2:16).

JUDGMENT, DAY OF (See Judgment).

JUDGMENT HALL, palace of governor, as of Pilate (Matt. 27:27; Mark 15:16; John 18:28), or of Herod at Caesarea (Acts 23:35).

JUDGMENT SEAT (platform), bench or seat where a judge sits to hear arguments and pleas and delivers sentence (Matt. 27:19; John 19:13; Acts 18:12). Also refers to judgment seat of Christ before which all believers will stand (Rom. 14:10; II Cor. 5:10).

JUDGMENT, THE LAST (See Judgment).

JUDGMENTS, THE (See Judgment).

JUDGMENTS OF GOD (See Judgment).

JUDITH (jōō'dĭth). 1. Wife of Esau (Gen. 26:34). 2. Heroine of apocryphal book of Judith.

JULIA (jōōl'yà), Christian at Rome to whom Paul sent greetings (Rom. 16:15).

JULIUS (jōōl'yŭs), Roman centurion to whom Paul was entrusted (Acts 27:1,3).

JUNIA, JUNIAS (jōō'nĭ-à, jōō'nĭ-ăs), kinsman and fellow prisoner of Paul (Rom. 16:7).

JUNIPER (See Plants).

JUPITER (jōō'pĭ-tẽr), chief of the Roman gods; called Zeus by Greeks (Acts 14:12, 13; 19:35).

JUSHAB-HESED (jōō-shăb-hē'sĕd), son of Zerubbabel (I Chron. 3:20).

JUSTIFICATION (jŭs'tĭ-fĭ-kā'shŭn, **to absolve, set right**), judicial act of God, by which, on basis of meritorious work of Christ, righteousness is imputed to a re-pentant sinner and received by him through faith, so that the sinner is absolved from his sin, released from its penalty, and restored as righteous. Acts 13:38,39; Rom. 3:24-26; 4:5-8.

JUSTUS (jŭs'tŭs, **just**). 1. Surname of Joseph Barsabas (Acts 1:23-26). 2. Surname of Titus, of Corinth (Acts 18:7). 3. Surname of Jesus, an early Hebrew Christian at Rome (Col. 4:11).

JUTTAH (jŭt'á), town of Judah (Josh. 15: 55; 21:16). Now called Jutta.

K

KAB (See Cab, also Weights and Measures).

KABZEEL (kăb'zĕ-ĕl), city in S Judah near border of Edom (Josh. 15:21). Site unknown. Called Jekabzeel in Neh. 11:25.

KADESH (kā'dĕsh, **be holy**), also known as En-mishpat (Gen. 14:7), place c. 70 miles S of Hebron, in vicinity of which Israel wandered for 37 years (Deut. 1:46; Num. 33:37,38; Deut. 2:14); Miriam died there (Num. 20:1); Moses sent spies to Palestine from there (Num. 13:21-26; Deut. 1:19-25); Moses displeased God there by striking instead of speaking to rock (Num. 20:2-13). Often called Kadesh-barnea (Num. 32:8; Deut. 2:14).

KADESH-BARNEA (See Kadesh).

KADMIEL (kăd'mĭ-ĕl), head of family of Levites who returned with Zerubbabel (Ezra 2:40; Neh. 7:43; 10:9).

KADMONITES (kăd'mŏn-īts), ancient Arab tribe between Egypt and Euphrates (Gen. 15:18-21).

KAIN (kān). 1. Town in Judah (Josh. 15: 57), Cain in KJV. 2. Tribal name; KJV has "Kenite" (Num. 24:22; Judg. 4:11).

KALLAI (kăl'ā-ī), high priest (Neh. 12:20).

KAMON (See Camon).

KANAH (kā'ná). 1. Brook flowing between Ephraim and Manasseh into Mediterranean (Josh. 16:8; 17:9). 2. City c. 8 miles SE of Tyre, near boundary of Manasseh (Josh. 19:28).

KAREAH (ká-rē'á), father of two men who warned Gedaliah of his danger (II Kings 25:23, KJV has Careah; Jer. 40:8).

KARKA (kär'ká), place on S boundary of Judah (Josh. 15:3). KJV has Karkaa.

KARKOR (kär'kŏr), place E of Jordan where Gideon defeated Midianites (Judg. 8:10). Exact location unknown.

KARTAH (kär'tá), city in Zebulun (Josh. 21:34).

KARTAN (kär'tăn), city in Naphtali (Josh. 21:32). Kirjathaim in KJV of I Chron. 6:76.

KEDAR (kē'dẽr). 1. Son of Ishmael (Gen. 25:13). 2. Tribe descended from Kedar; they were nomads (Ps. 120:5; S. of Sol. 1:5).

KEDEMAH (kĕd'ē-má), son of Ishmael (Gen. 25:15).

KEDEMOTH (kĕd'ē-mŏth), place E of Jordan given to Reuben (Num. 21:21-32; Deut. 2:26).

KEDESH (kē'dĕsh). 1. Town in S Judah (Josh. 15:23); city of refuge (Josh. 20:7; 21:32). 2. City of Issachar (I Chron. 6:72). 3. City of refuge in Naphtali NW of Lake Huleh (Josh. 19:37; Barak and Deborah assembled Israelites there (Judg. 4:6-10).

KEDESH NAPHTALI (See Kedesh).

KEDRON (See Kidron).

KEHELATHAH (kē'hē-là'thá), encampment of Israelites (Num. 33:22,23).

KEILAH (kē-ī'lá). 1. City in Shepheleh rescued from Philistines by David (Josh. 15:44; I Sam. 23:1-13). 2. Descendant of Caleb (I Chron. 4:19).

KELAIAH (kē-lā'yá), also Kelita; Levite who divorced foreign wife (Ezra 10:23).

KELITA (See Kelaiah).

KEMUEL (kĕm'ū-ĕl). 1. Son of Nahor; uncle of Laban and Rebekah (Gen. 22:21). 2. Prince of Ephraim (Num. 34:24). 3. Father of Hashabiah, leading Levite (I Chron. 27:17).

KENAN (kē'năn), great-grandson of Adam (I Chron. 1:2). In KJV of Gen. 5:9-14 Cainan.

KENATH (kē'năth), Amorite city in region of Bashan in kingdom of Og (Num. 32:42; I Chron. 2:22,23).

KENAZ (kē'năz). 1. Grandson of Esau (Gen. 36:11,15). 2. Father of Othniel (Josh. 15:17; Judg. 1:13; 3:9-11). 3. Grandson of Caleb (I Chron. 4:15).

KENEZITE, KENIZZITE (kē'nĕz-īt, kē'nĭz-īt), descendants of Kenaz (Gen. 15:19). Caleb (Num. 32:12) and Othniel (Josh. 15:17) were Kenizzites.

KENITES (kē'nīts). Bedouin Midianite smiths related to Kenizzites (Gen. 15:19). Saul advised them to separate from Amalekites (I Sam. 15:6). Moses' father-in-law was a Kenite (Judg. 1:16), and so was Hobab, son of Raguel (Judg. 1:16; 4:11).

KENIZZITES (See Kenezite).

KENOSIS (kē-nō'sĭs, **emptying**), a term applied to Christ's taking the form of a servant in the incarnation (Phil. 2:7).

KERCHIEF (See Dress).

KEREN-HAPPUCH (kĕr'ĕn-hăp'ŭk), daughter of Job born after trial (Job 42:14,15).

KERIOTH (kĕr'ĭ-ŏth). 1. City in S Judah (Josh. 15:25), same as Kerioth-hezron (not "Kerioth and Hezron" as in KJV). 2. City of Moab (Amos 2:1-3; Jer. 48:24,41).

KEROS (kē'rŏs), ancestor of Nethinim who

returned with Zerubbabel (Ezra 2:44; Neh. 7:47).

KETTLE, cooking vessel or basket (I Sam. 2:14).

KETURAH (kĕ-tū'rà), Abraham's 2nd wife; mother of six sons, ancestors of Arabian tribes (Gen. 25:1-6; I Chron. 1:33).

KEY; Oriental keys made of wood. Figuratively, a symbol of authority (Isa. 22:20-22; Matt. 16:19).

KEZIA, KEZIAH (kĕ-zī'à), daughter of Job born after trial (Job 42:14).

KEZIZ (kĕ'zĭz), valley near Beth-hoglah in Benjamin (Josh. 18:21).

KIBROTH-HATTAAVAH (kĭb'rŏth-hă-tā'à-và), encampment of Israelites c. 30 miles NE of Sinai; there they gorged themselves on quail (Num. 11:34,35; 33:16,17; Deut. 9:22).

KIBZAIM (kĭb-zā'ĭm), town in Ephraim (Josh. 21:22). Jokmean in I Chron. 6:68.

KID (See Animals: Goats).

KIDNEY (kĭd'nĕ), used with surrounding fat as burnt offering (Exod. 29:13,22; Lev. 3:4,10,15; 4:9); regarded as seat of the emotions, translated "reins" (Job 19:27; Ps. 7:9).

KIDRON (kĭd'rŏn), valley along E side of Jerusalem, joins Valley of Hinnom, and extends 20 miles to Dead Sea; burial ground (II Kings 23:6); dumping place for idols and their altars (I Kings 15:13; II Chron. 29:16; 30:14); David crossed it when he fled Absalom (II Sam. 15:23); Jesus crossed it on way to Gethsemane (John 18:1, KJV Cedron).

KINAH (kī'nà), city in extreme S of Judah (Josh. 15:21,22); site uncertain.

KINE (See Animals: Cattle).

KING, earliest king mentioned in Bible is Nimrod (Gen. 10:8-12); Israel had kings from Saul to Zedekiah (c. 1020-587 B.C.), many wicked, only a few really godly; Israelites regarded David as their greatest king; God is regarded as King (Ps. 5:2; 10:16; 18:50; 54); in the prophets we find the concept of a messianic king (Isa. 32:1; 33:17; Jer. 23:5); there are many references to foreign kings in both Testaments.

KINGDOM OF GOD, the sovereign rule of God manifested in Christ to defeat His enemies, creating a people over whom He reigns, and issuing in a realm or realms in which the power of His reign is experienced. All they are members of the kingdom of God who voluntarily submit to the rule of God in their lives. Entrance into the kingdom is by the new birth (John 3:3-5); two stages in the kingdom of God: present and future in an eschatological sense; Jesus said that His ability to cast out demons was evidence that the kingdom of God had come among men (Matt. 12:28); the term "kingdom of heaven" is used synonymously with "kingdom of God" in the Bible.

KINGDOM OF HEAVEN (See Kingdom of God).

KINGDOM OF ISRAEL (See Israel).

KINGDOM OF JUDAH (See Judah).

KINGS, I AND II, BOOKS OF. These are named in English by subject-matter: four centuries of kings of Israel, from David (his death in 930 B.C.) to Jehoiachin (in Babylon, after 561); provide a sequel to books of Samuel, which embrace the reigns of Saul and David; the two books were originally written as a unit, whĭch was divided in two at the time of the LXX translation; shows how God rewards the good and punishes the wicked. Outline: 1. Solomon's reign (I Kings 1-11). 2. Kings of Israel and Judah (I Kings 12-II Kings 18). 3. Kings of Judah to exile (II Kings 18-25).

KING'S GARDEN, near Pool of Siloam (II Kings 25:4; Jer. 39:4; 52:7; Neh. 3:15).

KING'S HIGHWAY, ancient N and S road E of the Jordan through Edom and Moab (Num. 20:17; 21:22). The road is still in use.

KING'S VALE, OR DALE, Valley of Shaveh E of Jerusalem (Gen. 14:17; II Sam. 18:18).

KINSMAN (kĭnz'màn, near relative), in OT: one who has a right to redeem or avenge; one too closely related for marriage; a neighbor, friend, or acquaintance; in the NT, one of the same race (Luke 14:12; John 18:26; Rom. 9:3).

KIR (kŭr), place to which Assyrians carried inhabitants of Damascus captive (II Kings 16:9; Amos 1:5). In Isa. 22:6 "Kir of Moab."

KIR OF MOAB (See Kir).

KIR-HARASETH (kŭr-hăr'à-sĕth), capital of Moab when Jehoram, king of Israel, made war on Mesha, king of Moab (II Kings 3:4-25). Modern Kerak.

KIRIATH, KIRJATH (kĭr'ĭ-àth, kĭr'jàth, city), city of Benjamin (Josh. 18:28).

KIRIATHAIM, KIRJATHAIM (kĭr'ĭ-à-thā'im). 1. Town in Moab N of Arnon; assigned to Reuben (Num. 32:37; Josh. 13:19). 2. City of Gershonite Levites in Naphtali (I Chron. 6:76). Kartan in Josh. 21:32.

KIRIATH-SEPHER (kĭr'ĭ-àth-sē'fĕr), Debir (Josh. 15:15).

KIRIOTH (kĭr'ĭ-àth), town of Moab (Jer. 48:24,41; Amos 2:2).

KIRJATH (See Keriath).

KIRJATH-ARBA (kĭr'jàth-àr'bà, city of Arba), ancient name for Hebron (Gen. 23:2; Josh. 14:15; 15:54; 20:7).

KIRJATH-ARIM (kĭr'jàth-à'rĭm) (See Kirjath-Jearim).

KIRJATH-HUZOTH (kĭr'jàth-hū'zŏth), city near Bamoth-baal (Num. 22:39).

KIRJATH-JEARIM (kĭr'jàth-jē'à-rĭm, city of woods), one of four Gibeonite towns mentioned in Josh. 9:17; at SW corner of boundary of Benjamin; called Baale-judah in II Sam. 6:2, Kiriatharim in Ezra 2:25.

KIRJATH-SANNAH (kĭr'jàth-sàn'à), Debir (Josh. 15:49).

KISH (kĭsh, bow, power). 1. Benjamite; father of Saul (I Sam. 9:1,3; 10:11,21), Cis in KJV of Acts 13:21). 2. Benjamite (I Chron. 8:30; 9:36). 3. Levite (I Chron. 23:21,22; 24:29). 4. Levite who assisted Hezekiah (II Chron. 29:12). 5. Cousin of Esther (Esth. 2:5).

KISHI (kĭsh'ĭ), Merarite Levite (I Chron. 6:44), Kushaiah in I Chron. 15:17.

KISHION (kĭsh'ĭ-ŏn), city of Issachar (Josh. 19:20; 21:28 KJV Kishon; in I Chron. 6:72 called Kedesh).

KISHON, KISON (kĭ'shŏn, kĭ'sŏn, curving), stream which flows from Mt. Tabor and Mt. Gilboa westward through Plain of Esdraelon and enters Bay of Acre N of Mt. Carmel (Josh. 19:11; I Kings 18:40; Ps. 83:9).

KISHON RIVER (See Kishon).

KISS, affectionate greeting among people, both male and female, expressing friendship, love, passion, worship, respect, etc.; a formal greeting among early believers (Rom. 16:16; I Cor. 16:20; II Cor. 13:12).

KITHLISH (kĭth'lĭsh), town in lowlands of Judah (Josh. 15:40); site unknown.

KITRON (kĭt'rŏn), town in Zebulun (Judg. 1:30).

KITTIM (kĭt'ĭm). 1. Descendants of Javan (Gen. 10:4; I Chron. 1:7). 2. KJV Chittin; Cyprus (Isa. 23:1,12; Jer. 2:10; Ezek. 27:6).

KNEADING TROUGH, shallow vessel for kneading dough with hands (Exod. 8:3).

KNEE, bowing the knee or kneeling regarded as act of reverence (Gen. 41:43; II Kings 1:13) and subjection (Isa. 45:23; Phil. 2:10).

KNIFE, sharp-edged cutting instrument, in primitive times made of flint (Josh. 5:2,3); metal knives not used in Israel until time of later monarchy; used for all sorts of cutting purposes.

KNOP (nŏp). 1. Knob ornamenting candlestick in tabernacle (Exod. 25:31-36; 37:17-22). 2. Ornaments carved on walls of Solomon's Temple (I Kings 6:18).

KOA (kō'à), people E of Tigris, between Elam and Media (Ezek. 23:23).

KOHATH, KOHATHITES (kō'hăth, -ĭts), son of Levi (Gen. 46:11), descendants (Kohathites) included priestly family of Aaron (Exod. 6:18-20).

KOLAIAH (kō-lā'yà). 1. Benjamite (Neh. 11:7). 2. Father of false prophet Ahab (Jer. 29:21).

KORAH, KORAHITE (kō'rà, -ĭt). 1. Son of Esau (Gen. 36:5,14,18; I Chron. 1:35). 2. Grandson of Esau (Gen. 36:16). 3. Descendant of Caleb (I Chron. 2:43). 4. Levite from whom the Korahites were descended (Exod. 6:24; I Chron. 6:22). In KJV also Korhites, Korahites. 5. Son of Izhar and grandson of Kohath (Exod. 6:21,24; I Chron. 6:37; 9:19).

KORE (kō'rē). 1. Korahite (I Chron. 9:19; 26:1,19). 2. Levite (II Chron. 31:14).

KOZ (kŏz). 1. Priest whose descendants returned from exile (Ezra 2:61; Neh. 7:63). 2. Ancestor of Meremoth, who helped repair wall (Neh. 3:4,21).

KUSHAIAH (kū-shā'yà), Merarite Levite (I Chron. 15:17); called Kishi in I Chron. 6:44.

L

LAADAH (lā'à-dà), Judahite (I Chron. 4:21).

LAADAN (lā'à-dăn). 1. Ancestor of Joshua (I Chron. 7:26). 2. Levite (I Chron. 23: 7-9; 26:21).

LABAN (lā'băn, white). 1. Nephew of Abraham; lived in Haran; brother of Rebekah (Gen. 24:29); uncle of Jacob, to whom he gave his daughters Rachel and Leah in marriage (Gen. 29). 2. Place in Plains of Moab (Deut. 1:1).

LABOR. Bible refers to labor as honorable (Ps. 128:2; Prov. 21:25; I Thess. 4:11); laborers protected by laws (Deut. 24:14). Creative work of God described as labor (Gen. 2:2). Onerous labor the result of the curse (Gen. 3:17-19).

LACE, cord used to bind high priest's breastplate to the ephod (Exod. 28:28,37; 39:21,31).

LACHISH (lā'kĭsh), Canaanite royal city and Judean border fortress, occupying strategic valley 25 miles SW of Jerusalem; identified with Tell ed-Duweir, a mound excavated by J. K. Starkey from 1932 to 1938. Joshua captured it (Josh. 10:31-33; Deut. 7:2); burned c. 1230 B. C.; fortified by Rehoboam (II Chron. 11:9); besieged by Sennacherib in 701 B. C. (II Chron. 32:9); destroyed by Nebuchadnezzar together with Jerusalem (II Kings 24,25; Jer. 34:7); resettled after exile (Neh. 11:30). Lachish Letters (ostraca) from time of Jeremiah reveal much about city.

LADDER, mentioned only in Gen. 28:12 in English Bible, where it means "staircase."

LAEL (lā'ĕl), father of Eliasaph (Num. 3:24).

LAHAD (lā'hăd), Judahite (I Chron. 4:2).

LAHAI-ROI (See Beer-Lahai-Roi).

LAHMAM (lă'măm), town in Judean Shephelah (Josh. 15:40), perhaps same as modern el-Lahm.

LAHMI (là'mī), brother of Goliath (I Chron. 20:5).

LAISH (lā'ĭsh). 1. City in upper Jordan valley and renamed Dan by Danites (Judg. 18:7,14,27,29). Called Leshem in Josh. 19:47, Laish in Isa. 10:30. 2. Father of Phalti (I Sam. 25:44; II Sam. 3:15).

LAKUM, LAKKUM (lā'kŭm), town of Naphtali (Josh. 19:33), location unknown.

LAMB, used for food (Deut. 32:14; Amos 6:4) and for sacrifices (Gen. 4:4; 22:7). esp. at Passover (Exod. 12:3-5). Sacrificial lambs typical of Christ (John 1:29; Rev. 5:6,8).

LAMB OF GOD, Jesus called the Lamb of God by John the Baptist (John 1:29,36), emphasizing redemptive character of work of Christ. In Revelation the lamb is often used as a symbol of Christ.

LAME (See Diseases).

LAMECH (lā'mĕk). 1. Son of Methusael (Gen. 4:18-24); father of Tubal, Jubal, Tubalcain, and Naamah. 2. Son of Methuselah (Gen. 5:25-31); father of Noah.

LAMENTATIONS, BOOK OF. Author not stated, but ancient authorities ascribe it to Jeremiah. LXX, Vulgate, and English Bible place it after Jeremiah, but in Heb.

Bible it appears between Ruth and Ecclesiastes. Title accurately designates contents; the book bewails the seige and destruction of Jerusalem, and sorrows over the sufferings of the inhabitants during this time; makes poignant confession of sin on behalf of the people and their leaders, acknowledges complete submission to the Divine will, and prays that God will once again favor and restore His people. Five poems (the first four consisting of acrostics based on Heb. alphabet) make up the five chapters.

LAMP. Archaeology has recovered many specimens in a great variety of forms. Most were oil-fed and had a wick. There were no candles in ancient times, and therefore no candlesticks. In tabernacle and Temple the lamps were of gold (Exod. 25:31-40; 37:17-24) and burned olive oil (Exod, 27:20). Often used figuratively for God's Word (Ps. 119:105), God's guidance (II Sam. 22:29), God's salvation (Isa. 62:1), etc.

LANCE (See Arms, Armor).

LANDMARK, object used to mark boundary of a field; not to be removed (Deut. 19:14; 27:4,5).

LANE, alley of a city (Luke 14:21).

LANGUAGES. Many different languages spoken in OT times. Israelites spoke Hebrew when they entered Palestine and at least as late as the time of Nehemiah, and it remained the literary language permanently. In colloquial use it was replaced by Aramaic. The chief languages in NT Palestine: Aramaic (Hebrew), Greek, Latin (John 19:20).

LAODICEA (là-ŏd'ĭ-sē'à), city in Lycus valley of Asia Minor, founded by Antiochus II (261-246 B. C.); prosperous commercial city (Col. 2:1; 4:15; Rev. 1:11; 3:14-22). Church there condemned for lukewarmness (Rev. 3:14-22).

LAODICEA, CHURCH AT (See Laodicea).

LAODICEANS, EPISTLE TO, letter mentioned by Paul in Col. 4:16; could be a lost letter of Paul's or the Epistle to the Ephesians. An apocryphal Epistle to the Laodiceans consisting of 20 verses exists.

LAPPED, LAPPETH. Heb. verb used to indicate alertness (Judg. 7:5-7) and disgust (I Kings 21:19; 22:38).

LAPPIDOTH (lăp'ĭ-dŏth), husband of Deborah the prophetess (Judg. 4:4).

LAPWING (See Birds).

LASCIVIOUSNESS (là-sĭv'ĭ-ŭs-nĕs), shameless immorality (Mark 7:22; II Cor. 12:21; Gal. 5:19).

LASEA (là-sē'à), seaport town on S coast of Crete; visited by Paul (Acts 27:8).

LASHA (lā'shà), place near Sodom and Gomorrah (Gen. 10:19). Site not identified.

LASHARON (là-shā'rŏn), Canaanite town (Josh. 12:18).

LATCHET (lăch'ĕt, sandal-thong), strap to fasten sandal to foot. Often used figuratively (Gen. 14:23; Isa. 5:27; Mark 1:7).

LATIN (lăt'ĭn), language of the Romans (John 19:20).

LATTICE (lăt'ĭs), latticework used for privacy, ventilation, decoration (Judg. 5:28; II Kings 1:2; translated "casement," Prov. 7:6).

LAUGHTER (làf'tèr), used to express joy (Gen. 21:6; Luke 6:21), derision (Ps. 2:4), disbelief (Gen. 18:13).

LAVER (là'vèr, basin), vessel containing water, located between altar and door of tabernacle, at which priests washed hands and feet before ministering (Exod. 30:17-22).

LAW. 1. Ten Commandments given to Moses (Exod. 20:3-17; Deut. 5:6-21), summarized God's requirements of man. 2. Torah, first five books of OT (Matt. 5:17; Luke 16:16). 3. OT (John 10:34; 12:34). 4. God's will in words, acts, precepts (Exod. 20:1-17; Ps. 19). OT Jews manifested their faith in Jehovah by observing the law. Christ fulfilled the law; respected, loved it, and showed its deeper significance (Matt. 5: 17-48). Purpose of OT law to prepare way for coming of Christ (Gal. 3:24). Law shows man's sinfulness, but cannot bring victory over sin (Rom. 3-8; Gal.). Jesus' summary of the law: it demands perfect love for God and love for one's neighbor comparable to that which one has for himself (Matt. 22:35-40).

LAW OF MOSES (See Law).

LAWGIVER. God is the only absolute lawgiver (James 4:12); instrumentally, Moses bears this description (John 1:17; 7:19).

LAWYER, a professional interpreter of the written and oral law; also called scribe (Matt. 22:35; Luke 10:25).

LAYING ON OF HANDS, symbolic act signifying impartation of inheritance rights (Gen. 48:14-20), gifts and rights of an office (Num. 27:18,23); dedication of animals (Lev. 1:4), priests (Num. 8:10), people for special service (Acts 6:6; 13:3).

LAZARUS (lăz'à-rŭs, God has helped). 1. Brother of Martha and Mary; raised from dead by Jesus (John 11:1-12:19). 2. Beggar who died and went to Abraham's bosom (Luke 16:19-31).

LEAF; leaf of a tree, page of a book, leaf of a door. Metaphorically, green leaves symbolize prosperity, and dry leaves ruin and decay (Ps. 1:3; Prov. 11:28; Job 13:25; Isa. 1:30).

LEAH (lē'à), Laban's daughter and Jacob's first wife (Gen. 29:21-30).

LEASING (lēz'ing), obsolete KJV word for falsehood (Ps. 4:2; 5:6).

LEATHER (lĕth'èr), designates the tanned hide of animals. Skins were used for rough clothing, as well as for armor, bags, sandals, and writing materials (Lev. 13:48; Ezek. 18:10; Matt. 3:14; Heb. 11:37).

LEAVEN (lĕv'ĕn), substance used to make dough rise (Exod. 12:15,20); could not be used in meal offerings (Lev. 2:11) or in Passover (Lev. 2:11; Exod. 12); symbol of moral influence, whether good or bad (Matt. 13:33; 16:6).

LEBANA, LEBANAH (lē-bā'nà, white), ancestor of family which returned from exile (Ezra 2:45; Neh. 7:48).

LEBANON (lĕb′å-nŭn, white), mt. range extending in a NE direction for 100 miles along the Syrian coast, from Tyre to Arvad, and the country which bears its name. Between the Lebanon and Anti-Lebanon ranges there is a valley known as Coele (hollow) Syria. Some peaks reach 10,000 feet. Mt. Herman (9383 ft.) is southernmost spur of Anti-Lebanons. Formed N boundary of Palestine (Deut. 1:7). Heavily wooded; known especially for cedars (Judg. 9:15; I Kings 5:6).

LEBAOTH (lĕ-bā′ŏth), town in S Judah (Josh. 15:32); also called Beth-lebaoth (Josh. 19:6) and probably, Beth-birei (I Chron. 4:31).

LEBBAEUS (lĕ-bē′ŭs), one of Christ's apostles, also called Thaddaeus (Matt. 10:3) and Judas (Luke 6:16; Acts 1:13).

LEBONAH (lĕ-bō′nà), town N of Bethel between Shiloh and Shechem (Judg. 21:19).

LECAH (lē′kà), son of Er (I Chron. 4:21).

LEEKS (See Plants).

LEES (lĕz, something preserved), sediment of wine (Isa. 25:6). Also used figuratively to describe blessings of Messianic times, spiritual lethargy, inevitability of God's judgment (Jer. 48:11; Ps. 75:8).

LEFT, used with a variety of meanings: simple direction; North (Gen. 14:15); lesser blessing (Gen. 48:13-19), weakness (Judg. 3:15,21, etc.).

LEGION (lĕ′jŭn). 1. Largest single unit in Roman army, including infantry and cavalry. 2. Vast number (Matt. 26:53; Mark 5:9).

LEHABIM (lĕ-hā′bĭm), 3rd son of Mizraim (Gen. 10:13) and descendants, the Libyans (Ezek. 30:5; 38:5).

LEHI (lē′hī, jawbone), place where Samson killed 1000 Philistines with a jawbone of ass (Judg. 15:9,14).

LEMUEL (lĕm′ū-ĕl), king, otherwise unknown, to whom his mother taught the maxims in Prov. 31:2-9; probably Solomon (Prov. 31:1).

LENTILE, LENTIL (See Plants).

LEOPARD (See Animals).

LEPER (See Diseases).

LEPROSY (See Diseases).

LESHEM (lē′shĕm), city renamed Dan, at extreme N of Palestine (I Sam. 3:20); variant of Laish.

LETTER, designates an alphabetical symbol, rudimentary education (John 7:15), written communication, the external (Rom. 2:27,29), Jewish legalism (Rom. 7:6; II Cor. 3:6). In ancient times correspondence was privately delivered. Archaeology has uncovered many different kinds of letters.

LETTUSHIM, LETUSHIM (lĕ-tū′shĭm), 2nd son of Dedan, grandson of Abraham (Gen. 25:3).

LEUMMIM (lĕ-ŭm′ĭm), 3rd son of Dedan (Gen. 25:3).

LEVI (lē′vī, joined). 1. Jacob's third son by Leah (Gen. 29:34; 35:23); avenged seduction of his sister Dinah (Gen. 34). 2, 3. Ancestors of Jesus (Luke 3:24-29). 4. See Matthew.

LEVIATHAN (See Animals).

LEVIRATE MARRIAGE (lĕv′ĭ-rāt), Jewish custom according to which when an Israelite without male heirs died the nearest relative married the widow, and the first born son became the heir of the 1st husband (Deut. 25:5-10).

LEVITES (lĕ′vĭts), name given to descendants of Levi through his sons Gershon, Kohath, Merari (Exod. 6:16-25; Lev. 25:32); became substitutes for fellow-Israelites in duties pertaining to God (Num. 3:11-13; 8:16); three-fold organization: top echelon occupied by Aaron and his sons, and they alone were priests in the restricted sense; middle echelon consisted of some Levites not of Aaron's family, who had the privilege of bearing the tabernacle (Num. 3:27-32); bottom echelon, comprised all members of the families of Gershon and Merari, who had lesser duties in the tabernacle (Num. 3:21-26, 33-37). Priests were Levites belonging to Aaron's family, but Levites were not necessarily priests. Levites received no tribal territory; 48 cities were assigned to them (Num. 35), and they were supported by tithes (Lev. 27:30-33; Num. 18:21-24).

LEVITICUS (lĕ-vĭt′ĭ-kŭs, relating to the Levites), 3rd book of the Pentateuch; authorship ascribed to Moses by tradition; describes duties of priests and Levites; emphasizes holiness of God and the need to approach Him through proper channels. Outline: 1. Sacrifices and offerings (1-7). 2. Duties of priests (8-10). 3. Cleanliness and holiness (11-22). 4. Feasts (23). 5. Promises and warnings (25-27).

LEVY (lĕv′ē, tribute), people conscripted to perform forced labor for another (I Kings 5:13,14; 9:21).

LIBATION (lĭ-bā′shŭn), pouring out of wine or some other liquid as an offering to a diety as an act of worship (Exod. 29:40, 41; Jer. 44:17-25).

LIBERTINES (lĭb′ĕr-tēnz), freedmen (Acts 6:9).

LIBERTY, freedom, whether physical, moral, or spiritual. Israelites who had become slaves were freed in year of jubilee (Lev. 25:8-17). Through Christ's death and resurrection the believer is free from sin's dominion (John 1:29; 8:36; Rom. 6,7), Satan's control (Acts 26:18), the law (Gal. 3), fear, the second death, future judgment.

LIBNAH (lĭb′nà). 1. Encampment of Israel (Num. 33:20,21), site unknown. 2. Canaanite city, near Lachish, captured by Joshua (Josh. 10:29-32); became Levitical city (Josh. 21:13; I Chron. 6:57).

LIBNI (lĭb′nī). 1. Son of Gershon (Exod. 6:17; Num. 3:18,21). 2. Levite (I Chron. 6:29).

LIBNITES (lĭb′nĭts), descendants of Libni (Num. 3:21; 26:58).

LIBRARIES. Libraries, both public and private, were not uncommon in ancient times in the Oriental, Greek, and Roman worlds.

The Dead Sea Scrolls is one example of an ancient library that has survived to modern times.

LIBYA (lib'ĭ-à), ancient Greek name for N Africa W of Egypt (Ezek. 30:5; Acts 2:10).

LICE (See Insects).

LIEUTENANTS (lū-tĕn'ănts), official title of satraps governing large provinces of the Persian empire (Ezra 8:36; Esth. 3:12; 8:9; 9:3).

LIFE, refers to physical life (Gen. 6:17; Exod. 1:14), spiritual life (Rom. 8:6; Col. 3:3), eternal life (Eph. 2:5-10). Christ the source of all life (John 1:4; 11:25; Col. 3:4).

LIFE, THE BOOK OF, figurative expression denoting God's record of those who inherit eternal life (Phil. 4:3; Rev. 3:5; 21:27).

LIGHT. Created by God (Gen. 1:3); Jesus the light of the world (John 1:4-9); God is light (I John 1:5); symbol of spiritual illumination (II Cor. 4:6; Eph. 5:14); Word of God is light (Ps. 119:105); disciples of Christ are lights (Matt. 5:14).

LIGHTNING, used both literally and symbolically in Bible; a symbol of speed (Ezek. 1:14) and of dazzling brightness (Dan. 10:6; Matt. 28:3).

LIGN-ALOES (See Plants).

LIGURE (See Minerals).

LIKHI (lik'hĭ), Manassite (I Chron. 7:19).

LILY (See Plants).

LINE, usually a measuring line (II Sam. 8:2; Ps. 78:55); a portion (Ps. 16:6); sound made by a musical chord (Ps. 19:4).

LINEN, thread or cloth prepared from the fiber of flax; used as far back as the Stone Age; used for garments (Gen. 41:42; Ezek. 9:2; Mark 14:51), especially for apparel of priests, Levites, and royal personages (Exod. 28:5-42; II Chron. 5:12; II Sam. 6:14); temple veil made of it (II Chron. 3:14); symbol of wealth (Luke 16:19); purity (Rev. 19:8,14).

LINTEL, horizontal beam forming the upper part of doorway (Exod. 12:22,23).

LINUS (lī'nŭs), Roman friend of Paul (II Tim. 4:21).

LION (See Animals).

LITTER, portable couch or sedan borne by men or animals (Isa. 66:20).

LITTLE OWL (See Birds).

LIVER, considered center of life and feeling (Prov. 7:23); used especially for sacrifice (Exod. 29:13) and divination (Ezek. 21:21).

LIVING CREATURES, apparently identical with cherubim (Ezek. 1:5-22; 3:13; Rev. 4: 6-9).

LIZARD (See Animals).

LO-AMMI (lō-ăm'ĭ, not my people), symbolic name for Hosea's 3rd child (Hos. 1:9,10; 2:23).

LOCK, LOCKS. 1. Beams of wood or iron used for fastening gates or doors (Neh. 3:3; S. of Sol. 5:5). 2. Hair of the head (Judg. 16:13,19).

LOCUST (See Insects).

LOD (lŏd), town of Benjamin (I Chron.

8:12); Lydda of the NT.

LO-DEBAR (lō-dē'bär), town in Gilead E of the Jordan (II Sam. 9:4,5; 17:27ff).

LODGE, temporary shelter erected in a garden for a watchman guarding ripening fruit (Isa. 1:8).

LOFT, upper chamber or story of a building (I Kings 17:19; Acts 20:9).

LOGIA, Greek word for non-Biblical sayings of Christ, such as those in the so-called Gospel of Thomas discovered in 1945.

LOGOS, philosophical and theological term translated "Word" referring to the dynamic principle of reason operating in the world, and forming a medium of communion between God and man. In the NT the concept is found principally in Johannine contexts (John 1:1ff; Rev.19:13).

LOIN, part of body between ribs and hip bones. It is the place where the girdle was worn (Exod. 12:11; II Kings 1:8) and the sword fastened (II Sam. 20:8).

LOIS (lō'ĭs), Timothy's grandmother (II Tim. 1:5).

LOOKING-GLASS (See Mirror).

LORD, a term applied to both men and God, expressing varied degrees of honor, dignity, and majesty; applied also to idols (Exod. 22:8; Judg. 2:11,13); used of Jesus as Messiah (Acts 2:36; Phil. 2:9-11; Rom. 1:4; 14:8).

LORD'S DAY, the day especially associated with the Lord Jesus Christ; a day consecrated to the Lord; the 1st day of the week, commemorating the resurrection of Jesus (John 20:1-25) and the pouring out of the Spirit (Acts 2:1-41); set aside for worship (Acts 20:7).

LORD'S PRAYER, THE, prayer taught by Jesus as a model of how His disciples should pray (Matt. 6:9-13; Luke 11:2-4).

LORD'S SUPPER, instituted by Christ on the night of His betrayal immediately after Passover feast to be a memorial of His death and a visible sign of the blessings of salvation that accrue from His death. Goes by various names: body and blood of Christ (Matt. 26:26,28), communion of the body and blood of Christ (I Cor. 10:16), bread and cup of the Lord (I Cor. 11:27), breaking of bread (Acts 2:42; 20:7), Lord's Supper (I Cor. 11:20). Not to be observed unworthily (I Cor. 11:27-32).

LO-RUHAMAH (lō-rŏŏ-hà'mà, not pitied), symbolic name given to Hosea's daughter (Hos. 1:6,8; 2:4,23).

LOT (lŏt, covering). 1. A means of deciding an issue or of determining the divine will in a matter; often used in ancient times, both by heathens and Jews (Esth. 3:7; Jonah 1:7). 2. That which is assigned by lot, as a share or inheritance (Deut. 32:9; Josh. 15:1).

LOT (lŏt, envelope, covering), son of Haran and nephew of Abraham (Gen. 11:31; 12:5); went with Abraham to Canaan (Gen. 11: 27-32; 12:4,10; 13:1); settled near Sodom (Gen. 13:5-13); rescued by Abraham (Gen. 14:1-12); left Sodom (Gen. 19); ancestor of

Moab and Ammon (Gen. 19:36-38).

LOTAN (lō'tăn), son of Seir (Gen. 36:20, 22,29).

LOVE, presented in Scripture as the very nature of God (I John 4:8,16) and the greatest of the Christian virtues (I Cor. 13:13); essential to man's relations to God and man (Matt. 22:37-39); Christ the unique object of the Father's love (John 17:24); God's love for man manifested in redemption wrought for him (John 3:16; Rom. 5:8-10; love created in believer by Holy Spirit (Rom. 5:5; Gal. 5:22); chief test of Christian discipleship (John 13:35; I John 3:14); Christian must love his enemy as well as his brother (Matt. 5:43-48; I John 3:14).

LOVE FEAST, a common meal eaten by early Christians in connection with the Lord's Supper to express and deepen brotherly love (I Cor. 11:18-22,33,34; Jude 12).

LOVING-KINDNESS, the kindness and mercy of God toward man (Ps. 17:7; 26:3).

LUBIM (lū'bĭm), probably the Libyans; always mentioned in conjunction with Egyptians or Ethiopians (II Chron. 12:3; 16:8; Nah. 3:9).

LUCAS (lū'căs), same as Luke (Philem. 24).

LUCIFER (See Satan, Devil).

LUCIUS (lū'shĭ-ŭs). 1. Christian from Cyrene (Acts 13:1). 2. Kinsman of Paul (Rom. 16:21).

LUD, LUDIM (lŭd, lū'dĭm), either one or two nations of antiquity. Lud was the kingdom of Lydia in Asia Minor (Gen. 10:22; I Chron. 1:17). Ludim are also listed as descendants of Mizraim or Egypt (Gen. 10:13).

LUHITH (lū'hĭth), town of Moab (Isa. 15:5).

LUKE, GOSPEL OF. Third book of NT,

written, according to tradition, by Luke the beloved physician and co-worker of Paul. Preface to Acts shows that the Gospel was written before it, somewhere c. A. D. 58-60; both books were done by the same person, as tradition and internal evidence show. The author states in the preface (1:2) that he collected his material from eyewitnesses. Outline: 1. Thirty years of private life (1-4:13). 2. Galilean ministry of Jesus (4:14-9:50). 3. Journey from Galilee to Jerusalem (9:51-19:44). 4. Last days of Jesus in Jerusalem, His crucifixion and burial (19:45-23:56). 5. Resurrection and appearances of the risen Lord and His ascension (24:1-53).

LUNATIC (See Diseases).

LUTE (See Musical Instruments).

LUZ (lŭz, turning aside). 1. Town on N boundary of Benjamin (Josh. 16:2; 18:13). 2. Hittite town (Judg. 1:26).

LYCAONIA (lĭk'ȧ-ō'nĭ-ȧ), district in central plain of Asia N of Taurus range (Acts 14:6,11).

LYCIA (lĭsh'ĭ-ȧ), province of SW Asia Minor (Acts 21:2; 27:5).

LYDDA (lĭd'ȧ), town c. 30 miles NW of Jerusalem (Acts 9:32-38).

LYDIA (lĭd'ĭ-ȧ), Paul's first convert in Europe; resided in Philippi; sold purple dyes; Paul stayed at her house (Acts 16:14,15,40).

LYRE (See Musical Instruments).

LYSANIAS (lĭ-sā'nĭ-ăs), tetrarch of Abilene (Luke 3:1).

LYSIAS (lĭs'ĭ-ăs), tribune of Roman soldiers in Jerusalem; rescued Paul and sent him to Caesarea (Acts 23:12-33).

LYSTRA (lĭs'trȧ), city in Lycaonia (Acts 14:6-21).

M

MAACAH, MAACHAH (mā'ȧ-kȧ, oppression). 1. Son of Nahor, brother of Abraham (Gen. 22:24). 2. Wife of David; mother of Absalom (II Sam. 3:3; I Chron. 3:2). 3. Father of Achish, king of Gath (I Kings 2:39). 4. Wife of king Rehoboam (II Chron. 11:20-22). 5. Concubine of Caleb, son of Hezron (I Chron. 2:48). 6. Wife of Machir, the son of Manasseh (I Chron. 7:14-16). 7. Wife of Jeiel (I Chron. 8:29; 9:35). 8. Father of Hanan (I Chron. 11:43). 9. Father of Shephatiah (I Chron. 27:16).

MAACHAH (mā'ȧ-kȧ, oppression), country on edge of Syrian desert N of Gilead (II Sam. 10:6-19).

MAACHATHI, MAACHATHITES (mȧ-ăk'ȧ-thī, mȧ-ăk'ȧ-thĭts), people of the nation of Maachah, in the region of Bashan (Deut. 3:14; Josh. 12:5; 13:11; II Sam. 23:34; I Chron. 4:19).

MAADAI (mā'ȧ-dā'ī), Israelite who married a foreign woman (Ezra 10:34).

MAADIAH (mȧ-ȧ-dī'ȧ), chief priest who returned from exile with Zerubbabel (Neh. 12:5).

MAAI (mā-ā'ī), priest who blew trumpet at

dedication of wall (Neh. 12:36).

MAALEH-ACRABBIM (mā'ȧ-lē-ȧ-krăb'ĭm). area assigned to tribe of Judah (Josh. 15:3).

MAARATH (mā'ȧ-răth), city in Judah, near Hebron (Josh. 15:59).

MAASEIAH (mā'ȧ-sē'yȧ, work of Jehovah). 1. Levite musician (I Chron. 15:18,20). 2. Army captain who assisted Jehoiada in overthrowing Athaliah (II Chron. 23:1). 3. Officer of Uzziah (II Chron. 26:11). 4. Son of Ahaz, king of Judah (II Chron. 28:7). 5. Governor of Jerusalem in Josiah's reign (II Chron. 34:8). 6. Priest who married foreign woman (Ezra 10:18). 7. Another priest who married foreign woman (Ezra 10:21). 8. Another priest who married foreign woman (Ezra 10:22). 9. Israelite who married foreign woman (Ezra 10:30). 10. Father of Azariah (Neh. 2:23). 11. Priest; assistant of Ezra (Neh. 8:4). 12. Man who explained law to people (Neh. 8:7). 13. Chief who sealed covenant with Nehemiah (Neh. 10:25). 14. Descendant of son of Baruch (Neh. 11:5). 15. Benjamite (Neh. 11:7). 16. Priest who blew trumpet at dedication of wall (Neh. 12:41). 17. Another priest who took part in dedication of wall (Neh. 12:42). 18. Priest; father of Zephaniah (Jer. 21:1; 37:3). 19. Father of Zedekiah (Jer. 29:21). 20. Gatekeeper of temple (Jer. 35:4). 21. Ancestor of Baruch (Jer. 32:12).

MAASIAI (må-ås'i-ī), priestly family after exile (I Chron. 9:12).

MAATH (mā'åth), ancestor of Christ (Luke 3:26).

MAAZ (mā'åz), descendant of Jerahmeel (I Chron. 2:27).

MAAZIAH (må-å-zī'å). 1. Head of 24th course of priests (I Chron. 24:18). 2. Priest who sealed covenant with Nehemiah (Neh. 10:8).

MACCABEES (måk'å-bēs, hammer?), Hasmonean Jewish family of Modin that led revolt against Antiochus Epiphanes, king of Syria, and won freedom for the Jews. The family consisted of the father, Mattathias, an aged priest, and his five sons: Johanan, Simon, Judas, Eleazar, Jonathan. The name Maccabee was first given to Judas, perhaps because he inflicted sledgehammer blows against the Syrian armies, and later was also used for his brothers. The revolt began in 168 B. C. The temple was recaptured and sacrifices were resumed in 165 B. C. The cleansing of the temple and resumption of sacrifices have been celebrated annually ever since in the Feast of Dedication. The Maccabees served as both high priests and kings. The story of the Maccabees is told in two books of the Apocrypha, I and II Maccabees. The following were the most prominent of the Maccabees: Judas (166-160 B. C.), Jonathan (160-142 B. C.), Simon (142-134 B. C.), John Hyrcanus (134-104 B. C.), Aristobulus (104-103 B. C.), Alexander Jannaeus (103-76 B. C.), Alexandra (76-67 B. C.), Aristobulus II (66-63). In 63 B. C. the Romans took over when Pompey conquered the Israelites.

MACEDONIA (mås'ē-dō'nI-à), country N of Greece in Balkan Peninsula first ruled by Philip (359-336 B. C.) and then by his son Alexander the Great (336-323 B. C.); became Roman province in 168 B. C.; often visited by Paul (Acts 16:9-12; 17:1-15; 20:1-6; Rom. 15:26; I Cor. 16:5; II Cor. 1:16; 2:13; 7:5; 8:1; 9:2; 11:9; Phil. 4:15; I Thess. 1:7; 4:10; I Tim. 1:3).

MACHAERUS (må-kē'rŭs), fortress stronghold built by Alexander Janneus (90 B. C.?) and used as a citadel by Herod Antipas; located on E of Dead Sea; John the Baptist was put to death there (Matt. 14:3ff).

MACHBENAH (måk-bē'nå), place in Judah (I Chron. 2:49). "Father" may mean "founder."

MACHBENAI (måk'bå-nī), Gadite (I Chron. 12:13).

MACHI (mā'kī), Gadite; father of Geuel, one of 12 spies (Num. 13:15).

MACHIR (mā'kīr, sold). 1. Eldest son of Manasseh, son of Joseph (Gen. 50:23; Num. 27:1; 32:39,40); Machirites descended from him (Num. 26:29). 2. Man who brought

provisions to David when he fled from Absalom (II Sam. 17:27).

MACHNADEBAI (måk-nåd'ē-bī), Israelite who divorced foreign wife (Ezra 10:40).

MACHPELAH (måk-pē'lå), field bought by Abraham as burial place for Sarah (Gen. 23:19,20). Abraham, Isaac, Rebekah, Leah, and Jacob also buried there (Gen. 25:9; 49:30,31; 50:13).

MADAI (måd'å-ī), people descended from Japheth (Gen. 10:2; I Chron. 1:5).

MADIAN (See Midian).

MADMANNAH (måd-mån'nå). 1. Town in S Judah 8 miles S of Kirjath-sepher (Josh. 15:31). 2. Grandson of Caleb (I Chron. 2:48,49).

MADMENAH (måd-mē'nå), town of Benjamin (Isa. 10:31); location uncertain.

MADON (mā'dŏn), Canaanite city near modern Hattin (Josh. 11:1; 12:19).

MAGBISH (måg'bish), name of man or place (Ezra 2:30).

MAGDALA (måg'då-là), town on NW shore of Sea of Galilee, 3 miles N of Tiberias (Matt. 15:39). Dalmanutha in Mark 8:10. Home of Mary Magdalene.

MAGDALEN, MAGDALENE (See Mary).

MAGDIEL (måg'dī-ĕl), chief of Edom (Gen. 36:43; I Chron. 1:54).

MAGI (mā'jī), originally a religious caste among the Persians; devoted to astrology, divination, and interpretation of dreams. Later the word came to be applied generally to fortune tellers and exponents of esoteric religious cults throughout the Mediterranean world (Acts 8:9; 13:6,8). Nothing is known of the magi of the Nativity story (Matt. 2); they may have come from S Arabia.

MAGIC, the art or science of influencing or controlling the course of nature, events, and supernatural powers through occult science of mysterious arts (Gen. 41:8; Exod. 7:11,22; 8:7,18; Acts 19:19). Includes necromancy, exorcism, dreams, shaking arrows, inspecting entrails of animals, divination, sorcery, astrology, soothsaying, divining by rods, witchcraft (I Sam. 28:8; Ezek. 21:21; Acts 16:16).

MAGICIANS (See Magic).

MAGISTRATE (måj'is-trāt, judge, ruler), chief official in government of Roman colony (Acts 16:20,22,35,36,38).

MAGNIFICAT (måg-nif'ī-kåt), song of praise by Mary recorded in Luke 1:46-55.

MAGOG (mā'gŏg, land of Gog?). 1. Son of Japheth (Gen. 10:2; I Chron. 1:5). 2. Land of Gog; various identifications: Scythians, Lydians, Tartars of Russia. Used symbolically for forces of evil (Rev. 20:7-9).

MAGOR-MISSABIB (mā'gŏr-mis'å-bīb), name given to Pashur by Jeremiah (Jer. 20:3).

MAGPIASH (måg'pī-åsh), Israelite who sealed covenant with Nehemiah (Neh. 10:20).

MAGUS, SIMON (See Simon).

MAHALAH (mà-hā'là), child of Hammoleketh (I Chron. 7:18).

MAHALALEEL(mà-hā'là-lē'ĕl), son of Kenan

(Gen. 5:12,13,15,16,17; I Chron. 1:2; Luke 3:37).

MAHALATH (mă-hà-lăth). 1. Daughter of Ishmael (Gen. 28:9). 2. Wife of Rehoboam (II Chron. 11:18). 3. Musical term in heading of Ps. 53 and 88.

MAHALI (ma'hà-lī), son of Merari (Exod. 6:19).

MAHANAIM (mă'hà-nă'ĭm, two hosts), town in Gilead E of the Jordan on boundary between Gad and Manasseh; assigned to Levites (Josh. 21:38); angels met Jacob there (Gen. 32:2); David fled there from Absalom (II Sam. 17:24; 19:32); capital of Israel for a short time (II Sam. 2:8). Exact location uncertain.

MAHANEH-DAN (mă'hà-nĕ-dăn, camp of Dan). 1. Place between Zorah and Eshtaol (Judg. 13:25). 2. Place W of Kirjath-jearim (Judg. 18:12).

MAHARAI (mà-hăr'à-ī), Zerahite captain in David's army (II Sam. 23:28; I Chron. 11:30).

MAHATH (mă'hăth). 1. Kohathite; ancestor of Heman the singer (I Chron. 6:35). 2. Levite who helped Hezekiah (II Chron. 29:12; 31:13).

MAHAVITE (mă'hà-vīt), family name of Eliel, one of David's warriors (I Chron. 11:46).

MAHAZIOTH (mà-hà'zĭ-ŏth, visions), son of Heman (I Chron. 25:4,30).

MAHER-SHALAL-HASH-BAZ (mă'hĕr-shăl'ăl-hăsh'băz, the spoil speeds, the prey hastens), symbolic name Isaiah gave his son (Isa. 8:1,3).

MAHLAH (mă'là, disease). 1. Daughter of Zelophehad (Num. 26:33; 27:1ff; 36; Josh. 17:3ff). 2. Daughter of Hammoleketh (I Chron. 7:18).

MAHLI (măh'lī). 1. Levite; son of Merari (Exod. 6:19; Num. 3:20; Ezra 8:18). 2. Son of Mushi (I Chron. 6:47; 23:23; 24:30).

MAHLITE (măh'līt), descendant of Mahli, son of Merari (Num. 3:33; 26:58; I Chron. 23:22).

MAHLON (mà'lŏn), son of Elimelech (Ruth 1:2,5; 4:9,10).

MAHOL (mă'hŏl), father of Calcol and Darda, men famous for wisdom (I Kings 4:31).

MAID, MAIDEN. 1. Female slave (Exod. 2:5; 21:20,26). 2. Virgin (Exod. 22:16; Judg. 19:24). 3. Girl (Exod. 2:5; Ruth 2:8,22,23). 4. Girl of marriageable age (Gen. 24:43; Exod. 2:8; Ps. 68:25; S. of Sol. 1:3; 6:8; Prov. 30:19; Isa. 7:14). 5. Maid servant (Gen. 16:2,3,5,6,8).

MAIL, COAT OF (See Armor).

MAIMED (See Diseases).

MAKAZ (mă'kăz), town near Beth Shemesh (I Kings 4:9).

MAKHELOTH (măk-hē'lŏth), encampment of Israel in wilderness (Num. 33:25,26).

MAKKEDAH (măk-kè'dà), town near Libnah and Azekah (Josh. 10:16ff); assigned to Judah (Josh. 15:41).

MAKTESH (măk'tĕsh), place; location unknown (Zeph. 1:11).

MALACHI (măl'à-kī, messenger of Jehovah or my messenger), prophet of Judah who lived c. 450-400 B. C.; author of OT book

which bears his name; nothing known of him beyond what is said in his book; contemporary of Nehemiah (Mal. 2:11-17; Neh. 13:23-31). Principal themes of book: sin and apostasy of Israel; judgment that will fall upon the faithless and blessing upon the faithful. Outline: 1. Sins of the priests (1:1-2:9). 2. Sins of the people (2:10-4:1). 3. Coming of the Sun of Righteousness (4:2-6).

MALCHAM, MALCAM (măl'kăm, either **Milcom**, an idol of the Moabites and Ammonites (Zeph. 1:5; Jer. 49:3) or their king (Amos 1:15; Jer. 49:1); maybe both.

MALCHIAH, MALCHIJAH (măl-kī'à, măl-kī'jà). 1. Gershonite (I Chron. 6:40). 2. Ancestor of Adaiah (I Chron. 9:12; Neh. 11:12). 3. Priest (I Chron. 24:9). 4. Israelite who married foreign woman (Ezra 10:25). 5. Another who did same thing (Ezra 10:25). 6. Another who did same thing (Ezra 10:31). 7. Son of Harim (Neh. 3:11). 8. Son of Rechab (Neh. 3:14). 9. Goldsmith (Neh. 3:31). 10. Man who assisted Ezra (Neh. 8:4). 11. Israelite who sealed covenant with Nehemiah (Neh. 10:3). 12. Priest (Neh. 12:42). May be same as No. 11. 13. Father of Pashur who helped arrest Jeremiah (Jer. 21:1; 38:1). 14. Son of King Zedekiah (Jer. 38:6).

MALCHIEL (măl'kī-ĕl), son of Beriah (Gen. 46:17; Num. 26:45; I Chron. 7:31).

MALCHIJAH (See Malchiah).

MALCHIRAM (măl-kī'răm), son of Jeconiah (I Chron. 3:18).

MALCHI-SHUA (măl-kī-shōō'à), son of King Saul (I Sam. 14:49; 31:2, KJV Melchi-shua; I Chron. 8:33; 9:39).

MALCHUS (măl'kŭs), servant of high priest whose ear Peter cut off with sword (John 18:10).

MALEFACTOR (măl'ĕ-făk'tĕr, evil doer), evil doer (John 18:30; Luke 23:32,33,39).

MALELEEL (See Mahaleel).

MALLOTHI (măl'ŏ-thī), son of Heman; temple musician (I Chron. 25:4,26).

MALLOW (See Plants).

MALLUCH (măl'lŭk, counselor). 1. Levite; ancestor of Ethan (I Chron. 6:44). 2. Man who married foreign woman (Ezra 10:29). 3. Another such man (Ezra 10:32). 4. Priest who came with Zerubbabel (Neh. 12:2). 5. Chief of people who sealed covenant (Neh. 10:27).

MALTA (See Melita).

MAMMON (măm'ŭn, riches), Aramaic word for riches (Matt. 6:24; Luke 16:11,13).

MAMRE (măm'rè, strength). 1. Amorite (Gen. 14:13,24). 2. Place a few miles N of Hebron where oak trees grew (Gen. 13:18; 18:1; 23:17,19).

MAN. Created by God in His image and likeness (Gen. 1:26,27); has body, soul, spirit (Matt. 6:25; Gen. 2:7; 41:8); dependent upon God (Matt. 6:26-30); fell into sin (Gen. 3; Rom. 5); subject to death (Rom. 5:12, 17); saved through faith in Christ (Rom. 3:21,22). New man denotes the regenerated individual (Eph. 2:15; 4:24); natural man, the unregenerated individual (I Cor. 2:14);

inner man, the soul (Rom. 7:22; Eph. 3:16); outward man, the body (II Cor. 4:16).

MAN OF SIN (See Antichrist).

MAN, SON OF, a phrase used by God in addressing Daniel (Dan. 8:17) and Ezekiel (over 80 times); by Daniel in describing a personage he saw in a night vision (Dan. 7:13,14); and many times by Jesus when referring to Himself, undoubtedly identifying Himself with the Son of Man of Daniel's prophecy and emphasizing His union with mankind (Luke 9:56; 19:10; 22:48; John 6:62).

MANAEN (măn′á-ĕn, comforter), foster-brother of Herod Antipas; Christian leader in church at Antioch (Acts 13:1).

MANAHATH (măn′á-hăth). 1. Edomite; son of Shobal (Gen. 36:23; I Chron. 1:40). 2. Town in Edom (I Chron. 8:6), site unknown

MANAHETHITES (má-nä′hăth-īts). 1. Descendants of Shobal, son of Caleb (I Chron. 2:52). 2. Descendants of Salma, son of Caleb (I Chron. 2:54).

MANASSEH (má-năs′sĕ, one who forgets). 1. Son of Joseph and Asenath (Gen. 41: 50,51). 2. Tribe descended from Manasseh (Gen. 50:23; Num. 26:28-34); half of tribe settled E of Jordan (Num. 32:33-42); the other half, W of Jordan (Josh. 17:5-10). 3. Priest named Moses whose name was changed to Manasseh because he dishonored God (Judg. 18:30). 4. 14th king of Judah; son and successor of Hezekiah; idolater (II Kings 21:1-7; 23:11); persecuted those faithful to Jehovah (II Kings 21:6); brought his country to ruin (Jer. 15:4); carried captive to Babylon (II Chron. 33:11) and later allowed to return (II Chron. 33: 10-13),15-17). 5. Man who married foreign wife (Ezra 10:30). 6. Another such man (Ezra 10:33).

MANASSEH, TRIBE OF (See Manasseh 2).

MANASSES (má-năs′ĕz), name used in NT for "Manasseh" (Matt. 1:10; Rev. 7:6).

MANASSITES (má-năs′īts, forgetting), descendants of Joseph's son Manasseh (Gen. 41:51).

MANEH (See Weights and Measures).

MANGER (măn′jēr), stall or trough for cattle (Luke 2:7-16; 13:15).

MANNA (măn′á), food resembling hoar frost miraculously provided Israel by God in the desert (Num. 11:9; Exod. 16:14-36); cannot be identified with any known natural substance.

MANOAH (má-nō′á, rest), father of Samson (Judg. 13).

MANSIONS, abiding places (John 14:2).

MANSLAYER, person who has killed another human being accidentally; could find asylum in cities of refuge (Num. 35; Deut. 4:42; 19:3-10; Josh. 20:3).

MANTLE, usually a large, sleeveless, outer garment (I Kings 19:19), or such a garment with sleeves (Isa. 3:22).

MANUSCRIPTS, DEAD SEA (See Dead Sea Scrolls).

MAOCH (mā′ŏk), father of Achish who protected David (I Sam. 27:2; 29:1-11).

MAON (mā′ŏn). 1. Descendant of Caleb (I Chron. 2:42-45). 2. Town S of Hebron (I Sam. 23:24-28; 25:1-3).

MAONITES (mā′ŏn-īts), enemies of Israel, called Menuhim, probably from Arabian peninsula (Judg. 10:11,12; Ezra 2:50).

MARA (mā′rá, bitter), name Naomi called herself (Ruth 1:20).

MARAH (mā′rá, bitterness), spring of bitter water in wilderness of Shur (Exod. 15: 22-25; Num. 33:8,9).

MARALAH (măr′á-lá), town 4 miles from Nazareth on border of Zebulun (Josh. 19:11).

MARANATHA (măr′á-năth′á, our Lord comes!), expression of greeting and encouragement after a solemn warning (I Cor. 16:22, RSV).

MARBLE (See Minerals).

MARCUS (măr′kŭs), Roman name of John Mark, kinsman of Barnabas (Acts 13:13; 15:39).

MARESHAH (má-rē′shà, possession). 1. Father of Hebron (I Chron. 2:42). 2. Grandson of Judah (I Chron. 4:21). 3. Important city of Judah between Hebrew and Gaza (Josh. 15:44); fortified by Rehoboam (II Chron. 11:5-12).

MARI, ancient city of Euphrates Valley, discovered in 1933 and subsequently excavated. 20,000 cuneiform tablets have been found, throwing much light upon ancient Syrian civilization. Mari kingdom was contemporary with Hammurabi of Babylon and the Amorite tribes of Canaan, ancestors of the Hebrews.

MARK, a word with various meanings: a special sign or brand (Gen. 4:15; Gal. 6:17), a sign of ownership (Ezek. 9:4,6; Rev. 7: 2-8), signature (Job 31:35 RSV), a target (I Sam. 20:20), a form of tattooing banned by the Lord (Lev. 19:28), a goal to be attained (Phil. 3:14), a particular brand denoting the nature or rank of men (Rev. 13:16).

MARK, JOHN (mark, a large hammer), author of 2nd Gospel. John was his Jewish name, Mark (Marcus) his Roman; called John (Acts 13:5,13), Mark (Acts 15:39), "John, whose surname was Mark" (Acts 12:12,25; 15:37); lived in Jerusalem (Acts 12:12-17); relative of Barnabas (Col. 4:10); accompanied and then deserted Paul on 1st missionary journey (Acts 12:25,13:13); went with Barnabas to Cyprus after Paul refused to take him on 2nd missionary journey (Acts 15:36-39); fellow-worker with Paul (Philem. 24); recommended by Paul to church at Colosse (Col. 4:10); may have been young man of Mark 14:51,52. Early tradition makes him the "interpreter" of Peter in Rome and founder of the church in Alexandria.

MARK, GOSPEL OF, 2nd of the four Gospels, and the shortest. Both early tradition and internal evidence of the Gospel make John Mark the author; probably written between c. 64-69 in Rome at the request of Roman Christians who wanted a record of Peter's preaching about Jesus.

Characteristics of the Gospel: rapidity of action, vividness of detail, and picturesqueness of description. Outline: 1. Baptism and temptation of Jesus (1:1-13). 2. Galilean ministry (1:14-9:50). 3. Ministry in Perea (10). 4. Passion Week and resurrection (11-16).

MARKET, place in ancient cities for sale of goods, recreation and fellowship, public business, courtroom, and forum (Matt. 11: 16,17; 20:3,6; Mark 12:38; Acts 16:19; 17:17).

MAROTH (mā'rŏth), town probably in plain W of Jerusalem (Mic. 1:12).

MARRIAGE, an intimate, personal, life-long union to which a man and woman consent (Gen. 1:26-31; 2:18-25; Matt. 19:5); the creation of God (Matt. 19:3-6); objects of marriage – procreation (Gen. 1:28; 29:32), loving companionship (Gen. 2:18-24); intended to be monogamous (Matt. 19:5; I Tim. 3:2); divorce permitted, but not part of God's plan (Matt. 19:3-9), allowable where marriage is violated by fornication (Matt. 5:31,32; 19:3-10; Mark 10:2-12; Luke 16:18); Israelites forbidden to marry Canaanites (Deut. 7:3,4), and there were legal restrictions on marrying other foreigners (Deut. 23:3-8); polygamy practiced in OT times, but it is nowhere approved (Gen. 30; I Kings 11:3); foreign wives divorced by Jews after exile (Ezra 9,10); husband and wife equal partners, but wife to be obedient to husband (I Cor. 19:9); symbolic of union between God and Israel (Jos. 2:19; Jer. 3:14; 31:32), and between Christ and the Church (II Cor. 11:2; Eph. 5:23; Rev. 21: 2,9).

MARROW, heart of the bone (Job 21:24), used figuratively of good things (Ps. 63:5; Isa. 25:6).

MARSENA (mär-sē'nà), counselor of King Ahasuerus (Esth. 1:10-14).

MARS HILL (Hill of Ares), hill in Athens dedicated to Ares, god of war (Acts 17: 16-34).

MARSH, swamp lands (Ezek. 47:11).

MARTHA (mär'thà, lady), sister of Lazarus and Mary of Bethany (Luke 10:38-41).

MARTYR (mär'tẽr, witness), one who dies to bear witness to a cause (Acts 22:20; Rev. 17:6).

MARY (mâr'ĭ). Miriam in OT. 1. See Mary, The Virgin. 2. Mother of James and Joses (Matt. 27:56; Mark 15:40; Luke 24:10), probably the mother of Clopas (John 19:25); witnessed crucifixion and visited grave on Easter morning (Matt. 27:56; 28:1). 3. Mary Magdalene; Jesus cast seven demons out of her (Mark 16:9; Luke 8:2); followed body of Jesus to grave (Matt. 27:61) and was first to learn of the resurrection (Matt. 28:1-8; Mark 16:9). 4. Mary of Bethany; sister of Lazarus and Martha; lived in Bethany (John 11:1); commended by Jesus (Luke 10:42); anointed feet of Jesus (John 12:3). 5. Mother of John Mark; sister of Barnabas (Col. 4:10); home in Jerusalem meeting place of Christians (Acts 12:12). 6. Christian at Rome (Rom. 16:6).

MARY THE VIRGIN, wife of Joseph (Matt. 1:18-25); kinswoman of Elizabeth, the mother of John the Baptist (Luke 1:36); of the seed of David (Acts 2:30; Rom. 1:3; II Tim. 2:8); mother of Jesus (Matt. 1:18, 20; Luke 2:1-20); attended to ceremonial purification (Luke 2:22-38); fled to Egypt with Joseph and Jesus (Matt. 2:13-15); lived in Nazareth (Matt. 2:19-23); took twelve-year-old Jesus to temple (Luke 2:41-50); at wedding in Cana of Galilee (John 2:1-11); concerned for Jesus' safety (Matt. 12:46; Mark 3:21,31ff; Luke 8:19-21); at the cross of Jesus (John 19:25ff), where she was entrusted by Jesus to care of John (John 19:25-27); in the Upper Room (Acts 1:14). Distinctive Roman Catholic doctrines about Mary: Immaculate Conception (1854) and Assumption of Mary (1950).

MASCHIL (mås'kil), word of uncertain meaning found in titles of Psalms 32, 42, 44, 45, 52, 54, 55, 74, 78, 88, 89, 142.

MASH, son of Aram (Gen. 10:22,23); called "Meshech" in I Chron. 1:17.

MASHAL (mā'shål), village in Asher (Josh. 19:26); called "Misheal" in Josh. 19:26, and "Mishal" in Josh. 21:30. Location unknown.

MASON (See Occupations and Professions).

MASREKAH (màs'rē-kà), royal city of King Samlah, in Edom (Gen. 36:31,36; I Chron. 1:47).

MASSA (màs'à), tribe descended from Ishmael near Persian Gulf (Gen. 25:14; I Chron. 1:30).

MASSAH (màs'à), site of rock in Horeb from which Moses drew water (Exod. 17:1-7; Deut. 6:16; 9:22); connected with Meribah (Deut. 33:8).

MASTER, word with a variety of meanings: ruler, lord, master of servant or slave (Gen. 24:9); prince, chief (I Chron. 15:27); owner (Exod. 22:8); teacher (Matt. 8:19); overseer (Luke 5:5); guide (Matt. 23:10); steersman (Acts 27:11).

MATHUSALA (See Methuselah).

MATRED (mā'trĕd), mother of Mehetabel, wife of Hadar (Gen. 36:39), who is called "Hadad" in I Chron. 1:50.

MATRI (mā'trĭ), head of Benjamite family (I Sam. 10:21).

MATTAN (màt'àn). 1. Priest of Baal (II Kings 11:18; II Chron. 23:16f). 2. Father of Shephatiah, who cast Jeremiah into prison (Jer. 38:1-28).

MATTANAH (màt'à-nà), encampment of Israel in wilderness (Num. 21:18).

MATTANIAH (màt'à-nī'à, gift from Jehovah). 1. Original name of King Zedekiah (II Kings 24:17). 2. Chief choir leader and watchman (Neh. 11:17; 12:8,25). 3. Levite (II Chron. 20:14). 4. Son of Elam (Ezra 10:26). 5. Son of Zattu (10:27). 6. Son of Pahath-Moab (10:30). 7. Son of Bani (Ezra 10:37). 8. Grandfather of Hanan (Neh. 13:13). 9. Son of Heman; head musician (I Chron. 25:4,5,7,16). 10. Levite who assisted Hezekiah (II Chron. 29:13).

MATTATHA (See Mattathah).

MATTATHAH (màt'à-thà), man who divorced

foreign wife (Ezra 10:33).

MATTATHIAS (măt´á-thī´ás, gift of Jehovah). 1. Assistant of Ezra, spelled Mattathiah (Neh. 8:4). 2. Name borne by two ancestors of Christ (Luke 3:25,26). 3. Priest; founder of Maccabee family (I Macc. 2). See also I Macc. 11:70; 16:14-16; II Macc. 14:19.

MATTENAI (măt´ē-nā´ī). 1. Priest of the restoration (Neh. 12:19). 2. Two priests under Ezra who divorced foreign wives (Ezra 10:33,37).

MATTHAN (măt´hăn), grandfather of Joseph, Mary's husband (Matt. 1:15).

MATTHAT (măt´thăt), two ancestors of Jesus (Luke 3:24,29).

MATTHEW (măth´ū), son of Alphaeus (Mark 2:14); tax collector, also called Levi (Mark 2:14; Luke 5:27); called by Jesus to become disciple (Matt. 9:9; Mark 2:14; Luke 5:27) and gave feast for Jesus; appointed apostle (Matt. 10:3; Mark 3:18; Luke 6:15; Acts 1:13).

MATTHEW, GOSPEL OF, unanimously ascribed to Matthew the Apostle by early church fathers; date and place of origin are unknown, although there is good reason to believe it was written before A. D. 70. Outline: 1. Birth and early years of the Messiah (1:1-4:16). 2. Galilean ministry of Jesus (4:17-18:35). 3. Perean ministry (19, 20). 4. Passion Week and resurrection (21-28). Characteristics: a didactic Gospel; shows fulfilment of OT prophecies in Christ; stresses Christ as King; structure of Gospel woven around five great discourses.

MATTHIAS (mă-thī´ás, gift of Jehovah), apostle chosen by lot to take place of Judas (Acts 1:15-26); had been follower of Christ (Acts 1:21,22).

MATTITHIAH (măt´ī-thī´á, gift of Jehovah). 1. Korahite Levite (I Chron. 9:31). 2. Levite; son of Jeduthun (I Chron. 15:18,21; 16:5; 25:3,21). 3. Son of Nebo who put away foreign wife (Ezra 10:43). 4. Assistant of Ezra (Neh. 8:4).

MATTOCK (măt´ŭk), single-headed pickaxe with point on one side and broad edge on other side (I Sam. 13:20,21; Isa. 7:25).

MAUL, war club or club used by shepherds (Prov. 25:18).

MAW, one of the stomachs of a ruminating animal (Deut. 18:3).

MAZZAROTH (See Astronomy).

MEADOW (mě´dō). 1. Place where reeds grow (Gen. 41:2,18). 2. Pasture land (Judg. 20:33).

MEAH (mě´á), tower in Jerusalem (Neh. 3:1; 12:39).

MEAL, ground grain used for both food and sacrificial offerings (Gen. 18:6; Lev. 2:1).

MEAL OFFERING (See Offerings).

MEALS, in Bible times usually two meals were served during the day; there were no set times for meals; foods consisted of vegetables, fruits, and meat; spices were freely used; knives, forks, and spoons were not used; people usually reclined at meals; food was cooked over charcoal, sticks,

thorns, or grass.

MEARAH (mě-á´rá), town in NE Palestine belonging to Zidonians (Josh. 13:4).

MEASURE (See Weights and Measures).

MEAT (See Food).

MEAT OFFERING (See Offerings).

MEBUNNAI (mě-bŭn´ī), one of David's bodyguard (II Sam. 23:27), called Sibbechai in II Sam. 21:18.

MECHERATHITE (mě-kě´răth-īt), description of Hepher (I Chron. 11:36).

MEDAD (mě´dăd, affectionate), one of 70 elders appointed to assist Moses (Num. 11:24-30).

MEDAN (mě´dăn), son of Abraham by Keturah (Gen. 25:2; I Chron. 1:32).

MEDEBA (mě´ē-bá), ancient town E of Jordan, c. 16 miles SE of entrance of Jordan to the Dead Sea (Num. 21:30; Josh. 13:9).

MEDES, MEDIA (mědz, mě´dī-á), inhabitants of the land of Media, W and S of the Caspian Sea. The people were a strong power for a long period (II Kings 17:6; 18:11; Esth. 1:19; Dan. 5:28).

MEDIA (See Medes).

MEDIATION (See Mediator).

MEDIATOR (mě´dī-á´těr, middle man), one who brings about friendly relations between two or more estranged people (I Sam. 2:25; Job 33:23). Christ is the mediator of the new covenant between God and man (I Tim. 2:5; Heb. 8:6; 9:15; 12:24).

MEDICINE (See Diseases).

MEDITERRANEAN SEA (měd´ī-tě-rá´ně-ăn), referred to in Scripture as "the sea" (Num. 13:29), "the great sea" (Josh. 1:4), "the uttermost sea" (Deut. 11:24), "hinder sea" (Deut. 34:2 RSV), "Sea of the Philistines" (Exod. 23:31).

MEEKNESS, mildness of temper; a humble, submissive attitude of heart; a willingness to submit to God's will (Num. 12:3; Ps. 10:17; Isa. 29:19; Matt. 5:5; II Cor. 10:1; Eph. 4:2; Col. 3:12; James 1:21). A mark of true discipleship (I Peter 3:15).

MEGIDDO (mě-gĭd´ō, place of troops), city on the Great Road linking Gaza and Damascus, connecting the coastal plain and the Plain of Esdraelon (Josh. 12:21; 17:11; Judg. 1:27; 5:19); fortified by Solomon (I Kings 9:15); wounded Ahaziah died there (II Kings 9:27); Josiah lost life there in battle with Pharaoh Necho (II Kings 23:29, 30; II Chron. 35:20-27). Large-scale excavations have revealed a great deal of material of great archaeological value.

MEGIDDON (See Megiddo).

MEHETABEL (mě-hĕt´á-bĕl). 1. Daughter of Matred, wife of King Hadar (Gen. 36:39). 2. One who sought to betray Nehemiah (Neh. 6:10-13).

MEHIDA (mě-hī´dá), ancestor of Nethinim who returned from exile (Ezra 2:52; Neh. 7:54).

MEHIR (mě´hĭr), son of Chelub (I Chron. 4:11).

MEHOLATHITE (mě-hō´lá-thīt), native of Meholah, in Jordan valley near Beth-shan

MEHUJAEL (mē-hū'jà-ĕl), descendant of Cain; father of Methusael (Gen. 4:18).

MEHUMAN (mē-hū'măn), eunuch of Ahasuerus, king of Persia (Esth. 1:10).

MEJARKON (mē-jàr'kŏn), place in Dan between Gath-rimmon and Rakkon (Josh. 19:46).

MEKONAH (mē-kō'nà), town in S Judah near Ziklah (Neh. 11:28).

MELATIAH (mĕl-à-tī'àh), Gibeonite (Neh. 3:7).

MELCHI (mĕl'kī), name of two ancestors of Jesus (Luke 3:24,28).

MELCHIAH (See Malchiah).

MELCHISEDEC (See Melchizedek).

MELCHI-SHUA (mĕl'kī-shōō'à), son of King Saul (I Sam. 31:2).

MELCHIZEDEK, MELCHISEDEK (mĕl-kīz'ĕ-dĕk, king of righteousness), priest and king of Salem (Jerusalem); blessed Abram in the name of Most High God and received tithes from him (Gen. 14:18-20); type of Christ, the Priest-King (Heb. 5:6-10; 6:20; 7).

MELEA (mē'lē-à), ancestor of Jesus (Luke 3:31).

MELECH (mē'lĕk, king), son of Micah (I Chron. 8:35; 9:41).

MELICU (See Malluch).

MELITA (mĕl'ĭ-tà), island of Malta, c. 60 miles S of Sicily; scene of Paul's shipwreck (Acts 27,28).

MELODY (See Music).

MELON (See Plants).

MELZAR (mĕl'zàr, overseer), Persian word for steward (Dan. 1:11,16).

MEMBER, any feature or part of the body (Job 17:7; James 3:5).

MEMPHIS (mĕm'fĭs), capital city of Egypt, on W bank of Nile c. 20 miles S of modern Cairo; its destruction foretold by prophets (Isa. 19:13; Jer. 2:16; 44:1; 46:14,19; Ezek. 30:13,16; all RSV). See also Noph.

MEMUCAN (mē-mū'căn), wise man at Persian court who advised Ahasuerus to punish Queen Vashti (Esth. 1:13-22).

MENAHEM (mĕn'à-hĕm, comforted), 16th king of Israel; evil; slew his predecessor, Shallum (II Kings 15:13-22).

MENAN (mē'năn), ancestor of Jesus (Luke 3:31).

MENE, MENE, TEKEL, UPHARSIN (mē'nē, mē'nē, tē'kĕl, ū-fàr'sĭn), four Aramaic words of uncertain interpretation, but probably meaning ''numbered, numbered, weighed, and found wanting,'' which suddenly appeared on the walls of Belshazzar's banquet hall (Dan. 5).

MENI (mē'nī, fate, destiny), probably Canaanite god of good luck or destiny (Isa. 65:11). Translated ''number'' in KJV.

MEONENIM (mē-ŏn'ē-nĭm), plain near Shechem named for a diviner's tree (Judg. 9:37), exact site unknown.

MEONOTHAI (mē-ŏn'ō-thī), descendant of Judah through Caleb (I Chron. 4:13,14).

MEPHAATH (mĕf'à-ăth), Levitical city in Reuben (Josh. 13:18; 21:37).

MEPHIBOSHETH (mē-fĭb'ō-shĕth). Meribaal in I Chron. 8:34; 9:40. 1. Son of Saul and Rizpah (II Sam. 21:8). 2. Son of Jonathan; grandson of Saul; crippled in accident; honored and provided for by David (II Sam. 4:4; 9:6-13; 16:1-4; 19:24-30; 21:7).

MERAB (mē'răb), daughter of King Saul (I Sam. 14:49; 18:17-19; II Sam. 21:8 where ''Merab'' should be read instead of ''Michal'').

MERAIAH (mē-rā'yà), priest (Neh. 12:12).

MERAIOTH (mē-rā'yŏth, rebellious). 1. High priest (I Chron. 6:6,7). 2. Priest; ancestor of Hilkiah (I Chron. 9:11). 3. Another priestly ancestor of Helkai (Neh. 12:15). May be same as ''Meremoth'' in Neh. 12:3.

MERARI (mē-rā'rī, bitter), youngest son of Levi; progenitor of Merarites (Num. 3:17, 33-37; Josh. 21:7,34-40).

MERATHAIM (mĕr-à-thā'ĭm, rebellion), symbolic name for Babylon (Jer. 50:21).

MERCHANDISE, MERCHANT (See Commerce).

MERCURIUS (mĕr-kū'rĭ-ŭs, Gr. Hermes), son of Zeus; messenger of the Greek gods. People of Lystra called Paul ''Mercury'' (Acts 14:12).

MERCURY (See Mercurius).

MERCY. 1. Forbearance from inflicting punishment upon an adversary or a law-breaker. 2. Compassion which causes one to help the weak, sick, or poor; cardinal Christian virtue (Matt. 5:7; James 2:1-13).

MERCY SEAT (See Tabernacle).

MERED (mē'rĕd), Judahite who married daughter of one of the Pharaohs (I Chron. 4:17,18).

MEREMOTH (mĕr'ē-mŏth, elevations). 1. Priest who returned from exile (Neh. 12:3). 2. Another priest who returned from exile (Ezra 8:33; Neh. 3:4,21). 3. Man who divorced foreign wife (Ezra 10:36). 4. Priest who signed covenant with Nehemiah (Neh. 10:5).

MERES (mē'rĕz), Persian prince (Esth. 1:14).

MERIBAH (mĕr'ĭ-bà, contention). 1. Place NW of Sinai where God gave Israelites water from rock (Exod. 17:1-7). 2. Place near Kadesh-barnea where God also gave Israelites water from a rock. Because of Moses' loss of temper God did not permit him to enter the Promised Land (Num. 20:1-13).

MERIB-BAAL (mĕr'ĭb-bā'ăl, Baal contends), son of Jonathan (I Chron. 8:34; 9:40). May be same as Mephibosheth.

MERIBAH-KADESH (See Meribah).

MERODACH (mē-rō'dăk), Marduk, the chief god of the Babylonians (Jer. 50:2).

MERODACH BALADAN (mē-rō'dăk-băl'à-dăn, Marduk has given a son), twice king of Babylon (722-710; 703-702 B. C.); invited Hezekiah to join conspiracy against Assyria (II Kings 20:12-19; Isa. 39:1-8).

MEROM (mē'rŏm, high place), place near head-waters of Jordan river where Joshua defeated N coalition (Josh. 11:5,7). Identified with Lake Huleh.

MERONOTHITE (mē-rŏn'à-thīt), inhabitant

of Meronoth, a region in Galilee, given to Naphtali (I Chron. 27:30).

MEROZ (mē'rŏz), town in Galilee not far from Nazareth (Judg. 5:23).

MESECH (See Meshech).

MESHA (mē'shà). 1. Place in S Arabia (Gen. 10:30). 2. Benjamite (I Chron. 8:9). 3. Descendant of Judah (I Chron. 2:42). 4. King of Moab in days of Ahab, Ahaziah, and Jehoram (II Kings 3:4).

MESHACH (mē'shăk), Babylonian name given to Mishael, prince of Judah (Dan. 1:3-7).

MESHECH (mē'shĕk, tall). 1. Son of Japheth (Gen. 10:2). 2. People descended from the preceding (Ezek. 27:13; 38; 39). 3. Grandson of Shem (I Chron. 1:17); "Mash" in Gen. 10:23. 4. Tribe mentioned in Ps. 120:5. May be same as 2.

MESHELEMIAH (mē-shĕl'ē-mī'à), father of Zechariah (I Chron. 9:21; 26:1,2,9); "Shelemiah" in I Chron. 26:14.

MESHEZABEEL (mē-shĕz'à-bēl, God delivers). 1. Ancestor of Meshullam (Neh. 3:4). 2. Covenanter with Nehemiah (Neh. 10:21). 3. Judahite (Neh. 11:24).

MESHILLEMITH (See Meshillemoth).

MESHILLEMOTH (mē-shĭl'ē-mŏth). 1. Father of Berechiah (II Chron. 28:12). 2. Priestly ancestor of Amashsai (Neh. 11:13). "Meshillemith" is another spelling of the same name (I Chron. 9:12).

MESHULLAM (mē-shŭl'ăm, reconciled). 1. Grandfather of Shaphan (II Kings 22:3). 2. Son of Zerubbabel (I Chron. 3:19). 3. Leading Gadite (I Chron. 5:13). 4. Chief Benjamite (I Chron. 8:17). 5. Father of Sallu (I Chron. 9:7). 6. Benjamite of Jerusalem (I Chron. 9:8). 7. Priest (I Chron. 9:11; Neh. 11:11). 8. Ancestor of priest (I Chron. 9:12). 9. Kohathite (II Chron. 34:12). 10. Israelite who returned with Ezra (Ezra 8:16). 11. Man active in matter of putting away foreign wives (Ezra 10:15). 12. Divorced foreign wife (Ezra 10:29). 13. Son of Berechiah; helped rebuild Jerusalem wall (Neh. 3:4,30; 6:18). 14. Another repairer of wall (Neh. 3:6). 15. Helper of Ezra (Neh. 8:4). 16. Priest (Neh. 10:7). 17. Priest who sealed covenant (Neh. 10:20). 18. Benjamite (Neh. 11:7). 19. Priest (Neh. 12:13). 20. Possibly the same man (Neh. 12:33). 21. Another priest (Neh. 12:16). 22. Levite (Neh. 12:25).

MESHULLEMETH (mē-shŭl'ē-mĕth), wife of King Manasseh; mother of King Amon (II Kings 21:19).

MESOBAITE (mē-sō'bà-ĭt), name of place otherwise unknown (I Chron. 11:47).

MESOPOTAMIA (mĕs'ō-pō-tà'mi-à, middle river), area between the Tigris and Euphrates rivers, a region which in the Hebrew is called Aram, Aram-Neharaim, or Padan-Aram; now practically coextensive with modern Iraq (Gen. 24:10; Deut. 23:4; Judg. 3:8-11; I Chron. 19:6; Acts 2:9; 7:2).

MESS, any dish of food sent to the table (Gen. 43:34; II Sam. 11:8; Heb. 12:16).

MESSIAH (mē-sī'à, anointed one); the basic meaning of the Heb. mashiah and the Gr. Christos is "anointed one." In the OT the word is used of prophets, priests, and kings who were consecrated to their office with oil. The expression "the Lord's anointed" and its equivalent is not used as a technical designation of the Messiah, but refers to the king of the line of David, ruling in Jerusalem, and anointed by the Lord through the priest. With the possible exception of Dan. 9:25,26 the title "Messiah" as a reference to Israel's eschatological king does not occur in the OT. It appears in this sense later in the NT, where He is almost always called "the Christ." The OT pictures the Messiah as one who will put an end to sin and war and usher in universal righteousness and through His death will make vicarious atonement for the salvation of sinful men. The NT concept of the Messiah is developed directly from the teaching of the OT. Jesus of Nazareth is the Messiah; He claimed to be and the claim was acknowledged by His disciples (Luke 4:18,19; Acts 4:27; 10:38).

MESSIAS (See Messiah).

METALS (See Minerals of the Bible).

METEYARD (mēt'yàrd), archaic word for "measures of length" (Lev. 19:35).

METHEG-AMMAH (mē'thĕg-ăm'à), town David took from Philistines (II Sam. 8:1).

METHUSAEL (mē-thū'sà-ĕl), father of Lamech (Gen. 4:18).

METHUSELAH (mē-thū'zĕ-là), son of Enoch; father of Lamech; lived 969 years (Gen. 5:21-27).

MEUNIM (mē-ū'nĭm), people who lived in Arab city near Petra (I Chron. 4:41, translated "habitations"). "Mehunims" in II Chron. 26:7 KJV; "Mehunim" in Ezra 2:50, where they are counted among the "Nethinim" at the return.

MEZAHAB (mĕz'à-hăb), grandfather of Mehetabel (Gen. 36:39; I Chron. 1:50).

MIAMIN (mī'à-mĭn). 1. Israelite who divorced foreign wife (Ezra 10:25). 2. Priest who returned with Zerubbabel (Neh. 12:5). 3. "Mijamin" in I Chron. 24:9 and Neh. 10:7 is the same word in Hebrew.

MIBHAR (mĭb'hàr), one of David's mighty men (I Chron. 11:38).

MIBSAM (mĭb'săm). 1. Ishmaelite patriarch (Gen. 25:13). 2. Descendant of Simeon (I Chron. 4:25).

MIBZAR (mĭb'zàr), descendant of Esau (Gen. 36:42).

MICAH (mī'kà, who is like Jehovah?). 1. Ephraimite whose mother made an image for which he secured a priest; both image and priest were later stolen by the tribe of Dan (Judg. 17,18). 2. Reubenite (I Chron. 5:5). 3. Grandson of Jonathan (I Chron. 8:34; 9:40). 4. Levite (I Chron. 23:20). 5. Father of one of Josiah's officers, called "Achbor" in II Kings 22:12 and "Abdon" in II Chron. 34:20. 6. Prophet Micah, the Morashthite; prophesied in reigns of Jotham, Ahaz, and Hezekiah (Mic. 1:1; Jer. 26:18). 7. Son of Imlah (II Chron. 18:14), usually called Micaiah. 8. Simeonite (Judith 6:15).

MICAH, BOOK OF, 6th of the Minor Prophets; comes from late 700's; predicts fall of Samaria which occurred in 722, but has much to say of the sins of Jerusalem in days of Hezekiah c. 700 B. C. Outline: 1. Desolation of Samaria and Jerusalem foretold (1:1-3:12). 2. Eventual blessings for Zion (4:1-8). 3. Invasions and deliverance by the Davidic ruler (4:9-5:15). 4. Condemnation for sins (6:1-7:6). 5. Eventual help from God (7:7-20).

MICAIAH (mĭ-kā'yà, who is like Jehovah?), prophet living in Samaria c. 900 B. C. who predicted the death of King Ahab (I Kings 22; II Chron. 18).

MICHA (mī'cà, who is like Jehovah?). 1. Grandson of Jonathan (II Sam. 9:12). 2. Levite covenanter (Neh. 10:11). 3. Another Levite (Neh. 11:17). 4. Another (Neh. 11:22; "Micah" in I Chron. 9:15).

MICHAEL (mī'kĕl, who is like Jehovah?). 1. Father of Sethur (Num. 13:13). 2. Two Gadites (I Chron. 5:13,14). 3. Gershonite (I Chron. 6:40). 4. Issachar chief (I Chron. 7:3). 5. Benjamite (I Chron. 8:16). 6. Manassite who joined David at Ziklag (I Chron. 12:20). 7. Father of Omri of Issachar (I Chron. 27:18). 8. Son of Jehoshaphat (II Chron. 21:2). 9. Father of Zebadiah (Ezra 8:8). 10. Archangel (Jude 9).

MICHAH (See Micah, Micha).

MICHAIAH (mĭ-kā'yà, who is like Jehovah?). 1. Father of Achbor (II Kings 22:12-14). 2. Daughter of Uriel of Gibeah (II Chron. 13:2). 3. Prince of Judah (II Chron. 17:7). 4. Ancestor of priest in Nehemiah's time (Neh. 12:35). 5. Priest (Neh. 12:41). 6. Grandson of Shaphan the Scribe (Jer. 36:11-13).

MICHAL (mī'kàl, contraction of Michael), daughter of Saul; wife of David; scoffed at David when he danced before the Lord (I Sam. 14:49; 18:20,27; 19:11-17; 25:44; II Sam. 3:13,14; 6:16-23; I Chron. 15:29).

MICHMAS, MICHMASH (mĭk'màs, mĭk'màsh, hidden place), place in Benjamin c. 8 miles NE of Jerusalem; Jonathan led Israelites to victory over Philistines there (I Sam. 13; 14; Neh. 11:31).

MICHMETHAH (mĭk'mē-thà), place on border of Ephraim and Manasseh (Josh. 16:6; 17:7).

MICHRI (mĭk'rī), Benjamite (I Chron. 9:8).

MICHTAM (mĭk'tàm), word of uncertain meaning found in the titles of six psalms (16,56-60).

MIDDIN (mĭd'ĭn), city in Judah in wilderness just W of Dead Sea (Josh. 15:61).

MIDDLE WALL, barrier between Court of the Gentiles and the Court of the Jews in the temple in Jerusalem (Eph. 2:14).

MIDIAN, MIDIANITES (mĭd'ĭ-àn). 1. Son of Abraham by Keturah (Gen. 25:1-6). 2. Descendants of Midian (Judg. 7:13).

MIGDAL-EL (mĭg'dàl-ĕl), city in Naphtali (Josh. 19:38).

MIGDAL-GAD (mĭg'dàl-gàd), city in Judah c. 24 miles W of Hebron (Josh. 15:37).

MIGDOL (mĭg'dŏl). 1. Encampment of Israelites in wilderness (Exod. 14:2; Num. 33:7). 2. Place N of Egypt where many Jews practiced idolatry (Jer. 44:1-14; 46:14).

MIGRON (mĭg'rŏn, precipice), Benjamite town (I Sam. 14:2; Isa. 10:28).

MIJAMIN (mĭj'à-mĭn). 1. Priest in David's time (I Chron. 24:9). 2. Covenanter priest (Neh. 10:7). 3. Priest who returned from exile (Neh. 12:5). 4. Man who divorced foreign wife (Ezra 10:25).

MIKLOTH (mĭk'lŏth). 1. Benjamite (I Chron. 8:32; 9:37,38). 2. One of David's rulers (I Chron. 27:4).

MIKNEIAH (mĭk-nē'yà), Temple musician (I Chron. 15:18,21).

MILALAI (mĭl-à-lā'ĭ), Levite; musician (Neh. 12:36).

MILCAH (mĭl'kà, counsel). 1. Daughter of Haran; sister of Lot (Gen. 11:27-29; 22: 20-23). 2. Daughter of Zelophehad (Num. 36:11-12; Josh. 17:3,4).

MILCOM (See Moloch).

MILDEW, fungus growth destructive of grains and fruits (Deut. 28:22; I Kings 8:37; Amos 4:9; Hag. 2:17).

MILE (See Weights and Measures).

MILETUS (mĭ-lē'tŭs), Ionian coastal city, 36 miles S of Ephesus; for centuries a great sea power; visited by Paul (Acts 20: 15,17; II Tim. 4:20, KJV has "Miletum").

MILK (See Food).

MILL, apparatus used to grind any edible grain — wheat, barley, oats, rye, etc. — into flour. It was made of two stones, the top one revolving around the one on bottom, with the grain ground between them (Exod. 11:5; Num. 11:7,8; Deut. 24:6; Jer. 25:10; Matt. 24:41).

MILLENNIUM, the Latin word for "1000 years." It comes from Rev. 20:1-15 where the expression appears six times. It refers to a period when Christ rules upon earth and Satan is bound.

MILLET (See Plants).

MILLO (mĭl'ō, fulness), mound built up with earth and stones. 1. Ancient fortification in or near Shechem (Judg. 9:6,20). 2. Filled-in fortification just N of Mt. Zion (II Sam. 5:9; I Kings 9:15,24; 11:27; I Chron. 11:8; II Chron. 32:5).

MINA (See Weights and Measures).

MIND, in Scripture often meaning "heart," "soul," in the NT often used in ethical sense (Rom. 7:25; Col. 2:18).

MINERALS OF THE BIBLE. The science of minerology is a recent one, and did not exist in ancient times. It is often impossible to be certain that when a mineral name is used in the Bible, it is used with the same meaning as that attached in modern minerology. The following minerals are mentioned in the Bible. 1. Precious stones: adamant (Ezek. 3:9; Zech. 7:12), agate (Exod. 28:19), amber (Ezek. 1:4,27; 8:2), amethyst (Exod. 28:19; Rev. 21:20), bdellium (Num. 11:7), beryl (Dan. 10:6), carbuncle (Isa. 54:12), carnelian (same as sardius), chalcedony (Rev. 21:19), chrysolyte (Rev. 21:20), coral (Job 28:18), chrysoprasus (Rev. 21:20), crystal (Job 28:17), diamond (Exod. 28:18), emerald (Exod. 28:18), jacinth (Rev. 9:17), jasper (Ezek. 28:13), ligure (Exod. 28:19), onyx (Gen. 2:12), pearl (Job 28:18), ruby (Job 28:18), sapphire (Exod. 24:10), sardius (Exod. 28:17), sardonyx (Rev. 21:20), topaz (Exod. 28:17). 2. Metals: gold (Gen. 2:11,12), silver (Matt. 10:9), iron (Num. 31:22), copper or "brass" (Gen. 4:22), lead (Exod. 15:10), tin (Num. 31:22), mercury (quicksilver), translated "dross" (Ps. 119:119). 3. The common minerals: alabaster (Matt. 26:7), brimstone (sulfur) (Gen. 19:24), marble (I Chron. 29:2), nitre (Prov. 25:20; Jer. 2:22), water.

MINES, MINING, ancient occupation of man; described in Job 28:1-11; Deut. 8:9; I Kings 7:13-50.

MINGLED PEOPLE, in Exod. 12:38 the reference is to non-Israelite people who left Egypt with the Israelites. In Jer. 25:20 and 50:37 the term is used for the mixed blood of certain of Israel's enemies.

MINIAMIN (min'ya-min). 1. Levite (II Chron. 31:15). 2. Head of family of priests (Neh. 12:17). 3. Priest in Nehemiah's time (Neh. 12:41).

MINISTER. 1. One who serves or waits on another as when Joshua was a minister to Moses (Exod. 24:13; Josh. 1:1); not a menial or one who works for wages. 2. One in the service of the state or God, like priests and Levites (Exod. 28:43; Num. 3:31) or Paul administering the gospel to the Gentiles (Rom. 15:16). 3. The representative and servant of a master; used especially for God's minister in the gospel (I Thess. 3:2; Eph. 6:21).

MINNI (min'i), kingdom which later probably came to be known as Armenia (Jer. 51:27).

MINNITH (min'ith), Ammonite town (Judg. 11:33; Ezek. 27:17).

MINSTREL, in the OT a player upon a stringed instrument; in the NT a piper (I Sam. 16:23; Matt. 9:23).

MINT (See Plants).

MIPHKAD (mif'kad), name of one of the gates of Jerusalem (Neh. 3:31).

MIRACLES, literally, an event which causes wonder. In Christian theology a miracle is (1) an extraordinary event, unexplainable in terms of ordinary natural forces; (2) an event which causes the observers to postulate a super-human personal cause; (3) an event which gives implications much wider than the event itself. Purpose of miracles is revelation and edification (John 20:31). Miracles are recognized by faith as being from God. They are outside the operation of known laws (John 4:48; Acts 2:19; II Cor. 12:12).

MIRIAM (mir'i-ăm). 1. Sister of Aaron and Moses; saved life of the baby Moses (Exod. 2:4,7,8); prophetess (Exod. 15:20); criticized Moses for his marriage (Num. 12); buried at Kadesh (Num. 20:1). 2. Judahite (I Chron. 4:17).

MIRMA (mûr'mà), Benjamite (I Chron. 8:10).

MIRROR, ancient mirrors were made of polished metal (Exod. 38:8; Job 37:18; I Cor. 13:12; James 1:23).

MISGAB (mis'gàb), town in Moab (Jer. 48:1).

MISHAEL (mish'à-ĕl, who is like God?). 1. Cousin of Moses and Aaron (Exod. 6:22; Lev. 10:4). 2. Man who stood by Ezra at reading of the law (Neh. 8:4). 3. Prince of Judah taken captive by Nebuchadnezzar (Dan. 1:6,7; 3:19-30).

MISHAL (mi'shăl), Levitical city in Asher (Josh. 21:30); "Misheal" in Josh. 19:26 and "Mashal" in I Chron. 6:74.

MISHAM (mi'shăm), son of Elpaal (I Chron. 8:12).

MISHEAL (See Mishal).

MISHMA (mish'mà). 1. Son of Ishmael (Gen. 25:14; I Chron. 1:30). 2. Simeonite (I Chron. 4:25ff).

MISHMANNAH (mish-măn'à), Gadite (I Chron. 12:10).

MISHRAITES (mish'rà-īts), family of Kirjath-jearim in Judah (I Chron. 2:53).

MISPERETH (mis'pĕ-rĕth), one who returned with Zerubbabel (Neh. 7:7); "Mispar" in Ezra 2:2.

MISREPHOTH-MAIM (mis'rĕ-fŏth-mā'ĭm), place near Sidon and Tyre (Josh. 11:8; 13:6).

MIST. 1. Steamy vapor rising from ground (Gen. 2:6). 2. Dimness of vision (Acts 13:11). 3. Description of false teachers (II Peter 2:17).

MITE (See Money).

MITER (See Dress, also Priesthood).

MITHCAH (mith'kà), desert encampment (Num. 33:28,29).

MITHNITE (mith'nit), patronymic designation of Joshaphat (I Chron. 11:43).

MITHRAISM (mith'rà-izm), cult of Mithras, Persian sun-god, widely disseminated in the Roman Empire in the 1st cent. A. D.

MITHREDATH (mith'rĕ-dàth, given by Mithras). 1. Treasurer of Cyrus (Ezra 1:8). 2. Persian officer in Samaria who slandered Jews (Ezra 4:7).

MITYLENE (mit-ĭ-lē'nè), chief city of Lesbos (Acts 20:14).

MIXED MULTITUDE, non-Israelites who travelled and associated with children of Israel (Num. 11:4-6; Neh. 13:3).

MIZAR (mi'zàr), hill near Mt. Hermon (Ps. 42:6).

MIZPAH (miz'pà, watchtower). 1. As a common noun, "watchtower" (II Chron. 20:24; Isa. 21:8). 2. Heap of stones erected in Gilead by Jacob as witness of covenant with Laban; Mizpah blessing spoken there (Gen. 31:44-49). 3. Unidentified region mentioned in Josh. 11:3 and 11:8. 3. City in Gilead (Josh. 13:26). 4. Town in Judah (Josh. 15:38). 5. Town in Benjamin (Josh. 18:26).

MIZPAR (mĭz'pàr), co-worker of Zerubbabel (Ezra 2:2). "Mispereth" in Neh. 7:7.

MIZPEH (Mizpah).

MIZRAIM (mĭz'rā-ĭm). 1. Son of Ham (Gen. 10:6,13; I Chron. 1:8,11); progenitor of Egyptians, people of N Africa, Hamitic people of Canaan. 2. Usual Hebrew word for "Egypt," always so translated in RSV.

MIZZAH (mĭz'à), grandson of Esau (Gen 36:13,17).

MNASON (nā'sŏn), Cypriot Christian with house in Jerusalem (Acts 21:16).

MOAB (mō'ăb, seed). 1. Grandson of Lot. 2. People descended from Moab; also their land E of Jordan (Num. 21:13-15); refused Israel passage to Canaan (Judg. 11:17,18); sent Balaam to curse Israel (Num. 22-24); subdued by David (II Sam. 8:2,12; I Chron. 18:2,11); denounced by prophets (Isa. 15-16; Jer. 9:26; Ezek. 25:8-11; Amos 2:1; Zeph. 2:8-11). Ruth was a Moabitess (Ruth 1:4).

MOABITE STONE, THE, black basalt stele, 2 by 4 ft., inscribed by Mesha, king of Moab, with 34 lines in the Moabite language (practically a dialect of Hebrew), giving his side of the story recorded in II Kings 3.

MOADIAH (See Maadiah).

MOLADAH (mŏl'à-dà), town c. 10 miles E of Beersheba (Neh. 11:26).

MOLE (See Animals).

MOLID (mō'lĭd), Judahite (I Chron. 2:29).

MOLOCH, MOLECH (mō'lŏk, mō'lĕk), heathen god worshiped especially by Ammonites by sacrifice of children; worship forbidden the Israelites (Lev. 18:21; 20:1-5); places of worship set up by Solomon for heathen wives (I Kings 11:7); sanctuary built in valley of Hinnom by Manasseh (II Chron. 33:6); abolished by Josiah (II Kings 23:10); denounced by prophets (Jer. 7:29-34; 19:1-13; Ezek. 20:26-39; Amos 5:26).

MOLTEN SEA (See Tabernacle).

MONEY. No money coined in Israel until after the Exile. Before that exchange of values was made by bartering; this was followed by the weight system (Gen. 23:16; I Chron. 21:25). Israelites were compelled to use the coinage of their pagan conquerors. Among coins used were the drachma (equiv. of a day's pay), stater, assarion, lepton and kodrantes (widow's mite), denarius.

MONEY CHANGER, one who changed foreign currency into sanctuary money at a profit (Matt. 21:12).

MONOTHEISM (mŏn'ō-thē-ĭzm, one god), belief that there is but one God.

MONSTERS (See Animals).

MONTH (See Calendar, Time).

MOON (See Astronomy).

MORASTHITE (mō-răs'thĭt), inhabitant of Moresheth (Jer. 26:18; Mic. 1:1).

MORDECAI (mōr'dĕ-kī, from **Marduk,** chief god of Babylon). 1. Judahite leader (Ezra 2:2; Neh. 7:7). 2. Benjamite; foster father of Esther (Esth. 2:6); deported from Judah (Esth. 2:6); saved Ahasuerus from murder plot (Esth. 2:19-23); saved Jews from Haman's plot and instituted Feast of Purim (Esth. 3:10).

MOREH, HILL OF (mō'rĕ), hill in plain of Jezreel (Judg. 7:1).

MOREH, OAK OF (KJV, "Plain of Moreh"), place near Shechem (Gen. 12:6).

MORESHETH-GATH (mō'rĕsh-ĕth-găth, possession of Gath), town c. 5 miles W of Gath in the Shephelah (Mic. 1:1; Jer. 26:18).

MORIAH (mō-rī'à), place to which Abraham went to offer up Isaac (Gen. 22:2). Solomon built temple on Mt. Moriah (II Chron. 3:1), but it is not certain whether it is the same place.

MORNING SACRIFICE (See Offerings).

MORSEL, a meal (Heb. 12:16).

MORTAL, MORTALITY. A mortal is a being subject to death (Rom. 8:11; I Cor. 15:53,54).

MORTAR. 1. Bowl-shaped vessel of stone in which grain and spices were crushed with a pestle (Num. 11:8). 2. Substance, like cement, used to bind bricks or stones together in a wall. Sometimes, mud, clay, or bitumen was used (Nah. 3:14; Ezek. 13:10,11,14,15).

MOSAIC, picture or design made by setting tiny squares or cones of varicolored marble, limestone, or semiprecious stones in some medium such as plaster to tell a story or to form a decoration.

MOSERAH (mō-sē'rà), in KJV "Mosera," encampment of Israelites in wilderness (Deut. 10:6).

MOSES (mō'zĭz, **drawn out),** Hebrew deliverer from slavery, leader, lawgiver, statesman, prophet. Exact dates for life of Moses are dependent upon the date of the Exodus, which some scholars fix c. 1440 B. C., and others as late as 1225 B. C. Born in Egypt of Israelite parents; saved from death and adopted by Pharaoh's daughter (Exod. 2:1-10); educated in Egypt (Acts 7:22); compelled to flee to Midian, where he married Zipporah, daughter of Jethro (Exod. 2:11-25); 40 yrs. later called by God to be leader of Israel (Exod. 3;4); led Israelites out of Egypt and gave them the Law at Mt. Sinai (Exod. 5-25); led Israel through 40 yrs. wilderness wanderings; opposed by Aaron and Miriam (Num. 12); opposed by Korah, Dathan, and Abiram (Num. 16); sinned at Meribah (Num. 20); named Joshua as his successor (Num. 27); died on Mt. Nebo (Deut. 34). Authorship of Pentateuch attributed to him in NT; compared to Christ (Acts 3:22; Heb. 3).

MOSES, ASSUMPTION OF, anonymous Jewish apocalyptic book, probably written early in 1st century A. D.; gives prophecy of future of Israel.

MOSES, LAW OF (See Law).

MOST HIGH, name applied to God (Gen. 14:18,19,20,22; Ps. 7:17).

MOTE, particle of dust or splinter of wood that might enter the eye (Matt. 7:3-5; Luke 6:41,42).

MOTH (See Insects).

MOTHER (See Family, Marriage).

MOUNT, MOUNTAIN; much of Palestine is hilly or mountainous. Lebanon system begins at NE corner of Mediterranean and extends through Palestine. Highest mts. found in Syria N of Palestine (c. 9100 feet above sea level). Ancient peoples often regarded mts. as holy places. In Scripture mts. are symbolic of eternity (Gen. 49:26), strength and stability; sometimes pride (Isa. 2:14) and the Messianic reign (Isa. 2:2).

MOUNT OF BEATITUDES, site of the Sermon on the Mount (Matt. 5-7); exact location unknown.

MOUNT EPHRAIM (See Ephraim).

MOURN, MOURNING. OT contains warnings against pagan mourning rites (Deut. 14: 1,2; Lev. 19:27,28); Israelite priests not allowed to take part in mourning ceremonies (Lev. 21:1-4,10,11). Mourners rent clothes (II Sam. 1:2); sprinkled earth or ashes upon head (Josh. 7:6); wore sackcloth (Isa. 22:12); wore hair loose (Lev. 10:6). Professional mourners were hired (Jer. 9:17-22; Amos 5:16; Matt. 9:23); mourning lasted at least seven days (I Sam. 31:13).

MOUSE (See Animals).

MOUTH, has various connotations: literal mouth, language, opening; sometimes personified (Ps. 119:108; Prov. 15:14; Rev. 19:15).

MOWING. This was done by hand with a short sickle—originally of flint, later of metal. The king's mowings were the portion of the harvest taken by the king as taxes (Amos 7:1).

MOZAH (mō'zà), town of Benjamin (Josh. 18:26), site uncertain.

MUFFLER (See Dress).

MULBERRY TREE (See Plants).

MULE (See Animals).

MUMMIFICATION (See Embalm).

MUPPIM (mŭp'ĭm), son or descendant of Benjamin (Gen. 46:21). Called Shupham (Num. 26:39) and Shuppim (I Chron. 7: 12,15). Shephuphan of I Chron. 8:5 may be same person.

MURDER, forbidden on penalty of death (Gen. 9:4-6; Exod. 21:14; Lev. 24:17; Deut. 19:11-13); a murdered man's nearest relative had the duty to pursue the slayer and kill him (Num. 35:19), but the slayer could flee to a city of refuge, where he would be tried and then either turned over to the avenger or be protected (Num. 35:9-34; Deut. 19:1-10).

MURRAIN (See Diseases).

MUSHI, MUSHITES (mū'shī, mū'shīts), Merarite Levite; progenitor of Mushites (Exod. 6:19; Num. 3:20; 26:58; I Chron. 6:19,47; 23:21,23).

MUSIC, existed from earliest times (Gen. 4:21); used for varied occasions: feasts (II Sam. 19:35), weddings (Jer. 7:34), funerals (Matt. 9:23); David organized sacred Levitical choir (I Chron. 6:31-48; II Chron. 29:25), and this was continued by subsequent kings. Instruments: lyre (Gen. 4:21); pipe or flute (Job 21:12; 30:31; Ps. 150:4); tambourine or timbrel (Ps. 8:12; 149:3; 150:4); bell (Exod. 28:33-35), shofar (horn) (Josh. 6:20); trumpet (Num. 10:1,2,9,10); harp (I Sam. 10:5; psaltery (Ps. 33:2; 144:9); oboe (I Kings 1:40); sistra or rattle, wrongly translated "cornets" (II Sam. 6:5); cymbals (I Chron. 15:16,19,28); organ (Gen. 4:21); shalishim a term of uncertain meaning (I Sam. 18:6); music and hymnody an important part of the Christian life (Eph. 5:19; Col. 3:16).

MUSTARD (See Plants).

MUTHLABBEN (mŭth-lăb'ĕn), expression of doubtful meaning; probably name of the tune to which Ps. 9 was sung (Ps. 9 title).

MUZZLE. Mosaic law forbade muzzling of oxen when they were treading out the grain (Deut. 25:4).

MYRA (mī'rà), seaport of Lycia (Acts 27:5).

MYRRH (See Plants).

MYRTLE (See Plants).

MYSIA (mĭsh'ĭ-à), district occupying NW end of Asia Minor bounded by the Aegean, the Hellespont, the Propontis, Bithynia, Phrygia, and Lydia. In 133 B.C. it fell to the Romans and they made it a part of the province of Asia. Traversed by Paul (Acts 16:7,8).

MYSTERY, a divine truth once hidden, but now revealed in the gospel (Rom. 16:25, 26; Eph. 1:9; 3:3,5,10; 6:19; Col. 4:3,4).

MYSTERY RELIGIONS, a cult of certain deities which involved a private ceremonial of initiation, and a secret ritual; little is known about the rites of worship and initiation, for the initiates made vows of secrecy, but it is quite certain that the worship had to do with sin, ritual uncleanness, purification, regeneration, and spiritual preparation for another life.

N

NAAM (nā'ăm), son of Caleb (I Chron. 4:15).

NAAMAH (nā'à-mà, pleasant). 1. Daughter of Lamech and Zillah (Gen. 4:22). 2. Wife of Solomon; mother of Rehoboam (I Kings 14:21,31). 3. Town in Judah (Josh. 15:41), site unknown.

NAAMAN (nā'à-măn, pleasant). 1. Grandson of Benjamin (Gen. 46:21), progenitor of Naamites (Num. 26:40). 2. Commander of Benhadad II, king of Syria; healed of leprosy by Elisha (II Kings 5:1-27).

NAAMATHITE (nā'à-mà-thīt), inhabitant of

Naamah (Job 2:11; 11:1; 20:1; 42:9).

NAAMITES (nā'à-mīts), descendants of Naaman, grandson of Benjamin (Num. 26:40).

NAARAH (nā'à-rà). 1. Wife of Ashur (I Chron. 4:5f). 2. Place on border of Ephraim (Josh. 16:7).

NAARAI (nā'à-rī), one of David's mighty men (I Chron. 11:37).

NAARAN (nā'à-răn), town N of Jericho (I Chron. 7:28); "Naarah" in Josh. 16:7 ARV).

NAARATH (See Naaran).

NAASHON, NAASSON (See Nahshon).

NABAL (nā′băl, fool), rich sheepmaster of Maon in Judah who insulted David and was saved from vengeance by his wife Abigail, who after Nabal's death became David's wife (I Sam. 25:1-42).

NABATEA, NABATEANS (năb′à-tē′ăn), Arabian tribe named in Apocrypha but not in Bible. Their king Aretas IV controlled Damascus when Paul was there (II Cor. 11:32). Capital was Petra.

NABONIDAS, NABONIDUS (năb′ō-nī′dŭs), last ruler of Neo-Babylonian Empire, 556-539 B. C.; his son Belshazzar (Dan. 5; 7:1; 8:1) was co-regent with him from the 3rd year of his reign.

NABOPOLASSAR (năb′ō-pō-lăs′àr), first ruler of the Neo-Babylonian Empire, 626-605 B. C. Allied with Medes and Scythians, he overthrew the Assyrian Empire, destroying Nineveh in 612 B. C., as prophesied by Zeph. 2:13-15.

NABOTH (nā′bŏth), Israelite whose vineyard King Ahab obtained through fraud of Jezebel (I Kings 21:1-24; II Kings 9: 21-26).

NACHON, NACON (nā′kŏn), Benjamite at whose threshing floor Uzzah was smitten for touching the ark (II Sam. 6:6). Called "Chidon" in I Chron. 13:9.

NACHOR (nā′kŏr), grandfather of Abraham; in genealogy of Jesus (Luke 3:34).

NADAB (nā′dăb). 1. Son of Aaron (Exod. 6:23); accompanied Moses up Mt. Sinai (Exod. 24:1,2,9-15); priest (Exod. 28:1); he and brother Abihu offered strange fire on altar and were killed (Lev. 10:1-7; Num. 3:4; 26:61). 2. Great-grandson of Jerahmeel (I Chron. 2:26,28,30). 3. Benjamite (I Chron. 8:30; 9:36). 4. 2nd king of Israel; son and successor of Jeroboam; wicked; slain by Baasha, who succeeded him on throne (I Kings 14:20).

NAGGAI, NAGGE (năg′ī, năg′ĕ), ancestor of Christ (Luke 3:25).

NAHALAL, NAHALLAL, NAHALOL (nā′hà-lăl, nā′hà-lŏl), town in Zebulun (Josh. 19:15).

NAHALIEL (nà-hā′lĭ-ĕl), encampment of Israelites between Mattanah and Bamoth (Num. 21:19).

NAHAM (nā′hăm), descendant of Judah through Caleb (I Chron. 4:19).

NAHAMANI (nā′hà-mā′nī), leader who returned from exile (Neh. 7:6,7).

NAHARAI, NAHARI (nā′hà-rī), Beerothite, Joab's armorbearer (II Sam. 23:37).

NAHASH (nā′hăsh). 1. Ammonite king defeated by Saul (I Sam. 11:1,2; 12:12). 2. Ammonite king whose son insulted David's messengers, and David avenged the insult (II Sam. 10; I Chron. 19). 3. Father of Abigail and Zeruiah (II Sam. 17:25).

NAHATH (nā′hăth). 1. Son of Reul, son of Esau (Gen. 36:13,17; I Chron. 1:37). 2. Descendant of Levi (I Chron. 6:26). 3. Levite (II Chron. 31:13).

NAHBI (nā′bī), spy of Naphtali (Num. 13:14).

NAHOR (nā′hòr). 1. Grandfather of Abraham (Gen. 11:22-26; I Chron. 1:26,27). 2.

Brother of Abraham (Gen. 11:26-29; 22:20,23; 24:15,24,47; 29:5).

NAHSHON (nā′shŏn), leader of tribe of Judah (Num. 1:7; 2:3; 10:14); sister Elisheba married Aaron (Exod. 6:23, KJV "Naashon"). In genealogies of Jesus the KJV has "Naasson" (Matt. 1:4; Luke 3:32).

NAHUM, THE ELKOSHITE (nā′hŭm); name is a shortened form of **Nehemiah**. Author of Book of Nahum; native of Elkosh; prophesied between 663 and 606 B. C. (Nah. 1:1; 3:8-11).

NAHUM, BOOK OF, a book predicting the downfall of Nineveh, the capital of Assyria. Written between 663 and 612 B. C. Outline: 1. Poem concerning the greatness of God (1:1-15). 2. Poem detailing the overthrow of Nineveh (2:1-3:19).

NAIL. 1. Finger-nail (Deut. 21:12; Dan. 4:33; 7:19). 2. Tent-pin (Judg. 4:21,22; 5:26); peg driven in wall to hang things on (Ezra 9:8; Isa. 22:23-25). 3. Nails of metal – iron, bronze, gold (I Chron. 22:3; II Chron. 3:9).

NAIN (nā′in), modern Nein, a village of Galilee (Luke 7:11-17).

NAIOTH (nā′ŏth), place in or near Ramah of Benjamin where Samuel lived with a band of prophets (I Sam. 19:18-20:1).

NAKED. 1. Without any clothing (Gen. 2:25; 3:7-11). 2. Poorly clad (Job 22:6). 3. Without an outer garment (John 21:7). Often used figuratively for spiritual poverty (Rev. 3:17) and lack of power (Gen. 42:9).

NAMES. Names of God reveal His nature and attributes (Exod. 3:13-15; 33:19; Ps. 8:1; I Tim. 6:1). In OT times names compounded with El (God) or Jeho-, -iah (Jehovah) were common. Messiah was given significant names: Immanuel, **God with us**; Jesus, **Saviour**. Miracles wrought in Christ's name (Acts 3:16). In patriarchal times names often indicated character, function, or destiny. By NT times both personal and family names were common or descriptive phrases were added.

NANNAR (năn′năr), name given at Ur to Babylonian moon-god Sin.

NAOMI (nā′ō-mī), wife of Elimelech of Bethlehem; mother-in-law of Ruth (Ruth 1:1-4:22).

NAPHISH (nā′fish), son of Ishmael; progenitor of tribe, probably the Nephushesim (Gen. 25:15; I Chron. 1:31; 5:19).

NAPHTALI (năf′tà-lī). 1. Son of Jacob by Bilhah (Gen. 30:8; 46:24). 2. Tribe of Naphtali; located in N Palestine (Josh. 19:32-39). Home of Barak (Judg. 4:6); one of Solomon's revenue districts (I Kings 4:15); conquered by Ben-hadad (I Kings 15:20).

NAPHTUHIM (năf-tū′hĭm), tribe of Egypt (Gen. 10:13; I Chron. 1:11).

NAPKIN (năp′kin), cloth for wiping off perspiration (Luke 19:20; John 11:44; 20:7).

NARCISSUS (nàr-cĭs′ŭs), Roman friend whose household Paul greeted (Rom. 16:11).

NARD (See Plants, Spikenard).

NATHAN (nā′thăn, **God has given**). 1. Prophet during reigns of David and Solomon; told David that not he but Solomon was to build the temple (II Sam. 7; I Chron. 17); rebuked David for sin with Bathsheba (II Sam. 12:1-25); helped get throne for Solomon (I Kings 1:8-53); wrote chronicles of reign of David (I Chron. 29:29) and Solomon (II Chron. 9:29); associated with David in arranging musical services for house of God (II Chron. 29:25). 2. Son of David (II Sam. 5:14; I Chron. 14:4). 3. Father of Igal (II Sam. 23:36). 4. Judahite (I Chron. 2:36). 5. Israelite who returned from exile (Ezra 8:16). 6. Man who put away foreign wife (Ezra 10:39).

NATHANAEL (nà-thǎn'à-ĕl, God has given), disciple of Jesus (John 1:45-51); identified commonly with Bartholomew. Church Fathers use the two names interchangeably.

NATHAN-MELECH (nà'thǎn-mē'lĕk, king's gift), officer of Josiah (II Kings 23:11).

NATIONS, usually means "Gentiles" (Exod. 34:24; Isa. 43:9; Jer. 10:1-25); a few times, Israelites (Gen. 12:2; Deut. 32:28).

NATURAL. 1. Full of sap (Deut. 34:7). 2. Animal, sensuous (I Cor. 15:44), unconverted (I Cor. 2:14), birth (James 1:23).

NATURE, the entire compass of one's life (James 3:6); the inherent character of a person or thing (Rom. 1:26; 2:14; 11:21-24); disposition (II Peter 1:4).

NAUGHTINESS (See Sin).

NAUM, NAHUM (nā'ŭm, nā'hŭm), ancestor of Christ (Luke 3:25).

NAVE (nāv), hub of a wheel (I Kings 7:33).

NAVEL (nā'vĕl); muscle, body (Prov. 3:8); umbilical cord not cut (Ezek. 16:4).

NAZARENE (nǎz'à-rēn). 1. Inhabitant of Nazareth (Matt. 2:23). 2. A Christian (Acts 24:5).

NAZARETH (nǎz'à-rĕth), town in lower Galilee belonging to tribe of Zebulun, the home town of Mary, Joseph, and Jesus (Mark 1:9; Matt. 4:13; Luke 1:26; 2:4,51; 4:16-44).

NAZARETH DECREE, an inscription on a slab of white marble, dating c. A. D. 40 to 50, by Claudius Caesar, found in Nazareth, decreeing capital punishment for anyone disturbing graves and tombs.

NAZIRITE, NAZARITE (nǎz'ĭ-rīt, consecrated), an Israelite who consecrated himself or herself and took a vow of separation and self-imposed abstinence for the purpose of some special service. The Nazirite vow included a renunciation of wine, prohibition of the use of the razor, and avoidance of contact with a dead body. The period of time for the vow was anywhere from 30 days to a lifetime (Num. 6:1-21; Judg. 13:5-7; Amos 2:11,12).

NEAH (nē'à), town in Zebulun (Josh. 19:13).

NEAPOLIS (nē-ǎp'ō-lĭs), seaport city of Philippi; visited by Paul (Acts 20:3-5).

NEARIAH (nē'à-rī'à). 1. Descendant of David (I Chron. 3:22). 2. Descendant of Simeon (I Chron. 4:42).

NEBAI (nē'bī), signer of the covenant with Nehemiah (Neh. 10:19).

NEBAIOTH, NABAJOTH (nē-bā'yŏth, nē-bā'jŏth). 1. Son of Ishmael (Gen. 25:13; 28:9; 36:3). 2. N Arabian tribe, perhaps same

as Nabataeans (Isa. 60:7).

NEBALLAT (nē-bǎl'ǎt), Benjamite town, four miles NE of Lydda (Neh. 11:34).

NEBAT (nē'bǎt), father of Jeroboam I, 1st king of Israel (I Kings 12:15).

NEBO (nē'bō). 1. Babylonian god of science and learning (Isa. 46:1). 2. Mt. from which Moses beheld Promised Land (Deut. 34:1ff). 3. Town repopulated after exile (Ezra 2:29; Neh. 7:33); site unknown.

NEBUCHADNEZZAR, NEBUCHADREZZAR (nĕb'ū-kàd-nĕz'ẽr, nĕb'ū-kàd-rĕz'ẽr). 1. 4th Dynasty ruler of Old Babylonian Empire (c. 1140 B. C.). 2. Ruler of Neo-Babylonian empire (605-562 B. C.); son of Nabopolassar; conquered Pharaoh Necho at Carchemish (605 B. C.); destroyed Jerusalem and carried Jews into captivity (587 B. C.) (II Kings 25:1-21); succeeded by son Evil-Merodach. Often mentioned in OT (I Chron. 6:15; II Chron. 36; Ezra 1:7; 2:1; 5:12,14; 6:5; Neh. 7:6; Esth. 2:6; Jer. 21:2; 52:4; Dan. 1-5).

NEBUSHASBAN (nĕb'ū-shǎs'bǎn, Nebo, save me), chief officer of Nebuchadnezzar (Jer. 39:11-14).

NEBUZARADAN (nĕb'ū-zàr-ā'dǎn, Nebo has given seed), Nebuchadnezzar's general when the Babylonians besieged Jerusalem (II Kings 25:1,11,12,20; Jer. 52:12ff); conducted captives to Babylon.

NECHO, NECHOH, NECCO (nē'kō), pharaoh of Egypt, 609-595 B. C.; defeated Josiah at battle of Megiddo (II Kings 23:29; II Chron. 35:20ff); defeated by Nebuchadnezzar at battle of Carchemish (II Kings 24:7).

NECK, term often used in Bible with literal and figurative meanings (Exod. 32:9; Deut. 9:13; Ps. 75:5; Acts 7:51).

NECKLACE, ornamental chain worn around the neck (Isa. 3:19).

NECROMANCER, NECROMANCY (nĕk'rō-mǎn-sẽr, nĕk'rō-mǎn-sè), consulting with the dead; forbidden by Mosaic law (Deut. 18:10,11); King Saul consulted with Witch of Endor (I Sam. 28:7-25).

NEDABAIAH (nĕd'à-bī'à), descendant of King David (I Chron. 3:18).

NEEDLE'S EYE, expression used by Jesus in Matt. 19:24. He meant that it is absurd for a man bound up in his riches to expect to enter the kingdom of God.

NEEDLEWORK, art of working in with the needle various kinds of colored threads in cloth (Judg. 5:30; Ps. 45:14).

NEESING (nē'zing), Elizabethan English for "sneezing" or "snorting" (Job 41:18).

NEGEB (nĕg'ĕb, dry), the desert region lying to the S of Judea, sometimes translated "the south" (Gen. 12:9; 13:1; 20:1; Num. 13:29; I Sam. 27:5f).

NEGINAH (See Music).

NEHELAMITE (nē-hĕl'à-mīt), designation of Shaiah, a false prophet (Jer. 29:24,31,32).

NEHEMIAH (nē'hĕ-mī'à, Jehovah has comforted). 1. Leader of Jews who returned with Zerubbabel (Ezra 2:2; Neh. 7:7). 2. Son of Azbuk; helped rebuild walls of Jerusalem (Neh. 3:16). 3. Son of Hachaliah; governor of Persian province of Udah after 444 B. C.; cupbearer to King Artaxerxes of Persia (Neh. 1:11; 2:1); rebuilt walls of Jerusalem (Neh. 1-4;6); cooperated with Ezra in numerous reforms (Neh. 8); nothing known of the end of his life.

NEHEMIAH, BOOK OF. Closes history of the Biblical period. Closely allied to the Book of Ezra, it was attached to it in the old Jewish reckoning. Gives the history and reforms of Nehemiah the governor from 444 to c. 420 B. C. Outline: 1. Nehemiah returns to Jerusalem (1;2). 2. Building despite opposition (3:1-7:4). 3. Genealogy of the first returning exiles (7:5-73). 4. Revival and covenant sealing (8:1-10:39). 5. Dwellers at Jerusalem and genealogies (11:1-12:26). 6. Dedication of the walls (12: 27-47). 7. Final reforms (13:1-31).

NEHILOTH (nē'hĭ-lŏth), musical term found in title to Ps. 5. May mean "wind instrument."

NEHUM (nē'hŭm), chief of Judah who returned with Zerubbabel; also called "Rehum" (Ezra 2:2; Neh. 7:7).

NEHUSHTA (nē-hŭsh'tà), mother of King Jehoiachin of Judah (II Kings 24:8; 24:12; Jer. 29:2).

NEHUSHTAN (nē-hŭsh'tăn), name given by King Hezekiah to brazen serpent he destroyed (II Kings 18:4).

NEIEL (nē-ī'ĕl), boundary town between Zebulun and Asher (Josh. 19:27). Perhaps Neah (v. 13).

NEIGHBOR. Commandments 6-10 deal with duties toward one's neighbor. In OT neighbor meant one who lived nearby, a fellow Israelite (Exod. 20:16,17); in the NT a neighbor referred to anyone for whom Christ died – all men (Luke 10:25-37). Both Testaments teach "Thou shalt love thy neighbor as thyself (Lev. 19:18c; Matt. 19:19).

NEKEB (nē'kĕb), town on NW border of Naphtali (Josh. 19:33); site uncertain.

NEKODA (nē-kō'dà), head of a family of Nethinim who could not prove Israelitish descent (Neh. 7:50,62; Ezra 2:60).

NEMUEL (nĕm'ū-ĕl). 1. Brother of Dathan and Abiram (Num. 26:9). 2. Son of Simeon (Gen. 46:10; Num. 26:12; I Chron. 4:24). "Jemuel" is a variant.

NEPHEG (nē'fĕg). 1. Brother of Korah, Dathan, and Abiram (Exod. 6:21). 2. Son of David (II Sam. 5:15; I Chron. 3:7; 14:6).

NEPHEW, grandson (Judg. 12:14), descendant (Job 18:19; Isa. 14:22), grandchild (I Tim. 5:4).

NEPHILIM (nĕf'ĭ-lĭm), antediluvians (Gen. 6:4); aboriginal dwellers in Canaan (Num. 13:32,33); not angelic fallen beings (Deut. 1:28).

NEPHISH (See Naphish).

NEPHISHESIM (nē-fish'ē-sĭm), family of Nethinim (Ezra 2:50; Neh. 7:52).

NEPHTHALIM (See Naphtali).

NEPHTOAH (nĕf-tō'à), spring and town on border of Judah and Benjamin (Josh. 15:9; 18:15); two miles NW of Jerusalem; modern Lifta.

NEPHUSIM (nē-fū'sĭm), variant reading of Nephishesim (Ezra 2:50).

NER (nŭr, lamp). 1. Father of Abner (I Sam. 14:50; 26:14). 2. Grandfather of King Saul (I Chron. 8:33).

NEREUS (nē'rūs), Roman Christian (Rom. 16:15).

NERGAL (nûr'găl), Babylonian deity of destruction (II Kings 17:30).

NERGAL-SHAREZER (nûr'găl-shà-rē'zĕr), son-in-law of Nebuchadnezzar (Jer. 39:3-13).

NERI (nē'rĭ), ancestor of Christ (Luke 3:27).

NERIAH (nē-rī'à), father of Baruch, the scribe of Jeremiah (Jer. 32:12,16; 36:4; 43:3).

NERIGLISSAR (See Nergal-Sharezer).

NERO (nē'rō), 5th Roman emperor (A. D. 54-68); killed many Christians when Rome burned in A. D. 64; called "Caesar" in Acts 25:11; Phil. 4:22.

NEST. Disturbance of nest with mother and young forbidden (Deut. 22:6).

NETHANEEL (nē-thăn'ē-ĕl, **God has given**). 1. Prince of Issachar (Num. 1:8; 2:5). 2. Son of Jesse (I Chron. 2:14). 3. Priest; played trumpet before ark (I Chron. 15:24). 4. Levite (I Chron. 24:6). 5. Son of Obededom (I Chron. 26:4). 6. Prince of Judah (II Chron. 17:7). 7. Wealthy Levite (II Chron. 35:9). 8. Man who divorced foreign wife (Ezra 10:22). 9. Priest (Neh. 12:21). 10. Levite musician (Neh. 12:36).

NETHANIAH (nĕth'à-nī'à). 1. Father of Ishmael who murdered Gedaliah (Jer. 40:8-41:18). 2. Chief singer (I Chron. 25:2,12). 3. Levite (II Chron. 17:8). 4. Father of Jehudi (Jer. 36:14).

NETHINIM (nĕth'ĭ-nĭm, **given ones**), large group of servants who performed menial tasks in the temple (I Chron. 9:2; Ezra 2:43-58; 8:17-20; Neh. 7:46-56); probably descended from Midianites (Num. 31:47), Gibeonites (Josh. 9:23), and other captives. They are usually listed with priests, Levites, singers, and porters (Ezra 2:70).

NETOPHAH, NETOPHATHITES (nē-tō'fà, nē-tō'fà-thīts), village of Judah and its inhabitants; c. three miles S of Jerusalem (II Sam. 23:28,29; I Chron. 2:54; 9:16; Neh. 12:28).

NETTLE (See Plants).

NETWORK, white cloth (Isa. 19:9), ornamental carving upon pillars of Solomon's temple (I Kings 7:18,42), a grate for the great altar of burnt-offerings at the tabernacle (Exod. 27:4; 38:4).

NEW BIRTH, the beginning of spiritual life in a believer (John 3:3,5,6; II Cor. 5:17; I Pet. 1:23). See REGENERATION.

NEW MOON (See Calendar, Feasts).

NEW TESTAMENT, a collection of 27 documents regarded by the church as inspired and authoritative, consisting of four Gospels, the Acts of the Apostles, 21 epistles, and the Book of Revelation. All were written during the apostolic period, either by apostles or by men closely associated with apostles. The Gospels tell the story of the coming of the Messiah, the 2nd person of the Trinity, to become the Saviour of the world; the Acts of the Apostles describe the beginnings and growth of the church; the epistles set forth the significance of the person and work of Christ; while the Book of Revelation tells of the consummation of all things in Jesus Christ. The formation of the NT canon was a gradual process, the Holy Spirit working in the church and guiding it to recognize and choose those Christian books God wanted brought together to form the Christian counterpart of the Jewish OT. By the end of the 4th century the NT canon was practically complete.

NEW YEAR (See Feasts, Feast of Trumpets).

NEZIAH (nĕ-zī'à), one of the Nethinim whose descendants returned from Captivity (Ezra 2:54; Neh. 7:56).

NEZIB (nĕ'zĭb), village in Judah c. 10 miles NW of Hebron (Josh. 15:43).

NIBHAZ (nĭb'hăz), god of Avites (II Kings 17:31).

NIBSHAN (nĭb'shăn), town in S of Judah (Josh. 15:62).

NICANOR (nĭ-kā'nòr), one of the seven deacons chosen by apostolic church (Acts 6:5).

NICODEMUS (nĭk'ō-dē'mŭs, victor over the people), Pharisee; member of the Sanhedrin; came to Jesus at night for conversation (John 3); spoke up for Jesus before Sanhedrin (John 7:25-44); brought spices for burial of Jesus (John 19:39-42).

NICOLAUS, NICOLAS (nĭk'ō-lā'ŭs, nĭk'ō-làs), one of the first seven deacons chosen by the apostolic church (Acts 6:5).

NICOPOLIS (nĭ-cŏp'ō-lĭs, city of victory), city of Epirus situated on Gulf of Actium, founded by Augustus Caesar (Titus 3:12).

NIGER (ni'jèr, black), surname of Symeon, leader of the church at Antioch (Acts 13:1-3).

NIGHT (See Time).

NIGHT HAWK (See Birds).

NILE (nil, meaning not certainly known), main river of Egypt and of Africa, 4,050 miles long; in the KJV usually called "The River," but never the "Nile;" begins at Lake Victoria and flows northward to the Mediterranean; annual overflow deposits rich sediment which makes N Egypt one of the most fertile regions in the world. Moses was placed on the Nile in a basket of bulrushes; turning of the Nile into blood was one of the 10 plagues (Exod. 7:20,21); on its bank grows the papyrus reed from which the famous papyrus writing material is made. Also called "Sihor" in KJV (Isa. 23:3).

NIMRAH (nĭm'rà), city in Gilead, c. 10 miles NE of Jericho (Num. 32:3); "Beth-nimrah" in Num. 32:36.

NIMRIM (nĭm'rĭm), place in Moab, probably SE of Dead Sea (Isa. 15:6; Jer. 48:34).

NIMROD (nĭm'rŏd), son of Cush; hunter, ruler, builder; founded Nineveh and kingdoms in Shinar (Gen. 10:8-12; I Chron. 1:10; Micah 5:6).

NIMRUD (nĭm'rŭd), ancient Calah in As-

syria, founded by Nimrod.

NIMSHI (nĭm'shī), father of Jehu (I Kings 19:16; II Kings 9:2,14).

NINEVEH, NINEVE (nĭn'ĕ-vĕ), ancient city, founded by Nimrod (Gen. 10:11,12), on banks of Tigris; for many years capital of Assyrian empire; kings who strengthened and beautified it: Sennacherib, Esarhaddon, Ashurbanipal; destroyed in 612 B. C. by Babylonians, Scythians, and Medes; many treasures have been discovered in its ruins by archaeologists.

NISAN (See Calendar).

NISROCH (nĭs'rŏk), god worshipped at Nineveh in whose temple Sennacherib was slain (Isa. 37:36-38).

NITER (ni'tèr), mixture of washing and baking sodas found in deposits around alkali lakes of Egypt. Used to make soap (Jer. 2:22; Mal. 3:2).

NO (nō, city of the god Amon), capital of Upper Egypt, c. 400 miles S of Cairo; fuller name, "No-amon," (Jer. 46:25); classical writers called it Thebes.

NOADIAH (nō'à-dī'à). 1. Levite who returned to Jerusalem after exile (Ezra 8:33). 2. False prophetess who tried to terrorize Nehemiah (Neh. 6:14).

NOAH (nō'à, rest). 1. Son of Lamech (Gen. 5:28,29); righteous in a corrupt age (Gen. 6:8,9; 7:1; Ezek. 14:14); warned people of Flood 120 years (Gen. 6:3); built ark (Gen. 6:12-22); saved from flood with wife and family, together with beasts and fowl of every kind (Gen. 7:8); repeopled earth (Gen. 9:10); lived 950 years. "Noe" in Matt. 24:37; Luke 3:36. 1. Daughter of Zelophehad (Num. 26:33; 27:1; 36:11; Josh. 17:3).

NOB (nŏb), town of priests in Benjamin near Jerusalem (Isa. 10:32). David fled for refuge to it; Saul destroyed it because of the people's hospitality to David (I Sam. 21:1).

NOBAH (nō'bà). 1. Manassite; took Kenath from Amorites (Num. 32:42). 2. Town near which Gideon defeated Midianites (Judg. 8:11).

NOBAI (See Nebai).

NOBLEMAN, one belonging to a king (John 4:46-53); or one well born (Luke 19:12-27).

NOD (nŏd, wandering), region E of Eden to which Cain went (Gen. 4:16).

NODAB (nō'dăb), tribe of Arabs, probably Ishmaelites E of the Jordan (I Chron. 5:19).

NOE (See Noah).

NOGAH (nō'gà), son of David (I Chron. 3:7).

NOHAH (nō'hà), son of Benjamin (I Chron. 8:2).

NON (See Nun).

NOON (See Time).

NOPH (nŏf), better known as Memphis, city S of Cairo (Isa. 19:13; Jer. 2:16; 46:19).

NOPHAH (nō'fà), city of Moab (Num. 21:30).

NORTH, often merely as a point of the compass; but sometimes a particular country, usually Assyria or Babylonia (Jer. 3:18;

46:6; Ezek. 26:7; Zeph. 2:13).

NOSE, NOSTRILS, sometimes used figuratively to mean "anger" (Gen. 27:45; Exod. 32:19).

NOSE JEWEL (See Dress).

NOVICE (nŏv'ĭs, **newly-planted**), a recent convert (I Tim. 3:6).

NUMBERS. Hebrews did not use figures to denote numbers. They spelled numbers out in full; from 2nd cent. B. C. they used Hebrew letters of the alphabet for numbers. Numbers were often used symbolically; some had special religious significance (Deut. 6:4; Gen. 2:2; Exod. 20:3-17), esp. 1,3,7,10,12,40,70; 666; 1,000).

NUMBERS, BOOK OF, 4th book of the Pentateuch; called **Numbers** because Israelite fighting force was twice numbered (1:2-46; 26:2-51). Hebrew title is **In the Wilderness** because the book describes the 40-year wilderness wandering of the Israelites after the arrival at Sinai (Exod. 19). Outline: 1. Additional legislation; organization of the host (1-10:11). 2. March from Sinai to Kadesh-Barnea (10:12-12:16). 3. Debacle at Kadesh (13;14). 4. Wanderings in wilderness (15-21:11). 5. Conquest of Trans-Jordan and preparations to enter Canaan (21:12-36:13).

NUN (nŭn), father of Josh. (Exod. 33:11).

NURSE (See Occupations and Professions).

NUT (See Plants).

NYMPHAS (nĭm'fàs), Christian in Laodicea (Col. 4:15).

O

OAK (See Plants).

OATH (ōth), a solemn appeal to God, a person, or an object to witness the truth of a statement or of the binding character of a promise (Gen. 21:23; 42:15; Matt. 5:34). Some oaths were simple; some, elaborate. Various formulas and ceremonies were used (Gen. 14:22; 24:2; I Sam. 20:23; Jer. 34: 18,19). Christ condemned indiscriminate and light taking of oaths (Matt. 5:33-37). The apostles gave oaths (II Cor. 11:31; Gal. 1:20).

OBADIAH (ō'bà-dī'à, **servant of Jehovah**). 1. Governor of Ahab's household (I Kings 18:3-16). 2. Judahite (I Chron. 3:21). 3. Chief of Issachar (I Chron. 7:3). 4. Son of Azel (I Chron. 8:38). 5. Levite who returned from captivity (I Chron. 9:16) called "Abda" in Neh. 11:17. 6. Gadite soldier (I Chron. 12:9). 7. Father of Ishmaiah, prince of Zebulun (I Chron. 27:19). 8. Prince of Judah (II Chron. 17:7). 9. Merarite Levite (II Chron. 34:12). 10. Jew who returned from captivity (Ezra 8:9). 11. Priestly covenanter with Nehemiah (Neh. 10:5). 12. Gate-keeper in Jerusalem (Neh. 12:25). 13. Prophet who wrote Book of Obadiah.

OBADIAH, BOOK OF, 4th of the minor prophets. Subject—the destruction of Edom, which from time immemorial had been hostile to Israel. The book is undated, but a probable date is late in the 8th century B. C., during the reign of Ahaz of Judah, when Edom and the Philistines were associated in warfare against Judah (verse 19). Outline: 1. Judgment pronounced upon Edom (1-14). 2. Israel's restoration in the day of Jehovah (15-21).

OBAL (ō'bàl), son of Joktan (Gen. 10:28); "Ebal" in I Chron. 1:22.

OBED (ō'bĕd, **worshiper**). 1. Early Judahite (I Chron. 2:37,38). 2. One of David's heroes (I Chron. 11:47). 3. Levitical gate-keeper (I Chron. 26:7). 4. Father of captain who helped make Joash king (II Chron. 23:1). 5. Son of Ruth and Boaz; grandfather of David (Ruth 4:21,22; Matt. 1:5; Luke 3:32).

OBED-EDOM (ō'bĕd-ē'dŏm, **one who serves Edom**). 1. Man of Gath in whose home David had the ark of God placed for three months (II Sam. 6:10-12). 2. Levite musician (I Chron. 15:18-24). 3. Son of Jeduthun; door-keeper of tabernacle (I Chron. 16:38). 4. Treasurer (I Chron. 26:15); may be same as No. 3. 5. Descendant of No. 4 who kept treasury in Amaziah's time (II Chron. 25:24).

OBEDIENCE. Supreme test of faith is obedience to God (I Sam. 28:18). Faith and obedience are linked throughout the Bible (Gen. 22:18; Rom. 1:5; I Peter 1:14). Christ Himself obeyed the Father (Phil. 2:8). Children are to obey their parents (Col. 3:20); Christians are to obey the state (Rom. 13:1-7).

OBEISANCE (ō-bā'sàns), the act of bowing low or of prostrating one's self in token of respect or submission (Gen. 43:28; Exod. 18:7; II Sam. 1:2).

OBIL (ō'bil), Ishmaelite; keeper of David's camels (I Chron. 27:30).

OBLATION (See Offerings).

OBOTH (ō'bōth), encampment of Israel E of Moab (Num. 21:10,11; 33:43).

OCCUPATIONS AND PROFESSIONS: apothecary; artificer—a worker with any materials, as carpenter, smith, engraver, etc. (Gen. 4:22; Isa. 3:3); author; baker; barber; beggar; butler; carpenter; chamberlain, an officer to look after the personal affairs of a sovereign; clerk; confectioner, a female perfumer or apothecary (I Sam. 8:13); coppersmith, counselor; doctor of the law (Acts 5:34,40); diviner, one who obtains or seems to obtain secret knowledge, particularly of the future; dyer; farmer; fisherman; fuller, one who washed or bleached clothing (I Kings 18:17; Isa. 7:3); herdsman; hunter; judge; lawyer (Matt. 22:35); Luke 7:30); magician; mason; musician; nurse; physician; plowman; porter—a gate-keeper; potter; preacher; priest; prophet(-ess); publican—collector of Roman revenue; rabbi—teacher of Jewish law; recorder; robber; ruler; sailor; saleswoman (Acts 16:14); schoolmaster; scribe; seer; senators—elders of Israel (Ps. 105:22); sergeant—Roman lictors who attended the chief magistrates when they appeared in public (Acts 16: 35,38); servant; servitor; sheepmaster; sheep-shearer; shepherd; silversmith; singer; slave; smith; soldier; sorcerer; spinner; steward; tanner; taskmaster; tax collector; teacher; tent-maker; tetrarch; tiller; town clerk; treasurer; watchman; weaver; wizard; writer.

OCHRAN, OCRAN (ŏk'răn), prince of the tribe of Asher (Num. 1:13; 7:72).

ODED (ō'dĕd, he restored). 1. Father of Azariah the prophet (II Chron. 15:1). 2. Prophet of Samaria in days of Ahaz (II Chron. 28:9-15).

ODOR (ō'dẽr), pleasant or unpleasant smell (Gen. 8:21; Lev. 1:9-17; John 11:39). Also used figuratively (Rev. 5:8).

OFFENSE (ŏ'fĕns'), used in a variety of ways; injury, hurt, damage, occasion of sin, stumbling block, infraction of law, sin, transgression, state of being offended.

OFFERINGS. Biblical prescriptions regarding the various kinds of offerings arose from the need for purification from sin or the desire of the worshiper to enter into fellowship with God. Offerings were derived from both animal and vegetable kingdoms. Types of offerings: sin offering – for acts of unconscious transgression, mistakes or other inadvertencies (Lev. 4:1-35; 6:24-30); trespass offering, or guilt offering, signified expiation and restitution, and availed for inadvertent offenses, false swearing and improper dealings with a neighbor; peace offering – symbolized right spiritual relations with God; meal offering, or meat offering; drink offering, or libation, accompanied many of the sacrifices (Exod. 29:40f); wave offering, heave offering (Exod. 29:24-28; Lev. 7:14).

OFFICER, holder of an official position (I Kings 4:7; Luke 12:58).

OFFSCOURING, contemptuous word for sweepings, scraps, filth, dung, etc. (Lam. 3:45; I Cor. 4:13).

OG (ŏg), Amorite king of Bashan (Deut. 31:4; Josh. 2:10; I Kings 4:19); giant; defeated by Israelites (Deut. 3:1-13).

OHAD (ō'hăd), son of Simeon (Gen. 46:10).

OHEL (ō'hĕl), son of Zerubbabel (I Chron. 3:20).

OHOLAH, OHOLIBAH (ō-hō'lȧ, ō-hōl'ĭ-bȧ), symbolic names for Samaria and Jerusalem (Ezek. 23 RSV).

OIL, in Bible almost always olive oil; a prime article of food; used for making soap, anointing wounds, cosmetics, official inauguration to high office, light. Symbolic of the Holy Spirit. Ps. 23:5; 104:15.

OIL TREE (See Plants).

OINTMENTS AND PERFUMES. Usually made of perfumed olive oil; used for anointing hair, skin, anointing dead bodies (Esth. 2:3-12; Matt. 26:6-13; Luke 23:56).

OLD GATE, gate in NW corner of Jerusalem in Nehemiah's time (Neh. 3:6).

OLD TESTAMENT. Bible from Genesis to Malachi; composed of 39 books – five of law, 12 of history, five of poetry, five of major prophets, and 12 of minor prophets. Classification of our present Hebrew Bibles is different – five of law, eight of prophets, and 11 of miscellaneous writings; these 24 contain all our 39 books. All of these books were regarded by Israelites as Scripture, inspired and authoritative, before the 1st century A. D. They appeared over a period of c. 1000 years. The authors of many of them are unknown.

OLIVE (See Plants).

OLIVES, MOUNT OF, (called Olivet in two KJV contexts: II Sam. 15:30; Acts 1:12). A ridge, c. 1 mile long, with four identifiable summits, E of Jerusalem, beyond the Valley of Jehoshaphat, through which flows the Kidron stream. Gethsemane, Bethphage, and Bethany are on its slopes (II Sam. 15:30; Zech. 14:4; Matt. 21:1; 24:3; 26:30; Mark 11:1; 13:3; 14:26; Luke 19:29,37; 22:39; John 8:1; Acts 1:12).

OLYMPAS (ō-lĭm'pȧs), Christian in Rome to whom Paul sent greetings (Rom. 16:15).

OMAR (ō'mȧr), grandson of Esau (Gen. 36:11,15).

OMEGA (ō-mē'gȧ), last letter of the Greek alphabet.

OMER (See Weights and Measures).

OMNIPOTENCE (ŏm-nĭp'ō-tĕns), attribute of God which describes His ability to do whatever He wills (Job 42:2; Jer. 32:17; Matt. 19:26).

OMNIPRESENCE (ŏm'nĭ-prĕz'ĕns), attribute of God by virtue of which He fills the universe in all its parts and is present everywhere at once (Ps. 139:7-12; Jer. 23:23, 24; Acts 17:27,28).

OMNISCIENCE (ŏm-nĭsh'ĕns), attribute by which God perfectly and eternally knows all things which can be known, past, present, and future (Prov. 15:11; Ps. 147:5; Isa. 46:10).

OMRI (ŏm'rē). 6th king of Israel (c. 886-874 B. C.); commander-in-chief under Elah, son of Baasha; proclaimed king after murder of Elah; transferred capital to Samaria; evil influence in land (I Kings 16:25,26). 2. Benjamite (I Chron. 7:8). 3. Judahite (I Chron. 9:4). 4. Prince of Issachar (I Chron. 27:18).

ON (ŏn). 1. Delta city of Egypt, called by the Greeks "Heliopolis" (City of the Sun). "Aven" in Ezek. 30:17; "Bethshemesh" in Jer. 43:13. Joseph married Asenath, daughter of the priest of On. Worship of the Sun-god was centered there. 2. Reubenite chief (Num. 16:1).

ONAM (ō'năm). 1. Horite (Gen. 36:23). 2. Great-grandson of Judah (I Chron. 2:26,28).

ONAN (ō'năn, strong), son of Judah; refused to consummate a levirate marriage and was therefore slain (Gen. 38:4-10).

ONESIMUS (ō-nĕs'ĭ-mŭs, profitable), runaway slave of Philemon of Colossae; converted through Paul, who wrote Epistle to Philemon in his behalf (Col. 4:9; Philem.)

ONESIPHORUS (ŏn'ė-sif'ō-rŭs, profitbringer), Ephesian Christian who ministered to Paul in prison in Rome (II Tim.

1:16-18; 4:19).

ONION (See Plants).

ONLY-BEGOTTEN, title applied to our Lord by John (John 1:14,18; 3:16,18; I John 4:9) and once in Hebrews (11:17) in connection with His uniqueness.

ONO (ō'nō, strong), town in Benjamin, c. 6 miles SE of Joppa (I Chron. 8:12; Neh. 6:2; 11:35).

ONYCHA (ŏn'ĭ-kà), incense ingredient probably made from a certain mussel (Exod. 30:34).

ONYX (See Minerals).

OPHEL (ō'fĕl, hill), S end of temple hill in Jerusalem (II Chron. 33:14; Neh. 11:21).

OPHIR (ō'fēr). 1. Son of Joktan (Gen. 10:29). 2. Land occupied by the descendants of Ophir, SW Arabia, source of gold; important way-station for ships from India which brought ivory, apes, peacocks, almug trees (I Kings 10:11,12,22; Job 22:24; 28:16).

OPHNI (ŏf'nī), city in N Benjamin, c. 2-1/2 miles NW of Bethel (Josh. 18:24).

OPHRAH (ŏf'rà, hind). 1. Town in Benjamin (Josh. 18:23), c. 3 miles NE of Bethel. 2. Town in Manasseh where Angel of Jehovah talked with Gideon (Judg. 6:24). 3. Son of Meonothai (I Chron. 4:14).

ORACLE (ŏr'à-k'l). 1. An utterance from deity (II Sam. 16:23). 2. Utterance of prophecy, translated "burden" (Isa. 14:28; 15:1; Ezek. 12:10; Nah. 1:1). 3. Holy of Holies in the temple (I Kings 6:5f).

ORATOR. 1. Isa. 3:3 (KJV) has "eloquent orator," where ASV correctly reads "skilful enchanter." 2. A public speaker, esp. an advocate (Acts 24:1).

ORDAIN, ORDINATION, act of conferring a sacred office upon someone, as: deacons (Acts 6:6), missionaries (Acts 13:3); elders (Acts 14:23). OT priests were ordained to office (Exod. 28:41; 29:9).

OREB AND ZEEB (ō'rĕb, zē'ĕb, raven and wolf), two princes of the Midianites slain by Gideon, the first at the rock of Oreb, the second at the wine-press of Zeeb (Judg. 7:24,25; Ps. 83:11).

OREB, ROCK OF (See Oreb and Zeeb).

OREN (ō'rĕn), son of Jerahmeel (I Chron. 2:25).

ORGAN (See Musical Instruments).

ORION (See Astronomy).

ORNAMENT (See Dress).

ORNAN (ŏr'năn), Jebusite prince (called "Araunah" in II Sam. 24:16ff) whose

threshing-floor David purchased (I Chron. 21:15-25).

ORONTES (ō-rŏn'tēz), chief river in Syria, almost 400 miles long, rises in Anti-Lebanon range, and flows N for most of its course.

ORPAH (ŏr'pà, neck), Moabite woman whom Chilion, son of Naomi, married (Ruth 1:4, 14; 4:9,10).

OSEE (See Hosea).

OSHEA (See Joshua).

OSNAPPAR (See Ashurbanipal).

OSPRAY (See Birds).

OSSIFRAGE (See Birds).

OSTIA (ŏs'tĭ-à), the port of Rome, on the Tiber mouth, some 16 miles from the city.

OSTRACA (ŏs'trà-kà), inscribed fragments of pottery, or potsherds. Some important ancient documents have come down to us in this form (e.g. the Lachish Letters).

OSTRICH (See Birds).

OTHNI (ŏth'nī), son of Shemaiah (I Chron. 26:7).

OTHNIEL (ŏth'nĭ-ĕl), son of Kenaz, the brother of Caleb; captured Debir (Josh. 15:13-19; Judg. 1:11-15); delivered Israelites from king of Mesopotamia (Judg. 3:8-11).

OUCHES (ouch'ĕz). 1. Settings for precious stones on high-priest's ephod (Exod. 28:11). 2. A rich texture inwrought with gold thread or wire (Ps. 45:13).

OVEN; ancient ovens were primitive – often a hole in the ground coated with clay and in which a fire was made. The dough was spread on the inside and baked. Sometimes ovens were made of stone, from which the fire is raked when the oven is very hot, and into which the unbaked loaves are placed (Hos. 7:4-7).

OVERSEER; inspector (Gen. 39:4,5), foreman (I Chron. 2:18), bishop, overseer (Acts 20:28).

OWL (See Birds).

OWNER OF A SHIP, ship-owner or the sailing-master of a ship engaged in state service (Acts 27:11).

OX (See Animals, Cattle).

OX GOAD, pointed stick used to urge the ox to further effort (Judg. 3:31).

OZEM (ō'zĕm). 1. Son of Jesse (I Chron. 2:15). 2. Son of Jerahmeel (I Chron. 2:25).

OZIAS (See Uzziah).

OZNI (ŏz'nī), son of Gad and father of the Oznites (Num. 26:16).

P

PAARAI (pā'à-rī), one of David's mighty men (II Sam. 23:35). Called "Naarai" in I Chron. 11:37).

PADAN-ARAM (pā'dăn-ā'răm, plain of Aram), region near head of fertile crescent; sometimes called simply "Mesopotamia;" in Gen. 48:7, "Padan" only. Gen. 31:18.

PADON (pā'dŏn), one of the Nethinim who returned from Babylon (Ezra 2:44; Neh. 7:47).

PAGIEL (pā'gĭ-ĕl), chief of Asher in wilderness (Num. 7:72).

PAHATH-MOAB (pā'hăth-mō'ăb, governor of Moab), head of one of the leading families of Judah; descendants returned from exile (Ezra 2:6; 8:4; 10:30; Neh. 3:11; 9:38; 10:14).

PAI (See Pau).

PALACE. Palaces have been found all over the Biblical world by archaeologists. Some were made of stone; some were fortress palaces; some were constructed over important wells or springs of water.

PALAL (pā'lăl), son of Uzai (Neh. 3:25).

PALESTINE (păl'ĕs-tīn). The name is derived from Philistia, an area along the S seacoast occupied by the Philistines (Ps. 60:8); original name was Canaan (Gen. 12:5); after the conquest it came to be known as Israel (I Sam. 13:19), and in the Greco-Roman period, Judea. The land was c. 70 miles wide and 150 miles long, from the Lebanon mts. in the N to Beersheba in the S. The area W of the Jordan was 6,000 sq. m.; E of the Jordan, 4,000 sq. m. In the N, from Acco to the Sea of Galilee, the distance is 28 miles. From Gaza to the Dead Sea in the S the distance is 54 miles. The land is divided into five parts: the Plain of Sharon and the Philistine Plain along the coast; adjoining it, the Shepheleh, or foothills region; then the central mt. range; after that the Jordan valley; and E of the Jordan the Transjordan plateau. The varied configuration of Palestine produces a great variety of climate. The Maritime Plain has an annual average temperature of 57 degrees as Joppa; Jerusalem averages 63 degrees; while Jericho and the Dead Sea area have a tropical climate. As a result, plants and animals of varied latitudes may be found. The winter season, from Nov. to April, is mild and rainy; the summer season, from May to October, is hot and dry. Before the conquest the land was inhabited by Canaanites, Amorites, Hittites, Horites, and Amalekites. These were conquered by Joshua, judges, and kings. The kingdom was split in 931 B. C.; the N kingdom was taken into captivity by the Assyrians in 722 B. C.; the S kingdom by the Babylonians in 587 B. C. From 587 B. C. to the time of the Maccabees the land was under foreign rule by the Babylonians, Persians, Alexander the Great, Egyptians, and Syrians. In 63 B. C. the Maccabees lost control of the land to the Romans, who held it until the time of Mohammed. In NT times Palestine W of the Jordan was divided into Galilee, Samaria, and Judea; and E of the Jordan into the Decapolis and Perea.

PALLU, PALLUITE (păl'ū, păl'ū-it), son of Reuben spelled Phallu (Gen. 46:9); progenitor of the Palluites (Num. 26:5).

PALMER WORM, probably a kind of locust (Joel 1:4; 2:25; Amos 4:9).

PALM TREE (See Plants).

PALMYRA (See Tadmor).

PALSY (See Diseases).

PALTI (păl'tī). 1. Spy from Benjamin (Num. 13:9); "Phalti" in KJV of I Sam. 25:44. 2. Man to whom Saul gave Michal, David's wife (I Sam. 25:44).

PALTIEL (păl'tĭ-ĕl, God delivers). 1. Prince of Issachar (Num. 34:26). 2. Once "Phaltiel" in KJV (II Sam. 3:15), the same as Palti 2.

PALTITE (păl'tīt), one of David's mighty

men (II Sam. 23:26); "Pelonite" in I Chron. 11:27; 27:10.

PAMPHYLIA (păm-fĭl'ĭ-à), Roman province of S Asia Minor extending along Mediterranean coast 75 miles and 30 miles inland to Taurus mts. (Acts 2:10; 13:13; 14:24; 15:38; 27:5).

PANNAG (păn'ăg), meaning uncertain; perhaps an article of trade (Ezek, 27:17).

PAP (păp), breast (Luke 11:27; Rev. 1:13).

PAPER (See Papyrus, Writing).

PAPHOS (pā'fŏs), capital of the island of Cyprus; visited by Paul (Acts 13:6-13).

PAPYRUS (pà-pī'rŭs), reed which grows in swamps and along rivers or lakes, especially along the Nile; from 8-12 feet tall; used to make baskets, sandals, boats, and especially paper – the most common writing material of antiquity. The NT books were undoubtedly all written on papyrus (Job 8:11; Isa. 18:2).

PARABLE (păr'à-b'l, likeness). 1. Proverbial saying (I Sam. 10:12; 24:14); prophetic figurative discourse (Num. 23:7,18,24); poem (Num. 21:27-30; Ps. 49:5; 78:2); riddle (Ps. 49:4; Ezek. 17:2). 2. A story in which things in the spiritual realm are compared with events that could happen in the temporal realm; or, an earthly story with a heavenly meaning (Matt. 13; Luke 15). Differs from fable, myth, allegory, proverb. Characteristic teaching method of Jesus.

PARACLETE (păr'à-klēt, advocate), one who pleads another's cause. Used by Christ of the Holy Spirit in John's Gospel (14: 16,26; 15:26; 16:7) and of Christ in I John 2:1.

PARADISE (păr'à-dīz, park) (Eccl. 2:5); forest (Neh. 2:8); orchard (S. of Sol. 4:13); home of those who die in Christ (Luke 23:43). Exact location uncertain.

PARAH (pā'rà), city in Benjamin (Josh. 18:23).

PARALLELISM, a characteristic of OT Hebrew verse, which has neither rhyme nor meter, but parallelism – the repetition in successive phrases of similar or contrasting ideas.

PARALYSIS (See Diseases).

PARALYTIC (See Diseases).

PARAMOUR (păr'à-mŏŏr), male lover (Ezek. 23:20).

PARAN (pā'răn, ornamental), a wilderness area in the central area of the Sinaitic peninsula. Its boundaries are uncertain (Gen. 14:6; 21:21; Num. 10:12; 12:16; 13:26; I Sam. 25:1).

PARAN, MOUNT, unidentified peak in Paran (Deut. 33:2; Hab. 3:3).

PARBAR (pär'bär), some building on the W side of the temple area translated "suburbs" (I Chron. 26:18; II Kings 23:11).

PARCHED GROUND, mirage (Isa. 35:7).

PARCHMENT (See Writing).

PARDON, forgiveness. God demands a righteous ground for pardoning the sinner – the atoning work of Christ (Exod. 34:9; I Sam. 15:25,26; Isa. 55:7).

PARENT. The necessity of children honoring and obeying their parents is taught in both Testaments (Exod. 20:12; Lev. 19:3; Eph. 6:1; Col. 3:20). Parents are expected to love and care for their children and not to provoke them to wrath (II Cor. 12:14; Eph. 6:4; Col. 3:21).

PARENTAL BLESSINGS, very important in OT times; often prophetic of a child's future (Gen. 27:4,12,27-29).

PARMASHTA (pàr'mȧsh'tȧ), son of Haman (Esth. 9:9).

PARMENAS (pàr'mē-nȧs), one of seven men chosen for daily ministration to the poor (Acts 6:5).

PARNACH (pàr'nȧk), father of Elizaphan the prince of Zebulun (Num. 34:25).

PAROSH (pā'rŏsh), one whose descendants returned from exile (Ezra 2:3; Neh. 7:8); **Pharosh** in KJV of Ezra 8:3.

PAROUSIA (pȧ-rōō'sĭ-ȧ, presence, coming), a Greek word frequently used in NT of our Lord's return (I Cor. 15:23; I Thess. 4:15; Matt. 24:3; I Thess. 3:13; II Peter 1:16; a visit of a person of high rank.

PARSHANDATHA (pàr'shȧn-dā'thȧ), son of Haman (Esth. 9:7).

PARTHIANS (pàr'thĭ-ȧnz), inhabitants of Parthia, a country NW of Persia and S of the Caspian Sea. At one time their empire extended from the Tigris to India. Known today as Iran. Acts 2:9.

PARTITION, MIDDLE WALL OF, probably the wall in the temple area in Jerusalem separating the court of the Gentiles from the courts into which only Jews might enter (Eph. 2:14).

PARTRIDGE (See Birds).

PARUAH (pȧ-rōō'ȧ), father of Jehoshaphat employed by Solomon (I Kings 4:17).

PARVAIM (pàr-vā'ĭm), place from which Solomon obtained gold (II Chron. 3:6).

PASACH (pā'sȧk), son of Japhlet (I Chron. 7:33).

PASDAMMIM (pȧs-dăm'ĭm), place in Judah between Shocoh and Azekah (I Chron. 11:13). "Ephesdammim" in I Sam. 17:1.

PASEAH (pȧ-sē'ȧ). 1. Son of Eshton (I Chron. 4:12). 2. Progenitor of Nethinim who returned from captivity (Neh. 3:6).

PASHUR (pȧsh'hẽr). 1. Son of Immer (Jer. 20:1); chief governor of temple; put Jeremiah in stocks (Jer. 20:1-6). 2. Son of Melchiah who with others sought to have Jeremiah put to death (Jer. 21:1; 38:1,4). Father of Gedaliah (Jer. 38:1).

PASSAGE, ford of a river (Gen. 32:23), mountain pass (I Sam. 13:23), a crossing (Josh. 22:11).

PASSION OF CHRIST (See Christ, Jesus).

PASSOVER, FEAST OF (See Feasts).

PASTORAL EPISTLES. A common title for I and II Timothy and Titus, which were written by the apostle Paul to his special envoys sent on specific missions in accordance with the needs of the hour. I Timothy was written to Timothy at Ephesus while Paul was still traveling in the coastal regions of the Aegean Sea; Titus was written to Titus in Crete, probably from Nicopolis or some other city in Macedonia;

II Timothy, from Rome toward the end of the second imprisonment. The epistles concern church organization and discipline, including such matters as the appointment of bishops and deacons, the opposition of heretical or rebellious members, and the provision for maintenance of doctrinal purity.

The authorship of these Epistles has been disputed because of differences in vocabulary and style from the other epistles ascribed to Paul, and because their references to his travels do not accord with the itineraries described in Acts. The differences though real, have been exaggerated, and can be explained on the basis of a change of time, subject-matter, and destination. These are letters written by an old man to his understudies and successors at the close of his career, and for churches that have passed the pioneering stage. The historical references can be fitted into Paul's biography if he were released from the first imprisonment mentioned in Acts, and if he resumed traveling before his final imprisonment and execution. There is no theological discrepancy between the Pastorals and the other epistles, for while these emphasize good works, they emphasize also salvation by faith (Titus 3:5).

Background: Released from the first imprisonment, Paul left Titus on Crete to organize the churches (Titus 1:5) and went to Ephesus, where he stationed Timothy (I Tim. 1:3,4). Proceeding to Macedonia, he wrote to Timothy and Titus. Evidently Paul had visited the Ionian cities just before his last arrest, for he mentions Troas, Corinth, and Miletus (II Tim. 4: 13,20). He had been deserted by most of his friends (4:10,11) and had already stood trial once (4:16).

Outlines: I Timothy: 1. Personal Testimony, 1:1-20; 2. Official Regulations, 2:1-4:5; 3. Administrative Counsel, 4:6-6:21. Titus: Church Administration, 1:1-16; 2. Individual Conduct, 2:1-3:8; Personal Advice, 3:9-15. II Timothy: 1. Memories of the Past, 1:1-18; 2. Mandate for the Future, 2:1-26; 3. Menace of Apostasy, 3:1-17; 4. Memoranda for Action, 4:1-22.

PATARA (pȧt'ȧ-rȧ), seaport on SW coast of Lycia (Acts 21:1,2).

PATHROS (pȧth'rŏs), country of Upper Egypt (Isa. 11:11; Jer. 44:1,15; Ezek. 29:14; 30:14).

PATHRUSIM (pȧth-rōō'sĭm), inhabitants of Pathros, Egypt (Gen. 10:13f; I Chron. 1:11f).

PATIENCE, endurance under trials; longsuffering, one of the fruits of the Spirit (Gal. 5:22).

PATMOS (pȧt'mŏs), island, 15 miles in circumference, off the coast of Asia Minor, c. 28 miles S of Samos; apostle John banished there (Rev. 1:9).

PATRIARCHS, PATRIARCHAL AGE (pā'trĭ-ȧrk), name given in NT to those who founded the Hebrew race and nation: Abraham (Heb. 7:4), sons of Jacob (Acts 7: 8,9), David (Acts 2:29). The term is now commonly used to refer to the persons whose names appear in the genealogies and covenant-histories before the time of Moses (Gen. 5,11).

PATROBAS (păt'rō-băs), Roman Christian to whom Paul sent greetings (Rom. 16:14).

PAU (pā'ū), capital city of king Hadar of Edom (Gen. 36:39); "Pai" in I Chron. 1:50.

PAUL (pôl, little). Hebrew name was Saul; always so called until his clash with Bar-Jesus at Paphos (Acts 13:9), after which he is always called Paul. Jews of the dispersion often had both a Hebrew and a Roman name. **Background.** Benjamite Jew (Phil. 3:5); son of a Pharisee (Acts 23:6); inherited Roman citizenship from father (Acts 22:28); native of Tarsus (Acts 21:39); educated in Jerusalem under Gamaliel (Acts 22:3; 26:4,5); tentmaker (Acts 18:3); present at stoning of Stephen (Acts 7:58; 26:10,11). **Conversion and Early Activities.** Converted on way to Damascus to persecute Christians (Acts 9; 22; 26); preached Christ in Damascus (Acts 9:20-22); visit to Arabia (Gal. 1:17); fled from Damascus (Acts 9: 23-25; Gal. 1:17); held in suspicion by Christians in Jerusalem (Acts 9:26-28); sent to Tarsus by Jerusalem Christians (Acts 9:30); brought to Antioch by Barnabas (Acts 11:20-26); took famine collection to Jerusalem with Barnabas (Acts 11:29,30). **Missionary Journeys.** Sent by church at Antioch on missionary journey with Barnabas and Mark (Acts 13,14); attended Jerusalem Council over Judaizing question (Acts 15); second missionary journey to Asia Minor, Macedonia, and Greece (Acts 15:36-18:22); third missionary journey (Acts 18:23-21:16); arrest in Jerusalem and hearings (Acts 21:17-23:30); imprisonment in Caesarea (Acts 23:31-26:32); sent to Rome (Acts 27,28); imprisoned for at least two years in Rome (Acts 28:30); released from prison; further missionary activities, during which he wrote I Timothy and Titus; 2nd Roman imprisonment (II Timothy); death at Rome c. 67 A. D. (II Tim. 1:8,14; 4). Author of at least 13 NT epistles.

PAULUS, SERGIUS (pô'lŭs, sûr'jĭ-ŭs), Roman proconsul of Cyprus; became Christian through Paul (Acts 13:6-12).

PAVEMENT, THE, courtyard outside palace in Jerusalem where Pilate passed public sentence on Jesus (John 19:13).

PAVILION (pả-vil'yŭn, booth, tent), movable tent or canopy (I Kings 20:12; Jer. 43:10). Figuratively of God's protection (Ps. 27:5) or majesty (Job 36:29 ASV).

PEACE, in OT times the usual word of greeting (II Kings 9:18); spirit of tranquillity and freedom from either inward or outward disturbance (Num. 6:26; I Kings 4:24; Acts 9:31 ASV); peace with God brought through a right relation with God in Christ (Eph. 2:14-17).

PEACE OFFERING (See Offerings).

PEACOCK (See Birds).

PEARL, formed within the bodies of certain mollusks; symbol of spiritual truths (Matt. 7:6). In Bible the word often means precious stones (I Tim. 2:9; Rev. 17:4).

PEDAHEL (pĕd'ȧ-hĕl), prince of Naphtali appointed by Moses to apportion Palestine (Num. 34:28).

PEDAHZUR (pĕ-dā'zĕr), prince of Manasseh; father of Gamaliel (Num. 1:10; 2:20).

PEDAIAH (pĕ-dā'yȧ, **Jehovah redeems**). 1. Grandfather of Jehoiakim (II Kings 23:36). 2. Father of Zerubbabel (I Chron. 3:18). 3. Father of Joel, chief of Manasseh (I Chron. 27:20). 4. Man who helped build wall of Jerusalem (Neh. 3:25). 5. Benjamite, father of Joed (Neh. 11:7). 6. Levite; temple treasurer (Neh. 13:13).

PEEP, cry of a bird (Isa. 10:14) and noise made by wizards uttering sounds that are supposed to come from the dead (Isa. 8:19).

PEKAH (pē'kȧ, **to open**), son of Remaliah the 18th king of Israel; murdered Pekahiah; reigned 734-714 B. C. (II Kings 15:27); made league with Damascus against Judah (II Kings 15:37,38); became subject to Assyria (II Kings 15:29); murdered by Hoshea (II Kings 15:25-31; II Chron. 28:5-15).

PEKAHIAH (pĕk'ȧ-hī'ȧ, **Jehovah has opened**), Israel's 17th king; son of Menahem; wicked and idolatrous (II Kings 15: 24); murdered by Pekah (II Kings 15:22-25).

PEKOD (pē'kŏd), Aramaean tribe living to E and near mouth of the Tigris (Jer. 50:21; Ezek. 23:23).

PELAIAH (pē-lā'yȧ). 1. Judahite (I Chron. 3:24). 2. Levite who helped Ezra and Nehemiah (Neh. 8:7; 10:10).

PELALIAH (pĕl-ȧ-li'ȧ), priest; father of Jeroham and Amzi (Neh. 11:12).

PELATIAH (pĕl-ȧ-ti'ȧ, **Jehovah has delivered**). 1. Grandson of Zerubbabel (I Chron. 3:21). 2. Simeonite military leader (I Chron. 4:42). 3. Man who sealed covenant with Nehemiah (Neh. 10:22). 4. Prince of Israel; Ezekiel prophesied against him (Ezek. 11:2,13).

PELEG (pē'lĕg, **division**), son of Eber (Gen. 10:25; 11:16-19); "in his days was the earth divided" (Gen. 10:25).

PELET (pē'lĕt). 1. Son of Jahdai (I Chron. 2:47). 2. Benjamite; joined David at Ziklag (I Chron. 12:3).

PELETH (pē'lĕth). 1. Father of On who conspired against Moses and Aaron (Num. 16:1). 2. Jerahmeelite (I Chron. 2:33).

PELETHITES (pĕl'ē-thīts, **courier**), part of David's bodyguard (II Sam. 8:18; 15:18; 20:7,23; I Kings 1:38,44; I Chron. 18:17).

PELICAN (See Birds).

PELLA (pĕl'ȧ), city E of the Sea of Galilee; one of the cities forming the Decapolis.

PELONITE (pĕl'ō-nīt), title of two of David's mighty men, Helez and Ahijah (I Chron. 11:27,36).

PEN (See Writing).

PENCE (See Money).

PENDANT (See Dress).

PENIEL, PENUEL (pē-ni'ĕl, pē-nū'ĕl, **face of God**). 1. Place where Jacob wrestled with angel of Jehovah (Gen. 32:24-32), not far from Succoth. 2. Son of Hur (I Chron. 4:4). 3. Son of Shashak (I Chron. 8:25).

PENINNAH (pē-nin´á), one of Elkanah's wives; taunted Hannah (I Sam. 1:2-7).

PENKNIFE, small knife to sharpen pens or writing reeds (Jer. 36:23).

PENNY (See Money).

PENTATEUCH, THE (pĕn´tà-tòŏk, law or teaching), 1st five books of the Bible; covers period of time from creation to end of the Mosaic era; authorship attributed to Moses in Scripture. Outline: 1. Era of beginnings (Gen. 1:1-11:32). 2. Patriarchal period (Gen. 12:1-50:26). 3. Emancipation of Israel (Exod. 1:1-19:2). 4. Religion of Israel (Exod. 19:3-Lev. 27:34). 5. Organization of Israel (Num. 1:1-10:10). 6. Wilderness wanderings (Num. 10:11-22:1). 7. Preparations for entering Canaan (Num. 22:2-36:13). 8. Retrospect and prospect (Deut.).

PENTECOST (pĕn´tē-kŏst, 50th day). 1. Jewish Feast of Weeks (Exod. 34:22; Deut. 16:9-11), also called the Feast of Harvest (Exod. 23:16) and the Day of First-Fruits (Num. 28:26), which fell on the 50th day after the Feast of the Passover. The feast originally celebrated the dedication of the first-fruits of the corn harvest, the last Palestinian crop to ripen. The ritual of the feast is described in Lev. 23:15-21. 2. The Christian Pentecost fell on the same day as the Jewish Feast of Weeks. The coming of The Holy Spirit (Acts 2) transformed the Jewish festival into a Christian anniversary, marking the beginning of the Christian church.

PEOR (pē´ŏr, opening). 1. Mt. in Moab near town of Paal-Peor (Deut. 3:29). 2. Contraction for Baal-Peor (Num. 25:18; 31:16; Josh. 22:17). See Baal-Peor.

PERAEA (pē-rē´á), name given by Josephus to the region E of the Jordan; known in the Gospels as "beyond Jordan" (Matt. 4:15,25; Mark 3:7,8); the word "Peraea" does not occur in the Bible.

PERAZIM, MOUNT (pĕr´à-zīm), usually identified with Baal-perazim, where David obtained a victory over the Philistines (II Sam. 5:20; I Chron. 14:11).

PERDITION (pĕr-dĭ´shŭn, destruction), in the NT the word refers to the final state of the wicked, one of loss or destruction (John 17:12; Phil. 1:28; II Thess. 2:3; I Tim. 6:9).

PERDITION, SON OF, phrase used to designate Judas Iscariot (John 17:12) and the "man of sin" who is the Antichrist (II Thess. 2:3).

PEREA (See Peraea).

PERES (pē´rĕs, divided), one of the words written on a wall for Belshazzar and interpreted by Daniel (Dan. 5:1-29).

PERESH (pē´rĕsh), son of Machir (I Chron. 7:14,16).

PEREZ (pē´rĕz), son of Judah by Tamar (Gen. 38:29); ancestor of Perezites (Num. 26:20, KJV "Pharzites"), David and Jesus (Ruth 4:12; Matt.1:3). Called "Pharez" in

Gen. 46:12; Num. 26:20,21.

PEREZ-UZZA (pē´rĕz-ŭz´á, breach of Uzzah), name of place where Uzzah was struck dead for touching the ark of God (II Sam. 6:8).

PERFECT, PERFECTION, complete, finished; ritually clean victim of sacrifice (Exod. 12:5); uprightness of character (Gen. 6:9; 17:1; "undefiled," Ps. 119:1); absolute perfection (God).

PERFUME, for personal use (Prov. 7:17; 27:9; S. of Sol. 3:6; Isa. 3:20,24 RSV) and for incense (Exod. 30:34-38).

PERGA (pûr´gà), chief city of Pamphilia of Asia Minor (Acts 13:13,14; 14:24,25).

PERGAMUM, PERGAMOS (pûr´gà-mŭm, pûr´gà-mòs), city of Mysia in Asia Minor (Rev. 1:11; 2:12-17). Modern Bergama.

PERIDA (pē-rī´dà), servant of Solomon (Neh. 7:57); "Peruda" in Ezra 2:55.

PERIZZITE (pĕr´i-zīt), aborigines of Canaan (Gen. 13:7; 34:30; Exod. 3:8,17; 23:23; 33:2; 34:11; Deut. 20:17; Josh. 3:10; 24:11; Judg. 1:4).

PERJURY (pĕr´jĕr-ē), false swearing; forbidden by God (Lev. 19:12; Ezek. 16:59).

PERSECUTION (pĕr´sē-qū´shŭn); Christ foretold that His disciples would be persecuted (Matt. 10:23,24). The apostolic church was persecuted by the Jews (Acts 14:22; I Peter 4:13,14). Nero was the first Roman official who persecuted the Christians on a large scale. Christianity did not become a legal religion in the Roman empire until A. D. 323, when Constantine legalized it. Until then Roman emperors and governors persecuted Christians whenever they chose to do so.

PERSEPOLIS (pĕr-sĕp´ō-lĭs), capital of Persia, 30 miles NE of modern Shiraz; founded by Darius I (521-486 B. C.); destroyed by Alexander the Great in 331 B. C.

PERSEVERANCE (pûr-sē-vēr´áns); the word is found only in Eph. 6:18, where it is used in connection with prayer. The theological doctrine of the perseverance of the saints holds that the truly regenerated cannot ever fall away from Christ so as to lose their salvation. Both Calvinists and Arminians seek support for their view in the Scriptures, both sides often using the same passages, but interpreting them differently.

PERSIA (pûr´zhà), geographically, Persia comprised the Iranian plateau, bounded by the Tigris valley on the W and S, the Indus valley on the E, and by the Armenian ranges and the Caspian Sea to the N, comprising c. one million square miles. Cyrus founded the empire by defeating Media and Babylonia, and it dominated Asia from 539 to 331 B. C. Cyrus the Great permitted the Jews to return from the Babylonian captivity (II Chron. 36:22, 23; Ezra 1); Darius I authorized the rebuilding of the temple (Ezra 6); Xerxes I was probably the Ahasuerus of the book of Esther; and Artaxerxes I permitted additional exiles to return (Ezra 7:8; Neh.

2:1-8).

PERSIS (pûr'sĭs), Christian woman at Rome to whom Paul sent a greeting (Rom. 16:12).

PERUDA (See Perida).

PESHITTA (pĕ-shĕt'tà), ancient Syriac translation of the Bible.

PESTILENCE (pĕs'tĭ-lĕns), plague sent by divine providence (Exod. 5:3; Jer. 14:12; Matt. 24:7).

PESTLE (pĕs''l), an instrument used to grind in a mortar (Prov. 27:22).

PETER (pē'tẽr, rock), apostle; original name was Simon, or Simeon (Acts 15:14); native of Bethsaida (John 1:44); son of Jonah (Matt. 16:17); with his father and his brother Andrew he followed trade of fisherman (Mark 1:16); married (Mark 1:30; I Cor. 9:5); introduced to Jesus by Andrew (John 1:40-42); called to full time association with Jesus (Mark 1:16-20; Luke 5: 1-11); called to be apostle (Mark 3:13-19; Luke 6:12-16); witnessed raising of Jairus' daughter (Mark 5:37; Luke 8:51); witnessed transfiguration (Matt. 17:1; Mark 9:2); confessed Messiahship and unique Sonship of Jesus at Caesarea Philippi (Matt. 16:13-16; Mark 8:27-29); did not understand Christ's need to die (Matt. 16:22; Mark 8:32); with Jesus in Gethsemane (Matt. 26:37; Mark 14: 33); denied Jesus at high priest's palace (Matt. 26:69-75; Mark 14:70-72); Christ appeared to him personally on resurrection day (Luke 24:34; I Cor. 15:5); told by Jesus to feed His sheep (John 21:1-23); preached at Pentecost (Acts 2:14-40); leader in early church (Acts 1-12; 15); author of I and II Peter; according to tradition was put to death by Nero at Rome (c. 64-67).

PETER, FIRST EPISTLE OF; written by Peter the apostle (1:1); written from "Babylon" possibly Rome (5:13); destination—Christians "in Pontus, Galatia, Cappadocia, Asia, and Bithynia" (1:1); date of writing—probably in the middle 60's; purpose – to encourage Christians who had been undergoing persecution. Outline: 1. Salutation (1:1,2). 2. Nature of salvation (1:3-12). 3. Experience of salvation (1:13-25). 4. Obligations of salvation (2:1-10). 5. Ethics of salvation (2:11-3:12). 6. Confidence of salvation (3:13-4:11). 7. Behavior of the saved under suffering (4:12-5:11). 8. Concluding salutations (5:12-14).

PETER, SECOND EPISTLE OF, written by Peter the apostle (1:1); destination – same as I Peter (3:1); place of writing is uncertain, but probably Rome; time of writing was toward the end of Peter's life; occasion – the threat of apostasy. Outline: 1. Salutation (1:1). 2. Character of spiritual knowledge (1:2-21). 3. Nature and perils of apostasy (2:1-22). 4. Doom of the ungodly (3:1-7). 5. Hope of believers (3:8-13). 6. Concluding exhortation (3:14-18).

PETHAHIAH (pĕth'à-hī'à). 1. Head of 19th course of priests (I Chron. 24:16). 2. A Levite (Neh. 9:5). 3. Jewish counselor of King Artaxerxes (Neh. 11:24).

PETHOR (pē'thòr), home of Balaam in Mesopotamia, perhaps W of Carchemish (Num. 22:5; Deut. 23:4).

PETHUEL (pē-thū'ĕl), father of the prophet Joel (Joel 1:1).

PETRA (pē'trà, rock, cliff), capital city of the Nabataeans mentioned indirectly (Judg. 1:36; II Kings 14:7; Isa. 16:1).

PEULETHAI, PEULTHAI (pē-ŭl'ē-thī, pē-ŭl'thī), Levite; porter of tabernacle (I Chron. 26:5).

PHALEC (fā'lĕk), Gr. form of Heb. Peleg (Luke 3:35).

PHALLU (See Pallu).

PHALTI (fāl'tī). 1. Spy from Benjamin to search out Canaan (Num. 13:9). 2. Son-in-law of Saul (I Sam. 25:44). KJV has "Phaltiel" in II Sam. 3:15.

PHALTIEL (fāl'tĭ-ĕl). 1. Prince of Issachar (Num. 34:26). 2. Son-in-law of Saul (II Sam. 3:15). "Phalti" in I Sam. 25:44.

PHANUEL (fà-nū'ĕl, face of God), father of Anna the prophetess (Luke 2:36).

PHARAOH (fâr'ō), title of Egyptian rulers. Twenty-six separate dynasties of pharaohs have been recorded, extending from Menes, 3400 B. C. to Psamtik III, deposed at the Persian conquest in 525 B. C. Individual names were given the pharaohs at birth: Pharaoh Neco, Pharaoh Hophra, etc. Pharaohs mentioned in OT contexts: 1. Contemporaries of Abraham (Gen. 12:10-20). 2. Pharaohs mentioned in connection with Joseph (Gen. 39:1; 40:2ff; 43; 45:16-21; 47:1-11). 3. Pharaohs who oppressed Israelites in Egypt (Exod. 1-15). 4. Daughter of the Pharaoh, whom Mered married (I Chron. 4:18). 5. Pharaoh Sheshonk I (945-924 B. C.) – reigned during Solomon's reign (I Kings 3:1; 9:16,24; 11:1). 6. Pharaoh of Sennacherib's day (II Kings 19:21; Isa. 36:6). 7. Pharaoh Neco (II Kings 23:29-35). 8. Pharaoh Hophra (Ezek. 29:2-3).

PHARES, PHAREZ (fā'rĕz), Judah's twin son by his daughter-in-law, Tamar (Gen. 38:29; I Chron. 2:4).

PHARISEES (făr'ĭ-sēz), prominent sect of the Jews in Christ's time; opposed Jesus and His teachings; plotted His death (Matt. 12:14); were denounced by Him (Matt. 23). Characteristic teachings: belief in oral as well as written law; resurrection of the body; belief in the existence of spirit world; immortality of the soul; predestination; future rewards and punishment based upon works. Matt. 9:11-14; 12:1-8; 16:1-12; 23; Luke 11:37-44; Acts 15:5; 23:6-8.

PHAROSH (See Parosh).

PHARPAR (fâr'pàr), river of Damascus (II Kings 5:12).

PHARZITE (fâr'zit), descendant of Pharez, son of Judah (Num. 26:20).

PHASEAH (See Paseah).

PHASELIS (fà-sē'lis), Rhodian colony in Lycia (I Macc. 15:23).

PHASELUS (fà-sĕl'ūs), Latinization of Phasael, alternatively Phasaelus, the son of Antipater the Idumaean, and brother of Herod the Great.

PHEBE (See Phoebe).

PHENICE, PHOENIX (fē-nī'sē, fē'nĭks), town on the S coast of Crete (Acts 27:12). Phenice is also used as a term for Phoenicia.

PHICHOL (fī'kŏl), captain of Abimelech's army (Gen. 21:22,32; 26:26).

PHILADELPHIA (fĭl'à-dĕl'fĭ-à, brotherly love), city of Lydia in Asai Minor (Rev. 1: 11; 3:7-13).

PHILEMON (fī-lē'mŏn, loving), convert of Paul at Colosse; Epistle to Philemon written to him.

PHILEMON, EPISTLE TO, written by Paul during his 1st Roman imprisonment, and addressed to "Philemon . . . Apphia . . . Archippus, and the church in your house." It deals with Philemon's runaway slave, Onesimus, who was converted through Paul, established in the faith by him, and then sent back to Philemon with a plea that Onesimus be forgiven for the wrong done to his master. The slave had apparently absconded with some of his master's money, which he had squandered; and Paul suggests that Philemon not insist on getting his money back, and if he did then Paul would repay it.

PHILETUS (fī-lē'tŭs, worthy of love), false teacher in the church at Ephesus (II Tim. 2:17).

PHILIP (See Herod).

PHILIP THE APOSTLE (fĭl'ĭp, lover of horses), native of Bethsaida, the same town as Andrew and Peter (John 1:44); undoubtedly first a disciple of John the Baptist (John 1:43); brought his friend Nathanael to Jesus (John 1:45); called to apostleship (Matt. 10:3; Mark 3:18; Luke 6:14); faith tested by Jesus before feeding of 5,000 (John 6:5,6); brought Greeks to Jesus (John 12:20-23); asked to see the Father (John 14:8-12); in upper room with 120 (Acts 1:13).

PHILIP THE EVANGELIST (fĭl'ĭp, lover of horses), chosen one of the seven deacons (Acts 6:5); a Hellenist, or Greek-speaking Jew; preached in Samaria (Acts 8); Ethiopian eunuch converted through him (Acts 8:26-40); Paul stayed at his home in Caesarea, where he lived with his four unmarried daughters who were prophetesses (Acts 21:8,9).

PHILIP (fĭl'ĭp, lover of horses). 1. King of Macedonia; father of Alexander the Great; founder of city of Philippi in Macedonia (I Macc. 1:1). 2. Philip V, king of Macedonia (I Macc. 8:5). 3. Governor of Jerusalem under Antiochus, regent of Syria (II Macc. 5:22). 4. Herod Philip. Married Herodias (Matt 14:3; Mark 6:17; Luke 3:19). 5. Herod Philip II, tetrarch of Batanaea, Trachonitis, Gaulanitis, and parts of Jamnia. Best of Herods (Luke 3:1).

PHILIPPI (fī-lĭp'ī), city of Macedonia, founded by Philip II, father of Alexander the Great, in 358 B. C.; scene of the famous battle of Philippi in 42 B. C.; made Roman colony by Octavian; first European city to hear a Christian missionary (Acts 16).

PHILIPPIANS, EPISTLE TO THE (fī-lĭp'ī-

ănz), letter written by Paul in prison, probably from Rome, although this is not stated, to thank the church for the gift of money sent him by the hands of Epaphroditus, who subsequently became seriously ill and was nursed back to health by Paul, who now sends him back to Philippi with this letter. There is no word of criticism of the church; the main emphasis is one of joy and triumphant faith. 1. Greetings and thanksgiving (1:1-11). 2. Progress of the gospel (1:12-20). 3. Working and suffering for Christ (1:21-30). 4. Exhortation to humility (2:1-13). 5. Exhortation to the Christian life (2:14-18). 6. Personal remarks involving Timothy and Epaphroditus (2: 19-30). 7. Exhortations and warnings (3: 1-4:9). 8. Thanksgiving (4:10-20). 9. Final greeting (4:21-22).

PHILISTINES (fī-lĭs-tēnz); in KJV "Palestina" in Exod. 15:14; Isa. 14:29,31; "Palestine" in Joel 3:4. A people who inhabited the Philistine plain of Palestine during the greater part of OT times. Their country extended from Joppa to S of Gaza, and had five great cities: Ashdod, Gaza, Ashkelon, Gath, and Ekron (Josh. 13:3; I Sam. 6:17). They came from Caphtor (Jer. 47:4; Amos 9:7), which may be Crete or the islands of the Aegean. They were non-Semitic, perhaps Aryans, and came to Palestine in large numbers about the time of the judges. Eventually the whole land of Canaan was given the name of the small area along the coast where the Philistines lived. They brought with them a knowledge of metal working, which the Hebrews did not have until the time of David, and therefore they dominated the Israelites until the time of David (Judg. 13:1). Deliverance for Israel came through various deliverers: Shamgar (Judg. 3:31), Samson (Judg. 13-16), Samuel (I Sam. 7:1-14); they were defeated by Jonathan (I Sam. 14) and subjugated by David (I Sam. 17;18). During the divided monarchy they regained their power (I Kings 15:27; II Chron. 21:16; 28:18). Sargon (722-705 B. C.) deported some of them and set over them an Assyrian governor.

PHILOLOGUS (fī-lŏl'ō-gŭs), Christian in Rome to whom Paul sent a salutation (Rom. 16:15).

PHILOSOPHY. Epicureans and Stoics are mentioned in the NT (Acts 17:18). In Col. 2:8 Paul deprecates false philosophy.

PHINEHAS (fĭn'ē-às, mouth of brass). 1. Son of Eleazar and grandson of Aaron (Exod. 6:25; I Chron. 6:4,50; 9:20; Ezra 7:5; 8:2), who slew Zimri and Cozbi at God's command (Num. 25:6-15; Ps. 106:30). 2. Son of Eli; sinful priest (I Sam. 1:3; 2:12-17, 22-25,27-36; 3:11-13). He and his brother were killed by Philistines (I Sam. 4). 3. Father of Eleazar who returned from exile (Ezra 8:33).

PHLEGON (flē'gŏn), believer in Rome to whom Paul sent a greeting (Rom. 16:14).

PHOEBE, PHEBE (fē'bē, pure), deaconess

at Cenchrea, highly commended by Paul; delivered Epistle to the Romans (Rom. 16:1,2).

PHOENICIA, PHENICIA (fē-nĭsh'ĭ-à), country along Mediterranean coast, c. 120 miles long, extending from Arvad or Arados to Dor, just S of Carmel. The Semitic name for the land was Canaan. The term Phoenicia is from a Greek word meaning "dark red," perhaps because the Phoenicians were the discoverers of the crimson-purple dye derived from the murex shell-fish. The people were Semites who came in a migration from the Mesopotamian region during the 2nd millennium B. C. They became great seafarers, establishing colonies at Carthage and Spain, and perhaps even reached England. They were famous shipbuilders (Ezek. 27:9) and carpenters (I Kings 5:6). Its most famous cities were Tyre and Sidon. Its religion was polytheistic and immoral, and was brought to Israel by Jezebel (I Kings 16:31; 18:19). Hiram, one of their kings was friendly with David and Solomon (II Sam. 5:11; I Kings 5:1-12; II Chron. 2:3-16), and another Hiram helped Solomon in the building of the temple in Jerusalem (I Kings 7:13-47; II Chron. 2: 13,14). Jesus healed a Syrophoenician woman's daughter in its regions (Mark 7:24-30). Paul visited Christians there (Acts 15:3; 21:2-7).

PHRYGIA (frĭj'ĭ-à), province in SW Asia Minor which once included the greater part of Asia Minor; obtained by Rome in 133 B. C. Paul preached there on his 2nd and 3rd missionary journeys (Acts 16:6; 18:23).

PHURAH, PURAH (fū'rà), servant of Gideon (Judg. 7:10,11).

PHUT (fūt), 3rd son of Ham (Gen. 10:6; I Chron. 1:8); descendants lived in Africa between Ethiopia (Cush) and Egypt (Mizraim) (Gen. 10:6); many were mercenary soldiers (Ezek. 27:10; Jer. 46:9).

PHUVAH, PUA, PUAH (fū'và, pū'à). 1. Son of Issachar (Gen. 46:13; Num. 26:23; I Chron. 7:1). 2. Father of Tola the judge (Judg. 10:1).

PHYGELLUS (fĭ-jĕl'ŭs), Christian of the province of Asia who turned away from the apostle Paul (II Tim. 1:15).

PHYLACTERY (See Dress).

PHYSICIAN (See Occupations and Professions).

PI-BESETH (pĭ-bē'sĕth), (See Phi-Beseth).

PICTURES, occurs three times in KJV: Num. 33:52, perhaps stone idols are meant; Prov. 25:11, inlaid work in gold and silver; Isa. 2:16, perhaps the carved figureheads of ships.

PIETY (pī'ĕ-tē), religious duty.

PIGEON (See Birds).

PI-HAHIROTH (pī'hà-hī'rŏth), place in NE Egypt where Egyptian army overtook Israelites (Exod. 14:2,9; Num. 33:7).

PILATE (pī'lầt), 5th procurator of Judea (A. D. 26-36). He tried Jesus, and although he found Him innocent, he yielded to Jewish pressure to have Him crucified

(Matt. 27; Mark 15; Luke 23; John 18; Acts 3:13). Eusebius says he ended his life by suicide.

PILDASH (pĭl'dăsh), son of Nahor (Gen. 22:22).

PILEHA (pĭl'ē-hà), man who sealed covenant with Nehemiah (Neh. 10:24).

PILGRIM (pĭl'grĭm), sojourner in a strange place (Heb. 11:13-16; I Peter 2:11).

PILGRIMAGE (pĭl'grĭ-mĭj). 1. Jews were expected to make pilgrimages to the temple in Jerusalem for the great feasts (Ps. 120-134; Acts 2:5-11). 2. The NT describes Christians as pilgrims (Heb. 11:13; I Peter 2:11).

PILLAR (pĭl'ẽr). 1. Stone pillars were often set up as a memorial (Gen. 28:18; 31:45; 35:20; II Sam. 18:18). 2. Pillars as supports of buildings (I Kings 10:12). 3. Pillar of cloud and fire which guided Israel in the wilderness (Exod. 13:21; 14:19-24). 4. In the NT the word occurs figuratively, of God (I Tim. 3:15); of men (Gal. 2:9; Rev. 3:12); and of an angel's legs (Rev. 10:1).

PILLAR OF CLOUD AND FIRE. God guided Israel out of Egypt and through the wilderness by a pillar of cloud by day and fire by night (Exod. 13:21,22). The pillar of cloud rested over the tent of meeting outside the camp whenever the Lord met Moses there (Exod. 33:7-11). The cloud and fire were divine manifestations.

PILLOW (pĭl'ō), stone pillow for Jacob (Gen. 28:11,18); bolster in I Sam. 19:13; cushion for the head (Mark 4:38).

PILOT (pī'lŭt), mentioned among the skilled craftsmen of Tyre (Ezek. 27:8,27,28,29).

PILTAI (pĭl'tī), priest (Neh. 12:17).

PIM (See Weights and Measures).

PIN, tent peg (Judg. 4:21; 5:26); stick for beating up woof in the loom (Judg. 16: 13,14); crisping pins (Isa. 3:22) were probably bags or purses.

PINE (See Plants).

PINNACLE (pĭn'à-k'l), on a building, a turret, battlement, pointed roof or peak. Satan tried to get Jesus to cast Himself down from the pinnacle of the temple (Matt. 4:5,6; Luke 4:9).

PINON (pī'nŏn), chief of Edom of the family of Esau (Gen. 36:40,41; I Chron. 1:52).

PIRAM (pī'răm), Canaanite king of Jarmuth (Josh. 10:1-11).

PIRATHON (pĭr'à-thŏn), town of Ephraim where Abdon (Judg. 12:13-15) and Benaiah (II Sam. 23:30; I Chron. 11:31; 27:14) lived.

PIRATHONITE (See Pirathon).

PISGAH (pĭz'gà), mt. on NE shore of Dead Sea (Num. 21:20). Balak brought Balaam to the top of Pisgah (Num. 23:14), and Moses viewed the Land of Promise from the top of Pisgah (Deut. 3:17).

PISHON, PISON (pī'shŏn, pī'sŏn), river of Eden (Gen. 2:11). It cannot be identified.

PISIDIA (pĭ-sĭd'ĭ-à), Roman province in S Asia Minor just N of Pamphilia; visited twice by Paul (Acts 13:14; 14:24).

PISON (See Pishon).

PISPA, PISPAH (pĭs'pà), Asherite (I Chron. 7:38).

PIT (pĭt), bitumen deposit "slime pits" (Gen. 14:10); deep place (Matt. 12:11; Gen. 37:20-29); well or cistern (Jer. 14:3; Luke 14:5); earthen vessel (Lev. 11:33); death, grave, or Sheol (Job 33:18; Isa. 14:15; Num. 16:30,33).

PITCH. 1. Asphalt or bitumen (Gen. 14:10; Exod. 2:3). 2. To encamp (Gen. 12:8; 31:25; Exod. 17:1; Num. 1:51; Josh. 8:11).

PITCHER, earthenware water jar (Gen. 24: 14-20; Mark 14:13; Luke 22:10).

PITHOM (pī'thŏm), Egyptian store city in valley between the Nile and Lake Timsah; dedicated to the sun-god Atum (Exod. 1:11).

PITHON (pī'thŏn), descendant of King Saul (I Chron. 8:35; 9:41).

PITY (pĭ'tĕ), tender, considerate, compassionate feeling for others; attribute of God (Ps. 103:13; Jonah 4:11; James 5:11); required of believers (Isa. 1:17; Matt. 18: 23-35).

PLAGUE (See Diseases).

PLAGUES OF EGYPT, 10 in number, they were the means by which God induced Pharaoh to let the Israelites leave Egypt: water turned into blood, lice, flies, murrain upon cattle, boils upon man and beast, hail, locusts, darkness, death of the first-born (Exod. 7-11).

PLAIN, broad stretch of level land (Gen. 11:2; Ezek. 3:22).

PLAISTER (See Plaster).

PLAITING (See Dress).

PLANE, scraping tool (Isa. 44:13).

PLANE TREE (See Plants).

PLANTS OF THE BIBLE. The following plants are mentioned in the Bible. Some of them are not identifiable. Algum tree (II Chron. 2:8; 11:9); almond (Exod. 25: 33-36); almug tree probably identical with algum (I Kings 10:11,12); aloes (Ps. 45:8; John 19:39); translated "odours"; amomum, (Rev. 18:13); anise (Matt. 23:23); apple (S. of Sol. 2:3),—many think that the apricot is meant; aspalathus (Ecclesiastes 24:15); balm (Ezek. 27:17); barley (Hos. 3:2); bdellium (Num. 11:6,7); beans (Ezek. 4:9); box tree (Isa. 41:19; 60:13); bramble (Judg. 9:14,15); brier (Ezek. 28:24); bul-rush (Exod. 2:3); bush (burning bush) (Exod. 3:2,3); camphire (S. of Sol. 1:14); cassia (Exod. 30:22-25); cedar of Lebanon (Ezek. 31:3,5); chestnut (plane tree) (Gen. 30:37); cinnamon (Exod. 30:23); cockle (Job 31:40); coriander (Exod. 16:31); corn (wheat) (Deut. 8:8); cotton (Esth. 1:5,6 RSV); cucumber (Num. 11:5); cummin (Isa. 28:26, 27); cypress (Isa. 44:14); desire (caper) (Eccl. 12:5); dove's dung (II Kings 6:25); ebony (Ezek. 27:15); eelgrass (Jonah 2:5); elm (Hos. 4:13); flag (Exod. 2:3,5); fig (Gen. 3:6,7); fir (Isa. 60:13); fitches (Isa. 28:25-27); flax, source of linen (Luke 23: 52,53); frankincense (Matt. 2:11); galbanum (Exod. 30:34-36); gall (Matt. 27:34); garlic (Num. 11:5); gourd (Jonah 4:5-7); grape (Gen. 40:10,11); green bay tree (Ps. 37:35); hemlock (Hos. 10:4); herbs, bitter herbs (Exod. 12:8); hyssop (I Kings 4:33); juni-

per (I Kings 19:3,4); leeks (Num. 11:5); lentil (Gen. 25:29,30,34); lilies (of the field) (Luke 12:27); lily (S. of Sol. 5:13); locusts (Matt. 3:4); mallows (Job 30:1,3,4); mandrake (Gen. 30:14-16); melon (Num. 11:5); millet or "pannag" (Ezek. 4:9; 27:17); mint (Luke 11:42); mulberry tree (II Sam. 5: 23,24); mustard (Matt. 13:31,32); myrrh (OT) (Gen. 37:25,26,27), (NT) (Matt. 2:11); myrtle (Zech. 1:7,8); nettle (Job 30:7); nuts (wal-nut) (S. of Sol. 6:11); nuts (pistachio) (Gen. 43:11); oak (holly oak) (Gen. 35:8); oak (valonia oak) (Zech. 11:2); oil tree (Isa. 41:19); olive (Exod. 27:20); onion (Num. 11:5); onycha (Exod. 30:34,35); palm (date) (Num. 33:9); pannag (millet) (Ezek. 4:9; 27:17); parched corn (wheat, q.v.); pine tree (fir) (Isa. 60:13); plane tree (chest-nut, q.v.); pomegranate (I Sam. 14:2); pop-lar (Gen. 30:37); pulse (II Sam. 17:28); reed (Job 40:15,20-22); rie, rye (spelt) (Exod. 9:32); rolling thing (rose of Jericho) (Isa. 17:13); rose (narcissus) (Isa. 35:1); rose of Sharon (S. of Sol. 2:1,2); rue (Luke 11:42); rush (flag) (Exod. 2:3); saffron (S. of Sol. 4:14); shittah tree (Isa. 41:18; Exod. 25:10); spices (Gen. 43:11); spikenard (Mark 14:3); stacte (storax) (Exod. 30:34); strange vine (vine, q.v.); sweet cane (sugar cane) (Isa. 43:24); sweet cane (calamus, sweet calamus) (Jer. 6:20); sycamine (Luke 17:6); sycamore (Amos 7:14); tares (Matt. 13:25); teil (turpentine tree, q.v.); thistles (II Kings 14:9); thorns (crown of thorns) (Mark 15:17); thorns (Isa. 7:19); thyine wood (Rev. 18:12); turpentine tree (teil tree) (Isa. 6:13); vine (true) (Gen. 40:9-11); vine (wild vine, vine of Sodom, q.v.); vine of Sodom (Deut. 32:23),—it is uncertain what plant is intended; water lily (I Kings 7:19, 22,26); weeds (eelgrass, q.v.); wheat (Gen. 41:22); wild gourd (II Kings 4:39); willow (aspen) (Ps. 137:2); willow "withes" (Judg. 16:7-9); wormwood (Lam. 3:15,19).

PLASTER (plăs'tĕr); in Egypt stone build-ings, even the finest granite, were plas-tered, inside and out, to make a smooth surface for decoration (Deut. 27:2,4). The poor used a mixture of clay and straw. In Palestine an outside clay coating would have to be renewed after the rainy season.

PLASTER, MEDICINAL, in Isa. 38:21 a cake of figs applied to a boil.

PLEDGE, personal property of a debtor held to secure a payment (Gen. 38:17-18). Law of Moses was concerned with protection of the poor. A pledged outer garment had to be restored at sunset for a bed cover-ing (Exod. 22:26,27); a widow's clothing could not be taken (Deut. 24:17); a hand-mill or its upper millstone could not be taken (Deut. 24:6).

PLEIADES (plē'yà-dēz), stars in constella-tion Taurus (Job 9:9; 38:31).

PLINY (plĭn'ē), Caius Plinius Caecilius Sec-undus, called "the Younger," Roman gov-ernmental official, famous as the author of literary letters covering all manner of subjects, one of which contains a description of the Christian church in Bithynia, a province which Pliny governed in A. D. 112. The letter, together with the reply of the emperor Trajan are important evidence for the official attitude towards the Christians.

PLOWMAN (See Occupations and Professions).

PLOW, PLOUGH. The ancient plow consisted of a forked stick, the trunk hitched to the animals which drew it, the branch braced and terminating in the share, which was at first the sharpened end of the branch, later a metal point. It was ordinarily drawn by a yoke of oxen (Job 1:14; Amos 6:12). Such a plough did not turn over the soil; it did little more than scratch the surface.

PLOWSHARE (plou′shâr, the blade of a plow), to beat swords into plowshares was symbolic of an age of peace (Isa. 2:4); to beat plowshares into swords portended coming war (Joel 3:10).

PLUMB LINE (plŭm līn), a cord with a weight, the plummet, tied to one end; used in testing whether a wall is perpendicular (Amos 7:7-9; II Kings 21:13; Isa. 28:17).

POCHERETH (pŏk′ē-rĕth), servant of Solomon whose descendants returned from exile with Zerubbabel (Ezra 2:57; Neh. 7:59).

POET (pō′ĕt, a maker); Paul quotes from pagan poets in Acts 17:28; I Cor. 15:32; and Titus 1:12. A great deal of the OT is written in the form of poetry.

POETRY (pō′ĕt-rē); Hebrew poetry is marked by a distinctive vocabulary and syntax. Hebrew rhythm is irregular as compared with English. Rhyme is rare. The most obvious feature of Hebrew poetic form is its parallelism. The three principal varieties are: synonymous, in which the meaning of both members is similar (Ps. 15: 1; 24:1-3); antithetic, in which the meanings of the members are opposed (Ps. 37:9; Prov. 10:1); and synthetic, in which the noun corresponds to noun, verb to verb, and member to member, and each member adds something new (Ps. 19:8,9). Acrostic poems were favorites (Ps. 9:10; 34; 37). Short poems are embedded in the OT historical books (Exod. 15:1-18,21; Judg. 15:16). The Gospel of Luke has a number of poems (1:46-55; 1:68-79; 2:14; 2:29-32).

POETS, PAGAN, QUOTATIONS FROM. NT quotations from pagan poets are confined to Paul. Acts 17:28 contains a quotation from Cleanthes. Titus 1:12 is a quotation from Epimenides. I Cor. 15:33 is a quotation from Menander.

POISON, a substance producing a deadly effect, like the venom of reptiles (Deut. 32:24,33; Job 20:16; Ps. 58:4). Vegetable poisons were known in antiquity: hemlock (Hos. 10:4 RSV); wild gourd (II Kings 4: 39,40). A poisoned drink is referred to in Mark 16:18.

POLE (pōl), standard on which the brazen serpent was displayed (Num. 21:8,9).

POLITARCH (pŏl′ĭ-tärk), city magistrate of Thessalonica (Acts 17:6,8). Sixteen epi-

graphical inscriptions with the word have been discovered.

POLL (pōl, skull, head), as a verb, "to shear;" as a noun, "head." Mic. 1:16; Num. 1:2-22.

POLLUTION (pŏ-lū′shŭn), ceremonial or moral defilement, profanation, and uncleanness (Exod. 20:25; II Pet. 2:20).

POLLUX (pŏl′ŭks), with Castor, one of the Twin Brothers, sons of Zeus and patrons of sailors (Acts 28:11).

POLYGAMY (See Marriage).

POMEGRANATE (See Plants).

POMMEL (pŭm′′l), bowl-shaped part of the capitals of the temple pillars (II Chron. 4:12,13).

PONTIUS PILATE (See Pilate).

PONTUS (pŏn′tŭs, sea), Roman province of N Asia Minor along the Black Sea (Acts 2:9; I Pet. 1:1).

POOL, reservoir of water, natural or artificial (II Kings 18:17; 20:20; Neh. 2:14; Isa. 7:3).

POOR. The Mosaic law made specific provisions for the benefit of the poor: gleaning (Lev. 19:9,10); sabbatical year (Exod. 23:11); year of jubilee (Lev. 25:25-30); laws on usory and pledges (Exod. 22:25-27); prompt wages (Deut. 24:14). Both Testaments show God's love and care for the poor (Ps. 9:18; 12:5; Eccl. 5:8). Wilful neglect leading to poverty is not condoned (Prov. 13:4-18). Apostles asked Paul and Barnabas to remember the poor (Gal. 2:10). James has some sharp words about the relations of rich and poor (James 1:9-11; 2:1-9).

POPLAR (See Plants).

PORATHA (pō-rā′thà), son of Haman (Esth. 9:8).

PORCH, an area with a roof supported by columns: vestibule (I Kings 7:6ff), colonnade (Judg. 3:23), place before a court (Mark 14:68), gateway (Matt. 26:71).

PORCIUS (See Festus).

PORCUPINE, PORPOISE (See Animals).

PORTER (See Occupations and Professions).

PORTION (pōr′shŭn), a part; less than the whole of anything; share (Num. 31:30,47; Neh. 8:10,12).

POST (pōst). 1. Part of a doorway (I Kings 6:33). 2. One who conveys a message speedily (Job 9:25).

POT, utensil of metal or clay for holding liquids or other substances (II Kings 4:38).

POTENTATE (pō′těn-tāt, mighty one), person with great power and authority (I Tim. 6:15).

POTIPHAR (pŏt′ĭ-fẽr, whom Re has given), officer of Pharaoh; purchased Joseph; cast him into prison (Gen. 39:1-20).

POTIPHERAH (pō-tif′ẽr-à, one given by the sun-god), Egyptian priest of On (Gen. 41:45,50; 46:20).

POTSHERD (pŏt′shûrd), piece of earthenware (Job 2:8).

POTTAGE (pŏt′ij, boiled), stew of vegetables and meat (Gen. 25:29,30,34; II Kings 4:38,39).

POTTER (See Occupations and Professions).

POTTER'S FIELD, piece of ground which the priests bought with the money Judas received for betraying our Lord (Matt. 27:7).

POTTER'S GATE, gate in wall of Jerusalem (Jer. 19:2).

POTTERY, one of the oldest of crafts in Bible lands. Place where potter's clay was dug was called "potter's field" (Matt. 27:7). Pottery was shaped by hand on a potter's wheel, powered by foot or by an apprentice (Jer. 18:3-6), then dried and baked in a kiln. Many different items were made: bowls, basins, and cups; cooking pots; jars; decanters, flasks, and juglets; lamps; ovens; braziers; dishes. Thousands of objects have been found by the archaeologists. Careful study has been made of the historical development of pottery styles, so that experts can date and place pottery with considerable accuracy.

POUND (See Weights and Measures).

POWER. Many kinds of power are referred to in the Bible: man's, Satan's, military, official, Christ's. The word is used in two senses: ability to act (Luke 1:35; 5:17) and the authority to act (Acts 5:4; Rom. 9:21).

PRAETOR (prē'tòr), originally the highest Roman magistrate; later, officials elected to administer justice; under the principate the office declined in prestige, power, and functions.

PRAETORIAN GUARD (prē-tò'rĭ-ăn), guard of imperial palace or provincial governor called "Caesar's household" (Phil. 1:13; 4:22).

PRAETORIUM (prē-tò'rĭ-ŭm), in the Gospels it refers to the temporary palace or headquarters of the Roman governor while in Jerusalem (Matt. 27:27; Mark 15:16; John 18:28,33); in Acts 23:35, the palace of Herod at Caesarea.

PRAISE, broad term for words or deeds which exalt or honor people, God, or gods (Prov. 27:21; Exod. 15:11; Judg. 16:24). Book of Psalms is filled with praise; Psalms 113-118 are called the Hallel, the praises. Praise for redemption dominates the NT (Luke 2:13,14; Rev. 19:5-7).

PRAYER. Prayer is a necessity to man because he is incurably religious. It is a universal phenomenon; but while not exclusively Christian, it is most real in Christianity because the Christian life is a life of fellowship with God. In no other religion do we find such prayers as are found uttered by men like Moses, David, and Paul. In Biblical religion the relationship between God and man is genuinely interpersonal. Some things are brought to pass only as man prays (I Tim. 2:1-4). Prayer is essentially communion; God desires man's fellowship, and man needs the friendship of God. As a many-faceted phenomenon, prayer includes the following elements: communion, adoration, thanksgiving, confession, petition, intercession, submission. The pivotal factor in prayer is attitude.

Posture, language, place or time do not matter. Man's heart must be en rapport with God. Jesus has left us an unsurpassed and perfect example of the importance of prayer in one's life. The following principles are regulative in prayer. 1. Prayer avails only as it is made in faith (Heb. 11:6; Matt. 17:20); in the name of Jesus (John 14:13; 15:16); in keeping with the will of God (I John 5:14,15); under the direction and dynamic of the Holy Spirit (Jude 20); by a suppliant who has confessed and renounced sin (Ps. 66:18; Isa. 59:1,2); by a forgiving heart (Matt. 6:14-15); in a context of harmonious relationships on the human level (Matt. 5:23,24; 18:19); with persistence (Luke 11:5-8; 18:1-8). From the standpoint of human responsibility, prayer is the major element in the outworking of God's redemptive program (I Tim. 2:1-4). Neglect of prayer is sin (I Sam. 12:23).

PREACHER, PREACHING (See Occupations and Professions).

PREDESTINATION (See Election).

PRESBYTERY (prĕz'bĭ-tēr-ē). 1. Organized body of Jewish elders in Jerusalem (Acts 22:5). 2. Christian elders (I Tim. 4:14).

PRESIDENTS (prĕz'ĭ-dĕnts), administrative officers in Darius' kingdom (Dan. 6:2-7).

PRESS, crowd (Mark 2:4; Luke 8:19).

PRESS FAT (prĕs făt), the vat or vessel used to collect the liquid from pressed grapes (Hag. 2:16).

PRICK (a goad), any slender pointed thing, like a thorn (Num. 33:55); goad of conviction (Acts 9:5).

PRIEST, PRIESTHOOD. The NT word for "priest" is related to a word meaning "holy," and indicates one who is consecrated to and engaged in holy matters. The Heb. word for priest is of uncertain origin, but seems originally to have meant a "seer," as well as one who has to do with divine things. A priest is a minister of any religion, whether heathen (Gen. 41:45; Acts 14:13) or Biblical (Matt. 8:4; I Pet. 2:5,9). Originally, individuals were priests (Gen. 4:3,4); later, fathers of families (Gen. 12:7; 13:18); at Sinai God through Moses designated Aaron, his sons, and his descendants priests (Exod. 28:1). The Aaronic priests had to meet very rigid standards (Lev. 21:16-24); in the sanctuary they ministered in special garments, and adhered to a definite ritual. They were divided into 24 courses, each serving a week at a time (I Chron. 24:1-19). They represented the people before God, offering sacrifices and praying in their behalf. The chief, or high, priest supervised the priests, offered a sin offering (Lev. 4) and sacrificed on the Day of Atonement (Lev. 16), and ascertained the will of God by the Urim and Thummim (Num. 27:21; Neh. 7:65). The Levites served as assistants to the Aaronic priests (Num. 3). In the NT Jesus Christ is described as a high priest after the order of Melchizedek (Heb. 5:10,20-7:17). The Aaronic priesthood is abolished in Him (John 14:6; I Tim. 2:5,6; Heb. 5:7-10). The sacrifice He offered was Himself, and it never needed to be repeated. By His death He made atonement for the sins of men once for all. The

NT teaches the priesthood of all believers; they share in Christ's priestly activity, bringing the word to men and bringing men to Christ (Eph. 2:18; Heb. 10: 19-25; 13:15; I Pet. 2:5,9; Rev. 1:5,6).

PRINCE, PRINCESS. A prince is a leader, an exalted person clothed with authority. A princess is the daughter or wife of a chief or king. The prince may be the head of a family or tribe, a ruler, governor, magistrate, satrap, or royal descendant (Num. 22:8; I Sam. 18:30). He may also be a spiritual ruler (Isa. 9:6) or the ruler of demons (Matt. 9:34).

PRINCIPALITIES (prins'sĭ-păl'ĭ-tēz). 1. Rule; ruler (Eph. 1:21; Titus 3:1). 2. Order of powerful angels and demons (Rom. 8:38; Eph. 6:12).

PRINT, a mark made by pressure (Lev. 19: 28; John 20:25).

PRISCA, PRISCILLA (prĭs'kà, prĭ-sĭl'à), Priscilla (diminutive of Prisca) was the wife of the Jewish Christian, Aquila, with whom she is always mentioned in the NT; tentmakers; had church in their house; taught Apollos; assisted Paul (Acts 18:2, 26; Rom. 16:3; I Cor. 16:19; II Tim. 4:19).

PRISON. Prisoners were often put in dry wells or cisterns (Gen. 37:24; Jer. 38:6-13) or dungeons which were part of a palace (I Kings 22:27). The Herods and the Romans had royal prisons (Luke 3:20; Acts 12:4; 23:10,35). Jesus foretells imprisonment for His disciples (Luke 21:12). Disobedient spirits are now in prison (I Pet. 3:19). Satan will be imprisoned (Rev. 20:7).

PROCHORUS (prŏk'ō-rŭs), one of the first deacons (Acts 6:5).

PROCONSUL (prō'kŏn-sŭl), Roman official who served as deputy consul in a Roman province; term of office usually one year; Sergius Paulus and Gallio were proconsuls (Acts 13:7; 18:12).

PROCURATOR (prō'kū-rā'tèr), governor of a Roman province appointed by the emperor; often subject to imperial legate of a larger political area. Pilate, Felix, Festus were procurators (Matt. 27:2; Acts 23:24; 26:30).

PROFANE (prō-fān'), to desecrate or defile (Exod. 31:14; Lev. 19:8,12; Ezek. 22:26; Matt. 12:5); common as opposed to holy (Ezek. 28:16; 42:20); godless, unholy (Heb. 12:16).

PROMISE. 1st promise of the Redeemer (Gen. 3:15); promise repeated to Abraham (Gen. 12:2,7); promise made to David that his house would continue forever (II Sam. 7:12,13,28). Jesus' promise of the Spirit fulfilled at Pentecost. There are hundreds of promises made to believers (James 2:5; I Tim. 4:8; II Pet. 3:9).

PROPHECY, PROPHETS, a spokesman for God. OT prophets were not interpreters of God's will; they uttered the actual words which God gave them. Two aspects to their work: forthtelling and foretelling. There were schools of the prophets, but little is known of them (I Sam. 19:19,20; II Kings 2:3,5; 4:38; 6:1). There were true and false prophets (Jer. 28:1ff). The prophets of the OT were of two kinds: the former, who wrote an interpretative history of the background of the period in which the great writing prophets lived and worked; the latter, also called writing prophets – Isaiah, Jeremiah, Ezekiel, Daniel and the Twelve Minor Prophets.

PROPHETESS, a woman who exercised the prophetic gift in ancient Israel or in the early Christian church (Exod. 15:20; Judg. 4:4; II Kings 22:14; Isa. 8:3; Acts 21:8,9).

PROPITIATION (prō-pĭsh'ĭ-ā'shŭn, to cover), to appease the wrath of God so that His justice and holiness will be satisfied and He can forgive sin. Propitiation does not make God merciful; it makes divine forgiveness possible. For this, an atonement must be provided; in OT times, animal sacrifices; now, the death of Christ for man's sin. Through Christ's death propitiation is made for man's sin (Rom. 3:25; I John 2:2; 4:10).

PROSELYTE (prŏs'ē-lit), in OT times a foreign resident (Exod. 20:10; Deut. 5:14); in the NT, a person of Gentile origin who had accepted the Jewish religion, whether living in Palestine or elsewhere (Matt. 23:15; Acts 2:10; 6:5; 13:43). A distinction was apparently made between uncircumcised proselytes, i.e., those who had not fully identified themselves with the Jewish nation and religion; and circumcised proselytes, those who identified themselves fully with Judaism.

PROSTITUTE (prŏs'tĭ-tūt), harlot (Lev. 19: 29; Deut. 23:17). The term is often used by the OT prophets to refer to religious unfaithfulness (Isa. 1:21; Jer. 2:20). In ancient heathen worship a special class of prostitutes was connected with the temples.

PROVENDER (prŏv'ĕn-dèr), feed, as grain or hay fed to cattle, horses, and the like (Gen. 24:25,26; 42:27; Judg. 19:19,21).

PROVERB (prŏv'ûrb), pithy saying, comparison or question expressing a familiar or useful truth (Gen. 10:9; I Sam. 10:12; Proverbs).

PROVERBS, BOOK OF, best representative of Wisdom literature of ancient Israel; claims Solomonic authorship for bulk of book (1:1; 10:1); not a mere collection of ancient maxims for success, but a compendium of moral instruction, dealing with sin and holiness. Author gives instruction on life and holiness in proverbial form. Outline: 1. Introduction (1:1-9). 2. Sin and righteousness personified and contrasted (1:10-9:18). 3. Single-verse contrasts of sin and righteousness (10:1-22:16). 4. Miscellaneous and longer contrasts (22:17-29:27). 5. Righteousness in poems of climax (30:1-31:31).

PROVIDENCE (prŏv'ĭ-dĕns), the universal sovereign reign of God; God's preserving and governing all His creatures, and all their actions (Job 9:5,6; 28:25; Ps. 104: 10-25; 145:15; 147:9; Matt. 4:4; 6:26-28; Luke 12:6,7; Acts 17:25-28). General providence includes the government of the entire universe, especially the affairs of men. Special providence is God's particular care over the life and activity of the believer (Rom. 8:28).

PROVINCE (prŏv'vĭns), unit of an empire, like those of the Roman empire. In Persia they were called satrapies. Rome's provinces were divided into two categories: imperial, those requiring a frontier army, and ruled by a legate appointed by the emperor; senatorial, those presenting no major problems, and ruled by someone appointed by the Senate – a proconsul (Acts 13:7).

PROVOCATION (prŏv'ô-kā'shŭn), any cause of God's anger at sin (I Kings 15:30; 21:22; Ezek. 20:28; Neh. 9:18,26).

PRUNING HOOK, agricultural tool used in the cultivation of the vine (Isa. 2:4; Joel 3:10).

PSALMS, THE BOOK OF (săms); the Heb. designation means "praises;" the Greek "Psalmoi" means "songs sung to the accompaniment of stringed instruments." This is the longest book in the Bible, and consists of 150 psalms. Author's names are almost always given in the titles: Moses (90), David (3-9, 11-32, 34-41, 51-65, 68-70, 86, 101, 103, 108-110, 122, 124, 131, 133, 138-145), Solomon (72,127), Asaph (50, 73-83), sons of Korah (42, 44-49, 84, 85, 87, 88), Heman (88), Ethan (89). Many of the psalm titles include musical terms in Hebrew, some designating ancient melodies, others preserving musical instructions. The meaning of some of these terms is uncertain or unknown. Hebrew Psalter is divided into five books: 1. 1-41. 2. 42-72. 3. 73-89. 4. 90-106. 5. 107-150. Each of the psalms exhibits the formal character of Heb. poetry. This consists, not primarily in rhyme, but in a parallelism of thought. Most of them possess a lyric, singing quality.

PSALMS OF SOLOMON, one of the pseudepigrapha, consisting of 18 psalms in imitation of the canonical psalms, probably written between 64 and 46 B. C.

PSALMODY (See Music).

PSALTER (See Music, Psalms).

PSALTERY (See Music, Psalms).

PSEUDEPIGRAPHA (sū'dē-pĭg'rȧ-fȧ), books not in the Heb. canon or the Apocrypha, ascribed to earlier Jewish authors. They were written chiefly during the intertestamental period.

PTOLEMAIS (See Accho).

PTOLEMY (tŏl'ē-mē), common name of the 15 Macedonian kings of Egypt whose dynasty extended from the death of Alexander the Great in 323 B. C. to the murder of Ptolemy XV, son of Julius Caesar and Cleopatra in 30 B. C.: Ptolemy I, Soter (323-285 B. C.); Ptolemy II, Philadelphus (285-246 B. C.); LXX translated, Golden Age of Ptolemaic Egypt; Ptolemy III (c. 246-222 B. C.); Ptolemy IV, Philopator (222-205 B. C.); Ptolemy V, Epiphanes (205-181 B. C.); Ptolemy VI, Philometor (181-145 B. C.); Ptolemy VII, Physcon (145-117 B. C.); Ptolemy XI was the last of the male line of Ptolemy I, killed by Alexandrians; Ptolemy XII (51-47 B. C.) fled to Rome; Ptolemy XIII had Cleopatra to wife.

PUA (pū'ȧ), son of Issachar (Num. 26:23); also spelled "Puah" and "Phuva" (Gen. 46:13; I Chron. 7:1).

PUAH, PUVAH (pū'ȧ, pū'vȧ), Hebrew midwife who refused to obey edict to destroy infant sons of Hebrew women (Exod. 1:15-20).

PUBLICAN (See Occupations and Professions).

PUBLIUS (pŭb'lĭ-ŭs), chief person on island of Malta (Melita) in Mediterranean; helped Paul (Acts 27:27-44; 28:7-10).

PUDENS (pū'dĕnz), Roman Christian (II Tim. 4:21).

PUHITES (pū'hĭts), family descended from Caleb (I Chron. 2:50,53).

PUL (pŭl, pōōl). 1. King of Assyria, Tiglath-pileser III, who invaded Israel (II Kings 15:19; I Chron. 5:26). 2. Tribe or place in Africa (Isa. 66:19); may be Put.

PULPIT (pŭl'pĭt), platform used primarily as a position from which to speak (Neh. 8:4).

PULSE (See Plants).

PUNISHMENT. Death was the punishment for striking or reviling a parent, blasphemy, sabbath breaking, witchcraft, adultery, rape, incestuous connection, kidnaping, idolatry (Exod. 21:15,17; Lev. 24:14,16,23, Num. 15; 32-36). Capital punishment was by stoning (Deut. 22:24); Romans introduced beheading (Matt. 14:10) and crucifixion (Mark 15:21-25). Other forms of punishment: sawing asunder, cutting with iron harrows, stripes, burning, sword. Punishment in kind was a common principle (Exod. 21:23-25). Christ procured forgiveness for man by bearing punishment for sin (Acts 2:38; 10:38-43).

PUNISHMENT, EVERLASTING, is taught in Scripture for those who reject God's love revealed in Christ (Matt. 25:46; Dan. 12:2). In Matt. 25:46 the word *aionion* (translated "everlasting" and "eternal") applies to the destiny of both the saved and the lost. Final place of everlasting punishment is called the "lake of fire" (Rev. 19:20; 20:10,14,15); also called "the second death" (Rev. 14:9-11; 20:6). "Hell" in Scripture translates **Hades**, the unseen realm where the souls of all the dead are. Gehenna is the place of punishment of Hades; paradise is the place of blessing of Hades (Luke 16:19-31). The reason for eternal punishment is the rejection of the love of God in Christ (John 3:18,19).

PUNITES (pū'nĭts), descendants of Puvah, of the tribe of Issachar (Num. 26:23; I Chron. 7:1).

PUNON (pū'nŏn), Israelite encampment E of Edon (Num. 33:42,43).

PUR (pŭr, lots), lot cast to destroy Jews in time of Esther (Esth. 3:7; 9:26). Feast of Purin is a Jewish festival commemorating the deliverance of the Jews from mass murder by Haman.

PURA (See Phurah).

PURIFICATION (pūr'ĭ-fĭ-cā'shŭn). For Israelites religious purity was both ceremonial and ethical. Ceremonial purification was required for four acts: birth of a child

(Lev. 12:2ff); contact with a corpse (Num. 19:11-14); certain diseases, such as leprosy (Lev. 13:8); a running sore (Lev. 15:1-15). Jews were expected to be racially pure (Deut. 23:3; Ezra 10:1-14). Jesus taught that purity comes from the heart (Matt. 5:27f; 19:3-9; Mark 10:2-12; I Cor. 5:9-13; 6:18-20).

PURPLE, a color highly esteemed in ancient times; because of its costliness, it became a mark of distinction to wear robes of purple. Royalty was so dressed. The color included various shades between crimson and violet. Exod. 25:4; 26:36; 28:15; 35:6; Judg. 8:26; II Chron. 2:14.

PURSE, finely finished leather pouch. In Matt. 10:9 the reference is to the Oriental girdle worn around the waist.

PURTENANCE (pūr′tē-nàns), entrails (Lev. 1:9).

PUT (pŭt). 1. Son of Ham (Gen. 10:6). 2. Libya (Isa. 66:19; Ezek. 27:10; 38:5; Nah. 3:9). Put has also been taken to signify Egypt.

PUTEOLI (pŭ-tē′ō-lē, little wells or springs), seaport of Italy, eight miles W of Naples; nearest harbor to Rome (Acts 28:13,14). Modern Pozzuoli.

PUTIEL (pū′tĭ-ĕl), father-in-law of Eliezer (Exod. 6:25).

PUVAH (See Phuvah).

PYGARG (See Animals).

PYRAMIDS (pĕĕr′à-mĭds), tombs with superstructures of pyramidal form made for the interment of royalty in Egypt. C. 80 survive.

PYRRHUS (pĭr′ŭs), father of Sopater (Acts 20:4).

Q

QUAIL (See Birds).

QUARANTANIA (kwŏr′ăn-tā′nĭ-à), mt. where according to tradition Satan tempted Jesus to worship him (Matt. 4:8-10); Tell es-Sultan, a short distance W of OT Jericho.

QUARRIES (kwŏr′ĕz, graven images), in Judg. 3:19,26 the reference is probably to graven images.

QUARTUS (kwŏr′tŭs), Corinthian Christian (Rom. 16:23).

QUATERNION (kwà-tĕr′nĭ-ŭn), Roman guard of four soldiers (Acts 12:4).

QUEEN. 1. Dowager queen (I Kings 11:19; II Kings 10:13). 2. King's wife (I Kings 10:1; Esth. 1:9; 2:22). 3. King's wife distinguished from his concubines (Neh. 2:6).

QUEEN OF HEAVEN, female deity, probably Ashtoreth, goddess of love and fertility (Jer. 7:18; 44:17-25).

QUICKSANDS, sandbanks off shores of N Africa S of Crete; very treacherous (Acts 27:17).

QUIRINIUS (kwĭ-rĭn′ĭ-ŭs), governor of Syria when the emperor Augustus issued a decree for the census in which Joseph enrolled (Luke 2:2). It is quite certain that he was governor of Syria A. D. 6-9 and that a census was ordered for that period; but there is no clear evidence that he was governor and ordered a census 14 years prior to that. However, an inscription survives which states that Quirinius governed Syria twice.

QUOTATIONS FROM PAGAN POETS (See Poets, Pagan).

QURUN HATTIN (See Hattin, Horns of; Beatitudes, Mount of).

R

RA (See Re).

RAAMAH (rā′à-mà), son of Cush and grandson of Ham (I Chron. 1:9); descendants were tribe in SW Arabia (Gen. 10:7; Ezek. 27:22).

RAAMIAH (rā′à-mī′à, Jehovah has thundered), Israelite who returned from captivity with Zerubbabel (Neh. 7:7); "Reelaiah" in Ezra 2:2.

RAAMSES (rā-ăm′sĕz), Egyptian store city built by Israelites (Exod. 1:11); probably the modern San el Hagar in NE part of Delta.

RABBAH, RABBATH (răb′à, răb′ăth). 1. Town in Judah (Josh. 15:60); not now identifiable. 2. Capital of Ammon, represented today by Amman, capital of Jordan, 22 miles E of Jordan (Josh. 13:25; II Sam. 11:1; 12:27-29; I Chron. 20:1; Jer. 49:2,3). Subsequently captured by Ptolemy Philadelphus (285-247 B. C.), who changed its name to Philadelphia; became one of the cities of the Decapolis. Twice spelled "Rabbath" (Deut. 3:11; Ezek. 21:20).

ABBATH-AMMON (See Rabbah).

RABBI (See Occupations and Professions).

RABBITH (răb′ĭth), town in tribe of Issachar (Josh. 19:20).

RABBONI (răb-bō′nĭ), variant of Rabbi, the Heb. word for Master (John 20:16).

RAB-MAG (răb′măg), title of Babylonian prince (Jer. 39:3); same as "Nergalsharezer" (Jer. 39:3).

RABSARIS (răb′sà-rĭs), title of high Assyrian and Babylonian official (II Kings 18: 17ff; Jer. 39:13).

RABSHAKEH (răb′shà-kĕ), title of high Assyrian governmental official (II Kings 18: 17-37; 19:4-8; Isa. 36; 37:4,8).

RACA (rà′kà, empty, worthless), term of contempt and scorn (Matt. 5:22).

RACE. Racing was a popular sport in ancient times especially among the Greeks (I Cor. 9:24; Heb. 12:1; II Tim. 4:7).

RACHAB (See Rahab).

RACHAL (rā′căl), town in Judah (I Sam. 30:29).

RACHEL (rā′chĕl, ewe), daughter of Laban; wife of Jacob; mother of Joseph and Benjamin (Gen. 29:6,16,18; 30:1-9).

RADDAI (răd'ā-ī), son of Jesse (I Chron. 2:14).

RAGAU (rā'gò), Greek form of Reu, ancestor of Christ (Luke 3:35).

RAGUEL, REUEL (rà-gū'ĕl, rōō'ĕl), father-in-law of Moses (Num. 10:29); KJV has "Reuel" in Exod. 2:18.

RAHAB (rā'hăb, broad), harlot of Jericho who hid Israelite spies (Josh. 2:1); mother of Boaz; great-grandmother of King David (Matt. 1:5; Ruth 4:18-21); shining example of faith (Heb. 11:31). 2. Mythical monster of the deep; enemy of Jehovah (Job 9: 13 RSV; Ps. 89:10); applied to Egypt (Ps. 87:4; Isa. 30:7; 51:9).

RAHAM (rā'hăm), son of Shema (I Chron. 2:44).

RAHEL (See Rachel).

RAIMENT (See Dress).

RAIMENT, CHANGES OF (See Dress).

RAIN. In Palestine the rainy season extends from October to April; the dry season, from May to October. The early rain occurs in October and November (Ps. 84:6; Isa. 30:23; Jer. 5:24); the latter rain in March and April (Job 29:23; Prov. 16:15; Jer. 3:3; 5:24; Zech. 10:1). Crops are therefore planted so that they will grow during the rainy season. "Rain" is often used in the OT in a figurative sense. Abundance of rain denotes the rich blessing of Jehovah upon His people (Deut. 28:12); lack of rain is a sign of God's displeasure (Deut. 28:23,24). In Canaanite religion Baal was conceived as the god of rain, and was therefore ardently worshipped.

RAINBOW, sign of God's covenant with man that He would not again allow a universal flood (Gen. 9:8-22).

RAISINS (See Food).

RAKKATH (răk'ăth), fortified city in Naphtali (Josh. 19:35); probably near Sea of Galilee on site of Tiberias.

RAM (See Animals, Sheep).

RAMA, RAMAH (rā'mà, height). 1. Ramah-Arael, city of Naphtali (Josh. 19:36). 2. Rhama-Ramah, town in Asher (Josh. 19:29). 3. Ramah Iamah, city in Benjamin (Judg. 4:5; Isa. 10:28-32). 4. Ramah-Aramathaim, birthplace of prophet Samuel (I Sam. 1:19; 2:11). 5. Ramah-of-the-South, see Ramath-Lehi below.

RAMATH-LEHI (rā'măth-lē'hĭ), place where Samson cast away jawbone of ass after slaughter of Philistines (Judg. 15:17).

RAMATH-MIZPEH (rā'măth mĭz'pĕ, heights or watchtower), N boundary line of Gad (Josh. 13:26). Also called Mizpeh, Galeed, and Jegar-Sahadutha.

RAMATH (RAMAH) OF THE SOUTH (rā'măth, Ramoth of the south), city in S Judah alloted to tribe of Simeon (Josh. 19:8).

RAMATHAIM-ZOPHIM (See Ramah).

RAMATHITE (See Ramah).

RAMESSES (rà-ăm'sĕz, various other spellings, e.g., Rameses, Ramses), name of 11 Egyptian pharaohs, of whom Ramesses II (c. 1301-1234 B. C.) was the most famous, many scholars holding that he was the pharaoh of the Exodus. Some of these pharaohs must have had at least indirect influence on Israelite life, but none of them is mentioned in the OT.

RAMIAH (rà-mī'à), descendant of Parosh; divorced foreign wife (Ezra 10:25).

RAMOTH (rā'mŏth, height). 1. Precious stone of uncertain variety, translated "coral" (Job 28:18; Ezek. 26:16). 2. Israelite who divorced foreign wife (Ezra 10:29). 3. City of refuge in Gad (I Kings 4:13; 22:1-37); also called Ramoth-Gilead (Josh. 20:8; 21:38).

RAMS' HORNS (See Musical Instruments, Shofar).

RAMS' SKINS, skins of sheep; used for clothing of shepherds and covering for tabernacle (Exod. 25:5).

RANSOM (răn'sŭm), price paid for recovery of a person or thing (Lev. 19:20); reparation paid for injury or damages (Exod. 22:10-12). In NT it signifies the redemptive price paid by Christ for the salvation of His people (Mark 10:45; I Tim. 2:5,6).

RAPHA (rā'fà). 1. Son of Benjamin (I Chron. 8:2). 2. Descendant of Saul (I Chron. 8:37).

RAPHU (rā'fū), father of spy Palti (Num. 13:9).

RAS SHAMRA (ràs shàm'rà), modern name of mound marking the site of ancient city of Ugarit, located on Syrian coast opposite island of Cyprus; an important commerical center; destroyed by Sea Peoples who overran the area c. 1200 B. C.; reached peak of prosperity in 15th-14th centuries B. C. Several hundred clay tablets forming part of scribal library were found from 1929 through 1936: personal and diplomatic correspondence; business, legal, and governmental records; veterinary texts, and, most important religious literature. These throw a great deal of light upon Canaanite religion, culture, and Hebrew literary style; and show striking similarities between Canaanite and Hebrew systems of worship. They clarify our knowledge of the world in which Israel developed.

RASOR, RAZOR (rā'zèr). Priests of Israel were not permitted to cut their beard (Lev. 21:5). Nazarites could not use the razor as long as their vows were upon them (Num. 6:5).

RAVEN (See Birds).

RE, RA (rà), Egyptian sun-god. Joseph married daughter of the priest of On of the cult of Re (Gen. 41:45).

REAIAH, REAIA (rè-ā'yà). 1. Judahite (I Chron. 4:2). 2. Reubenite (I Chron. 5:5). 3. Family name of a company of Nethinim (Ezra 2:47; Neh. 7:50).

REAPING, in ancient times done either by pulling up grain by roots or cutting it with sickle. Stalks then bound into bundles and taken to threshing floor. Term often used figuratively of deeds that produce their own harvest (Prov. 22:8; Hos. 8:7; I Cor. 9:11; Gal. 6:7,8).

REBA (rē'bà), Midianite chieftain slain at command of Moses (Num. 31:8; Josh. 13:21).

REBEKAH, REBECCA (rē-bĕk'à), wife of Isaac; sister of Laban; mother of Esau and Jacob (Gen. 22:20-24; 24; 25:21-26).

RECAH, RECA (rē'kà), unknown place in tribe of Judah (I Chron. 4:12).

RECHAB (rē'kăb, horseman). 1. Benjamite who with brother slew Ishbosheth, son of Saul (II Sam. 4:2-12). 2. Father of Jehonadab (II Kings 10:15; Jer. 35:6-19). 3. Father of Malchiah (Neh. 3:14).

RECHABITES (rĕk'à-bīts), Israelites who sought return to nomadic life and abstention from wine (Jer. 35).

RECONCILIATION (rĕk'ŏn-sĭl-ĭ-ā'shŭn), change of relationship between God and man based on changed status of man through the redemptive work of Christ. Enmity between God and sinful man removed by death of Christ, and appropriated by sinner through faith (Acts 10:43; II Cor. 5:18,19; Eph. 2:16).

RECORDER (See Occupations and Professions).

RED, blood-like or blood-red color (Exod. 25:5; 26:14; 35:7; Zech. 1:8; Rev. 6:4).

REDEEMED, REDEEMER (See Redemption).

REDEMPTION (rē-dĕmp'shŭn, to tear loose; a ransom), deliverance from the enslavement of sin and release to a new freedom by the sacrifice of the Redeemer, Jesus Christ. The death of Christ is the redemptive price. The word contains both the ideas of deliverance and the price of that deliverance, or ransom. Rom. 3:24; Gal. 3:13; Eph. 1:7; I Pet. 1:18,19.

REDEMPTION OF LAND. In Heb. society, any land which was forfeited through economic distress could be redeemed by the nearest of kin. If not so redeemed, it returned to its original owner in the year of Jubilee (Lev. 25:24-34).

RED HEIFER, ashes of red heifer were used for removal of certain types of ceremonial uncleanness (Num. 19:9).

RED SEA, 1,350 mile long oceanic gulf extending from Indian Ocean to Gulf of Suez. Has two arms: Gulf of Suez and Gulf of Aqabah. "Red Sea" may refer to either arm (Num. 33:10,11; I Kings 9:26) or the entire Red Sea (Exod. 23:31), or the nearby lakes. The Red Sea of Exod. 13:17,18 should be rendered "Reed Sea." It is improbable that the Red Sea is meant. More likely the reference is to a body of water near Goshen which the Egyptians themselves referred to as Reed Sea.

REED (rēd). 1. Tall flags, rushes, grasses; sometimes used figuratively for fickleness (Matt. 11:7), weakness (Isa. 42:3), or uncertain support (I Kings 18:21). 2. A Hebrew unit of measurement, equal to six cubits (Ezek. 40:5).

REELAIAH (rē'ĕl-ā'yà), head of family that returned with Zerubbabel (Ezra 2:2; Neh. 7:7). Nehemiah has "Raamiah."

REFINE, REFINER (See Occupations).

REFUGE, CITIES OF, six cities on either side of the Jordan which were set aside for the asylum of the accidental slayer (Num. 35:6,

11-32; Deut. 4:43; 19:1-13; Josh. 20); Bezer (Benjamin), Ramoth-Gilead (Gad), Golan (Manasseh), Hebron (Judah), Shechem (Ephraim), Kedesh (Naphtali).

REGEM (rē'gĕm), descendant of Caleb (I Chron. 2:47).

REGEM-MELECH (rĕg'ĕm mē'lĕk), member of delegation sent to inquire of Zechariah concerning propriety of fasting (Zech. 7:2).

REGENERATION (rē-jĕn-ẽr-ā'shŭn), spiritual change wrought in the heart of man by the Holy Spirit in which his inherently sinful nature is changed so that he can respond to God in faith and live in accordance with His will (Matt. 19:28; John 3:3,5,7; Titus 3:5). It extends to the whole nature of man, altering his governing disposition, illumining his mind, freeing his will, and renewing his nature.

REHABIAH (rē'hà-bī'à), son of Eliezer, grandson of Moses (I Chron. 23:17; 24:21; 26:25).

REHOB (rē'hŏb). 1. Northern limit searched by spies (Num. 13:21). 2. Two towns in Asher (Josh. 19:28; 19:30). 3. Father of Hadadezer, king of Aram (II Sam. 8:3,12). 4. Levite; signed covenant with Nehemiah (Neh. 10:11).

REHOBOAM (rē'hō-bō'ăm), son of Solomon and Naamah (I Kings 14:21,31); lost 10 N tribes; became king of Judah and Benjamin (I Kings 12:14); lost fortified cities to King Shishak of Egypt (II Chron. 12:1-4).

REHOBOTH (rē-hō'bŏth). 1. City near Nineveh in Assyria (Gen. 10:11). 2. Well dug by Isaac in Valley of Gerar (Gen. 26:9-22). 3. Home of Saul ("Shaul" in I Chron. 1:48), king of Edom (Gen. 36:37). Location unknown.

REHUM (rē'hŭm, beloved). 1. Israelite who returned with Ezra (Ezra 2:2). 2. Officer of Artaxerxes' court (Ezra 4:7-24). 3. Man who helped repair walls of Jerusalem (Neh. 3:17). 4. Israelite who signed covenant (Neh. 10:25). 5. Priest who returned with Zerubbabel (Neh. 12:3).

REI (rē'ĭ), loyal member of David's court (I Kings 1:8).

REINS (rāns), inward parts; kidneys as seat of emotions (Ps. 7:9; 26:2; Jer. 17:10; Job 19:27).

REKEM (rē'kĕm). 1. King of Midian (Num. 31:1-8). 2. Son of Hebron; Judahite (I Chron. 2:42-44).

RELIGION, man's recognition of his relation to God and the expression of that relation in faith, worship, and conduct; may be correct or not (Acts 26:5; James 1:26,27). Biblical religion primarily a thing of heart and life rather than ritual.

REMALIAH (rĕm'à-lī'à), father of King Pekah (II Kings 15:25).

REMETH (rē'mĕth), city in Issachar (Josh. 19:17-21); probably Ramoth of I Chron. 6:73 and Jarmuth of Josh. 21:29.

REMMON (See Rimmon).

REMNANT. 1. People who survived political or military crises (Josh. 12:4; 13:12). 2. Spiritual kernel of Israel who would survive God's judgment and become the germ of the new people of God (Isa. 10:20-23; 11:11,12; Jer. 32:38,39; Zeph. 3:13; Zech. 8:12).

REMON METHOAR (rĕm'ŏn-mĕth'ō-àr), town on border of Zebulun (Josh. 19:13).

REMPHAN (rĕm'făn), pagan deity worshiped by Israelites in wilderness (Acts 7:43); probably Chiun, or Saturn (Amos 5:26).

REPENTANCE (rē-pĕn'tăns), change of mind and of heart with regard to sin, so that there is a turning away from sin (Matt. 27:3; II Cor. 7:9,10). Repentance is necessary to salvation (Matt. 3:2,8; 4:17).

REPHAEL (rĕ'fā-ĕl), Levite; tabernacle gate-keeper (I Chron. 26:7).

REPHAH (rē'fā), grandson of Ephraim (I Chron. 7:23-25).

REPHAIAH (rē-fā'yà). 1. Descendant of David (I Chron. 3:21; "Rhesa" of Luke 3:27). 2. Son of Ishi (I Chron. 4:42-43). 3. Grandson of Issachar (I Chron. 7:2). 4. Descendant of Jonathan (I Chron. 9:40-43). 5. Son of Hur, a builder (Neh. 3:9).

REPHAIM (rĕf'ā-ĭm, mighty), giant people who lived in Canaan even before Abraham's time (Gen. 14:5; 15:20; Josh. 12:4; 13:12; 17:15).

REPHAIM, VALLEY OF (rĕf'ā-ĭm, vale of giants), fertile plain S of Jerusalem, three miles from Bethlehem (Isa. 17:4,5; I Chron. 14:9).

REPHIDIM (rĕf'ĭ-dĭm, plains), encampment of Israelites in wilderness; there Moses struck a rock to secure water (Exod. 17:1-7; 19:2); battle with Amalekites took place there (Exod. 17:8-16).

REPROBATE (rĕp'rō-bāt), moral corruption, unfitness, disqualification, disapproved (Rom. 1:28; I Cor. 9:27).

RESEN (rē'sĕn), town founded by Nimrod (Gen. 10:8-12) between Nineveh and Calah.

RESERVOIR, place where water is collected and kept for use when wanted, chiefly in large quantities. Because most of W Asia was subject to periodic droughts, and because of frequent sieges, reservoirs and cisterns were a necessity (II Chron. 26:10; 18:31; Eccl. 2:6).

RESHEPH (rē'shĕf), descendant of Ephraim (I Chron. 7:25).

REST, a word of frequent occurrence in the Bible. God commanded 7th day to be day of rest (Exod. 16:23; 31:15) and that the land was to have its rest every 7th year (Lev. 25:4). God promises rest to those who trust in Him (Matt. 11:28; Heb. 4).

RESURRECTION (rĕz-ū-rĕk'shŭn, a raising), the arising to life of a dead body. The Bible does not teach an abstract immortality of the soul, but the redemption of body and soul together. OT passages which speak of a resurrection of the body: Isa. 25:8; 26:19; Job 14:13-15; Dan. 12:2; Ps. 16:9-11; NT passages: John 5:25,28,29; Acts 24:15; I Thess. 4:16,17; I Cor. 15; Rev. 20:12ff. Christ first to rise (I Cor. 15); resurrection to be universal (II Cor. 5:10); new body to be spiritual, incorruptible, per-

fectly adapted to the new mode of existence, recognizably the same, but no longer subject to space-time limitations (Luke 24; John 20).

RESURRECTION OF JESUS CHRIST. The resurrection of Jesus Christ is the heart of the Christian faith. The NT is, if anything, even more resurrection-oriented than it is cross-centered. In Christ's teaching His resurrection is never divorced from His crucifixion. The two form a redemptive complex (Matt. 16:21; 20:18,19; Mark 8:31; 9:31; 10:33,34; Luke 24:26; John 10:17,18). In apostolic preaching the resurrection proves that Jesus is the true Messiah (Acts 2:12-36; 3:12-18; 4:10; 5:29-32; 10:39-43; 13:29-37; 17:23-31). The resurrection established Jesus as the Son of God with power (Rom. 1:4). By virtue of it He became Head of the Church (Eph. 1:19-23) and cosmic Sovereign (Phil. 2:9-11), and entered upon His ministry as High Priest (Rom. 8:34). The resurrection is an integral part of the whole redemptive process. It is a guarantee that life continues after death (John 11:25,26; 14:19), as well as a guarantee of judgment to come (Acts 17:31). It is not to be thought of as the survival of the soul of Jesus, or the continuation of the principles for which Jesus stood, but an actual historical event – the reappearance of Jesus in bodily, physical form, but with a body changed and incorruptible, not subject to disease and death.

REU (rē'ū), son of Peleg (Gen. 11:19), called "Ragau" in Luke 3:35.

REUBEN (rōō'bĕn, See a son!), eldest son of Jacob and Leah (Gen. 29:32); brought mandrakes to mother (Gen. 30:14f); committed incest (Gen. 35:22); saved Joseph from death (Gen. 37:19-22; 42:22); offered sons a surety for Benjamin (Gen. 42:37); tribe settled E of Jordan (Num. 1:20,21; 32; Josh. 13:15-23).

REUBENITES (rōō'bĕn-īts), descendants of Reuben, son of Jacob; settled in Gilead; supported King David (I Chron. 12:37); taken into Assyrian captivity (I Chron. 5:26).

REUEL (rōō'ĕl, God is friend). 1. Son of Esau (Gen. 36:4,10). 2. Father-in-law of Moses (Exod. 2:16-22), probably same as Jethro (Exod. 3:1). 3. Father of Eliasaph called Deuel in Num. 1:14) (Num. 2:14). 4. Benjamite (I Chron. 9:8).

REUMAH (rōō'mà), concubine of Nahor, brother of Abraham (Gen. 22:20-24).

REVELATION (rĕv-ē-lā'shŭn), the doctrine of God's making Himself and relevant truths known to men. Revelation is of two kinds: general and special. General revelation is available to all men, and is communicated through nature, conscience, and history. Special revelation is revelation given to particular people at particular times (although it may be intended for others as well), and comes chiefly through the Bible and Jesus Christ.

REVELATION, BOOK OF THE, last book in the Bible; only NT book exclusively prophetic in character; apocalyptic; tradition says it was written by John the apostle; written on island of Patmos, where John was imprisoned for his faith, either shortly after the death of Nero or at the close of the 1st century; addressed to seven churches of the Roman province of Asia; written to correct evils in the churches and to prepare them for the events that were about to confront them. Outline: 1. Christ the critic of the churches (1:1-3:22). 2. Series of seals, trumpets, and bowls; God's judgment upon a world controlled by evil (4: 1-16:21). 3. Overthrow of evil society, religion, and government in the destruction of Babylon and the defeat of the beast and his armies by Christ (17:1-21:8). 4. Establishment of the city of God, the eternal destiny of His people (21:9-22:5). Epilogue: Appeal and invitation (22:6-21).

REVELLING, any extreme intemperance and lustful indulgence, usually accompanying pagan worship (Gal. 5:21; I Pet. 4:3).

REVILE, REVILER, REVILING; to revile is to address with opprobrious or contumelious language; to reproach (Exod. 21:17; Zeph. 2:8; Mark 15:32; I Cor. 6:10).

REVISED VERSIONS (See Bible, English version).

REWARD, something given in recognition of a good or bad act (Ps. 9:8; Jer. 40:5; Mic. 7:3; I Tim. 5:18).

REZEPH (rē'zĕf), important caravan center in ancient times (II Kings 19:8-12; Isa. 37:12).

REZIA (rē-zī'ȧ), descendant of Asher (I Chron. 7:39); also Rizia.

REZIN (rē'zĭn). 1. King of Syria (735-732 B. C.); fought with Israel against Judah (Isa. 7); defeated and killed by Tiglath-pileser (II Kings 16:9). 2. Founder of a family of Nethinims (Ezra 2:43,48).

REZON (rē'zŏn), king of Damascus (I Kings 11:23-25). Probably same as Hezion in I Kings 15:18.

RHEGIUM (rē'jĭ-ŭm), Greek colony on toe of Italy (Acts 28:13). Modern Reggio.

RHESA (rē'sȧ), son of Zerubbabel; ancestor of Christ (Luke 3:27).

RHODA (rō'dȧ), servant or slave girl in home of Mary, John Mark's mother (Acts 12:13).

RHODES (rōdz, rose), island on SW tip of Asia Minor; commercial center until crippled by Rome in 166 B. C.; famous for Colossus, a statue of Helios; Paul stopped off there (Acts 21:1).

RIBAI (rī'bī), Benjamite; father of Ittai (II Sam. 23:29; I Chron. 11:31).

RIBLAH (rĭb'lȧ). 1. City on boundary of Canaan and Israel, N of Sea of Galilee (Num. 34:11). 2. Important town on E bank of Orontes River 50 miles S of Hamath, in Assyrian province of Mansuate. In this place Pharaoh Necho (609 B. C.) put King Jehoahaz II of Judah in chains, and Nebuchadnezzar killed the sons of King Zedekiah of Judah (587 B. C.) and put out his eyes, and then carried him off in chains to Babylon (II Kings 25:6f; Jer.

39:5-7). It is possible that the two Riblahs may be the same.

RIDDLE (hidden saying, proverb), any dark saying of which the meaning is not immediately clear and must be found by shrewd thought (Num. 12:8; Prov. 1:6). It may be a parable (Ps. 49:4) or something for men to guess (Judg. 14:12-19), or just a hard question (I Kings 10:1; II Chron. 9:1).

RIGHTEOUSNESS, the quality of rightness or justice; an attribute of God. As a result of the fall, man is corrupt and lacking in righteousness (Rom. 3:23), and incapable of making himself righteous (Rom. 3:19,20). In justification man is declared righteous through the imputed righteousness of Jesus Christ when he has faith (II Cor. 5:21). In sanctification man is progressively made righteous in character and conduct (I John 1:7-9).

RIMMON (rĭm'ŏn, pomegranate). 1. City in S Judah (Josh. 15:32); "En-rimmon" in Neh. 11:29.

RIMMON-METHOAR (rĭm'ŏn-mĕ'thō-àr), Levitical city in Zebulun (Josh. 19:13).

RIMMON PAREZ (See Rimmon-Perez).

RIMMON-PEREZ (rĭm'ŏn pĕ'rĕz), "Parez" in KJV; encampment of Israelites in wilderness (Num. 33:16-19).

RIMMON, ROCK OF, fortress to which 600 Benjamites fled after escaping slaughter (Judg. 20:45,47; 21:13), near Jeba or Gibeah.

RING (See Dress).

RING, worn as adornment (James 2:2); signet ring became seal of authority (Gen. 41:42,43; Luke 15:22); signet rings originally worn on a chain around neck, but later put on hand.

RING-STREAKED, mottled of color, characterizing Laban's sheep (Gen. 30:35; 31:8,12).

RINNAH (rĭn'ȧ), son of Shimon of Judah (I Chron. 4:20).

RIOT, squander in evil ways (Prov. 23:20; 28:7); waste (Titus 1:6; I Pet. 4:4); revelry (Rom. 13:13); luxury (II Pet. 2:13).

RIPHATH (rī'fȧth), son of Gomer (Gen. 10:3).

RISSAH (rĭs'ȧ, ruins), encampment of Israelites in wilderness (Num. 33:21); site unknown.

RITHMAH (rĭth'mȧ), encampment of Israelites in wilderness (Num. 33:18).

RIVER, may refer to large streams (Gen. 2:10-14), the Nile (Gen. 41:1; II Kings 19:24), winter torrent the bed of which is dry in summer (Amos 6:14), fountain stream (Ps. 119:136). Used figuratively for abundance of good or evil (Job 20:17; Isa. 43:2).

RIVER OF EGYPT, brook on SW border of Palestine flowing into Mediterranean Sea (Gen. 15:18; Num. 34:5); now Wadi el Arish.

RIZPAH (rĭz'pȧ, hot stone), concubine of Saul (I Sam. 3:7); Abner accused of incest with her (II Sam. 3:7b).

ROADS, may refer to paths or highways; hundreds of allusions to roads in Bible; road robbers quite common (Matt. 11:10; Luke 10:30); Romans built highways throughout empire, some of which are still in use; used by traders, travelers, and armies; Paul used Roman roads on his missionary journeys; the statement, "All roads lead to Rome," shows how well provided the Roman empire was with roads.

ROBBERY, illegal seizure of another's property; forbidden by law (Lev. 19:13); highways unsafe (Judg. 5:6; Luke 10:30; II Cor. 11:26); houses built to resist robbers; even priests sometimes turned to pillage (Hos. 6:9); denounced by prophets (Isa. 61:8; Ezek. 22:29); withholding tithes and offerings from God's storehouse regarded as robbery (Mal. 3:8).

ROBE (See Dress).

ROBINSON'S ARCH, remains of ancient Jerusalem masonry, named for American archaeologist Edward Robinson, who discovered it in 1838. Giant stones, projecting from SW wall of Temple enclosure, are evidently part of an arch of a bridge or viaduct that in Herod's time connected Jerusalem's western hill with the eastern hill.

ROBOAM (See Rehoboam).

ROCK, natural fortress (Judg. 20:45,47), mountain (I Sam. 23:25,26); Moses smote rock for water (Exod. 17:6); sometimes used figuratively: referring to God (II Sam. 22:2), Peter (Matt. 16:18), believers (I Pet. 2:5).

ROD, branch, stick, staff; symbol of authority (Exod. 4:2,17,20; 9:23; 14:16); chastisement symbolized by rod (Mic. 5:1); Messianic ruler (Isa. 11:1); affliction (Job 9:34).

RODANIM (rŏd'à-nĭm), tribe descended from Javan, son of Japheth (I Chron. 1:7).

ROE, ROEBUCK (See Animals).

ROGELIM (rŏ'gĕ-lĭm), town near Mahanaim whose citizens assisted David (II Sam. 17:27,29; 19:31).

ROHGAH (rŏ'gà), descendant of Asher (I Chron. 7:34).

ROLL, sheets of papyrus or parchment (made of skin) sewn together to make long sheet of writing material which was wound around a stick to make a scroll (Isa. 34:4; Jer. 36; Ezek. 3:1-3; Rev. 5; 10:1-10).

ROLLER, anything that turns or revolves (Isa. 17:13).

ROMAMTI-EZER (rŏ-màm'tĭ-ê'zèr), son of Neman; temple musician (I Chron. 25:4,31).

ROMAN EMPIRE. City of Rome founded 753 B. C.; a monarchy until 509 B. C.; a republic from 509 to 31 B. C.; empire began in 31 B. C., fell in 5th cent. Rome extended hold over all Italy and eventually over whole Mediterranean world, Gaul, half of Britain, the Rhine-Danube rivers, and as far as Parthia. Augustus, the first Roman emperor, divided Roman provinces into senatorial, which were ruled by proconsuls (Acts 13:7; 18:12; 19:38) and imperial, ruled by governors (Matt. 27:2; Luke 2:2; Acts 23:24). Moral corruption was responsible for the decline and fall of the Roman Empire. Roman reservoirs, aqueducts, roads, public buildings, statues survive. Many Roman officials are referred to in

the NT, including the emperors Augustus (Luke 2:1), Tiberius (Luke 3:1), Claudius (Acts 11:28), Nero (Acts 25:11,12).

ROMANS, EPISTLE TO THE, written by Paul during his three months stay in Corinth on his 3rd missionary journey (Acts 20: 2,3; Rom. 1:1; 15:25-27). He planned to visit Spain after a brief stay in Jerusalem, and he hoped to stop off in Rome on his way to Spain (Rom. 1:10,11; 15:14-33). He had never been in Rome before, and in this epistle he clearly set forth the message of the gospel which he preached. Outline: 1. Introduction (1:1-15). 2. Sinfulness of man, including both Gentiles and Jews (1:16-3:20). 3. Justification by faith (3: 21-5:21). 4. Sanctification (6-8). 5. Israel and world salvation (9-11). 6. Details of Christian conduct (12-15:13). 7. Concluding remarks, Greetings (15:14-16:27).

ROME, capital of Roman Empire; founded in 753 B. C.; Paul imprisoned there twice (Acts 28; II Tim. 4).

ROOM. 1. Chamber in a house (Acts 1:13). 2. Place or position in society (Matt. 23:6; Luke 14:7,8; 20:46).

ROOT. Usually used in figurative sense. 1. Essential cause of something (I Tim. 6:10). 2. Source or progenitor (Isa. 11:10; Rom. 15:12). 3. Foundation or support of something (I Kings 19:30; Job 5:3). 4. Injured roots means loss of life or vitality (Job 31:12; Isa. 5:24).

ROPE, often mentioned in Bible (II Sam. 17:7-13; I Kings 20:31,32; Ps. 118:27; John 2:15).

ROSE (See Plants).

ROSETTA STONE, inscribed basalt slab, found on Rosetta branch of the Nile, in 1799, with text in hieroglyphic, demotic, and Greek. It furnished the key for the decipherment of Egyptian hieroglyphics.

ROSH (rŏsh, head). 1. Son of Benjamin (Gen. 46:21). 2. Chief of three nations that are to invade Israel during the latter days (Ezek. 38:2; 39:1 ASV).

ROW, ROWERS (See Ship).

RUDDY, red or fair complexion (I Sam. 16:12).

RUDE (untrained, ignorant of rules), technically not trained (II Cor. 11:6).

RUDIMENTS (rŏo'dĭ-mĕnts, first principles or elements of anything), elements (Gal. 4:3,9; II Pet. 3:10,12), first principles (Heb. 5:12), physical elements of the world (II Pet. 3:10,12).

RUE (See Plants).

RUFUS (rŏo'fŭs). 1. Brother of Alexander and son of Simon of Cyrene who bore the cross (Mark 15:21). 2. Friend of Paul (Rom. 16:13).

RUHAMAH (rŏo-hà'mà, to be pitied), Hosea's daughter by Gomer (Hos. 2:1).

RULER, word used to translate several Heb. and Gr. words meaning king, captain, exalted one, overlord, magistrate, etc. (Gen. 45:8; Prov. 23:1; Ezra 9:2; Neh. 2:16; Dan. 5:7; Acts 17:6,8).

RUMAH (rŏo'mà), home of Pedaiah, whose

daughter Zebudah bore Jehoiakim to Josiah king of Judah (II Kings 23:36), perhaps Arumah near Shechem, or Rumah in Galilee.

RUSH (See Plants).

RUTH (rōŏth), Moabitess who married a son of Elimelech and Naomi of Bethlehem (Ruth 1:1-4); ancestor of Christ (Matt. 1:5); Book of Ruth is about her.

RUTH, BOOK OF, historical romance narrating story of Ruth, Moabitess, ancestor of David and Christ. She first married a son of Elimelech and Naomi of Bethlehem (Ruth 1:1-4). When her husband died, she returned with her mother-in-law to Judah (1:7), where she married Boaz, a kinsman of Naomi (2:20-23), after a nearer kinsman of Naomi had declined to do so (4:6,13).

RYE (See Plants).

S

SABA, SABAEANS (sā′bà, sà-bē′ănz). Saba is mentioned in Gen. 10:7 and I Chron. 1:9 as a son of Cush. The Sabaeans were a merchant people who in early times lived in SW Arabia in a region bordering Ophir and Havilah. Romans called it **Arabia Felix.** Sabaean raiders killed Job's flocks and servants (Job 1:15). They were slave traders (Joel 3:8). One of the Sabaean monarchs was the famous Queen of Sheba (I Kings 10:1,4,10,13; II Chron. 9:1,3,9,12).

SABACHTHANI (sà-bàkh′thà-nē), a word in the utterance of Jesus on the cross, "My God, my God, why hast Thou forsaken me?" (Matt. 27:46; Mark 15:34).

SABAOTH, THE LORD OF (săb′à-ŏth, hosts), the same as "the Lord of hosts" (Rom. 9:29; James 5:4); probably means that all created agencies and forces are under the command and leadership of Jehovah.

SABBATH (săb′àth, rest), the weekly day of rest and worship for the Jews; instituted at creation (Gen. 2:3); Mosaic institution (Exod. 16:23-30; 20:8-11; Lev. 19:3; 30; 23:3; Deut. 5:12-15); prophets always exalted sabbath (Isa. 56:2,4; 58:13; Jer. 17:21-27; Ezek. 20:12-24); wilful sabbath-breakers were put to death (Num. 15:32-36); scribes formulated innumerable legal restrictions regarding the sabbath and came into conflict with Jesus because He disregarded some of their absurd restrictions (Matt. 12:1-14; Mark 2:23-3:6; Luke 6:1-11; John 5:1-18). Early Christians kept the 7th day as a sabbath, but also met for worship on the first day of the week in celebration of the resurrection of Christ. As the split between the Jews and Christians widened, they came gradually to meet for worship only on the first day; typical of man's entrance into God's rest through Jesus Christ (Heb. 4; Col. 2:16,17).

SABBATH, COVERT FOR THE, obscure expression found in II Kings 16:18; may refer to a colonnade in the temple compound.

SABBATH, MORROW AFTER THE, expression of uncertain meaning found in Lev. 23:11; may refer to the ordinary weekly sabbath or the first day of the Passover on whatever day of the week it might fall.

SABBATH, SECOND AFTER THE FIRST, expression of uncertain meaning found in Luke 6:1. Many explanations have been suggested.

SABBATH DAY'S JOURNEY, journey of limited extent (3,000 feet) which the scribes thought a Jew might travel on the sabbath without breaking the Law (Acts 1:12).

SABBATICAL YEAR (See Feasts).

SABBEUS (sè-bē′ûs), man who divorced foreign wife (I Esdras 9:32); "Shemaiah" in Ezra 10:31.

SABTA, SABTAH (săb′tà), son of Cush (Gen. 10:7; I Chron. 1:9); perhaps also a place in S Arabia.

SABTECHA, SABTECHAH (săb′tè-kà), son of Cush (Gen. 10:5-7); descendants probably lived in S Arabia.

SACAR (sā′kàr). 1. Father of Ahiam (I Chron. 11:35); "Sharar" in II Sam. 23:33. 2. Son of Obed-edom (I Chron. 26:4).

SACKCLOTH (săk′klŏth), coarse dark cloth made of goat's hair worn by mourners (II Sam. 3:31; II Kings 19:1,2), often by prophets (Isa. 20:2; Rev. 11:3), and by captives (I Kings 20:31).

SACRAMENT (săk′rà-mĕnt), symbolic rite instituted by Christ setting forth the central truths of the Christian faith: death and resurrection with Christ and participation in the redemptive benefits of Christ's mediatorial death. Roman Catholic Church has seven sacraments; Protestant Church has two, baptism and the Lord's Supper.

SACRIFICE (săk′rĭ-fĭs), a religious act belonging to worship in which offering is made to God of some material object belonging to the offerer—this offering being consumed in the ceremony, in order to attain, restore, maintain, or celebrate friendly relations with the deity; expresses faith, repentance, and adoration; main purpose of the sacrifice is to please the deity and to secure His favor. Practiced from ancient times (Gen. 4:4f; 8:20f; 12:7,8; 13: 4,18; 15:4f; 26:25; Job 1:5; 42:7-9). Before building of temple in Jerusalem sacrifices were offered by heads of families. Sacrifices have not been offered by Jews since the destruction of the temple by the Romans in A. D. 70. In Mosaic sacrifices only certain kinds of animals and fowl could be offered. Sacrifices were of two kinds, animal and vegetable. Animal sacrifices: Sin Offering (Lev. 4:1-35; 6:24-30), Guilt Offering (Lev. 5:14-6:7), Burnt Offering (Lev. 1), Peace Offering (Lev. 3). Vegetable sacrifices: Meat Offerings (Lev. 2: 1-16; 6:14-18), Drink Offerings (Num. 6:17; 15:1-12). All OT sacrifices point forward to and are a type of the sacrifice of Jesus Christ (Heb. 9:10).

SACRILEGE (săk'ri-lĕj), in Rom. 2:22 it means to rob temples.

SADDLE (săd'l, *riding seat*), getting a beast ready for riding (Gen. 22:3; Num. 22:21; Judg. 19:10; II Sam. 16:1; 17:23). Asses were not ridden with saddles; when carrying heavy burdens they had a thick cushion on their back.

SADDUCEES (săd'yū-sēz), Jewish religious sect in the time of Christ. Beliefs: acceptance only of the Law and rejection of oral tradition; denial of resurrection, immortality of the soul, spirit world (Matt 12:18; Luke 20:27; Acts 23:8); supported Maccabeans; a relatively small group, but generally held the high priesthood; denounced by John the Baptist (Matt. 3:7,8) and Jesus (Matt. 16:6,11,12); opposed Christ (Matt. 21:12f; Mark 11:15f; Luke 19:47) and the apostolic church (Acts 5:17,33).

SADOC (sā'dŏk). 1. Ancestor of Ezra (II Esdras 1:1). 2. Descendant of Zerubbabel and ancestor of Jesus (Matt. 1:14).

SAFFRON (See Plants).

SAIL (See Ship).

SAILOR (See Occupations and Professions).

SAINT. 1. A member of God's covenant people Israel, whether a pious layman (II Chron. 6:41; Ps. 16:3) or someone like a priest who is consecrated to God (Ps. 106:16; I Peter 2:5). 2. A NT believer, belonging exclusively to God (Acts 9:13; I Cor. 16:1; II Cor. 1:1). The saints are the Church (I Cor. 1:2), people called out of the world to be God's own people. Throughout the Bible the saints are urged to live lives befitting their position (Eph. 4:1; Col. 1:10).

SALA, SALAH (sā'là), son of Arphaxad (Gen. 10:24; 11:13ff; I Chron. 1:18,24; Luke 3:35,36).

SALAMIS (săl'à-mis), city on E coast of Cyprus. Paul and Barnabas preached there (Acts 13:5).

SALATHIEL (sà-lā'thi-ĕl, **I have asked God**), son of Jeconiah, king of Judah (Matt. 1:12), or of Neri (Luke 3:27). He may have been the real son of Neri, but only the legal heir of Jeconiah.

SALCAH (săl'kà), city on NE boundary of Bashan (Deut. 3:10; Josh. 12:5; 13:11); now known as Salkhad.

SALCHAH (săl'kà), another spelling of Salcah.

SALEM (sā'lĕm, **peace**), name of city of which Melchizedek was king (Gen. 14:18; Heb. 7:1,2); probably Jerusalem.

SALIM (sā'lim), place near Aenon W of Jordan (John 1:28; 3:23,26; 10:40).

SALLAI (săl'ā-i). 1. Benjamite chief (Neh. 11:8). 2. Priestly family (Neh. 12:20), called "Sallu" in verse 7.

SALLU (See Sallai).

SALMA (săl'mà), son of Caleb (I Chron. 2:51; 2:54).

SALMON (săl'mŏn), father of Boaz the husband of Ruth (Ruth 4:20,21; I Chron. 2:11;

Matt. 1:4,5; Luke 3:32).

SALMONE (săl-mō'nē), promontory forming E extremity of Crete (Acts 27:7).

SALOME (sà-lō'mē, fem. of Solomon). 1. Wife of Zebedee and mother of James and John (Matt. 27:56; Mark 15:40; 16:1); ministered to Jesus (Mark 15:40,41); present at the crucifixion of Jesus (Matt. 27:56); came to tomb to anoint body of Jesus (Mark 16:1). 2. Daughter of Herodias; as a reward for her dancing she obtained head of John the Baptist (Matt. 14:3-11; Mark 6:17-28). Her name is not given in the Gospels.

SALT, used in ancient times for seasoning and preserving food (Job 6:6; Isa. 30:24 RSV; Matt. 5:13), as an antiseptic in medicine (Ezek. 16:4), and with offerings of all kinds (Lev. 2:13; Ezek. 43:24). Captured cities were sometimes destroyed and sown with salt (Judg. 9:45). Covenants were sometimes made with salt (Num. 18:19; II Chron. 13:5). Christ's disciples called "the salt of the earth" (Matt. 5:13; Mark 9:50; Luke 14:34).

SALT, CITY OF, city in wilderness of Judah, between Nibshan and Engedi (Josh. 15:62); site uncertain.

SALT, COVENANT OF, a covenant confirmed with sacrificial meals at which salt was used (Lev. 2:13; Num. 18:19).

SALT SEA (See Dead Sea).

SALT, VALLEY OF, valley between Jerusalem and Edom in which great victories were won over the Edomites (II Sam. 8:13; II Kings 14:7; II Chron. 25:11).

SALU (sā'lū), father of Zimri (Num. 25:14).

SALUTATION (săl-ū-tā'shŭn), a greeting given either orally (Luke 1:29,41,44) or in writing (I Cor. 16:21; Col. 4:18; II Thess. 3:17). Greetings in the Bible sometimes included acts as well as words, like prostrations, kneeling, kissing of the hand, etc. Every situation in life had its own particular kind of salutation. Paul's epistolary salutations are usually of rich spiritual fulness.

SALVATION (săl-vā'shŭn), deliverance from any kind of evil, whether material or spiritual. Theologically, it denotes (1) the whole process by which man is delivered from all that interferes with the enjoyment of God's highest blessings, (2) the actual enjoyment of those blessings. In the OT the deliverance may be from defeat in battle (Exod. 15:2), trouble (Ps. 34:6), enemies (II Sam. 23:36-38), violence (II Sam. 22:3), reproach (Ps. 57:3), exile (Ps. 106:47), death (Ps. 6:4), sin (Ezek. 36:29). God is often spoken of as Saviour (Isa. 43:3,11; Jer. 14:8). The most important of the human conditions for salvation was trust in God. In the NT salvation usually means deliverance from sin through entrance upon a new divine life, and it is through faith in the incarnate Son of God (John 3:16; Eph. 2:13-18). Salvation brings not merely deliverance from future punishment, but also from sin as a present power (Rom. 6). It includes all the redemptive blessings we have in Christ, chiefly conversion, regeneration, justification, adoption, sanctification and glorification. In some sense, the doctrine of salvation extends beyond man so as to affect the universe (I Cor. 15:28).

SAMARIA (sȧ-mâr'ĭ-ȧ, watch tower). 1. Another name for the N kingdom of Israel, founded when the 10 N tribes refused to acknowledge Rehoboam, the son of Solomon, as their king. It extended from Bethel to Dan, and from the Mediterranean to Syria and Ammon. Important cities: Shechem, Samaria, Sychar, Shiloh, Bethel. 2. Capital of N kingdom built by Omri c. 5-1/2 miles NW of Shechem; rebuked for luxury and corruption (I Kings 18:3; 21; Isa. 7:9; Jer. 31:5; Ezek. 23:33; Hos. 8:5; Amos 3:1-22). Modern Sebastiyeh.

SAMARITAN PENTATEUCH (See Samaritans).

SAMARITANS (sȧ-mĕr'ĭ-tȧns). 1. The inhabitants of the region of Samaria (II Kings 17:26; Matt. 10:5; Luke 9:52; 10:33; John 4:9,30,40; Acts 8:25). After the captivity of the N kingdom colonists from Babylonia, Syria, Elam, and other Assyrian territories (II Kings 17:24-34) intermarried with remnants of Jews in Samaria; held in contempt by the Jews (Neh. 4:1-3; Matt. 10:5; John 4:9-26). 2. The sect which derived its name from Samaria, a term of contempt with the Jews (John 8:48). Religion of the Samaritans was based on the Pentateuch alone.

SAMGARNEBO (săm'gär-nĕb'bō), chief army officer of Nebuchadnezzar (Jer. 39:3).

SAMLAH (săm'là), king of Edom (Gen. 36:36,37; I Chron. 1:47,48).

SAMOS (sā'mŏs, height), island off W Asia Minor near Lydia (Acts 20:15).

SAMOTHRACE (săm'ō-thrās, Samos of Thrace), island in NE Aegean between Troas and Neapolis (Acts 16:11).

SAMSON (săm'sŭn), Danite hero; son of Manoah; birth the result of special providence; life-long Nazirite; married Philistine woman in Timnath, who was later given to another, and in revenge Samson burned Philistine fields; killed many Philistines; performed many feats of strength; finally betrayed by Delilah; died by pulling down pillars of temple of Dagon; judge of Israel 20 years (Judg. 13-16; Heb. 11:32).

SAMUEL (săm-ū'ĕl, name of God or God has heard), last of the judges (I Sam. 7:15) and first of the prophets after Moses (II Chron. 35:18; Jer. 15:1), a seer (I Sam. 9:9) and priest (I Sam. 2:18,27,35); son of Elkanah and Hannah (I Sam. 1:19,20); birth the result of special providence; brought up by Eli (I Sam. 3); anointed Saul (I Sam. 10) and David (I Sam. 16:13) as kings; possible author of Biblical books which bear his name; died at Ramah (I Sam. 25:1).

SAMUEL, BOOKS OF. Historical books named after the outstanding figure of the early section. I and II Samuel were once one book; the LXX divided in into two. Author's name not given, but Jewish tradition ascribes the work to the prophet Samuel, although it tells of Samuel's death and all of the events of I Sam. 25-31 and II Sam. occurred after Samuel's death. The books of Samuel present the establishment of the kingship in Israel. Outline: 1. Samuel as Judge (I Sam. 1-7). 2. Saul as King (I Sam. 8-II Sam. 1). 3. David as King (II Sam. 2-24).

SANBALLAT (săn-băl'ăt, the god Sin (moongod) has given life), very influential Samaritan who tried unsuccessfully to defeat Nehemiah's plans for rebuilding the walls of Jerusalem (Neh. 4:1ff; 6:1-14; 13:28).

SANCTIFICATION (sănk-ti-fi-kā'shŭn, separation, setting apart), to separate from the world and consecrate unto God. To sanctify anything is to declare that it belongs to God. It may refer to persons, places, days and seasons, and objects used for worship (Exod. 13:2; 19:5,6; 29:27,44; Lev. 27:14,16; Num. 3:12; Neh. 13:19-22). In an ethical sense it means the progressive conformation of the believer into the image of Christ, or the process by which the life is made morally holy. Sanctification is through the redemptive work of Christ and the work of the indwelling Holy Spirit. It begins at regeneration and is completed when we see Christ.

SANCTUARY (săngk'tū-ȧ-rē, holy place). 1. The tabernacle or temple, where God established His earthly abode. 2. Judah (Ps. 114:2). 3. Place of asylum (I Kings 2:28f). 4. In plural, idolatrous shrines (Amos 7:9). 5. Earthly sanctuary a type of the heavenly sanctuary, in which Christ is high priest and sacrifice (Heb. 10:1-18).

SAND, found in desert and shores of large bodies of water; symbolic of numberlessness, vastness (Gen. 22:17; Jer. 33:22; I Kings 4:29), weight (Job 6:3), and instability (Matt. 7:26).

SANDAL (See Dress).

SANHEDRIM, SANHEDRIN (săn'hē-drim, săn'hē-drin, council), highest Jewish tribunal during Greek and Roman periods; its origin is unknown; lost its authority when Jerusalem fell to the Romans in A. D. 70; in time of Jesus it had authority only in Judaea, but its influence was recognized even in the Diaspora (Acts 9:2; 22:5; 26:12). Composed of 70 members, plus the president, who was the high priest; members drawn from chief priests, scribes, and elders (Matt. 16:21; 27:41; Mark 8:31; 11:27; 14:43,53; Luke 9:22); the secular nobility of Jerusalem; final court of appeal for all questions connected with the Mosaic law; could order arrests by its own officers of justice (Matt. 26:47; Mark 14:43; Acts 4:3; 5:17f; 9:2); did not have right of capital punishment in time of Christ (John 18:31,32).

SANSANNAH (săn-săn'à), town in S of Judah (Josh. 15:31), identical with Hazar-susah (Josh. 19:5).

SAPH (săf), Philistine giant slain by one of

David's heroes (II Sam. 21:18; I Chron. 20:4).

SAPHIR (sā'fĕr, glittering), town probably in SW Palestine (Micah 1:10-15).

SAPPHIRA (să-fī'rà, beautiful), wife of Ananias; struck dead at Peter's feet because she lied (Acts 5:1-10).

SAPPHIRE (See Minerals).

SARA, SARAH, SARAI (sâr'à, princess). 1. Wife of Abraham; mother of Isaac (Gen. 11:29; 21:2,3); originally named Sarai; twice passed off by Abraham as his sister (Gen. 12:10-20; 20:1-18); induced Abraham to take Hagar as concubine (Gen. 16:1-7) and later to banish her (Gen. 21:9-21); buried at Machpelah (Gen. 23); praised for her faith (Heb. 11:11) and obedience (I Pet. 3:6). 2. Daughter of Raguel, the wife of Tobias (Tob. 3:7,17).

SARAPH (sā'răf), Judahite (I Chron. 4:22).

SARDINE (See Mineral).

SARDIS (sâr'dĭs), chief city of Lydia; famous for arts and crafts; patron of mystery cults (Rev. 1:11; 3:1-6).

SARDITE (sâr'dĭt), descendant of Sered (Gen. 46:14; Num. 26:26).

SARDIUS, SARDONYX (See Minerals).

SAREPTA (să-rĕp'tà), Phoenician town eight miles S of Sidon (Luke 4:26; I Kings 17:9,10).

SARGON (sâr'gŏn, the constituted king). 1. Sargon I, king and founder of early Babylonian empire (2400 B. C.). Not referred to in Bible. 2. Sargon II (722-705 B. C.), Assyrian king (Isa. 20:1); successor of Shalmaneser who captured Samaria (II Kings 17:1-6); defeated Egyptian ruler So (II Kings 17:4); destroyed Hittite empire; succeeded by his son Sennacherib.

SARID (sā'rĭd), village on boundary of Zebulun (Josh. 19:10,12), probably modern Tell Shadud, N of Megiddo.

SARON (See Sharon).

SARSECHIM (sâr'sĕ-kĭm), prince of Nebuchadnezzar who entered Jerusalem when it fell (Jer. 39:3).

SARUCH (See Serug).

SATAN (sā'tăn, adversary). 1. As a common noun: enemy or adversary (I Sam. 29:4; I Kings 5:4; 11:14; Ps. 38:20; 109:6). 2. As a proper noun: the chief of the fallen spirits, the grand adversary of God and man (Job 1:6,12; 2:1; Zech. 3:1); hostile to everything good. Names and descriptive designations by which he is known: devil (Matt. 4:1; Luke 4:2), accuser of the brethren (Rev. 12:9,10), adversary (I Pet. 5:8), Beelzebub (Matt. 12:24), Belial (II Cor. 6:15), deceiver of the whole world (Rev. 12:9), the great dragon (Rev. 12:9), the evil one (Matt. 13:19,38), the father of lies (John 8:44), god of this world (II Cor. 4:4), murderer (John 8:44), the old serpent (Rev. 12:9), the prince of this world (John 12:31; 14:30), prince of the powers of the air (Eph. 2:2), the tempter (Matt. 4:5; I Thess. 3:5). Not an independent rival of God, but is able to go only as far as God permits (Job 1:12; 2:6; Luke 22:31); basically evil; story of his origin not told, but he was originally good; fell through pride (I Tim. 3:6); ruler

of a powerful kingdom standing in opposition to God (Matt. 12:26; Luke 11:18); ever seeks to defeat the divine plans of grace toward mankind; defeated by Christ at Calvary; will some day be cast into the lake of fire to be eternally doomed (Matt. 25:41; Rev. 20:1-3, 7-10).

SATRAP (sā'trăp), viceroy in Persian empire who ruled several small provinces (satrapies), each having its own governor. In KJV "lieutenant" in Ezra 8:36; Esth. 3:12; 8:9; 9:3, "prince" in Dan. 3:2,3,27; 6:1-7).

SATYR (săt'ĕr), lascivious deity, half man and half goat, in Mediterranean mythology (Isa. 13:21; 34:14).

SAUL (sôl, asked of God). 1. First king of Israel; son of Kish; Benjamite; anointed king by Samuel (I Sam. 8-10); chosen king by Israelites (I Sam. 10:17-27); defeated Israel's enemies: Ammonites, Philistines, Moabites, Amalekites (I Sam. 11-14); disobeyed God and was rejected by Him (I Sam. 13:1-14; 15); jealous of David because of his greater popularity and sought to kill him (I Sam. 16-26); ended his own life after being wounded in battle (I Sam. 31). 2. Hebrew name for Paul (Acts 13:9).

SAVIOUR (săv'yŏr, deliverer), one who saves, delivers, or preserves from any evil or danger, whether physical or spiritual, temporal or eternal; term applied both to men (Judg. 3:9,15; II Kings 13:5; Neh. 9:27; Obad. 21) and God (Ps. 44:3,7; Isa. 43:11; 45:21; 60:16; Jer. 14:8; Hos. 13:4). In NT it is never applied to man, but only of God and Christ (Luke 1:47; I Tim. 1:1; 2:3; 4:10; Titus 1:3). Saviour is pre-eminently the title of the Son (Titus 1:4; 2:13; 3:6; II Tim. 1:10; II Pet. 1:1; I John 4:10).

SAVOR, SAVOUR (sā'vŏr), taste (Matt. 5:13; Luke 14:34), smell (Joel 2:20). Also used metaphorically (II Cor. 2:14; Eph. 5:2; Phil. 4:18).

SAVORY MEAT, meals made by Jacob and Esau for their father Isaac prior to receiving his blessing (Gen. 27:4,9,14,17,31).

SAW. Ancient saws were made of flint, bronze, or iron. Stone was sawed as well as wood (I Kings 7:9).

SCAB (See Diseases, Skin).

SCAFFOLD, platform (II Chron. 6:13).

SCALE. 1. Only fish having fins and scales were permitted as food for Hebrews (Lev. 11:9-12). 2. Instrument for weighing (Isa. 40:12; Prov. 16:11; 20:23).

SCALL (See Diseases, Skin).

SCAPEGOAT, the 2nd of two goats for which lots were cast on the Day of Atonement (Lev. 16:8,10,26). The first was sacrificed as a sin offering, but the second had the people's sins transferred to it by prayer and was then taken into the wilderness and released.

SCARLET, probably a bright rich crimson. Scarlet cloth was used for the hangings of the tabernacle (Exod. 25:4), high priest's vestments (Exod. 39:1), royal or expensive apparel (II Sam. 1:24). Sins are "as scarlet" (Isa. 1:18).

SCARLET (See Plants).

SCEPTER (sĕp'tẽr), rod held in the hands of kings as a token of authority (Gen. 49:10; Num. 24:17; Ps. 45:6).

SCEVA (sē'và), chief priest living in Ephesus whose seven sons were exorcists (Acts 19:14-17).

SCHISM (sĭz'm, rent or division), a formal division inside a religious group (I Cor. 12:25).

SCHOOL, place or institution devoted to teaching and learning. In the early history of Israel the home was the primary agency for religious training, which was imparted chiefly through conversation, example, and imitation. All teaching was religiously oriented. Samuel instituted a school of the prophets (I Sam. 19:19,20). During the Babylonian captivity the synagogue had its origin. It was a place of teaching, never of sacrifice. Later an elementary school system was developed with the synagogue attendant (Luke 4:20) as the teacher. Memorization had a prominent place. Teachers had an important part in the work of the church (James 3:1; Rom. 12:7).

SCIENCE, knowledge (Dan. 1:4; I Tim. 6:20).

SCOFF, mock, deride (II Kings 2:23; Ezek. 22:5; Hab. 1:10).

SCOFFER, one who derides, mocks (II Pet. 3:3).

SCORPION (skòr'pĭ-ŏn), insect of the arachnid (spider-like) type, with poisonous stinger in its tail (Deut. 8:15; Ezek. 2:6; Luke 10:19). Punishment with scorpions probably referred to ships or scourges (I Kings 12:11; II Chron. 10:11).

SCOURGE (skûrj, whip), the act or the instrument used to inflict severe pain by beating. Mosaic law authorized scourging of a culprit, but limited it to 40 strokes (Deut. 25:3). Administered by local synagogue authorities (Matt. 10:17) or by the Sanhedrin (Acts 5:40). Among the Romans either rods (Acts 16:22) or whips (Matt. 27:26) were used. Also used figuratively for "affliction" (Josh. 23:13; Job 5:21).

SCREECH OWL (See Birds).

SCRIBES (See Occupations and Professions).

SCRIBES, JEWISH, class of learned men who made the systematic study of the law and its exposition their professional occupation. Also called "lawyers" (Matt. 22:35), "doctors of the law" (Luke 5:17), "rabbis" (Matt. 23:8). They devoted themselves to the preservation, transcription, and exposition of the law. To safeguard the sanctity of the law they gradually developed an extensive and complicated system of teaching, known as "the tradition of the elders" (Matt. 15:2-6). All higher instruction was in their hands. They often served as judges in Jewish courts and were an important element in the membership of the Sanhedrin (Matt. 26:57). They were laymen, not priests. Most of them followed some trade, as they were not expected to receive money

for their teaching. They fiercely opposed Jesus (Mark 2:16) and were denounced by Him (Matt. 23). They played an important part in His death (Matt. 26:57) and also persecuted the early church (Acts 4:5; 6:12).

SCROLL, book made of papyrus or smoothed skins of animals sewn together to make a long strip which was wound around sticks at both ends (Isa. 34:4; Jer. 36; Ezek. 3: 1-3; Rev. 5; 10:1-10). They varied in length from a few feet to 35 feet. The codex form of book was not used until the 2nd century A. D.

SCROLLS, DEAD SEA (See Dead Sea Scrolls).

SCULPTURE (See Art).

SCURVY (See Diseases, Skin).

SCYTHIAN (sĭth'ĭ-àn), a nomadic people, savage and uncivilized, living N and E of the Black Sea (Col. 3:11).

SEA, used in several ways in the Bible. 1. The ocean (Gen. 1:10). 2. Almost any body of water, salt or fresh, like the sea of Galilee (Matt. 4:18). 3. Rivers, like the Nile (Isa. 18:2) and the Euphrates (Isa. 21:1). 4. The basin in Solomon's temple was called a sea (I Kings 7:23-26).

SEA, BRAZEN, the great basin in Solomon's temple where the priests washed their hands and feet preparatory to temple ministry (I Kings 7:23-26; II Chron. 4:2-6).

SEA OF GLASS, a glassy sea before the throne of God (Rev. 4:6; 15:2).

SEA OF JAZER. No such sea is known; perhaps a scribal error for "city of Jazer" (Jer. 48:32).

SEA MEW (See Birds, Cuckoo).

SEA MONSTER, any great fish of the sea (Gen. 1:21; Job 7:12; in KJV "whale").

SEASON (See Time, Calendar).

SEAT, chair, stool, throne (I Sam. 20:18; Luke 1:52).

SEBA (sē'bà), people descended from Cush (Gen. 10:7) who lived in S Arabia. Same as Sheba.

SEBAT (sē'bàt), 11th month of the Hebrew year (Zech. 1:7); corresponded to our February.

SECACAH (sē-kā'kà), village in wilderness of Judah (Josh. 15:61); location unknown.

SECHU (sē'kū), village near Ramah (I Sam. 19:22).

SEAL, device bearing a design, name, or some other words so made that it can impart an impression in relief upon a soft substance like clay or wax; used as a mark of authority and authenticity on letters, etc., (I Kings 21:8), to ratify a covenant (Jer. 32:11-14), to protect books and other documents (Jer. 32:14), to furnish proof of deputed authority and power (Gen. 41:42), to seal doors (Matt. 27:66), as an official mark of ownership. Also used figuratively (Deut. 32:34; Job 14:17).

SECOND COMING OF CHRIST, THE, the doctrine that Christ will some day return to earth personally, bodily, and visibly as the climax and culmination of His redemptive work, to usher in that Kingdom which will eventually result in God being all in all (Acts 1:11; Rom. 8:19-23; I Cor. 15:23-28; Eph. 1:14).

SECT (sĕkt, sect, party, school), religious group with distinctive doctrine: Sadducees (Acts 5:17), Pharisees (Acts 15:5; 26:5), Christians (Acts 24:5; 28:22).

SECUNDUS (sē-kŭn'dŭs), Thessalonian Christian friend of Paul (Acts 20:4).

SECURITY, the theological teaching which maintains the certain continuation of the salvation of those who are saved; also known as the perseverance of the saints (John 10:28; Rom. 8:38,39; Phil. 1:6; II Thess. 3:3; I Pet. 1:5).

SEDUCER (sē-dūs'ẽr), false teacher, deceiver, perhaps through the use of magical arts (II Tim. 3:13).

SEED. 1. Agricultural—propagative portion of a plant. 2. Physiological—semen (Lev. 15:16ff). 3. Figurative—descendants (Gen. 13:16).

SEEDTIME (See Agriculture).

SEER (See Prophet).

SEGUB (sē'gŭb). 1. Son of Hiel; died when his father set up the gates of Jericho (I Kings 16:34). 2. Son of Hezron (I Chron. 2:21,22).

SEIR (sē'ẽr), Horite; ancestor of inhabitants of the land of Seir (Gen. 26:20; I Chron. 1:38).

SEIR, LAND OF and **MOUNT** (sē'ẽr). 1. Alternate names for the region occupied by the descendants of Edom or Esau. Originally called the land of Seir (Gen. 32:3); later called Edom (Gen. 36:8,9); extends S from Moab on both sides of the Arabah c. 100 miles; mountainous; in Greek period called Idumea. Mt. Seir c. 3500 feet high. "Seir" also used for people who lived in Mt. Seir (Ezek. 25:8). 2. Region on border of Judah W of Kirjath-jearim (Josh. 15:10).

SEIRAH, SEIRATH (sē-ī'ra, sē-ī'răth), town in Ephraim, probably in SE part (Judg. 3:26).

SELA (sē'la), Edomite city called Petra by Greeks (II Kings 14:7; Isa. 42:11); capital of the Nabateans.

SELAH (sē'la, to lift up), term of uncertain meaning found frequently in Psalms; probably for instruction to singers or musicians (Ps. 9:16; Hab. 3:3,9,13).

SELA-HAMMAHLEKOTH (sē'la-ha-ma'lē-kŏth), cliff in wilderness of Maon (I Sam. 23:28).

SELED (sē'lĕd), Judahite (I Chron. 2:30).

SELEUCIA (sē-lū'shĭ-a), seaport of Syrian Antioch, founded by Seleucus I in 300 B.C. (Acts 13:4).

SELEUCIDS (sē-lū'sĭds), a dynasty of rulers of the kingdom of Syria (included Babylonia, Bactria, Persia, Syria, and part of Asia Minor), descended from Seleucus I, general of Alexander the Great. It lasted from 312 to 64 B.C., when the Romans took it over. One of them, Antiochus Epiphanes, precipitated the Maccabean War by trying forcibly to Hellenize the Jews.

SELVEDGE (sĕl'vĕj), the edge of each of the two curtains which covered the boards of the tabernacle (Exod. 26:4; 36:11).

SEM (See Shem).

SEMACHIAH (sĕm'a-kī'a), Levite gatekeeper (I Chron. 26:7).

SEMEI (sĕm'ē-ī). 1. Man who put away foreign wife (I Esdras 9:33), probably same as Shimei in Ezra 10:33.

SEMEIN (sĕm'ē-in), ancestor of Christ (Luke 3:26).

SEMITES (sĕm'īts), a diverse group of ancient peoples whose languages are related, belonging to the Semitic family of languages; their world was the Fertile Crescent: principal Semitic peoples of ancient times: Akkadians—including Babylonians and Assyrians; Arameans; Canaanites—including Edomites, Ammonites, Moabites, Hebrews; Arabs; Ethiopians.

SENAAH (sē-nā'a), descendants of Senaah (sometimes spelled Hassenaah); returned with Zerubbabel (Ezra 2:35; Neh. 7:38).

SENATE (sĕn'ăt, council of elders), Sanhedrin (Acts 5:21).

SENATOR (See Occupations and Professions).

SENEH (sē'nĕ), crag 3-1/2 miles SE of Michmash (I Sam. 14:4,5).

SENIR (sē'nĭr), Amorite name of Mt. Hermon (Deut. 3:9; S. of Sol. 4:8); also spelled "Shenir" in KJV.

SENNACHERIB (sē-năk'ẽr-ĭb, Sin (moongod) multiplied brothers), king of Assyria (705-681 B.C.); son and successor of Sargon II; great builder and conqueror; invaded Judah in time of Hezekiah, but his army was miraculously destroyed (II Kings 18; 19; Isa. 36; 37). Accounts of his campaigns recorded on clay prisms survive.

SENSUAL (sĕn'shū-ăl, pertaining to the soul), physical life (I Cor. 15:44), carnal (I Cor. 2:14; Jude 19), wisdom characterizing the unregenerate mind (James 3:15).

SENUAH (See Hasenuah).

SEORIM (sē-ō'rĭm), descendant of Aaron; head of 4th course of priests (I Chron. 24:1-8).

SEPHAR (sē'fär), border of Joktan in S Arabia (Gen. 10:30).

SEPHARAD (sē-fā'răd), place of unknown location to which Sargon deported Jews (Obad. 20).

SEPHARVAIM, SEPHARVITE (sĕf'ăr-vā'ĭm, sē'fär-vīt), place from which Assyrians brought colonists to live in Samaria (II Kings 17:24,31); probably located in region of Hamath.

SEPTUAGINT (sĕp'tū-a-jĭnt), translation of the OT into Greek prepared in Alexandria in 2nd and 3rd centuries B.C.

SEPULCHRE (See Tomb).

SEPULCHRE, CHURCH OF THE HOLY, the church professedly covering the tomb where Jesus was buried, built by Constantine in A.D. 325.

SERAH (sē'ra), daughter of Asher (Gen. 46:17; I Chron. 7:30); "Sarah" in Num. 26:46.

SERAIAH (sē-rā'ya). 1. Son of Kenaz (I

Chron. 4:13). 2. Scribe (II Sam. 8:17). 3. Son of Asiel (I Chron. 4:35). 4. Man sent to arrest Jeremiah and Baruch (Jer. 36:26). 5. High priest when Nebuchadnezzar captured Jerusalem (II Kings 25:18-21; Jer. 52:24-27). 6. Prince carried into captivity (Jer. 51:59-64). 7. Son of Tanhumeth (II Kings 25:23; Jer. 40:8). 8. Priest who returned with Zerubbabel (Ezra 2:2; Neh. 12:1); called Azariah in I Chron. 9:11 and Neh. 7:7.

SERAPHIM (ser'à-fĭm, burning ones), celestial beings whom Isaiah saw standing before the enthroned Lord (Isa. 6:2,3,6,7).

SERAPIS (sē-rā'pĭs), Graeco-Egyptian god widely worshipped in Mediterranean world; not mentioned in Bible.

SERED (sē'rĕd), founder of tribal family (Gen. 46:14; Num. 26:26).

SERGEANT (See Occupations and Professions).

SERGIUS PAULUS (sûr'jĭ-ŭs pô'lŭs), Roman proconsul (KJV "deputy") of Cyprus (Acts 13:7-12).

SERMON ON THE MOUNT, the 1st of six extended discourses of Jesus given in the Gospel of Matthew (5-7). It contains Christ's instruction to His disciples for godly living in the present world.

SERPENT (See Animals, Reptiles).

SERUG (sē'rŭg), great-grandfather of Abraham (Gen. 11:20,22f; I Chron. 1:26); "Saruch" in KJV of Luke 3:35.

SERVANT, used of slave, wage servant. Israelites acquired slaves through purchase (Lev. 25:44,45) and war (Num. 31:25-47). Israelites could become slaves through poverty (Exod. 21:1-11; Lev. 25:39,47; II Kings 4:1), theft (Exod. 22:3), and birth (Exod. 21:4). Mosaic law protected servants (Exod. 20:10; Lev. 25:55). Slaves and servants often referred to in NT (Mark 1:20; John 18:10-18; Acts 12:13-15).

SERVANT OF JEHOVAH, agent of the Lord like patriarchs (Exod. 32:13); Moses (Num. 12:7f), prophets (Zech. 1:6), and others. Chiefly used as a title for the Messiah in Isaiah 40-66. NT applies the Servant-passages to Christ (Isa. 42:1-4; Matt. 12:16-21).

SERVICE, refers to all sorts of work from the most inferior and menial to the most honored and exalted (Lev. 23:7f; Num. 3:6ff).

SERVITOR (See Occupations and Professions).

SETH (sĕth), Adam's 3rd son (Gen. 4:25,26; 5:3-8; Luke 3:38). 2. Moabites (Num. 24:17).

SETHUR (sē'thẽr), spy of Asher (Num. 13:2,13).

SEVENEH (sĕ-vē'nĕ), Egyptian town located on 1st cataract of Nile, known today as Aswan (Ezek. 29:10; 30:6 ASV).

SEVENTY, THE, disciples sent on preaching mission by Jesus (Luke 10:1).

SEVENTY WEEKS, THE, name applied to period of time (probably 490 years) referred to in Dan. 9:24-27. It has been interpreted in many different ways.

SEVEN WORDS FROM THE CROSS, the seven sentences spoken by Jesus from the cross. No one Gospel gives them all.

SHAALABBIN (shā'à-lăb'ĭn), town between Ir-shemesh and Aijalon (Josh. 19:42).

SHAALBIM (shā-ăl'bĭm), town, probably in central Palestine, won by Danites from Amorites (Judg. 1:35).

SHAALBONITE (See Shaalbim).

SHAAPH (shā'ăf). 1. Son of Jahdai (I Chron. 2:47). 2. Son of Caleb (I Chron. 2:49).

SHAARAIM (shā'à-rā'ĭm). 1. Town in Judah (Josh. 15:36; I Sam. 17:52). 2. Town in Simeon (I Chron. 4:31); "Sharuhen" in Josh. 19:6 and "Shilhim" in Josh. 15:32.

SHAASHGAZ (shā-ăsh'găz), chamberlain in court of Ahasuerus (Esth. 2:14).

SHABBETHAI (shăb'ĕ-thī, Sabbath-born), Levite who favored divorcing foreign wives (Ezra 10:15); interpreter of Law (Neh. 8:7f).

SHACHIA (shà-kī'à), Benjamite (I Chron. 8:10).

SHADDAI (shăd'ī), name (exact meaning unknown) for God often found in OT (Gen. 17:1; 28:3; 43:14; Num. 24:4,16; Ps. 68:14).

SHADOW, used literally, figuratively (I Chron. 29:15; Ps. 17:8; Isa. 30:3), theologically (Col. 2:17; Heb. 8:5; 10:1).

SHADRACH (shā'drăk), Babylonian name given to Hananiah (Dan. 1:3,7).

SHAFT, shank of the golden candelabrum (Exod. 25:31); used in Messianic sense in Isa. 49:2.

SHAGE (shā'gē), father of Jonathan, one of David's mighty men (I Chron. 11:34).

SHAHARAIM (shā'hà-rā'ĭm), Benjamite (I Chron. 8:8-11).

SHAHAZIMAH (shā'hà-zī'mà), town in Issachar between Tabor and the Jordan (Josh. 19:22).

SHALEM (shā'lĕm), town near Shechem (Gen. 33:18).

SHALIM, LAND OF (shā'lĭm), region probably near N boundary of Benjamin's territory (I Sam. 9:4).

SHALISHAH (shà-lī'shà), region near Mt. Ephraim (I Sam. 9:4).

SHALLECHETH, THE GATE OF (shăl'ĕ-kĕth), W gate of Solomon's Temple (I Chron. 26:13-16).

SHALLUM, SHALLUN (shăl'ŭm, shăl'ŭn, recompense). 1. Son of Naphtali (I Chron. 7:13), "Shillem" in Gen. 46:24 and Num. 26:48f. 2. Son of Shaul (I Chron. 4:25). 3. Son of Sisamai (I Chron. 2:40f). 4. Son of Kore; chief of gatekeepers (I Chron. 9:17,19,31; Neh. 7:45), "Meshelemiah" in I Chron. 26:1 and "Shelemiah" in I Chron. 26:14. 5. Son of Zadok (I Chron. 6:12f), "Meshullam" in I Chron. 9:11 and Neh. 11:11. 6. King of Israel (II Kings 15:10-15). 7. Father of Jehizkiah (II Chron. 28:12). 8. Husband of the prophetess Huldah (II Kings 22:14). 9. King of Judah (I Chron. 3:15), better known as Jehoahaz II. 10. Uncle of Jeremiah (Jer. 32:7). 11. Father of Maaseiah (Jer. 35:4). 12. Levite who divorced foreign wife (Ezra 10:24). 13. Man who divorced foreign wife (Ezra 10:42).

14. Ruler who helped build Jerusalem walls (Neh. 3:12). 15. Builder of walls of Jerusalem (Neh. 3:15).

SHALMAI (shăl'mī), ancestor of Nethinim that returned with Zerubbabel (Ezra 2:46; Neh. 7:48).

SHALMAN (shăl'măn), either contraction of Shalmaneser or the Moabite king Salmanu (Hos. 10:14).

SHALMANESER (shăl'măn-ē'zĕr, **the god Shulman is chief**), title of five Assyrian kings, of whom one is mentioned in OT, another refers to an Israelitish king. 1. Shalmaneser III (859-824 B. C.); son of Ashurnasirpal; inscription left by him says that he opposed Benhadad of Damascus and Ahab of Israel, and made Israel tributary. 2. Shalmaneser V (726-722 B. C.), son of Tiglath-pileser; received tribute from Hoshea; besieged Samaria and carried N tribes into captivity (II Kings 17:3; 18:9), "Shalman" in Hos. 10:14.

SHAMA (shā'mà), one of David's mighty men (I Chron. 11:44).

SHAMARIAH (See Shemariah).

SHAMBLES, meat market (I Cor. 10:25).

SHAME, SHAMEFACEDNESS, shame is a feeling brought about by a sense of guilt (Ezra 9:7), impropriety (Exod. 32:25), or disillusionment through false confidence (Ps. 97:7); shamefacedness in I Tim. 2:9 denotes sexual modesty.

SHAMED (shā'mĕd), son of Elpaal (I Chron. 8:12).

SHAMER (shā'mĕr). 1. Father of Bani (I Chron. 6:46). 2. Son of Heber; head of Asherite clan (I Chron. 7:34).

SHAMGAR (shăm'gàr), son of Anath; judge; slew 600 Philistines with an oxgoad (Judg. 3:31).

SHAMHUTH (shăm'hūth), David's 5th divisional commander of the army (I Chron. 27:8).

SHAMIR (shā'mĕr, **sharp point**). 1. Town in Judah c. 13 miles SW of Hebron (Josh. 15:48). 2. Town in Ephraim; home of Tola (Judg. 10:1f). 3. Temple attendant (I Chron. 24:24).

SHAMMA (shăm'à), son of Zophah (I Chron. 7:37).

SHAMMAH (shăm'à, **waste**). 1. Grandson of Esau (Gen. 36:13,17; I Chron. 1:37). 2. Brother of David (I Sam. 16:9; 17:13); also called Shimea (I Chron. 20:7), Shimeah (II Sam. 13:3,32), and Shimei (II Sam. 21:21). 3. One of David's mighty men (II Sam. 23:11), "Shage" in I Chron. 11:34. 4. Another of David's mighty men (II Sam. 23:33); also called Shammoth (I Chron. 11:27) and Shamhuth (I Chron. 27:8). May be same as 3.

SHAMMOTH (shăm'ŏth), one of David's mighty men (I Chron. 11:27); apparently same as Shammah (II Sam. 23:25) and Shamhuth (I Chron. 27:8).

SHAMMUA (shă-mū'à, **renowned**). 1. Son of Zaccur; Reubenite spy (Num. 13:4). 2. Son of David and Bath-sheba (II Sam. 5:14, KJV has Shammuah; I Chron. 14:4). 3.

Levite; father of Abda (Neh. 11:17), "Shemaiah" in I Chron. 9:16. 4. Priest (I Chron. 24:14; Neh. 12:6,18), "Bilgai" in Neh. 10:8.

SHAMSHERAI (shăm'shē-rī), son of Jeroham (I Chron. 8:26).

SHAPHAM (shā'făm), Gadite chief (I Chron. 5:12).

SHAPHAN (shā'făn, **rock rabbit**), state scribe and secretary under Josiah (II Kings 22: 3-20; II Chron. 34:8-28); read newly-discovered book of the Law before Josiah (II Chron. 34:18); carried Josiah's message to prophetess Huldah (II Chron. 34:20-28).

SHAPHAT (shā'făt, **he has judged**). 1. Simeonite spy (Num. 13:5). 2. Father of Elisha the prophet (I Kings 19:16,19). 3. Gadite chief in Bashan (I Chron. 5:12). 4. Herdsman of David (I Chron. 27:29). 5. Son of Shemaiah (I Chron. 3:22).

SHAPHER (shā'fĕr), encampment of Israelites in wilderness (Num. 33:23).

SHAPHIR (See Saphir).

SHARAI (shà-rā'ī), man who divorced foreign wife (Ezra 10:10,40,44).

SHARAIM (shà-rā'ĭm), town in Judah (Josh. 15:36).

SHARAR (shā'rĕr), father of one of David's mighty men (II Sam. 23:33), "Sacar" in I Chron. 11:35.

SHARE, plowshare (I Sam. 13:20).

SHAREZER (shà-rē'zĕr, **protect the king**). 1. Son of Assyrian king Sennacherib (II Kings 19:37; Isa. 37:38). 2. Contemporary of Zechariah the prophet (Zech. 7:2, "Sherezer" in KJV).

SHARON (shăr'ŭn). 1. Palestine coastal plain between Joppa and Mount Carmel (I Chron. 27:29; Isa. 35:2). 2. Suburbs of Sharon possessed by tribe of Gad (I Chron. 5:16). 3. Lassharon q.v. (Josh. 12:18). 4. Figuratively of fruitfulness, glory, peace (Isa. 35:2; 65:10).

SHARONITE (shăr'ŭn-it), man of Sharon (I Chron. 27:29).

SHARUHEN (shà-rōō'hĕn), Simeonite town in Judah's territory (Josh. 19:6). Apparently the same as Silhim (Josh. 15:32) and Shaarim (I Chron. 4:31). Now identified with Tell el-Far'ah.

SHASHAI (shā'shī), man who divorced foreign wife (Ezra 10:40).

SHASHAK (shā'shăk), Benjamite (I Chron. 8:14f).

SHAUL, SHAULITES (shā'ŭl, shăl'ū-līts, **asked**). 1. King of Edom (Gen. 36:37f, Saul in KJV; I Chron. 1:48f). 2. Son of Simeon (Gen. 46:10; Exod. 6:15). 3. Descendant of Levi (I Chron. 6:24).

SHAVEH, VALLEY OF (shā'vĕ, **plain**), valley where, after rescuing his nephew Lot, Abraham met the king of Sodom (Gen. 14:17).

SHAVEH-KIRIATHAIM (shā'vĕ-kĭr-yà-thā'ĭm, **plain of Kiriathaim**), plain where Chedorlaomer smote the Emim (Gen. 14:5), probably on E of Dead Sea (Num. 32:37).

SHAVING, priests and Nazirites were prohibited from shaving (Lev. 21:5; Num. 6:5); Hebrews generally wore beards. Shaving was often done for religious reasons, as an act of contrition (Job 1:20), consecration for Levites (Num. 6:9; 8:7), cleansing for lepers (Lev. 14:8f; 13:32ff); also as an act of contempt (II Sam. 10:4).

SHAVSHA (shăv′shà), David's secretary of state (I Chron. 18:16), "Shisha" in I Kings 4:3; "Seraiah" in II Sam. 8:17; "Sheva" in II Sam. 20:25.

SHEAF, a handful of grain left behind by the reaper, gathered and bound by women and children, and later taken to the threshing-floor (Jer. 9:22; Ruth 2:7,15). Some sheaves were left behind for the poor (Deut. 24:19).

SHEAL (shē′ăl), man who divorced foreign wife (Ezra 10:29).

SHEARIAH (shē′à-rī′à), son of Azel; descendant of Jonathan (I Chron. 8:38; 9:44).

SHEARING HOUSE, (binding house of the shepherds), place between Jezreel and Samaria where Jehu slaughtered 42 members of the royal house of Ahaziah, king of Judah (II Kings 10:12-14).

SHEAR-JASHUB (shē′ăr-jà′shŭb, remnant shall return), symbolic name of Isaiah's oldest son (Isa. 7:3; 8:18).

SHEALTIEL (shē-ăl′tī-ĕl, I have asked God), father of Zerubbabel (Ezra 3:2,8; 5:2).

SHEBA (shē′bà, seven, an oath). 1. Chief of a Gadite family (I Chron. 5:13). 2. Town allotted to Simeon (Josh. 19:2). 3. Benjamite who led a rebellion against David (II Sam. 20:1). 4. Son of Raamah (Gen. 10:7; I Chron. 1:9). 5. Son of Joktan; probable founder of kingdom of Sabeans (Sheba) in S. Arabia (Gen. 10:28). 6. Grandson of Abraham by Keturah (Gen. 25:1-3; I Chron. 1:32); descendants may have founded kingdom of Sheba.

SHEBAH (shē′bà, seven, oath), name of well dug by Isaac's servants. Town of Beer-sheba named from this well (Gen. 26:31-33).

SHEBAM (shē′băm), town in Reuben (Num. 32:3), called "Shibmah" in Num. 32:38; E of Dead Sea, but exact location unknown.

SHEBANIAH (shĕb′à-nī′à). 1. Trumpeter priest (I Chron. 15:24). 2. Levite who signed covenant with Nehemiah (Neh. 9:4,5; 10:10). 3. Another Levite who signed covenant (Neh. 10:12). 4. Priest who signed covenant (Neh. 10:4). 5. Priest (Neh. 12:14).

SHEBARIM (shĕb′à-rīm), place near Ai to which Israelite soldiers were chased (Josh. 7:5).

SHEBAT (See Sebat).

SHEBER (shē′bĕr), son of Caleb (not famous spy) (I Chron. 2:48).

SHEBNA (shĕb′nà). 1. Steward of Hezekiah (Isa. 22:15-21). 2. Scribe who faced Rabshakeh (Isa. 36:3-37:2; II Kings 18).

SHEBUEL (shē̆b-bū′ĕl). 1. Levite treasurer (I Chron. 23:16; 26:24); "Shubael" in I Chron. 24:20. 2. Son of Heman (I Chron. 25:4); called "Shubael" in I Chron. 25:20.

SHECANIAH, SHECHANIAH (shĕk-à-nī′à, dweller with Jehovah). 1. Head of 10th course of priests in days of David (I Chron.

24:11). 2. Levite (II Chron. 31:15). 3. Descendant of David (I Chron. 3:21,22). 4. Man who returned with Ezra (Ezra 8:3). 5. Another such man (Ezra 8:5). 6. Man who proposed to Ezra that foreign wives be put away (Ezra 10:2-4). 7. Keeper of E gate of Jerusalem in time of Nehemiah (Neh. 3:29). 8. Father-in-law of Tobiah the foe of Nehemiah (Neh. 6:18). 9. Chief priest who returned with Zerubbabel (Neh. 12:3).

SHECHEM (shē′kĕm, shoulder). 1. Ancestor of Manassites (Num. 26:31). 2. Son of Shemidah; Gileadite (I Chron. 7:19). 3. City in hill country of Ephraim near S border of Manasseh, 41 miles N of Jerusalem, at E end of pass between Mts. Ebal and Gerizim; one of chief cities of Canaanites during most of 2nd millennium B. C.; first place visited by Abraham (Gen. 12:6); Jacob bought ground there (Gen. 33:18-20); Joseph buried there (Josh. 24:32); scene of Abimelech's abortive attempt to found a kingdom (Judg. 9); Jeroboam I established his first royal residence there (I Kings 12:25). Site is Tell Balatah, just E of Nablus; archaeologists have excavated the ruins.

SHECHINAH (See Shekinah).

SHEDEUR (shĕd′ē-ĕr), Reubenite; father of Elizur (Num. 1:5; 2:10; 7:30; 10:18).

SHEEP (See Animals).

SHEEPCOTE, SHEEPFOLD, enclosure for protection of sheep (Num. 32:16; Judg. 5:16; I Sam. 24:3).

SHEEP GATE, gate of Jerusalem (Neh. 3: 1,32).

SHEEP MARKET, RV and RSV have "sheep gate" (John 5:2).

SHEEPMASTER (See Occupations and Professions).

SHEEP-SHEARER (See Occupations and Professions).

SHEERAH (See Sherah).

SHEET, large piece of linen (Acts 10:11; 11:5).

SHEHARIAH (shē-hà-rī′à), son of Jeroham; Benjamite (I Chron. 8:26).

SHEKEL (See Money).

SHEKINAH (shē-kī′nà, dwelling of God), the visible presence of Jehovah (Isa. 60:2; Matt. 17:5; Acts 1:9; Rom. 9:4).

SHELAH, SHELANITE (shē′là, shē′là-nīt). 1. Son of Arpachshad (Gen. 10:24). "Salah" in KJV; "Sala" in Luke 3:35 KJV. 2. Son of Judah (Gen. 38:5-26).

SHELEMIAH (shĕl-ē-mī′à, friend of Jehovah). 1. Doorkeeper of tabernacle (I Chron. 26:14); in previous verses of this chapter he is called "Meshelemiah." 2. Son of Cushi (Jer. 36:14). 3. Man sent to arrest Jeremiah (Jer. 36:26). 4. Father of man whom Zedekiah sent to Jeremiah to ask his prayers (Jer. 37:3). 5. Son of Hananiah (Jer. 37:13). 6. Two men who divorced foreign wives (Ezra 10:39,41). 7. Father of Hananiah (Neh. 3:30). 8. Priest; treasurer (Neh. 13:13).

SHELEPH (shē′lĕf), son of Joktan (Gen. 10:26).

SHELESH (shē′lĕsh), son of Helem (I Chron. 7:35).

SHELOMI (shē-lō′mī), father of Ahihud, Asherite prince (Num. 34:27).

SHELOMITH, SHELOMOTH (shē-lō′mith, shē-lō′mŏth). 1. Daughter of Dibri; her son was killed for blasphemy (Lev. 24:10-12,23). 2. Cousin of Moses (I Chron. 23:18). 3. Gershonite Levite (I Chron. 23:9). 4. Descendant of Moses (I Chron. 26:25). 5. Child of Rehoboam (II Chron. 11:20). 6. Daughter of Zerubbabel (I Chron. 3:19). 7. Ancestor of a family that returned with Ezra (Ezra 8:10).

SHELUMIEL (shē-lū′mī-ĕl), Simeonite chief in days of Moses (Num. 1:6; 7:36).

SHEM (shĕm, name, fame), son of Noah; progenitor of Semitic race (Gen. 11:10).

SHEMA (shē′mà, fame, rumor). 1. Town in S Judah (Josh. 15:26). 2. Son of Hebron (I Chron. 2:44). 3. Son of Joel (I Chron. 5:8). 4. Benjamite (I Chron. 8:13). 5. Assistant of Ezra (Neh. 8:4). 6. Hebrew name for Deut. 6:4.

SHEMAAH (shē-mā′à, fame), father of Ahiezer and Joash, soldiers of David (I Chron. 12:3).

SHEMAIAH (shē-mā′yà, Jehovah has heard). 1. Simeonite prince (I Chron. 4:37). 2. Reubenite (I Chron. 5:4), possibly same as Shema of verse 8. 3. Chief Levite (I Chron. 15:8,11). 4. Levite scribe (I Chron. 24:6). 5. Son of Obed-edom (I Chron. 26: 4,6,7). 6. Prophet who forbade Rehoboam to war against Israel (I Kings 12:22-24). 7. Descendant of David (I Chron. 3:22). 8. Merarite Levite (I Chron. 9:14; Neh. 12:18). 9. Levite who returned from exile (I Chron. 9:16). "Shammua" in Neh. 11:17. 10. Levite (II Chron. 17:8). 11. Levite who cleansed temple (II Chron. 29:14). 12. Levite who assisted in distribution of food (II Chron. 31:15). 13. Levite in days of Josiah (II Chron. 35:9). 14. Levite who returned with Ezra (Ezra 8:13). 15. One whom Ezra sent back for ministers (Ezra 8:16), possibly same as preceding. 16. Priest who divorced foreign wife (Ezra 10:21). 17. Another priest who did the same thing (Ezra 10:31). 18-23. Men who played various roles in Nehemiah's rebuilding and dedication of the Jerusalem wall (Neh. 3:29; 6:10ff; 10:8; 12: 6,18,34,35,36,42). 24. Father of Uriah the prophet (Jer. 26:20). 25. False prophet who fought against Jeremiah (Jer. 29:24-32). 26. Father of Delaiah, prince in days of Jehoiakim (Jer. 36:12).

SHEMARIAH (shĕm-à-rī′à, Jehovah keeps). 1. One of David's mighty men (I Chron. 12:5). 2. Son of Rehoboam, king of Judah (II Chron. 11:19). 3. Man who put away foreign wife (Ezra 10:32). 4. Another man who put away foreign wife (Ezra 10:41).

SHEMEBER (shĕm-ē′bĕr), king of Zeboiim, a city near the Dead Sea (Gen. 14:2).

SHEMER (shē′mĕr). 1. Asherite (I Chron. 7:34). 2. Merarite Levite (I Chron. 7:34). 3. Man who sold hill to Omri, king of Israel (1 Kings 16:24).

SHEMIDA, SHEMIDAH (shē-mī′dà), Gileadite; founder of clan of Shemidaites (Num. 26:32).

SHEMIDAITES (shē-mī′dà-īts), family descended from Shemida (Num. 26:32; Josh. 17:2).

SHEMINITH (shĕm′ī-nith), musical term of uncertain meaning possibly "octave" (I Chron. 15:21; Ps. 6; 12 titles).

SHEMIRAMOTH (shē-mir′à-mŏth). 1. Levite; singer (I Chron. 15:18,20). 2. Teaching Levite (II Chron. 17:8).

SHEMUEL (shē-mū′ĕl, name of God). 1. Simeonite (Num. 34:20). 2. Samuel; spelled "Shemuel" in KJV of I Chron. 6:33. 3. Issachar chief (I Chron. 7:2).

SHEN (shĕn, pointed rock), unidentified site near which Samuel erected the stone "Ebenezer" (I Sam. 7:12).

SHENAZAR (shē-nāz′àr), son of Jeconiah (I Chron. 3:18).

SHENIR (shē′nĕr), Amorite name for Mt. Hermon (I Chron. 5:23).

SHEOL (shē′ŏl), the OT name for the place of departed souls, corresponding to the NT word "Hades." When translated "hell" it refers to the place of punishment, but when translated "grave" the reference is to the souls of good men. It often means the place or state of the soul between death and resurrection. The clearest indication of different conditions in Sheol is in Christ's parable of the rich man and Lazarus (Luke 16:19-31).

SHEPHAM (shē′fàm), place in NE of Canaan, near Sea of Galilee (Num. 34:10,11).

SHEPHATIAH (shĕf′à-tī′à, Jehovah is judge). 1. Son of David (II Sam. 3:4). 2. Son of Reuel (I Chron. 9:8). 3. One of David's mighty men (I Chron. 12:5). 4. Simeonite prince (I Chron. 27:16). 5. Son of King Jehoshaphat (II Chron. 21:2). 6. Founder of family which returned with Zerubbabel (Ezra 2:4). 7. One of children of Solomon's servants whose descendants returned with Zerubbabel (Ezra 2:57). 8. One whose descendants returned with Ezra (Ezra 8:8). May be same as the preceding. 9. Son of Mahalaleel (Neh. 11:4). 10. Prince who wanted Jeremiah to be put to death for prophesying (Jer. 38:1).

SHEPHELAH, THE (shē-fē′là, low country), hilly country between mountains of Judah and the maritime plain S of the plain of Sharon, extending through the country of Philistia along the Mediterranean (Josh. 12:8).

SHEPHER (See Shapher).

SHEPHERD (See Occupations and Professions).

SHEPHI, SHEPHO (shē′fī, shē′fō), early descendant of Seir (Gen. 36:23; I Chron. 1:40). "Shepho" in Genesis, "Shephi" in I Chron.

SHEPHUPHAN (shē-fū′fàm), grandson of Benjamin (I Chron. 8:5).

SHERAH (shē′rà), daughter of Ephraim; descendants built three villages (I Chron. 7:24).

SHERD (See Potsherd, Ostraka).

SHEREBIAH (shĕr-ē-bī′à). 1. Levite prominent in Ezra's time (Ezra 8:18,24). 2. Covenanter with Nehemiah (Neh. 10:12). 3.

Levite who returned with Zerubbabel (Neh. 12:8). 4. Chief Levite (Neh. 12:24).

SHERESH (shē'rĕsh), grandson of Manasseh (I Chron. 7:16).

SHEREZER (shē-rē'zẽr), man sent from Bethel to Jerusalem to inquire whether days of mourning should be continued (Zech. 7:2).

SHESHACH (shē'shăk), perhaps a cryptogram for "Babel" or "Babylon" (Jer. 25:26; 51:41).

SHESHAI (shē'shī), son of Anak (Num. 13:22; Josh. 15:14; Judg. 1:10).

SHESHAN (shē'shăn), descendant of Judah whose daughter married an Egyptian (I Chron. 2:31,34).

SHESHBAZZAR (shĕsh-băz'ẽr), Jewish prince whom Cyrus made governor and who helped lay the foundation of the temple (Ezra 1:8,11; 5:14,16). May be same as Zerubbabel.

SHETH (shĕth). 1. Third son of Adam and Eve (I Chron. 1:1). 2. Designation for Moab (Num. 24:17).

SHETHAR (shē'thär), Persian prince (Esth. 1:14).

SHETHAR-BOZENAI, SHETHAR-BOZNAI (shē'thär-bŏz'ē-nī, shē'thär-bŏz'nī), Persian official who tried to hinder Jews (Ezra 5:3,6).

SHEVA (shē'và). 1. David's scribe (II Sam. 20:25), perhaps same as "Seraiah" in 8:17. 2. Son of Caleb (I Chron. 2:49).

SHEWBREAD, SHOWBREAD (See Tabernacle).

SHIBAH (shī'ba), well from which Beersheba was named (Gen. 26:33); in KJV "Shebah."

SHIBBOLETH (shĭb'bō-lĕth, ear of grain; stream), word differently pronounced on the two sides of the Jordan, and was used by the men of Gilead to determine whether the speaker was of Ephraim or not (Judg. 12:5,6).

SHIBMAH, SIBMAH (shĭb mà), city taken by tribe of Reuben from Moabites (Num. 32:38).

SHICRON, SHIKKERON (shĭk'rŏn, shĭk'ē-rŏn), town on N boundary of Judah (Josh. 15:11).

SHIELD (See Armor).

SHIGGAION (shĭ-gā'yŏn), musical term of unknown meaning found in heading of Ps. 7.

SHIGIONOTH (shĭg-ĭ-ō'nŏth), plural of Shiggaion. Heading of Habakkuk's psalm (Hab. 3:1).

SHIHON, SHION (shī'ŏn), town on border of Issachar, near Nazareth (Josh. 19:19).

SHIHOR, SIHOR (shī'hŏr, sī'hŏr), may refer to the Nile, a stream which separated Egypt from Palestine, or a branch of the Nile (Josh. 13:3; I Chron. 13:5; Isa. 23:3; Jer. 2:18).

SHIHOR-LIBNATH (shī'hŏr-lĭb'nàth), small stream on S border of Asher (Josh. 19:26).

SHIKKERON (See Shicron).

SHILHI (shĭl'hī), father-in-law of Jehoshaphat, king of Judah (I Kings 22:42).

SHILHIM (shĭl'hĭm), town in S of Judah

in Joshua's time (Josh. 15:32).

SHILLEM, SHILLEMITE (shĭl'ĕm, shĭl'ĕm-īt), son of Naphtali (Gen. 46:24) and his descendants (Num. 26:49); "Shallum" in I Chron. 7:13.

SHILOAH (See Siloam).

SHILOH (shī'lō). 1. City in Ephraim, c. 12 miles N and E of Bethel where the tabernacle remained from the time of Joshua to the days of Samuel (Judg. 21:19; I Sam. 4:3);. Benjamites kidnapped wives (Judg. 21:15-24); residence of Eli and Samuel (I Sam. 3); home of the prophet Ahijah (I Kings 14); a ruin in Jeremiah's time (Jer. 7:12,14). 2. Word of uncertain meaning regarded by many Jews and Christians as a reference to the Messiah (Gen. 49:10).

SHILONI, SHILONITE (shĭ-lō'nī, shī'lō-nīt). 1. Inhabitant of Shiloh (I Kings 11:29). 2. Ancestor of Maaseiah (Neh. 11:5).

SHILSHAH (shĭl'shà), Asherite; son of Zophah (I Chron. 7:37).

SHIMEA (shĭm'ē-à). 1. Brother of David (I Chron. 20:7). 2. Son of David and Bathsheba (I Chron. 3:5). 3. Merarite Levite (I Chron. 6:30). 4. Gershonite Levite (I Chron. 6:39). No. 1 is probably the same as "Shimma" (I Chron. 2:13 KJV), "Shamma" (I Sam. 16:9), "Shimeah" (II Sam. 21:21 KJV), and "Shimei" (II Sam. 21:21 ASV, RSV).

SHIMEAH (shĭm'ē-à). 1. Brother of David (II Sam. 13:3). 2. Benjamite (I Chron. 8:32), "Shimeam" in I Chron. 9:38.

SHIMEAM (See Shimeah).

SHIMEATH (shĭm'ē-àth), Ammonitess; son helped assassinate king Joash of Judah (II Chron. 24:26; II Kings 12:21).

SHIMEATHITES (shĭm'ē-àth-īts), Kenite family of scribes living in Jabez (I Chron. 2:55).

SHIMEI (shĭm'ē-ī, famous). 1. Son of Gershon (Num. 3:18; I Chron. 23:7), "Shimi" in KJV Exod. 6:17. 2. Gershonite Levite (I Chron. 23:7-10). 3. Faithful soldier of David (I Kings 1:8). 4. One of Solomon's purveyors of food (I Kings 4:18). 5. Grandson of Jehoiachin (I Chron. 3:19). 6. Simeonite (I Chron. 4:26,27). 7. Son of God (I Chron. 5:4). 8. Early Merarite Levite (I Chron. 6:29). 9. Judahite (I Chron. 8:21), "Shimhi" in KJV. 10. Levite; head of 10th course of singers (I Chron. 25:17). 11. Overseer of David's vineyards (I Chron. 27:27). 12. Descendant of Heman who helped clean temple (II Chron. 29:14). 13. Levite treasurer (II Chron. 31:12,13). 14. Levite who put away foreign wife (Ezra 10:23). 15. Man who divorced foreign wife (Ezra 10:33). 16. Another who put away foreign wife (Ezra 10:38). 17. Grandfather of Mordecai (Esth. 2:5). 18. Benjamite who cursed David (II Sam. 16:5-13; 19:16-23; I Kings 2:36-46).

SHIMEON (shĭm'ē-ŭn), divorced foreign wife (Ezra 10:31).

SHIMHI (See Shimei).

SHIMI (See Shimei).

SHIMITE (shĭm'īt), descendant of Shimei

(Num. 3:21 KJV; ASV "Shimeites").

SHIMMA (shĭm'ä), son of Jesse (I Chron. 2:13 KJV), "Shammah" in I Sam. 16:9.

SHIMON (shī'mŏn), Judahite (I Chron. 4:20).

SHIMRATH (shĭm'rȧth), son of Shimei; Benjamite (I Chron. 8:21).

SHIMRI (shĭm'rī). 1. Son of Shemaiah; Simeonite (I Chron. 4:37). 2. Father of Jediael and Joha, two of David's mighty men (I Chron. 11:45). 3. Merarite Levite. "Simri" in KJV of I Chron. 26:10. 4. Levite who assisted in cleansing the temple (II Chron. 29:13).

SHIMRITH (shĭm'rĭth, watchful), Moabitess; mother of Jehozabad who helped slay Joash, king of Judah (II Chron. 24:26), "Shomer" in II Kings 12:21.

SHIMROM, SHIMRON (shĭm'rŏm, shĭm'rŏn, guard). 1. Son of Issachar (Gen. 46:13), "Shimrom" in KJV of I Chron. 7:1. 2. Town in N Canaan whose king fought Joshua (Josh. 11:1ff), "Shimron-Meron" in Josh. 12:20.

SHIMRON-MERON (shĭm'rŏn-mē'rŏn), town in N Canaan conquered by Joshua (Josh. 12:20).

SHIMSHAI (shĭm'shī, sunny), scribe who tried to hinder Jews in rebuilding temple (Ezra 4:8).

SHINAB (shī'nȧb), king of Admah, Canaanite city later destroyed (Gen. 14:2).

SHINAR (shī'när), alluvial plain of Babylonia in which lay cities of Babel, Erech, Accad, and Calneh (Gen. 10:10); tower of Babel built there (Gen. 11:1-9); Amraphel, king of Shinar, invaded Canaan (Gen. 14:1); Jews exiled to Shinar (Zech. 5:11); Nebuchadnezzar transported Temple treasures to Shinar area (Dan. 1:2).

SHION (shī'ŏn), town in Issachar (Josh. 19:19), KJV has "Shihon."

SHIPHI (shī'fī), Simeonite prince (I Chron. 4:37).

SHIPHMITE (shĭf'mīt), patronymic of Zabdi, vineyard overseer (I Chron. 27:27).

SHIPHRAH (shĭf'rà), Hebrew midwife who saved Hebrew boy babies (Exod. 1:15-21).

SHIPHTAN (shĭf'tȧn), father of Kemuel, prince of Ephraim (Num. 34:24).

SHIPS. The Israelites were an agricultural, not a sea-going, people because the coastline of Palestine was harborless. Small fishing boats and ferryboats were used on the Sea of Galilee and the Jordan (Matt. 4:21; 9:1; 14:22). Solomon had a fleet at Ezion-geber (I Kings 9:26-28), but it was composed of Phoenician ships and manned by Phoenician crews. Jehoshaphat's fleet was shipwrecked (II Chron. 20:35-37). Phoenicians were the great navigators of the ancient world, travelling as far as Cornwall for tin, and to the Canaries. Egyptian boats were often built of bundles of papyrus (Isa. 18:2). Romans used triremes and quinqueremes for warships, and large ships (up to 3250 tons burden) to transport grain from Egypt. Paul travelled on one of these ships that carried 276 people when it was shipwrecked (Acts 27). Travelling by ship on the Mediterranean in the fall of the year was very dangerous, as Paul's experience shows.

SHISHA (shī'shȧ), father of two of Solomon's secretaries (I Kings 4:3); may be identical with Seraiah (II Sam. 8:17), Sheva (II Sam. 20:25), and Shavsha (I Chron. 18:16).

SHISHAK (shī'shȧk), Egyptian king, founder of 22nd dynasty (950-929 B. C.), gave refuge to Jeroboam (I Kings 11:40); invaded Jerusalem in reign of Rehoboam (I Kings 14:25f).

SHITRAI (shĭt'rī), Sharonite herdsman of David (I Chron. 27:29).

SHITTAH TREE (See Plants).

SHITTIM (shĭt'ĭm), wood which comes from Acacia tree; wood is hard, fine-grained; used for tabernacle and its furniture (Exod. 25:5-28).

SHITTIM (place), contraction of Abel-shittim, last stop of Israel before crossing the Jordan (Num. 25:1; 33:49); thence Joshua sent two spies to Jericho (Josh. 2:1); there Balaam tried to curse Israel (Num. 22:1; 25:1-3).

SHIZA (shī'zȧ), Reubenite (I Chron. 11:42).

SHOA (shō'ȧ, rich), people mentioned in association with Babylonians, Chaldeans, and Assyrians (Ezek. 23:23). May be Sutu of Amarna letters.

SHOBAB (shō'bȧb). 1. Grandson of Hezron (I Chron. 2:18). 2. Son of David (I Chron. 3:5).

SHOBACH (shō'bȧk), Syrian general defeated by David (II Sam. 10:16-18); "Shophach" in I Chron. 19:16.

SHOBAI (shō'bī), Levite gatekeeper whose descendants returned with Zerubbabel (Ezra 2:42; Neh. 7:45).

SHOBAL (shō'bȧl). 1. Chief of Horites (Gen. 36:20,23,29). 2. Ephrathite; founder of Kiriath-jearim (I Chron. 2:50,52). 3. Grandson of Judah (I Chron. 4:1,2).

SHOBEK (shō'bĕk), Israelite chief who covenanted with Nehemiah to keep law (Neh. 10:24).

SHOBI (shō'bī), prince of the Ammonites (II Sam. 17:27).

SHOCHO (shō'kō), city in Judah, built by Rehoboam (II Chron. 11:7); KJV has "Shoco."

SHOE (See Dress).

SHOE LATCHET (See Dress).

SHOFAR (See Music, Musical Instruments).

SHOHAM (shō'hȧm), Merarite Levite (I Chron. 24:27).

SHOMER (shō'mĕr, keeper). 1. Father of Jehozabad, conspirator of Joash of Judah (II Kings 12:20,21; II Chron. 24:25,26). 2. Great-grandson of Asher (I Chron. 7:32); "Shamer" in verse 34 KJV.

SHOPHACH (shō'fȧk), Syrian general slain by David (I Chron. 19:16,18), "Shobach" in II Sam. 10:16.

SHOPHAN (shō'fȧn), 2nd half of Atroth-shophan, city of Gad (Num. 32:35).

SHOPHAR (See Music, Musical Instruments).

SHORE, the land where it meets the sea (Josh. 15:2; Judg. 5:17; Matt. 13:2).

SHOSHANNIM (shō-shăn'ĭm, lilies), found in titles of Pss. 45, 69, 80 and in Ps. 60 in the singular; may refer to lily-shaped musical instrument or tune known as "Lilies."

SHOULDER, used both literally and figuratively. The shoulder of a sacrificed ox or sheep went to the priest as his portion (Deut. 18:8); the sacred furniture of the tabernacle had to be carried upon the shoulders (Num. 7:6-9). "To pull away the shoulder" (Zech. 7:11) is to refuse to obey.

SHOULDER PIECE. 1. Part of the ephod in which the front and the back were joined together (Exod. 28:7,8). 2. Piece of meat taken from shoulder of animal (Ezek. 24:4).

SHOVEL, tool used to take ashes from altar (Exod. 27:3); for sanitary purposes (Deut. 23:13); or for winnowing (Isa. 30:24).

SHOWBREAD, SHEWBREAD (See Tabernacle).

SHRINE, dwelling for a god (Acts 19:24).

SHROUD, generally the dress for the dead, but also a bough (Ezek. 31:3), where ASV has "a forest-like shade."

SHRUB (See Plants).

SHUA (shōō'à, prosperity). 1. Canaanite whose daughter became Judah's wife (Gen. 38:2,12). 2. Heber's daughter (I Chron. 7:32).

SHUAH (shōō'äh, depression). 1. Son of Abraham by Keturah (Gen. 25:2; I Chron. 1:32). 2. See Shua 1. 3. Chelub's brother (I Chron. 4:11).

SHUAL (shōō'ăl, fox). 1. Son of Zophar (I Chron. 7:36). 2. District near Michmash (I Sam. 13:17).

SHUBAEL (shōō'bà-ĕl), name of two Levites (I Chron. 24:20; 25:20). Also called "Shebuel."

SHUHAM, SHUHAMITE (shōō'hăm, shōō'hăm-ĭt), son of Dan (Num. 26:42), also called "Hushim" (Gen. 46:23). Dan's descendants are called "Shuhamites."

SHUHITE (shōō'hĭt, native of Shuah), descendant of Shuah I (Job 2:11; 8:1; 18:1; 25:1).

SHULAMITE (shōō'lăm-ĭt, peaceful), probably native of Shunem (S. of Sol. 6:13).

SHUMATHITES (shōō'măth-ĭts), family of Kirjath-jearim (I Chron. 2:53).

SHUNAMMITE (shōō'năm-ĭt, native of Shunem). 1. Designation of woman whose son Elisha was raised from dead (II Kings 4:12). 2. Designation of Abishag (I Kings 1:3; 2:17-22).

SHUNEM (shōō'nĕm), city of Issachar (Josh. 19:18), 3-1/2 miles N of Jezreel; site of Philistine encampment before battle (I Sam. 28:4); home of Abishag, David's nurse (I Kings 1:3); home of woman who befriended Elisha (II Kings 4:8-37).

SHUNI, SHUNITE (shōō'nĭ, shōō'nĭt), son of Gad; progenitor of Shunites (Gen. 46:16; Num. 26:15).

SHUPHAM, SHUPHAMITE (shōō'făm, shōō'făm-ĭt), son of Benjamin and progenitor of Shuphamites (Num. 26:39). May be same as Shephuphan of I Chron. 8:5.

SHUPPIM (shū'pĭm). 1. Benjamite (I Chron. 7:12,15). 2. Levite gatekeeper (I Chron. 26:16).

SHUR (shōōr, wall), locality S of Palestine and E of Egypt (Gen. 16:7; 20:1).

SHUSHAN (shōō'shăn). Babylonian city; later capital of Persian empire (Neh. 1:1; Esth. 1:2; Dan. 8:2). Code of Hammurabi found there. Greeks called it "Susa."

SHUTHELAH, SHUTHALHITE (shōō-thē'là, shōō-thăl'hĭt). Son of Ephraim (Num. 26:35,36); descendants called "Shuthalnites" (I Chron. 7:20,21). 2. Son of Zabad; father of Ezer and Elead (I Chron. 7:21).

SHUTTLE (shŭt'l), part of weaving loom; used as a figure of the shortness of life (Job 7:6).

SIA (sĭ'à), progenitor of Nethinim that returned with Zerubbabel (Neh. 7:47); "Siaha" in Ezra 2:44.

SIAHA (sĭ'à-hà) (See Sia).

SIBBECAI, SIBBECHAI (sĭb'ē-kī, sĭb'ē-kī), one of David's mighty men, designated "Hushathite" (II Sam. 21:18; I Chron. 11:29; 20:4; 27:11); slew Philistine Saph (II Sam. 21:18).

SIBBOLETH (See Shibboleth).

SIBMAH (sĭb'mà), town E of Jordan; assigned to Reuben (Josh. 13:19). Probably same as Shebam (Num. 32:3) or Shibmah (Num. 32:38).

SIBRAIM (sĭb-rà'ĭm), place on N boundary of Palestine (Ezek. 47:16).

SICHEM (sĭ'kĕm), same as Shechem.

SICILY (sĭs'ĭ-lè), island lying off the toe of Italy; visited by Paul (Acts 28:12). See Syracuse.

SICK, SICKNESS (See Diseases).

SICKLE (sĭk'l, reaping hook), tool used for cutting grain, sometimes also for pruning (Deut. 16:9; Joel 3:13; Mark 4:29). Used figuratively for God's judgment (Rev. 14:14).

SIDDIM, VALE OF (sĭd'ĭm, valley of the fields), place at SE end of Dead Sea (Gen. 13:10; 14:3,10).

SIDON (sĭ'dŏn), (sometimes "Zidon" in KJV). 1. Ancient Phoenician city situated on Mediterranean promontory about 20 miles N of Tyre; assigned to Asher, but never conquered (Judg. 1:31); helped Solomon build temple (I Kings 5:6; I Chron. 22:4); cult of Baal and Ashtoreth corrupted Israel (I Kings 11:5); native city of Jezebel who married Ahab (I Kings 16:31-33); denounced by prophets (Jer. 27:3; Joel 3:4-6); visited by Christ (Mark 7:24,31); Paul stopped there (Acts 27:3). Modern Saida in Lebanon. 2. Canaan's son (Gen. 10:15; I Chron. 1:13).

SIEGE (See Warfare).

SIEVE (sĭv), sifting device for grain; made of reeds, horsehair, or strings (Isa. 30:28; Amos 9:9). Also used figuratively (Luke 22:31).

SIGN, something addressed to the senses to attest the existence of a divine power: miracles (Exod. 4:8), rainbow (Gen. 9:12, 13), circumcision (Rom. 4:11), miracles of Jesus (John 3:2; 4:54).

SIGNET (See Seal).

SIHON (sī'hŏn), king of the Amorites who opposed Israel on their journey from Egypt to Palestine and was killed by them (Num. 21:21-31; Deut. 1:4).

SIHOR (sī'hŏr, turbid), body of water mentioned in connection with Egypt (Josh. 13:3; Isa. 23:3). Should be spelled "Shihor." Identity uncertain; may be the Nile or the Brook of Egypt.

SILAS (sī'lăs, asked), Jerusalem Christian; delivered letter of Jerusalem Council (Acts 15:22,23); went with Paul on 2nd missionary journey (Acts 16-18:22). Shortened form of Silvanus (I and II Thess. 1:1; II Cor. 1:19; I Pet. 5:12).

SILK, imported from China by Phoenicians (Prov. 31:22; Ezek. 16:10,13; Rev. 18:12).

SILLA (sil'à), unknown place below Millo (II Kings 12:20).

SILOAH, SHILOAH (See Siloam).

SILOAM (sī-lō'ăm), reservoir located within the city walls of Jerusalem at the S end of the Tyropoean Valley; receives water through 1,780-foot tunnel from En-rogel (John 9:7); constructed by Hezekiah in 8th cent. B. C. "Shiloah" in Isa. 8:6; "Shelah" (KJV "Siloah") in Neh. 3:15. Modern Birket Silwan.

SILOAM, TOWER OF (sī-lō'ăm), probably part of fortification system of Jerusalem wall, near pool of Siloam (Luke 13:4).

SILOAM, VILLAGE OF (sī-lō'ăm), not mentioned in Bible; modern village (Silwan) situated across valley E of the Spring Gihon.

SILVANUS (See Silas).

SILVER (See Minerals).

SILVERSMITH (See Occupations and Professions).

SIMEON (sĭm'ē-ŭn, perhaps hearing). 1. Son of Jacob by Leah (Gen. 29:33); he and brother Levi massacred Hivites in Shechem (Gen. 34:24-31); kept as hostage by Joseph (Gen. 42:24). 2. Tribe founded by Simeon; assigned extreme S of Canaan (Josh. 19:1-9); eventually probably absorbed by Judah. 3. Ancestor of Jesus (Luke 3:30). 4. Devout Jew who took the infant Jesus into his arms and praised God (Luke 2:25,34). 5. Simon Peter (Acts 15:14). 6. Christian leader in church at Antioch, surnamed Niger (Acts 13:1,2).

SIMEONITE, member of tribe of Simeon.

SIMILITUDE (sī-mĭl'ĭ-tūd, likeness), pattern, resemblance, similarity (Num. 12:8; II Chron. 4:3; Ps. 106:20; Heb. 7:15).

SIMON (sī'mŭn, hearing). 1. Son of Jonas; brother of Andrew; apostle (Matt. 4:18; 16:17,18). See Peter. 2. Apostle; Simon the Canaanite (Matt. 10:4; Mark 3:18), or "the Zealot" (Luke 6:15; Acts 1:13). 3. Leper of Bethany (Matt. 26:6; Mark 14:3). 4. Brother of Jesus (Matt. 13:55; Mark 6:3). 5. Simon of Cyrene; helped Jesus carry cross (Matt. 27:32). 6. Pharisee in whose house woman anointed Jesus' feet (Luke 7:40,43,44). 7. Father of Judas Iscariot (John 6:71; 12:4; 13:2,26). 8. Simon Magus, sorcerer at Samaria; tried to buy power of conferring Holy Spirit on others (Acts 8:14-24). 9. Tanner at Joppa (Acts 9:43; 10:6,17).

SIMON MACCABEUS (sī'mŭn măk'à-bē-ŭs), Hasmonaean ruler in Palestine (143-134 B. C.).

SIMON MAGUS (See Simon).

SIMPLE, naive; easily led into wrong-doing (Ps. 19:7; 119:130; Prov. 7:7).

SIMRI (sĭm'rĭ), Levite; doorkeeper (I Chron. 26:10).

SIN, anything in the creature which does not express, or which is contrary to, the holy character of the Creator. The first sin in the universe was an act of free will in which the creature deliberately, responsibly, and with adequate understanding of the issues, chose to corrupt the holy, godly character with which God originally endowed His creation. Sin in the human race had its origin in Adam and Eve (Gen. 3), but sin in the universe had its origin in angelic beings who rebelled against the creator and whose nature, as a result, became fixed in evil (II Pet. 2:4; Jude 6). Adam and Eve were created with a holy, godly nature, in fellowship with God; as a result of their sin their nature became corrupt; they became hostile to God and guilty before Him; and they involved the whole human race in their corruption and guilt (Rom. 5:12f). The essence of sin is living independently of God. The solution to the problem of sin is found in Christ, in the redemption provided by Him (Rom. 3:21-8:39).

SIN, Egyptian city on E arm of the Nile (Ezek. 30:15,16).

SIN, WILDERNESS OF, wilderness through which the Israelites passed between Elim and Mt. Sinai (Exod. 16:1; 17:1; Num. 33: 11,12).

SIN OFFERING (See Offerings).

SINA (See Sinai).

SINAI (sī'nī, meaning uncertain). 1. Sinai Peninsula W of the Wilderness of Paran between the Gulf of Akabah and Suez on the E and W respectively (Exod. 19:1). 2. Mount Sinai (Exod. 19:20), on which Mosaic Law was given, also called Horeb (Exod. 3:1; 17:6; Deut. 1:6; 4:10), covenant ratified at base (Exod. 19:1-25; 24:1-18), nation of Israel organized (Exod. 20-Num. 10). Exact location is disputed.

SINEW (sī'nū), tendon, in contrast to bone structure (Gen. 32:32; Job 40:17; Ezek. 37:6-8).

SINGING (See Song; Music).

SINGLE EYE, eye that is clear, sound, and healthy, with the connotation generous (Matt. 6:22).

SINIM (sī'nĭm), remote, unknown area (Isa. 49:12); RSV reads Syene.

SINITES (sī'nĭts), tribe descended from Canaan (Gen. 10:17).

SION, MOUNT (sī'ŭn, lofty), designation of Mt. Hermon (Deut. 4:48).

SIPHMOTH (sĭf'mŏth), place in S Judah (I Sam. 30:28), not identified.

SIPPAI (sĭp'ī), man slain by Sibbechai (I

Chron. 20:4).

SIRACH, SON OF (sī'răk), supposed author of Ecclesiasticus; wrote c. 190-170 B. C.

SIRAH (sī'rà), well, c. 1 mile N of Hebron (II Sam. 3:26).

SIRION (sīr'ĭ-ŏn), name given to Mt. Hermon by Zidonions (Deut. 3:9), "Shirion" in Ps. 29:6.

SISMAI, SISAMAI (sĭs'mĭ, sĭs'à-mĭ), son of Eleasah; Judahite (I Chron. 2:40).

SISERA (sĭs'ĕr-à). 1. Captain of army of Jabin, king of Hazor; defeated in battle by Barak; slain by Deborah (Judg. 4:5; I Sam. 12:9; Ps. 83:9). 2. Ancestor of Nethinim who returned with Zerubbabel (Ezra 2:53; Neh. 7:55).

SISTER. 1. Full or half sister (Gen. 20:12; Deut. 27:22). 2. Wife (S. of Sol. 4:9). 3. Woman of same country or tribe (Num. 25:18). 4. Blood relatives (Matt. 13:56; Mark 6:3). 5. Female fellow Christian (Rom. 16:1; II John 13).

SITNAH (sit'nà, hostility), well dug by Isaac between Gerar and Rehoboth (Gen. 26:21).

SIVAN (sĕ-vàn), name of 3rd month of Heb. sacred year (May-June) (Esth. 8:9).

SKIN, skins of animals used as bottles for water and wine, articles of clothing, shoes.

SKIRT (See Dress).

SKULL (See Golgotha).

SKY, clouds, firmament; also used figuratively (Deut. 33:26).

SLANDER, malicious utterance designed to hurt or defame (Lev. 19:16; Ezek. 22:9; Eph. 4:31).

SLAVE, SLAVERY (See Servant).

SLEEP. 1. Physical rest (Ps. 4:8; John 11:13). 2. Death (I Cor. 11:30; I Thess. 4:13). 3. Spiritual indolence (Matt. 25:5; Rom. 13:11).

SLIME, bitumen; used as cement for bricks and for waterproofing (Gen. 6:14; 11:3; Isa. 34:9; Exod. 2:3).

SLIP, cutting from a plant (Isa. 17:10).

SLOTHFUL, indolent, lazy; slothfulness censured (Prov. 6:6-9; Matt. 25:26).

SLOW, always refers to the passions in the OT (Neh. 9:17; Ps. 103:8; 145:8).

SLUGGARD (See Slothful).

SMITH (See Occupations and Professions).

SMYRNA (smĭr'nà), ancient seaport on W coast of Asia Minor 40 miles N of Ephesus; seat of important Christian church (Rev. 1:11; 2:8-11).

SNARE, device for catching birds and animals (Ps. 124.7); also used figuratively (Ps. 91:3).

SNOUT, long, projecting nose of a beast, as of a pig (Prov. 11:22).

SNOW, falls in elevated areas of Palestine in January and February, but soon melts; Mt. Hermon covered with snow even in summer; used for cooling purposes. Used figuratively for righteousness and purity (Isa. 1:18; Ps. 51:7; Matt. 28:3; Rev. 1:14).

SNUFF, panting for wind (Jer. 14:6), contempt for God's sacrifices (Mal. 1:13).

SO, king of Egypt with whom Hoshea, king of Israel, made an alliance, so bringing down the wrath of Assyria upon Israel (II Kings 17:4); not identified.

SOAP, in a modern sense was unknown in OT times, but fullers made a cleansing material compounded from vegetable alkali (Jer. 2:22; Mal. 3:2).

SOCHO, SOCOCH, SOCOH (sō'kō, branches). 1. Town in Judah (Josh. 15:35) NW of Adullam; identified with Khirbet Shuweikeh. 2. Another city by this name 10 miles SW of Hebron (Josh. 15:48). 3. Son of Heber (I Chron. 4:18).

SOCKET (See Tabernacle).

SODI (sō'dī), father of Zebulun spy (Num. 13:10).

SODOM (sŏd'ŭm), with Admah, Gomorrah, Zeboiim, and Zoar one of the "Cities of the Plain," located on S portion of Dead Sea; probably water covers the remains. Lot lived there (Gen. 13:1-13); destroyed because of its wickedness (Gen. 19); symbol of vice, infamy, and judgment (Isa. 1:9,10; 3:9; Jer. 23:14; Lam. 4:6; Ezek. 16:46; Matt. 10:15; Rev. 11:8). "Sodoma" in KJV Rom. 9:29.

SODOMA (See Sodom).

SODOMITE (See Sodomy).

SODOMY (sŏd'ŭm-ĕ, male temple prostitute), unnatural sexual perversion for which Sodom became noted (Gen. 19:5). Forbidden by Law (Deut. 23:17); fastened itself upon Israel (I Kings 14:24) and ancient heathen world (Rom. 1:26f); practiced even in temple (II Kings 23:7).

SOLDER (sō'dĕr, joint), metallic substance used to join metals together (Isa. 41:7).

SOLDIER (See Occupations and Professions, also Warfare).

SOLOMON (sŏl'ō-mŭn, peaceable), 3rd and last king of united Israel; son of David and Bathsheba (II Sam. 12:24; I Chron. 3:5); anointed king in David's advanced age (I Kings 1); revenged himself upon Abiathar, Shimei, Adonijah, and Joab (I Kings 2); married daughter of Pharaoh (I Kings 3:1); prayed for understanding heart and became noted for his wisdom (I Kings 3:5-28; 10:1-10; II Chron. 1:3-12); with help of Hiram king of Tyre built the temple and his palace (I Kings 5-8; II Chron. 2-7); conscripted labor for building projects (I Kings 5:13-17; 9:19-21); became fabulously wealthy through widespread trade (I Kings 10:11-29); naturalist (I Kings 4:33); author of proverbs, songs, psalms, Song of Solomon, Book of Proverbs, Ecclesiastes; his many wives caused him to compromise with heathenism; when he died, the 10 N tribes refused to acknowledge his son Rehoboam as king, and chose as their ruler Jeroboam, former superintendent of public works under Solomon. A man of outstanding gifts and opportunities, he died a failure.

SOLOMON, SONG OF, full title is "The song of songs which is Solomon's (1:1); the last of the five OT poetic books in the English Bible. Also called Canticles, from Latin Canticum Canticorum (1:1). Authorship attributed by book itself and by tradition to Solomon. Outline: 1. The mutual admiration of the lovers (1:2-2:7). 2. Growth in love (2:8-3:5). 3. The marriage (3:6-5:1). 4. Longing of the wife for her absent husband (5:2-6:9). 5. The beauty of the Shulammite bride (6:10-8:4). 6. The wonder of love (8:5-8:14). There is great diversity and much overlapping among interpretations of the book. Various views are: 1. Allegorical, 2. Typical, 3. Literal, 4. Dramatic, 5. Erotic-literary, 6. Liturgical, and 7. Didactic-moral. Commonly held interpretation by Jews is that the bridegroom represents God; the Shulammite bride, the Jewish people. Many Christians hold that the bridegroom is Christ; the Shulammite bride, the Church.

SOLOMON'S POOLS, three pools near Jerusalem from which water was brought by means of aqueducts to Jerusalem (Eccl. 2:6). They are still in use.

SOLOMON'S PORCH, colonnade built by Solomon on E side of the temple area (John 10:23; Acts 3:11; 5:12).

SOLOMON'S SERVANTS, slaves used by Solomon in his temple for menial tasks; their descendants returned from Babylon under Zerubbabel (Ezra 2:55,58; Neh. 7:57; 60; 11:3).

SOLOMON'S TEMPLE (See Temple).

SON. 1. Any human offspring regardless of sex (Gen. 3:16). 2. Male descendant (I Kings 9:20; Mal. 3:6). 3. Member of a guild or profession (II Kings 2:3,5; Neh. 3:8). 4. Spiritual son (I Tim. 1:18). 5. Address to younger man (I Sam. 3:6). 6. Follower (Num. 21:29; Deut. 14:1). 7. Adopted son (Exod. 2:10). 8. Native (Lam. 4:2). 9. Possessor of a quality (I Sam. 25:17; Luke 10:6). 10. Used of Christ in a unique sense.

SON OF GOD, a title of Jesus referring to His co-equality, co-eternity, con-substantiality with the Father and the Spirit in the eternal Triune Godhead (John 5:18,23,36). Christ claimed to be eternal, co-equal and of the same substance as the Father. He is uniquely God's son.

SON OF MAN. 1. A member of the order of humanity (Ezek. 2:1,3,8ff; Dan. 8:17). 2. Used in a Messianic sense in Dan. 7:13,14. Jesus applies the term to Himself many times in the Gospels (Matt. 8:20; 9:6; 10:23; 11:19; 12:8, etc.). Sometimes He uses it in connection with His earthly mission, but He also uses it when describing His final triumph as Redeemer and Judge (Matt. 16:27f; 19:28; 24:30; 25:31). He appears to identify Himself with the Son of Man of Dan. 7:13,14.

SONG. Singing played a prominent part in the worship and national life of the Hebrews (Exod. 15; Psalms), and also in the early church (Eph. 5:19; Col. 3:16).

SONG OF DEGREES (See Music).

SONG OF SONGS (See Song of Solomon).

SONG OF THE THREE HEBREW CHILDREN, an addition to the book of Daniel found in the OT Apocrypha. Author is unknown; written c. 164 B. C.

SONS OF GOD, CHILDREN OF GOD, any personal creatures of God: angelic beings (Job 1:6; 2:1; 38:7); the entire human race (Acts 17:28); the regenerate as distinguished from the unregenerate (I John 3:10). The "sons of God" in Gen. 6:1-4 are probably human beings, with special emphasis upon man's nature as created in the image of God.

SONS OF THE PROPHETS, members of prophetic guilds or schools; gathered around great prophets like Samuel and Elijah for common worship, united prayer, religious fellowship, and instruction of the people (I Sam. 10:5,10; II Kings 4:38,40). In the times of Elijah and Elisha they lived together at Bethel, Jericho, and Gilgal (II Kings 2:3,5; 4:38).

SOOTHSAYER, SOOTHSAYING, one claiming power to foretell future events (Josh. 13:22; Jer. 27:9), interpret dreams (Dan. 4:7), and reveal secrets (Dan. 2:27).

SOP (morsel of bread), bread to dip food from a common platter (Ruth 2:14; Prov. 17:1; John 13:26).

SOPATER (sŏ'pȧ-tẽr), Berean Christian; companion of Paul (Acts 20:4; Rom. 16:21).

SOPHERETH (sŏ'fē-rĕth), descendants of Solomon's servants who returned from captivity with Zerubbabel (Ezra 2:55).

SORCERER, SORCERY, one who claimed to have supernatural power or knowledge. Sorcery condemned by prophets (Isa. 47:9; Mal. 3:5).

SORE (See Diseases).

SOREK (sŏ'rĕk, vineyard), valley in Philistine territory c. 8-1/2 miles S of Joppa (Judg. 16:4).

SOSIPATER (See Sopater).

SOSTHENES (sŏs'thē-nĕz). 1. Ruler of the synagogue at Corinth; beaten by crowd in presence of Gallio (Acts 18:17). 2. Christian friend of Paul (I Cor. 1:1). May be same as 1.

SOTAI (sŏ'tī), servant of Solomon whose descendants returned from captivity (Ezra 2:55; Neh. 7:57).

SOUL, the non-material ego of man in its ordinary relationships with earthly and physical things; the immortal part of man (Matt. 10:28).

SOUTH, the Negeb, an indefinite area lying between Palestine and Egypt (Gen. 12:9; 13:1; I Sam. 27:8-12; II Chron. 28:18).

SOVEREIGNTY OF GOD, the supreme authority of God. He is not subject to any power or law which could be conceived as superior to or other than Himself (Isa. 45:9; Rom. 9:20,21).

SOWER, SOWING (See Agriculture).

SPAIN, westernmost peninsula of Europe. Paul hoped to visit this Roman province (Rom. 15:24,28).

SPAN (See Weights and Measures).

SPARROW (See Birds).

SPECKLED, mottled in color (Gen. 30:25-43).

SPICE, aromatic vegetable compound used for toilet, embalming, anointing, medicine and religious ceremonies (Gen. 37:25; 43:11; S. of Sol. 4:14; Mark 16:1; John 19:39,40).

SPIES, secret scouts (Gen. 42:9; Josh. 6:23;

I Sam. 26:1-4; II Sam. 15:7-10; Luke 20:20).

SPIKENARD (See Plants).

SPINDLE, implement used in spinning (Exod. 35:25; Prov. 31:19).

SPINNING (See Occupations and Professions).

SPIRIT (breath, wind, spirit), the non-material ego in special relationships; the self is generally called "spirit" when the direct relationship of the individual to God is the point of emphasis (Rom. 8:15,16).

SPIRIT, HOLY (See Holy Spirit).

SPIRITS IN PRISON, those who in the days of Noah refused his message (I Pet. 3:18-20; 4:6).

SPIRITUAL GIFTS, extraordinary gifts of the Spirit given to Christians to equip them for the service of the Church (Rom. 12: 6-8; I Cor. 12:4-11; 28-30; Eph. 4:7-11).

SPIT, SPITTLE, SPITTING; spitting in the face an act of gross insult (Num. 12:14; Deut. 25:9; Matt. 26:67; Mark 14:65).

SPOIL, plunder taken from the enemy in war; pillage; booty (Num. 31:27; Josh. 22:8).

SPOKES, rods connecting the rim of a wheel with the hub. Basins for washing of sacrifices were set on bases moving upon wheels. The spokes were part of these wheels (I Kings 7:27-33).

SPONGE (See Animals).

SPOT, blemish, blot (S. of Sol. 4:7; Job 11:15; Lev. 24:19f; Prov. 9:7; Jude 23).

SPOUSE (See Marriage).

SPREAD, SPREADING, scatter, disperse (Matt. 21:8; Mark 1:28).

SPRINKLING; sprinkling of blood, water, and oil formed a very important part of the act of sacrifice (Exod. 24:6-8; Lev. 14; Num. 8:7).

STABLE, enclosure to lodge and feed animals (Ezek. 25:5).

STACHYS (stā′kis), Roman Christian (Rom. 16:9).

STACTE (stăk′tē, drop), fragrant ingredient used in incense (Exod. 30:34).

STAFF, STAVES (See Rod).

STAIRS, steps leading to an upper chamber (I Kings 6:8; Acts 21:40) or some other elevated place (Ezek. 40:6; 43:17).

STAKE, tent-pin or tent-pole (Exod. 27:19; Isa. 33:20).

STALL, place for care of livestock, or compartment in a stable for one animal (II Chron. 32:28). Solomon's barns provided stalls for 4,000 horses (II Chron. 9:25).

STAR (See Astronomy).

STAR OF THE WISE MEN (See Astronomy).

STATURE, natural height of an animal body (II Sam. 21:20; Isa. 45:14; Luke 19:3).

STEEL (See Minerals).

STELE (stē′lē, erect block or shaft), narrow, upright slab of stone with an inscription cut on it to commemorate an event, mark a grave, or give a votive likeness of a deity. Prevalent especially in Egypt and Greece.

STEPHANAS (stĕf′á-năs, crown), Corinthian Christian (I Cor. 16:15,16,17).

STEPHEN (stē′věn, crown), one of seven deacons of apostolic church (Acts 6:1-6);

preached in Jerusalem synagogue, and put to death by Sanhedrin, becoming the 1st Christian martyr (Acts 7); Paul held clothes of those who stoned him.

STEWARD (See Occupations and Professions).

STOCK. 1. Wooden idol worshiped by apostate Israel (Isa. 44:19; Jer. 2:27). 2. Family (Lev. 25:47; Isa. 40:24; Acts 13:26; Phil. 3:5). 3. Instrument of punishment in which head, hands, and feet were fastened (II Chron. 16:10; Jer. 20:2; Job 13:27).

STOICISM (stŏ′ĭ-sĭzm), school of philosophy founded by the Greek Zeno; system of pantheistic monism; regarded virtue as highest good; ethics were austere; unmoved by pleasure or pain (Acts 17:18).

STONE, abundant in Palestine; used for building (I Kings 5:17; Amos 5:11), land-marks (Josh. 15:6), walls of city, altars, memorials, weapons (I Sam. 17:40), idols (Isa. 57:3-7). Often used figuratively (Exod. 15:5,16; I Sam. 25:37; Ezek. 11:19; Dan. 2:34; Matt. 21:42).

STONES, PRECIOUS (See Minerals).

STONING, the ordinary form of capital punishment prescribed by Hebrew law (Lev. 20:2) for blasphemy (Lev. 24:16), idolatry (Deut. 13:6-10), desecration of sabbath (Num. 15: 32-36), human sacrifice (Lev. 20:2), occultism (Lev. 20:27). Execution took place outside city (Lev. 24:14; I Kings 21:10,13; Acts 7:58).

STOOL, three or four-legged seat (Exod. 1: 16; II Kings 4:10).

STORE CITIES, supply depots for provisions and arms (I Kings 9:15-19; II Chron. 8:4-6; 16:4).

STOREHOUSE, place for keeping treasures, supplies, and equipment (Deut. 28:8; I Chron. 29:16; II Chron. 31:10; Mal. 3:10).

STORK (See Birds).

STOVE, household stoves usually made of clay; were small and portable, burning charcoal; the well-to-do had metal stoves or braziers (Jer. 36:22f RSV).

STRAIGHT STREET, street in Damascus (Acts 9:11).

STRAKES, archaic word for "streaks" (Gen. 30:37; Lev. 14:37).

STRANGER. 1. Foreigner who put himself under protection of Israel and Israel's God, who submitted to many requirements of the law of Israel, and who was therefore given certain privileges (Exod. 20:10; 22:21). 2. Foreigner who did not have cultus-fellowship with Israel (Ezek. 44:7-9). 3. People entirely different from, or even hostile to, Israel (Isa. 1:7; Ezek. 11:9).

STRANGLE, to deprive of life by choking. Israelites were forbidden to eat flesh from strangled animals (Lev. 17:12). At the Jerusalem council even Jewish Christians were forbidden to eat such meat (Acts 15:20).

STREAM OF EGYPT (See River of Egypt).

STRIKER, a pugnacious person (I Tim. 3:3; Titus 1:7).

STRINGED INSTRUMENTS (See Music).

STRIPES, wounds inflicted by scourges for

punishment (Exod. 21:25); authorized by Jewish law for certain offenses (Deut. 25:2,3) and practiced also by Romans (Matt. 27:26).

STRONG DRINK (See Wine).

STUBBLE, stalks of grain left after reaping (Exod. 5:10-14). Figurative for wayward Israel (Isa. 47:14).

STUMBLING BLOCK, anything that causes a person to trip or fall. Figuratively, any cause of material or spiritual ruin (Ezek. 14:3,4; Jer. 18:15; Rom. 14:13; I Cor. 8:9).

SUAH (sū'à), descendant of Asher (I Chron. 7:36).

SUBURB, lands near cities used for pasturage of animals (Josh. 21:2,42; Ezek. 45:2).

SUCCOTH (sŭk'ŏth, booths or huts). 1. Place E of Jordan near Zarethan where Jacob built booths (Gen. 32:22); assigned to Gadites (Josh. 13:27); Gideon punished town severely (Judg. 8:5-16). 2. 1st encampment of Israel after leaving Rameses (Exod. 12: 37; 13:20; Num. 33:5).

SUCCOTH BENOTH (sŭk'ŏth bē'nŏth), pagan idol brought into Samaria after Assyria had captured it (II Kings 17:24-30).

SUCHATHITES (sū'kăth-its), inhabitants of Sucah or Socah (I Chron. 2:55); site unknown.

SUETONIUS (swē-tō'nĭ-ŭs), Roman writer (c. A. D. 69-140), famous for his **Lives of the Caesars**.

SUKKIM (sŭk'ĭ-im), soldiers of unknown identity who joined Shishak in his invasion of Judah (II Chron. 12:3).

SUKKOTH (See Feasts).

SULPHUR (See Minerals).

SUMER (sū'mèr), one of two political divisions, Sumer and Akkad, originally comprising Babylonia.

SUN, early recognized by people for what it does for man, hence it was worshiped by Hebrews (II Kings 21:3,5; 23:5) and by others (Job 31:26,27); fosters agriculture (Deut. 33:14) and burns vegetation (Jonah 4:8); directions determined by sun (Isa. 45:6; Ps. 50:1). Used metaphorically: glory of Christ compared to it (Matt. 17:2); also saints (Matt. 13:43); darkened sun a symbol of calamity (Ezek. 32:7; Joel 2:10,31).

SUN, WORSHIP OF. Worship of the sun found varied forms in the ancient world. Even the Israelites at times worshiped sun images (Lev. 26:30; Isa. 17:8). Shamash was a great sun god of the ancient Middle East. Phoenicia worshiped a sun Baal, Baal-hammon. In Egypt the center of sun worship was On, or Heliopolis, where the sun was called Re.

SUNDAY, first day of the week, commemorating the resurrection of Jesus (John 20:1-25) and the Day of Pentecost (Acts 2:1-41). For a time after the ascension of Jesus the Christians met on 7th and 1st days of the week, but as the Hebrew Christian churches declined in influence, the tendency to observe the Hebrew sabbath slowly passed. The disciples at Troas worshiped on the first day (Acts 20:7). Paul

admonished the Corinthians to lay by in store as God had prospered them, doing it week by week on the first day (I Cor. 16:2). The term "Lord's Day" occurs in Rev. 1:10.

SUPERSCRIPTION (sū'pèr-skrĭp'shŭn, inscription). 1. The wording on coins (Matt. 22:20). 2. Words written on board attached to the cross naming the crime of which the condemned was accused (Mark 15:26; Luke 23:38; John 19:19-20).

SUPERSTITIOUS (sū'pèr-stĭsh'ŭs), used in Acts 17:22 with the sense "very religious," as ASV and RSV have it.

SUPH, SUPHAH (sŏŏf), KJV has "The Red Sea" for both these words (Num. 21:14; Deut. 1:1). Suph is an unidentified region E of the Jordan; Supha, probably the region of the Red Sea.

SUPPER, LORD'S (See Lord's Supper).

SUPPLICATION (See Prayer).

SURETY, SURETYSHIP (shŏŏr'tē, shŏŏr'ē-tē-ship). 1. One who makes himself responsible for the obligations of another is a surety (Prov. 6:1; 11:15; 17:18; 20:16). 2. Guarantee; security for payment (Gen. 44:32).

SURFEITING (sûr'fĕt-ing, drinking-bout), over-indulgence of food or drink; dissipation (Luke 21:34).

SUSA (See Shushan).

SUSANCHITES (sū-săn'kĭts), colonists from Susa or Shushan planted in Samaria by Assyrians (Ezra 4:9,10).

SUSANNA (sū-zăn'à, lily). 1. Woman who ministered to Christ (Luke 8:1-3). 2. Heroine of **The History of Susanna**, in the OT Apocrypha.

SWADDLING BAND, bands of cloth in which a new born baby was wrapped (Luke 2:7, 12). Used figuratively in Job 38:9.

SWALLOW (See Birds).

SWAN (See Birds).

SWEAR (See Oath).

SWEAT, perspiration (Gen. 3:19; Ezek. 44:18; Luke 22:44).

SWEAT, BLOODY, physical manifestation of the agony of Jesus in Gethsemane (Luke 22:44). Christ's sweat did not become blood, but became "as it were" great drops of blood.

SWELLING (swĕl'ing), usually "pride," meaning the flooding of Jordan in spring (Jer. 12:5; 49:19; 50:44); in Ps. 46:3, the tumult of a stormy sea.

SWINE (See Animals).

SYCAMINE (See Plants).

SYCAMORE, SYCOMORE (See Plants).

SYCHAR (sī'kàr), village 1/2 mile N of Jacob's well, on E slope of Mt. Ebal (John 4:5).

SYCHEM (See Shechem).

SYENE (sī-ē'nē), Egyptian town on border of Egypt and Ethiopia (Ezek. 29:10; 30:16); the present-day Aswan.

SYMBOL, that which stands for or represents something else; a visible sign or representation of an idea or quality or of another object. In the Bible there is found symbolism of numbers (Rev. 1:4; Jer. 49:36;

Rev. 13:18), colors (Rev. 6:5,6; 7:14), and actions (I Sam. 15:27,28; I Kings 11:29,30).

SYMEON (See Simeon).

SYNAGOGUE (sĭn'å-gŏg, place of assembly), Jewish institution for the reading and exposition of the OT, which originated perhaps during the Babylonian exile (Ezra 8:15; Neh. 8:2; 9:1). It means both a community of persons organized for a religious purpose, and also the building in which gatherings for such purposes were held (Matt. 4:23). Functions were: worship and instruction, provide place where adults and children could learn the Law, social center - for the discussion of community problems, funerals, legal transactions. There were synagogues all over the Mediterranean world. Synagogues had a reading platform with lectern, case for sacred books, seats for congregation, lamps and trumpets, and officers who were responsible for the services. The NT has many references to the synagogue. Services included prayer, reading of the Scriptures, sermon, and benediction. Synagogue officials were: ruler of the synagogue, responsible for the building, general oversight of the public worship, appointing of persons to read the Scriptures, pray, and address the congregation; the minister or attendant, who took care of the building, furniture, and rolls of Scripture (Luke 4:20). The congregation was divided, the men on one side and the women on the other. The more prominent members took the front seats. No single individual was appointed to do the preaching. Any competent worshiper might be invited by the ruler to bring the sermon for the day (Luke 4:16,17; Acts 13:15). The form of worship of the synagogue was adopted by the Christian church.

SYNAGOGUE, MEN OF THE GREAT, or of the Great Assembly, a college of learned men supposedly organized by Nehemiah after the Return from Exile (Neh. 8-10), to which Jewish tradition attributed the origination and authoritative promulgation of many ordinances and regulations.

SYNOPTIC PROBLEM (See Gospels).

SYNTICHE, SYNTYCHE (sĭn'tĭ-chē, fortunate), Christian woman at Philippi (Phil. 4:2).

SYRACUSE (sĭr'å-kūs), town on E coast of Sicily (Acts 28:12).

SYRIA (sĭr'ĭ-å), abbreviation of "Assyria" or possibly from the Babylonian "Suri;" "Aram" in OT, after the Aramaeans who occupied the area in the 12th cent. B. C.; boundaries varied over the centuries, but generally included area S of Taurus Mts., N of Galilee and Bashan, W of Arabian desert, and E of the Mediterranean; chief cities: Damascus, Antioch, Byblos, Aleppo, Palmyra, and Carchemish; conquered by David (II Sam. 10:6-19), but became independent under Solomon (I Kings 11:23-25); often in conflict with Jews (I Kings 15:18-20; 20; 22; II Kings 6:8-33; 7; 9:14,15; 10:32, 33; 13); Romans made it a province in 64 B. C.; played prominent part in early Church (Acts 11:26; 13:1-3).

SYRIA MAACHAH (See Maachah).

SYRIAC, language of Syria. KJV uses "Aramaic" (II Kings 18:26; Ezra 4:7; Isa. 36:11; Dan. 2:4).

SYRIAC VERSIONS (See Texts and Versions).

SYRIAN (sĭr'ĭ-ån). 1. Language of Syria; see Syriac. 2. People of Syria (II Sam. 8:5, etc.).

SYROPHOENICIAN (sī'rō-fē-nĭsh'ån), inhabitant of region near Tyre and Sidon (Mark 7:26).

SYRTIS (sûr'tĭs), banks of quicksand off the coast of Libya (Acts 27:17).

T

TAANACH (tā'å-năk), fortified city of Canaan five miles SE of Megiddo; assigned to Manasseh (Judg. 1:27; 5:19; Josh. 12:21; 17:11; I Chron. 7:29). Modern Taanach.

TAANATH-SHILOH (tā'å-nāth-shi'lō, approach to Shiloh), town on NE border of Ephraim (Josh. 16:6), c. 10 miles E of Shechem.

TABBAOTH (tå-bā'ŏth, rings), family of temple servants who returned with Zerubbabel (Ezra 2:43; Neh. 7:46).

TABBATH (tăb'åth), place probably E of the Jordan between Jabesh-gilead and Succoth (Judg. 7:22).

TABEAL, TABEEL (tā'bē-ål, tā'bē-ĕl). 1. Father of man whom Rezin of Damascus and Pekah of Israel attempted to place on throne of Judah (Isa. 7:6 KJV "Tabeal"). 2. Persian official in Samaria (Ezra 4:7).

TABERAH (tăb'ē-rå, burning), encampment of Israel in wilderness where fire of Lord consumed some complainers (Num. 11:1-3; Deut. 9:22); site unidentified.

TABERNACLE (tăb'ẽr-năk-'l, tent), portable sanctuary that served as a place of worship for the Israelites from the time of the wilderness wanderings until the building of the temple by Solomon; typified God dwelling with His people (Exod. 25:8); variously called (Exod. 25:9; 26:9; 33:7; 39:32; I Chron. 6:48; 9:23; 17:5; II Chron. 24:6); described in Exod. 25:10-27:19,35-38); tabernacle stood in a court 150 feet long and 75 feet wide, the sides of which were covered with linen curtains, which were fastened to 60 supporting pillars of bronze. Within the court were the great altar of burnt offering (Exod. 27:1-8) and the bronze laver used by the priests for ritual ablutions (Exod. 30:17-21).

The tabernacle, which stood at the W end of the court, was a wooden structure 45 by 15 feet, divided by a heavy veil into two parts, a holy place and a most holy place. This was covered on the inside with embroidered linen tapestry and on the outside with double blankets of skin. The holy place contained the table of showbread, a golden candlestick, and the altar of incense. The most holy place, or Holy of Holies, had in it only the ark of covenant, a small box-like structure of wood covered with gold in which there were the tablets of the law, a pot of manna, and Aaron's rod (Exod. 25:16,22; Heb. 9:4). The tabernacle was set up at Sinai the beginning of the second year after leaving Egypt (Exod. 40:2,17); for 35 years it stood at Kadesh, and always preceded the Israelites when on the march (Num. 10:33-36). Later it was stationed at Gilgal (Josh. 4:19), Shiloh (Josh. 18:1), Nob (I Sam. 21:1), Gibeon (I Chron. 16:39; 21:29). David moved it to Jerusalem. It was superseded by the building of the temple. The old tabernacle was but a shadow of the true ideal (Heb. 8:5; 10:1).

TABITHA (tăb'ĭ-thà, gazelle), Christian woman in Joppa; befriended poor widows; raised from dead by Peter (Acts 9:36-43).

TABLE. 1. Table for food (Judg. 1:7; I Kings 2:7). 2. Lord's table – Lord's Supper (I Cor. 10:21). 3. "Serving tables" (Acts 6:2) refers to distribution of food, etc., to the Christian poor. 4. Tabernacle and Temple were provided with various tables. 5. Stone tablets on which Law was written (Exod. 24:12). 6. Tables were also tablets on which messages were written (Luke 1:63).

TABLE OF SHEWBREAD, the 12 loaves of consecrated unleavened bread placed on a table in the Holy Place in the Tabernacle and Temple (Exod. 25:30; Lev. 24:5-9).

TABLES OF THE LAW, stone tablets on which Moses wrote the 10 commandments (Exod. 24:3,4; 31:18; Deut. 4:13; 5:22).

TABLET (See Dress).

TABOR (tā'bẽr). 1. Mt. in Galilee 6 miles E of Nazareth (Josh. 19:22); Barak gathered his soldiers there to fight Sisera (Judg. 4:6-14); Gideon's brothers killed (Judg. 8:18-21). 2. Plain of Tabor (I Sam. 10:3), probably in Benjamin. 3. City in Zebulun for Merarite Levites (I Chron. 6:77).

TABRET, timbrel (I Sam. 10:5).

TABRIMMON, TABRIMON (tăb-rim'ŏn), father of Benhadad, king of Syria (I Kings 15:18); "Tabrimon" in KJV.

TACHE (tăch, clasp), clasp (Exod. 26:6; 36: 13,18).

TACHMONITE, TACHEMONITE (tăk'mŏ-nĭt), family of David's chief captain (II Sam. 23:8); same as Jashobeam, a Hachmonite (I Chron. 11:11).

TACKLING, either hawsers (Isa. 33:23) or furniture (Acts 27:19) of a ship.

TADMOR (tăd'mŏr), city in desert NE of Damascus (I Kings 9:18; II Chron. 8:4), a fabulously rich trade metropolis later called Palmyra. Magnificent ruins have been excavated.

TAHAN, TAHANITE (tā'hăn, tā'hăn-ĭt). 1. Son of Ephraim (Num. 26:35). 2. Descendant of Ephraim (I Chron. 7:25).

TAHAPANES, TAHPANHES (tà-hăp'à-nēz), fortress city at E edge of the Nile Delta

to which Jews fled after the fall of Jerusalem (Jer. 2:16, KJV has "Tahapanes"; 43:7-9; 44:1; 46:14). Ezek. 30:18 has "Tehaphnehes."

TAHASH (tā'hăsh), son of Nahor and Reumah (Gen. 22:24), KJV has "Thahash."

TAHATH (tā'hăth, below). 1. Kohathite Levite (I Chron. 6:24,37). 2. Encampment of Israel in desert (Num. 33:26,27). 3. Ephraimite (I Chron. 7:20).

TAHPENES (tà'pĕn-ĕz), Egyptian queen contemporary with Solomon (I Kings 11:19,20).

TAHREA (tä'rē-à), grandson of Mephibosheth (I Chron. 9:41); called "Tarea" in 8:35.

TAHTIM-HODSHI (tā'tim-hŏd-shī), place E of Jordan in the land of the Hittites (II Sam. 24:6).

TALE, sigh (Ps. 90:9), number (Exod. 5:8, 18), count (I Chron. 9:28), slander (Ezek. 22:9), idle talk (Luke 24:11), talebearing, slander (Lev. 19:16; Prov. 11:13).

TALITHA CUMI (tă-lē'thà-kŏō'mē), Aramaic for "damsel, arise" (Mark 5:41).

TALMAI (tăl'mī). 1. Son of Anak (Num. 13:22; Josh. 15:14). 2. King of Geshur; father-in-law of David (II Sam. 3:3; 13:37; I Chron. 3:2).

TALMON (tăl'mŏn), Levite porter whose descendants returned with Zerubbabel (I Chron. 9:17; Ezra 2:42; Neh. 7:45).

TALMUD (tăl'mŭd), collection of Jewish tradition of the early Christian centuries; two forms: Palestinian and Babylonian.

TAMAH (tā'mà), temple servant whose descendants returned from captivity (Neh. 7:55); "Thamah" in Ezra 2:53.

TAMAR (tā'mẽr, palm tree). 1. Wife of Er, then of Onan; mother of Perez and Zerah (Gen. 38); Matt. 1:3 KJV "Thamar." 2. Daughter of David; abused by half-brother Amon (II Sam. 13:1-33). 3. Daughter of Absalom (II Sam. 14:27). 4. Unidentified borderland site in restored Israel (Ezek. 47:19; 48:28). 5. City in Syria, more commonly known as Tadmor, later Palmyra.

TAMIR (See Tadmor).

TAMMUZ (tăm'ŭz), fertility god worshiped in Mesopotamia, Syria, and Palestine; corresponded to Osiris in Egypt and Adonis of the Greeks (Ezek. 8:14).

TANACH (See Taanach).

TANHUMETH (tăn-hū'mĕth), a Netophathite (II Kings 25:23; Jer. 40:8).

TANIS (See Zoar).

TANNER, TANNING. Tanning is the conversion of skin into leather by removing the hair and soaking it in tanning solution (Exod. 25:5; 26:14; Acts 10:6).

TAPHATH (tā'făth), Solomon's daughter (I Kings 4:11).

TAPPUAH (tă-pū'à). 1. City in lowland of Judah (Josh. 12:17; 15:34). 2. Town on boundary of Ephraim (Josh. 16:8); modern Sheikh Abu Zarad. 3. Judahite (I Chron. 2:43).

TARAH (tā'rà), encampment of Israel in wilderness (Num. 33:27,28).

TARALAH (tăr'à-là), city of Benjamin between Irpeel and Zelah (Josh. 18:27).

TAREA (tā'rē-à), descendant of King Saul (I Chron. 8:35); "Tahrea" in I Chron. 9:41.

TARES, probably bearded darnel, a poisonous plant; resembles wheat (Matt. 13:25-30).

TARPELITES (tàr'pĕl-ĭts), people sent as colonists to Samaria by Assyrians (Ezra 4:9,10).

TARSHISH (tàr'shĭsh). 1. Son of Javan (Gen. 10:4). 2. Place in W Mediterranean, perhaps in Spain or Tunisia (II Chron. 9:21; 20:36,37; Ps. 72:10). 3. "Ships of Tarshish"; large, sea-going trade ships (I Kings 9:26; 10:22; 22:48; II Chron. 9:21). 4. Great-grandson of Benjamin (I Chron. 7:10). 5. Persian prince (Esth. 1:14).

TARSUS (tàr'sŭs), capital of Cilicia, 10 miles from Mediterranean; maritime city; educational center; home of Paul (Acts 9:11, 30; 11:25; 21:39; 22:3).

TARTAK (tàr'tăk), god worshiped by Avvites, colonists in Samaria (II Kings 17:31).

TARTAN (tàr'tăn), commander-in-chief of the Assyrian army (Isa. 20:1; II Kings 18:17). A title, not a proper name.

TASKMASTERS, one who burdens another with labor; overseer (Exod. 1:11; 3:7; 5:6,10,13).

TATTENAI, TATNAI (tăt'ē-nī, tăt'nī), Persian governor ordered to assist Jews in rebuilding the temple (Ezra 5:3,6; 6:6,13).

TAVERN, an inn (Acts 28:15).

TAVERNS, THREE, place, c. 33 miles SE of Rome where Paul met Roman Christians (Acts 28:15).

TAXES, charges imposed by governments, either political or ecclesiastical, upon the persons or the properties of their members or subjects. Hebrews did not pay taxes during nomadic period. Under the theocracy of Israel every man paid a half shekel for the support of tabernacle worship (Exod. 30:13; 38:25,26). Under the kings heavy taxes were imposed, so that when Solomon died the N tribes rebelled (I Kings 12). The Ptolemies, Seleucidae, and the Romans farmed out the taxes (Matt. 17:24; 22:17).

TEACHER, TEACHING. In Christ's time boys received instruction in synagogues. In the NT the teacher was one of the Christian orders (Eph. 4:11). The NT presents Jesus as a teacher come from God (John 3:2).

TEBAH (tē'bà), nephew of Abraham (Gen. 22:24).

TEBALIAH (tĕb-à-li'à), Merarite Levite (I Chron. 26:11).

TEBETH (tē'bĕth), 10th Jewish month (Dec.Jan.).

TEETH, often used figuratively (Job 16:9; Ps. 58:6; Lam. 2:16).

TEHINNAH (tē-hin'à), Judahite (I Chron. 4:12).

TEIL TREE (tēl), oak (Isa. 6:13).

TEKEL (tē'kĕl), weighed (Dan. 5:25).

TEKOA, TEKOAH, TEKOITE (tē-kō'à, -ĭt), city of Judah 12 miles S of Jerusalem (II Sam. 14:2,4,9); home of Amos (Amos 1:1). Modern Taku'a. Inhabitant of Tekoa.

TEL-ABIB (tĕl-à'bĭb, **grain heap**), place on

Chebar river where Ezekiel lived (Ezek. 3:15).

TELAH (tē'là), Ephraimite (I Chron. 7:25).

TELAIM (tē-lā'ĭm), place where Saul mustered army against Amalek (I Sam. 15:4); may be same as Telem (Josh. 15:24) in Judah.

TELASSAR (tē-lăs'ĕr), city in Mesopotamia (Isa. 37:12); not identified.

TELEM (tē'lĕm). 1. City of Judah near Edom (Josh. 15:24). 2. Porter who divorced foreign wife (Ezra 10:24).

TEL-HARESHA, TEL-HARSA (tĕl'hà-rē'shà, tĕl'hàr'sà), place in Babylonia (Ezra 2:59; Neh. 7:61).

TELL (tĕl), mound or heap of ruins which marks the site of an ancient city and is composed of accumulated occupational debris, usually covering a number of archaeological or historical periods and showing numerous building levels or strata (Deut. 13:16; Josh. 18:28 RSV; Jer. 30:18).

TELL EL AMARNA (tĕl-ĕl-à-màr'nà), city built as capital of Egypt by Akhnaton (c. 1387-1366 B. C.); more than 350 clay tablets, representing official correspondence from rulers in W Asia to Akhnaton, found there in 1887.

TEL-MELAH (tĕl-mē'là), Babylonian town, probably not far N of Persian Gulf (Ezra 2:59; Neh. 7:61).

TEMA (tē'mà). 1. Son of Ishmael (Gen. 25:12-16). 2. Place in Arabian desert (Job 6:19).

TEMAN (tē'màn). 1. Grandson of Esau (Gen. 36:11). 2. Edomite chief (Gen. 36:42). 3. City in NE Edom (Jer. 49:7).

TEMANI (tĕm'ē-nī), inhabitant of Teman (Gen. 36:34).

TEMENI (tĕm'ē-nī), son of Ashur (I Chron. 4:6).

TEMPERANCE, self-control (Acts 24:25; Gal. 5:23; II Pet. 1:6; I Cor. 9:25); chastity, in Acts 24:25.

TEMPLE, name given to complex of buildings in Jerusalem which was the center of the sacrificial cult for the Hebrews. Three temples stood successively on Mt. Moriah (II Chron. 3:1) in Jerusalem: Solomon's, Zerubbabel's, and Herod the Great's. Material for Solomon's collected by David (II Sam. 7; I Chron. 17; 28:12-19); built with help of Hiram, king of Tyre; consisted of three sections: porch through which temple proper was entered; Holy Place – 60 feet long, 30 feet wide, 45 feet high; Holy of Holies – a 30 foot cube; stone walls were covered with paneling of cedar overlaid with gold; Holy Place contained 10 golden lampstands (I Kings 7:49), 12 tables of shewbread, and an incense altar (I Kings 7:48); Holy of Holies contained two wooden cherubim overlaid with gold and the ark of the covenant, a box overlaid with gold, its lid called the mercy seat (Lev. 16:14,15); on W, E, and S sides were three stories of rooms for officials and storage; on the N was a portico with two pillars called Jachin and Boaz; around the temple was an inner court for priests, and in it were the great altar for sacrifices and the laver used by priests for ceremonial washing; around the inner court was an outer court for Israel (I Kings 6,7; II Chron. 3,4). Solomon's temple was burned by the Babylonians (II Kings 25: 8-17; Jer. 52:12-23). Temple of Zerubbabel was less magnificent (Ezra 6). This was later rebuilt and enlarged by Herod the Great. It had four courts: for priests, Jewish males, women, and Gentiles. Herod began the work 20 B. C. The temple was burned when Jerusalem fell to the Roman armies in A. D. 70.

TEMPTATION (trial, proof), has two meanings: any attempt to entice into evil; a testing which aims at spiritual good (Gen. 3:5; 22:1-2).

TENONS (tĕn'ŭns, hands), projections in tabernacle boards to hold the boards in place (Exod. 26:17).

TENT, temporary dwelling generally made of goat's hair cloth stretched over poles; sometimes used figuratively (Gen. 9:27; Isa. 13:20).

TERAH (tĕ'rà). 1. Son of Nahor (Gen. 11: 24,25); father of Abraham, Nahor, Haran (Gen. 11:26); idolater (Josh. 24:2); went as far as Haran with Abraham (Gen. 11: 24-32). 2. Encampment of Israelites in wilderness (Num. 33:27,28), KJV has "Tarah."

TERAPHIM (tĕr'à-phĕm), household idols; images in human form (Gen. 31:19,32-35; I Sam. 19:13; Ezek. 21:21; Zech. 10:2).

TERESH (tĕ'rĕsh), chamberlain of Xerxes of Persia (Esth. 2:21).

TERRACE, steps leading up to temple (II Chron. 9:11).

TERROR, extreme fear or dread; or sometimes, the one who causes such agitation (Gen. 35:5; Ps. 55:4; II Cor. 5:11).

TERTIUS (tûr'shĭ-ŭs), scribe of Paul (Rom. 16:22).

TERTULLUS (tĕr-tŭl'ŭs), diminutive of Tertius; lawyer employed by Jews to state their case against Paul before Felix (Acts 24:1).

TESTAMENT. 1. Covenant (Heb. 8:6-10; 9:1,4). 2. Testamentary disposition, or will (Heb. 9:16,17). 3. Books of the Bible, containing the Old and New covenants.

TESTAMENTS OF THE TWELVE PROPHETS, apocryphal document that claims to report the last words of the 12 sons of Jacob; probably written c. 2nd cent. B. C.

TESTIMONY. 1. Ten Commandments (Exod. 25:16; 27:21; II Kings 11:12). 2. Divine commands (Deut. 4:45; 6:17). 3. Witness; legal evidence (Ruth 4:7).

TETRARCH, petty prince, ruler of a small district (Matt. 14:1; Luke 3:1; 9:7; Acts 13:1).

TEXTS AND VERSIONS (OLD TESTAMENT). The original manuscripts of the OT have all been destroyed; the oldest manuscripts that survive are the famous Dead Sea Scrolls found in 1947 and later

in caves along the Dead Sea, dating from 250 B. C. to c. A. D. 70; all the OT books except Esther are represented, most of them in fragmentary form. The oldest versions of the OT are: (1) Greek, Septuagint (250-100 B. C.), versions made in the 2nd cent. A. D. by Aquila, Theodotion, and Symmachus, and a translation made by Origen c. A. D. 240; (2) Aramaic (1st to 9th cent. A. D.); (3) Syriac (2nd or 3rd cent. A. D.); (4) the Latin (3rd and 4th centuries A. D.); (5) Coptic, Ethiopic, Gothic, Armenian, Georgian, Slavonic, Arabic (2nd to 10th centuries).

TEXTS AND VERSIONS (NEW TESTAMENT). Greek manuscripts whether of a portion or of the whole of the NT total nearly 4700. Of these c. 70 are papyri, 250 uncials, 2500 minuscules, and 1800 lectionaries; the earliest is a fragment of the Gospel of John and dates c. A. D. 125. The oldest NT versions are (1) Latin (2nd to 4th centuries), (2) Syriac (2nd to 6th centuries), (3) Coptic (2nd and 3rd centuries), (4) Gothic, Armenian, Georgian, Ethiopic, Arabic, Persian, Slavonic (4th to 9th centuries). A great deal of evidence for the text of the NT is also found in the writings of the early Church Fathers, principally in Greek, Latin, and Syriac.

THADDAEUS (thà-dē'ŭs), one of the 12 apostles (Matt. 10:3; Mark 3:18). This name does not appear in Luke 6:16 and Acts 1:13, where the name "Judas, son of James" (RSV) occurs instead. Little is known about him.

THAHASH (See Tahash).

THAMAH (See Tamah).

THAMAR (See Tamar).

THANK OFFERING (See Offerings).

THARA (See Terah).

THARSHISH (See Tarshish).

THEATER, place for dramatic performances (Acts 19:29,31).

THEBES (thĕbz), capital of Egypt during 18th dynasty called "No" in the Bible; on E bank of Nile; famous for temples; cult center of god Amon (Jer. 46:25); denounced by prophets (Jer. 46:25; Ezek. 30:14-16).

THEBEZ (thē'bĕz), city in Ephraim c. halfway from Beth-Shean to Shechem; Abimelech, son of Gideon, slain there (Judg. 9:50; II Sam. 11:21).

THELASAR (thē-lā'sẽr), KJV spelling for "Telassar" (II Kings 19:12); in Mesopotamia.

THEOCRACY, a government in which God Himself is the ruler; God's intention for the people of Israel (I Sam. 8:4-9; 12).

THEOPHANY, visible appearance of God, generally in human form (Gen. 3:8; 4; 28:10-17).

THEOPHILUS (thē-ŏf'ĭ-lŭs), man to whom Gospel of Luke and Acts of the Apostles are addressed (Luke 1:3; Acts 1:1). Nothing is known of him.

THESSALONIANS, EPISTLES TO (thĕs-à-lŏ'nĭ-ànz), written by Paul in Corinth c. A. D. 51 during Paul's 2nd missionary journey, not long after he had founded the church. First epistle written to encourage the Thessalonians' growth as Christians and to settle a question that was troubling them, whether those of their number who had died would miss some of the blessings of the second coming of Christ. Outline: 1. Conversion of the Thessalonians (1:1-10). 2. The ministry of Paul at Thessalonica (2). 3. Paul's concern and prayer for the church (3). 4. Problems of the church: moral instruction, the Lord's coming, ethical duties (4:1-5:22). 5. Conclusion (5:23-28). 2nd Thessalonians was written to correct some misconceptions concerning the 2nd coming of Christ. Outline: 1. Comfort in persecution (1). 2. Signs of the day of Christ: apostasy, revelation of the man of sin, preservation of God's people (2). 3. Spiritual counsel (3).

THESSALONICA (thĕs'á-lō-nī'ká), chief city of Macedonia; founded in 332 B. C. by Cassander, officer of Alexander the Great; port city on Thermaic Gulf; ruled by politarchs; visited by Paul who built church there (Acts 17:1-8).

THEUDAS (thū'dás), Jew who led rebellion against Rome (Acts 5:36,37).

THIEF, THIEVES, in Mosaic law punishment of thieves was very severe (Exod. 22:1-4).

THIGH, to put one's hand under the thigh of another was to enhance the sacredness of an oath (Gen. 24:2,9; 47:29).

THIMNATHAH (thĭm'ná-thá), town on N boundary of Judah three miles SW of Beth-shemesh (Josh. 19:43). Modern Tibnah.

THISTLE, exists in many varieties in Palestine. Used figuratively for trouble, desolation, judgment, wickedness (Num. 33:55; Prov. 24:31; 15:19; Isa. 5:6; II Cor. 12:7).

THOMAS (tŏm'ás, twin), one of the 12 apostles; also called Didymus (Greek for twin); doubted the resurrection of Jesus (John 20:24,25); with apostles in upper room after ascension of Jesus (Acts 1:13). Tradition says he preached in Parthia, Persia, and India.

THOMAS, GOSPEL OF, Gnostic gospel consisting entirely of supposed sayings of Jesus; dated c. A. D. 140; found at Naj Hamadi in Egypt in 1945.

THORN, many varieties grow in Palestine; an undesirable yield of the soil (Gen. 3:18); used for fuel (Exod. 22:6; Ps. 58:9); symbol of vexation (Num. 33:55), misfortune (Ezek. 2:6), God's judgment on evil people (Nah. 1:10). Crown of thorns placed on head of Christ (Matt. 27:29).

THORN IN THE FLESH, Paul's description of a physical ailment from which he prayed to be relieved (II Cor. 12:7). What it was is not known.

THOUSAND, often used symbolically in the Bible. In OT sometimes means "many" (I Sam. 21:11; II Chron. 15:11), "family" (Num. 10:4).

THOUSAND YEARS, the millennium (Rev. 20:1-4).

THRACE (thrás), kingdom and later a Roman province, in SE Europe, E of Mace-

donia (II Macc. 12:35).

THREE HOLY CHILDREN, SONG OF, apocryphal additions to the OT book of Daniel; probably written in 1st cent. B. C.

THREE TAVERNS, stopping place on Via Appia, c. 33 miles from Rome (Acts 28:15).

THRESHING, done in two ways: by beating sheaves with rod or flail, by trampling them under the feet of oxen (Isa. 28:27); done out-of-doors on the ground.

THRESHING FLOOR, place where grain was threshed, usually clay soil packed to a hard, smooth surface (Deut. 25:4; Isa. 28:27; I Cor. 9:9).

THRESHOLD, piece of wood or stone at the bottom of a door, and has to be crossed on entering a house.

THRONE, chair of state occupied by one in authority or of high position, like a high priest, judge, governor, or king (Gen. 41:40; II Sam. 3:10; Neh. 3:7; Ps. 122:5; Jer. 1:15; Matt. 19:28).

THUMB, either the great toe of the foot or the thumb of the hand (Exod. 29:20; Lev. 8:23).

THUMMIM (See Urim and Thummim).

THUNDER, noise that follows a lightning discharge; considered by Jews to be revelation of God's power (Job 37:2-5; 40:9; Ps. 18:13; 29:2-9).

THUNDER, SONS OF, title given James and John by Jesus (Mark 3:17).

THUTMOSE (also Tuthmosis, Thotmes), name of four kings of Egypt of 18th dynasty, centering in Thebes. Under their rule Egypt attained her greatest power.

THYATIRA (thī'á-tī'rá), city in Roman province of Asia, on boundary of Lydia and Mysia; noted for weaving and dyeing (Acts 16:14 ; Rev. 2:18-29).

TIAMAT (tī'á-mät), mythical monster in Babylonian-Assyrian creation story.

TIBERIAS (tī-bē'rĭ-ás), city on W shore of Sea of Galilee; built by Herod Antipas, and named for the emperor Tiberius; famous health resort; after A. D. 70 it became a center of rabbinic learning. Modern Tabariyeh.

TIBERIAS, SEA OF (See Sea of Galilee).

TIBERIUS (tī-bēr'ĭ-ŭs), 2nd Roman emperor (A. D. 14-37); reigning emperor at time of Christ's death (Luke 3:1).

TIBHATH (tĭb'háth), city of Zobah, E of Anti-Lebanon Mountains (I Chron. 18:7-9); "Betah" in II Sam. 8:8.

TIBNI (tĭb'nĭ), son of Ginath; unsuccessful competitor for throne of Israel (I Kings 16:21).

TIDAL (tī'dál), king of Goiim; confederate of Chedorlaomer (Gen. 14:1-17).

TIGLATH-PILESER (tĭg'láth-pī-lē'zèr), famous Assyrian king (1114-1074 B. C.); great conqueror; received tribute from king Azariah of Judah and king Menahem of Samaria (II Kings 15:19,20); Ahaz secured his help against Pekah of Israel and Rezin of Syria; deported Transjordanian Israelites (I Chron. 5:6,26); Ahaz gave tribute to him (II Chron. 28:20,21).

TIGRIS (ti'grĭs), one of the two great rivers of the Mesopotamian area; 1,150 miles long ("Hiddekel" Dan. 10:4).

TIKVAH (tĭk'và). 1. Father-in-law of the prophetess Huldah (II Kings 22:14). 2. Father of Jahaziah (Ezra 10:15).

TILE, slab of burnt clay used for writing and roofing (Ezek. 4:1-8; Luke 5:19).

TILGATH-PILNESER (See Tiglath-Pileser).

TILING, clay roofing (Luke 5:19).

TILON (ti'lŏn), son of Shimon (I Chron. 4:20).

TIMBREL, percussion instrument like a tambourine (Exod. 15:20; Judg. 11:34; II Sam. 6:5; I Chron. 13:8; Ps. 81:2).

TIME. In the early Biblical period time was marked by sunrise and sunset, phases of the moon, and location of a few constellations; but there were no names for days and months, and no accurate knowledge of years. Ancient people had no method of reckoning long periods of time. They dated from great and well-known events, like the founding of Rome (753 B. C.), the beginning of the Olympian games (766 B. C.), the founding of the Seleucid dynasty (312 B. C.), the Exodus, the Babylonian Exile, the earthquake (Amos 1:1). The starting point in the Maccabean age was the beginning of the Seleucid era (312 B. C.). The year was lunar (354 days, 8 hours, 38 seconds), divided into 12 lunar months, with seven intercalary months added over 19 years. The Hebrew month began with the new moon. Early Hebrews gave the months names; later they used numbers; and after the Exile they used Babylonian names. The sacred year began with Nisan (March-April); the secular year, with Tishri (September-October). Months were divided by the Jews into weeks of seven days, ending with the Sabbath (Exod. 20:11; Deut. 5:14, 15). Days were divided into 24 hours of 60 minutes of 60 seconds. The Roman day began at midnight and had 12 hours (John 11:9); the Hebrew day was reckoned from sunset. Night was divided into watches. At first the Hebrews had three watches; in the time of Christ there were four. Various kinds of clocks were used: sundials, shadow clocks, water clocks.

TIMES, OBSERVER OF, person who has a superstitious regard for days regarded as lucky or unlucky, as decided by astrology (Deut. 18:9-14).

TIMEUS, TIMAEUS (tĭ-mē'ŭs), father of Bartimaeus (Mark 10:46).

TIMNA (tĭm'nà, **holding in check**). 1. Concubine of Eliphaz (Gen. 36:12). 2. Sister of Lotan (Gen. 36:22). 3. Chieftain of Edom (Gen. 36:40), KJV has "Timnah." 4. Son of Eliphaz (I Chron. 1:36).

TIMNAH (tĭm'nà). In KJV eight times "Timnath" (Gen. 38:12-14; Judg. 14:1-5), once "Thimnathah" (Josh. 19:43). 1. Town on border of Judah, c. three miles SW of Beth-Shemesh (Josh. 15:10); site at Tibnah. 2. Town in hill country of Judah (Josh. 15:57). Location unknown.

TIMNATH (See Timnah).

TIMNATH-HERES (See Timnath-Serah).

TIMNATH-SERAH (tĭm'năth-sē'rà), village in Ephraim (Josh. 19:50); Joshua buried there (Josh. 24:30); probably Tibnah, 12 miles NE of Lydda. Same as Timnath-heres (Judg. 2:9).

TIMNITE (tĭm'nĭt), native of Timnah (Judg. 15:3-6).

TIMON (ti'mŏn), one of seven deacons (Acts 6:5).

TIMOTHEUS (See Timothy).

TIMOTHY (tĭm'ō-thĕ, honoring God), companion and assistant of Paul; son of Jewess and Greek (Acts 16:1-3); received religious training from mother and grandmother (II Tim. 1:5; 3:15); lived at Lystra or Derbe, where he was converted before Paul's 2nd missionary journey (c. A. D. 48); taken by Paul as his assistant on 2nd missionary journey (Acts 16:1-4); set apart for church work (II Tim. 1:6); circumcised (Acts 16:3); constant companion of Paul, who used him in a variety of tasks (Acts 16:12; 17:14; 19:22; 20:3-6; II Cor. 1:1; Phil. 1:1; Col. 1:1; I Thess. 1:1; 3:2; II Thess. 1:1; Philemon 1). I and II Timothy addressed to him. Head of the church at Ephesus (I Tim. 1:3); set free from prison (Heb. 13:23).

TIMOTHY, EPISTLES TO (See Pastoral Epistles).

TINKLING, sound of small bells worn by women on chain fastened to anklets (Isa. 3:16).

TIPHSAH (tĭf'sà). 1. City on Euphrates (I Kings 4:24). 2. Town, apparently not far from Tirzah (II Kings 15:16); possibly modern Tappuah.

TIRAS (ti'ràs), son of Japheth (Gen. 10:2; I Chron. 1:5).

TIRATHITE (ti'răth-ĭt), family of scribes in Jabez (I Chron. 2:55).

TIRE (headdress), ornamental headdress (Ezek. 24:17,23; Isa. 3:20 – KJV "bonnet;" 61:10, KJV "ornaments").

TIRHAKAH (tûr'hà-kà), Egyptian king, 3rd of the 25th dynasty; defeated by Sennacherib (II Kings 19:9; Isa. 37:9), and later by Esarhaddon and Assurbanipal.

TIRHANAH (tûr'hà-nà), son of Caleb and Maacah (I Chron. 2:48).

TIRIA (tĭr'ĭ-à), son of Jehaleleel (I Chron. 4:16).

TIRSHATHA (tûr-shà'thà, revered), title of governor of Judah under Persians (Ezra 2:63; Neh. 7:65,70; 8:9; 10:1).

TIRZAH (tûr'zà). 1. Daughter of Zelophehad (Num. 26:33; Josh. 17:3). 2. Town six miles E of Samaria (Josh. 12:24); capital of N kingdom until time of Omri (I Kings 14:17; 15:21,33; 16:6); probably Tell el-far'ah.

TISHBITE (tĭsh'bĭt), designation of Elijah (I Kings 17:1); probably to be identified with modern el-Istib, little W of Mahanaim.

TITHE (tĭth, tenth), 10th part of one's income set aside for a specific use, to the government or ecclesiastics. Its origin is unknown, but it goes back far beyond the time of Moses, and it was practiced in lands from Babylonia to Rome. Abraham gave tithes to Melchizedek (Gen. 14:20; Heb. 7:2,6); Jacob promised tithes to God (Gen. 28:22); Mosaic law required tithing of all produce of land and herds (Lev. 27:30-33); used for support of Levites and priests (Num. 18:21-32); additional tithes may have been required at certain times (Deut. 12:5-18; 14:22-29); there were penalties for cheating in tithing (Lev. 27:31; Deut. 26:13-15). Pharisees tithed even herbs (Matt. 23:23; Luke 11:42).

TITTLE (tit'l, horn), small, horn-shaped mark used to indicate accent in Hebrew (Matt. 5:18; Luke 16:17).

TITUS (ti'tus), convert, friend, and helper of Paul (Titus 1:4); Greek, son of Gentile parents (Gal. 2:3); Paul refused to allow him to be circumcised (Gal. 2:3-5); travelled to Jerusalem with Paul and Barnabas; sent to Corinth by Paul (II Cor. 2:13; 8:6,16; 12:18); rejoined Paul in Macedonia (II Cor. 7:6,13,14); organized churches in Crete (Titus 1:4,5); met Paul at Nicopolis (Titus 3:12).

TITUS, EPISTLE TO (See Pastoral Epistles).

TITUS, FLAVIUS VESPASIANUS, Roman emperor (A. D. 79-81); captured and destroyed Jerusalem in A. D. 70.

TITUS JUSTUS (See Justus).

TIZITE (ti'zit), designation of Toha, one of David's soldiers (I Chron. 11:45).

TOAH (tō'a), ancestor of Samuel (I Chron. 6:34); "Nahath" in I Chron. 6:26 and "Tohu" in I Sam. 1:1.

TOB (tob), district in Syria, extending NE from Gilead, to which Jephtha fled (Judg. 11:1-3).

TOB-ADONIJAH (tŏb-ăd-ō-ni'ja), Levite sent by Jehoshaphat to teach law to Judah (II Chron. 17:7-9).

TOBIAH, TOBAJAH (tō-bi'a, tō-bi'ja, Jehovah is good). 1. See Tob-Adonijah. 2. Family that could provide proofs of being Israelites (Ezra 2:60; Neh. 7:61,62). 3. Ammonite who opposed Nehemiah (Neh. 2:10,19; 13:4ff). 4. Exile who returned to Jerusalem (Zech. 6:9-15).

TOBIT, BOOK OF (See Apocrypha).

TOCHEN (tō'kĕn), town of Simeon (I Chron. 4:32).

TOGARMAH (tō-gà'ma), descendant or group descended from Japheth (Gen. 10:3; I Chron. 1:6; Ezek. 38:6).

TOHU (tō'hū), ancestor of Samuel (I Sam. 1:1).

TOI (tō'ē), king of Hamath who congratulated David for victory over Hadadezer (II Sam. 8:9-11).

TOKEN, sign (Exod. 13:9,16; Num. 17:10).

TOLA (tō'la). 1. Son of Issachar (Gen. 46: 13). 2. Judged Israel 23 years (Judg. 10:1,2).

TOLAD (tō'lăd), city of Simeon (I Chron. 4:29).

TOMB, a burial place or sepulchre. Most Hebrew burying sites were unmarked; some kings were buried in a vault in Jerusalem (II Sam. 2:32; Neh. 2:3); tombs of NT

times were either caves or else were dug into stone cliffs; doors were circular, weighing from one to three tons (Luke 24:2; John 20:1).

TONGS, snuffers (Exod. 25:38; Num. 4:9), instrument for taking hold of something (Isa. 6:6; 44:12).

TONGUE. 1. Organ of speech (Job 27:4). 2. Organ of the body (Judg. 7:5). 3. Language or dialect (Gen. 10:5,20; Deut. 28:49). 4. People or race having a common language (Isa. 66:18; Dan. 3:4). 5. Often used figuratively (Ps. 64:3; 140:3).

TONGUES, CONFUSION OF, punishment by God for arrogant attempt to build tower reaching to heaven (Gen. 11:1-9).

TONGUES OF FIRE, one of phenomena which occurred at outpouring of Holy Spirit on day of Pentecost; symbolic of Holy Spirit who came in power on the Church (Acts 2:3).

TONGUES, GIFT OF, a spiritual gift mentioned in Mark 16:17; Acts 2:1-13; 10:44-46; 19:6; I Cor. 12,14. The gift appeared on the day of Pentecost with the outpouring of the Holy Spirit on the assembled believers (Acts 2:1-13). The phenomenon appeared again in the home of Cornelius (Acts 10: 44-11:17), at Ephesus (Acts 19:6), and in the church at Corinth (I Cor. 12,14). Instruction regarding the use of tongues is given by Paul in I Cor. 12-14.

TOOLS, The following kinds are mentioned in the Bible; cutting, boring, forks and shovels, carpentry, drawing, measuring, tilling, metal-working, stone-working.

TOOTH, Both human and animal teeth are mentioned (Num. 11:33; Deut. 32:24); figurative use is common: cleanness of teeth, famine (Amos 4:6), gnashing of teeth, rage and despair (Job 16:9), oppression (Prov. 30:14), plenty (Gen. 49:12).

TOPHEL (tō'phĕl, cement), place in wilderness where Moses addressed Israelites (Deut. 1:1); may be modern el-Tafeleh, 15 miles SE of Dead Sea.

TOPHET, TOPETH (tō'phĕt, tō'phĕth), place in valley of Hinnom where human sacrifices were made to Molech (Jer. 7:31) defiled by Josiah (II Kings 23:10); used as dumping place for refuse.

TORAH (tō'rà, instruction, law), divine law; the Pentateuch; the entire Jewish Scriptures (John 10:34).

TORMENTOR, probably jailer (Matt. 18:34).

TOU (tō'oō), (See Toi).

TOW (tō), short fibers of flax or hemp (Judg. 16:9; Isa. 1:31; 43:17).

TOWEL, cloth for wiping and drying (John 13:4,5).

TOWER, lofty structure used for purposes of protection or attack (II Chron. 14:7; 26:9; Isa. 23:13; Matt. 21:33).

TOWN, in ancient times large cities had towns or villages surrounding them for protection (Num. 21:25,32; Josh. 15:45-47); sometimes it means an unwalled town (Deut. 3:5; I Sam. 16:4).

TOWN CLERK, official in Graeco-Roman

cities of the 1st century, as at Ephesus (Acts 19:35).

TRACHONITIS (trăk-ō-ni'tis, **rough region**), area of c. 370 sq. miles S of Damascus; tetrarchy of Philip (Luke 3:1).

TRADE AND TRAVEL. Trade in the OT. Ur of the Chaldees a trading port; Egypt, from earliest times, a great trading nation (Gen. 37:25); first organized commerce of Hebrew people was under Solomon, who formed a partnership with the great mercantile cities of Tyre and Sidon (I Kings 9:27,28; 10:11); after the death of Solomon Israel again became an agricultural nation. **Trade in the NT.** Jewish trade and commerce have small place in the Gospels. All through NT times trade, in the wider sense of the word, was in the hands of Rome and of Italy. **Travel.** Motives for travel: trade, colonization, exploration, migration, pilgrimage, preaching, courier service, exile. Travel had serious hazards (II Cor. 11:25-27; Acts 27,28); was facilitated by wonderful Roman roads, some of which still are used. Regular passenger service by land or sea was unknown.

TRADE GUILDS, societies of tradesmen organized chiefly for purpose of social intercourse (Acts 19); not trade unions in the modern sense.

TRADITION (trà-di'shŭn, **a giving over**), by word of mouth or in writing. 1. Interpretations of OT Law (Matt. 15:1-9; Gal. 1:14). 2. Gospel truths handed down by apostles (Luke 1:2; Rom. 6:17; I Cor. 11:2,23; 15: 3-9; II Pet. 2:21).

TRAIN. 1. Retinue of a monarch (I Kings 10:2). 2. Skirt of a robe (Isa. 6:1). 3. To discipline (Titus 2:4 RSV).

TRAJAN (trā'jăn), Roman emperor (A. D. 98-117); able soldier; progressive ruler.

TRANCE (a throwing of the mind out of its normal state), mental state in which the senses are partially or wholly suspended and the person is unconscious of his environment while he contemplates some extraordinary object (Acts 10:9-16; 22:17-21).

TRANSFIGURATION (trăns-fig-ū-rā'shŭn), name given to event when Jesus was visibly glorified in the presence of three select apostles (Matt. 17:1-8; Mark 9:2-8; Luke 9:28-36).

TRANSGRESSION (trăns-grĕ'shŭn), breaking of a law (Prov. 17:19; Rom. 4:15).

TRANSJORDAN, TRANS-JORDAN (trănsjŏr'dăn), large plateau E of Jordan, comprised in modern Hashemite Kingdom of Jordan; in NT times, the Peraea and the Decapolis; in OT times, Moab, Ammon, Gilead, and Bashan. Associated with Moses; Joshua; the tribes Reuben, Gad, and Manasseh; David; Nabataeans.

TRANSLATE, to remove from one place to another (I Sam. 3:10; Heb. 11:5).

TRANSPORTATION, in ancient times done chiefly by camels, donkeys, horses, and boats.

TRAVAIL (trăv'āl), pangs of childbirth (Gen.

35:16; 38:27; I Sam. 4:19), trouble (Isa. 23:4; 54:1), to be weak or sick (Jer. 4:31), weariness (Exod. 18:8).

TRAVEL (See Trade and Travel).

TREASURE, a collection of objects of value, including stores of provisions (Jer. 41:8; Ezek. 28:4; Dan. 11:43; Matt. 12:35; Acts 8:27).

TREASURER, one trusted with charge of treasure or treasures.

TREE. Palestine in ancient times far more wooded than today; over 25 different kinds of trees have been identified as having grown in the Holy Land; trees venerated by heathen people; Hebrews forbidden to plant a tree near a sacred altar (Deut. 16:21).

TREE OF KNOWLEDGE, special tree in garden of Eden, set apart by the Lord as an instrument to test the obedience of Adam and Eve (Gen. 2:9,17).

TREE OF LIFE, another special tree in the garden of Eden; its fruit conferred immortality on persons eating it (Gen. 2:9; 3: 22,25; Rev. 22:2).

TRENCH, rampart, intrenchment (II Sam. 20:15; I Sam. 17:20, 26:5).

TRESPASS (trĕs'păs), violation of the rights of others, whether of God or of man.

TRESPASS OFFERING, sacrifice of a ram for the purpose of expiation of sins against others; in addition to the sacrifice, restitution had to be made (Lev. 5:16; 6:5; Num. 5:7,8).

TRES TABERNAE (See Three Taverns).

TRIAL OF JESUS, betrayed by Judas into the hands of the Jewish religious leaders, Jesus was first brought before Annas, former high priest, and father-in-law of the current high priest Caiaphas, for a brief examination (John 18:13); then at cockcrowing time he appeared before the Sanhedrin in the palace of Caiaphas, where He was questioned and had indignities heaped upon Him (Mark 14:60-65; Luke 22:63-64); at dawn He appeared before the Sanhedrin again and was condemned to death (Luke 22:66-70); next He was brought by the Sanhedrin before Pilate, who after an examination pronounced Him innocent (John 18:33-38), but the Jews would not hear of His being released, and Pilate therefore sent Him to Herod Antipas, who was also present for the Passover, on the plea that He belonged to Herod's jurisdiction. Herod, however, merely mocked Jesus and returned Him to Pilate uncondemned (Luke 23:2-12); Pilate then gave the Jews the opportunity of choosing for release either Barabbas or Jesus, and the Jews chose Barabbas; another attempt by Pilate to have Jesus released met with failure, for the Jews threatened him if he did not carry out their wishes; after the Roman soldiers scourged and mocked Him, Jesus was crucified (Mark 15:16-20).

TRIBE, TRIBES, the tribes of Israel were descended from the 12 sons of Jacob, with Joseph's sons, Ephraim and Manasseh, forming two, while no tribal territory was allotted to Levi (Gen. 48:5; Num. 26:5-51; Josh. 13:7-33; 15-19). The leaders of the tribes are called by various names: princes, rulers, heads, chiefs (Exod. 34:31; Num. 1:16; Gen. 36:15ff); before the Israelites entered the promised land two tribes, Reuben and Gad, and half of Manasseh chose to settle on the E side of the Jordan (Num. 32:33). During the period of the Judges in Israel the tribes were each one a law unto themselves. When David became king over the whole land the 12 tribes were unified. He appointed a captain over each tribe (I Chron. 27:16-22). The captivities wiped out tribal distinctions.

TRIBULATION, GREAT TRIBULATION (trib-ū-lā´shŭn), a period of suffering sent from God upon earth at the end time because of its awful wickedness (Dan. 12:1; Matt. 24:21).

TRIBUTE, enforced contributions to individuals, governments, or institutions – like the Temple: took the form of human labor (Exod. 5; Josh. 16:10) and enforced contributions of precious things, commodities, or slaves (I Kings 20:1-7; II Kings 17:1-6).

TRINITY (trin´ĭ-tĭ), theological term for the one only, the living and true God, who subsists in Three Persons: Father, Son, and Holy Spirit (Matt. 3:13-17; 28:19), although in essence He is one – undivided and indivisible (John 10:30; I Tim. 2:5).

TRIUMPH (to lead in triumph), celebration of victory; in Roman times a magnificent procession in honor of a victorious general (II Cor. 2:14; Col. 2:15).

TROAS (trō´ăs), a chief city and port of the Roman Province of Asia, on the Aegean coast, c. 10 miles from the ruins of ancient Troy; known as Alexandria Troas (Acts 16:8; 20:5; II Cor. 2:12). This general area is also sometimes called Troas.

TROGYLLUM (trō-jĭl´ĭ-ŭm), promontory thrusting SW from Asian mainland N of Miletus, opposite island of Samos (Acts 20:15).

TROPHIMUS (trŏf´ĭ-mŭs, **nourishing**), Gentile Christian of Ephesus (Acts 21:29) and companion of Paul (II Tim. 4:20).

TRUTH, correspondence of the known facts of existence with the sum total of God's universe; may be known by general and

special revelation – but only so much as God chooses to reveal. God has made known all that man needs to know for life and salvation. Truth is manifested supremely in Christ (John 1:14,17; 14:6); those who turn away from Him choose to live in error.

TRYPHENA (trī-fē´nå, **dainty**), Christian woman friend of Paul's in Rome (Rom. 16:12).

TRYPHOSA (trī-fō´så, **delicate**), another Christian woman friend of Paul's in Rome (Rom. 16:12).

TUBAL (tū´bål), tribe descended from Japheth (Gen. 10:2; Isa. 66:19).

TUBAL-CAIN (tū´bål-kān), son of Lamech and Zillah; worker in brass and iron (Gen. 4:22).

TUNIC, shirt-like garment worn by men and women under other clothes in Bible times.

TURBAN, man's brimless headdress formed by winding cloth around head or a tight-fitting cap.

TURTLE, TURTLEDOVE, bird found in Palestine and used by poor people for sacrifice (Lev. 12:6-8; Luke 2:24).

TWELVE, THE (See Apostles).

TYCHICUS (tĭk´ĭ-kŭs, **fortuitous**), Asian Christian and close friend and valued helper of Paul (Acts 20:4; Col. 4:7-9; II Tim. 4:12; Titus 3:12).

TYRANNUS (tĭ-răn´ŭs, **tyrant**), Greek teacher in whose school Paul preached after he was expelled from the synagogue (Acts 19:9).

TYRE, TYRUS (tīr, tĭ´rŭs, **rock**), Phoenician port S of Sidon and N of Carmel; founded by Sidon (Isa. 23:2,12); assigned to Asher, but never occupied (Josh. 19:29; II Sam. 24:7); first built on mainland, but later on a nearby island; David and Solomon in friendly alliance with its kings (I Kings 9:10-14; II Chron. 2:3-16); powerful merchant city (Isa. 23:8); famous especially for dyes, glassware, and metal works; Carthage founded by Tyrian colonists; denounced by prophets (Isa. 23:1-17; Jer. 27:3; Ezek. 26-28); Jesus visited region and was well received (Mark 7:24-31); Paul stayed there seven days (Acts 21:3-7).

TYROPEON VALLEY, valley in Jerusalem separating W and E hills and joining Kidron and Hinnom valleys on the S.

U

UCAL (ū´kål), obscure word; usually taken as son or pupil of Agur (Prov. 30:1).

UEL (ū´ĕl), man who divorced foreign wife (Ezra 10:34).

UGARIT (ū´gȧ-rīt), ancient city on N Syrian coast, 40 miles SW of Antioch; also called Ras Shamra; great commercial and religious center; hundreds of tablets known as "Ras Shamra Tablets" discovered there.

UKNAZ (ŭk´năz), son of Jephunneh (I Chron. 4:15), KJV has "even Kenaz."

ULAI (ū´lī), river in Elam near Susa on whose bank Daniel saw vision (Dan. 8:2,16).

ULAM (ū´lăm). 1. Manassite (I Chron. 7: 16,17). 2. Descendant of Eshek (I Chron. 8:39,40).

ULLA (ū´lå), Asherite (I Chron. 7:39).

UMMAH (ŭm´å), city of Asher (Josh. 19:30).

UNCIAL LETTERS, large letters, like capitals. Early Greek manuscripts of NT written in uncials.

UNCIRCUMCISED (ŭn-sûr´kŭm-sizd). 1. One who has not submitted to Jewish rite of circumcision. 2. Gentiles (Gen. 34:14; Judg. 14:3; Rom. 4:9). 3. One whose heart is not open to God (Jer. 4:4; 6:10; Acts 7:51).

UNCLE. 1. Brother of one's father or mother (II Kings 24:17). 2. Any kinsman on father's side (Lev. 10:4; Amos 6:10).

UNCLEAN, UNCLEANNESS. 1. Two kinds of uncleanness: moral and ceremonial. 2. Foods regarded as unclean in OT: animals that did not chew the cud and part the hoof; animals and birds which eat blood or carrion; anything strangled or that died of itself (Lev. 11:1-8; 26-28); water creatures without scales and fins (Lev. 11:9-12); insects without hind legs for jumping (Lev. 11). 3. Other forms of ceremonial uncleanness: contact with the dead (Lev. 11:24-40; 17:15; Num. 19:16-22); leprosy (Lev. 13; 14; Num. 5:2); sexual discharge (Lev. 15: 16-33); childbirth (Lev. 12:6-8). In Christianity uncleanness is moral, not ceremonial.

UNCTION (ŭngk'shŭn, **anointing**), act of anointing (I John 2:20).

UNDEFILED, any person or thing not tainted with moral evil (Ps. 119:1; Heb. 7:26; 13:4; I Pet. 1:4).

UNDERSETTERS, supports of the laver in Solomon's temple (I Kings 7:30,34).

UNICORN (ū'nĭ-kôrn), fabulous animal; horned; strong; wild; difficult to catch; may be wild ox (Num. 23:22; 24:8; Deut. 33:17; Job 39:9f; Ps. 29:6).

UNITY, togetherness, fellowship (Gen. 13:6; Judg. 19:6; Eph. 4:13).

UNKNOWN GOD, inscription on an altar at Athens dedicated to an unknown god that worshipers did not want to overlook (Acts 17:23).

UNKNOWN TONGUE, charismatic gift of speaking in tongues (I Cor. 14:2,4,13,14, 19,27).

UNLEARNED, illiterate (Acts 4:13; II Pet. 3:16); non-professional (I Cor. 14:16,23f).

UNLEAVENED, unmixed with yeast (I Cor. 5:7,8).

UNLEAVENED BREAD, bread made without yeast (Exod. 12:8).

UNLEAVENED BREAD, FEAST OF (See Feasts).

UNNI (ŭn'ī). 1. Levite; musician (I Chron. 15:18,20). 2. Levite; musician (Neh. 12:9). "Unno" is the correct spelling.

UNPARDONABLE SIN, blasphemy against the Holy Spirit (Matt. 12:31,32; Mark 3:28, 29; Luke 12:10), probably the sin of decisively and finally rejecting the testimony of the Holy Spirit regarding the person and work of Jesus Christ.

UNTEMPERED MORTAR, mortar made of clay instead of slaked lime.

UPHARSIN (ū-fär'sĭn), "divisions" or "divided" (Dan. 5:24-28).

UPHAZ (ū'făz), place where gold was obtained (Jer. 10:9; Dan. 10:5); location unknown. Perhaps "Ophir" should be read.

UPPER CHAMBER, UPPER ROOM, room built on wall or roof of a house; scene of our Lord's last supper (Mark 14:15; Luke 22:12).

UR (ûr), father of Eliphal (I Chron. 11:35).

UR OF THE CHALDEES, city in S Mesopotamia, c. 140 miles SE of old Babylon; early home of Abraham (Gen. 11:28,31; 15:7; Neh. 9:7).

URBANE (ûr'băn, **polite**), Roman Christian (Rom. 16:9).

URI (ū'rī). 1. Father of Bezaleel (Exod. 31:2; 35:20; 38:22; I Chron. 2:20; II Chron. 1:5). 2. Father of Geber (I Kings 4:19). 3. Temple porter who put away foreign wife (Ezra 10:24).

URIAH, URIAS (ū-rī'á, ū-rī'ăs, **Jehovah is light**). 1. Hittite; husband of Bathsheba (II Sam. 11:3). 2. High priest during reign of Ahaz of Judah, for whom he built a pagan altar in the temple (II Kings 16: 10-16). 3. Priest who aided Ezra (Neh. 8:4). 4. Father of Meremoth (Ezra 8:33; Neh. 3:4). 5. Son of Shemaiah, a prophet of Kirjath-jearim (Jer. 26:20-23).

URIEL (ū'rĭ-ĕl, **God is light**). 1. Kohathite Levite (I Chron. 6:24). 2. Chief of Kohathites who assisted in bringing the ark from house of Obed-Edom (I Chron. 15: 5,11). 3. Father of Michaiah, wife of Rehoboam (II Chron. 13:2).

URIJAH (ū-rī'já, **Jehovah is light**). 1. Prophet who predicted destruction of Judah and was slain (Jer. 26:20). 2. See Uriah 2 and 3.

URIM AND THUMMIM (ū'rĭm and thŭm'im, **lights and perfections**), objects, not specifically described, placed in breastplate of high priest by which he ascertained the will of God (Exod. 28:30; Lev. 8:8).

USURY, charging of interest on money loaned; law forbade loaning of money to a brother Jew for interest (Exod. 22:25; Deut. 23:19), but permitted lending money to a stranger with interest (Deut. 23:20). Jesus did not condemn receiving reasonable rates of interest for money loaned (Matt. 25:27; Luke 19:23).

UTHAI (ū'thī). 1. Son of Ammihud (I Chron. 9:4). 2. Man who returned with Ezra (Ezra 8:14).

UZ (ŭz). 1. Son of Nahor (Gen. 22:21), KJV has "Huz." 2. Son of Aram (Gen. 10:23; I Chron. 1:17). 3. Son of Dishan (Gen. 36:28). 4. Country in which Job lived (Job 1:1); site uncertain.

UZAI (ū'zī), father of Palal (Neh. 3:25).

UZAL (ū'zăl), son of Joktan (Gen. 10:27; I Chron. 1:21); founded Uzal, capital of Yemen.

UZZA (ŭz'á, **strength**). 1. Son of Shimei (I Chron. 6:29). 2. Son of Ehud (I Chron. 8:7). 3. Owner or caretaker of garden in which Manasseh and Amon were buried (II Kings 21:18,26). 4. One whose children returned under Zerubbabel (Ezra 2: 49; Neh. 7:51).

UZZA, GARDEN OF, garden in which Manasseh and his son were buried (II Kings 21:18,26).

UZZAH (ŭz'á, **strength**), son of Abinadab; slain for touching the Ark to steady it when the oxen carrying it stumbled (II Sam. 6:3-8; I Chron. 13:6-11).

UZZEN-SHERAH (ŭz'ĕn-shĕ'ē-rá), town built by Ephraim's daughter Sheerah (I Chron. 7:24).

UZZI (ŭz'ī, strong). 1. Descendant of Aaron (I Chron. 6:5,51; Ezra 7:4). 2. Grandson of Issachar (I Chron. 7:2,3). 3. Benjamite (I Chron. 7:7). 4. Father of Elah (I Chron. 9:8). 5. Overseer of Levites (Neh. 11:22). 6. Priest in family of Jedaiah (Neh. 12:19).

UZZIAH (ŭ-zī'à, Jehovah is strength). 1. Son of Amaziah; 11th king of Judah (II Kings 14:21); ruled 52 years; successful king; struck with leprosy for burning incense to the Lord (II Chron. 26:16-21). 2. Kohathite Levite (I Chron. 6:24). 3. Father of Jehonathan (I Chron. 27:25). 4. Man who put away foreign wife (Ezra 10:16-21). 5. Father of man who returned after Exile (Neh. 11:4).

UZZIEL, UZZIELITE (ŭ-zī'ĕl, ŭ-zī'ĕl-īt, God is strength). 1. Kohathite Levite (Exod. 6:18,22; Lev. 10:4). 2. Son of Ishi; Simeonite (I Chron. 4:42). 3. Head of Benjamite family (I Chron. 7:7). 4. Son of Heman (I Chron. 25:4). 5. Levite who helped in cleansing temple (II Chron. 29:14-19). 6. Son of Harhaiah (Neh. 3:8). Anyone descended from Uzziel, the Levite, was known as an Uzzielite (Num. 3:27; I Chron. 26: 23; 15:10).

V

VAGABOND (to wander), word used in curse pronounced upon Cain (Gen. 4:12,14), imprecatory prayer of David (Ps. 109:10), and professional exorcists (Acts 19:13).

VAJEZATHA (và-jĕz'à-thà), son of Haman (Esth. 9:9).

VALE, VALLEY, low-lying ground; plain, ravine, gorge, a wadi (Deut. 34:6; Josh. 10:40; Luke 3:5).

VALLEY GATE, gate in Jerusalem walls (Neh. 2:13; 3:13; 12:31,38); location uncertain.

VANIAH (và-nī'à), man who divorced foreign wife (Ezra 10:36).

VANITY, emptiness, evanescence, worthlessness, futility, unprofitableness (Job 7:3; Ps. 39:5,6; I Sam. 12:21; II Kings 17:15; Eph. 4:17; II Pet. 2:18); never used in KJV in sense of conceit or undue self-esteem.

VASHNI (vàsh'nī, weak), eldest son of Samuel (I Chron. 6:28); in I Sam. 8:2 Joel is named as Samuel's first-born. The Hebrew text is probably corrupt here.

VASHTI (vàsh'tī, beautiful woman), wife of Ahasuerus; queen of Persia; divorced (Esth. 1:19).

VEIL. 1. Fabric used for concealment or for protection against elements (Gen. 24:65; I Cor. 11:4-16). 2. In tabernacle and temple a beautiful, hand-woven veil separated the holy place from the holy of holies (Exod. 26:31-37).

VEIN (source), mine (Job 28:1).

VENGEANCE, any punishment meted out in the sense of retribution (Judg. 15:7; Jer. 11:20; 20:12).

VENISON (game of any kind), any game taken in hunting (Gen. 25:28; 27:5ff).

VERMILION (vĕr-mil'yŭn), brilliant red color (Jer. 22:14; Ezek. 23:14).

VERSIONS OF THE SCRIPTURES (See Bible, also Texts and Versions).

VESSEL, any material thing which may be used for any purpose, whether it be a tool, implement, weapon, or receptacle (Hos. 13:15). In the NT it is sometimes applied to persons (Rom. 9:20-24; II Tim. 2:20,21).

VESTRY, place where royal or ceremonial vestments were kept (II Kings 10:22).

VESTURE, archaic word for garments (Gen. 41:42; Deut. 22:12; Ps. 22:18). Sometimes used metaphorically (Ps. 102:26; Heb. 1:12).

VIA DOLOROSA, traditional route which our Lord traveled on the day of His crucifixion from the judgment seat of Pilate to the place of His crucifixion (Matt. 27:26,31,33).

VIAL, flask or bottle (I Sam. 10:1); shallow bowl or basin (Rev. 5:8; 21:9).

VICTUAL (vit'l), food.

VILLAGE. Villages were usually grouped around a fortified town to which the people could flee in time of war (II Chron. 8:18).

VINE, trailing or climbing plant: grapes, melons, gourds (Num. 13:23f; Jonah 4:6ff). Grapes flourished in Palestine. See Plants.

VINEGAR, sour liquid obtained from acetous fermentation in wine or other strong drink; forbidden to Nazirites (Num. 6:3); offered to Jesus on cross (Mark 15:36; John 19:29), was different from "wine mixed with myrrh" that he had refused earlier (Mark 15:23).

VINEYARD. Soil of Palestine has always been very favorable to the cultivation of grapes (Num. 13:20,24); vineyards usually surrounded with a protecting wall to keep out animals and thieves (Num. 22:24); also had tower for watchman (Mark 12:1), winepress hollowed out of a flat rock, and a vat into which the wine flowed from the winepress (Isa. 1:8; 5:1-7; Matt. 21:33-41); gleanings left to the poor (Lev. 19:10); wine stored in new goatskin bags (Matt. 9:17) or in large pottery jars. Grapes were eaten fresh, made into jelly, dried into raisins or cakes for future eating (I Sam. 25:18), and made into wine. Pulp was placed in vat with water and allowed to ferment to make vinegar or poor grade of wine (Ps. 69:21; Matt. 27:48). Every seventh year the vines were allowed to lie fallow (Exod. 23:11; Lev. 25:3). Figuratively, the vine symbolized prosperity and peace (I Kings 4:25; Mic. 4:4; Zech. 3:10) and the chosen people Israel.

VINEYARDS, PLAIN OF THE, Abel-cheramim, village of the Ammonites E of Jordan (Judg. 11:33).

VIPER, any poisonous snake of the genus Vipera; used as a symbol of evil (Isa. 30:6; Matt. 12:34; Luke 3:7).

VIRGIN. 1. Young unmarried woman (Gen. 24:16; Exod. 22:16f). 2. Young woman of

marriageable age, whether married or not (Gen. 24:43; S. of Sol. 1:3; 6:8; Isa. 7:14).

VIRGIN BIRTH, the NT teaching that Jesus Christ entered into the stream of human life without the mediation of an earthly father, born not of sexual intercourse but as a result of the supernatural overshadowing of the Holy Spirit (Matt. 1:18-25; Luke 1:26-2:7).

VIRTUE, righteousness, goodness, chastity (Prov. 31:10f); power (Mark 5:30; Luke 6:19; 8:46).

VISION, sight presented to the mind through a dream, vision, or other nonobjective stimulus. Most visions in Scripture convey revelations from God. This is especially true of prophets (Dan. 10:7; Acts 9:7; 10:3).

VISITATION, divine visit for purpose of rewarding or punishing people for their deeds (Jer. 10:15; Luke 19:44; I Pet. 2:12).

VOPHSI (vŏf'si), spy from Naphtali (Num. 13:14).

VOW, voluntary promise to God to perform some service or do something pleasing to Him, in return for some hoped-for benefits (Gen. 28:20-22; Lev. 27:2,8; Num. 30:3; Judg. 11:30); or to abstain from certain things. Jesus condemns the abuse of vows (Matt. 15:4-6; Mark 7:10-13).

VULGATE, Latin version of the Bible, prepared by Jerome in 4th century.

VULTURE, name given to several kinds of large birds of prey, usually feeding on carrion; unclean for the Jews (Lev. 11:14; Deut. 14:13).

W

WADI (wä'dē), valley which forms the bed of a stream during the winter, but which dries up in hot season (Gen. 26:19).

WAFERS, thin cakes (Exod. 16:31; I Chron. 23:29).

WAGES, pay given for labor; in early times often paid in kind (Gen. 29:15,20; 30:28-34); Mosaic law required daily payment (Lev. 19:13; Deut. 24:14,15); withholding wages condemned (Jer. 22:13; Mal. 3:5; James 5:4).

WAGON, vehicle with wheels used for carrying goods as well as persons (Gen. 45: 19,21; 46:5).

WAIL, in ancient funeral processions wailing relatives and hired mourners and musicians preceded body to grave (Jer. 9:17-21; Amos 5:16; Matt. 9:23).

WALK, in NT used uniformly in figurative sense and refers to the whole manner of life and conduct (Eph. 2:2,10; 5:2,8,15) and the observance of laws or customs (Acts 21:21).

WALL. All over the East the walls of houses were built of sun-baked mud brick; stone little used; every ancient city had enormous walls surrounding it. Symbol of truth and strength (Jer. 15:20), protection (Zech. 2:5), salvation (Isa. 26:1).

WAR. For Israelites war had a religious significance; priests often accompanied Israel's armies into battle; battles were begun with sacrificial rites (I Sam. 7:8-10; 13:9), and after consulting the divine oracle (Judg. 20:18ff; I Sam. 14:37); blowing of trumpet throughout land announced call to arms (Judg. 3:27). Weapons included slings, spears, javelins, bows and arrows, swords, and battering-rams. Strategical movements included ambush (Josh. 8:3ff), feint (Judg. 20:20ff), flank movement (II Sam. 5:22f), surprise attack (Josh. 11:1f), raid (I Chron. 14:9), foray (II Sam. 3:22), foraging to secure supplies (II Sam. 23:11). Wars sometimes settled by single combat (I Kings 11:15). Prisoners sold into slavery or killed (Deut. 20:16-18; Amos 1:6,9); booty equally divided (I Sam. 30:24,25).

WASHING, frequent bathing necessary in Bible lands; hands washed before meals, feet after journey (Gen. 18:4; Exod. 30: 19,21; Judg. 19:21).

WATCH, man or group of men set to guard a city, crops, etc. (Neh. 4:9; Matt. 27:62-66).

WATCHES OF THE NIGHT, divisions into which hours of the night were divided. Jews had a threefold division; Romans, fourfold (Judg. 7:19; Mark 6:48).

WATCHMAN, one who guards a city or headquarters of an army (I Sam. 14:16; II Sam. 18:24-27).

WATER. Because of its scarcity in Palestine, it is much appreciated; absence of water very serious (I Kings 17:1ff; Jer. 14:3); rivers mostly small; people dependent upon springs and fountains; cisterns a necessity; drinking water carried in goatskins and often sold in streets. Water used for ceremonial washings (Lev. 11:32; 16:4; Num. 19:7). Used as symbol of cleansing of the soul from sin (Ezek. 16:4,9; 36:25; John 3:5).

WATER OF BITTERNESS, water mingled with dust which a woman suspected of unfaithfulness was expected to drink to prove her innocence (Num. 5:12-31).

WATER OF JEALOUSY (See Water of Bitterness).

WATER OF SEPARATION, water for removal of impurity (Num. 19:9,13,20,21; 31:23).

WATERPOT, earthen jars for carrying or holding water (John 4:28).

WATERSPOUT, cataract (Ps. 42:7).

WAVE OFFERING, sacrificial portion waved before the Lord.

WAY, often used metaphorically to describe conduct or manner of life (Exod. 32:8; Deut. 5:33). In NT, God's plan of salvation (Matt. 3:3), Christianity or Judaism (Acts 9:2; 19:9; 22:4).

WAYFARING MAN, traveler (Judg. 19:17; II Sam. 12:4; Isa. 33:8; 35:8).

WEALTH, abundance of possessions whether material, social, or spiritual. In early history of Israel wealth consisted largely of flocks and herds, silver and gold, brass, iron, and clothing (Josh. 22:8). God taught Israel that He was the giver of their wealth

(Deut. 8:18); taught them to be liberal (Prov. 11:24). Jesus did not condemn wealth, but stressed the handicap of wealth to one wanting to enter the kingdom of God (Matt. 19:24; Luke 16:19-31).

WEAN, WEANING, to wean is to accustom a child to depend upon other food than its mother's milk; celebrated by a feast (Gen. 21:8) and with an offering (I Sam. 1:24).

WEAPON (See Arms, Armor).

WEASEL, a small, carnivorous animal, allied to the ferret; for Israelites, unclean (Lev. 11:29).

WEATHER. There is no Hebrew word corresponding to "weather," but the Israelites were keenly aware of weather phenomena. The great topographical diversity of Palestine assures a variety of weather on a given day: on the top of Mt. Hermon (9,000 feet above sea level) there is snow on the ground the year round; while at Jericho in summer (1300 feet below sea level) the heat is very oppressive, and the region around the Dead Sea (1290 feet below sea level) is intolerable. On the coast even the hottest summer day is made bearable by refreshing breezes from the Mediterranean.

WEAVING, known in very early times; Jabal, an antediluvian, is called "the father of such as dwell in tents and have cattle" (Gen. 4:20), implying that the weaving of cloth for tents was then known; cloth made into garments, tents, curtains for shrines, etc.; Paul; Aquilla, and Priscilla did weaving (Acts 18:2,3); guilds of weavers existed in NT times; materials used for weaving included sheep's wool, goats' hair, camels' hair, flax, hemp, and ramie.

WEDDING, a joyous occasion, celebrated with music, feasting, drinking of wine, joking; after the Exile written contracts were drawn up and sealed; bridegroom went to bride's home with friends and escorted her to his own house (Matt. 25:7); festive apparel expected of guests; festivities lasted one or two weeks (Gen. 29:27; Judg. 14:12).

WEDGE, literally "tongue" (Josh. 7:21,24). Occurrence of word in Isa. 13:12 is an error. ASV properly renders "golden wedge" as "pure gold."

WEEDS (See Plants).

WEEK (See Calendar; Time).

WEEKS, FEAST OF, Pentecost, celebrated 50 days after sheaf waving on 16th Nisan (Exod. 34:18-26).

WEIGHTS AND MEASURES. Balances used for scales (Lev. 19:36; Prov. 16:11) and stones for weights (Lev. 19:36). Some Biblical measures: 1. **Liquid.** Log equals 2/3 pint; hin equals 12 logs, or one gallon; bath equals six hins, or six gallons; cor equals 10 baths, or 60 gallons. 2. **Dry.** Cab equals two plus pints; omer equals 1-4/5 cabs, or four pints; seah equals 3-1/3 omers, or 1/5 bushel; ephah equals three seahs, or 3/5 bushel; homer equals 10 ephahs, or 6-1/4 bushels.

3. **Length.** Finger equals ¾ inches; palm equals four fingers, or three inches; span equals three palms, or nine inches; cubit equals two spans, or 18 inches; fathom equals four cubits, or six feet; furlong equals ⅛ mile. 4. **Weights.** Gerah equals nine grains; beqa equals 10 gerahs, or 88 grains; shekel equals two beqas, or .4 ounces; talent equals 60 manehs, or 75.5 pounds.

WELL, hole dug in earth down to watertable, and usually surrounded by a wall of stone; at times cause of strife (Gen. 21:25); sometimes owned in common (Gen. 29:2,3); digging of new wells an occasion for rejoicing; sometimes clogged by enemies (Gen. 26:15,16).

WEST, used figuratively with "east" to denote great distance (Ps. 103:12).

WHALE. 1. Any large sea animal (Gen. 1:21; Ezek. 32:2). 2. Sea monster (Matt. 12:40). Great fish in Jonah 1:17.

WHEAT, most commonly used for flour, but other grains used in emergency or by the poor (Ezek. 4:9,10); ground between stones.

WHEELS, with spokes were early known (Exod. 14:25); potters' wheels (Jer. 18:3); cistern wheels (Eccles. 12:6).

WHELP, the young of a dog or a beast of prey; a cub (Gen. 49:9; Deut. 33:22; Jer. 51:38; Nah. 2:11,12).

WHIP, generally a lash attached to a handle; figurative use (I Kings 12:14).

WHIRLWIND, any violent wind, not necessarily a whirling one (Ezek. 1:4; Hos. 8:7; James 3:4); figurative use (Prov. 1:27; Isa. 5:28; Jer. 4:13).

WHORE, prostitute or harlot; whoredom, a capital crime (Gen. 38:24); often used figuratively for apostasy and idolatry (Exod. 34:15f; Lev. 17:7; Deut. 31:16; Judg. 2:17; I Chron. 5:25; Hos. 1:2).

WIDOWS, protected by Law (Exod. 22:22; Deut. 27:19; Ps. 94:6; Ezek. 22:7; Mal. 3:5); shared in tithe of the third year (Deut. 14:29; 26:12); had other special rights (Deut. 16:11,14; 24:19-21); permitted to engage in levirate marriage (Deut. 25:5,6; Matt. 22:23-30); wore special garb (Gen. 38:14,19); taken care of by church in apostolic times (Acts 6:1; James 1:27; I Tim. 5:4,9,10).

WIFE (See Family, Marriage).

WILDERNESS, either a barren desert or an uncultivated region suitable for pasturage and occupied by nomads; an empty waste (Job 24:5; Mal. 1:3; Matt. 14:13; Heb. 11:38).

WILLOW, type of tree growing along brook or near water; several species in Palestine; symbol of joy (Lev. 23:40; Job 40:22), sorrow (Ps. 137:2).

WILLOWS, BROOK OF THE, brook on boundary of Moab (Isa. 15:7).

WILLS, statements, oral or written in form, to which law courts give effect, by which property may be disposed of after death (Heb. 9:16,17).

WINDOW, in Palestine window openings were narrow, high up in walls, and usually fitted with latticework (Judg. 5:28; II Kings 1:2;

Prov. 7:6).

WINDS. In Palestine E wind is stormy, wrecks ships, withers growing things (Gen. 41:6; Ps. 48:7); N wind brings rain, is refreshing, or stormy (Prov. 25:23 RSV); S wind brings heat (Luke 12:55), helps growth (Ps. 78:26; Job 37:17); W wind brings rain (I Kings 18:43-45; Ps. 148:8). Also used symbolically for transiency of life (Job 7:7) and of the wicked (Prov. 10:25); disorder of war (Jer. 18:17).

WINE, priests forbidden to drink wine on duty (Lev. 10:9); Nazirites could not touch it (Num. 6:3,20); abuse of wine condemned (Prov. 4:17; 31:4,5). In OT times wine not diluted; in NT times mixed with much water. Used as medicine (I Tim. 5:23). Over-indulgence warned against (I Tim. 3:8; Titus 2:3). Jesus made water into wine at Cana (John 2:2-11); "fruit of the vine" used in Last Supper (Matt. 26:29).

WINEPRESS, trough, usually of stone, in which grapes were pressed by men treading them, and from which juice flowed into vat (Judg. 6:11; Neh. 13:15; Isa. 63:2,3); figurative use (Lam. 1:15; Rev. 14:19,20).

WINESKIN, made of tanned whole skins of animals (Matt. 9:17).

WING, often used figuratively (Ps. 18:10; 55:6; 68:13; Prov. 23:5; Matt. 23:37).

WINNOWING, separating kernels of threshed grain from chaff; done by shaking bunches of grain into breeze-stirred air so that the kernels fall to the ground, while the chaff is blown away by the wind (Ruth 3:2; Isa. 30:24).

WINTER, in Palestine is usually short and mild, but in higher regions brings snow and hail (Gen. 8:22; Ps. 74:17; Zech. 14:8).

WINTERHOUSE. The wealthy had separate residences for hot and cold seasons (Amos 3:15).

WISDOM, attribute of God (Prov. 3:19); in Hebrew thought characterized by such virtues as industry, honesty, sobriety, chastity, concern for good reputation; includes technical skill (Exod. 28:3), military prowess (Isa. 10:13), shrewdness (I Kings 2:6); given to men through fear of the Lord (Ps. 111:10; Job 28:28); personified (Prov. 8; Matt. 11:19); Jesus is wisdom (I Cor. 1:30; Col. 2:2,3); wisdom of believers contrasted with wisdom of world (I Cor. 1:19-26).

WISDOM OF JESUS, SON OF SIRACH (See Apocrypha).

WISDOM OF SOLOMON (See Apocrypha).

WISE MEN. 1. Men of understanding and skill in ordinary affairs (Prov. 1:5; Job 15:2; Ps. 49:10); came to be recognized as a distinct class, listed with priests and prophets in Jer. 18:18, and also found outside Palestine (Gen. 41:8; Exod. 7:11; Dan. 2:12-5:15). 2. The magi (Matt. 2:1ff); astrologers; came from East; number and names are legendary.

WITCH, one (usually a woman) in league with evil spirits who practices the black art of witchcraft; condemned by law (Exod.

22:18; Deut. 18:9-14; I Sam. 28:3,9; II Kings 23:24; Isa. 8:19; Acts 19:18,19).

WITHE, strong, flexible willow or other twig (Judg. 16:7-9).

WITHERED HAND, hand wasted away through some form of atrophy (Mark 3:1-6).

WITNESS, one who may be called to testify to an event at which he was present; things may be witnesses (Gen. 31:44-52; Deut. 31:19-21,26; Josh. 22:27-34; Isa. 19:20); bearing false witness condemned (Exod. 20:16; Deut. 5:20); disciples of Christ witness to Him (John 15:27).

WITNESS OF THE SPIRIT, direct, immediate, personal communication by the Holy Spirit that we are children of God (Rom. 8:15,16) or some other truth (Acts 20:23; I Tim. 4:1).

WIZARD, magician or sorcerer, male or female (Lev. 19:31; 20:6,27; I Sam. 28:3,9; Isa. 8:19).

WOLF, figuratively, of the wicked (Ezek. 22:27; Matt. 10:16); false teachers (Matt. 7:15; Acts 20:29).

WOMAN, created by God as helpmeet of man (Gen. 2:18-24); in OT times often tireless drudges; primary function in Biblical times that of wife and mother; Hebrew legislation protected (Deut. 15:12; 23:17; 24:1-5,17); Jesus showed sympathy for women (Matt. 9:18-26; Luke 10:38-42); women prominent in early church as prophetesses, deaconesses, teachers, fellow workers with apostles; first convert in Europe a woman (Acts 16:13-15).

WOOL, fleece of sheep and some other animals; mixing wool and linen forbidden (Lev. 19:19; Deut. 22:11).

WORD, WORD OF THE LORD, usually the will, purpose, or plan of God revealed to individuals through visions (Gen. 15:1), theophanies (Gen. 18:1f), a voice (I Sam. 3:4); came through patriarchs (Gen. 15:1), Moses (Exod. 4:30); prophets (Num. 22:38; Isa. 1:10); Jesus Christ (John 1:1; I John 1:1; Rev. 19:13; Heb. 1:2); apostles.

WORLD. 1. Universe (John 1:10). 2. Human race (Ps. 9:8; 96:13; Acts 17:31). 3. Unregenerate humanity (John 15:18; I John 2:15). 4. Roman Empire (Luke 2:1).

WORM, creeping, boneless animal (Exod. 16:24; Isa. 51:8; Acts 12:23); used metaphorically of man's insignificance (Job 25:6; Isa. 41:14).

WORMWOOD, bitter plant which grows in wastelands (Deut. 29:18); symbolic of bitter experience (Prov. 5:4).

WORSHIP (bow down, to prostrate, do obeisance to), the honor, reverence, and homage paid to superior beings or powers, whether men, angels, or God; used especially of divine honors paid to a deity; when given to God, involves acknowledgement of divine perfections; may be private or public, involving a cultus. Four stages of development in Bible: patriarchs worshipped by building altars and sacrificing (Gen. 12:7,8; 13:4); organized worship in Temple ritual, with complex ritual and system of sacrifices; synagogue, which began during Exile; Christian, consisting of preaching (Acts 20:7), reading of Scripture (James 1:22), prayer (I Tim. 2:8), singing (Eph. 5:19), baptism and Lord's Supper (Acts 2:41; I Cor. 11:18-34), and almsgiving (I Cor. 16:1,2).

WRATH. 1. Anger of men (Gen. 30:2; I Sam. 17:28); may be evil (II Cor. 12:20) or reaction to evil (I Sam. 20:34); work of the flesh (Gal. 5:20). 2. Anger of God – reaction of righteous God against sinful people and evil in all forms (Deut. 9:7; Isa. 13:9; Rom. 1:18; Eph. 5:6; Rev. 14:10,19).

WRESTLE. To contend by grappling with an opponent (Gen. 32:24,25); used figuratively (Gen. 30:8; Eph. 6:12).

WRITING, invented in Mesopotamia, probably by Sumerians, at least as early as 2500 B. C.; they had a primitive, nonalphabetic linear writing, not phonetic but pictographic, ideas being recorded by means of pictures or sense-symbols, rather than by sound-symbols. The next stage in the history of writing was the introduction of the phonogram, or the type of sign which indicates a sound, and afterward came alphabetic scripts. Egyptians first developed an alphabetic system of writing. Hebrews derived their alphabet from Phoenicians. Semitic writing dating between 1900 and 1500 B. C. has been found at Serabit el-Khadim in Sinai. Greeks received their alphabet from Phoenicians and Aramaeans. Writing first mentioned in Bible in Exod. 17:14. Ten Commandments written with finger of God (Exod. 31:18; 32:15,16). Ancient writing materials: clay, wax, wood, metal, plaster (Deut. 27:2,3; Josh. 8:32; Luke 1:63); later, parchment (II Tim. 4:13) and papyrus (II John 12). Instruments of writing: reed, on papyrus and parchment; stylus, on hard material (Exod. 32:4).

X

XERXES (zûrk′sĕz), king of Persian Empire from 486-465 B. C.; same as Ahasuerus, mentioned in Ezra, Esther and Daniel.

Y

YAHWEH (yä′wĕ) (See YHWH below).

YARMUK, WADI EL, stream six miles SE of Sea of Galilee flowing into Jordan; marked S boundary of kingdom of Bashan.

YARN, found in KJV of I Kings 10:28 and II Chron. 1:16; correctly rendered in RSV by the proper name "Kue," the old Assyrian name given to Cilicia, in SE Asia Minor.

YEAR (See Calendar).

YHWH (Yăhwĕh), the Hebrew name for God, Jehovah; known as tetragrammaton, four consonants standing for ancient Hebrew name for God, Yahweh.

YODH (yŏd), 10th letter of Hebrew alphabet, pronounced much like English "y."

YOKE, wooden frame for joining two draft animals; a wooden bar held on neck by thongs around neck (Num. 19:2; Deut. 21:3). Yoke of oxen is a pair (I Sam. 14:14; Luke 14:19). Often used figuratively to denote subjection (I Kings 12:4,9-11; Isa. 9:4); removal of yoke denotes deliverance (Gen. 27:40; Jer. 2:20; Matt. 11:29,30).

YOKEFELLOW (yoked together), person united to another by close bonds, as in marriage or labor (Phil. 4:3).

YOM KIPPUR, Hebrew for "Day of Atonement." (See Feasts).

Z

ZAANAIM (zā′a-nā′ĭm), probably same as Zaanannim in Josh. 19:33, c. three miles NE of Mount Tabor (Judg. 4:11); modern Khan et-Tujjar.

ZAANAN (zā′a-năn), place in Shephelah of Judah (Micah 1:11), site uncertain.

ZAANANNIM (See Zaanaim).

ZAAVAN (zā′a-văn), son of Ezer (Gen. 36:27; I Chron. 1:42).

ZABAD (zā′băd, Jehovah has given). 1. Son of Nathan (I Chron. 2:36). 2. Son of Shimeath; conspired against King Joash; killed by Amaziah (II Chron. 24:26). 3. Ephraimite (I Chron. 7:21). 4-6. Three Israelites who put away foreign wives (Ezra 10:27,33,43).

ZABBAI (zăb′ā-ĭ). 1. Man who put away foreign wife (Ezra 10:28). 2. Father of Baruch (Neh. 3:20).

ZABBUD (zăb′ŭd), man who accompanied Ezra to Jerusalem (Ezra 8:14).

ZABDI (zăb′dĭ, God has given). 1. Achan's grandfather (Josh. 7:1,17). 2. Benjamite (I Chron. 8:19). 3. Man in charge of David's wine cellars (I Chron. 27:27). 4. Ancestor of Mattaniah (Neh. 11:17).

ZABDIEL (zăb′dĭ-ĕl, God has given). 1. Father of Jashobeam (I Chron. 27:2).

ZABUD (zā′bŭd), son of Nathan (I Kings 4:5).

ZABULON (See Zebulun).

ZACCAI (zăk′ā-ī), ancestral head of family that returned with Zerubbabel (Neh. 7:14; Ezra 2:9).

ZACCHAEUS (ză-kē′ŭs, pure), chief publican; climbed sycamore tree to see Jesus, and became His disciple (Luke 19:8).

ZACCUR (zăk′ûr, remembered). 1. Father of Reubenite spy, Shammua (Num. 13:4). 2. Simeonite (I Chron. 4:26), "Zacchur" in KJV. 3. Son of Merari (I Chron. 24:27). 4. Son of Asaph; musician (I Chron. 25:1,2; Neh. 12:35). 5. Son of Imri who helped rebuild walls of Jerusalem (Neh. 3:2). 6. Man who sealed covenant with Nehemiah (Neh. 10:12). 7. Father of Hanan (Neh. 13:13).

ZACCHUR (See Zaccur).

ZACHARIAH (zăk'a-rī'á, Jehovah has remembered), 14th king of Israel; last of the house of Jehu; slain by Shallum his successor (II Kings 10:30; 15:8-10).

ZACHARIAS (zăk'a-rī'ás, Jehovah has remembered). 1. Father of John the Baptist (Luke 1:5); righteous priest; angel announced to him he would have a son (Luke 1:5-80). 2. Son of Barachias; slain between altar and temple (Matt. 23:35; Luke 11:51).

ZACHER (zā'kēr), son of Jehiel (I Chron. 8:31; 9:37).

ZADOK (zā'dŏk, righteous), 1. Son of Ahitub; priest who helped David (II Sam. 8:17; I Chron. 12:28); helped bring ark to Jerusalem (I Chron. 15:11-13); supported David against Absalom (II Sam. 15:24-36; 17:15); made high priest by Solomon (I Kings 2:35). 2. Father of Shallum (I Chron. 6:12). 3. Father of Jerusha (II Kings 15:33; II Chron. 27:1). 4. Man who aided in constructing walls of Jerusalem (Neh. 3:4; 10:1). 5. Son of Immer; also aided in rebuilding walls (Neh. 3:29). 6. Scribe (Neh. 13:13). May be same as 5 or 6.

ZAHAM (zā'hăm), son of Rehoboam (II Chron. 11:19).

ZAIR (zā'ir), village E of Dead Sea where Joran smote Edomites (II Kings 8:21).

ZALAPH (zā'lăf), father of man who aided Nehemiah repair walls (Neh. 3:30).

ZALMON (zăl'mŏn, dark). 1. One of David's mighty men (II Sam. 23:28), called "Ilai" in I Chron. 11:29. 2. Forest near Shechem (Judg. 9:48).

ZALMONAH (zăl-mōn'á), encampment of Israelites in wilderness, SE of Edom (Num. 33:41,42).

ZALMUNNA (zăl-mŭn'á), king of Midian killed by Gideon (Judg. 8:4-21; Ps. 83:11).

ZAMZUMMIM (zăm-zŭm'im, murmurers), race of giants (Deut. 2:20); lived E of Jordan; called Rephaim (II Sam. 5:18,22); may be same as "Zuzims" (Gen. 14:5).

ZANOAH (zá-nō'á, rejected). 1. Town in Shephelah of Judah (Josh. 15:34); identified with Khirbet Zanu', 10 miles W of Jerusalem. 2. Town in mountains of Judah, 10 or 12 miles SW of Hebron (Josh. 15:56); identified with Zenuta.

ZAPHENATH-PANEAH (zăf'ē-năth-pà-nē'á, one who furnishes the sustenance of the land), name given to Joseph by Pharaoh (Gen. 41:45).

ZAPHON (zā'fŏn), territory E of Jordan assigned to Gad (Josh. 13:27); modern Amateh.

ZARA (zā'rá), Greek for Hebrew Zerah, mentioned in ancestry of Christ (Matt. 1:3).

ZAREAH (See Zorah).

ZAREATHITE (See Zorah).

ZARED (See Zered).

ZAREDA (See Zarethan).

ZAREPHATH (zăr'ē-făth, refinement), town eight miles S of Sidon, 14 miles N of Tyre (I Kings 17:9,10; Luke 4:26); ruins survive S of modern Sarafand.

ZARETHAN (zăr'ē-thăn), place near Bethshean and Adam (Josh. 3:16); KJV has "Zaretan;" "Zeredah" in II Chron. 4:17. Exact site not ascertained.

ZARETH-SHAHAR (zā'rēth-shā'hàr), city in Reuben (Josh. 13:19); not identified.

ZARHITES, THE (zăr'hits), descendants of Zerah, son of Judah (Num. 26:13,20; Josh. 7:17; I Chron. 27:11,13).

ZARTANAH (zàr-tā'ná), city in Jordan valley (I Kings 4:12); location uncertain.

ZARTHAN (zăr'thăn). 1. Place between Succoth and Zarthan (I Kings 7:46); "Zeredathah" in II Chron. 4:17. 2. Place of uncertain location (Josh. 3:16).

ZATTHU (See Zattu).

ZATTU (zā'tū), head of family that returned with Zerubbabel (Neh. 10:14; Ezra 10:27).

ZAVAN (See Zaavan).

ZAZA (zā'zá), Jerahmelite (I Chron. 2:33).

ZEALOT (zĕl'ŭt, zealous one), member of Jewish patriotic party started to resist Roman aggression; violent; fanatical; Simon the Zealot, an apostle (Luke 6:15; Acts 1:13).

ZEBADIAH (zĕb'a-dī'á, Jehovah has bestowed). 1. Benjamite (I Chron. 8:15). 2. Another Benjamite (I Chron. 8:17). 3. Ambidextrous Benjamite soldier of David (I Chron. 12:1,2,7). 4. Korahite door keeper (I Chron. 26:2). 5. Son of Asahel (I Chron. 27:7). 6. Levite sent by Jehoshaphat to teach law to residents of Judah (II Chron. 17:8). 7. Son of Ishmael; head of Jehoshaphat's affairs (II Chron. 19:11). 8. Son of Michael; returned with Ezra (Ezra 8:8). 9. Son of Immer; priest who divorced foreign wife (Ezra 10:20).

ZEBAH (zē'bá, sacrifice), king of Midian defeated and slain by Gideon (Judg. 8:10,12, 18,21; Ps. 83:11).

ZEBAIM (zē-bā'im, gazelles), native dwelling place of "sons of Pochereth" who returned with Zerubbabel (Ezra 2:57; Neh. 7:59).

ZEBEDEE (zĕb'ē-dē), father of James and John (Matt. 4:21; Mark 1:19; fisherman; husband of Salome (Matt. 27:56; Mark 15:40).

ZEBINA (zē-bī'ná), man who put away foreign wife (Ezra 10:43).

ZEBOIIM, ZEBOIM (zē-boi'im, zē-bŏ'im). 1. City in vale of Siddim destroyed with Sodom and Gomorrah (Gen. 10:19; 14:2,8; Deut. 29:23; Hos. 11:8). 2. Ravine in Benjamin not far from Michmash (I Sam. 13:18; Neh. 11:34).

ZEBOIM, VALLEY OF (zē-bŏ'im), see under Zeboiim, No. 2.

ZEBUDAH (zē-bū'dá, given), Josiah's wife; mother of Jehoiakim (II Kings 23:36).

ZEBUL (zē'bŭl, dwelling), ruler of Shechem (Judg. 9:28,30,38); adviser to Abimelech.

ZEBULONITE (See Zebulun).

ZEBULUN (zĕb'û-lŭn, habitation). 1. Son of Leah and Jacob (Gen. 30:19,20). 2. Tribe of Israel springing from Zebulun; assigned to area between Sea of Galilee and Mediterranean; Christ carried on ministry there (Matt. 4:12-16). 3. City in Asher between

Bethdagon and valley of Jiphthahel (Josh. 19:27).

ZEBULUNITE (See Zebulun).

ZECHARIAH (zĕkʹa̍-rīʹȧ, Jehovah remembers). 1. Reubenite chief (I Chron. 5:7). 2. Korhite, son of Meshelemiah (I Chron. 9:21; 26:2,14). 3. Benjamite (I Chron. 9:37). 4. Levite; musician (I Chron. 15:20; 16:5). 5. Priest; trumpeter (I Chron. 15:24). 6. Levite (I Chron. 24:25). 7. Merarite Levite (I Chron. 26:11). 8. Manassite chief; father of Iddo (I Chron. 27:21). 9. Prince who taught in cities of Judah (II Chron. 17:7). 10. Father of prophet Jahaziel (II Chron. 20:14). 11. Son of Jehoshaphat; killed by Jehoram (II Chron. 21:2-4). 12. Son of Jehoiada, the high priest; stoned (II Chron. 24:20-22). 13. Prophet in reign of Uzziah (II Chron. 26:5). 14. Father of Abijah (II Chron. 29:1). 15. Levite; son of Asaph (II Chron. 29:13). 16. Kohathite who assisted in repair of temple in days of Josiah (II Chron. 34:12). 17. Temple ruler (II Chron. 35:8). 18. Man who returned with Ezra (Ezra 8:3). 19. Another man who returned with Ezra (Ezra 8:11). 20. Adviser of Ezra (Neh. 8:4; Ezra 8:15,16). 21. Man who divorced foreign wife (Ezra 10:26). 22. Judahite (Neh. 11:4). 23. Another Judahite (Neh. 11:5). 24. Son of Pashhur; aided rebuilding of walls (Neh. 11:12). 25. Son of Iddo; priest (Neh. 12:16). 26. Priest; son of Jonathan; trumpeter (Neh. 12:35,41). 27. Son of Jeberechiah (Isa. 8:2). 28. Prophet; son of Berechiah and grandson of Iddo (Zech. 1:1); returned with Zerubbabel; contemporary with Haggai.

ZECHARIAH, BOOK OF. The author a contemporary of Haggai; began to prophecy in 520 B.C.; deals with destiny of God's people. Contents: 1. Series of eight symbolic night-visions (1-6). 2. Prophecies spoken two years later than the above; exhortations and warnings (7,8). 3. Judgment and mercy; the coming day of the Lord (9-14).

ZEDAD (zēʹdăd), city on N boundary of Palestine (Num. 34:8; Ezek. 47:15).

ZEDEKIAH (zĕdʹḗ-kīȧ, Jehovah is righteous). 1. Son of Chanaanah, leader of 400 false prophets during reign of Ahab (I Kings 22:19-24; II Chron. 18:10). 2. Last king of Judah; son of Josiah and Hamutal (II Kings 24:18); made king by Nebuchadnezzar, but rebelled and was severely punished (II Kings 24:20; 25:1-7). 3. Son of Jeconiah (I Chron. 3:16). 4. Son of Maaseiah; false prophet among Jews in Babylon (Jer. 29:21-23). 5. Son of Hananiah; prince of Israel (Jer. 36:12). 6. High official who sealed covenant with Nehemiah, translated Zidkijah (Neh. 10:1).

ZEEB (zēʹĕb, wolf), prince of Midian slain by Gideon's men (Judg. 7:25).

ZELAH (zēʹlȧ), town in Benjamin; site of family sepulchre of Saul (II Sam. 21:14).

ZELEK (zēʹlĕk), Ammonite; one of David's mighty men (II Sam. 23:37; I Chron. 11:39).

ZELOPHEHAD (zĕ-lōʹfē-hȧd), Manassite who

had five daughters but no sons; this led to law of female inheritance (Num. 27: 1-11; 36:1-12).

ZELOTES (See Zealot).

ZELZAH (zĕlʹzȧ), town in S border of Benjamin (I Sam. 10:2).

ZEMARAIM (zĕmʹȧ-rāʹĭm). 1. Town c. four miles N of Jericho assigned to tribe of Benjamin (Josh. 18:22). 2. Mountain in Ephraim upon which King Abijah rebuked King Jeroboam (II Chron. 13:4).

ZEMARITES (zĕmʹȧ-rīts), tribe of Canaanites (Gen. 10:18).

ZEMIRA (zḗ-mīʹrȧ), grandson of Benjamin (I Chron. 7:8).

ZENAN (zēʹnȧn), place in lowland of Judah (Josh. 15:37); same as Zaanan (Micah 1:11).

ZENAS (zēʹnȧs), Christian lawyer in Crete (Titus 3:13).

ZEPHANIAH (zĕfʹȧ-nīʹȧ, hidden of Jehovah). 1. Ancestor of prophet Samuel (I Chron. 6:36). 2. Author of book of Zephaniah (Zeph. 1:1); of royal descent; principal work done in Josiah's reign; contemporaries were Nahum and Habakkuk. 3. Priest, son of Maaseiah (II Kings 25:18-21; Jer. 21:1); slain by Nebuchadnezzar. 4. Father of a Josiah to whom God sent the prophet Zechariah (Zech. 6:10).

ZEPHANIAH, BOOK OF, 9th of the Minor Prophets and the last before the 70 years' captivity of Judah; denounced evils of his time; prophecy dated in reign of Josiah (639-608 B. C.). Outline: 1. Judgment on Judah and Jerusalem (1-2:3). 2. Judgment on Philistia, Moab, Ammon, Assyria (2:4-15). 3. Judgment on Jerusalem (3:1-8). 4. Effects of judgment (3:9-13). 5. Restoration of Israel (3:14-20).

ZEPHATH (zēʹfăth), Canaanite city c. 22 miles SW of S end of Dead Sea; destroyed by tribes of Judah and Simeon and renamed "Hormah" (Judg. 1:17).

ZEPHATHAH (zĕfʹȧ-thȧ), valley near Mareshah in W part of Judah (II Chron. 14:10).

ZEPHI (zēʹfī), grandson of Esau (I Chron. 1:36); "Zepho" in Gen. 36:11,15.

ZEPHO (See Zephi).

ZEPHON (zēʹfŏn), Gadite from whom family of Zephonites descended (Num. 26:15); "Ziphion" in Gen. 46:16.

ZEPHONITES (See Zepho).

ZER (zēr), city NW of Lake Galilee (Josh. 19:35), assigned to Naphtali.

ZERAH (zēʹrȧ, rising). 1. Son of Judah (Gen. 38:30); Zarhites descended from him (Num. 26:20). 2. Cousin of preceding; son of Simeon (Num. 26:13). 3. Gershonite Levite (I Chron. 6:21). 4. Another Gershonite Levite, but later (I Chron. 6:41). 5. Grandson of Esau through Reuel (Gen. 36:13,17). 6. Father of Jobab (Gen. 36:33). 7. King of Ethiopia (II Chron. 14:9); defeated in battle by Asa.

ZERAHIAH (zĕr-ȧ-hīʹȧ, Jehovah is risen). 1. Levite in ancestry of Ezra (I Chron. 6:6,51). 2. Leader of 200 who returned with Ezra (Ezra 8:4).

ZERED (zēʹrĕd), valley between Moab and

Edom; encampment of Israel in wilderness wanderings (Num. 21:12, KJV has "Zared;" Deut. 2:13,14).

ZEREDA (zĕr-ĕ′dȧ), birthplace of Jeroboam of Ephraim (I Kings 11:26); site unknown.

ZEREDATHAH (See Zarthan).

ZERERATH (zĕr′ĕ-răth), part of valley of Jezreel to which Midianites fled from Gideon (Judg. 7:22).

ZERESH (zē′rĕsh, **golden**), wife of Haman the Agagite (Esth. 5:10,14; 6:13).

ZERETH (zē′rĕth), early descendant of Judah through Helah (I Chron. 4:7).

ZERI (zē′rī), son of Jeduthun; musician (I Chron. 25:3).

ZEROR (zē′rŏr), Benjamite; great-grandfather of King Saul (I Sam. 9:1).

ZERQA (zĕr′kȧ), modern name for ancient river Jabbok. Also "Zerka."

ZERUAH (zē-roō′ȧ), widow of Nebat, father of King Jeroboam of Israel (I Kings 11:26).

ZERUBBABEL (zĕ-rŭb′ȧ-bĕl, **shoot of Babylon**), son of Shealtiel; grandson of King Jehoiachin (Ezra 3:2; Hag. 1:1; Matt. 1:12); appointed governor of Judah by Cyrus (Ezra 1:1,11; 5:14); rebuilt temple (Hag. 1:12-2:4).

ZERUIAH (zĕr′ōō-ī′ȧ), sister of David and mother of Joab, Abishai and Asahel (II Sam. 17:25).

ZETHAM (zē′thăm), Gershonite Levite; son of Ladan (I Chron. 23:8).

ZETHAN (zē′thăn), Benjamite; son of Jediael (I Chron. 7:10).

ZETHAR (zē′thȧr), chamberlain of Xerxes (Esth. 1:10).

ZEUS (zūs), chief of Greek gods, corresponding to Roman Jupiter (Acts 14:12,13; 19:35). See also RSV.

ZIA (zī′ȧ), early Gadite (I Chron. 5:13).

ZIBA (zī′bȧ, **plant**), member of Saul's household staff (II Sam. 9:2); appointed by David to work for Mephibosheth; slandered Mephibosheth (II Sam. 19:24-30).

ZIBEON (zĭb′ē-ŭn), Hivite; grandfather of Aholibama, wife of Esau (Gen. 36:2,14).

ZIBIA (zĭb′ĭ-ȧ), early descendant of Benjamin (I Chron. 8:9).

ZIBIAH (zĭb′ĭ-ȧ), woman of Beersheba who married King Ahaziah; mother of King Joash (II Kings 12:1; II Chron. 24:1).

ZIDDIM (zĭd′ĭm), fortified city of Naphtali, c. 1-1/2 miles N of Horns of Hattin (Josh. 19:35).

ZIDKIJAH (See Zedekiah).

ZIDON (zī′dŏn, **fishery**), in KJV usually Zidon in OT, and always Sidon in NT; Canaanite city 22 miles N of Tyre (Gen. 10:15,19); chief gods were Baal and Ashtoreth (I Kings 11:5,33; II Kings 23:13); father of Jezebel a king of Zidon (I Kings 16:31); modern Saida.

ZIDONIANS (See Zidon).

ZIF (zĭf), 2nd month of old Hebrew calendar, corresponding to Iyyar in later Jewish calendar (I Kings 6:1,37).

ZIGGURAT (zĭg′ŏŏ-răt, **pinnacle**), temple tower of the Babylonians, consisting of a lofty structure in the form of a pyramid, built in successive stages, with staircases on the outside and a shrine at the top.

ZIHA (zī′hȧ). 1. Head of family of Nethinim that returned with Zerubbabel (Ezra 2:43; Neh. 7:46). 2. Ruler of Nethinim (Neh. 11:21).

ZIKLAG (zĭk′lăg), town probably in S Judah, between Beersheba and Debir (Josh. 15:31); for long a Philistine city; given by Achish, king of Gath, to David (I Sam. 27:1-7); later became property of kings of Judah.

ZIKRI (zĭk′rī). 1. Levite; cousin of Aaron and Moses (Exod. 6:21). 2. Benjamite; son of Shashak (I Chron. 8:23). 3. Benjamite of family of Shemei or Shema (KJV "Shimhi") (I Chron. 8:19). 4. Benjamite; son of Jeroham (I Chron. 8:27). 5. Ancestor of Mattaniah who returned from captivity (I Chron. 9:15); "Zabdi" in Neh. 11:17. 6. Descendant of Eliezer (I Chron. 26:25). 7. Father of Eliezer; Reubenite (I Chron. 17:16). 8. Father of Amasiah; soldier (II Chron. 17:16). 9. Father of Elishaphat (II Chron. 23:1). 10. Ephraimite; killed son of Ahaz (II Chron. 28:7). 11. Father of Joel, the overseer of Benjamites (Neh. 11:9). 12. Descendant of Abijah; priest (Neh. 12:17).

ZILLAH (zĭl′ȧ), wife of Lamech; mother of Tubal-cain (Gen. 4:19-22).

ZILPAH (zĭl′pȧ), handmaid of Leah; mother of Gad and Asher (Gen. 29:24; 30:9-13).

ZILTHAI (zĭl′thī). 1. Early Benjamite (I Chron. 8:20). 2. Manassite soldier (I Chron. 12:20).

ZIMMAH (zĭm′ȧ), Gershonite Levite (I Chron. 6:20,42,43).

ZIMRAN (zĭm′răn), son of Abraham and Keturah (Gen. 25:2; I Chron. 1:32).

ZIMRI (zĭm′rī). 1. Prince of Simeon; slain by Phinehas, grandson of Aaron, for committing adultery with Midianite woman (Num. 25:14). 2. 5th king of N kingdom; murdered King Elah; ruled seven days (c. 876 B. C.); overthrown by Omri (I Kings 16:8-20). 3. Son of Zerah; grandson of Judah (I Chron. 2:6). 4. Benjamite; father of Moza (I Chron. 8:36; 9:42). 5. Unknown tribe in East (Jer. 25:25).

ZIN (zĭn), wilderness the Israelites traversed on way to Canaan (Num. 13:21); near borders of Canaan; bounded by Edom and Paran on the S (Josh. 15:1-3).

ZION (zī′ŭn), one of the hills on which Jerusalem stood; originally a Jebusite fortress (II Sam. 5:6-9); captured by David and ark brought to it (II Sam. 6:10-12); later the name was extended to take in Mount Moriah (Isa. 8:18; 18:7; 24:23; Micah 4:7), and still later it was used for the whole of Jerusalem (II Kings 19:21; Ps. 48; 69:35). Also used figuratively for Jewish Church and polity (Ps. 126:1; 129:5) and for heaven (Heb. 12:22; cf. Rev. 14:1).

ZIOR (zī′ôr), town in S Judah probably near Hebron (Josh. 15:54).

ZIPH (zĭf). 1. City in Negeb, probably c. four miles S by E from Hebron (Josh. 15:55). 2. Wilderness named from above city where David hid (I Sam. 23:14-24; 26:

1,2). 3. City in W Judah (II Chron. 11:8).
4. Calebite family name (I Chron. 2:42).
5. Judahite (I Chron. 4:16).

ZIPHAH (zi'fà), son of Jehaleleel (I Chron. 4:16).

ZIPHIMS (See Ziphites).

ZIPHION (See Zephon).

ZIPHITES (zif'its), inhabitants of Ziph (I Sam. 23:19; 26:1-5).

ZIPHRON (zif'rŏn), place on N border of Canaan, probably not far from Homs (Num. 34:9).

ZIPPOR (zip'ŏr), father of Balak, king of Moab (Num. 22:3,4).

ZIPPORAH (zi-pō'rà, bird), daughter of Jethro or Reuel, priest of Midian; 1st wife of Moses (Exod. 2:21); mother of Gershom and Eliezer (Exod. 18:1-6).

ZITHRI (zith'ri), Kohathite Levite; cousin of Aaron and Moses (Exod. 6:22).

ZIV (See Zif).

ZIZ (ziz, shining), cliff near W side of Red Sea on way from Engedi to Tekoa (II Chron. 20:16).

ZIZA (zi'zà, abundance). 1. Simeonite; son of Shiphi (KJV "Ziphi") (I Chron. 4:37-41). 2. Son of Rehoboam and brother of Abijah, kings of Judah (II Chron. 11:20).

ZIZAH (zi'zà), son of Shimei (I Chron. 23:11); called "Zina" in preceding verse.

ZOAN (zō'àn), ancient Egyptian city E of the Delta (Num. 13:22; Ps. 78:12,43; Isa. 19:11,13; 30:4; Ezek. 30:14). Greeks called it "Tanis." Extensive ruins survive near San, c. 18 miles SE of Damietta.

ZOAR (zō'èr, little), ancient Canaanite city near SE part of Dead Sea; formerly called "Bela" (Gen. 14:2); saved from destruction through prayer of Lot (Gen. 19:20-22); refuge of Lot.

ZOBA, ZOBAH (zō'bà), important Aramaean state N of Damascus (II Sam. 8:3,5); enemy of Israel (I Sam. 14:47; II Chron. 8:3); "Zoba" in KJV.

ZOBEBAH (zō-bē'bà), Judahite (I Chron. 4:8).

ZOHAR (zō'hàr). 1. Hittite; father of Ephron from whom Abraham purchased field of Machpelah (Gen. 23:8; 25:9). 2. Son of Simeon, 2nd son of Jacob (Gen. 46:10; Exod. 6:15); "Zerah" in Num. 26:13 and I Chron. 4:24.

ZOHELETH (zō'hĕ-lĕth, serpent), stone or ledge by En-rogel (I Kings 1:9).

ZOHETH (zō'hĕth), Judahite (I Chron. 4:20).

ZOPHAH (zō'fà), Asherite (I Chron. 7:35,36).

ZOPHAI (zō'fi), ancestor of Samuel the prophet (I Chron. 6:26); "Zuph" in vs. 35.

ZOPHAR (zō'fèr), friend of Job (Job 2:11).

ZOPHIM (zō'fim), field near Pisgah (Num. 23:14).

ZORAH (zō'rà), city c. 15 miles W of Jerusalem on borders of Judah and Dan (Josh. 15:33; 19:41).

ZORATHITES (zō'rà-thits), inhabitants of Zorah (I Chron. 2:53); (KJV has Zoreathites).

ZOREAH (See Zorah).

ZORITES (zō'rits), Judahite family (I Chron. 2:54).

ZOROBABEL (See Zerubbabel).

ZUAR (zū'èr), father of Nethaneel; Issacharite (Num. 1:8; 2:5).

ZUPH (zūf, honeycomb). 1. Ancestor of the prophet Samuel (I Chron. 6:35); "Zophai" in I Chron. 6:26. 2. District in Benjamin, near N border (I Sam. 9:5); location unknown.

ZUR (zūr, rock). 1. King of Midian slain by Israel (Num. 25:15; 31:8). 2. Son of Jeiel (I Chron. 8:30,33).

ZURIEL (zū'ri-èl), son of Abihail, prince of Merarite Levites in wilderness (Num. 3:35).

ZURISHADDAI (zū'ri-shàd'i), father of Shelumiel; Simeonite (Num. 1:6; 2:12; 7:36,41; 10:19).

ZUZIM (zū'zim), primitive race of giants, defeated by Chedorlaomer and allies (Gen. 14:5); erroneously called "Zuzims" in KJV.

The so-called Tomb of *Absalom* outside the southeast corner of the Jerusalem city wall, in the Kidron Valley.
© MPS

Ruins of Tekoah, the birthplace of the prophet *Amos*.
© MPS

Ruins of the so-called Tower of Babel at Birs-Nimrud in Babylonia. © MPS

The site of Gordon's Calvary.

Remains of the city walls of ancient *Jericho.* © MPS

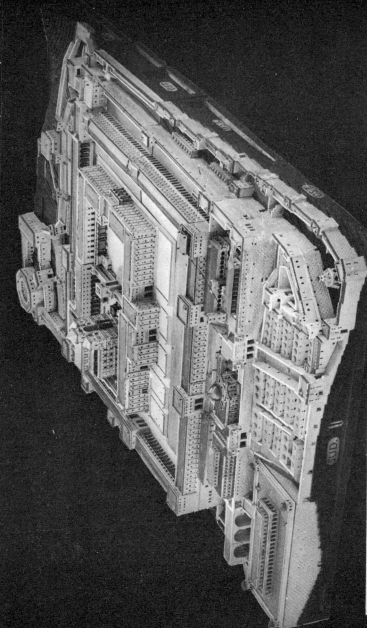

The majestic temple of Solomon and its environs (after Dr. Shick's model), the crowning achievement of the united Israelite kingdom under David and Solomon. © MPS

A pillar of salt on Jebel Usdum (Hill of Sodom), the mountain of salt on the western shore of the Dead Sea. This pillar of salt is known as "Lot's Wife." © MPS

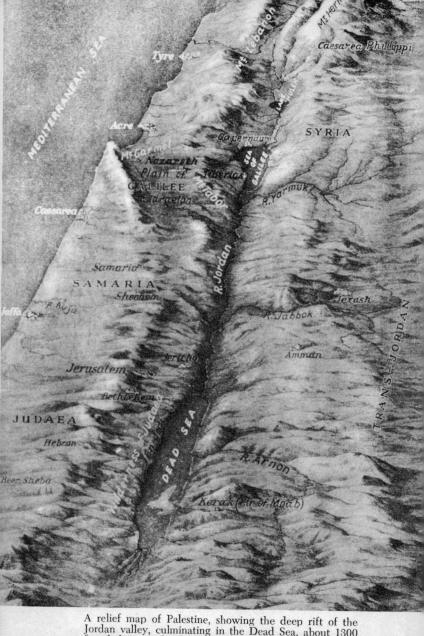

A relief map of Palestine, showing the deep rift of the Jordan valley, culminating in the Dead Sea, about 1300 feet below sea level. This is a reproduction of a map made by the Palestine Exploration Fund. © MPS

Near the top of the great pyramid of Cheops, showing the size of the stone blocks used in its construction. © MPS

Along the *Via Dolorosa* (the "sorrowful way") in Jerusalem. © MPS